Race, Law and Education in the Post-Desegregation Era

Four Perspectives on Desegregation and Resegregation

Kevin Brown

Professor of Law, Charles A. Whistler Faculty Fellow
and Director of the Hudson & Holland Scholars Programs
Indiana University-Bloomington

Carolina Academic Press

Durham, North Carolina

Library of Congress Cataloging-in-Publication Data

Brown, Kevin Dion.
Race, law, and education in the post-desegregation era / by Kevin Brown.
p. cm.
Includes bibliographical references.
ISBN 1-59460-025-2 (alk. paper)
1. Segregation in education--Law and legislation--United States.
2. Discrimination in education--Law and legislation--United States.
3. United States--Race relations. I. Title.

KF4155.B678 2004
379.2'63'0973--dc22

2004018302

Carolina Academic Press
700 Kent Street
Durham, North Carolina 27701
Telephone (919) 489-7486
Fax (919) 493-5668
E-mail: cap@cap-press.com
www.cap-press.com

Printed in the United States of America

This book is dedicated to my four children: Nichole, Crystal, Shayla and Devin. Contained within this book is all the wisdom that a father can convey to his children. This book is also dedicated to the rainbow of my life, my wife Dianne. Without her support, encouragement and patience I could not have completed this book.

Contents

Preface

This book is intended to address the era of the desegregation of public schools that occurred in American society over the past fifty years. Thus, it discusses the rise of desegregation from the Supreme Court's 1954 decision in *Brown v. Board of Education* to the fall of desegregation beginning in the late 1980s to the current educational reform movement of expanding school choice. These developments are discussed primarily in terms of there implications for African-American schoolchildren because they were designated as the principal beneficiaries of desegregation. But this book is an examination of the desegregation of American education from the vantage point of this, the Post-Desegregation Era. Thus, while this book discusses the history of race relations, the desegregation of public schools and the current educational situation of African-American schoolchildren, this book is not about those issues. Rather this book is intended to discuss and reveal the most significant realization about racial phenomena and racial issues that stems from the experience of the desegregation of American society. This realization also constitutes the core experience of the Post-Desegregation Era.

To understand and experience something, it must be conceptualized against a *sub silento* background of a much larger set of ideas. These larger unseen, and often unperceived, background sets of ideas provide the conceptual contexts to place given events into "proper" context. The comprehension of racial and ethnic phenomena are merely a subset of this basic limit of human understanding. Thus, the comprehension of any particular racial or ethnic phenomena is always done against a background of a much larger set of ideas about race and ethnicity that structures and limits the perception of such a phenomena and the types of arguments that are persuasive to resolve a given racial or ethnic dispute. And just as important, there have always been multiple sets of background ideas about race and ethnicity in American society in which to comprehend a given racial phenomena and discuss a given racial issue. As a result, there are always multiple understandings of racial phenomena and thus multiple solutions to given racial conflicts. While these different background sets of ideas could be viewed as different points of view or different perspectives, this book will refer to these larger diverse sets of ideas as the following: "discourses"; "patterns of understanding"; "systems of meaning"; or "cognitive frameworks."

When reexamining the desegregation era of public education from the vantage point of the Post-Desegregation Era, it must be acknowledged initially that this reexamination can not provide only one objective and truthful interpretation, but rather multiple interpretations. It is the recognition that racial phenomena are understood against the background of different discourses that is both the most significant realization of the Desegregation Era and the core experience of the Post-Desegregation Era. Thus, how to comprehend the desegregation of public schools, as well as the history of race relations and the current educational situation of African-American schoolchildren, will largely be a function of the discourse upon which the comprehension is based. In order to reveal the structures and limits of thinking about race, this book discusses these racial issues within the conceptual limits of four different patterns of understanding referred to as Traditional Americanism, African-American Centralism, Colorblind Individualism and American Collectivism, which provide alterative understandings of these racial issues.

There is a philosophy woven into this book. Despite the fact that understandings of separate racial phenomena ostensibly appear as detached and distinct occurrences, our appreciation of them is never in such isolation. The comprehension of racial phenomena that force themselves into our consciousness is the comprehension of a part of a much larger pattern of understanding that is present to provide structure for and limitation of what is consciously perceived. There is also a hope that is woven into this book as well. To be constantly aware of multiple interpretations of racial phenomena requires an acculturation into a broader horizon of knowledge for which new, and hopefully, better solutions to racial conflicts can be conceived, developed and implemented.

Acknowledgments

The genesis of this book began with a law review article that I published over a decade ago. I would like to acknowledge my indebtedness to the many colleagues both at Indiana University and in the legal academy who have commented upon various drafts of portions of this book, especially the following individuals: Alexander Aleinikoff, A. B. Assensoh, John Baker, Pat Baude, Craig Bradley, Trevor Brown, Wendy Brown, Paulette Caldwell, Dan Conkle, Anthony Cook, John Dayton, Judy Failer, Richard Fraher, Bryant Garth, Don Gjerdingen, Dwight Greene, Linda Greene, Carol Greenhouse, Matthew Gutwein, Lynne Henderson, Stephanie Jones, Daniel Kobil, Brian Landsberg, Douglas Laycock, John Lucaites, Alan Mathewson, Martha McCarthy, Michael Middleton, Martha Minnow, John Pratter, David Rabban, Lauren Robel, John Scanlan, Theodore Shaw, David Smith, Leland Ware, David Williams and Susan Williams.

I would also like to thank the following law students at Indiana University School of Law or the University of Texas School of Law for their invaluable research and editorial assistance: Glenda Alexander, Margaret Allen, Silvia Biers, Vivek Boray, Daletta Briggs, Carmen Brun, Robyn Carr, John Dayton, Scott Gilchrist, Victor Katz, Olivia Phillips, Cheryl Peebles, Clarence Pollard, Alex Sharma, Tina Speagle, Scott Timberman and Daniel Trammel. I would, however, like to especially acknowledge the extraordinary research and editorial assistance of Andrija Samardzich. Further I would like to thank the many students in my Race, American Society and the Law courses over the years at Indiana University School of Law, the University of Texas School of Law and the University of Alabama School of Law for their many insights and suggestions that I incorporated into my thinking and, thus, this book. But I would especially like to thank the following students in my Fall 2003 Seminar on Antidiscrimination in Education: Nathalie Collins, Shakeba DuBose, David Giampetroni, Nathaniel Sinn and Kristine Zeabart. Finally, I would like to acknowledge Deborah Eads, Krystie Herndon, Marjorie Young and Peggy Wilkes for their secretarial assistance on this book.

Race, Law and Education in the Post-Desegregation Era

Introduction

Supreme Court opinions reveal their consequences and yield their secrets only with the passage of time and the development of American society. The Supreme Court candidly recognized this reality seventeen years after it delivered its opinion in *Brown v. Board of Education.*[1] "Nothing in our national experience prior to 1955 prepared anyone for dealing with changes and adjustments of the magnitude and complexity encountered since then."[2] Over fifty years have elapsed since the Supreme Court rendered its historic opinion on May 17, 1954. The passage of time allows us to put perspective into a reexamination of the opinion that launched American society into the Desegregation Era and became the catalyst for astonishing changes not only in public education, but also in race and ethnic relations throughout American society. Having passed the Golden Anniversary of *Brown*, we can also reflect on the developments of the educational situation of African-American schoolchildren, who were designated as the principal beneficiaries of the Court's opinion, with the benefit of hindsight that comes from being more than fifty years removed from that historic day.

I. Changes in American Society Resulting from *Brown v. Board of Education*

At the time the Supreme Court delivered its opinion in *Brown v. Board of Education,* people of African descent were called Negroes or colored out of respect; and were called coon, darkie and even black as an insult. Neither America nor her descendants from Africa had undergone the Civil Rights Movement, the Black Consciousness Movement, the Multicultural Movement nor the Diversity Movement. The Court's opinion in *Brown v. Board of Education* preceded by ten years the passage of the Civil Rights Act of 1964, which has been the most sweeping piece of civil rights legislation in the country's history. It also preceded by eleven years the Voting Rights Act of 1965, which helped to secure the right to vote for most Negroes living in the South where the majority of them still resided. At the time of the Court's opinion in 1954, most Negroes in the South had been disenfranchised for the entire twentieth century. Segregation and conscious racial discrimination were the explicit law of the land in many areas of the country. Where segregation and conscious racial discrimination were not the law, they still formed part of customary American business, educational, political and social practice. Discrimination, based on race in employment, merchandising stores, eating establishments, places of entertainment, hotels and motels, was generally accepted as a fact of life. Negroes seldom occupied positions above the most menial levels in American businesses and corporations. Even lower level management positions were, for the most part, unobtainable. What became known as the "glass ceiling" in the 1980s was a firmly implanted, outright concrete barrier in the 1950s. In 1954 only a handful of Negroes attended the prestigious colleges and universities of this country and almost none of them taught there. No man of color had been elected mayor of a major U.S. city in the twentieth century. There were only four Negroes serving in Congress, none of whom had been elected from any of the eleven states that made up the former Confederacy since 1900. In 1954 many places in the country maintained separate water fountains, waiting rooms, transportation facilities, rest rooms, schools, hospitals and cemeteries for whites and coloreds.

But America has now lived with the Court's opinion in *Brown* for over fifty years. Many of the people of African descent who were once called "Negroes" as a term of respect in 1954 would be offended to be called a "Negro" today. Conversely to call such a person "black" is not an insult, but a sign of respect. In most circles, the term used is "African-American", an expression no one considered using in 1954. The America of today is not the one that existed before the Civil Rights Movement and the Black Consciousness Movement, but is instead more than thirty-five years removed from the beginnings of those movements. It is not the America that preceded the Multicultural and Diversity Movements, but an America immersed in those movements. This is not the America that existed before the Civil Rights Act of 1964, but an America that is over forty years removed from that historic piece of legislation. Nor is this the America that existed before the Voting Rights Act of 1965, but forty years after it. Conscious racial discrimination in employment, merchandising stores, eating establishments, places of entertainment, hotels and motels is illegal. A number of successful and highly visible discrimination suits have been won by African-American victims of discrimination.[3] Texaco, for example, paid out $176 million, then the largest amount ever paid in a racial discrimination suit, to settle the class action claims of over 1,400 African American employees.[4] In 1999, a $12 million settlement was reached in a class action racial discrimination lawsuit brought by African-Americans against United Parcel Service.[5] African-Americans Robert Johnson and Ophra Winfrey are on the list of the wealthiest Americans. Richard Parsons of AOL Time Warner and Stanley O'Neal of Merrill Lynch are among those African-Americans who have run and currently run some of America's most powerful corporations. Black athletes like Tiger Woods, Michael Jordan and LeBron James are among the highest paid marketing personalities in American history. African-Americans not only attend prestigious colleges and universities, but in the 2002–03 academic year, constituted 7% of the undergraduate population at Harvard and 7.2% at Yale.[6] African-Americans are highly regarded members of faculties and administrative bodies at almost all of America's elite educational institutions. In 1999 there were over 9,000 African-American elected officials, including 451 mayors of major U.S. cities.[7] Even though there are no black Senators, there are thirty-seven blacks elected to the House of Representatives,[8] constituting nearly 8.5% of the members of the lower house of Congress. President George W. Bush, Jr. has five African-Americans serving in powerful positions in his administration, Secretary of Education Rod Paige; Secretary of State Colin Powell; National Security Advisor Condoleeza Rice; Federal Trade Commission Chairman Michael Powell and Secretary of Housing and Urban Development Alphonso Jackson. Since President Bush received only 8% of the African-American vote, these appointments are not *quid pro quo* for African-American electoral support, but arguably represent appointment of the best persons for the positions.[9] Americans no longer live with "white only" and "colored only" signs etched above water fountains, waiting rooms, transportation facilities, rest rooms, schools, hospitals and cemeteries; nor have they for the past thirty years. Even in contexts where it is not illegal to consciously discriminate on the basis of race, the general American ethos considers conscious racial discrimination wrong or in bad taste.[10]

In spite of these significant achievements, African-Americans still lag far behind non-Hispanic whites in terms of political, economic, educational and social welfare and health conditions. When adjusted for inflation, the per capita income of African-Americans, for example, increased by 250% from 1967 to 2000. Yet, this increase left blacks earning only 65% of that of non-Hispanic white per capita income in 2000.[11] According to the U.S. Census Bureau, in 1966 41.8% of the black population,[12] 50.6% of black children under the age of 18 and 55.1% of blacks over the age of 65 lived below the poverty line.[13] In 2001 these percentages had decreased to 22.7%,[14] 30.2% and 21.9%, respectively.[15] For non-Hispanic white Americans, however, the corresponding 2001 figures were 7.8%,[16] 9.5% and 8.1%,[17] respectively. The percentage of blacks ages 18 to 24 enrolled in higher education increased from 13% in

1967 to 31.3% in 2001.[18] However, the percentage of non-Hispanic whites enrolled in college increased over the same period from 26.9% to 39.3%.[19] The college completion rate for blacks over the age of 25 increased from 4.5% in 1970 to 16.5% in 2000.[20] But the non-Hispanic white completion rate increased from 11.6% to 28.1%.[21] In addition, African-Americans continue to earn significantly less than their non-Hispanic white counterparts with the same levels of educational attainment. For example, blacks who are high school graduates, have a bachelors degree or a professional degree earn only 83.1%, 79.8% and 73% respectively of their non-Hispanic white counterparts.[22] In 1965, 1% of all law students were black and over one-third of them were enrolled in one of the four law schools that had been established for blacks. Two percent of all medical students were black with 75% of them enrolled in one of the two all-black medical schools in the country, Howard University or Meharry Medical College.[23] In 1998, however, African-Americans constituted 4.3% of lawyers and judges, 4.9% of physicians, 4.1% of engineers and 5.8% of college and university teachers.[24] As impressive as the increase in these percentages is, because one out of every eight Americans is black, these percentages are considerably less than what is necessary to reach proportionate representation. The 2000 census shows that 10.6% of those employed in executive, administrative or managerial positions are African-Americans. But in 2002, blacks constituted 47.8% of the 1,848,700 persons in either state or federal prison or local jails.[25] Ten percent of African-American men between the ages of 25 and 29 were incarcerated at the end of 2001, in contrast to only 1.2% of non-Hispanic white men in the same age group.[26] The infant mortality rate for blacks has fallen from 22.2 per 1,000 live births to 14.6 between 1980 and 1999. But this figure is still far higher than the non-Hispanic white infant mortality rate which fell from 10.9 to 5.8 over the same period.[27] The life expectancy of black males increased by over eight years from 1970 to 2000 and that of black females by nearly seven years. Yet, the figures from 2000 still have black males living six and one-half years less than non-Hispanic white males (68.3 and 74.8) and black females living five years less than non-Hispanic white females (75.0 and 80.0).[28]

Though not a result of the Court's school desegregation jurisprudence, the changing racial and ethnic demographics is another dramatic development that has occurred in American society over the past fifty years. When *Brown* was decided, America thought of itself primarily as a biracial society. As late as 1970, Latinos were still classified in American society in terms of their racial group and not ethnicity. Thus, 98.5% of Americans were classified as either black or white.[29] According to the 2000 census data, African-Americans comprise 12.3% of the population, but Latinos comprise 12.5% and Asians another 3.6% of the population.[30] It has been estimated that by the year 2040, one-half of the U.S. population will be African-American, Latino American, Native American and/or Asian American. The public schools are already well on their way to those percentages. In 2001–02 school year only 60.3% of public schoolchildren were non-Hispanic white, 17.2% black, 17.1% Latino, 4.2% Asian, and 1.2% Native American.[31] The nature of the changing racial and ethnic characteristics of American society has made the old biracial view of American society that existed in 1954 obsolete. In addition, with the world becoming more and more connected, Americans are increasingly brought into contact with racial and ethnic groups from around the world who have different perspectives and views about America and American society. Cross racial and ethnic interchanges are increasingly becoming a part of everyday life in American society.

In brief, Americans today live in a society that has been fundamentally altered by the Desegregation Era sparked by *Brown v. Board of Education.* Many of the changes in race relations that have occurred since 1954 can accurately be described as, stunning. All but the most obstinate observer of race relations acknowledges significant improvement in the social, political, economic and educational conditions of African-Americans. Race is currently less of a factor in limiting the opportunities of blacks than at any other time in this country's collective past. Despite the success of many individual African-Americans, however, as a group, blacks continue to lag far behind non-Hispanic whites in virtually all aggregate statistics related to social welfare. America's national agenda is thus unable to escape conscious deliberations on racial matters. America is torn between recognizing and congratulating herself over the obvious progress on race relations during the Desegregation Era and being demoralized and dispirited over the lack of success.

II. Public Education Has Moved into the Post-Desegregation Era

Decisions by the Supreme Court, especially in the context of race and race relations, contribute to either broadening or restricting notions of American racial equality. Supreme Court opinions like *Dred Scott v. Sandford,*[32] *Plessy v. Ferguson,*[33] *Brown v. Board of Education* and *Regents of the University of California v. Bakke*[34] have helped to shape the thinking of all Americans about race. These opinions help all Americans organize their experiences with people from different races. The principal reason for the dramatic influence of Supreme Court opinions on American thinking about race is that law is a powerful mechanism through which our society carries out its normative choices.[35] Since the courts are the final arena for resolving disputes in American society, the public discourse of judges, especially Supreme Court justices, is given a preferred meaning and assumed to more accurately reflect reality. Many Americans believe in the myth of an impersonal judiciary divining its decisions based upon some notion of objective truth.[36] They, therefore, view the law as an autonomous and legitimate means of mediating social disputes.[37] As Professor Wasby has pointed out, the principal belief about the Supreme Court—which is still believed by many Americans—is that the Supreme Court does not make, but only finds the law.[38] The Court's opinions operate to validate particular conceptions of society, by legitimizing certain concrete social arrangements.[39] Thus, Supreme Court opinions not only reflect the final solution to a given social problem, but also function as powerful "symbolic declarations to guide, influence, and endorse" policies made outside of a strictly judicial forum.[40]

As the twenty-first century unfolds, it is clear that the assimilation vision forged during the turbulent 1950s and 1960s, with its emphasis on integration and racial balancing as solutions to black/white racial conflict, has run its course. Three developments, all derived from the Supreme Court's equal protection jurisprudence, make it especially clear that American public education has moved into a Post-Desegregation Era.

The first development is the increasing resegregation of public schools. The scope and extent of school desegregation were principally the products of the Supreme Court's interpretations of the rights of black schoolchildren derived from the equal protection clause. After opinions that embraced the use of race in order to bring about the greatest possible degree of actual desegregation, the Court began to back away from its commitment to desegregate American education in the 1970s. Second, the Supreme Court has not fully embraced a colorblind approach to interpreting the equal protection clause. Nevertheless, the Supreme Court has firmly rejected the notion embedded in its opinion in *Brown v. Board of Education* which interpreted the equal protection clause as including a special concern about improving the educational environment of black schoolchildren. The Supreme Court's decisions over the past thirty years reflect a strong preference for viewing issues regarding racial and ethnic discrimination against a background of assumptions that requires government to treat all citizens as individuals. Third, even though respect for individuality is the basis for the resolution of equal protection challenges involving race, interpreting social phenomena involving racial issues based upon the notion that all people should be viewed as individuals is not the only valid understanding. The Supreme Court's decision to uphold the University of Michigan law school's affirmative action program in *Grutter v. Bollinger*[41] strongly implies this point. As the Court noted in *Grutter*, the educational process is more enlightening when important social phenomena are understood through multiple perspectives that include those of minorities with a history of discrimination.

School desegregation decrees originating in the 1960s, 1970s and 1980s were some of the most important means used to desegregate American society. In the 1968–69 school year, 23.4% of black students attended majority white schools nationwide, but in the 1972–73 this percentage had increased to 36.4%.[42] It reached its zenith of 37.1% in the 1980–81 school year. Also, in the 1968–69 school year 64.3% of black students were in schools that were 90% or more minority. But, that percentage decreased to 38.7% four years later.[43] This figure continued to decrease through the 1970s to the mid-1980s reaching its nadir of 32% in 1988.[44] But after opinions requiring school districts to aggressively pursue desegregation, the Supreme Court's commitment waned. By the 1990s, the Court had turned its attention to issues regarding the termination of school desegregation decrees. Over the past seventeen years, a number of school desegregation decrees have been terminated. The termination of school desegregation decrees allows local school districts to return to race neutral student assignment policies, including neighborhood schools. Since school assignment policies are no longer motivated by a desire to maintain racial and ethnic integration, segregation inevitably increases.

In addition to the termination of school desegregation decrees, a number of lower federal courts have recently addressed challenges to the use of racial classifications to foster integrated student bodies when desegregation was not required to remedy a constitutional violation. The Supreme Court has not directly addressed this issue. Lower federal courts, however, have analyzed these uses of racial classifications by public schools under strict scrutiny as required by the Supreme Court's 1995 opinion in *Adarand Constructors, Inc. v. Pena.*[45] Many of these lower court decisions have struck down the school desegregation plans presented to them.[46] Lower federal courts have generally agreed that diversity as articulated by Justice Powell in his opinion in *Bakke*—and reaffirmed by the Supreme Court in *Grutter*—is a compelling interest. But since the goal of these desegregation plans was to promote racial and ethnic balancing, as opposed to individual diversity, the means was not narrowly tailored to the compelling state interest. Nothing more cogently demonstrates the end of the Desegregation Era in public education than federal courts, which had encouraged the use of racial classifications to foster integration of public schools, finding desegregation plans as violations of the same provision of the Constitution that previously required them.

The impact of these changes in the constitutional view of school desegregation can be seen in increasing rates of racial and ethnic segregation in the public schools. The percentage of African-American schoolchildren attending majority-white schools has decreased from its peak of 37.1% in the

1980–81 school year to 31.2% in the 1996–97 school year to the 28.4% in 2000. The percentage of African-Americans in schools that are 90% or more minority has also increased. This percentage has gone from its lowest figure of 32% in 1988 to 35% in 1996–97 to 37.4% in 2000.[47] For Latinos, segregation has been increasing since the 1968–69 school year. At that time 54.8% of Latino students were in majority-minority schools and only 23.1% were in schools that were at least 90% minority. In 2000, 76% of Latinos were in predominately minority schools and 37.0% were in schools that were over 90% minority.[48]

The second and third developments that point to the movement of American public education into the Post-Desegregation Era were at the core of what Justice Scalia called the Court's "split double header" in the University of Michigan affirmative action decisions in the Summer of 2003. In *Grutter v. Bollinger*[49] the Supreme Court upheld the affirmative action plan adopted by the University of Michigan Law School. But in *Gratz v. Bollinger*[50] the Court struck down the plan adopted by the University of Michigan's College of Literature, Science, and Arts. *Grutter* held that racial classifications could be used in an individualized admissions process as a means to pursue a critical mass of minority students from groups with a history of discrimination that would not be represented in significant numbers without such considerations. The Supreme Court rejected the affirmative action plan presented to it in *Gratz* because the plan did not provide for the individualized considerations that must be the core of a race-conscious admissions policy.

Justice O'Connor's opinion for the Court in *Grutter* noted that the benefits of enrolling a critical mass of underrepresented minority students are substantial.[51]

> The Law School's admission policy promotes "cross-racial understanding," helps to break down racial stereotypes, and "enables [students] to better understand persons of different races." These benefits are "important and laudable," because "classroom discussion is livelier, more spirited and simply more enlightening and interesting" when the students have "the greatest possible variety of backgrounds."[52]

For the first time, a majority of the justices on the Supreme Court recognized the tremendous educational value obtained from exposing people to the different perspectives derived from the experiences of minority groups with a history of discrimination. The benefit is substantial enough to constitute a compelling state interest. However, the Supreme Court also rejected the affirmative action plan presented to it in *Gratz* as not narrowly tailored because the plan lacked the individualized consideration that must be the core of a race-conscious admissions policy. Thus, the second development that indicates that America is in the Post-Desegregation Era is that interpretations of the equal protection clause are based upon a point of view centered around treating all people, regardless of race or ethnicity, as individuals. Even though this perspective is decisive for addressing equal protection rights, the third development is to make us aware that it this not the only valid understanding of a given social phenomena, including racial phenomena.

III. The Two Interwoven Objectives

This book discusses the development of the current educational situation of African-American schoolchildren with a full recognition that American education has moved into the Post-Desegregation Era. There are two interwoven objectives of this book. The first objective is to discuss the developments of the current educational situation of African-American schoolchildren fifty years after the Supreme Court's opinion in *Brown v. Board of Education. Brown* propelled American education into the Desegregation Era and made school integration the primary means of pursuing educational reform. In this, the Post-Desegregation Era, the driving force behind educational reform is expanding school choice. This book will discuss why expanding school choice makes sense in light of the current educational situation of black schoolchildren.

The second interwoven objective of this book is to advance the discussion of racial issues, particularly those involving African-American schoolchildren, through the Post-Desegregation Awareness. The Post-Desegregation Awareness is the conscious awareness that important social phenomena—including racial phenomena such as the development of the educational situation of black schoolchildren over the past fifty years—are more enlightening when they are comprehended from multiple perspectives or points of view. The Post-Desegregation Awareness is thus a conscious awareness that racial or ethnic phenomena are not understood as separate, isolated and unconnected incidents. In American society, the comprehension of any particular racial or ethnic phenomena is always done against a *sub silentio* background of a much larger set of ideas about race and ethnicity that structures and limits the perception of such phenomena in alternative and conflicting ways. While these different interpretations could be viewed as different points of view or different perspectives, this book will refer to these larger diverse sets of ideas as the following: "discourses"; "patterns of understanding"; "systems of meaning"; or "cognitive frameworks." The principal means to accomplish the second interwoven objective of this book is by discussing the desegregation of public education initiated by the Court's opinion in *Brown* through to the current educational situation of African-Americans that has spawned the educational reform movements focusing on increased school choice within the conceptual boundaries of four different discourses: Traditional Americanism, African-American Centralism, Colorblind Individualism and American Collectivism.

Despite the dramatic change in the racial/ethnic demographics of American society, this book will focus on the experience of African-American schoolchildren over the past fifty years. I have chosen African-American schoolchildren because it was the desire to advance their educational interest that started America down the path of desegregation. Thus their educational interest had much to do with the development, then restriction and later termination of school desegregation. In addition, until recently, African-Americans have also constituted the single largest racial/ethnic minority group in the United States. As noted above, until as late as 1970, Latinos were classified in terms of their racial group. Throughout American history the primary background issue in addressing a legal conflict involving other racial or ethnic minority groups was often how similar to or different from African-Americans is the particular group.[53] An explanation of how American society has come to this current place regarding the education of black schoolchildren can shed some light on the general discussion about the educational situation of other racial/ethnic minority students. Finally, and perhaps most importantly, one of the most significant realizations of the Post-Desegregation Era is that diverse racial/ethnic groups possess cultural interpretations of their situation in American society from different points of view centered around that groups particular historical experiences. There are numerous racial/ethnic groups in the United States. All of the broadly recognized racial or ethnic groups in America: African-American, Asian, non-Hispanic white, Latino or Native American—can be further subdivided. For example, Asian descendants in America are not a monolithic group. The experiences of Chinese in America, Hawaiians in America, South Asians in America, Japanese in America, Koreans in America, Vietnamese in America and so on are very different. The same is true of the experiences of groups in America that speak Spanish. The experience of Mexicans in America, Puerto Ricans in America, Cubans in America, Panamanians in America, Dominicans in America, Hondurans in America, Nicaraguans in America, Salvadoreans in America and so on are different. While discussing the current educational situation of one minority racial/ethnic group will yield insights for another, it is not a substitute. In order to do adequate justice to the current educational experience of a given racial/ethnic group it is necessary to deal with that particular groups experience in detail. Such a detailed treatment of so many racial/ethnic groups is beyond the scope of this book.

A. Current Educational Situation of African-American Schoolchildren

In discussing the current educational situation of African-American schoolchildren there are two crucial factors that are readily apparent. The first factor relates to the achievement gaps between black schoolchildren and non-Hispanic white schoolchildren in virtually every measure of academic achievement. Black schoolchildren trail their non-Hispanic white counterparts in performance on standardized tests and high school graduation/school dropout rates. Black students are twice as likely as their non-Hispanic white counterparts to be retained in grade during their educational career. When tracking is used to divide students based on presumed academic ability, black children are under represented in high ability skills groups and over represented in low ability skills groups.

The second factor that is exerting a tremendous influence on the current educational situation of black schoolchildren is the change in the background assumptions for interpreting the equal protection clause since *Brown v. Board of Education*. The current interpretation of the equal protection clause severely limits the ability to institute public educational policies and programs that use racial classifications. Thus, legislators and educators are increasingly forced to embrace educational reform proposals that are race-neutral. This has inevitably led to the third factor, increase in school choice. Choice is a racially neutral form of educational reform that can still be targeted in such a way as to disproportionately advantage poor minority urban schoolchildren.

1. Racial Gaps in Academic Achievement

There are three characteristics that lead to significant achievement gaps as reported on standardized tests that have proved especially persistent. Low-income children on average score lower on standardized tests than their middle-income and upper-income counterparts. Black, Latino and Native American children on average score lower than non-Hispanic white children. Children attending urban public schools on average score lower than children attending schools in the suburbs. Children with all three of these characteristics score on average lowest of all. Given the disproportionate number of African-American schoolchildren attending predominantly minority, low-income, urban schools—as a racial group—they congregate at the losing end of America's educational performance spectrum not only in regards to performance on standardized tests, but other measures of academic achievement.

Gaps on standardized tests can be noted on virtually all such tests used in public schools. For example, the Scholastic Achievement Test (SAT) scores of black children improved from 686 in 1975–76 school year to 857 in 2002–03.[54] Despite this improvement, according to the College Board's 2003 National Report profiling SAT test takers,[55] the gap between the SAT scores of African-Americans and that of non-Hispanic whites is still 206 points (1063 and 857, respectively).[56] After closing through the 1970s and 1980s,[57] the disheartening aspect is that this racial gap has actually increased over the past ten years.[58] There are also significant racial gaps between the performance of blacks and non-Hispanic whites on the ACT where the average composite score of African-Americans is 16.9 compared to non-Hispanic whites at 21.7.[59] This gap has held fairly consistent over the past seven years.[60]

While the SAT and the ACT are tests taken by students who desire to attend post-secondary education in order to get a look at the existence of racial gaps for a broader section of elementary and secondary students it is necessary to focus on different standardized tests. The National Assessment of Educational Progress is a program created by Congress in 1969. The purpose of the program has been to assess the trends in elementary and secondary student progress in certain academic areas, including reading, math and science. Since 1971 three age groups of students in school—9, 13 and 17 year olds—have been tested. In reading, all three black age groups showed progress in closing the gap with white students on the tests from 1971 to 1988. The reading test scores of black students was increasing, while the scores of white students remained essentially the same.[61] These gaps in reading test scores began to widen in the late 1980s, however, as the scores of all black age groups fell, the scores of whites showed a modest rise.[62] The gap in the performance of black students compared to white students on the science tests fell for all three age groups from 1970 to 1986, but these gaps also began to rise during the 1990s.[63] The gaps in the math scores have generally remained constant since 1990, but they continue to be substantial.[64]

Another significant measure of academic achievement where African-American students significantly trail their non-Hispanic white counterparts is in high school graduation/school dropout statistics. The disparity between high school graduation rates of blacks and non-Hispanic whites cannot be completely separated from the gaps in standardized tests because many states now require passing a standardized test in order to receive the high school diploma. More than half of the states have enacted measures that will require students to pass exit exams in order to get a high school diploma.[65]

According the Census Bureau in 2001, 13.8% of African-Americans between 18 and 24 had not completed—nor were they enrolled in—high school, compared to 13.4% of non-Hispanic whites.[66] However, official reports of dropout rates and high school graduation rates may significantly understate the problem. "Graduation rates based on reported enrollment suggest strongly that there are large numbers of 'missing' students that go completely unaccounted for in either official dropout or graduation rate reports."[67] High school dropout rate figures also include those who left school and later received GED credentials. A recent report on high school graduation rates released by the Civil Rights Project at Harvard University, the Urban Institute, Advocates for Children of New York and the Civil Society Institute developed a more accurate measure of high school graduation and dropout rates. The Report based graduation rates on what it called the "Cumulative Promotion Index" (CPI).[68] Each school district in the nation provides its actual enrollment data to the nation's Common Core of Data. The CPI uses this actual enrollment data to examine changes in enrollment and the likelihood of graduating with a high school diploma by combining the average success of groups of students moving from ninth grade to tenth grade, from tenth grade to eleventh grade, from junior year to senior year and from senior year to graduation. According to the Report only 68% of those who enter 9th grade graduate with a regular diploma in the 12th grade four years later. But there are vast differences between various racial/ethnic groups. The graduation rate for non-Hispanic whites is 74.9% and Asian/Pacific Islanders is 76.8%. In contrast, the graduation rates for African-Americans, Native Americans and Latinos are 50.2%, 51.1% and 53.2%, respectively.[69]

The relatively poor performance of African-Americans on standardized tests also contributes to other academic achievement gaps. Black schoolchildren are more likely to be retained in a grade during their academic careers than their non-Hispanic white counterparts. In 1999, 18% of black school students had been retained at least one time between kindergarten and 12th grade, which is double the rate of non-Hispanic whites.[70] "[R]etention in grade is the single most reliable predictor of a student eventually dropping out of school."[71] Black students are also overrepresented in the lower academic tracks or achievement skills groups and underrepresented in the higher academic tracks or achievement skills groups. For example, figures from 1998 reveal that non-Hispanic white high school graduates were almost 50% more likely to be in the highest academic placement in math than African-American high school graduates (45.1% to 30.4%, respectively) and blacks were considerably more likely to be in the two lowest math tracks than non-Hispanic whites (8.3% to 4.6%, respectively).[72] Black high school graduates were also less likely to be in advanced academic placements in English and science courses. Black high school graduates were 50% more likely to be in the least challenging English course than their non-Hispanic white counterparts (17.6% to 11.6%, respectively).[73] Approximately 64% of non-Hispanic white high school graduating students took at least one chemistry or physics course in high school, with 33.8% having taken at least two of these courses. In contrast, only 55% of African-Americans took at least one physics or chemistry course, with only 22.3% having taken at least two of these courses.[74] Due to the fact that these statistics of placement in academic courses are confined to high school graduates, they almost certainly understate the tracking gaps. These statistics do not account for the fact that blacks have higher high school dropouts rates than non-Hispanic whites. Black students are also more likely to be classified as having a disability. Almost 15% of African-American students compared to only 10.9% of non-Hispanic white students between the ages of 3 and 21 were served under the Individuals with Disabilities Education Act during the 1999–2000 school year.[75]

2. Change in the Background Assumptions for Interpreting the Equal Protection Clause since *Brown v. Board of Education*

In explaining why the Supreme Court struck down the segregation statutes presented in *Brown v. Board of Education,* Chief Justice Warren noted that segregation had psychologically damaged black schoolchildren in ways unlikely ever to be undone. Warren's opinion was consistent with a long line of Supreme Court cases interpreting the rights (or lack thereof) of African-Americans based upon the built-in assumption that in some way they were less than the relevant norm. What made *Brown* a break with the Supreme Court's past interpretations of the rights of blacks, however, was that it attributed the inferiority of blacks to environmental causes instead of ontological ones. When situated in a historical context, *Brown* was a very sanguine opinion because it suggested that there was a cure for—or at least a way to improve—black people. Blacks could be made better by enriching their social environment, particularly the educational environment of the young. Born out of this belief was a special concern for the educational interest of black schoolchildren. If their educational environment could be ameliorated, they could be improved as a people.

As noted before, three different trends in the interpretation of the equal protection clause, constrained, then halted and now is reversing the desegregation of public schools. After Supreme Court opinions embracing the use of race in order to bring about the greatest possible degree of actual desegregation, the Court began to back away from its commitment to desegregate American education in the 1970s. By the 1990s, the Court had turned its attention to issues regarding the termination of school desegregation decrees. This help to set the stage for the termination of school desegregation decrees and the concomitant institution of school assignment policies that were no longer motivated by a desire to maintain integrated student bodies. The third trend is represented by the decisions by lower federal courts upholding attacks on school desegregation policies when they can not be justified with reference to the compelling state interest of remedying the effects of the prior operation of a dual school system. These three trends all reflect a shift in the background assumptions for interpreting the rights derived from the equal protection clause. This shift was a movement away from viewing the equal protection clause in terms of a concern about improving the social environment of black schoolchildren, to viewing the equal protection clause as protecting the rights of individuals.

Outside the context of student assignments to public schools, this shift in interpreting the equal protection clause has also had dramatic consequences for the current educational situation regarding African-American schoolchildren. The shift in the background assumptions for deciding equal protection challenges involving the educational interest of black schoolchildren produces two significant consequences. First, unconstitutional discrimination is defined as racially motivated decision making which fails to treat a person as an individual, not as it was before—negative disparate effects on African-American schoolchildren generated by various educational policies and practices. But because educational policies and practices can almost always be justified based on legitimate educational concerns, it is difficult to prove that they were primarily motivated by discriminatory motives. Thus, the continued gaps in academic achievement between black and non-Hispanic white children derived from legitimate educational policies and practices are generally viewed for equal protection purposes as unfortunate byproducts of racially neutral educational decisions that do not raise constitutional concerns. Second, this shift severely limits the programs and policies that public school authorities can implement to attack racial achievement gaps in educational performance. Educational strategies that employ racial and ethnic classifications must survive strict scrutiny. Strict scrutiny is no longer viewed to be strict in appearance and fatal in fact.[76] Yet, outside of the need to remedy an existing equal protection violation or obtain the benefits derived from diversity in education, the use or racial classifications will seldom survive an equal protection challenge. Thus, legislators and educators interested in reducing the racial achievement gap are increasingly forced to advocate for the adoption of race-neutral educational policies and practices.

3. Increase in School Choice as a Principal Means of Pursuing Educational Reform

Given the above considerations—the racial gap in academic achievement, increasing levels of racial segregation in public schools and limits on the adoption or implementation of racially neutral educational policies or practices—politicians and educational reformist are increasingly forced to argue for policies and programs that are race-neutral and, therefore, not specifically targeted to the problems of black schoolchildren. One of the most significant racially neutral educational reform movements sweeping the country is increasing the educational choices of parents.

By choosing where to reside, parents exercise a tremendous amount of choice over what school their child attends. One of the major considerations in choosing where to live is the quality of the available schools. Families with financial means are able to leave a given school district by moving to another district. Due to this mobility, maintaining excellent schools is central to most affluent communities' appeal to those who can afford to live there and central to moderate-income communities' strategies to attract new tax-paying residents. In districts where people have the means to choose whether to leave or stay (i.e. the more affluent districts), the schools are predictably among the best. Thus, in terms of residential choice, the affluent parents of schoolchildren reap tremendous educational benefits for their children that comes from their considerable capacity to choose the school their children attend.

Under increased choice proposals all parents in a given school district, given school or schools in a given district, a given area of a given school district or below a particular income level are provided the limited opportunity to choose the school their child attends. Since choice is granted to parents with reference to a qualification unrelated to the race or ethnicity, it avoids the equal protection obstacle encountered by using racial classifications. But low-income parents of minority schoolchildren in urban areas are the ones who have the least capability to exercise the primary forms of school choice by moving into neighborhoods with good schools or by paying for private education. In theory, increasing racially neutral forms of school choice, therefore, should disproportionately advantage these parents and their children.

Although significant differences exist between public school choice and public funding of private education (i.e. school vouchers), both are born out of the same concerns. Advocates for increased choice generally assert that it will improve educational achievement in a number of ways. Increasing choice requires increasing the number and types of public or private schools. Increased choice also creates a competitive environment that forces schools to compete for students. As a result, increased school choice has the potential to produce new and innovative schools, including those that are particularly effective at responding to the educational needs of minority, low-income, urban school students. In a Darwinian competitive environment, schools that cannot demonstrate their ability to provide a good education will not survive. Increased school choice also reduces administrative burdens on educators. Educational decisions are driven increasingly down to the level of the individual school. This should allow educators to respond more effectively to the educational needs of students enrolled in their particular school.

These justifications explain why charter schools are one of the fastest growing forms of public school choice. Charter schools are public schools which are freed from many of the oversight procedures of normal public schools. Charter schools are intended to encourage experimentation, innovation and the development of alternative forms of education. Minnesota was the first state in the nation to pass charter school legislation in 1991.[77] As of January, 2003, there were nearly 2,700 charter schools operating in thirty-seven states with over 684,000 students enrolled.[78] Charter legislation will vary from state to state,[79] but it generally allows for private persons and institutions to develop and implement plans for a given school. Charter schools are considered public schools. They are, however, under less supervisory control by public educational officials and can often operate somewhat independently of public school authorities. Charter schools are intended to foster new approaches to education with innovative curriculum and instruction. The unique focus of charter schools forms the primary means of attracting parents and children to the school.

Another potential school choice option that looms on the educational horizon is public funding of private education or school vouchers. Currently, school vouchers are a relatively minor, but growing aspect of school choice. The attraction of public funding of private education has significantly increased, however, since the decision by the Supreme Court in the summer of 2002 in *Zelman v. Simmons-Harris.*[80] In *Zelman* the Court upheld a voucher program operated by Cleveland, Ohio against an establishment clause challenge. The law provided that low income students attending private schools could receive up to $2,250 for tuition. The maximum tuition voucher for other students was capped at $1,875. In the 1999–2000 school year, fifty-six private schools participated in the program. Forty-six (or 82%) of them were religiously affiliated. A General Accounting Office ("GAO") report of the program filed for the 1998–99 school year revealed that 70% of families with children participating in the program were headed by single mothers, with average family incomes of $18,750. A majority of the students who participated in the program, 73.4%, were minorities and 26.6% were white. The GAO Report also noted that approximately 3,400 voucher students were enrolled in private schools.[81]

Other than in Cleveland, at the time the Court upheld the voucher program in *Zelman,* only Milwaukee, Wisconsin and the state of Florida had recently adopted voucher programs in operation.[82] The Parental Choice Program in Milwaukee provided for school vouchers to students in the Milwaukee school district with family incomes below 175% of the poverty level. The vouchers were tied to the per pupil state aid or private school tuition, whichever was less. The value of the vouchers was $5,553 for the 2001–02 school year.[83] As of January 2002, there were 10,789 students participating in the program.[84] Florida was operating two voucher programs at the time of the Court's opinion in *Zelman.* The Opportunity Scholarships voucher program was passed by the Florida legislature in 1998. It allowed students who attended the lowest rated pubic schools in Florida to use state money to attend another public or private school. The amount of the voucher was tied to the state's share in the expenses of eligible students. For 2001–02, the average amount of the award was $3,500 to $3,900. As of the Fall 2001, only about 45 students attended private schools.[85] The second Florida program, the McKay Scholarship program, was serving only a few students in 2000–01 school year.[86] The McKay Scholarship program provides vouchers to special education students, to pay for private schooling. The amount of the vouchers varied from $4,500 to $21,000 depending upon the students and their particular disability.[87]

In April 2003, Colorado became the first state to pass a voucher program since the Court's decision in *Zelman.*[88] The Colorado voucher program seeks to provide up to $5,000 to students in kindergarten through 12th grade in districts with academic performance ratings of "low" or "unsatisfactory" on the Colorado School Accountability Report. To be eligible, however, the students must qualify for free or reduced-cost lunches. Initially about 3,500 students would be eligible under the program with as many as 20,000 eligible by the 2007–08 school year.[89] A voucher program has also recently been adopted for public school students in Washington D.C.[90] The plan provides for up to $7,500 for 2,000 low income students to fund private school education. Students attending schools identified as needing improvement or correction have priority. Since *Zelman,* Florida's McKay Scholarship program has expanded dramatically. This program went from serving only a few students in 2000–01 school year to an estimated 12,000 McKay Scholarships in the Fall of 2003.[91] Florida has also instituted a third voucher program that began in 2002.[92] This program is funded by state tax credits given to companies that donate money to nonprofit groups for scholarships for parents who meet income and other eligibility requirements. Companies can donate up to three-quarters of their state corporate-income taxes. About 20,000 students have applied for these tax-credit scholarships. The tax-credit scholarships provide the lesser of $3,500, or the total of the school's tuition, book and transportation costs.[93]

Zelman may not be the last word on the federal constitutionality of public funding of private school choice. But, for now, a well-crafted school voucher proposal can survive an establishment clause challenge brought under the First Amendment.[94] With regard to vouchers, however, *Zelman* is merely permissive. It removes a potential establishment clause objection to states that desire to provide school vouchers. But voucher programs may still be vulnerable to state constitutional challenges. Both the Cleveland and Milwaukee programs in operation at the time of the Court's decision in *Zelman* had to survive legal challenges brought under provisions of their respective state constitutions.[95] The Florida Opportunity Scholarship program initially survived a state constitutional challenge before the Supreme Court's opinion in *Zelman.* But on remand from the Florida Appeals Court, a Florida Circuit Court struck down this plan in August 2002 as violating the Florida constitution.[96] The state has appealed the ruling. The Circuit Court has allowed the program to operate until the appeal is resolved.[97] On June 28, 2004, the Colorado Supreme Court upheld a lower court ruling that struck down the Colorado voucher program. The high court concluded the program requires school districts to turn over a portion of locally raised funds to private schools, over which local school boards have no control. This violates the local-control provisions of the Colorado Constitution. Voucher supporters, however, are likely to introduce a new version of the legislation in the 2005 Legislature to conform to the ruling.[98]

Despite the claims that increased choice should lead to increased educational achievement, a consensus about such a result has not yet developed.[99] In order for diverse educational opportunities and a competitive environment for education to develop, a sufficient market for school choice must first be generated. Furthermore, the effects of increased choice may not be noticeable for a number of years after competitive market forces are in place. While charter schools currently exist, the charter school movement is only a dozen years old and considerably younger in many states. Although private schools have existed since the foundation of this country, one cannot easily compare the academic performance of private school students using school vouchers with their public school counterparts. The issue of bias in the determination of which former public school students use school vouchers to attend private schools or public schools of choice, like charter schools, has always been a problem in assessing the impact of choice on educational performance. Even if differences in income, parental education, neighborhood, hours spent studying and other relevant factors could be controlled for, selection bias would make comparisons between the academic performance of students in schools of choice as opposed to traditional public schools difficult. The students whose parents select charter schools or private schools funded with public funds are generally different from the ones whose parents do not. Families who are informed enough to select the school their child will attend have made a special effort that evinces their concern about their child's education and, more importantly, the wherewithal to advance that concern. A second form of selection bias is that operators of charter schools or private schools that accept school vouchers are likely to try to recruit the type of students that should do well in their educational programs. Thus, even if admission to the school is open to all, there is still likely to be biases in which students are recruited to attend a given charter school or private school accepting school vouchers. The existence of these biases makes it difficult to draw general conclusions about whether the better academic performance of students in charter schools or private schools is the result of the competitive environment created for the schools due to choice or the result of selection bias in the students who attend.

B. Post-Desegregation Awareness and the Four Discourses

The second interwoven objective of this book seeks to advance the discussion about racial issues, particularly those that involve African-American schoolchildren, by using the Post-Desegregation Awareness. This book will examine the desegregation of public education initiated by the Supreme Court's opinion in *Brown* through to the current educational situation of African-Americans that has spawned the educational reform movements focusing on increased school choice from four different discourses: Traditional Americanism, African-American Centralism, Colorblind Individualism and American Collectivism. Each of these patterns of understanding has its fundamental view of the social world, particular conception of moral and ethical behavior, understanding about the role of government and perspective on the role and treatment of African-Americans throughout American history. I have selected these four cognitive frameworks in order to capture the general cultural sense of the ways in which Americans think about racial issues. Thus, the ways in which each of these discourses perceives racial phenomena should be familiar to most Americans. We constantly encounter them when we discuss a range of racial issues involving African-Americans, including school desegregation, the academic performance of black students in public schools or the benefits of increasing school choice. While there is nothing intrinsic or inevitable about these four systems of meaning, I will stress throughout this book that Traditional Americanism for a long time dominated discussions regarding the determination of the legal rights (or lack thereof) of blacks through out much of American history. Over the past thirty years, however, the Supreme Court's equal protection jurisprudence has come to increasingly embrace Colorblind Individualism.

Historically the dominant beliefs in American society have not been the progressive individualist attitudes that began to emerge in the 1950s and 1960s. America's traditional culture ("Traditional Americanism")—traditional in the sense that its roots are deep in the history of American society—took for granted the conquest and extermination of the indigenous peoples found here, the exclusion and subordination of women, the repression of the immigrant European working class and the closeting of homosexuals. These beliefs were developed primarily from the perspective of able-bodied, Christian, Protestant, heterosexual, white males of Anglo-Saxon descent, having a degree of financial resources. When this traditional thinking was applied to people of African descent, blacks were considered to be members of a substandard racial group. Blacks were classified first as non-citizens and then as second-class citizens in North America for 300 years before the Court's decision in *Brown.* Within Traditional Americanism, non-Hispanic whites are conceptualized either as individuals or as a superior racial/ethnic group. The amalgamation of their actions, behaviors, attitudes, opinions and beliefs represents the implicit norm by which deviations are recognized. The salient feature of this cognitive framework, however, is its perception of blacks as "less than" the applicable norm. This discourse is always conscious of African-Americans, whether it is applied to the comprehension of blacks as individuals or as a group. For much of America's history the legal rights, or lack thereof, of African-Americans were determined based upon the embedded assumptions within this discourse. For example, the Supreme Court opinions in such infamous cases as *Dred Scott* and *Plessy v. Ferguson* relied on the presumptive inferiority of blacks as the basis of these decisions. Up until the 20th century, this system of meaning based the inferiority of blacks on either the Divine Will of God or the defective biology of a race of people having developed in the inhospitable climate of Africa. This belief made the oppression of blacks in the form of slavery, and later segregation, seem like these legally endorsed institutions were rational responses to the natural order of things. One of the manifestations of this belief before the *Brown* decision was the development and maintenance of legally separate and unequal public educational systems.

During the long struggle against racial oppression, African-Americans and those whites and others sympathetic to their cause, created a counter discourse to Traditional Americanism. The Africans who came to America were members of hundreds of different ethnic groups from thousands of different villages. In the American melting pot these diverse people were melded into one, African-Americans. Against the background of racial domination the descendants of the sons and daughters of the soil of Africa, along with others, formulated a counter discourse—"African-American Centralism"—to that of Traditional Americanism. This pattern of understanding provided an alternative explanation for the role and condition of blacks in American society. The fundamental focus behind this system of meaning was the desire to eradicate the racial domination of African-Americans. African-American Centralism sees the social world in terms of one major purpose, goal and objective—the liberation of black people from racial domination. Rather than viewing African-Americans as inferior as in Traditional Americanism, this pattern of understanding sees them as oppressed.

American culture has always had a strong belief in the sacredness of individual self-determination.[100] The essence of this pattern of understanding has been articulated with many variations by many thinkers. "Colorblind Individualism" is adequately summarized by Dr. Martin Luther King Jr.'s statement in his "I Have A Dream" speech that people be "judged not by the color of their skin, but the content of their character."[101] Colorblind Individualism views the social world as a collection of "Knowing Individuals." Knowing Individuals are viewed as autonomous, self-directed and free-willed people who know what they want in life and are capable of pursuing their self-determined goals and objectives.[102] They are capable of obtaining a self-reflective position separate from all of their beliefs, aims and attachments.[103] From this position, Knowing Individuals can assess and revise their beliefs, aims and attachments.[104] This capacity for self-reflection not only means that the attitudes, opinions and beliefs of Knowing Individuals are products of self-realization, but also that their objectives are self-formulated and their attachments in life are self-determined. The primary objective of this pattern of understanding is the advancement of individual self-determination. Much of the Supreme Court's explanation for the harm of racially motivated decision making by government over the past thirty years contained in the controlling opinions in cases like *Keyes v. School District No. 1*,[105] *Washington v. Davis*,[106] *Regents of the University of California v. Bakke*,[107] *Wygant v. Jackson Board of Education*,[108] *City of Richmond v. Croson*,[109] *Miller v. Johnson*,[110] *Adarand Constructors, Inc. v. Pena*,[111] *Gratz v. Bollinger*[112] and to a large extent *Grutter v. Bollinger*[113] rests upon the conception of the social world as a collection of Knowing Individuals.

The fourth and final cognitive framework, "American Collectivism," conceptualizes all citizens of the United States as constituting one group—American. Regardless of race, color, creed, national origin, gender, sexual orientation, condition of mental or physical disability, wealth, social status or education, Americans are united into one great people. The motto is accurately captured in the phrase "E Pluribus Unum"—out of many, one. The focus of this cognitive framework is furthering the collective interest of America. The primary goal, objective and concern is the best interest of the American collective. Within this discourse, the suffering of a portion of the American community is justified if it produces enough of a benefit for the entire community to outweigh that suffering. When attempting to determine what advances the best interest of American society, it is necessary to refer to the values that Americans hold sacred. Certain values have been at the core of American society from the founding of the nation. America has always valued liberty, equality, democracy and the pursuit of happiness. But the meanings of these fundamental American values change over time in response to both domestic and international developments. Each generation of Americans, therefore, has to define the meaning of these fundamental values to fit their current times. Thus, what is considered as advancing the best interest of American society is not necessarily the same from one generation of Americans to the next.

It is important to understand that these systems of meaning can and do structure the thoughts of any individual at any given place and time, including the reader's. Reverend Jesse Jackson, for instance, is reported to have said "[t]here is nothing more painful for me at this stage in my life than to walk down the street and hear footsteps and start to think about robbery and then look around and see it's somebody white and feel relieved. How humiliating."[114] In feeling a fear that blacks might be about to rob him, Jackson perceives African-Americans in terms of Traditional Americanism. Also, Justice Ginsburg firmly grounded her dissenting opinion in *Gratz v. Bollinger* in terms of what I have referred to as African-American Centralism. The fundamental desire of that discourse is the eradication of the continued oppression of African-Americans. In her opinion, Ginsburg states that "[a]ctions designed to burden groups long denied full citizenship stature are not sensibly ranked with measures taken to hasten the day when entrenched discrimination and its after effects have been extirpated."[115] Ginsburg goes on to quote Professor Stephen Carter,

> [T]o say that two centuries of struggle for the most basic of civil rights have been mostly about freedom from racial categorization rather than freedom from racial oppressio[n] is to trivialize the lives and deaths of those who have suffered under racism. To pretend... that the issue presented in *Regents of University of California v. Bakke,* was the same as the issue in *Brown v. Board of Education,* is to pretend that history never happened and that the present doesn't exist.[116]

In addition, the comprehension of racial phenomena by any one person is not limited to just one of these discourses at a given time. The human mind is far more flexible. Individuals can comprehend a given racial phenomena in more than one cognitive framework. In fact, the basic premise of this book is that our minds are capable of multiple comprehensions of any given racial phenomena.

Examining the statistics regarding the current condition of the African-American community noted above provides a quick example of how these different patterns of understanding produce alternative interpretations of the same racial phenomena. Traditional Americanism comprehends the continuing racial gap in the social statistics in terms of the inadequacy of blacks. Thus, the failure of a disproportionate number of African-Americans to earn a decent living, their poor performance in educational institutions, the propensity of black males to be involved in the criminal justice system and the failure of blacks to be more cognizant of their health concerns are understood as evidence of the continued existence of some defect in the being, biology and/or culture of African-Americans. Within the conceptual boundaries of African-American Centralism, the deficit condition revealed by the aforementioned socio-economic statistics is understood as evidence of the continued oppressive aspect of racial domination. The disproportionate numbers of blacks consigned to poverty, their lack of educational achievement, the disproportionate numbers of black males incarcerated and the poor health conditions of the black community are all understood as consequences of continued racial oppression. Colorblind Individualism would seek to minimize the focus on racial aspects of a given phenomena. People should be judged and understood as individuals and not as members of involuntary racial or ethnic groups. Colorblind Individualism would attribute as much of the differences in the socio-economic condition of blacks and non-Hispanic whites to non-racial factors such as age differences, differences in family structure, regional differences, educational differences and other considerations. Colorblind Individualism would interpret any racial differences remaining as of minimal importance because the real concerns are generally related to individuals, not to racial and ethnic groups. Group based statistics tell us nothing about the particular individual in a given situation being dealt with at any given time. Since American Collectivism is concerned with the best interest of the one American people, to focus on the parochial interest of a given group, like African-Americans, would miss the importance of the collective. Within the boundaries of this cognitive framework, the social statistics above must be interpreted within the larger context of what they mean for the best interest of the nation as a whole.

IV. Summary of the Following Chapters

This book is divided into three different Parts. Each of the four chapters in Part I will elaborate on one of the four discourses. Chapter One will develop Traditional Americanism. Chapter Two will explain African-American Centralism. Chapter Three will expound upon Colorblind Individualism. The final chapter in Part I, Chapter Four, will discuss American Collectivism. Each chapter in Part I will begin by discussing the view of the social world which each system of meaning is structured upon. This discussion of the conceptual structure will include discussions of the basic epistemology of each particular cognitive framework. Words commonly used to discuss racial issues like racism, racial oppression, racial discrimination and racial equality also draw their meaning from the basic structure of a given framework. These words will, therefore, have different meanings when they are understood against the conceptual background of these different cognitive frameworks. Each chapter will discuss the moral/ethical beliefs of each pattern of understanding. Since moral/ethical beliefs are derived from different views of the social world, what is considered moral/ethical behavior in one discourse could be condemned as immoral in another.

The majority of each of the first four chapters will present a version of the historical treatment of African-Americans as conceptualized by each particular pattern of understanding. The historical discussion is intended to set the stage for the discussion in Part II of the Supreme Court's decision in *Brown v. Board of Education* and the desegregation of public schools which it spawned. Thus, the historical treatment will include the time when Europeans first encountered Africans in the Fifteenth Century up to the time of the Court's decision in *Brown*.

The version of history in each cognitive framework will emphasize how the historical treatment of blacks was consistent with its general structure. Each version will be different, highlighting aspects of the history of the African-American experience that is highlighted within the conceptual boundaries of that particular discourse. Thus, Traditional Americanism's discussion of the historical experience of blacks will stress how the idea of blacks being "less than" was used throughout the African-American historical experience to justify their treatment as non-citizens during slavery and second-class citizens during segregation. Economic motivations played a significant part in the selection of blacks as the labor force to develop and cultivate the new world. But economic motivations alone can never suffice to provide the full explanation for institutions like slavery and segregation. People are motivated not just by material desires but also by psychological and spiritual longings. The historical discussion in Chapter One of Traditional Americanism will also discuss the religious, scientific and cultural justifications propounded throughout different historical eras to justify the view that blacks should be confined to the lowest level of society. African-American Centralism's historical discussion will emphasize the twin aspects of the experience of the black community—being subjected to various forms of racial oppression and struggling to overcome those forms of oppression. The historical experience of oppression and the concomitant struggle against it in Chapter Two begins on the coast of Africa where the African slaves first met their European purchasers. Blacks struggled against their oppression during the long years in which they were held in bondage in the United States, as well as, during segregation. Colorblind Individualism's treatment of history will focus on efforts to view blacks as Knowing Individuals. From the very beginning of colonization in North America, there was a nascent liberal religious tradition which viewed blacks as the sons and daughters of the first Adam. After the end of the Civil War, blacks were granted formal equality with regard to civil and political rights. But for the most part, the treatment of blacks as Knowing Individuals by Colorblind Individualism only occurred after the Supreme Court's opinion in *Brown v. Board of Education.* American Collectivism's version of history will emphasize how the treatment of blacks was consistent with a desire to advance the best interest of American society. At times the best interest of American society dictated favorable treatment of African-Americans. At other times the interest of blacks was sacrificed at the altar of the greater good for the country.

Part II consists of two chapters that address the rise of desegregation of public schools. The desegregation of public schools was largely created, directed and ultimately restricted and terminated by federal court interpretations of the equal protection clause. Chapter Five discusses the Supreme

Court's school desegregation jurisprudence that encouraged the desegregation of public schools. Chapter Five will start by discussing the four graduate and professional school decisions rendered by the Supreme Court between 1938 and 1950 before going on to discuss the Supreme Court's opinion in *Brown v. Board of Education.* While many states complied with the obligation to desegregate their public schools, the Court's opinion in *Brown* was met with massive resistance in many states of the former Confederacy. As a result, not much desegregation occurred in the Deep South during the first ten years after the *Brown* decision. Chapter Five will recount some of the resistance to school desegregation. The passage of the Civil Rights Act of 1964, however, had an important impact on school desegregation. One provision of the Civil Rights Act of 1964 authorized the Attorney General to intervene in or to initiate school desegregation lawsuits. With the enormous resources of the federal government being brought to bear on local school districts throughout the country, the pace of school desegregation litigation quickened. Another provision of the Civil Rights Act of 1964, Title VI, banned discrimination in all federally-aided programs. In order to be eligible for federal funds, public schools had to comply with regulations proscribing discrimination that were promulgated by the Department of Health, Education and Welfare. In its 1968 decision in *Green v. New Kent County*[117] the Supreme Court placed an obligation on school systems that had formerly operated a dual school system to desegregate and do it now. In discharging this duty, the Court demanded that school systems treat their students, teachers and administrators as members of racial groups in order to promote desegregation. Thus, the Court went beyond a race-neutral interpretation of *Brown* to compel the use of racial classifications by public schools. Three years later, the Court clarified the extent of the desegregation obligation it placed on school districts. In *Swann v. Charlotte Mecklenburg,*[118] the Court commanded school boards to achieve the greatest possible degree of actual desegregation. The Court also approved school busing as an appropriate tool to further that end. These developments set school desegregation in motion. The amount of desegregation in public schools increased significantly between 1964 and 1972. After the Court's opinion in *Swann,* however, the Court began a steady march away from its commitment to desegregate America's public schools. These decisions will be discussed in Chapter Seven of Part III.

One of the objectives of this book is to advance the discussion about racial issues involving African-American schoolchildren, by discussing those issues with a Post-Desegregation Awareness. Chapter Six will review the Supreme Court's school desegregation jurisprudence that encouraged the use of racial classifications in order to promote the desegregation of public schools through each of the four different cognitive frameworks—Traditional Americanism, African-American Centralism, Colorblind Individualism and American Collectivism—that are discussed more fully in Part I. As stated earlier, these discourses structure and limit the perception of given racial phenomena and the kinds of arguments that are considered persuasive in resolving a given racial conflict. However, these cognitive frameworks do not provide a definitive solution to a given racial conflict. Arguments could be made within each pattern of understanding for or against the use of racial classifications to further school desegregation. Since our society is celebrating, rather than lamenting, the Golden Anniversary of *Brown v. Board of Education,* Chapter Six will only present the type of arguments that would be generated within each of the four discourses which would argue for the use of racial classifications in order to promote desegregated education.

There are four chapters in Part III. Part III will sketch out how American society moved from the desegregation of public schools discussed in Part II to the current educational situation where one of the most significant educational reform movements is increasing school choice. The major premise of this Part is that the Supreme Court—and lower federal courts following its lead—changed the background assumptions for interpreting the equal protection clause to determine the rights of black schoolchildren. These changes have made increasing school choice one of the few strategies available for responding to the poor educational performance of black schoolchildren.

In explaining why the Supreme Court struck down the segregation statutes presented in *Brown v. Board of Education,* Chief Justice Warren noted that segregation had psychologically damaged black schoolchildren. Blacks could be made better by enriching their social environment, particularly the educational environment of the young. Born out of this belief was a special concern for the educational interest of black schoolchildren. If their educational environment could be ameliorated, they could be improved as a people. But beginning with its 1973 decision in *Keyes v. School District No. 1,*[119] the Court backed away from this interpretation of the equal protection clause and moved increasingly towards interpreting the equal protection rights of black schoolchildren based on treating all as individuals. The current underlying assumption for interpreting the equal protection clause is the notion that forms the core value and belief of Colorblind Individualism.

The effect of this shift on the current educational situation regarding African-Americans can not be overstated. Chapter Seven will discuss three trends over the last thirty years in the interpretation of the equal protection clause that constrained school desegregation, then halted and now is reversing the desegregation of public schools. The three trends are the waning of the Supreme Court's commitment to aggressively pursue integration in the 1970s; the impact of the termination of school desegregation decrees beginning in the 1990s; and lower federal court decisions striking down the use of racial and ethnic classifications to further integrated education starting in the mid 1990s. These three trends all reflect a shift in the cognitive framework against which the equal protection rights of black schoolchildren is interpreted within from Traditional Americanism to Colorblind Individualism. The effect of this shift has been that public schools for the past fifteen years have been resegregating. What is more, this resegregation is likely to continue for the foreseeable future. Chapter Eight extends the analysis of legal decisions interpreting the equal protection clause that was discussed in Chapter Seven to show that the same shift in background assumptions for interpreting the equal protection clause also occurred with regard to educational issues affecting black schoolchildren other than student school assignments.

Chapter Nine discusses why the expansion of school choice, both public and private, is one of the primary educational reform movements. There are three major considerations that are influencing the direction of public educational reforms for black schoolchildren. First, racial separation in public schools has been on the increase for the past fifteen years. Second, in almost all important indicia of academic achievement, African-American schoolchildren trail their non-Hispanic white counterparts. Third, the shift in the discourse for interpreting the equal protection clause has severely limited the ability of educators and politicians to employ racial classifications to attack the achievement gaps. Given the above three considerations, politicians and educational strategists desiring to reduce the racial academic achievement gaps are increasingly compelled to argue for policies and programs that are race neutral. The most obvious direction for responding to the educational situation of black schoolchildren in the Post-Desegregation Era will be to increase school choice. Increasing school choice is an obvious racially neutral educational reform that should disproportionately help black schoolchildren.

Chapter Ten concludes this part of the book by discussing the contemporary legal and educational situation of African-American schoolchildren in the Post-Desegregation Era. This contemporary situation is characterized by increasing public and private school choice against a background of resegregation of public schools. Consistent with the Post-Desegregation Awareness, however, this current situation will be viewed through each of the four different cognitive frameworks—Traditional Americanism, African-American Centralism, Colorblind Individualism and American Collectivism—that were discussed more fully in Part I.

Part I

The Four Discourses

With the passage of the Golden Anniversary of *Brown v. Board of Education*, we can reflect on perceptions about race in American society with the benefit of hindsight that comes both from being over fifty years removed from that historic day and from the realization that America has moved beyond the Desegregation Era. The Supreme Court's analysis in *Brown v. Board of Education* presumed that the physical facilities and other tangible factors of the public schools attended by black and white students were equal. Given the measurable equality of segregation in this context, the Court was forced to identify the harm resulting from segregation for the first time. In one of the most quoted phrases from *Brown*, the Court stated, "[t]o separate [African-American youth] from others of similar age and qualifications solely because of their race generates a feeling of inferiority as to their status in the community that may affect their hearts and minds in a way unlikely ever to be undone." The Court went on to quote approvingly from the district court in Kansas:

> Segregation of white and colored children in public schools has a detrimental effect upon the colored children. The impact is greater when it has the sanction of law; for the policy of separating the races is usually interpreted as denoting the inferiority of the negro group. A sense of inferiority affects the motivation of a child to learn. Segregation with the sanction of law, therefore, has a tendency to [retard] the educational and mental development of negro children....

In reading the Court's justification for striking down segregation with the cold reflection that comes fifty years after the opinion, the reality that the Court did not reject the fundamental belief in the inferiority of black people stands out. In its *de jure* segregation jurisprudence, the Supreme Court never repudiated the statements that the fundamental harm derived from segregation was the psychological damage to blacks. For example, in the 1968 decision in *Green v. New Kent County* the Court placed the burden upon school boards to affirmatively mix the races in public schools and do it now. In justifying this burden, the Court stated only that the constitutional rights of African-American schoolchildren noted in *Brown I* and *Brown II* required it. In the 1977 decision in *Milliken v. Bradley* (*Milliken II*) the Supreme Court approved the ordering of educational remedies to combat the effects of *de jure* segregated schools. In justifying these educational remedies the Court stated that

> [c]hildren who have been...educationally and culturally set apart from the larger community will inevitably acquire habits of speech, conduct, and attitudes reflecting their cultural isolation.... Pupil assignment alone does not automatically remedy the impact of previous, unlawful educational isolation; the consequences linger....

Thus, the Court's reasoning for approving educational remedies in *de jure* segregated schools rested upon the belief that racial isolation had damaged and would continue to damage only African-American children. The Court's second school desegregation termination opinion was delivered in the 1992 case of *Freeman v. Pitts.* In discussing the harm which remedies for the operation of a dual school system were directed at curing, Justice Kennedy's opinion for the Court quoted the above passages from *Brown,* which pointed to the psychological harm segregation inflicted on black children.

In a way, the Court's *Brown* opinion was consistent with a long line of Supreme Court cases interpreting the rights (or lack thereof) of African-Americans based on the assumption that in some way blacks were less than the requisite norm. This legal assumption justified both chattel slavery and segregation. But, when situated in a historical context, *Brown* was a fundamental break with the Supreme Court's jurisprudence that upheld slavery and "separate but equal" because it attributed the inferiority of blacks not to ontological causes, as had been done before, but to environmental ones. It was illogical to think of integrating public school students when the belief was that the abilities of African-Americans were largely fixed at birth and could not significantly improve through social engineering. However the view that the source of the "less than" nature of blacks results from environmental deficits was extraordinarily hopeful. If the black problem arose from a deficit social environment, then black people could be improved. The cure for their apparent substandard nature was to improve their social environment, especially that of black children.

While the legal system's resolution of a given social conflict is decisive in terms of determining legal rights and obligations, legal analysis does not produce the only valid understanding of a given social phenomena. One of the objectives of this book is to advance the discussion of racial issues, particularly those involving African-American schoolchildren, within the context of the Post-Desegregation Awareness. The Post-Desegregation Awareness is the conscious awareness that racial phenomena, like the Supreme Court's opinion in *Brown* and the school desegregation it generated, are not understood as separate isolated and unconnected incidents. Rather, as people we must comprehend the phenomena, including racial phenomena, that force themselves into our consciousness so as to make sense of the world. Despite the fact that understandings of separate phenomena ostensibly appear as detached and distinct occurrences, our appreciation of them is never in such isolation. To understand racial phenomena, like the Court's opinion in *Brown* and the school desegregation that it generated, we comprehend it against a *sub silentio* background of a much larger set of ideas regarding race and ethnicity which structure and limit our perception of a given racial phenomena. These larger diverse sets of ideas used to view given racial phenomena could be called perspectives or points of view, but in this book they will be referred to as the following: "discourses"; "patterns of understanding"; "systems of meaning"; or "cognitive frameworks."

Before discussing the Court's opinion in *Brown* and the school desegregation jurisprudence that it spawned with a Post-Desegregation Awareness, it is necessary to elaborate the four different discourses that will be used throughout this book. Each of the four chapters in this Part will elaborate on one of the four patterns of understanding—Traditional Americanism, African-American Centralism, Colorblind Individualism and American Collectivism. The discussion of these four cognitive frameworks is to capture a general sense of the ways in which Americans think about racial issues. Each of these discourses should be familiar to most Americans. They tend to represent the understandings that structure and limit much of the discussion of racial issues in American society. There is nothing intrinsic or inevitable about the four systems of meaning discussed in this Part I. But it must be stressed that Traditional Americanism for a long time dominated discussions about racial issues for purpose of determining the legal rights (or lack thereof) of blacks throughout much of American history. Over the past thirty years, however, the Supreme Court's equal protection jurisprudence has come to increasingly embrace Colorblind Individualism.

Each system of meaning has its own epistemology and provides its own mode of rationality, but that rationality operates only within the conceptual boundaries of the given cognitive framework. The definition of words that deal with interpretation of racial phenomena such as racism, racial oppression, racial discrimination and racial equality have different meanings within each of the respective patterns of understandings. Because each pattern of understanding is structured around different conceptions of the social world, it has different embedded values, beliefs and judgments for the same racial issue. Different views of the social world also produce different moral and ethical beliefs to govern interactions that people have with one another. These cognitive frameworks will also ascribe different roles and functions to government. After discussing the general outline of each of the different discourses, each of the following four chapters then presents a view of the historical treatment of the descendants of Africa in America up till the Supreme Court's school desegregation jurisprudence. Presenting America's racial history through four different systems of meaning also demonstrates how the same racial phenomena can be understood in radically different ways.

It is important to understand that these system of meaning can and do structure the thoughts of any discrete individual, including the reader's, at any given place and time. In addition, the comprehension of racial phenomena by any one person is not limited to just one of these discourses at a given time. The human mind is far more flexible than that. Individuals can comprehended a given racial phenomena in more than one cognitive framework. Thus, our minds are certainly capable of multiple apprehensions of racial phenomena.

Chapter One

The Discourse of Traditional Americanism

Historically the dominant beliefs in American society regarding racial or ethnic members of minority groups have not been the progressive individualist/liberal attitudes that began to emerge in the 1950s and 1960s. The dominant American beliefs about blacks, which their legal rights (or lack thereof) historically were constructed upon, was the belief in their ontological inferiority. From before the time the first blacks landed in Jamestown, Virginia, in 1619, until 1954, blacks were viewed as substandard beings. It was this belief that made the oppression of blacks in the form of slavery, and later segregation, seem as if these legally endorsed institutions were rational responses to the natural order. One aspect of this belief about African-Americans before *Brown* was the development and maintenance of separate and unequal public educational systems.

Within Traditional Americanism, black people are perceived as poor, lazy, lustful, ignorant and prone to aggressive and criminal behavior. Therefore, being classified as an African-American in Traditional Americanism results in the behaviors and actions of black individuals persistently being perceived in negative terms. One of the most significant signs of change in American society wrought by the Desegregation Era is that the discourse of Traditional Americanism is normally not explicitly used in public conversations regarding African-Americans. Thus, the expression of ideas about African-Americans within this pattern of understanding in an open and frank manner is somewhat incongruous in today's atmosphere of "political correctness." Traditional Americanism still provides an explanation of racial phenomena, but it functions more in very private conversations that are not normally aired for public consumption. It is also important to understand that Traditional Americanism also functions in terms of unarticulated or unconscious explanations of racial phenomena.

Despite the social and economic progress of African-Americans over the past fifty years, Americans continue to live in a country where racial inequality is the norm. This current inequality in the socio-economic condition of

African-Americans does not have to be traced to inherent flaws in the being, biology or culture of blacks as it was in the past. It can be attributed to socio-historical factors for which blacks should not be blamed. But African-Americans, as a social group, are materially worse off than their non-Hispanic white counterparts in almost every observable aspect. Statistics reveal that African-Americans score lower on standardized tests and do not obtain the same degree of educational success as non-Hispanic whites (proxies for intelligence). African-Americans earn less money and are more likely than non-Hispanic whites to be unemployed or live below the poverty line (proxies for indolence). And African-Americans constitute a much larger percentage of the prison population than the general population (proxies for tendencies toward violence and criminal behavior). Therefore, people who at times make negative judgments about individual African-Americans can, to a certain degree, rationalize those judgments by referring to "the facts." Thus, negative judgements of individual African-Americans may not appear to be rooted in irrational stereotyping, but appear to be rational judgments based on objective evidence detailing the social conditions of blacks.

Traditional Americanism, like all systems of meaning, can structure the thoughts of any discrete individual. Thus, thoughts of persons of any race, whether they are black, brown, red, yellow or white, can conceptualize racial phenomena within this horizon of knowledge.[1] Jesse Jackson, for example, is reported to have said, "[t]here is nothing more painful for me at this stage in my life than to walk down the street and hear footsteps and start to think about robbery and then look around and see it's somebody white and feel relieved."[2] Despite being a champion for the rights of blacks, at the moment when Jackson has this feeling he is unwittingly comprehending African-Americans in terms of Traditional Americanism. But when blacks are so comprehended, the sense of relief at discovering that the footsteps one hears is from a white person is understandable within this system of meaning.

Section I of this Chapter starts by describing the general structure of the discourse of Traditional Americanism. Section II discusses how this pattern of understanding was used throughout the African-American historical experience in America—until the Supreme Court's decision in *Brown v. Board of Education*—to justify the treatment of blacks as non-citizens during slavery and second-class citizens during segregation. The historical analysis begins with the Antebellum Period (which includes the colonial period to the Civil War), progresses to the era of the Civil War and Reconstruction and concludes with the period of disenfranchisement and the institution of separate but equal. Economic motivations played a significant part in the selection of blacks as the labor force to develop and cultivate the New World. But economic motivations alone can never suffice to provide full explanations of institutions like slavery and segregation. Section III will discuss the religious, scientific and cultural justifications propounded throughout history to justify the view that blacks constitute a substandard racial group whose natural position is at the lowest level of society.

I. The Conceptual Structure

For centuries, ministers, theologians, philosophers, scientists, academics, political leaders, judges, business people and media moguls developed and disseminated messages about the "less than" nature of black people. This belief has justified treatment by government and private entities that has consistently placed blacks at the lowest levels of American society. This section discusses the general structure of Traditional Americanism. It will begin by discussing the view of the social world upon which this system of meaning is structured and its embedded epistemology. The fundamental belief of Traditional Americanism is that blacks in some relevant way do not measure up to the specified or unspecified norm. This section will then discuss the moral beliefs derived from this system of meaning regarding how blacks should be treated. Next, the role of government will be discussed. When government performs its assigned functions, it should take account of the substandard nature of blacks. The last part of this section will contrast Traditional Americanism with the other three systems of meaning to demonstrate how this system of meaning will consistently interpret racial phenomena in different ways from the others.

A. Conception of the Social World

This pattern of understanding is not always conscious of the race of non-Hispanic whites as a group or as individuals. Thus, non-Hispanic whites can be conceptualized as individuals without regard to their race or as a superior racial/ethnic group. But, the amalgamation of their characteristics, traits, actions, behaviors, attitudes, opinions or beliefs constitutes the explicit or implicit norms from which deviations that require an explanation are recognized. The salient feature and abiding aspect of this cognitive framework when perceiving racial phenomena involving African-Americans, however, is its perception of blacks as less than the applicable norm.

From an epistemological standpoint, the race of blacks is always a part of the conceptualization of racial phenomena. Thus, this discourse is always conscious of the race of African-Americans, whether as individuals or as a racial group. The "less than" nature of blacks is also understood as infecting the institutions which they control and inhabit. For example, a predominately black elementary or secondary school, or college or university is generally considered an inferior educational institution. A predominately black neighborhood is generally considered a less desirable place to live, with lower property values than those in comparable neighborhoods.[3] The products made by a black person are thought to be of lesser quality, and the services rendered by a black person are thought to be performed with less skill and expertise.

B. Moral and Ethical Beliefs

Just because blacks are regarded as substandard beings does not mean that they should be treated with contempt or animosity. While the belief that the "less than" nature of blacks justifies oppressive structures such as slavery and segregation, at other times it justifies paternalistic attitudes and behaviors toward blacks aimed at helping them overcome their deficiencies. As Rudyard Kipling described in a poem written in 1899, *The White Man's Burden,* the superior races have an obligation to help the inferior races to the extent possible.[4] Thus, it is appropriate to confine inferior groups to their accustomed position in the social order, but it is also appropriate to treat blacks with paternalistic compassion and provide them with the assistance and guidance they are presumed to lack.

C. The Role of Government and Society

Within this cognitive framework, when government performs its assigned functions it should take into account the built in limitations of blacks. There is a long history of governmental action based on that premise. Until the Civil War, governments in states in which slavery was permitted incorporated the institution into their governing legal codes. As slaves, blacks were not only denied their personal liberty, but were also denied even basic legal rights. They could not sue nor be sued; testify in court; buy, sell, lease or rent property; enter into contracts; exercise the franchise; or hold political office. State militias and federal government troops were used to suppress slave insurrections. Runaway slaves were returned to their masters when caught by peace officers.

After the Civil War, three Amendments, the Thirteenth, Fourteenth and Fifteenth (the "Reconstruction Amendments"), were added to the Constitution. The Thirteenth Amendment formally abolished slavery. The Fourteenth Amendment granted African-Americans citizenship; prohibited the states from interfering with the privileges and immunities of citizens of the United States; proscribed states from depriving anyone of life, liberty and property without due process; and guaranteed to all the right to equal protection of the laws. The Fifteenth Amendment made it unconstitutional to deny the right to vote because of race, color or previous condition of servitude. In the 1873 decision by the Supreme Court in the *Slaughterhouse Cases,* the Court articulated the purpose of the Reconstruction Amendments:

> The one pervading purpose found in them all, lying at the foundation of each, and without which none of them would have been even suggested...was the freedom of the former slave race, the security and firm establishment of that freedom and the protection of the newly-made [freedmen] and [citizens] from the oppressions of those who had...exercised...dominion over [them].[5]

The Reconstruction Amendments not only abolished slavery, but granted blacks certain civil and political rights. Yet, not long after the Reconstruction Amendments were ratified, government policies and practices were employed to disenfranchise and segregate blacks. Due to the constitutional protections which prevented discrimination based on race, color or previous condition of servitude, schemes employed to disenfranchise African-Americans were required to be thinly veiled in racially neutral terms. One important method was the poll tax. Since blacks left slavery as illiterate, landless, penniless peasants, few of them could afford the payment of a tax as a prerequisite to being eligible to vote. Mandating literacy requirements also proved to be an effective means in which to disenfranchise black male voters. Voting registrars responsible for certifying voters would refuse to certify black males. For purposes of determining constitutional violations, their refusal was not based on race, but the racially neutral criteria that the black person seeking to register failed to demonstrate an ability to read or understand the political process. Nevertheless, excluding blacks from the political process was viewed as elevating the electorate and, thus, providing for better political decisions.

While the Reconstruction Amendments were viewed as granting civil and political equality to blacks, these Amendments were viewed as non-applicable to social rights. Social rights were distinguishable from civil and political rights. Where civil and political rights were asserted against government, social rights were asserted against fellow citizens. Thus, denying a black person the right to sit on a jury involved an infringement on his civil right. But governmental laws requiring segregation on railway cars, omnibuses, stagecoaches, steamboats, waiting rooms, restrooms, lecture halls, theaters and schools involved social rights. The justification for social segregation was based upon a realization that even if under the Reconstruction Amendments blacks were entitled to civil and political equality, that did not require social equality. As the Court stated in *Plessy v. Ferguson*, "if one race be inferior to the other socially, the constitution of the Untied States can not put them on the same plane."[6] Thus, segregation policies and practices instituted by government were normally understood as reasonable regulations of social rights that recognized the second-rate nature of blacks.

D. Contrasted with Other Systems of Meaning

Traditional Americanism and African-American Centralism generally have an antithetical relationship. There are two fundamental differences between the discourse of Traditional Americanism and African-American Centralism. While both cognitive frameworks consciously focus on the race of African-Americans, Traditional Americanism conceptualizes blacks as inferior. African-American Centralism, however, sees blacks as oppressed, not inferior. For example, both discourses readily recognize the deficit condition of the black community revealed by comparative social statistics between non-Hispanic whites and African-Americans in per capita income, employment, education and life expectancy. But these discourses derive the cause of the deficit conditions from different explanations. Traditional Americanism ascribes the source of the deficit conditions of the black community to some defect in African-Americans. African-American Centralism ascribes the source of the deficit conditions to some form of racism or racial discrimination. The second enduring difference concerns the perception of non-Hispanic whites. Traditional Americanism is sometimes conscious of the race of non-Hispanic whites and sometimes it is not. But African-American Centralism perceives the social world as a collection of racial and ethnic groups. Thus, it is always conscious of the race of non-Hispanic whites.

Colorblind Individualism views people primarily as individuals and does not attach any particular importance to their skin color. For Colorblind Individualism, the race of blacks is not relevant information. Thus, where Traditional Americanism would perceive a black person, Colorblind Individualism would perceive a person who happens to be black. For Colorblind Individualism, the use of black is as an adjective to describe a purely physical trait, but does not carry any useful information about that person's personality traits or characteristics. In discussions about a given racial issue, however, sometimes the position of Traditional Americanism can be advanced through arguments embracing Colorblind Individualism. In some situations keeping blacks "in their place" is accomplished almost as effectively by treating them as individuals—

and thus ignoring the impact that race has—as by consciously discriminating against them. For example, absent some other policy change, the elimination of affirmative action in selective college, university and graduate admissions programs always results in a significant reduction in the number of blacks who gain admission to selective institutions of higher learning. The results achieved by such "racially neutral" decision making could be similar to those achieved by a strict prohibition against the admittance of blacks altogether. But, at other times the effect of treating blacks as individuals undermines the idea that blacks should be kept at the bottom of the social order. Colorblind Individualism rejects race conscious discriminatory policies and practices which would include those maintained during slavery and segregation.

American Collectivism views all Americans regardless of race or ethnicity as comprising one people. When American Collectivism considers the situation of African-Americans, it is in a larger analysis of the interest of the entire American people. From the conceptual boundaries of Traditional Americanism, American Collectivism—like Colorblind Individualism—also swings a double edged sword. Sometimes advancing the interest of the nation will justify measures that maintain black people at the bottom of the social hierarchy. For example, the Founding Fathers accepted slavery in order to form "a more perfect union." But sometimes the national interest dictates ameliorative programs for black people. For example, President Abraham Lincoln executed the Emancipation Proclamation motivated by a desire to win the war against the Confederacy. Lincoln made it clear that his purpose was not to help nor hurt the slaves, but to save the Union.[7] Nevertheless, abolition proved to be a tremendous benefit to blacks.

II. History Blacks in America and the Legal System's Treatment of Them

The belief in the substandard nature of blacks predates the landing of the first Africans in British America at Jamestown, Virginia, in 1619. The Portuguese and the Spanish had been taking Africans out of Africa for 175 years before the first recorded landing of them in Virginia. Virtually since the first contact of Europeans with Africans in the Fifteenth Century, Europeans' (and then later Americans') dominant perceptions about blacks was that they were "less than" whites. It was thought in European countries and the British colonies that Africans came from a place where their history was largely the unrewarding gyrations of barbarous tribes in picturesque but, heretofore, irrelevant places of the earth.

This section discusses how this discourse was used from the Colonial Period up to the Supreme Court's school desegregation jurisprudence to justify the rights (or lack thereof) of blacks. This historical analysis starts with the Colonial Period, beginning with first contact by the Europeans with Africans on the west coast in the Fifteenth Century. It will then proceed to discuss the Antebellum Period. Then the discussion moves to the Civil War and the era of Reconstruction. It will then end with a discussion of the disenfranchisement of black male voters and the institution of "separate but equal" at the end of the Nineteenth and beginning of the Twentieth centuries.

A. The Colonial Period

The first major cargo of blacks to reach European shores directly from Africa arrived in Lagos, Portugal in 1444. Prince Henry the Navigator was among those present to observe the novel spectacle of the unloading of 235 slaves ranging from white Muslims to mulattoes to black Africans. One-fifth of the slaves were given to Prince Henry, who gave thanks for "saving so many new souls for God."[8]

Soon after Columbus's voyages of discovery, the Spanish experienced the need for an increasing labor force in the New World in order to mine silver and gold, plant spices and sugar and raise hides. While a few European slaves and indentured servants were sent to America by the Spanish, their numbers were inadequate to meet the labor needs. Early efforts to enslave enough of the native population to meet the labor demands generally proved unsuccessful. The first indigenous people that the Spanish—and later the Portuguese—attempted to enslave tended to come from hunter/gatherer civilizations. They did not adapt well to the rigors of repetitive, arduous and continuous work. In addition, diseases brought by the Europeans for which the indigenous people had no immunities devastated their population. The first major smallpox epidemic occurred only twenty-six years after Columbus first landed in the New World. This led the Spanish to start importing Africans. By as early as 1510 the Spanish concluded that the Africans were better workers and more likely to survive captivity than the natives.

The first successful colony planted in North America by the English was at Jamestown, Virginia in 1607. John Rolfe's casual reference to the arrival of black slaves in Jamestown, Virginia twelve years later is generally regarded as the first time Africans were imported into British North America.[9] The Norfolk-born first recorder of the Virginia Colony, wrote "About the last of August, came in a dutch man of warre that sold us twenty Negars. . . ."[10]

Throughout much of the seventeenth century, American landlords and planters preferred white European indentured labor to that of blacks. During the first hundred years of colonization "some 400,000 English left for the New World."[11] By the beginning of the eighteenth century, however, the availability of indentured servant supplies—those who were willing or who could be forced to come and work in America—proved insufficient.[12] Like the Portuguese and Spanish, the early English settlers also attempted to supply their additional labor needs by enslaving the native population. These efforts also proved unsuccessful.

The Africans first brought to British America were treated as indentured servants or apprentices for life. Their children were considered to be free. In 1661, however, Virginia became the first colony to provide by law for perpetual servitude of blacks.[13] Maryland joined Virginia's lead two years later, New York did so in 1706, and the rest of the other colonies followed suit thereafter.

B. The Antebellum Period

By the time the architects of the Constitution met in Philadelphia in 1787, blacks had been in North America for almost 170 years and Europeans had been taking Africans out of what they called the "Dark Continent" for over 340 years. The acceptance of slavery as an institution in the Constitution and recognition of the substandard nature of those who were enslaved was a foregone conclusion. At the heart of the Constitution was the protection of property and wealth. Nearly 20% of the population, almost one out of every five persons, was owned by another. Ownership of slaves constituted an important form of property, a tremendous amount of wealth and generated a significant portion of the income for many citizens of the new nation. A government constituted in part to protect property could not, consistent with that purpose, deprive so many of their most valuable assets. Not one of the fifty-five delegates present at the Constitutional Convention seriously advocated for the abolition of slavery.[14] But the issue of slavery intruded on many debates conducted by the delegates. Even though the term 'slave' or 'slavery' was artfully left out of the Constitution, at least seven provisions addressing slavery were included in the basic document that provided for the structure of American government.[15]

In discussing the condition of blacks during the Antebellum period, a significant factor to note is that throughout this period blacks were concentrated in the South. At the time of the Constitutional Convention over 93% of the slaves resided in the five southernmost states of Virginia, North Carolina,

South Carolina, Georgia and Maryland;[16] and on the eve of the Civil War 91% of blacks resided in the states that legalized slavery.[17] The Atlanta *Daily Intelligencer* captured the spirit of the southern perspective on the view of blacks during the Antebellum period.

> We can't see for the life of us how anyone understanding fully the great principle that underlies our system of involuntary servitude, can discover any monstrosity in subjecting a Negro to slavery of a white man. We contend on the contrary that the monstrosity, or, at least, the unnaturalness in this matter, consists in finding Negroes anywhere in white communities not under the control of the whites.[18]

Laws in slaveholding states supported the institution of slavery. The slave codes of the Antebellum South reflected the legal conclusion that slaves were property not persons. Thus, killing a slave was not considered murder, and rape of a female slave was only considered trespassing against her owner's property interest. Slaves were forbidden to leave the plantation without permission. Slaves suffered from a number of legal disabilities. Neither the oath nor the word of a slave was considered binding. Black slaves were generally forbidden from testifying in court, entering into contracts or owning property.

Though slaves were seldom able to challenge their confinement through frontal wars of liberation, the possibility of slave rebellions was an ever-present reality. The laws typically forbade blacks from congregating in large groups without white supervision, forbid them from carrying weapons and prevented them from striking a white person. South Carolina and Georgia passed acts that made it treason to aid a slave revolt. Slave patrols were set up to apprehend slaves out of place and return them to their masters or send them to jail. In addition, patrols would also visit the slave quarters periodically to ensure there were no weapons there. Virginia, Maryland, Georgia and North Carolina limited the nighttime religious meetings of blacks for fear that those meetings would be used to foment rebellion.[19]

Free blacks presented special problems in slaveholding states. Special laws were adopted to both restrict the rights and numbers of free blacks. Laws were enacted to make manumission difficult. To ensure that free blacks were denied the ability to elevate their social standing, states passed laws to prevent them from owning arms, participating in militia exercises and having sexual relations with whites.[20]

The most authoritative legal decision authored by the Supreme Court expressing the constitutional view of blacks and their rights during the antebellum period was Chief Justice Taney's 1857 opinion in *Dred Scott v. Sandford.*[21] In concluding that the slave and would-be free man, Dred Scott, could not sue in federal court to obtain his freedom, Chief Justice Taney found that people of African descent (slave or free) were not considered citizens within the definition of the Constitution. As a result, the federal courts were closed to them. In examining the beliefs of the Founding Fathers to determine if they considered any blacks to be capable of being a citizen of the United States, Taney wrote:

> [Blacks] had for more than a century before [the Declaration of Independence] been regarded as beings of an inferior order, and altogether unfit to associate with the white race, either in social or political relations; and so far inferior, that they had no rights which the white man was bound to respect....[22]

Taney went on to state in this opinion that blacks had been stigmatized with "deep and enduring marks of inferiority and degradation."[23]

Though blacks were not slaves in the North during most of the antebellum period, the dominant beliefs about them there were also structured around an acceptance of their second-rate nature. Blacks were locked into the bottom of the racial caste system by custom, if not by explicit law. Blacks were systematically separated from whites or excluded from railway cars, omnibuses, stagecoaches and steamboats.[24] They were segregated into secluded and remote corners of theaters and lecture halls; they could not enter most hotels, restaurants and resorts, except as servants; they prayed in separate pews; and partook of the sacrament of the Eucharist after whites. They were segregated in housing, schools, hospitals and cemeteries. Boston, Cincinnati, New York and Philadelphia had their segregated ghettoes. Indiana, Illinois and Oregon incorporated in their respective state constitutions provisions restricting the admittance of Negroes into their states. Free blacks could not testify as witnesses against whites in court, were excluded from jury service and could not become government officials.

Free blacks were also generally denied political equality in the North and border states. They were disenfranchised in Delaware in 1792, in Kentucky, Maryland and Ohio in 1799 and in New Jersey in 1807. Between 1814 and 1860, free blacks in Connecticut, New York, Iowa, Wisconsin, Minnesota, Pennsylvania, Indiana, Illinois and Michigan had the vote taken away from them altogether; denied to them as new states were incorporated into the Union; or had their exercise of the franchise severely restricted. By the eve of the Civil War only 6% of the African-Americans in the North lived in the five northernmost states—Massachusetts, New Hampshire, Vermont, Maine and Rhode Island— which allowed them to vote on equal terms with whites.[25]

There were always those Americans who saw slavery as the "great and foul stain," a canker which corrodes the moral and political will of the nation.[26] But even in the abolition movements in the North, the belief in the inferiority of the descendants of Africa was an accepted aspect of their policies. Many of those who believed that slavery was wrong, nevertheless, accepted the reality that blacks were incapable of being assimilated politically, socially or physically into white society. For example, Judge Samuel Sewall wrote a highly regarded pamphlet entitled, *The Selling of Joseph,* in 1700, which made the first reasoned critique of the slave trade and slavery itself. Despite criticizing slavery in his pamphlet, Sewall made it clear that "Blackamores" (as he called the Africans) seldom use their freedom well and they can never embody with whites and grow up into orderly families to help people the land.[27] Even the "Great Emancipator" Abraham Lincoln deeply believed in the inferiority of the black race. For example, Lincoln expressed this belief during his senatorial debates with Stephen A. Douglas in 1858.

> I will say, then, that I am not, nor ever have been, in favor of bringing about in any way the social and political equality of white and black races; that I am not, nor ever have been, in favor of making voters or jurors of negroes, nor of qualifying them to hold office, nor to intermarry with white people; and I will say, in addition to this, that there is a physical difference between the black and white races which I believe will forever forbid the two races living together on terms of social and political equality. And inasmuch as they cannot so live, while they do remain together there must be the position of superior and inferior, and I as much as any other man am in favor of having the superior position assigned to the white race.[28]

Many, if not most, who worked for the abolition of slavery viewed the institution of slavery more in terms of its detriment to the interest of whites, rather than blacks.[29] Many argued that slavery tended to bring out the baser elements of the nature of the slave-master. It was asserted that the domination of one person over another is fundamentally uncivilized. Such arbitrary power intoxicates the mind and corrupts the spirit of the slave master. Another argument against slavery was that it deprived whites of the enterprising spirit necessary to become productive. In the Antebellum South the idea of hard work and labor became associated with blacks. Thus, the concept of hard work was degraded and idleness spread among the white community. Idleness was thought to be the parent of vice and dissipation.

Slavery also proved to be inconsistent with free white labor. As early as 1716, a Quaker tract written in Massachusetts argued that the slave trade adversely affected white immigration.[30] White immigrants to the country would avoid the areas where black slavery dominated. They felt that their best chance for an improved life was in going to parts of the country not populated by the blacks. Slavery also negatively impacted the procreation rate of whites and positively contributed to the procreation rate of blacks. Daniel Raymond noted in a pamphlet printed in 1819 that the white population in the South did not increase as fast as that in the North. He also noted that free blacks have a lower birth rate than blacks who are in slavery. A slave population increases faster by procreation than the white population of a slave state and the white population of a non-slaveholding state increases faster than the white population in a slaveholding state.[31] Over time slavery leads to a reduction in the percentage of whites in a state and an increase in the percentage of blacks. Similarly, in the proportion that the slave population is decreased, the white population is increased. Since slavery was inconsistent with free white labor, the settlers of new areas of the country were presented with a choice. Either these newly settled areas would be populated primarily by free whites or black slaves.

Alexis de Tocqueville accurately described the effects of slavery that led so many to argue for abolition in his book, *Democracy in America,* published in 1844.

> As time went on, the Anglo-Americans left the Atlantic coast and plunged daily farther into the solitudes of the West.... [I]n all these circumstances the same fact stood out time and again: in general, the colony that had no slaves was more populous and prosperous than the one where slavery was in force.
>
> The farther they went, the clearer it became that slavery, so cruel to the slave, was fatal to the master.
>
> But the banks of the Ohio provided the final demonstration of this truth. . . .
>
> So the traveler who lets the current carry him down the Ohio till it joins the Mississippi sails, so to say, between freedom and slavery; and he has only to glance around him to see instantly which is best for mankind.
>
> On the left bank of the river the population is sparse; from time to time one sees a troop of slaves loitering through half-deserted fields; the primeval forest is constantly reappearing; one might say that society had gone to sleep; it is nature that seems active and alive, whereas man is idle.
>
> But on the right bank a confused hum proclaims from afar that men are busily at work; fine crops cover the fields; elegant dwellings

> testify to the taste and industry of the workers; on all sides there is evidence of comfort; man appears rich and contented; he works.[32]

As could therefore be expected, many abolitionists believed that freeing the slaves had to be accompanied by their emigration. In 1777 a Virginia legislative committee headed by Thomas Jefferson put forth a plan of gradual emancipation and deportation of the freed blacks. Several abolition organizations, such as the Connecticut Emancipation Society, had as one of their principal goals the colonization of the free negroes. In 1817, Henry Clay, Andrew Jackson and other slave holders met in Washington D.C. and founded the American Colonization Society. Some in the movement felt that African colonization would be the means of encouraging slave holders to free their slaves. This organization made plans to establish a colony of blacks in Africa with the aid of federal and state governments and to educate the public on the sagacity of emigration of the black race. By 1832 more than a dozen legislatures including slaveholding states of Maryland, Kentucky and Virginia gave approval to the Society. At first only free blacks were transported to Africa, but after 1827 some slaves were freed for the purpose of being taken to Liberia. By 1830 over 1,400 blacks had been resettled in this African colony. Over the life of the organization, the Society "repatriated" about 12,000 blacks.[33]

Even President Lincoln entertained hopes of the emigration of blacks up to the eve of signing the Emancipation Proclamation. Shortly before announcing his intention to issue the Emancipation Proclamation, Lincoln invited a group of prominent free blacks to the White House and urged them to support colonization. He told them that "Your race suffer greatly, many of them, by living among us, while ours suffer from your presence. In a word we suffer on each side. If this is admitted, it affords a reason why we should be separated."[34] In December 1862 Lincoln "signed an agreement with an entrepreneur of dubious character" who agreed to resettle 5,000 blacks on an island near Haiti.[35] Just days before issuing the Emancipation Proclamation, Lincoln proposed three constitutional amendments that called for gradual, voluntary emancipation culminating no later than the year 1900 and providing assistance to help colonize the freed slaves.

C. The Civil War and Reconstruction Era

While there were abolitionist movements and those who sought to restrict the spread of slavery, slavery was firmly rooted on American soil during the antebellum period. It took a national crisis of the magnitude that threatened the disintegration of the Union to terminate slavery. Such a crisis developed after the elections of 1860. Abraham Lincoln, though opposed to the institution of slavery, came into the Presidency emphasizing that he only wished to prevent its expansion. In an effort to avert the Civil War or the dissolution of the Union, in early 1861 Lincoln proposed a constitutional amendment, which was approved by both houses of Congress, to make slavery permanent in the existing southern states.[36] This effort, however, proved to be too little, too late to avoid secession. When President-Elect Lincoln arrived in Washington D.C. in late February of 1861, seven states had already seceded from the Union. Hostilities in the Civil War began with firing on Fort Sumter in April, 1861. Though Fort Sumter was captured by the rebels, defending the Fort cost the Union four more slaveholding states.

The belief in the inferiority of blacks affected the Union's effort to wage war against the rebellion. It was the desire to preserve the Union that provided the North with its initial reason to wage war against its southern neighbors. Lincoln and Congress were very clear that their initial aims and objectives for the war were to restore the Union as it had been, that is one which protected the institution of slavery. The position that the war was not being fought by the Union to eliminate slavery was also consistent with the initial theory which the Union government used to justify the war. Since secession was seen as illegal, the Confederate states were still legally in the Union, though under the temporary control of insurrectionists.[37] As a result Lincoln and the Union government were still bound by the constitutional guarantee that protected the institution of slavery. As W. E. B. Du Bois noted:

> To the Northern masses the Negro was a curiosity, a sub-human minstrel, willingly and naturally a slave, and treated as well as he deserved to be. He had not sense enough to revolt and help Northern armies, even if Northern armies were trying to emancipate him, which they were not. . . Negroes on the whole were considered cowards and inferior beings whose very presence in America was unfortunate.[38]

The negative beliefs about blacks in the North goes a long way to explain why Lincoln did not support arming African-Americans until 1863, almost two years after the surrender of Fort Sumter. Lincoln feared—as did many in the North—that if the Union sought to use armed blacks in combat, they would simply drop their guns, flee the battlefield and their weapons would be in Confederate hands in a few weeks.[39]

As the Civil War dragged on, conditions regarding abolition changed. It became readily apparent that the North would not easily defeat the Confederacy. In addition, Union causalities mounted on the battlefield. Thus, military necessities became paramount. Since slaves were such a large percentage of the population of the South, abolition would weaken the ability of the South to wage the war. Also, there were indications that foreign powers, France and Great Britain, might be willing to recognize the Confederacy and provide it with financial support. Both of these countries, however, had strong abolitionist movements. Those governments might be willing to assist the self-determination of the people of the southern United States who desired to leave the Union in order to establish their own nation, but intervening on the side of the Confederacy to assist slavery was a different matter. Thus, abolition of slavery was fully consistent with the continued belief in the "less than" nature of the descendants from Africa.

Lincoln's Emancipation Proclamation served the Union's war objectives. In addition, the Union also employed black troops in large numbers to help win the war. But the victory of the North on the battlefield did not translate into an acceptance of blacks as equals in the North or the South. As southern governments that participated in the rebellion were reconstituted in the Summer and Fall of 1865 the first order of legislative business was to address the status of the newly made freedmen. These southern legislators passed a series of laws which came to be known as the "Black Codes." The goal of the Black Codes was to introduce a system to ensure that the whites could continue to extract the labor of blacks as was done during slavery. The Black Codes were first adopted by the state of Mississippi in November of 1865, just one month before the Thirteenth Amendment abolishing slavery was added to the Constitution. Among the provisions in various Black Codes were ones which required the former slaves to sign labor contracts by the beginning of the year that could not be broken during that upcoming year. The contracts were normally executed with whites who owned agricultural land that needed farming. All black persons who were not gainfully employed as of the first of the year were considered vagrants and upon conviction were imprisoned. When their fines were paid by others they were entrusted to that person, usually a former master, until they worked off their fines. Orphaned black children were brought before the probate court and apprenticed to a person the white judge considered competent and suitable (usually a former master) until they reached the age of maturity. The kind of work which black people could engage in was severely limited. Blacks were prohibited from owning land to farm. Without a plot of land to produce crops for their own consumption, blacks would be compelled to work for others. Blacks were prohibited from owning fire arms. Interracial marriages were proscribed. None of the reconstituted state legislatures granted blacks the right to vote.

Because violence had been used to maintain blacks in their natural position of inferiority during slavery, it was also resorted to by whites in the South to reassert control over their former slaves. "The wave of counterrevolutionary terror that swept over large parts of the South...lacks a counterpart in the American experience."[40] For example, over 2,000 colored people were murdered around Shreveport, Louisiana in 1865. Black bodies could be seen floating down the Sabine River in Texas. In Pine Bluff, Arkansas, a black settlement was set ablaze and at least 20 of its inhabitants hanged.[41] Large numbers of blacks were attacked and murdered in the summer of 1866 in race riots throughout the South, including Norfolk, Memphis and New Orleans. Freedmen Bureau records in Texas listed some of the reasons for the over one thousand murders of blacks by whites between 1865 and 1868 as including, the victim "did not remove his hat," the victim "wouldn't give up his whiskey flask" and the desire of a murderer to "thin out the niggers a little."[42] Female teachers and white educators who sought to educate the freedmen were also attacked. For example, Alonzo B. Corliss, a physically challenged, northern born, white Quaker was driven from the state of North Carolina for teaching blacks how to read and write.[43] It was also during this period when organizations like the Knights of the White Camellia and the Ku Klux Klan were spawned. Nathan Bedford Forest, a celebrated war hero of the Confederacy, was the first Grand Dragon of the Ku Klux Klan and Robert E. Lee pledged his support for the invisible empire.[44]

When the Thirty-ninth Congress assembled in December of 1865, its first priority was reconstruction. Despite President Johnson's proclamation that the southern states had met his requirements for readmittance, Congress began its session by excluding any representatives from the States that joined the Confederacy. It also established a Joint Committee on Reconstruction by concurrent resolution of the House and the Senate. This fifteen-member committee was charged with investigating the conditions in the southern states and reporting back on whether those states were entitled to representation in Congress.

It was against the backdrop of the adoption of the Black Codes and violence in the South that Congress began to debate the Fourteenth Amendment when it returned into session in early 1866. Congress felt that the Black Codes were a way to reinstate slavery by the defeated states of the South. By the end of the Civil War, the abolition of slavery was recognized as one of the purposes of the war. By adopting the Black Codes, many in the North felt that the South was acting as if it had won the war. Congress was not prepared to let the rebellious states undo the Union's victory on the battlefield.

There were other reasons that Congress was eager to add another amendment to the Constitution. Congress had to address an anomaly created by the ratification of the Thirteenth Amendment. Prior to abolition, slaves counted as three-fifths of a person for purposes of determining a states representation in the lower house of Congress and votes in the Electoral College. Now that blacks were free they would count as a full person. Without adjustment, the ratification of the Thirteenth Amendment would increase the voting power of the states that had the most slaves before the Civil War.

In order to more clearly understand the Fourteenth Amendment it is necessary to understand how the concept of equal rights was viewed in post-Civil War jurisprudence. The legal system of post Civil War America viewed rights as falling into one of four categories. It distinguished among natural, civil, political and social rights.[45] Natural rights were those granted to a person by virtue of being a person and were necessary to secure the blessings of liberty. Many viewed these rights as being of divine origin.[46] These rights included the right to personal freedom, the enjoyment of family ties, the right to the fruits of one's own labor and the pursuit of one's happiness. Slavery was understood to be a violation of a person's natural rights. Also, it was generally agreed that in order to effectively exercise natural rights, a person also had to have civil rights. Civil rights included the legal capacity to buy, sell, rent, lease and own property, as well as to have legal rights enforced by courts. Civil rights also included the right to due process, to sue and be sued in courts of law, to be able to testify in a court of law and to share equally in the costs and benefits of government. Political rights were acquired only within a political system. These rights included the right to vote, hold political office and to participate in the political life of the community.

Civil and political equality could be distinguished from social equality. Civil and political rights were viewed as rights that were asserted by an individual only against the government. Social rights, however, were of an entirely different order. Social rights were asserted not against the government, but against one's fellow citizen. According to the legal thought of the time, government had nothing to do with guaranteeing social rights, except by enforcing the rights guaranteed by the common law. For blacks to have political and civil equality was to have the same basic rights against the government as whites.[47] The grant of civil and political equality, however, did not extend to something like the right to patronize the business of a private individual, to attend non-segregated public schools or the ability to sit next to those of a different race in public transportation facilities. In fact, two years before voting to adopt the Fourteenth Amendment, Congress permitted the establishment of segregated schools in the District of Columbia.[48]

Section one of the Fourteenth Amendment declared that blacks were citizens of the United States, with rights and privileges of citizens and provided that they were guaranteed due process and the equal protection of the laws. Congress, however, did not respect the abilities of the freedmen enough to grant them the right to vote in the Fourteenth Amendment. Section 2 dealt with the anomaly created by the abolition of slavery and was also intended to be an inducement to encourage the states to grant blacks the right to vote. Under this provision a state had to make a choice. If it enfranchised the freedmen, then they would count as whole persons in determining each state's representation in Congress and the Electoral College. But if a state refused to grant the right to vote to the freedmen over the age of twenty-one, then the state's representation would be reduced in proportion to the number such freedmen bore to the whole number of the male population over the age of twenty-one.[49] Thus, if one of the former states of the Confederacy enfranchised black males that state would increase its voting strength in Congress and the Electoral College over what had existed before the Civil War. But if a state chose not to grant the freedmen the right to vote, then the state would lose voting strength. It was estimated that not granting black males the right to vote would cost the states of the former Confederacy one third of their potential representatives in the lower house and substantial representation in the Electoral College.[50]

By the time the Fourteenth Amendment was sent to the states for ratification, the break between President Andrew Johnson and the Republicans in Congress was complete. Congress had overridden Johnson's veto of the extension to the Freedmen's Bureau and the Civil Rights Act of 1866. Though the President did not have to approve a Constitutional Amendment, Johnson made it clear that he opposed the Fourteenth Amendment.

During the fall elections of 1866, Johnson took to the campaign trail speaking against leading Republicans. But this strategy backfired. Johnson's indiscrete utterances and rude conduct on the campaign trail were considered unbecoming of the dignity of the office of the Presidency. He and those he campaigned for were resoundingly defeated at the polls. Republicans won the fall elections winning every northern state legislature, every gubernatorial seat and more than two-thirds of the seats in both houses of Congress. In addition, urged on by Johnson, all of the states of the former Confederacy—except Tennessee—rejected the Fourteenth Amendment.[51] Tennessee was thus the only state readmitted into the Union. None of the former eleven states of the Confederacy granted black males the right to vote.

The rejection of the Fourteenth Amendment led Congress to pass the First Reconstruction Act. The ten southern state governments that failed to ratify the Fourteenth Amendment were ordered disbanded and those states were divided into five military districts under commanders who were authorized to use the army to protect life and property. Congress specified the steps necessary for readmittance of these ten states back into the Union. These included the ratification of the Fourteenth Amendment and the holding of a convention that would draft a new constitution for the state which required universal manhood suffrage. After the election of 1868, Congress then adopted the Fifteenth Amendment which provided that "The right of citizens of the United States to vote shall not be denied or abridged by the United States or by any State on account of race, color, or previous condition of servitude."[52] The Fifteenth Amendment was ratified in 1870. Blacks were thus extended the franchise nationwide.

D. Disenfranchisement and the Institution of Segregation

Toward the end of the nineteenth century, segregation emerged as the dominant system to manage the substandard nature of blacks. As Yale law professor and former attorney with the NAACP Legal Defense and Education Fund Charles Black wrote "[s]egregation in the South comes down in apostolic succession from slavery and the *Dred Scott* case. The South fought to keep slavery, and lost. Then it tried the Black Codes, and lost. Then it looked around for something else and found segregation."[53]

The legal establishment of the institution of segregation and the continued maintenance of the economic and educational marginality of blacks in the South was preceded by their political disenfranchisement. What made disenfranchisement of African-Americans such an urgent matter for whites in the South was the number of potential black voters. According to the 1870 census figures, blacks constituted a majority of the population in three southern states: South Carolina (59%), Mississippi (54%) and Louisiana (50.1%). They were over 40% of the population in Florida (49%), Alabama (48%), Georgia (46%) and Virginia (42%).[54] If effective political control was to be reasserted by whites, it was necessary for them to contain the political power of blacks.

From the moment that black males were granted the right to vote, their political power was undermined. Blacks and whites sympathetic to their cause were shot and families terrorized to prevent blacks from voting.[55] In 1868 in the southwest Georgia village of Camilla, 400 armed whites, who were led by the local sheriff, attacked a black election parade killing scores of blacks. White gangs roamed New Orleans where they intimidated African-Americans and broke up Republican political meetings. In St. Landry Parish, plantations were invaded resulting in the deaths of 200 blacks.[56] The Ku Klux Klan, Knights of the White Camellia and the White Brotherhood attacked countless local black leaders, forcing them to flee their homes, whipping them, beating them and—if necessary—killing them. In 1867–68 constitutional conventions were held in the ten former states of the Confederacy that were not readmitted to the Union. At least one tenth of the black members who attended those conventions were assaulted, with seven actually being murdered.[57] In October 1870 whites broke up a campaign rally in Greene County, Alabama, killing four blacks and wounding fifty-four.[58] In that same month in Laurensville, South Carolina, 150 freedmen were chased from their homes, with thirteen being killed, including a black legislator and others known to be prominent in local politics.[59] In January 1871 "an assault on the Union county jail by 500 masked men... resulted in the lynching of eight black prisoners." In York County, South Carolina, "nearly the entire white male population joined the Klan." They committed "at least eleven murders and hundreds of whippings," which forced thousands of blacks to take cover in the woods each night to avoid being beaten.[60] In March 1871 in Meridian, Mississippi, a riot followed a court hearing in which 30 blacks were killed.

One of the bloodiest riots during Reconstruction took place in Colfax, Louisiana, on Easter Sunday, 1873. There, over 100 blacks who tried to defend themselves were killed. The federal government tried to hold some of those involved responsible for the murders committed. But convictions were secured for only three of the perpetrators under the Enforcement Act of 1870 passed by Congress. The main thrust of the Enforcement Act was to impose criminal penalties for interference with the rights of blacks to vote. Section 6 of the Act specified that it was a crime to go in disguise upon the public highway to violate the civil rights of another. These convictions, however, were later overturned by the Supreme Court in *United States v. Cruikshank*.[61] The Court invalidated the convictions because it found that the indictments were faulty because they failed to allege the denial of a specific federal right.

The Compromise of 1877 resolved the disputed presidential election of 1876. Under the Compromise, Rutherford B. Hayes, the Republican candidate, was elevated to the Presidency. Part of the Compromise was an agreement by the Republicans to withdraw the federal troops from the South. In 1878 Congress also forbade the use of armed forces in elections. Political violence against blacks, however, did not end when the federal troops pulled out of the South in 1877. As late as 1898, for example, violence was still being used to drive the last black influence out of the southern electoral process. During the 1898 election in North Carolina, the Red-Shirts used violence and intimidation to frighten Republicans and blacks in order to prevent them from voting.[62] That election led to congressional redistricting in North Carolina which made it impossible for George White, the last black in Congress, to win re-election in 1900. Another black would not be elected to Congress until 1928. Another African-American was not elected to Congress from one of the states of the former Confederacy until Barbara Jordan from Texas and Andrew Young from Georgia were elected to the House of Representatives in 1972.

When violence and intimidation were not enough to drive blacks from the political process, elections were rigged to prevent candidates sympathetic to the African-Americans from getting elected. To ensure that blacks remained in their social position at the bottom of the racial hierarchy, ballot boxes were stuffed, perjury was committed and elections were carried by fraud.[63] The success of these combined measures was obvious. Despite the high percentages of the black population in various states, the only state legislature they numerically controlled after the Civil War was the lower house of South Carolina, and for only a short period of time.

As the end of the Nineteenth Century approached, efforts to disenfranchise blacks were written into the law. In 1890 Mississippi became the first state to blaze that trail by amending its constitution to include several provisions to disenfranchise blacks. South Carolina followed suit in 1895, Louisiana in 1898, North Carolina in 1900, Alabama in 1901, Virginia in 1901 and 1902, Georgia in 1908 and Oklahoma in 1910. Four other southern states, Arkansas, Florida, Tennessee and Texas, accomplished effective disenfranchisement of the black males without the need to amend their constitutions.[64]

One of the amendments added to the constitution of Mississippi was a two year residency requirement because young blacks males tended to move frequently. People who committed bigamy and petty theft, crimes associated with blacks, were permanently disenfranchised, even though those who committed murder, rape or grand larceny were not. Mississippi also added a provision requiring eligible voters to pay a $2.00 annual poll tax. Since blacks left slavery as illiterate, landless and penniless peasants this tax disproportionately discouraged them from exercising the right to vote. All eleven states in the former Confederacy followed Mississippi's lead in adopting a poll tax. The border state of Delaware, which also possessed a large number of potential black voters, actually instituted a poll tax seventeen years before Mississippi.[65]

The most ingenious provision adopted by Mississippi to disenfranchise black voters was the literacy and understanding clause. This clause required that a perspective voter demonstrate his ability to read or understand the Constitution to the satisfaction of the voting registrar. Registrars routinely concluded that a prospective white voter was qualified to vote, but excluded a prospective black voter. The Supreme Court's 1898 opinion in *Williams v. Mis-*

sissippi approved these "racially neutral measures" aimed at disenfranchisement. The Supreme Court held that a state does not violate the Equal Protection Clause when it requires eligible voters to be able to read, write, interpret or understand any part of the Constitution.[66]

In the 1903 case of *Giles v. Harris*,[67] the Court addressed a situation where an Alabama registrar refused to list a black man on the voters' roll. The would be voter went to federal court seeking an injunction that would compel the registrar to register him and 6,000 similarly situated blacks. The Court, however, rejected this request concluding that it could not order such an injunction. In response to the plaintiff's allegation that the great mass of the white population intends to keep blacks from voting, the esteemed and honorable Justice Oliver Wendell Holmes wrote, "[i]f the conspiracy and the intent exist, a name on a piece of paper will not defeat them. Unless we are prepared to supervise the voting in that State by officers of the court, it seems to us that all that the plaintiff could get from equity would be an empty form."[68]

Literacy and understanding provisions became standard means in which to disenfranchise black male voters. Since these provisions could also operate to disenfranchise white voters as well, some states added a grandfather clause to these provisions. Louisiana was the first state to do so in 1898. Under grandfather clauses if a man's father or grandfather was on the electoral rolls as of January 1, 1867 or some other time before blacks were granted the right to vote, then such a male's right to vote was "grand fathered." The grandfathered voter did not have to pass a literacy or an understanding test to qualify to vote. The Supreme Court eventually struck down the grandfather clause in its 1915 opinion in *Guinn v. United States*,[69] however, by then the disenfranchisement of blacks in the South was complete.

Another disenfranchisement scheme was that of the white primary. Republicans, the party of Lincoln, lost their voting appeal in the South after Reconstruction. In states that instituted the primary system, the Democratic primary was more important than the general election. Texas led the way with the white only primary. Texas limited participation in the primary to white Democrats who were qualified under the constitution and the laws of Texas to vote. It was not until World War II that the Supreme Court finally put an end to the white primary system, definitively ruling it unconstitutional.[70]

E. Acceptance of Segregation in Public Education

As blacks were eliminated as an effective voting force in the South, state legislatures enacted what were considered sensible segregation policies into law. Prior to this time segregation existed in many aspects of southern society, but it generally was not part of the legal code. Segregation statutes made their first appearances in the area of transportation. Through the mid 1880s no state required segregation on railways. Florida passed the first such statute, separating passengers in first class, in 1887, followed by Mississippi in 1888. Until the late 1890s railroad car segregation was the only form of segregation required by law by a majority of the states in the South.[71]

Whatever constitutional concerns about segregation that existed were resolved by the Supreme Court in its 1896 opinion in *Plessy v. Ferguson*,[72] the preeminent case of the segregation era. In addressing an equal protection challenge to a statute requiring separate but equal accommodations, Justice Brown's opinion for the Court stated that "in the nature of things [the Fourteenth Amendment] could not have been intended to abolish distinctions based upon color, or to enforce social, as distinguished from political, equality." Brown goes on to note "[i]f one race be inferior to the other socially, the Constitution of the United States cannot put them upon the same plane." Thus, segregation was justified based on the notion that blacks were socially inferior to whites. According to the highest court of the land, this was a reality that even the Constitution could not overcome.

The Court's opinion in *Plessy* was in tune with the times. Politics and public opinion had turned against the attempts at equality fostered by the Reconstruction Amendments. Congress, in 1891, had defeated a bill that would have enlarged federal protection of blacks seeking to vote in federal elections, and three years after that it repealed virtually all the Reconstruction statutory protections for the voting rights of blacks. Furthermore, the *Plessy* case did not provoke the media reaction the way the Court's decisions in the Civil Rights Cases thirteen years earlier had.[73] The case was not even mentioned in many legal publications and the decision was not reported in the United States Supreme Court Reports.[74]

Three years after its decision in *Plessy*, the Court in a public education decision, signaled that the requirement of equality did not have to be taken literally. In *Cumming v. Richmond County Board of Education*,[75] the Supreme Court sanctioned a situation where the Richmond County Board of Education used taxpayers funds to defer a portion of the cost of the high school education for white students, but provided no financial assistance for black students seeking high school education. The Richmond County Board of Education maintained two public high schools—one for black children charging $10 per year tuition and one for white girls charging $15 per year tuition. There was a private high school for white boys and girls that also received financial assistance from the Board of Education. When a shortage of space developed for black children in primary schools, the Board of Education decided to convert the black high school into four elementary schools. This deprived 60 black high school students of an education, but provided space for up to 300 black primary school students. The black plaintiffs went to court alleging a violation of the Fourteenth Amendment. They sought to prevent the Board of Education from collecting any taxes to support the high schools which were operated for the exclusive benefit of the white population and to enjoin the Board from using any funds or property, then held by it or thereafter to come into its hands, for supporting such high schools.

In a unanimous decision authored by Justice Harlan, the Court concluded that the reason for closing the black high school was to provide educational opportunities for some 300 primary school students. The Court rejected the notion that there was any desire or purpose on the part of the Board to discriminate against any of the county's colored schoolchildren on account of their race. Justice Harlan also indicated that the relief sought by the black plaintiffs would impair the efficiency of the high schools provided for the white children. This result would take from the white children an educational privilege granted to them, without any benefit to the black children. The Court concluded by noting that under the circumstances disclosed, it could not say that this action by the state was a denial of rights conferred under the Fourteenth Amendment. While all admit that the benefits and burdens of public taxation must be shared by citizens without discrimination against any class on account of race, the education of the people in schools maintained by state taxation is a matter belonging to the respective states. Even though the facts of the *Cumming* case were somewhat unusual and the legal arguments made on behalf of the black community were mishandled, *Cumming* came to stand for the proposition that while separate could be separate, equality was not absolute.

In two other opinions, the Supreme Court endorsed segregation in education. In *Berea College v. Kentucky*,[76] the Court upheld the criminal conviction of an incorporated college that admitted both whites and blacks for instruction in violation of a state law which prohibited a corporation from instructing both races at the same institution. In so doing the Court rejected a claim that the state segregation law violated the Constitution. In *Gong Lum v. Rice*[77] the Court rejected an equal protection challenge by Martha Lum, a nine year old girl who was denied admission into the local school for whites because of her Chinese ancestry. A provision in the Mississippi constitution provided that separate schools be maintained for the children of the white and colored races. The Mississippi Supreme Court concluded that this provision had divided educable children into those of pure white or Caucasian race and those of colored races of brown, yellow and black.[78] Therefore, Martha Lum could not insist on being classified as white. Since the Legislature was not compelled to provide separate schools for each of the colored races, all were given the benefit of a unified colored school. Though a challenge to segregation in public education was not directly addressed by the Supreme Court in its decision, for the Court to affirm the decision of the Mississippi Supreme Court it had to assume the validity of segregation in public elementary education.

Once blacks were reduced to an insignificant political force, state legislatures were able to eliminate much of the money they felt was being wasted on the education of blacks. After 1890 support for black public schools declined drastically in comparison to white schools.[79] For example, per pupil expenditures in Alabama and North Carolina were about the same for black and white students in 1890 and about twice as much per pupil was spent on the education of white children as compared to black children in Florida, Mississippi and Louisiana. By 1910, however, Alabama was spending three times as much on the education of white children than it was spending on blacks, and North Carolina was spending twice as much. In Florida and Mississippi the ratio increased from approximately two-to-one to approximately four-to-one, and Louisiana spent five times as much on the education of white children as black children.[80] In 1917 the U.S. Bureau of Education published *Negro Education: A Study of Private and Higher Schools for Colored People in the United States.* The report, written by Thomas Jesse Jones in two volumes, was the most comprehensive survey of the conditions of segregated schools in its time. The report revealed that only 29% of what was spent on the education of white students was spent on the education of black ones. The gap in spending was even larger in the South.[81] In addition to less resources being spent on the education of blacks, their school year was shorter, their teacher-pupil ratio higher and black teachers were paid far less than their white counterparts. Disparities in per pupil expenditures continued up to the eve of the Supreme Court's decision in the school segregation cases. For example, in 1930 South Carolina actually spent eight times and in 1945 three times as much money for the education of whites than it did for the education of blacks.[82] In 1929 Mississippi spent nine times and in 1945 four and one-half times as much for the education of a white child than for a black child.[83]

III. Rationales for the Belief in the Inferiority of Blacks

Economic motivations played a significant part in the selection of blacks as the labor force used to develop and cultivate the New World and their subsequent continued subordination under segregation after the Civil War. But economic motivations alone can never suffice to explain institutions like slavery and segregation. People are motivated by more than material needs and desires. To rest the justifications for such exploitation on economic motives alone requires ignoring the emotional, psychological and spiritual dimensions of human nature. Throughout history religious, scientific and cultural justifications were propounded to justify blacks being confined to an inferior status. The Supreme Court normally did not explicitly base its legal decisions upholding slavery or segregation on religious or scientific rationales regarding racial differences. The propounding of these rationales by experts and their acceptance by the general public however, helped strengthen the perception that the Court's decisions upholding slavery and segregation were rational given the nature of things.

A. Rationales for Slavery

At the time of initial contact between Europeans and Africans in the Fifteenth Century, the Divine word of the Almighty was held sacrosanct in European societies. Proponents of slavery found support for the institution in the Old Testament. Thus, the original justifications for slavery and ontological racial differences were based upon the inviolable will of God. Long before the first Africans set foot on North American soil, Biblical justifications for placing blacks in a condition of servitude abounded.[84] Thus, it could be cogently argued that slavery could not be a sin against Divine law, because it had been sanctioned in the Bible by God's infallible word.[85] In addition, it was often argued that blacks were better off as slaves in the United States than they would have been if they had remained in Africa. Finally, scientific opinion also supported slavery by pointing to the inherent inferiority of the Africans and their descendants.

1. Religious Justifications for Slavery

Abraham, the Father of three Faiths, owned slaves. In Chapter 25 of Leviticus, God specifically authorized the Israelites to enslave the heathens among them, but not the descendants of Israel.[86] As long as the Europeans were enslaving heathens—which they considered the Africans to be—not only did the Almighty not prohibit it, but positively commanded it. In the New Testament, the Apostle Paul's epistles took slavery for granted.[87] Thus, it was argued that slavery could not be a sin against Divine law, because the Bible sanctioned it.[88]

Perhaps the primary religious justification for specifically enslaving blacks was derived from the curse Noah placed on the descendants of Ham. According to Genesis Chapter 9:21–27, Noah became drunk and was lying naked in a stupor in his tent when he was discovered by his son, Ham. Ham saw the nakedness of Noah and told his two brothers, Shem and Japheth. The other two brothers took a garment, laid it upon their shoulders, went backwards and covered their father. They never saw Noah's nakedness. When Noah awoke and realized what had happened, he blessed Shem and Japheth, but cursed the descendants of Ham to be servants to Shem and Japheth. Both Christians and Muslims had long come to believe that the descendants of Ham had been turned black. Oral stories of the Hebrews collected in the Babylonian Talmud from the second to the sixth century CE also stated that the descendants of Ham were cursed by being black.[89] The Ham legend was generally accepted in Christian communities by the 1500s and was used to justify the argument that the enslavement of blacks was the result of a divine curse, which no human had the right to alter.[90]

2. Slavery was Often Viewed as a Beneficial Institution for the Slaves

Even though the blacks were held in bondage by the British colonist and later America citizens, it was often asserted that they were better off than they would have been if left in Africa.[91] To begin with, Africa was a place where the divine light of Christianity had not yet penetrated. Many English, and later Americans, believed that blacks simply did not have souls, and thus, instructing them about Christianity would be pointless. Many English colonists and Americans, however, accepted the burden of instructing their slaves about Christianity. If blacks were not enslaved, then their chances for eternal salvation following the heathen practices of their people in Africa were remote. Slavery provided black people with the ability to reap the tremendous benefits of being exposed to the divine light of Christianity and the mercy of the Son of God.

To comprehend the other arguments advanced for why slavery benefitted blacks, it must be noted that slavery was quite common in Africa. In some areas the percentage of the populations that were held as slaves was quite large. For example, a traveler through Senegambia in west Africa recorded that the labor is universally performed by slaves and guessed that three quarters of the population were slaves. Among the Ashanti, the most powerful of the kingdoms of Guinea, every man of property had slaves. Most of the laboring performed there was done by slaves. A French visitor to Dahomey thought that two-thirds of the population there were slaves. In the Niger delta most of the people seemed to have been slaves.[92]

The slaves would not have been available to the Europeans without the cooperation of the African kings, merchants and nobles. While some slaves, about 1% or 2%, were stolen by Europeans, the overwhelming majority were procured as a result of the Africans' desire to sell them.[93] The Europeans found that they could trade manufactured goods and firearms for slaves with much less risk to themselves than by trying to steal blacks. By trading, the Europeans also could maintain good relations with the local powers of the area. As a rule, African leaders were neither threatened nor bullied into selling slaves, but did so willingly.

The Africans were also thought by the Europeans and the Americans to be barbarous and heathen slave masters. For many of the Africans, if they were not purchased by Europeans they would have been killed by their African slave masters. A former head of the East India Company, who had spent years in Africa, told the House of Commons that an African king assured him of this reality. The African king was reported to have stated that if the slave merchants did not purchase from him and others their prisoners taken in war, they would be killed.[94] Slaves were also sacrificed at the death of some of the kings in West Africa. Perhaps as many as a thousand met such an ignoble fate in 1824 at the death of the King of the Ashanti.[95] Lord John Russell told the House of Commons in London in 1846 that he believed "a third of the captives intended as slaves for the Atlantic crossing died during the land journey on their way to the coast" while they were in the hands of their black captors. Henry Wise, an American naval commodore indicated that "rapid marches" of the slaves from the interior of Africa to the coast seldom produced less than a 20% mortality rate.[96] Thus, it could be argued that purchasing blacks and bringing them to North America saved hundreds of thousands of them from an earlier death and barbaric treatment in Africa.

Slavery was also thought to improve blacks because it could make rational men out of savage animals and industrious serfs out of wanton idlers. Slavery found Africans in "benighted ignorance" and led them to "the threshold of light and knowledge." It clothed their barbarous "nakedness in civilized habiliments, and taught a jungle idolater of Christ and immortality."[97] A London magazine summarized this argument, saying that the inhabitants of Guinea:

> Are in the most deplorable state of slavery under the arbitrary powers of their princes both as to life and property. In the several subordinations to them, every great man is absolute lord of his immediate dependents. And lower still; every master of a family is proprietor of his wives, children and servants, and may consign them to death or a better market.... Such a state is contrary to nature and reason, since every human creature hath an absolute right to liberty...yet it is not in our power to cure the universal evil and set all the kingdoms of the world free from the domination of

> tyrants.... All that can be done in such a case is to communicate as much liberty and happiness as such circumstances will admit, and the people will consent to: and this is certainly by the Guinea trade. For by purchasing, or rather ransoming, the negroes from their national tyrants and transplanting them under the benign influences of the law and Gospel, they are advanced to much greater degrees of felicity, tho'not to absolute liberty.[98]

A very small percentage of the slaves that crossed the Atlantic Ocean ended up in North America. But, slaves were treated better in the United States than any other place in the world. One of the unique features of slavery here was that it expanded significantly by natural reproduction instead of by dependence on importing more slaves from Africa. By 1860 only a very small percentage of the 4 million slaves in the United States, the largest slave population in the New World, resulted from importation from Africa. The Portuguese and the Dutch, by contrast, typically sought to transfer twice as many male slaves to their colonies as female slaves. Planters in their colonies preferred slaves whom they could work hard and then discard without the trouble of having to rear families. "Most sugar plantations, from the beginning to the end of the slavery era, were undertakings which needed a constant annual replenishment [of slaves] to maintain the labor force."[99]

Slaves in the United States were often looked upon by their masters paternalistically. The established custom of slaveholding families was to share with their slaves the necessities and, not infrequently, the comforts of life. This paternalistic view originated from the relationships of lords and serfs that existed in the feudal societies of Europe. Slaves and masters were viewed as having reciprocal duties to one another. Masters provided slaves with food, clothing, shelter, medical care and care for the young and old. In return for the masters paternalistic protection and direction, they were to receive the labor of the slaves.

The material advantages of slavery for blacks did not exist only in comparison to blacks in Africa or their brethren in other parts of the New World, but also in comparison to the free blacks of the North. Many of those arguing that blacks were better off in slavery pointed to the 1840 census for support. The 1840 census revealed that the number of blacks who were deaf and dumb, blind, idiots, insane, paupers and in prison in the states that have freed the blacks was one out of six and in slaveholding states one out of every one hundred fifty-four (154).[100] The rate of insanity and feeblemindedness was eleven times higher among free blacks of the North than those in bondage in the South. As John C. Calhoun summarized the argument,

> the experience of more than half a century is to decide ... in all instances in which the States have changed the former relation between the two races, the condition of the African, instead of being improved, has become worse. They have invariably sunk into vice and pauperism, accompanied by the bodily and mental inflictions incident thereto—deafness, blindness, insanity and idiocy to a degree without example....[101]

3. Scientific Justifications for Slavery

Whether the issue was slavery,[102] disenfranchisement, segregation[103] or lynching, solid scientific evidence demonstrated the logical need for these measures. Racial differences were a subject of intense academic study in the United States and elsewhere. J. C. Nott (his textbook *Types of Mankind* written with G. R. Gliddon in 1854 was the contemporary best seller in the field of anthropology) summarized the general academic motivation for studying racial differences. Shortly before the *Dred Scott* decision, Nott wrote:

> The aim of studying racial differences is certainly a noble one, and its pursuit cannot be otherwise than instructive to the statesman and historian, and no less so to the general reader. In this country, it is particularly interesting and important, for not only is our immense territory the abode of the three best defined varieties of human species—the white, the negroe and the Indian—to which the extensive immigration of the Chinese on our Pacific coast is rapidly adding a fourth, but the fusion of diverse nationalities is nowhere more rapid and complete.[104]

Scientists began studying racial differences long before the Declaration of Independence. While the explanation for the inferiority of blacks has varied over the years, scientists have continuously concluded—based on presumed objective, rational and unbiased scientific evidence—that blacks in some relevant way are substandard beings.

The first use of the word race did not occur until 1606, and there were only five discussions relating to the varieties of mankind during the entire seventeenth century.[105] The first group of scientists to record racial differences, the natural scientists, blended religion in with their explanations of the differences of people. These first racial "scientists" were not so much seeking to develop scientific ideas as they were attempting to describe God's divine plan that could be discovered by studying nature.[106] They noted that nature delights in inequality. They envisioned the whole of nature as one gigantic ladder of being that went from the lowliest and simplest creatures to the most developed and complex ones. In the great chain of being, the African stood somewhere between Caucasians and the orangutan. The African, however, was viewed as having more in common with the beast of the field than with the advanced Caucasian race.

In 1684 Francois Bernier, a French physician, became the first person to authoritatively divide humans based on skin color. In 1735 Carolus Linnaeus, however, was the first one to formalize the racial hierarchy scientifically. Linnaeus divided humans into four races, Homo Europeaus, Homo Asiaticus, Homo Afer and Homo Americanus. He linked culture and biology together in a way that has survived to this very day. The characteristic traits Linnaeus noted were observable in Homo Europeaus were gentle, acute, inventive and governed by custom. He noted that the characteristic traits of Homo Afer were crafty, indolent, negligent and governed by caprice.[107] German anatomist and anthropologist Johann Blumenbach also worked out an influential racial classification. He listed Caucasians at the top of the human ladder with Asians, Africans, Native Americans and Polynesians at the lower rungs.[108]

By the end of the eighteenth century the inferiority of the blacks, derived from the scientific understanding about the differences in nature, was generally accepted as indisputable scientific fact. The first edition of the Encyclopedia Britannica in 1798 in its entry on "Negroes" asserted that they were a people of "idleness, treachery, revenge, cruelty, impudence, stealing, lying, debauchery, nastiness and intemperance." Blacks were also said to be "strangers to every sentiment of compassion" and were "an awful example of the corruption of man when left to himself."[109]

Throughout much of the latter part of the eighteenth and the nineteenth century, scientists espousing views of black inferiority were embroiled in a theoretical debate about the causes of this inferiority. Scientists writing before Darwin advanced one of two positions. There were those who were monogenist and accepted the validity of the Genesis account of creation of Adam and Eve. The monogenists argued that while all humans come from one source, since creation the races had diverged and developed their own capacities. Georges Louis Leclerc de Buffon, in his 1778 book *Natural History of Man,* argued that white was the real and natural color of man. Thus, the standard from which to judge was that of white skin. Given that the objective and neutral standard of the proper color of humanity was white skin, this meant that there must be an explanation for the aberration of black skin. While physician Benjamin Rush contended that the black hue of the negro was the result of leprosy,[110] the answer most often accepted by the monogenists was that black skin was an aberrant development caused by extensive exposure to the sun in hot climates.[111] Even with this climactic theory to explain racial differences, the monogenists were in two different camps regarding its implications. While admitting that racial differences had developed gradually over time, some argued that those differences were permanent now. Others argued that the climatic explanation implied an ability to reverse the influence of climate over time. Monogenists—taking their lead from de Buffon—were in agreement, however, that white was the natural color of mankind and that the black race was the one that had been negatively impacted by an inhospitable climate.

Other scientist rejected a literal interpretation of Genesis and adopted the position of polygeny. Polygeny had a significant number of followers in the United States. It asserted that the human races were derived from separate biological species. Blacks were, thus, another form of life all together different from whites. Louis Agassiz and Samuel Morton were the best known of the polygenist. Agassiz, a Harvard professor, founded and directed the Museum of Comparative Zoology. In the relative ranking of the races, Agassiz assigned the lower rung of the human ladder to blacks. He noted that Africa had never produced a regulated society that could benefit from the advantages afforded by civilization.[112] When asked if his theory of polygeny contradicted the account of creation of Adam in the Book of Genesis, Agassiz responded that the Genesis account spoke only of the creation of the Caucasian race.

Samuel Morton provided the empirical work used to buttress the theory of polygeny. Morton was a Philadelphia physician who had a reputation as a great data-gatherer. His work won him praise from the eminent jurist, Justice Oliver Wendell Holmes. Morton had a large collection of human skulls, over 1,000 at the time of his death. He published three major works on the sizes of human skulls between 1839 and 1849. His work proved that Caucasians had the largest skulls, followed by Mongolians, American Indians and then Africans. The differences in the skulls was evidence that Caucasians had different origins than those of other racial groups. In addition, since intellectual superiority was tied to cerebral volume, Caucasians were also the most intelligent group.[113] Implicit in Morton's empirical work is the notion that because the skulls of whites are larger, larger is better.

Following the well accepted position of the natural scientists about the inferiority of blacks was the science of physiognomy, the science of discovering temperament and character from outward physical appearance, especially the face. The Dutch anatomist, Pieter Camper, demonstrated that there exists a connection between facial and cranial measurements and personality traits and character. Camper showed that a beautiful face and a beautiful body were inseparably attached to a beautiful nature, beautiful character and beautiful soul. He proved that the optimal facial angle was one-hundred degrees. Since the facial angle of Europeans measured out at ninety-seven degrees, they were closest to the optimal angle. The facial angles of black people by contrast measured between sixty and seventy degrees. This placed them closer to apes and dogs than white human beings.[114]

In the mid-nineteenth century, Paul Broca, the founder of the Society of Anthropology of Paris, broke new ground in the understanding of how the human brain functions. He measured the shape of the head and developed a cephalic index. Broca demonstrated that variations in the human head shape were linked to significant differences in the races. Others went further to argue that poor cephalic index ratings corresponded with lower intelligence. But Broca agreed that black skin and wooly hair were associated with inferior intelligence, while white skin and straight hair were the equipment of the best group.[115]

In 1856 the first American translation of the four volume treatise on racial inequality written by French diplomat Count Joseph Arthur de Gobineau was published. Gobineau was considered the most influential thinker about racial differences of the nineteenth century.[116] Gobineau concluded his treatise by proclaiming that he had demonstrated that the various branches of the human family are distinguished by permanent and ineradicable differences, both mentally and physically. Their intellectual capacities, personal beauty and physical strength are different. He admitted the possibility that there may be special individuals of the degraded black race who could be found with active and vigorous minds that greatly surpass in fertility of ideas and mental resources of the average white peasantry and even some in the middle classes. Nevertheless, the general conclusion of the inferiority of the black race holds true. According to Gobineau, society should not allow the rare performances of exceptional individuals to undercut the general rule about racial capabilities.[117]

B. Rationales for Segregation

Concurrent with the end of slavery, scientific explanations regarding the differences between the races underwent a dramatic change. The publication on the eve of the Civil War of Charles Darwin's book, *Origin of Species,* in 1859 required scientists to rethink their theories explaining racial differences. Evolutionary theories eventually swept away the old monogenicist/polygenicist discussions about the source of racial differences.

There were three different groups of Social Darwinists. One group followed Charles Darwin's statement in his *Descent of Man,* published in 1871. Darwin wrote, "[a]t some future period, not very distant as measured by centuries, the civilized races of man will almost certainly exterminate and replace throughout the world the savage races."[118] By the 1890s, tough-minded racial Darwinists like Frederick Hoffman were exalting census statistics showing higher black mortality and lower black birth rates than those of whites as a demonstration of futility of egalitarian or even traditionally paternalistic approaches to black economic, social and political participation. Hoffman argued that emancipation from slavery had been the worst thing that ever happened to blacks, because as enslaved people at least their needs were met.[119] Nathaniel Shaler, a prominent social scientist and a dean at Harvard University, argued that blacks were inferior. He went on to assert that the law of natural selection meant their eventual extinction.[120] Lewis Henry Morgan also argued for the extinction proposition. He asserted that since the black race was in a lower stage of development than whites, when blacks were brought into contact with the superior white race they were unable to compete.[121] The eventual result will be the disappearance of the black race.

Social Darwinists who were not preaching the eventual extermination of the black race were not much more complimentary to blacks. Many evolutionary scientists of the day examined research into racial differences, like that done by Sanford Hunt. Hunt was a United States surgeon and pioneer in the field of anthropometrics—the study of the physical characteristics of the races—who updated the work of Samuel Morton. He studied the results of 405 autopsies during the Civil War. Hunt discovered that the average weight of the brain of a black person was five ounces lighter than that of the average brain of a white person.[122] By studying skulls that he had obtained from Ancient Egypt, Hunt also noted that these differences among racial types had existed for thousands of years. Ten years after the Supreme Court's opinion in *Plessy v. Ferguson,* a researcher at Johns Hopkins University replicated Hunt's findings. In an article published in the American Journal of Anatomy, he claimed that the skulls of blacks were smaller than those of whites and their brains were "less convoluted."[123] Therefore, blacks possessed deficient brains.

From this data, racially optimistic Social Darwinists argued that intelligence evolves slowly over a long period of time. Blacks were destined to evolve to the level of whites, but slowly. Though it would take hundreds of thousands of years, eventually blacks would make up the deficit and achieve biological equality with whites.

Another group of Social Darwinists turned the arguments of the optimistic ones on their head. They asserted that while blacks were evolving, so were whites. More importantly, however, whites were actually evolving at a faster rate than blacks. Thus, the gap between the two races was actually growing larger not smaller.[124] No matter how inferior blacks of the present seemed to whites of the present, the future would only see the situation grow worse.

The end of the Civil War and the abolition of slavery made it necessary for scientists to consider another problem brought about by the potential for racial mixing outside of the limits of slavery—miscegenation. Thomas Jefferson noted long before the abolition of slavery that blacks favor white beauty as uniformly as is the preference of the orangutan for the black women over those of his own species.[125] Benjamin Franklin also expressed the view of most Caucasians in the eighteenth century about interracial sex. He argued that white amalgamation with the other color produces a degradation to which no lover of his country, no lover of excellence in the human character can innocently consent.[126] Since sex with blacks was considered licentious and savage, anyone born of such an act inherited the very characteristics of the act.[127]

At the beginning of the nineteenth century, Jean Baptiste Lamarck developed an evolutionary theory that was to become important in the debates in the latter portion of the century about miscegenation. Lamarck noted that there was an unconscious striving of organisms to improve their species.[128] The male of a species has an instinctive drive to mate with the best female possible.[129] In many species males fight each other and the stronger one gets first choice of the females. In this way, the best male and female mate.

Lamarck laid the framework that post Darwinians would use to provide biological explanations of the propensity of black males to lust after white women. Driven by instinctive passions, burly black male beasts are a constant threat to white women, desirous of raping and attacking them. Segregating blacks in public schools, transportation and entertainment facilities and other aspects of life where close affinities across racial lines could be developed was deemed a necessary aspect of social policy. But more than social segregation was needed. Lynching black males, therefore, became an accepted social policy to combat this natural urge. From 1882 until 1927, 3,513 black men were lynched.[130] The primary justification for these lynchings was the uncontrollable sexual drive of black men that led them to lust after white women.

As the twentieth century dawned, scientists provided a new form of evidence for proving the substandard nature of the black race—intelligence testing. In 1904, Alfred Binet was commissioned by the minister of public education in France to develop techniques to identify children whose lack of success in normal classrooms suggested a need for some form of special education. Binet developed a series of short tasks, related to everyday problems that were intended to assess basic reasoning processes such as ordering, comprehension, invention and censure.[131] Binet, however, did not assert that he was measuring an innate, genetically inherited capacity. The theory that IQ is a product of heredity was an American product.[132] H. H. Goddard brought Binet's ranking scale of intelligence to America and reified it into a score about innate intelligence.

In 1916, Lewis Terman, a professor at Stanford University, revised Binet's scale and increased the number of tasks to be performed on the IQ test. He gave his revision the name, Stanford-Binet. Terman relentlessly emphasized that the IQ tests measured the limits of intelligence and the inevitability of those limits. "Practically all of the investigations which have been made of the influence of nature and nurture on mental performance agree in attributing far more to original endowment than to environment." [133] Terman argued that those whose IQs were below 100 should not be admitted to professions of prestige and monetary reward. Substantial success in such occupations probably took an IQ of 115 or 120. By identifying in advance those who were feeble-minded, Terman argued that intelligence testing could curtail crime, pauperism and industrial inefficiency. With the mentally infirm identified, appropriate measures could be adopted to control their socially destructive tendencies.

R. M. Yerkes, a Harvard University professor, convinced the U.S. Army to allow him to administer intelligence tests to all of its World War I recruits. Yerkes argued that he could assist in the war effort by efficiently identifying those people who should be leaders and those who should be commanded. Yerkes, Terman, Goddard and other colleagues developed the army's mental tests in the summer of 1917. As an army colonel, Yerkes presided over the administration of these tests to 1.75 million World War I recruits. One of Yerkes' lieutenants, E. G. Boring, selected 160,000 case files and produced results from this sample. His results confirmed that blacks were a mentally deficient race. He found that blacks were at the bottom of the intellectual scale, with a full 89% testing out at the level of morons or below.[134]

The source of the differences noted in intelligence testing set off a scientific debate. While the debaters accepted the premise that blacks were intellectually inferior, a disagreement developed about the cause of the inferiority. Yerkes, Terman, Goddard and others asserted that their measures of intelligence were markers of permanent, inborn limits. Thus, the mental infirmities that these tests revealed were generally not remediable by social intervention. Environmentalists rejected this biological determinism. They harkened back to Alfred Binet's original motivation by emphasizing the power of creative education to increase the achievements of all children, but especially those from deficient social environments. Mental testing for them was a way for enhancing the potential of those who test poorly through proper education and improving their physical and social environment. While the environmentalist accepted the intellectual inferiority of those who performed poorly on the intelligence tests, including most blacks, the environmentalist believed that social policy could be structured to remedy this deficiency. It was the growth of opponents to the inherited notions of intelligence that set the stage for the desegregation of public schools in American society in the 1950s and 1960s. The environmentalist triumphed in the Supreme Court's opinion in *Brown v. Board of Education.*

Conclusion

Traditional Americanism is structured on the abiding belief that in some relevant way blacks are less than the applicable norm. From the epistemological standpoint of this discourse, the race of blacks is always a part of the conceptualization of racial phenomena. Blacks, as individuals or as a people, are perceived as poor, lazy, lustful, ignorant and prone to aggressive and criminal behavior. Therefore, being comprehended as black in Traditional Americanism results in the behaviors and actions of blacks persistently being perceived in negative ways.

This Chapter has not only discussed the conceptual structure of Traditional Americanism, but it has also presented a historical analysis of how blacks have been perceived within this cognitive framework. Economic motivations played a significant part in the selection of blacks by the Europeans (and later the forefathers of the United States) as the labor force to develop and cultivate the New World and the subsequent continued subordination of blacks under segregation after the Civil War. The belief in the inferiority of blacks made their oppression in the form of slavery and later segregation, however, seem as if these legally endorsed institutions were rational responses to the natural order. One aspect of this belief about African-Americans before *Brown* was the development and maintenance of separate and unequal public educational systems.

This Chapter also discussed the religious, scientific and cultural justifications propounded to justify the confinement of blacks in an inferior status throughout the centuries. At the time of initial contact between Europeans and Africans in the Fifteenth Century, the divine word of the Almighty was held sacrosanct in European societies. Thus, the original justifications for slavery and ontological racial differences were rooted in interpretations of the inviolable will of God. Long before the first African set foot on North American soil, biblical justifications for placing blacks in a condition of servitude abounded. Later scientific evidence replaced religious justifications as the dominant form of proof for the continued belief in the less than nature of blacks.

Chapter Two

The Discourse of African-American Centralism

Against the background of 335 years of racial domination that preceded the Supreme Court's decision in *Brown v. Board of Education*, the descendants of the sons and daughters of the soil of Africa in the United States and those non-blacks sympathetic to their cause formulated a counter discourse to that based on the belief of blacks as the paradigmatic inferior group in the United States. The development of African-American Centralism was limited by and responsive to the racial oppression imposed on the black community. But, this pattern of understanding always rejected the "less than" thinking about blacks that forms the basis of Traditional Americanism. Thus, this system of meaning provides an antithetical interpretation of the behaviors, attitudes and experiences of African-Americans to that derived within Traditional Americanism. African-American Centralism was driven by the desire to eradicate the racial oppression of blacks. As a result, this pattern of understanding is structured around a view of the social world that conceptualizes African-Americans as oppressed, not inferior.

Section I of this Chapter will start by describing the general structure of African-American Centralism. Section II provides a retelling of the African-American historical experience in America until the Supreme Court's decision in *Brown v. Board of Education*. The historical emphasis of this discourse is on the twin aspects of the experience of the black community—being subjected to various forms of racial oppression and struggling to overcome those forms of oppression. The experience of and struggle against racial oppression began on the coast of Africa where the African slaves first met their European purchasers. While African-Americans developed their culture of struggle against racial oppression in North America, the Africans brought to the New World came with beliefs from Africa. Section II starts by discussing those beliefs of Africans that survived transplantation to the United

States and formed part of the basis of African-American Centralism. The historical discussion will then focus on the era of slavery, which includes the colonial period of British America, before progressing to the era of the Civil War and Reconstruction. The historical discussion will conclude with a treatment of the period of disenfranchisement and the institution of separate but equal.

I. The Conceptual Structure

Like with all Americans, the motto for African-Americans could also be "E Pluribus Unum" (out of many, one). The overwhelming majority of the current 39,000,000 members of the African-American community can be traced to the original 500,000 Africans who were delivered to the shores of what became the United States during the years of the Trans-Atlantic Slave Trade.[1] The Africans brought to North America were from a hundred different tribes and a thousand different villages. They included people from diverse African tribes such as the Adanse, Akwamu, the Akyem, the Asante, the Bambara, the Bantu, the Bono, the Dagomba, the Denkyira, the Efik, the Ewe, the Fante, the Fons, the Fulani, the Ga, the Gonja, the Hausa, the Ibo, the Mandingo, the Susu, the Twifo, the Yorba, the Wasa, the Wolof and other ethnic groups too numerous to name. They were brought together by the common trait of their race and compelled to live constantly and consistently under unfavorable material, psychological and spiritual conditions. In America these ethnically diverse people with their different languages, customs, religious beliefs and cultural heritages were melded into one group, African-Americans. Their ethnic differences were largely attenuated as a new cultural perspective was created.

This section addresses the concept of the social world embedded in this cognitive framework, which views blacks as a group struggling against racial subordination. It then discusses the epistemology of this system of meaning. Words related to racial issues like racism, racial discrimination and racial equality draw their meaning within this pattern of understanding from the notion that blacks are struggling against group-based oppression. While anyone, regardless of race or ethnicity, can comprehend racial phenomena and discuss racial issues within the confines of this discourse, African-American Centralism places special moral and ethical obligations on African-Americans to join the collective struggle against racial domination. African-American Centralism views government's role to include taking actions necessary to dismantle continuing structures of racial oppression. This section concludes with a discussion of the relationship of African-American Centralism to the other three patterns of understanding.

A. Conception of the Social World

Up until the Supreme Court's opinion in *Brown v. Board of Education,* the central historical fact of the experience of black people in America was that of a group of people who constantly dealt with racial oppression. In 1954, not only did racial oppression meet them in the segregated schools that their children attended, but it met them in every aspect of life. It met them in the farm field, at the factory or the office, when they applied for a job, when they had a job and when they lost a job. It met them in the market places where they bought goods or services from others or sold goods and services to others. It met them in the Church Building, the Kingdom Hall or the Tabernacle. It met them at the doctor's office, at the hospital and at the funeral home. It met them from the cradle to the grave.

African-American Centralism sees social life in terms of one major purpose, goal or objective—the liberation of black people from racial domination. The liberation sought is not abstract. It is liberation from domination in the material, spiritual and psychological conditions of the lives of black people. This system of meaning views the racial or ethnic groups as having ontological primacy. Thus, racial or ethnic groups have a life of their own. These groups are not limited to current racial or ethnic group members in being. Rather these groups include all of those nameless and faceless ancestors from the past and the unnamed and unborn progeny of the future. The current members of a given racial or ethnic group occupy the center stage in the human drama, but they are obligated to the past and obliged to the future. The benefits and the obligations of the grandparents are passed on to the parents, who in turn pass them on to the children.

Individuals are not viewed as discrete, distinct, autonomous or living a separate isolated existence, but as members of their respective racial or ethnic communities. As a result, within this discourse, liberation of individual blacks is irrelevant. Final victory over racial oppression can only occur when the African-American community is liberated from the clutches of racial oppression. Even though individual African-Americans may obtain material, spiritual or psychological success, their success does not obscure the oppression of the African-American community. Conversely, though individual whites might be disadvantaged by a lack of money, education, intelligence or social prestige, as a group whites are viewed as possessing undue advantages derived from the privilege of their racial membership. These advantages exist regardless of a given white individual's failure to recognize such benefits or—if recognized—the white person's sincere desire to disassociate him or herself from such benefits.

Though race is the central feature that unites black people, it is also the basis of their oppression. Because of this, fighting racial oppression produces a deep, abiding and enduring paradox. The central paradox of African-American Centralism is, has been and always will be the fact that race is what unites blacks as a people, but is also the basis of their oppression. This central paradox creates two inconsistent and divergent paths to the eradication of racial subordination. One path seeks liberation through strategies based upon the acceptance and perpetuation of racial distinctions. On this path, liberation is envisioned only within a context in which race maintains its importance. Strategies employed by this view seek to accomplish the elimination of racial oppression either through the redistribution of material, economic, educational, social and political power from dominant non-Hispanic white group to African-Americans or through the physical separation of blacks into communities and social institutions where the effective control is exercised by the black community. The other path seeks the liberation of the black community through the eradication of racial distinctiveness of all Americans.[2] Strategies employed with this emphasis seek to eradicate racial distinctiveness through either transcending all racial distinctions and blending all Americans into a melting pot or undermining and eliminating all racial and ethnic distinctions by focusing on individualism and true colorblindness. Thus, since what oppresses and what unites blacks is race, the eradication of racial subordination can employ strategies which either strengthen or attenuate racial distinctiveness. There is no permanent solution to this tension. Whether racial distinctiveness should be extolled or avoided will always depend upon the exigencies of a given situation at a given time. But it must be stressed that paths to pursue the eradication of racial subordination are not the ends themselves. The goal is the eradication of racial subordination, but there are different ways to try to bring it about.

B. Epistemology and the Meaning of Words Related to Racial Issues

From an epistemological standpoint blacks are conceptualized as oppressed, not as inferior. The race or ethnicity of various actors is also part of the conceptualization of racial phenomena. There are no colorblind understandings of racial issues. Individuals who are separate from his or her race or ethnicity (whether black, brown, red, white or yellow) do not exist within this system of meaning.

When words are used to discuss racial issues such as "racism," "racial oppression," "racial discrimination" and "racial equality," these definitions are based upon a view of society in terms of racial and ethnic groups, not individuals. The past and present distribution of economic, political, educational and social power vastly favors the non-Hispanic white majority. As a group, blacks seldom have the social or economic power or the resources to oppress the non-Hispanic white community. Thus, generally speaking, it is non-Hispanic whites (speaking in group terms), not blacks (speaking in group terms) who can be racist. "Racial oppression" occurs when non-Hispanic whites or those subservient to their interest exercise their dominant power to maintain the oppression of blacks as a group. "Racial discrimination" occurs when whites—or those subservient to their interest—use their dominant power to single out blacks for unfavorable treatment. This form of discrimination, however, is not to be understood in terms of the discrimination of a black individual as an individual. Rather it is discrimination of a black person as a member of an oppressed group of people. "Racial equality" is obtained when blacks exercise proportionate social and economic power on par with non-Hispanic whites. The success of individual blacks is necessary in order to obtain racial equality. But success for black individuals is not the goal, only a necessary aspect of group based racial equality.

C. Moral and Ethical Beliefs

African-Americans have suffered from a deep, enduring and abiding historical wrong. It is morally and ethically right to correct this wrong. Thus, moral and ethical behavior is judged in terms of its effectiveness in assuaging the continued oppression of blacks. People, deeds and ideas are weighed on a scale that seeks to determine whether they contribute to or hinder the liberation of African-Americans from the interminable clutches of racial subordination.

Anyone, regardless of their race or ethnicity, can perceive racial phenomena within this pattern of understanding and can assist in the pursuit of racial equality. But this system of meaning ascribes special moral obligations to those who are black. Regardless of personal predilections, every black individual is viewed as always linked to the struggle against racial oppression. Thus, the success of black intellectuals, black athletes, black entrepreneurs, black politicians, black movie stars, black professionals or black administrators is viewed as the success of the black community. Conversely their failures and the failures of other African-Americans including the black criminals, the poor academic performance of black students and the inadequate job productivity of black employees are viewed as the failures of the African-American community. As a result, every black person regardless of religious creed, social or economic status, level of education, gender, region of the country from which they come, sexual orientation or associational or political affiliations is under a never ceasing obligation to accord him or herself consistent with the best interest of the black community. Blacks also have a responsibility to fight for the liberation of the African-American community. This responsibility, however, is not a function of merely assisting someone with black skin. It is triggered only when it is necessary to aid in the struggle against one of the multitudinous forms of racial oppression. A black person who contributes to the political campaign of a black politician should do so because the success of the politician furthers the struggle for the liberation of the black community. If the black politician, however, consistently takes positions antithetical to the liberation of the black community, then other blacks should work for his or her defeat. A black person might have a moral obligation to patronize a black business establishment, even if the prices are higher than at a comparable non-black business establishment. Circulating money in the black community strengths the community. But if the black business discriminates against black customers and does not employ black individuals, then the obligation would be to avoid patronizing that business establishment.

This is not to say that black persons cannot pursue their individual interests. There is no negative moral implication to blacks pursuing their individual interests if that pursuit does not conflict with the interest of the black community. Since the struggle against racial subordination requires group efforts, however, those blacks who pursue their individual interests in ways contrary to the collective interest of African-Americans are violating the primary moral obligation imposed upon them by this system of meaning. Black people who place their individual interest above the interest of the group are displaying moral depravity and iniquity.

D. One Putative Function of Government

Liberating the black community from racial subordination probably requires sustained and costly governmental action. In addition, governments at all levels have participated in the oppression of black people. Thus, one of the functions of government should be to right the historical wrongs inflicted upon African-Americans. Designing and implementing policies and procedures that help dismantle the continued oppression of the African-American community would be viewed as one of the primary functions of government.

E. Contrasted with Other Systems of Meaning

Like Traditional Americanism, African-American Centralism always sees blacks as members of an involuntary group. But, African-American Centralism also always sees non-Hispanic whites as members of an involuntary racial group. Traditional Americanism is not as concerned with how whites are perceived, sometimes viewing them as individuals and other times as a superior racial group. Traditional Americanism always views the amalgamation of the actions, behaviors, attitudes, opinions or beliefs of non-Hispanic whites as constituting the implicit norm from which deviations require an explanation. African-American Centralism is cognizant of the reality that the implicit norm is not a race neutral norm, but one centered upon the characteristics, experiences and proclivities of non-Hispanic whites. The other enduring epistemological difference between this cognitive framework and Traditional Americanism is that African-American Centralism views blacks as oppressed, not inferior.

African-American Centralism's relationship with Colorblind Individualism is more complex than with Traditional Americanism. Perceiving racial phenomena within the conceptual boundaries of Colorblind Individualism, sometimes advances the attenuation of the oppression of blacks. At other times Colorblind Individualism contributes to that oppression. Colorblind Individualism abhors conscious considerations of race. When it is necessary to combat conscious racial discrimination against blacks the argument that people should be treated based on the content of their character and not the color of their skin is effective. But, when this argument is asserted within African-American Centralism it is asserted not as an end in itself, but as a means to attenuate racial oppression. The tendency of Colorblind Individualism to ignore race, however, can also work against the efforts of African-Americans to overcome other forms of racism, particularly cultural, unconscious or institutionalized forms. Non-Hispanic whites—including recent immigrants—benefit from contemporary institutional practices in education, business, employment, housing and politics that benefit them as a group. These same contemporary institutional practices place significant obstacles in the path of African-Americans.[3] Often times ignoring race ignores the privilege accorded to non-Hispanic whites and the obstacles placed in the path of blacks. Thus, Colorblind Individualism can also contribute to the continued oppression of African-Americans through obscuring the privilege accorded non-Hispanic whites due to their racial/ethnic group membership and obstacles which blacks encounter. Colorblind Individualism creates a conscious experience for non-Hispanic whites of being an individual. Perceiving the benefits of white privilege, however, requires the conscious realization of group membership. In addition, ignoring race may obscure the propitious effects of a given decision, determination, resolution, law, rule or regulation for non-Hispanic whites and at the same time obscure the oppressive aspects on the black community.

A good illustration of the double-edged relationship between African-American Centralism and Colorblind Individualism comes from varying statements made by Louisiana governor, Mike Foster, on the same day. In January, 1996, he signed an order banning affirmative action in agencies under his control and signed into law a bill declaring the birthday of Reverend Martin Luther King, Jr. a state holiday. Of these acts, one which hinders the fight against black oppression and the other which advances it, Foster said:

> This just says we've got to be color-blind. I do not believe I have any prejudice—never had in my opinion. I don't look at color.... Dr. King dedicated his life to the pursuit of equality and opportunity for all Americans. He believed all men should be judged by their character, not by the color of their skin.[4]

American Collectivism seeks to advance the best interest of the American society. Thus, the concerns of African-Americans are subsumed in a larger analysis that focuses on the concerns of the American collective. As with Colorblind Individualism, sometimes the interest of African-Americans can be effectively advanced through advancing the best interest of the American Collective. For example, when President Lincoln announced his intention to issue the Emancipation Proclamation, he made it very clear that his primary objective was to restore the Union. Lincoln publicly stated that his objective was neither to help nor hurt slavery. Thus, the issuance of the Emancipation Proclamation was justified as a measure to assist in overcoming the rebellion and saving the Union. Even though the Emancipation Proclamation was not motivated by a sense of benevolence to blacks, it was nevertheless a tremendous blessing to African-Americans in the struggle against racial domination. But at other times the best interest of the American Collective will justify the sacrifice of the interest of blacks at the altar of the national interest. For example, when the Founding Fathers debated the Constitution there was no serious discussion about freeing the slaves. In order for the former British colonies to unite into a nation, acceptance of slavery was a foregone conclusion. Thus, the sacrifice of the freedom of the slaves was necessary to advance the national interest. Regardless of the motives of the Founding Fathers to advance the interest of the nation, the effect of accepting slavery at the Constitutional Convention was to strengthen the oppression of blacks.

II. History of the African-American Experience

This section will focus on the historical experience of the black community. The history of the African-American experience within this discourse focuses primarily on the racial oppression of the black community and its concomitant struggle to overcome that oppression. The ability of blacks to fight against their oppression was always limited. But blacks have struggled against their oppression from the very beginning in whatever ways were possible.

The Africans who came to America brought with them their own practices and beliefs. In discussing the historical experience of the black community this section will begin by discussing those African beliefs that survived and helped to form the basis of the pattern of understanding of African-American Centralism. After discussing those beliefs, this section will focus on the oppression during the era of slavery and the concomitant struggles by blacks against it. It will then proceed to a discussion about efforts of blacks to assist in the end of slavery during the Civil War, despite encountering racism from the very nation they sought to assist. This section will also discuss the political, economic, educational, legal and social progress obtained during Reconstruction along with the concomitant struggle against efforts to prevent and constrain those victories. This section will conclude with struggles by blacks to overcome racial oppression during the Segregation Era.

A. Traditional African Beliefs

While African-Americans developed their culture in the New World, they brought with them their beliefs from Africa. Some of the 500,000 Africans transported to North America came from the east coast of Africa, principally from Madagascar and Mozambique. The overwhelming majority, however, were brought from an area on the west coast of Africa stretching from the Senegal River in the north to the Congo in the south.[5] These Africans were from many different ethnic and kinship groups. While many of them practiced Islam, a large portion of them viewed the cosmos through the perspective of traditional African religious beliefs. Different African ethnic groups have different religious beliefs and practices, but there is general agreement that certain beliefs make up what loosely can be termed traditional African religious beliefs.[6]

The West African by tradition was not an individual, but part of an expanded network of people beginning with the closest relations of the extended family, spreading out to a kinship group and then to a community. The common refrain of the typical African is the saying "I am, because we are: I exist because the community exists."[7] The kinship group was the most important organizing unit in their societies. The status of individuals and their roles were determined by their position in their kinship group. Individuals were part of, and depended upon, their kinship connections to provide the meaning for all of their social interactions.[8] A person's health, security and chance of immortality were all products of the kinship group.[9]

In addition to obligations to the kinship group, the socialization of the African individual included obligations to the broader community. Individuals were to understand themselves as an integral part of the whole and play their appropriate role in the broader society. This sense of being part of a community carries with it an acculturated sense of concern for others because they are members of the community. Although there were conflicts among individuals to be resolved, when the interest of the individual was pitted against that of the community, the community's interest took precedence.[10]

In African religious cosmology, the universe is composed of visible and invisible spheres. The visible world includes humanity, plants, animals and inanimate beings. The invisible world is the sphere of God and includes the ancestors and the spirits. For the African, death did not lead to dimensional doors on the other side of which was an afterlife of heavenly bliss, hellish torment, redemptive purgatory or oblivion. Instead, an aspect of the living person survived death to inhabit an afterlife populated by ancestral spirits. The ancestors are located in a spiritual realm between God and human beings. The world of the living was closely connected to the world of the ancestors and other spirits. Thus, the organic community for the African included the living and the dead.[11] The ancestors were considered the string in the net that held the fabric of the kinship group and the community together.[12]

Some of these African ideas survived to become part of the basis of African-American Centralism.[13] The concept of the individual as a member of a community and the idea that the community includes more than the living are two important aspects of African-American Centralism's view of the social world. Consistent with traditional African religious beliefs, African-American Centralism places ontological primacy on the black community and the community is understood as an organic unit that includes those who have come before and those yet to be.

B. The Era of Slavery

It takes great imagination for someone of today's generation to understand the suffering of those Africans captured for the Trans-Atlantic slave trade and reduced to the state of commodities. It was on the west coast of Africa that the slaves met their European transporters. Once sold to the Europeans, they were branded so that their new owners could readily identify them. They were also locked into dungeons, corrals or pens, known as barracoons, in the European forts located on the coast. The slaves were left in barracoons to wait for the arrival of the ships that would transport them to unknown parts of the world.

In those barracoons the slaves would come to realize that their promise of a carefree life filled with family, friends and community would never be. They would come to realize that they would no longer walk on familiar land, stare up at familiar skies, drink from familiar waters and imbibe the liquor of freedom. All of their dreams for the future were turned into nightmares.

When the transport ships bearing names like "The Liberty," "The Freedom," "The Gift of God," "The Justice" and "The Integrity" arrived on the west coast of Africa, the slaves were herded onboard for the trip to the New World.[14] The Middle Passage, as it was known, was a time of unimaginable and indescribable suffering. The slaves were often chained together in spaces that provided only 18 inches of headroom. They were often packed so tightly together that they could not move even when driven by the undeniable necessities of nature. Thus, they were compelled to lay in pools of their own vomit and excrement. The stench of the air was intolerable and the heat generated by so many closely packed bodies was unbearable. These transport ships normally carried a doctor who tried to treat sick slaves, unless he considered them contagious. In such cases the infected ones would be jettisoned overboard. It was thought better to throw away the "infected cargo," than to risk it "spoiling" the whole "freight."

Accounts have been rendered about the reality of being aboard a slave ship from the eyes of the slave transporters. These accounts provide only a modicum of the anguish that the slaves must have actually endured. The following exchange is from a British surgeon who served on one of those ships:

Question: Do the slaves appear dejected when they first come on board?

Trotter: Most of them at coming on board, show signs of extreme distress and some of them even looks of despair, this I attribute to a feeling for their situation, and regret at being torn from their friends and connections. The slaves in the night were often heard making howling melancholy noises, something expressive of extreme anguish. I found that it was occasioned by finding themselves in a slave room, after dreaming that they had been in their own country amongst their friends and relatives.

Question: Were the slaves much crowded in your ship in the Middle Passage?

Trotter: Yes, so much so that it was not possible to walk amongst them without treading on them.

Question: Had they room to turn themselves, or any sort to lie at ease?

Trotter: By no means; the slaves that are not out of irons are locked spoonways, according to the technical phrase, and closely locked to one another.

Question: Did the slaves appear to suffer from want of air?

Trotter: Yes; I have seen their breasts heaving and observed them draw their breath with all those laborious and anxious efforts for life which we observe in expiring animals subjected by experiment to foul air of different kinds. I have also seen them, when the tarpaulins were, through ignorance, or inadvertently thrown over the gratings, attempting to heave them up, and crying out Kickeraboo! Kickeraboo! Which signifies, 'we are dying.' On removing the tarpaulins and grating, I have seen them fly to the hatchways with all the signs of terror and dread of suffocation.[15]

Another British surgeon writing about his experience on a slave ship described the following:

> Some wet and blowing weather having occasioned the port-holes to be shut, and the grating to be covered, fluxes and fevers among the negroes ensued. While they were in this situation, my profession requiring it, I frequently went down among them, till at length their apartments became so extremely hot as to be only sufferable for a short time. But the excessive heat was not the only thing that rendered their situation intolerable. The deck, that is the floor of their rooms, was so covered with the blood and mucous which had proceeded from them in consequence of the flux (dysentery), that it resembled a slaughter-house. It is not in the power of the human imagination to picture to itself a situation more dreadful or disgusting.[16]

Any form of resistance on these transport ships was brutally punished. Yet, the struggle by blacks against their oppression began on these transport ships. During the Middle Passage, the captives resisted their captors in various ways. Shipping records are reaped with efforts by them to seize control of ships and direct them back to Africa. For many of these slaves, however, death represented the only viable form of resistance to oppression.[17] Many sought liberation from their racial domination by jumping over the sides of the ships. Since slave merchants remuneration depended upon "cargo" delivered, the slave transporters tried to prevent this form of "cargo loss" by placing nets around the transport ships. Other slaves sought to resist their oppression through starvation. In order to keep them alive, however, slave transporters would force their mouths open far enough to pour a soupy food mixture down their defiant throats. Despite efforts of slave merchants to keep as many slaves as possible alive, a significant number of Africans found liberation from slavery in their deaths aboard slave ships.[18]

Once delivered to America, the slaves were resold. The overwhelming majority of blacks would remain slaves in the South during the Antebellum Period. In 1860, for example, 92% of black people lived in the states that would comprise the Confederacy, the border states and the District of Columbia where slavery was legal.[19]

In the "Land of the Free" and the "Home of the Brave," Africans and their descendants experienced an onerous bondage. The slaves toiled in the fields raising cotton, tobacco, sugar or rice for only enough sustenance to perpetuate their lives. Their ability to marry and raise families was limited to the whims of businessmen who might sell them or their family members off as financial circumstances dictated.

The mechanisms put in place to control the slaves often kept them from successfully challenging their confinement by major wars of liberation. Despite measures to prevent their uprisings, blacks engaged in numerous armed insurrections directed at liberation from slavery. Many of the blacks brought to North America were purchased from the West Indies. There were more than a dozen major slave revolts that took place during the eighteenth century in Jamaica alone. There are also recorded revolts by black slaves on Long Island in 1708 and in New York City in 1712 and 1733.[20] South Carolina imported more black slaves directly from Africa than any of the other colonies (and later states). In September of 1739 a group of twenty black revolutionaries broke into a plantation warehouse and obtained guns, ammunition and supplies. They were determined to reach Florida where they believed they would be safe and free. Eventually more than sixty black freedom soldiers joined their ranks. But outnumbered and outgunned by the South Carolina militia, they were eventually defeated. By the time their rebellion was thwarted over twenty whites had been killed in action.[21]

Other insurgency actions conducted by black freedom fighters were led by known revolutionary figures such as Gabriel Prosser, Nat Turner and Denmark Vessey. Among the freedom fighters that attacked Harper's Ferry with John

Brown were several African-Americans including, John A. Copeland, Jr., Shields Green, Lewis Leary, Dangerfield Newby and Osborn Perry Anderson.[22] Historian Herbert Aptheker reported finding records of about 250 slave revolts and conspiracies.[23] Since the tendency in the Antebellum South was to suppress news of insurrections because such reports would create fear and panic, this number almost certainly understates the number of actual slave uprisings. Vincent Harding has also chronicled many efforts by the black slaves at armed liberation.[24]

Arson was another way that blacks struck back at their oppression in the Antebellum Period. Major fires set in many American cities such as Charleston, Albany, Newark, New York, Savannah and Baltimore were suspected of being set by the hands of black slaves.[25] There were also many surreptitious assassinations or poisonings of slave holders that were so cunning the perpetrators were never identified or, if identified, captured.

Blacks looked for opportune times to engage in their own personal liberation from slavery. There were numerous individual acts of self-liberation. Many escapees like Harriet Tubman, Elijah Anderson and John Mason returned and risked their own lives to assist their fellow blacks escape. The most prominent black spokesperson for abolition, Frederick Douglass, was a run away slave.[26] Eliza Parker's resistance to slavery received a good deal of publicity. She was tried twice for killing a slave owner attempting to repossess her under the Fugitive Slave Act.

During the Revolutionary War black slaves emancipated themselves in large numbers. Thomas Jefferson, for example, estimated that in 1778 Virginia lost over 30,000 slaves. A South Carolina historian estimated that between 1775 and 1783 his state lost at least 25,000 slaves and it was estimated that Georgia lost 75% of her 15,000 black slave population during the War.[27] The British also invited blacks to join their Army and fight against the Americans. The most important proclamation by the British came on June 30, 1779 by Commander-in-Chief Henry Clinton. He promised freedom to any black who reached the British lines. Thousands of blacks seized this opportunity for personal liberation.[28] Many of them were repatriated to Canada after the Revolutionary War.

Slaves who worked on small plantations were usually closely supervised by white masters. Those who worked on large plantations, with the exception of house slaves, had a much more distant relationship with their slave masters. In slave communities, blacks were loyal to each other and produced their own internal class structure and social hierarchy. The primary determinant of who was qualified to lead them was a given person's ability to manage and extract benefits from whites. As a result, blacks who were artisans, drivers or domestics tended to occupy leadership positions, because they were in the best position to learn how to deal with the slave masters and could, from time to time, assist runaways and rebels.[29]

Blacks resisted slavery in other noticeable ways. They tried to frustrate the efforts of their slave owners to extract work from them by refusing to work when they could or performing their chores in haphazard fashions. They fought any change in their work quotas, put rocks or dirt in the bottoms of their baskets to fatten loads, broke tools, damaged crops and mistreated animals. As W. E. B. DuBois pointed out:

> All observers spoke of the fact that the slaves were slow and churlish; that they wasted material and malingered at their work. Of course they did.... It was the answer of any group of laborers forced down to the last ditch. They might be made to work continuously but no power could make them work well.[30]

The negative stereotype of being shiftless and ignorant so often associated with blacks throughout history could be viewed as having its roots, at least in part, in the misinterpretation of their acts of rebellion as the result of their indolence and stupidity.

Even though whites exercised more supervision over the religious services of blacks during slavery, a counter form of Christianity developed among the black slaves. Black slaves would meet in secret churches removed from the presence of whites. In these invisible churches black ministers preached a brand of Christianity different from that which white ministers attempted to foster upon them. Black preachers discussed how whites misrepresented Christian principles. The true God—the one that black preachers said was worthy of worship—knew neither Jew nor Gentile, black nor white, slave nor free, but all were brothers and sisters in Christ Jesus.[31] Their bondage was not a product of God's design, but man's (the white man's) sin. God and Jesus abhorred slavery. During the Antebellum Period, African-Americans came to see themselves as God's chosen people. They were not the chosen in the sense that they replaced the Jews, but in the sense that the just and merciful God that African-Americans bowed down to chooses to assist the oppressed and downtrodden. As He came to Israel in its time of distress, He too would come to them. As God had delivered the children of Israel from the bondage of Pharaoh, He too would deliver them from slavery.

African-American involvement in the abolition movements of the North was one of the most visible forms of struggle against their oppression during the Antebellum Period. Blacks constantly asserted and preached the wickedness and evil of slavery and the desire of black people for emancipation. Educated and articulate blacks would appear as exhibits to demonstrate to white audiences the humanity of the descendants of the soil of Africa. Sometimes the writings of blacks—like David Walker's *Appeal to the Colored Citizens of the World But in Particular and Very Expressly to those of the United States of America* or speeches like the July 4th address of Frederick Douglass—were able to command the nation's attention for a time.

C. The End of Slavery, The Civil War and Reconstruction Era

After Fort Sumter was fired upon in April 1861, free blacks from the North rushed to recruiting stations to sign up for the upcoming war. In Providence, for example, a company of blacks offered to leave for the war front with the First Rhode Island Regiment. In Philadelphia two African-American regiments were quickly formed and began to train. In Pittsburgh the black Hannibal Guards offered their services. Jacob Dodson, a black scout who had fought Native Americans at the side of Kit Carson, wrote the Secretary of War that he knew of 300 reliable black citizens who desired to provide their services to protect the Nation's capitol city.[32] But direct attacks on slavery were not part of the North's initial war efforts. Thus, when black men sought to sign up for the Union army they were summarily rejected.

Despite the official opposition to enlisting blacks as soldiers, some of the Union generals, like Hunter, Lane and Butler, proceeded to organize blacks anyway.[33] Even though they initially did not fight, African-Americans still assisted the Union war effort. During the Civil War about 200,000 blacks worked for the Union army in non-military capacities.[34] They served as laborers, teamsters, cooks, carpenters, nurses and scouts for the Union forces. Blacks helped build forts, load and discharge cargo and build bridges. They were some of the best spies in the Union army. They knew the country better than white northern invaders. They also knew the rebels better and could move in and out of the rebels' encampment often without arousing suspicion.[35]

As the war dragged on Union casualties mounted and its effort to defeat the rebels bogged down. African-Americans continued to insist on being allowed to enter the fray. Their motivation to defeat and humiliate the Confederates was far greater than that of the white northerners. Blacks would be fighting for the best cause for which a person could ever take up arms, the freedom of their mothers, fathers, sisters, brothers, children and friends. By proving their patriotism and bravery on the battlefield they expected to win freedom for all black people.

Despite the lumbering and laggardly steps of the Union to add the cause of abolition as a reason for the conflict, blacks took advantage of the uncertainties and confusion of the war and freed themselves. Where Union troops were encamped in slave territory, black slaves came in search of freedom. Even when Abraham Lincoln issued the Emancipation Proclamation, blacks had to be proactive if they were going to seize the illusion of freedom that the Proclamation provided. The Proclamation excluded from its provisions the loyal slave states of Missouri, Kentucky, Delaware and Maryland, the anti-Confederate West Virginia area and certain other areas in the Confederacy that remained loyal to the Union.[36] Thus, the document long revered as abolishing slavery expressly excluded over one million black slaves from its provisions.[37] The slaves to whom it applied mostly resided in places of the rebellion that were under the control of the Confederacy. The Proclamation was not recognized in those areas.

Issuance of the Emancipation Proclamation cleared the way for enlisting blacks into the Union Army. After two years of efforts by Frederick Douglass and others to persuade him, Lincoln finally became an enthusiastic proponent for enlisting black soldiers in early 1863.

> The colored population is the great *available* and yet *unavailed* of force for restoring the Union. The bare sight of fifty-thousand armed, and drilled black soldiers on the banks of the Mississippi, would end the rebellion at once. And who doubts that we can present that sight, if we but take hold in earnest?[38]

But blacks had to struggle against racism when they were finally given a chance to vindicate their desires to free their race on the battlefield. Even though blacks fought in the Northern war effort, they were subjected to indignities and injustices in the army of the very Union they were fighting to preserve. Blacks were paid less than what white soldiers received.[39] Many Union soldiers and officers believed that blacks were not fit for combat. Many white soldiers felt that they were too superior a race to fight side by side with blacks. They also believed that blacks were too servile and cowardly to be good soldiers. As one white soldier put it, "the average plantation negro was a hard-looking specimen, with about as little of the soldier to be seen in him as there was of the angel in Michel Angelo's block of marble before he had applied his chisel."[40]

Despite having to face racism and prejudice within the ranks of the Union army, blacks volunteered and served with distinction and honor. The 250,000 free blacks in the North comprised a little more than 1% of the twenty-one million people in the North. Eighty-five percent of eligible black men in the North joined the armed struggle for the freedom of black people.[41] These brave black men were joined in the Union army by their brethren recently liberated. By the end of the war, African-Americans comprised 10% of the Union's armed forces. Official statistics show that almost 179,000 black soldiers served the Union army with 7,122 being officers.[42] An additional 29,000 served as sailors, comprising 25% of the Union seamen.[43] Approximately 37,300 blacks were killed during the conflict, accounting for over 10% of the Union war deaths.[44] This percentage is remarkably high given that blacks were not allowed to engage in armed conflict until two years into the war. It has been estimated that mortality rates of black troops was 40% higher than that of white troops.[45]

With the end of the Civil War, African-Americans were to learn the bitter lesson that the abolition of slavery was one issue and eradication of racial oppression another. After the end of hostilities, the whites in the South once again sought to employ violence and intimidation in order to re-assert dominion over blacks. Blacks resisted whenever they could. Because the Union needed black troops to win the war, when it trained them to fight for the Union, it also trained them to defend the black communities after the war. Black troops found themselves fighting whites who sought to constrain or abolish their new freedoms. In Vicksburg and Memphis, black troops clashed with Irish policemen. Clashes between black troops and white troops over the treatment of local black communities occurred in Charleston, Atlanta, Danville, Chattanooga and Jacksonville.[46] The successful response by black troops to the indignities afflicted upon black people caused whites in the South to raise up a giant cry to have the black troops discharged as soon as possible. President Andrew Johnson responded positively to these pleas.

As southern governments were reconstituted after the Civil War under President Johnson's reconstruction plan, they passed a series of measures which came to be known as the Black Codes. The Black Codes were first adopted by the state of Mississippi in November 1865. Despite the obvious thrust of the Black Codes to reimpose peonage upon blacks after the Confederacy's defeat on the battlefield, President Johnson in his December 1865 address to Congress stated that his plan for reconstruction and reconciliation of the country had been successfully accomplished.[47]

Johnson, a Tennessean and former slave owner, at one time promised a black audience that he would be their Moses and lead them to the promise land. As President, however, Johnson proved to be a white supremacist who sympathized with the plight of the southerners. In his December 1867 address to Congress, for example, he stated that blacks possessed less "capacity for government than any other race of people. No independent government of any form has ever been successful in their hands. On the contrary, wherever they have been left to their own devices they have shown a constant tendency to relapse into barbarism."[48] Johnson also warned that black suffrage would result in a tyranny such as this continent had never witnessed.

Blacks circumvented the racist President and took their claims for justice directly to Congress. Congress took control of the process of reconstruction. In 1867 Congress dissolved the newly reconstituted governments of ten of the former states of the Confederacy—all but Tennessee—and voided the Black Codes. Congress placed these states under military control and demand that they enfranchise black males.

Blacks made significant political, economic, educational, legal and social progress after the Civil War. During the ten years that followed the end of the Civil War, America enacted three new Amendments—the Thirteenth, Fourteenth and Fifteenth (the Reconstruction Amendments)—to the Constitution. In order to further delineate and protect the rights granted in the Reconstruction Amendments, Congress also passed five major civil rights measures, including the Civil Rights Act of April 9, 1866, the Enforcement Act of May 31, 1870, the Enforcement Act of February 28, 1871, the Enforcement Act of April 20, 1871 and the Civil Rights Act of 1875.[49]

Blacks registered to vote, organized political campaigns and elected many of their own to political office for the first time in the nation's history. On February 25, 1870, Hiram Revels became the first African-American to serve in Congress. He took his seat as the distinguished senator from Mississippi, filling the vacancy left by the resignation of the former Confederate President, Jefferson Davis. Joseph Rainey of South Carolina was the first black person to serve in the House of Representatives, taking the oath of office on December 12, 1870. Before the end of the nineteenth century, there were twenty African-Americans who served in the House and two in the Senate, including Blanche Bruce from Mississippi.

Blacks occupied many seats in various state legislatures and offices before the end of the nineteenth century. On December 9, 1872, P. B. S. Pinchback became the first black governor in American history when he was appointed to serve as governor of Louisiana. Six African-Americans served as lieutenant governor, two were state treasurers, four served as superintendents of education and eight as secretary of state.[50] More than 600 African-Americans occupied seats in southern legislatures before the withdrawal of federal troops from the South as part of the Compromise of 1877 which resolved the disputed 1876 Presidential election.[51] A few blacks were elected mayors of towns and cities and many more served on city and town councils.

African-Americans were not very successful at passing much legislation in Congress. At the state level, however, blacks were a very effective political force. These elected officials helped to expand suffrage, institute free public education in the South, improve the tax system and repeal laws that imprisoned people for debt.

From the very beginning of obtaining the franchise, however, blacks found themselves fighting to maintain the political power they had won. Many African-Americans successfully elected to political office were forced to defend their victory against subsequent challenges to the electoral process. Most of the blacks elected to Congress during the nineteenth century, for example, had to spend a good deal of their time and energy defending their elections against challenges of fraud and voting irregularities.[52] But fight they did. In 1872, for instance, Pinchback became the first person in U.S. history to be simultaneously elected to the House of Representatives and the Senate, but was never seated to either because of presumed election irregularities. Later that year he was appointed to succeed the then Louisiana governor, who had been suspended as a result of impeachment hearings.

D. Disenfranchisement and the Imposition of Segregation

An important turning point for the new freedmen's rights was the withdrawal of federal troops as part of the Compromise of 1877. This left the fate of blacks in the hands of their former slave masters. Although Southern Democrats pledged to protect the new legal rights of the freedmen, calling themselves redeemers they accelerated the process of eliminating blacks from the political process. The elimination of blacks from the political process led to the legal imposition of segregation.

Despite the efforts of the black community to fight against it, a number of schemes were enacted in the latter part of the nineteenth century and the early part of the twentieth century to disenfranchise black male voters. Many states followed the lead of Mississippi and added long residency requirements as a qualification for voting because young black males tended to move frequently. All southern states enacted a poll tax which disproportionately prevented blacks from voting due to the widespread poverty in the black community. The most infamous legal means used to disenfranchise black voters was the discriminatory application of the literacy and understanding clauses. These clauses required that a prospective voter demonstrate his ability to read or understand the Constitution to the satisfaction of the white voting registrar. White registrars routinely concluded that a prospective white voter was qualified to vote but excluded a prospective black voter. As late as the 1950s, for example, Alabama registrars were still ruling that blacks with Ph.D.s from Tuskegee University were illiterate.[53] The Supreme Court's 1898 opinion in *Williams v. Mississippi*[54] approved these "racially neutral measures" aimed at disenfranchisement.

In the last decade of the nineteenth century, segregation statutes began to proliferate. Just as blacks had fought against their oppression during slavery, so too they fought against this new form of oppression. African-Americans also used the separation imposed upon them to organize against the very force that sought to oppress them through that separation.

Blacks first encountered segregation in the "freer" soil of the North prior to the Civil War. Thus, the struggle against segregation had started before abolition. Segregation and the demeaning treatment that African-Americans received as a result of it spawned the first and most important institution in the African-American community, the Black Church. The Black Church has been the government, the social club, the secret order, the espionage system and the main political party in many black communities. Historically, the Black Church was the driving force used to organize efforts to liberate the black community. Major social protest movements by African-Americans tend to start in the Black Church. Most of the black community's political leaders have been men of the cloth. In addition, the church building has not only been the sanctum sanctorum, but also the lyceum, the gymnasium, the community forum, the conservatory of music and the place where the elocutionary, graphic and literary arts were developed.[55]

In 1794 a small group of black worshipers at St George's Methodist Church in Philadelphia were forcibly pulled from their knees while inadvertently praying in the white section. Refusing to submit to any more indignities, black parishioners left St. George's. They established the first black church in the United States, the Bethel African Methodist Episcopal Church, under the leadership of Richard Allen. Thereafter, independent African Methodist Churches where black people could worship without the demeaning attitudes of whites were organized along the Atlantic Coast. In 1816 several of these independent black churches met at a conference in Philadelphia and established the first African-American Christian denomination, the African Methodist Episcopal (AME) Church. Its first bishop was Richard Allen. Six years later the second denomination known as the African Methodist Episcopal Zion (AME Zion) Church was established with its first bishop being James Varick.

Once slavery ended, southern blacks were free to organize into their own religious denominations. The AME and the AME Zion churches were joined by the Christian Methodist Episcopal (CME was founded as the Colored Methodist Episcopal) Church, three major Baptist conventions (The National Baptist Convention, Inc., The National Baptist Convention of America and the Progressive Baptist Convention), The Church of God in Christ and dozens of smaller sects. These black church denominations represent 95% of the black Christians in the country today.[56]

Education was one of the greatest needs of a people recently coming out of slavery. Except in North Carolina, prior to the Civil War there was no general system of public education in the South. The first massive effort at constructing a public education system was the result of reconstruction efforts after the Civil War. During the drafting of the state constitutional conventions in the former Confederate states called to pave the way for readmission to the Union in 1867 and 1868, public education was one of the most important issues addressed. When public education was discussed the issue of school integration came up, but due to white resistance to integrated schools the heated debates that occurred in nearly every state convention were, to a large degree, only theoretical. Most of the state conventions eventually avoided the issue by tabling motions either to mandate or to prohibit segregated schools. Even though no state constitution required the schools be segregated, only two-Louisiana and South Carolina, forbade segregation in public schools. However, integration prevailed only for a short period of time in several Louisiana elementary schools, mostly in New Orleans and at the University of South Carolina. The ability to successfully integrate some schools in New Orleans resulted partially from its cosmopolitan ethnic heritage. Because of the spectrum of colors in New Orleans it was sometimes difficult to tell certain black students from white ones. Nevertheless, the efforts to integrate schools caused several thousands of white children to transfer to private schools or to drop out all together.[57] In 1873, the failure of integration at the University of South Carolina reflected the inability to bring about integrated education. Nearly all whites withdrew from the University, and by 1875, 90% of the students were black. The remaining whites were mostly sons of carpetbaggers or Northern missionaries.[58]

Recognizing that segregated education was better than ignorance, the black churches took the lead in founding educational institutions for African-Americans. By 1900, the Baptist churches supported eighty elementary and high schools. There were also eighteen Baptist institutions of post secondary education. The AMEs established six colleges between 1870 and 1886, the CMEs established four such institutions between 1878 and 1902 and the AME Zions founded a college in 1879.[59]

Booker T. Washington was one of the spearheads of the drive to educate African-Americans. Born a slave in 1856, at the age of twenty-five he founded Tuskegee Institute in the heart of Alabama's black belt. By 1901 Tuskegee had 109 full-time faculty members and 1,095 pupils. By the late 1890s, Washington had also created a powerful political organization known as the "Tuskegee Machine." Washington understood that blacks left slavery as illiterate, penniless peasants without the necessary knowledge and skills to make a decent living. The educational philosophy he stressed was the acquisition of skills and knowledge that could be used to generate gainful employment and financial independence.

Washington's educational philosophies have often been criticized for accepting the notion that blacks should start at the bottom of the social hierarchy. However, Washington developed his educational philosophy for a people who were coming out of slavery in an extremely hostile environment. Washington was an excellent public orator and discovered that he could be an effective fund-raiser for black education by parroting what white philanthropists wanted to hear. He was able to secure substantial financial aid from wealthy white individuals and corporations for his endeavors to uplift the black race.[60] Washington felt that because of the overwhelming prejudice against blacks, public protest against their oppression would only cause an angry white backlash. Nevertheless, he worked quietly behind the scenes against black disenfranchisement, segregation and the exclusion of blacks from juries.[61]

African-American women were important and significant participants and leaders in various organizations established by blacks after the Civil War. In addition, they organized to focus on problems confronting black females. In 1896 the National Association of Colored Women (NACW) was founded with Mary Church Terrell as its first president. The NACW focused on sexual abuse, attacks on the moral character of black women, lynching, education, inadequate health care, lack of child care services and poverty. By 1915 there were over 1,000 clubs nationwide and 50,000 sisters who were members.[62] Other major activists of this movement included Ida B. Wells and Mary McLeod Bethune.

During the Segregation Era, black professionals were excluded from white professional organizations. Black professionals, therefore, organized their own professional associations to assist in their development and that of the black community. Black newspaper editors established the Colored Press Association in 1880, black school teachers founded a national association in 1889 and black physicians followed suit in 1894 when they established the National Medical Association. The National Bar Association was started by black lawyers in 1903 and the National Bankers' Association was established in 1906.[63]

African-Americans also became entrepreneurs in large numbers after the Civil War. While there were many individual business successes, in general their large-scale successes were in fields where racism gave blacks an opportunity to serve their own people. Since whites considered blacks to be bad risks, African-Americans owned and operated successful insurance companies. Blacks established successful banks because white bankers often felt that their accounts would be too meager to manage. Madame C. J. Walker and Mrs. A. E. Malone became wealthy selling hair and skin care products for black people.[64] To assist collective business efforts of African-Americans in the face of racism, Booker T. Washington founded the Negro Business League in 1900. It functioned as the black Chamber of Commerce, providing assistance, encouragement and inspiration to its entrepreneurial members. It helped to increase the number of black business enterprises from 20,000 to 40,000 between 1910 and 1914.[65] This organization had over 600 chapters by 1915.

The largest mass movement of African-Americans during the Segregation Era sought to eradicate the oppression of blacks through separation from whites. In 1914 Marcus Garvey established a black nationalist self-help organization, the Universal Negro Improvement Association (UNIA). Garvey was from the same political vein as people like Paul Cuffe (who took thirty-eight blacks to Africa at his own expense in 1815), Edward Wilmont Blyden, Alexander Crummell (who preached the ability and obligation of African-Americans to uplift the continent of Africa through returning to it) and Martin Delaney. Garvey argued that America was so irredeemably oppressive and fundamentally racist that it was best for blacks in America to seek a new homeland. The goals of Garvey's organization were, after gaining economic and political control of black communities, to develop an independent black colony in Africa. By the early 1920s there were over 700 UNIA branches in North America and a membership of half a million.[66]

A. Phillip Randolph was the leader of the largest African-American labor union, the Brotherhood of Sleeping Car Porters. This organization won significant concessions from the railroad industry for black porters in the 1930s. Randolph and Grant Reynolds founded an organization called the League for Nonviolent Civil Disobedience to the Draft to protest segregation in the armed forces. Randolph testified in March 1948 before the Senate Armed Services Committee. In his testimony he stated that unless segregation and discrimination were banned he would personally advise Negroes to refuse to fight for a democracy that they could neither possess nor enjoy.[67] This pressure and the desire to win votes from blacks in key northern industrial states in the upcoming 1948 election helps to explain why President Harry Truman issued Executive Order 9981 requiring the desegregation of the military. In the November presidential election, Truman received 70% of the black vote. Blacks provided him with his margin of victory in California, Ohio and Illinois. The seventy-eight electoral votes in those states were enough to make the difference in the outcome of the election.[68]

African-Americans were very active in interracial organizations that were established to assist in the struggles against disenfranchisement, segregation and racial oppression of black people, such as the Urban League and the National Association for the Advancement of Colored People (NAACP). With emancipation the number of blacks moving to urban areas in the North began to increase. By the end of the Nineteenth Century, there were more than 60,000 African-Americans residing in New York. An additional 30,000 called Philadelphia and Chicago home. Blacks migrating from the rural South to the urban North encountered special problems. They were often confronted by virulent housing discrimination which restricted available options to poorly maintained accommodations at inflated rents. Blacks often confronted discrimination in hiring which made it difficult to find gainful employment. Prejudice from white employers and labor unions forced many of them into unskilled laborer and servant positions. Black women normally needed to work in order to support their families but they were often confined to low-paying jobs as domestic servants. This generated another significant problem for the black urban community, child-rearing.

The Urban League was formed in 1911 from a merger of three organizations in New York City. Established in 1906, the National League for the Protection of Colored Women (NLPCW) was an interracial organization founded to respond to the problem of prostitution among black women who migrated to the North. Black women from the rural South migrated without definite plans for respectable employment and accommodation. They were often forced into prostitution in order to survive. The NLPCW employed a two-prong strategy. They attempted to prevent helpless, friendless and penniless black women from being sent North by irresponsible agencies. The NLPCW also assisted those black women who actually migrated. They sought to secure for these women respectable lodging and adequate vocational training. The Committee for Improving the Industrial Condition of Negroes in New York (CIICN) was an interracial organization founded in 1906. This group sought to improve employment opportunities for blacks. Prejudice from white employers and labor unions forced blacks into unskilled laborer and servants positions. In order to open up new employment opportunities it was necessary to provide blacks with adequate training. CIICN worked with the Board of Education of New York City to open up more night schools in black areas. CIICN also set up its own vocational training programs in Harlem and cooperated with employment agencies to find job openings for blacks. The third organization was the Committee on Urban Conditions. It was founded in 1910 and drew on the personnel and programs of the other two. In 1911, these three organizations joined together and established the Urban League.

The Urban League from the beginning preached that cooperation was the best hope for peace between the races. Urban League stationary stated, "Let us work, not as colored people nor as white people for the narrow benefit of any group alone, but *together* as American citizens, for the common good of our common city, our common country."[69] The Urban League did not seek charity, but opportunities for blacks. The Urban League also conducted scientific investigations of conditions among urban blacks to provide a basis for effective reforms. By the end of World War I, the Urban League had eighty-one staff members in over thirty cities.

In 1905, at Niagara Falls, Canada, W. E. B. Du Bois organized a meeting of twenty-nine people from thirteen states and the District of Columbia. The Niagara Movement called for the abolition of discrimination based on race or color and a recognition of the principles of human brotherhood. It dedicated itself to obtaining the rights belonging to all Americans. The Niagara Movement had some successes during its five years of existence, including defeating local legislation that would have created racially segregated railroad cars in Massachusetts.[70]

The mission of the Niagara Movement was taken up by a new organization that developed out of a call that Oswald Garrison Villard, the grandson of abolitionist William Lloyd Garrison, took the lead in issuing. Among those who signed the Call were Ida B. Wells, Monroe Trotter, Bishop Alexander Walters and Du Bois. The Call urged all believers in democracy to join in a national conference for the renewal of the struggle for civil and political liberty. The NAACP grew out of that conference and was to become the major confrontational group that launched frontal attacks on the "separate but equal" policy of the segregation era.

While many who served on the national board of the NAACP were whites committed to the fight for racial equality, the organization was always in the forefront of developing black leadership. For example, by 1914 thirteen African-Americans were on the Board of Directors and most of them were originally members of the Niagara Movement.[71] This goal also led to the ascension of James Weldon Johnson to the position of NAACP secretary in 1917. Du Bois was assigned the position of the Director of Publications and Research. In that position he launched the publication of the *Crisis.* The *Crisis* was a popular magazine from its first publication, starting with 31,000 subscriptions in 1914 and quickly rising to 100,000 by 1918.[72] Du Bois wrote that the *Crisis'* editorial page "will stand for the rights of men, irrespective of color or race, for the highest ideals of American democracy, and for reasonable but earnest and persistent attempt to gain these rights and realize these ideals."[73] Through the magazine, Du Bois became an unrelenting opponent of racial inequality. The central theme of the *Crisis* editorials was that racial inequality was a function of social and economic caste. "The struggle for 'social equality' was absolutely essential to erod(ing) the walls of racial segregation and to expand(ing) political and economic opportunities for black Americans."[74]

Membership in local chapters of the NAACP was dominated by African-Americans. The NAACP experienced tremendous growth largely through the efforts of Du Bois' advocacy in the *Crisis.* In 1912 the NAACP had ten branches, but within four years it had expanded to thirty-seven, including six in the South and a total of 9,000 members. By 1919, the NAACP boasted over 300 branches and 88,000 members with 155 of these branches and 42,000 of these members in the South.[75]

From its inception, the NAACP advocated the power of direct action against racial oppression. It organized protests against the film *Birth of a Nation.* D. W. Griffith's epic film retold the story of Reconstruction as a time when whites in the South were ruled by a black indolent horde. Griffith portrayed the Ku Klux Klan as the saviors of the South who came and redeemed it from the barbarous hands of unschooled blacks. When Woodrow Wilson instituted his policy of segregation in the federal government, the NAACP vigorously opposed it. The organization sponsored mass rallies in northern cities. It also delivered petitions to the White House signed by both blacks and whites.

The NAACP also led the fight to prevent the appointment of racist judges to the federal bench. Sometimes these struggles were successful. For example, Herbert Hoover nominated John J. Parker of North Carolina to the United States Supreme Court. Parker had unsuccessfully run for governor on the Republican ticket in 1920. During his nominating speech he announced his support for the addition of the grandfather clause to the North Carolina voting laws and indicated that blacks had not yet reached that stage of development where they could share the burdens and responsibilities of government. Apprized of Parker's views, Hoover nevertheless refused to withdraw the nomination. The NAACP organized a campaign to defeat the nomination, sending telegrams to every NAACP branch, with special emphasis on those in the North and in border states where Negro voting was a growing political factor.[76] Mass meetings were called and representatives from the national office of the NAACP, including Du Bois, Arthur Springarn and Walter White, went on speaking tours to drum up support against the nomination. Parker's nomination was defeated in the Senate by a vote of 39 to 41.

The NAACP and later the NAACP Legal Defense and Educational Fund, Inc. ("LDF")[77] were very active in a number of litigation efforts attacking segregation, discrimination and disenfranchisement of blacks. One of the NAACP's first successful legal campaigns was challenging the adoption of housing segregation ordinances. In 1917 the NAACP convinced the Supreme Court in *Buchanan v. Warley*[78] to strike down a Louisville ordinance which required houses sold on blocks where the majority of the residents were white be sold to other whites and on blocks where a majority of residents were black be sold to other blacks. Unfortunately, those committed to housing segregation, used a legal maneuver to significantly attenuate the effect of this victory.

The Court's decision in *Buchanan* applied only to government efforts to segregate housing. Housing segregation pursuant to the desires of private individuals and entities was considered to be an entirely different matter. Thus, in order to get around the Court's decision, housing discrimination was privatized. Private owners of residential property began to place restrictive covenants on their property that limited subsequent resales to members of the same race. A racially restrictive covenant prevented a white person from selling his home to anyone other than another white person. It was not until 1948 in *Shelley v. Kraemer*[79] that the LDF convinced the Supreme Court to strike down these racially restrictive covenants because they violated the Fourteenth Amendment.

The NAACP and LDF were also actively involved in litigation to restore the rights of blacks to the franchise. As indicated earlier, starting in the 1890s, a number of provisions were enacted into state law aimed at eliminating blacks from the electoral process. The most infamous disenfranchising scheme was the enactment of literacy and understanding clauses. But literacy tests could also operate to keep whites from voting. Alabama, Georgia, Louisiana, North Carolina, Oklahoma, South Carolina and Virginia responded to this potential problem by adding to the literacy test statutes, a grandfather clause. Oklahoma's grandfather clause, for example, exempted from the literacy test those whose fathers or grandfathers were on the electoral roll as of January 1, 1866, a time before blacks could vote. What this meant was that many whites that could not pass any literacy test were "grand-fathered" in as voters while blacks were excluded. The NAACP, however, convinced the Supreme Court to strike down grandfather clauses in its 1915 decision in *Guinn v. United States.*[80]

Blacks were also disenfranchised through the use of the white primary. Due to the Republican Party's association with Lincoln and the North's efforts in the Civil War, abolition and reconstruction, whites in the states of the former Confederacy disdained the Republican Party. After Reconstruction, the Democratic Party came to dominate southern politics. The most significant election in the southern states that adopted the primary system was not the general election, but the Democratic Party primary. Some states passed laws that limited participation in the Democratic primary election to white voters. The Fifteenth Amendment prohibits states from denying or abridging the right to vote on account of race, color or previous condition of servitude. These states asserted that because the Democratic Party was a voluntary association, a limitation on who could vote in the primary was not state action. Thus, such discrimination was not banned by the Fifteenth Amendment. The NAACP was finally successful in getting the Supreme Court to strike down the white primary in the 1944 decision *Smith v. Allwright.*[81]

Conclusion

This chapter has discussed the discourse of African-American Centralism, a discourse structured around a view of the social world as one where African-Americans as a group are struggling to overcome their racial oppression. As a result, this pattern of understanding views the social world in terms of racial and ethnic groups. African-Americans are understood as oppressed, not inferior. It sees the non-Hispanic white racial/ethnic group as possessing a disproportionate amount of social, economic, educational and political power.

This Chapter has also briefly presented the view of the historical experience of African-Americans generated within the boundaries of this cognitive framework. Within this discourse the perception of history focuses on the twin aspects of the African-American experience, being subjected to racial discrimination and the struggle against it. The struggle against racial oppression has always been a feature of the lives of blacks in America. The genesis of the struggle can be traced back to the west coast of Africa where the African slaves first met their European purchasers. This struggle continued unabated until the Supreme Court's opinion in *Brown v. Board of Education*. Despite significant progress by African-Americans over the past fifty years, this struggle continues today.

Chapter Three

The Discourse of Colorblind Individualism

Today Colorblind Individualism is the dominant discourse which controls much of the public discussions about race in American Society. This system of meaning did not spring into existence all at once, but developed over a period of four hundred years. It is a compilation and mix of the points of view of many different liberal politicians and philosophers who have extolled the virtues and benefits of individuality and self-determination. Colorblind Individualism views the social world as one populated by Knowing Individuals. Knowing Individuals are free-willed, rational, autonomous and self-determined people who are capable of pursuing their self-formulated goals and objectives. Knowing Individuals are capable of reflecting upon and altering the opinions they express, the beliefs they hold, the aims they pursue and the attachments they form. Thus the opinions, beliefs, aims and attachments of Knowing Individuals are presumed to be the result of individual self-determinations.

Since the 1970s, the Supreme Court has moved towards embracing a view of the rights embodied in the equal protection clause in terms of society as a collection of Knowing Individuals. In cases like *Keyes v. School District No.1,*[1] *Washington v. Davis*[2] and *Village of Arlington Heights v. Metropolitan Housing Development Corp*,[3] the Supreme Court analogized government to Knowing Individuals. It concluded that the determination of unconstitutional governmental discrimination is based upon the motivations that produced the governmental action, as opposed to the effects of that action. In addition, the Supreme Court's current interpretation of the equal protection clause requires all racial classifications, whether imposed by a "federal, state, or local governmental actor,... be analyzed by a reviewing court under strict scrutiny. In other words, such classifications are constitutional only if they are narrowly tailored measures that further compelling governmental interests."[4] The Supreme Court has only recognized two interest as being compelling enough to justify the use of racial classifications. The Supreme Court has repeatedly stated that government has a compelling state interest in remedying the effects of identified acts of discrimination.[5] Thus, governmental bodies have the legal power to use racial classifications and regard individuals as members of racial and ethnic groups in a narrowly tailored manner in order to remedy the effects of identified acts of discrimination. The most obvious example of this is the treatment of public school students, faculty, administrators and staff as member of racial and ethnic groups under school desegregation decrees issued to remedy the operation of a *de jure* segregated school system. In the summer of 2003, a majority of the members of the Supreme Court upheld the affirmative action admissions plan adopted by the University of Michigan Law School in *Grutter v. Bollinger.*[6] In *Grutter,* the Court concluded that the benefits of diversity were a compelling state interest. The Court also stated that using racial classifications in an individualized admissions process to pursue a critical mass of minority students from underrepresented groups with a history of discrimination was narrowly tailored to advance the interest of diversity.

The Supreme Court has not formally adopted a colorblind approach to the equal protection clause. By basing the determination of unconstitutional discrimination on the discriminatory motives and limiting the use of racial classifications by government to those applications that survive strict scrutiny, however, much of the discussions regarding equal protection rights are based upon the limitations on government that are derived from the underlying assumptions of Colorblind Individualism's view of society as a collection of Knowing Individuals.

Section I of this Chapter describes the conceptual structure of Colorblind Individualism. Section II will present a version of the historical treatment of African-Americans as conceptualized by this pattern of understanding. This version of history will emphasize efforts to recognize and expand the treatment of blacks as self-determined, free-willed individuals in American society. During the colonial period, there was a nascent movement within certain religious organizations to view blacks as equal under the sight of God. The Revolutionary War spawned movements which led to the abolition of the Trans Atlantic Slave Trade and, in the North, slavery. After the Civil War, blacks obtained a measure of formal legal equality with respect to political and civil rights, though they were still deemed to be socially inferior. By the end of the nineteenth century, however, those who happen to be black were being legally disenfranchised through the use of various racially neutral practices. After effectively losing the right to vote, segregation statutes were enacted throughout the South. Despite the discrimination against those who happened to be black, under segregation they were closer to being treated as Knowing Individuals than they were during the antebellum period.

I. The Conceptual Structure

This section describes the basic conceptual structure of Colorblind Individualism, together with its view of the social world as a collection of Knowing Individuals and the concept of the Knowing Individual. To further explain how this system comprehends racial phenomena, this section illuminates the Knowing Individual's relationship to historically developed traditions, including those based on religious beliefs and racial or ethnic heritage. This section will then focus on the epistemology of this system of meaning. For this discourse, individuals are perceived without regard to unchosen characteristics like race, ethnicity, gender or sexual orientation. Words used to discuss racial issues such as racism, racial oppression, racial discrimination and racial equality draw their meaning from a perception of society as a collection of Knowing Individuals. Thus, basing judgements about an individual's personality traits and characteristics on race or ethnicity is considered irrational. Moral and ethical behavior is centered on respecting fellow individuals' rights of self-determination. Colorblind Individualism views the role of government as limited. Government's primary responsibility is to protect the rights of Knowing Individuals to pursue their self-determined goals and objectives without interfering with the rights of other Knowing Individuals to do the same. The last part of this section will discuss the relationship of this system of meaning with the other three—Traditional Americanism, African-American Centralism and American Collectivism.

A. Conception of the Social World and of the Knowing Individual

The defining idea of Colorblind Individualism is of society as a collection of Knowing Individuals. Knowing Individuals are free-willed, rational, autonomous, self-determined and able to pursue their self-formulated goals and objectives. They are capable of reflecting upon all of the opinions they express, the beliefs they hold, the aims they pursue and the attachments they form.[7] Thus the opinions, beliefs, aims and attachments of Knowing Individuals are products of self-determination, not acculturation.

Because Knowing Individuals are capable of self-reflection, it follows that there is a split in their personality. While there is a manifest self present to the outside world, Knowing Individuals also possess a hidden, deep and essential self. This part of the self is prior to all the manifest characteristics of the Knowing Individual, including race, ethnicity, gender, sexual orientation and socio-economic class.[8] This part of the self is the "real," "true" or "subject" self.

It is the source of the motivations and drives that propel the individual to express opinions, hold beliefs, pursue actions and generate attachments.

This system of meaning is built upon the ontological presupposition that the true self originates, within each person, as a separate, unique and distinct entity. Under this pattern of understanding any given person should seek to uncover his/her true self, decipher its predilections, separate it from that which might obscure or alienate it and then structure the remaining aspects of life so as to be consistent with its prescriptions.[9] The only constraint placed on these individual choices is that each Knowing Individual exercise self-restraint over his or her inclinations that would, if satisfied, directly interfere or create a substantial risk of interference with others' ability to pursue their self-determined goals and objectives.

For the Knowing Individual, the constant question about any important life decision is, "does this choice reflect who I really am?" Thus, Knowing Individuals should seek occupations or employment that reflect the character and interest of their true selves. Knowing Individuals should listen to their inner voice to determine whether to be a soldier, a doctor, a lawyer, a banker, a businessperson, a philosopher, a law professor, a garbage collector, a cashier or a farmer. Knowing Individuals should dress in clothes that reflect a sense of who they are or clothes they feel comfortable wearing. Leisure activities that Knowing Individuals engage in—from listening to certain kinds of music, attending certain theatrical performances, watching certain television programs, engaging in certain sporting activities and eating at certain restaurants—should be those that they enjoy or that provide some other self-determined benefit. Knowing Individuals should not seek relationships with friends because they have similar racial, ethnic, religious or socio-economic backgrounds. Rather they should establish relationships with others they share common interests with, they like or those who will assist them in obtaining any of their goals and objectives. Knowing Individuals should not choose a partner or a spouse because they feel constrained by an involuntary obligation or duty to select as a mate someone of their race, ethnicity, religion or someone that meets with their parents' approval. This does not mean that Knowing Individuals should ignore the racial, ethnic or religious backgrounds of their potential mate or their parents' preferences. It means only that racial or ethnic customs, religious edicts or parental preferences are merely advisory, not obligatory.

B. The Knowing Individual's Relationship to Historically Developed Traditions

The basic value of Colorblind Individualism is for Knowing Individuals to follow their self-generated goals and desires. This discourse abhors attempts to constrain self-determination due to historically developed traditions of belief. Since race (and often ethnicity) is generally a visible characteristic, evidence of a Knowing Individual's race is almost always present when that Knowing Individual is present. Consequently, this individual factor can often work to deny a Knowing Individual's ability to be self-determining.

Despite the fact that the race of a person is normally visible when the individual is present, Colorblind Individualism comprehends a person's attachment to their racial group as it would other voluntary affiliations based on other historically developed traditions. Affiliations to historically developed religious traditions, for example, provides an analogy to how Colorblind Individualism would treat racial and group affiliations. Within this discourse Knowing Individuals can choose to follow a religious tradition and thereby make it a salient aspect of their life. Thus, religious adherents would be viewed as voluntarily choosing their religious beliefs. Religious adherents, however, should still constrain their actions so that others can pursue their self-determined goals and objectives. Other Knowing Individuals do not have to agree with a person's choice of religious beliefs. They should, however, tolerate their choices in order not to interfere with religious adherents exercise of their rights of self-determination.

In the same way that self-determined religious beliefs of Knowing Individuals are tolerated by others, so should traditions or beliefs based on racial or ethnic heritage. The notion of respecting the rights of Knowing Individuals to be self-determining within Colorblind Individualism therefore, does not lead inexorably to ignoring or attempting to efface historically developed traditions based on racial or ethnic affiliations. Knowing Individuals should not be involuntarily constrained by beliefs associated with unchosen traits such as race or ethnicity. Also, people should not be acculturated to unreflectively follow the dictates of historically developed traditions ascribed to racial or ethnic heritages. Nor should Knowing Individuals be treated against their will as members of their racial or ethnic group. But, even though Knowing Individuals should not be compelled to view themselves as members of their racial or ethnic group, they should be allowed the freedom to choose whether to celebrate their racial or ethnic affiliations and heritages. As contradictory as it sounds, affiliations based on those characteristics should be converted into voluntary ones.[10] Some Knowing Individuals will choose to make their racial or ethnic identity a salient part of their individuality and to extol their racial or ethnic heritage. Knowing Individuals who voluntarily choose to celebrate their racial or ethnic heritage do not constitute an involuntary group. Rather they constitute a group that is the product of the choices made by Knowing Individuals who happen to share a similar skin color or ethnic background and desire to celebrate it. Recognizing

Knowing Individuals who choose to make their race or ethnicity a salient part of their identity or celebrate their racial or ethnic heritage as members of their racial or ethnic group does not deny their individuality. Rather it respects their right to self-determination.

C. Epistemology and the Meaning of Words Related to Racial Issues

The epistemology of this pattern of understanding is founded on the notion that involuntary physical qualities, such as race or ethnicity, generally should not be taken into account in determining personality traits and characteristics of a given person. When a person presumes that physical traits imply certain personality traits, the cognitive processes of the perceiver are distorted. Such a perceiver attributes undue importance to irrelevant information. Rather than evaluating another individual based on the qualities and characteristics that he or she actually possesses or manifests, the perceiver relies on stereotypes to make these judgements.[11] People should "not be judged by the color of their skin but by the content of their character."[12]

Within this cognitive framework, concepts for discussing issues such as racism, racial oppression, racial discrimination and racial equality are defined by focusing on the motivations of the actor. The actions of Knowing Individuals are determined by their motivations. However, Knowing Individuals are motivated by a lot of different considerations. Often times, Knowing Individuals arrive at decisions or engage in actions for non-racial reasons, but those decisions or actions may have a disparate negative effect on other Knowing Individuals who happen to be members of certain racial or ethnic groups. The Knowing Individuals who share such traits are not victims of racism or racial discrimination when the actions are motivated by non-racial concerns. It is not the consequences of a given decision or action that determines whether it is racist or racially discriminatory. Racial discrimination and racism only occur when the actor or decision-maker acts or arrives at a decision because of, and not in spite of, the racially discriminatory effect on a particular racial or ethnic group or individual. Anyone, including those who happen to be non-Hispanic white, black, Asian, Latino or Native American, can perpetrate or be a victim of racism and racial discrimination.

Racial equality exists where neither race nor ethnicity are used to differentiate Knowing Individuals. Race is neither used to help nor to harm people, but is ignored or overlooked. Within this pattern of understanding, the society that has obtained racial justice—and thus eliminated racial oppression—

is one where race is considered to be irrelevant and racial affiliations are completely voluntary.

D. Moral and Ethical Beliefs

The need to foster the self-determination of Knowing Individuals is the foundation of the moral and ethical beliefs of Colorblind Individualism. Knowing Individuals have the right to pursue any lifestyle they choose, so long as it respects the right of others to do the same. Thus, the choices that Knowing Individuals make are constrained by the obligation not to interfere with the ability of their fellow Knowing Individuals to do the same. Murder, rape, assault, battery, robbery and deception are wrong because they interfere with the victims' ability to pursue their self-determined objectives.

Once the respective relations to the material world have been determined, Knowing Individuals will find it beneficial to interact with one another to advance their own self-determined desires. The baker may find it helpful to provide bread to the cobbler in exchange for the cobbler providing shoes for the baker's family. These voluntary interactions in furtherance of Knowing Individuals' self-determined interest create mutual obligations between contracting parties. Knowing Individuals must perform the duties required by their voluntary agreement with others. Thus violating voluntarily entered into agreements is also immoral.

The commitment to self-determination creates an unresolved conflict concerning the treatment of involuntary characteristics like race and ethnicity. On one hand, for one Knowing Individual to discriminate against another because of the other's involuntary characteristics inhibits the other's ability to be self-determining. On the other hand, however, Knowing Individuals have the right to pursue their self-determined beliefs. If Knowing Individuals are denied the ability to discriminate against others based on involuntary characteristics they deem to be relevant, they are denied their right to be self-determining. There must be certain activities where Knowing Individuals can discriminate based on involuntary characteristics and other activities where this is not proper. For example, this discourse would frown upon someone who stated flatly that they would only date or marry an individual of a given race. But at the same time, it would recognize that the right of self-determination must include the right of the individual to decide who they will date or marry for whatever reasons, including racially discriminatory ones. But allowing a Knowing Individual to state that they would only serve whites at their lunch counter would probably be viewed as immoral. An important moral task within this discourse is to distinguish certain public activities where racial discrimination is inappropriate from certain private activities where it is, reluctantly, acceptable.

E. The Role of Government and Society

Society and government come into existence as a result of the free-willed, self-determined choices of Knowing Individuals. Knowing Individuals voluntarily give up their isolation and join society because it is the best way to advance the pursuit of their self-determined goals and objectives. The benefits derived from joining society are the pursuit by Knowing Individuals of their goals and objectives without undue interference by others and the security and firm establishment of the rights to enjoy and use their accumulated property. These benefits assure for each person a sphere which is immune from interference by others. In order to maximize these benefits, all Knowing Individuals must accept burdens. These burdens require that each Knowing Individual exercise restraint over their inclinations that, if satisfied, would directly interfere or create a substantial risk of interfering with the ability of others to pursue their goals and objectives.

The benefits derived from, and the burdens imposed by, joining society, provide the explanation for the primary roles and purposes of government. Government should have a limited purpose and character. The principal functions of government flow from its obligation to help ensure a society where people enjoy the liberty to pursue their self-determined goals and objectives without undue interference by others and ensure that Knowing Individuals are reasonably secure in the use, possession and enjoyment of their property. Government should also provide, through universal and impersonal laws, the means to resolve disputes that arise among Knowing Individuals in pursuit of their self-determined goals and objectives.

Beyond ensuring that one Knowing Individual does not unjustly interfere with the right of self-determination of other Knowing Individuals, government should be neutral with regard to competing conceptions of a good life. It is generally inconsistent with the role of government for it to formulate a certain morality for citizens or to direct society along a certain path in order to advance a given vision of the good society. Each Knowing Individual should be left to make the decision regarding what a good life is for him or herself subject to the constraint of respecting the rights of others. Thus, there are very few circumstances where government should sacrifice the interest of Knowing Individuals for the common good. Such a compelled sacrifice is normally inconsistent with the limited nature of government.

F. Contrasted with Other Systems of Meaning

This cognitive framework perceives racial phenomena in ways different from the other three discourses. It is far more apparent that the other three discourses are based more on historical contingencies than Colorblind Individualism. The belief in the inferiority of African-Americans, the fundamental basis of Traditional Americanism, is clearly attributable to historical events. In different countries around the world, groups other than African-Americans are branded as being inferior. In India, for example, the Dalits (also known as "outcastes" or "untouchables") have historically been viewed as inferior. In Japan, the Koreans are generally looked down upon. Even though blacks in the United States are viewed as inferior, some groups in other countries see American blacks as an extraordinarily powerful group. The Dalits in India and blacks in South Africa, for instance, came to associate their liberation struggle with that of African-Americans. Many members of these groups saw the liberation struggle by African-Americans as one to be emulated.[13] They viewed blacks as remarkably adept in their ability to gain and wield tremendous power in the United States. African-American Centralism is also the result of historical contingencies. Blacks in America are actually composed of descendants of hundreds of different African ethnic groups. Those ethnic groups tended to view the world in terms of their kinship or ethnic group as opposed to their race. But among their African-American descendants those former ethnic differences are seldom known or discussed. American Collectivism depends upon the historical contingency of the creation of the United States as a nation. This system of meaning depends upon historical events such as the Declaration of Independence by the British colonies from Great Britain and their success in the subsequent Revolutionary War. If the United States ceases to exist as a nation, this system of meaning will also cease to exist. While Colorblind Individualism developed over nearly four hundred years of religious, political, racial and ethnic conflict, the structure of this discourse is far more permanent. It could be asserted that human societies could always view themselves as a collection of Knowing Individuals.

Traditional Americanism at times views non-Hispanic whites as Knowing Individuals and at other times as members of a superior involuntary non-Hispanic white racial group. Traditional Americanism never views blacks as individuals, but always as members of a substandard involuntary group. Colorblind Individualism, however, always rejects viewing Knowing Individuals—whether white, black, brown, red or yellow—in terms of their involuntary racial or ethnic group membership. Thus, Colorblind Individualism perceives the use of race conscious policies and practices to perpetuate the oppression of a given racial group, such as slavery and segregation, as wrong.

Sometimes viewing society as a collection of Knowing Individuals will produce results similar to those generated by Traditional Americanism's conscious recognition of blacks as an inferior racial group. At other times the consequences of viewing society as a collection of Knowing Individuals will assist African-Americans in overcoming their racial oppression and thus be consistent with the basic goal of African-American Centralism. For example, those who happen to be black typically score considerably lower than those who happen to be white on standardized tests such as the SAT or ACT. Eliminating any considerations of race and basing admissions decisions of highly selective colleges, universities and graduate programs solely on objective academic credentials would almost be as effective in excluding those who happen to be black from admissions as a racially conscious rule that proscribed all blacks from being admitted to such institutions. The basic assumptions of Traditional Americanism could easily embrace the position that blacks should be excluded from highly selective colleges, universities and graduate programs because they are intellectually inferior. Thus, Traditional Americanism could advance arguments that all should be treated as Knowing Individuals in this instance as a way to reach the result that blacks should be excluded from highly selective colleges, universities and graduate programs. When arguments generated by Traditional Americanism take the form of arguments within Colorblind Individualism, there is still a significant difference in comprehending these arguments within the conceptual boundaries of Traditional Americanism as opposed to Colorblind Individualism. Traditional Americanism would argue for treating all as individuals in order to produce the desired ends of confining blacks to an inferior position. Colorblind Individualism would view treating all as Knowing Individuals as the end to be desired and not a means to some other objective.

Conversely, if the issue is one that deals with racially conscious discrimination against blacks, then an assertion that all should be treated as Knowing Individuals will be consistent with the goal of African-American Centralism of reducing racial oppression. For example, a boutique clothing store with expensive merchandise may want to exclude all blacks from admittance to the store because the owners feel that there are very few blacks who have the financial means to afford their merchandise. Requiring the store owner to treat all potential customers as Knowing Individuals and not members of racial groups will eliminate this form of racial discrimination. African-American Centralism could easily generate the view that the store owner's racially-exclusive admittance policy is an aspect of racial oppression that must be fought against. Thus, African-American Centralism could advance the argument that the store owner should treat all potential customers as individuals and not admit or exclude potential customers based on their race. Thus, African-American Centralism can make arguments identical to those generated within Colorblind Individualism. This was common during the Desegregation Era. Many Black leaders quoted Rev. Martin Luther King, Jr.'s plea that people be judged by the content of their character and not the color of their skin. African-American Centralism, however, employs these kinds of arguments as a means to pursue the goal of eradicating racial oppression. For Colorblind Individualism, the end would be a society of a collection of Knowing Individuals. Thus, even when African-American Centralism asserts arguments identical to those of Colorblind Individualism, these arguments mean something different than when advanced within Colorblind Individualism.

The view of the social world of American Collectivism is that there is one American people. When racial phenomena is conceptualized and racial issues analyzed within the boundaries of American Collectivism, the general interest of the American community is paramount. Judgements about what advances the best interest of American society, however, are bound up in the current meanings attached to fundamental values that Americans cherish. Certain values like liberty, equality, democracy and the pursuit of happiness have been basic values of the nation since the beginning. The meanings of these values, however, change over time. Americans of today hold the values related to individual self-determination for all, regardless of race or ethnicity, in much higher esteem than Americans of the past. Advancing the best interest of American society today does not lose sight of the interpretation of liberty and equality in terms of individual liberty, freedom and self-determination for all, regardless of race or ethnicity. For example, during the Desegregation Era, many national political leaders in American society were urging Americans to move beyond the focus on race and ethnicity and treat people as individuals. This provided a number of positive benefits for American society, including increasing the sense of social justice in the society, increasing the sense of Americans as one people, reducing the possibility of destructive racial conflicts and increasing the material wealth of the country by increasing the productivity and utilization of blacks in the economy. But the treatment of all as individuals was viewed within American Collectivism as a means to advancing the interest of the American community, not as pursuing the end of a society as a collection of Knowing Individuals. Thus, the same argument about judging people based on the content of their character and not the color of their skin is being perceived differently within the conceptual boundaries of the American Collectivism than it would be within the boundaries of Colorblind Individualism. Also, while American Collectivism views individual liberty and freedom as fundamental values, there are times when the individual's interest must be sacrificed for the benefit of the collective good. American Collectivism is willing to sacrifice the interest of a given individual in order to advance the interest of the nation.

II. History of Those Who Happened to be Black and the Legal System's Treatment of Them

This section discusses efforts to recognize blacks as individuals from the time they were first brought to America until the Supreme Court's opinion in *Brown v. Board of Education.* The development of Colorblind Individualism took place over centuries. During the colonial period, there was an incipient notion within religious circles that viewed blacks as individuals who were equal to whites in God's sight. The Revolutionary War helped to generate a movement to abolish the Trans-Atlantic Slave Trade and, in the North, slavery. After the Civil War, the Thirteenth, Fourteenth and Fifteenth Amendments were added to the Constitution. In order to articulate, expand and effectuate the rights granted by these Reconstruction Amendments, Congress also enacted five major civil rights bills between 1866 and 1875. These measures were aimed at granting blacks civil and political equality. By the end of the nineteenth century, however, those who happened to be black were facing efforts aimed at legal disenfranchisement. After effectively losing the right to vote, segregation statutes were enacted throughout the South. While the use of racial classifications embedded in segregation was inconsistent with the view of society as a collection of Knowing Individuals, those who happened to be black were closer to being treated as Knowing Individuals under segregation than they were during the Antebellum Period.

A. The Colonial Period

From the very beginning of colonization in North America, there was a nascent religious tradition which saw blacks as the sons and daughters of the first Adam, the brethren and sisters of the last Adam and the offspring of God.[14] In the sight of God all are the same, hence color did not matter.[15] Over one-hundred years before the Revolutionary War, Cotton Mather, the symbol of authoritarian puritanism and one of the founders of Yale University, "asserted the equality of slaves in the sight of God."[16] Richard Baxter, another English puritan, told slave holders in 1673 that slaves are "as good a kind as you;... [i]f their sin have enslaved them to you,... remember that they have immortal souls, and are equally capable of salvation with yourselves."[17] In 1676, William Edmundson—a Quaker and a friend and companion of George Fox, founder of the Society of Friends—sent a letter to Newport, Rhode Island.[18] In that letter he argued that slavery should be unacceptable to a Christian. The first publicly recorded protest against the slave trade came from German Mennonites in the colony founded by William Penn in 1688.[19]

In 1700, Chief Justice Samuel Sewall of Massachusetts published a highly regarded pamphlet entitled *The Selling of Joseph.* This pamphlet made the first reasoned critique of the slave trade and slavery itself. In it Sewall argued that the selling of Joseph by his brothers in the Old Testament was illegal. Sewall asserted that since Joseph's brothers had no right to sell him in the first place, no one who purchased Joseph could gain rightful title to him. Sewall advanced the same argument against the legitimacy and ownership of Africans who had been originally reduced to slavery in their native land. Since the Africans had not obtained legitimate title to the people they reduced to slavery, no subsequent purchaser of a slave could obtain legitimate title. Sewall went on to proclaim that "these Ethiopians [a common name used to refer to all Africans], as black as they are,... ought to be treated with ... respect...."[20]

The Quakers were one of the first religious groups in America to advocate for the abolition of slavery. At the 1754 annual meeting of the Society of Friends in Philadelphia, Quakers condemned the slave trade. They asserted that living at ease on the toil of others was inconsistent with both Christianity and common justice. Four years later, the group decided that since no master could be expected to resist the temptation to exploit slaves, no Quaker could keep a slave without risking damnation. At their 1759 annual meeting in London, the Quakers condemned both slavery and the practice of dealing in slavery. They "threatened to exclude from a place of responsibility within the Society of Friends anyone who participated in the [slave] trade."[21]

Despite the broad acceptance of slavery within the legal systems in the British colonies during the colonial period, there were always strands of legal thought that reflected an opposition to the institution. For example, Rhode Island passed a law in 1652 designed to convert slaves into indentured servants. "A slave was to be freed after ten years—or at age twenty-four" if acquired while in childhood. The law was apparently enforced throughout the seventeenth century.[22] More significantly, however, the English common law tradition eventually rejected slavery on English soil. During the reign of Queen Elizabeth, a slave brought back from Russia was declared free on the ground that England was too pure an air for slavery. Edward Chamberlayne wrote in his 1672 book, *The Present State of England,* that foreign slaves brought to England were *ipso facto* freed from slavery, though not from ordinary service. In the 1705 case of *Smith v. Brown and Cooper,* Chief Justice Sir John Holt ruled that "one may be a villein in England, but not a slave".[23] Thus, as soon as a Negro comes into England he becomes free. However, in 1729, Attorney-General Sir Philip Yorke and Solicitor-General Charles Talpor issued an opinion to a reply by West Indian planters that a slave in England was not automatically free, nor did baptism bestow freedom on him nor make any alteration in his temporal condition. Twenty years later, Lord Chancellor Yorke confirmed this opinion in *Pearne v. Lisle.* It was against the background of this uncertainty that Sir William Blackstone, in his *Commentaries on the Laws of England* published in 1765 and 1769, declared that "the law of England abhors, and will not endure the existence of slavery within this nation." The moment a slave sets foot on English soil he is protected by the laws and with regard to all natural rights, becomes *eo instanti,* a free-man.[24]

Blackstone's Commentaries were influential in America. After 1770, almost every American lawyer began his study of legal and political institutions with the *Commentaries.*[25] In 1772, Blackstone's view was confirmed by Lord Mansfield in the *Somerset case.* In that case, James Somerset, a slave brought to England from Jamaica, escaped and was recaptured. After his recapture he was placed on a ship bound for Jamaica where he was resold. The case came before the King's Bench where Lord Mansfield concluded that slavery was so odious that nothing could be suffered to support it if positive law about the matter did not exist.

B. Founding of the Republic and the Antebellum Period

Despite slavery's undefined status in England, there was no question under British law that slavery was legal in its colonies. Thus, slavery was legal in all thirteen colonies at the time the Declaration of Independence was signed. Nevertheless, the Founding Fathers of the American revolution were significantly influenced by beliefs about the importance of individual self-determination in establishing this country.

The origins of this cognitive framework can be seen in the political writings of John Locke, a man who had enormous influence on the Founding Fathers of America.[26] Locke's influence is evident in the Declaration of Independence. In seventeenth century England, Locke developed a defense of individual rights for political and legal purposes not rooted in classical or Biblical sources.[27] The essence of Locke's breakthrough was the view that the rights of individuals exist prior to the formation of society.[28] Before the formation of society, individuals exist in a state of nature in which they are free to acquire property and pursue their own plans and purposes, subject only to their own predilections. Individuals chose to form a society because it would aid them in the pursuit of their endeavors. Thus, society "comes into existence through the voluntary contract of individuals trying to maximize their own self-interest."[29] The proper role of society and government is to protect the rights of those individuals that are derived from the state of nature. Locke's theory made it possible to think about individual rights, without simultaneously acknowledging the subservience of individuals to an omnipotent God.[30] The Declaration of Independence, penned by Thomas Jefferson, reflected the influence of Locke:

> We hold these truths to be self-evident, that all men are created equal, that they are endowed by their Creator with certain inalienable Rights, that among these are Life, Liberty and the pursuit of Happiness. That to secure these rights, Governments are instituted among Men, deriving their just powers from the consent of the governed....[31]

While America failed to condemn slavery in the Declaration of Independence, in an earlier draft Jefferson inserted a provision criticizing King George III as the real promoter of the slave trade to North America. The clause read as follows:

> He [King George III] has waged cruel war against human nature itself, violating its most sacred rights of life and liberty in the persons of a distant people who never offended him, captivating and carrying them into slavery in another hemisphere, or to incur miserable death in their transportation thither. This piratical warfare, the opprobrium of INFIDEL powers, is the warfare of the CHRISTIAN King of Great-Britain. Determined to keep open a market where MEN would be bought and sold, he has prostituted his negative for suppressing every legislative attempt to prohibit or restrain this execrable commerce.[32]

The provision, however, was deleted from the Declaration at the insistence of representatives from South Carolina and Georgia.

Despite the failure to condemn slavery in the Declaration of Independence, the anomaly of a nation which accepted slavery fighting a war based on the assertion of the equality of all men did not escape the Founding Fathers.[33] Before the Revolutionary War, Thomas Jefferson noted in "A Summary View of the Rights of British America" that the abolition of slavery was the desire of the colonies. However, Britain had made it increasingly difficult because it consistently blocked all colonial efforts to put an end to the slave trade.[34] Thomas Paine said it was hypocrisy to both fight for freedom and uphold the institution of slavery. This sentiment was also echoed by Patrick Henry in a 1773 letter to Robert Pleasants, a Quaker in the forefront of the antislavery movement.[35] Henry Laurens, the President of the Continental Congress in 1777–78, was a former slave trader. He, however, retired from the trade and came to regard it as evil. The first President of the new republic, George Washington, told Jefferson that "among his first wishes was to see some plan adopted" to abolish slavery. Washington also freed his slaves in his will.[36] Other Founding Fathers such as John Adams and Alexander Hamilton also spoke out against slavery.[37]

The Revolutionary War loosened some forces for the abolition of servitude of blacks. As the Revolutionary War wound to a close, some Northern states abolished slavery within their borders. In 1780, Pennsylvania passed a law that led to the eventual abolition of slavery in that state. In 1781, Levi Lincoln argued on behalf of the black slave, Quock Walker, that it was the law of nature that all men be equal and free.[38] Accepting his argument, the Massachusetts judiciary in 1783 effectively ended slavery in that state.[39] Connecticut and Rhode Island also adopted laws that would gradually lead to the abolition of slavery in 1784. In 1785, New York broadened its manumission provisions, as did New Jersey the following year, making it easier for owners to free their slaves. Congress also sought to restrict slavery in the aftermath of the Revolutionary War. Article 6 of the Northwest Ordinance adopted by Congress under the Articles of Confederation in 1787, ordained that there "shall be neither slavery nor involuntary servitude in the said territory." The territory of the Northwest Ordinance eventually produced five free states: Ohio, Indiana, Michigan, Illinois and Wisconsin.

Despite these emancipation efforts, the legitimacy of the institution of slavery was enshrined into the fundamental law of the new nation when the Constitution of the United States was ratified. Though the Constitution accepted the legitimacy of slavery, it provided that Congress could abolish the Trans-Atlantic Slave Trade in 1808.[40] By 1794, all of the states had adopted legislation which prohibited the Trans-Atlantic Slave Trade as well as the importation of new slaves. At the earliest effective date possible under the Constitution, Congress made the abolition of the slave trade permanent.

Religious groups continued their advocacy against slavery after the adoption of the Constitution. For example, on February 3, 1790, Ben Franklin—as President of the Pennsylvania Abolition Society, an association of various citizens and religious dominations—wrote a public letter to Congress. The letter noted that the Christian religion and the political creed of the new nation accept the belief that all are formed by the same Almighty Being alike and as objects of His care are equally designed for enjoyment and happiness. The blessings of liberty, thus, should be administered to all without regard to color.[41] Many religious believers in the equality of men under God were also active in the revival of the abolitionist movement in the 1830s. William Lloyd Garrison was perhaps the most influential of the abolitionists.[42] Garrisonian abolitionists viewed their mission as one of establishing in the hearts of men a deep and broad conviction of the brotherhood of the human race. As they saw it, "God hath indeed made of one blood all nations of men... to dwell on all the face of the earth."[43]

In addition to religious, judicial and political actors seeking the abolition of slavery, in the field of economics, Adam Smith was its chief proponent. In his path breaking book, *The Wealth of Nations,* Smith laid the groundwork for modern economic theory. He advocated an economic system structured on the freedom of individuals to pursue their self-determined desires. Smith demonstrated that the economic system works best when people, motivated by only their own self-interest, are free to produce and trade goods or services. Economic order arises spontaneously within such a system without the need for central direction by a governmental agency. The food and drink of others will be provided by the butcher and the brewer due to their regard for their own self-interest. An invisible hand will be at work that advantages others when people seek to advantage themselves. Smith also argued that slavery was economically inefficient. He noted that if a man had no hope of gaining property he would work badly and such a poor worker could not be discharged. According to Smith, experience of all the ages and various nations indicated that work done by free labor is cheaper than that performed by slaves. The experience of the northern states, where the number of slaves was always small, tended to confirm Smith's economic argument for the abolition of slavery. Smith's argument, however, was rejected by the southern states, where slavery was simply too important.

While the North progressed to abolish slavery, in the South—where over 90% of those who happen to be black resided until the eve of the Civil War—the institution continued unabated.[44] The Supreme Court upheld the institution of slavery in its infamous 1857 *Dred Scott* decision. Thus, before the Civil War the likelihood that slavery would be abolished through existing legal means seemed remote. In order to abolish slavery, the Constitution would have to be amended which required the consent of three-fourths of the states, an unlikely prospect given the importance of slavery to so many states.

C. The Civil War and Reconstruction

Abolition of slavery came about in perhaps the only way it could have, through an armed conflict that reshaped the nation. Abraham Lincoln's election to the Presidency proved to be the catalyst. Though Lincoln had only pledged to limit the spread of slavery, and not abolish it in the states where it existed, his election was a defining moment for southern states. By the time President-Elect Lincoln arrived in Washington D.C. in late February of 1861, seven states had already seceded from the Union. Defending Fort Sumter in April of 1861 would cost the Union four additional states.

Slavery was the dividing social institution between the temperaments of the North and that of the South. Nevertheless, the desire to preserve the Union provided the North with its initial reason to wage war against its southern neighbors. But, it was not long before the Union was compelled to address the issue of slavery. Within eighteen months after the firing on Fort Sumter, Lincoln publicly announced his intention to issue the Emancipation Proclamation. On January 1, 1863, the Emancipation Proclamation was signed and took effect. With the execution of that document, the Civil War was converted into a struggle with a dual purpose, the preservation of the Union and the abolition of slavery.

Victory by the Union in the Civil War catapulted America into a transition period with regard to the rights of those who happened to be black. In December of 1865, the Thirteenth Amendment, which abolished slavery, was formally ratified and added to the Constitution. This was only eight months after Robert E. Lee surrendered to General Grant at the Courthouse in Appomattox. The abolition of slavery, however, did not mean that the freedmen were granted rights co-extensive with those of white males. The ratification of the Fourteenth Amendment in 1868 bestowed upon blacks the status of citizenship of the United States and the state where they resided; prohibited states from abridging their privileges or immunities as citizens of the United States; prohibited states from depriving them of life, liberty or property without due process; and granted them the equal protection of the laws. The Fourteenth Amendment, however, did not bestow on the freedmen political rights. It took the ratification of the Fifteenth Amendment, two years later, to constitutionalize the prohibition against discrimination in voting based on race, color or previous condition of servitude. The end of the Civil War, the ratification of the Reconstruction Amendments and the passage of five major civil rights bills[45] lessened the burdens placed on those who happened to be black due to the arbitrariness of birth and increased their ability to be self-determining. All these measures, however, were not enough to guarantee their treatment as Knowing Individuals.

Equal rights under post-Civil War jurisprudence did not mean equality in the way that equal protection jurisprudence comprehends equality today. The legal system of post-Civil War America distinguished among natural, civil, political and social equality. Natural rights were those granted to all as persons. These included the right to personal liberty and freedom which slavery violated. Civil rights included the legal capacity to buy, sell, rent, lease and own property; to have legal rights enforced by courts; to be granted the right to due process; to sue and be sued in courts of law; to be able to testify in court; and to share equally in the costs and benefits of government. Political rights were acquired only within a political system. These included the right to vote, hold political office and to participate in the political life of the community. Civil and political rights were viewed as rights asserted by an individual only against the state. Social rights were distinguished from civil and political rights. Social rights were viewed as asserted against one's fellow citizen, not the state. According to the legal thought of the time, government had nothing to do with guaranteeing social rights, except by enforcing the rights guaranteed by the common law. Political and civil equality meant that those who happened to be black would have the same basic rights against the state as those who happened to be white.[46] Civil and political equality, however, did not extend to rights like patronizing the business of a private individual, attending non-segregated public schools or sitting next to someone of a different race in transportation facilities. Those rights were deemed to implicate social rights, not rights asserted solely against the state. Two years before voting to adopt the Fourteenth Amendment, for example, Congress permitted the establishment of segregated schools in the District of Columbia.[47]

Slavery did more than hold blacks in physical bondage, it also deprived them of the ability to develop their minds, their personalities and their potential. At the time of emancipation many states had statutes aimed at discouraging teaching slaves how to read and write. Thus, over 95% were illiterate when slavery was abolished. While slaves, they were also denied the ability to accumulate wealth or property. Thus, the abolition of slavery left the overwhelming majority of former slaves illiterate, penniless and landless peasants. In the years following the end of the Civil War it became clear that those who happened to be black needed to be educated if they were to become competent to accept all of the rights and discharge all the responsibilities that come with being free. While those who happened to be black founded a number of schools on their own, many of those who happened to be white also believed that the best way to increase the ability of the former slaves to take care of themselves was through education. A Freedmen's Aid Society set up by the Methodist Church founded five colleges, two theological seminaries and two medical schools by 1878.[48] The Presbyterians—who had already founded Lincoln University in Pennsylvania for those who happened to be black in 1854 — set up three more colleges between 1867 and 1872 for the freedmen. The Congregationalists, through their agency the American Missionary Association, founded seven colleges for blacks between 1866 and 1869, and by 1876 the Association was running fourteen normal and high schools.

D. Disenfranchisement and the Institution of Segregation

Legally imposed segregation can not be defended within the conceptual boundaries of Colorblind Individualism. Since segregation is based on an involuntary trait, it is anathema to the fundamental beliefs of this discourse. Those who happened to be black, however, suffered less denial of self-determining individuality under segregation than they did under slavery. They were no longer kept in legal bondage and, at least in the most formal sense, obtained equal treatment with respect to political and civil rights. While the Supreme Court embraced the doctrine of "separate but equal," there were some very significant constitutional legal victories during this period for those who happened to be black.[49]

The distinction between social and civil rights explains what would otherwise appear to be two inconsistent opinions delivered by the Supreme Court soon after the ratification of the Fourteenth Amendment. In 1879 in *Strauder v. West Virginia*,[50] the Court struck down a law that restricted jury duty to only white males. But four years later, in the *Civil Rights Cases*,[51] the Supreme Court struck down provisions of the Civil Rights Act of 1875 that entitled all persons (especially those who happened to be black) to the full and equal enjoyment of accommodations, advantages, facilities and privileges of inns, public conveyances on land or water, theaters and other places of public amusement. The *Strauder* case was understood by the Court to be about rights considered to be civil in nature because they involved only the assertion of a right—the right to serve on a jury—against the state. In the *Civil Rights Cases*, the ban on private discrimination was viewed by the Court as Congress' effort to compel private individuals who did not want to associate with blacks to do so. The provisions of the Civil Rights Act of 1875 which were struck down involved what the Court considered to be an unjustified intrusion by Congress into the arena of social rights.

The primary legal case of the segregation era, *Plessy v. Ferguson*,[52] legitimated the doctrine of "separate but equal." In an opinion written by Justice Brown, the Supreme Court upheld a Louisiana statute that required all railway companies carrying passengers in their coaches in the state to provide equal but separate accommodations for the white and colored races. In *Plessy*, the Court was presented with an argument that the statute was motivated by a desire to assert the superiority of whites and the inferiority of blacks.[53] The Court specifically stated that "[t]he object of the [Fourteenth] amendment was undoubtedly to enforce the absolute equality of the two races before the law, but in the nature of things it could not have been intended to abolish distinctions based upon color, or to enforce social, as distinguished from political equality."[54] The Court noted that "if the civil and political rights of both races be equal one cannot be inferior to the other civilly or politically. If one race be inferior to the other socially, the Constitution of the United States cannot put them upon the same plane."[55] In effect, the Court at the same time recognized both the political and civil equality and the social inferiority of the African descendants.

Justice Harlan was the sole dissenter in *Plessy*.[56] In his dissent he formulated the classic colorblind interpretation of the Constitution. Harlan argued "in view of the Constitution,... [t]here is no caste here. Our Constitution is colorblind, and neither knows nor tolerates classes among citizens. . . ."[57] For him, one of the main problems with the Louisiana segregation statute was that it interfered with the personal freedom of citizens. The statute eliminated the ability of a white man and a black man to choose to occupy the same public conveyance on a public highway.[58] By preventing this, the government was infringing upon the personal liberty of Knowing Individuals to make a self-determined choice.

The enactment of segregation statutes was generally preceded by the disenfranchisement of voters who happened to be black males in the South. The Fifteenth Amendment prohibited infringing on the right to vote due to race, color or previous condition of servitude. The Fifteenth Amendment's prohibition against using race as a means to disenfranchise voters is consistent with the concerns about individual self-determination of this cognitive framework. Disenfranchisement based on race or color interferes with individual self-determination because such disenfranchisement bases the right to vote on a characteristics that individuals can not control. But, racially neutral disenfranchisement schemes that disproportionately prevented black males from voting are different.

The most significant statutory provisions used to disenfranchise those who happen to be black males were the poll tax and literacy and understanding eligibility requirements to the exercise of the franchise. Neither a poll tax nor literacy and understanding eligibility requirements are *per se* racially discriminatory. These requirements do not use an involuntary characteristic such as race or ethnicity to classify voters. The ability to pay the poll tax does not depend on race *per se*, but on financial means and willingness to pay the cost necessary to vote. Unlike race, literacy and understanding are not immutable characteristics. People can learn to read and can improve their understanding of political ideas and issues. Thus, a legislature could reasonably conclude that these two provisions help to elevate the general quality of the electorate and thereby lead to better political decisions. These provisions could reduce the corruption of the electoral process by excluding a large mass of ignorant voters who would be susceptible to demagoguery, pecuniary and other social influences, without being motivated by racial animus towards those who happened to be black. Due to the destitute financial condition of so many of the former slaves, the requirement of paying a poll tax would be a greater burden on them than it would on those who happened to be white. In addition, since so many of the former slaves were illiterate at the time of emancipation, literacy and understanding requirements were likely to be more burdensome on those who happened to be black. But the discriminatory effects of these racially neutral measures is not racial discrimination. Rather it is simply the unfortunate results of the application of racially neutral governmental policies and practices. Thus, in 1898, in the case of *Williams v. Mississippi*,[59] the Supreme Court upheld literacy and understanding requirements against constitutional challenges. Many registrars who happened to be white would administer the literacy and understanding requirements in a racially discriminatory manner. They would often opine that a voter who happened to be white was qualified to vote, while a voter who happened to be black and who could demonstrate equal or superior reading and comprehension abilities was not. These actions by registrars were racially discriminatory, but not literacy requirements *per se*.

Not all disenfranchisement schemes directed at those who happened to be black survived constitutional challenges. Legislators were aware that racially neutral literacy and understanding requirements could disqualify white voters as well as black ones. Some states sought to prevent the exclusion of voters who happened to be white by adopting what were called "grandfather clauses." The Supreme Court in the 1915 case of *Guinn v. United States*[60] struck down a grandfather clause adopted by Oklahoma. Under the Oklahoma provision, an exemption from the literacy requirement was provided for persons who had been eligible to register to vote prior to January 1866 or his lineal ancestor had been eligible to vote as of that date. January 1866 was prior to the ratification of the Fourteenth or Fifteenth Amendment, thus no black person would have qualified for the exemption from the literacy requirement under this clause. In striking down the Oklahoma grandfather clause, the Court noted that including voting standards of 1866 clearly violated the Fifteenth Amendment.

Blacks were also disenfranchised through the use of the white primary in a number of states. After Reconstruction, the Democratic Party dominated southern electoral politics. Thus, for states that used the primary system, the most important election was not the general election, but the Democratic

Party primary. Texas, for example, passed laws aimed at excluding blacks from participating in the Democratic primary election. In the 1927 case of *Nixon v. Herndon*,[61] the Supreme Court struck down the statute as violating the Fourteenth Amendment. The Court noted that the power to exclude blacks from participating in the Democratic primary was derived from a statute passed by the state legislature. As a result, the statute constituted a clear violation of the Fourteenth Amendment. Undeterred by the Court's decision, Texas enacted another statute which gave the power to the Executive Committee of a political party to determine who could vote in its primary. Under the statute the Executive Committee of the Democratic party limited voting in its primary to whites. The Supreme Court in *Nixon v. Condon*[62] struck down this statute as well. The Court concluded that since the Executive Committee acted upon the authority conveyed to it by the statute this also amounted to state action in violation of the Fourteenth Amendment. After the Court's decision in *Nixon v. Condon* the state Democratic convention adopted a resolution limiting membership in the state party and, thus, qualification for voting in the Democratic Party primary to whites. The Supreme Court initially upheld this change in its 1935 opinion in *Grovey v. Townsend*.[63] Since the requirement was that of the Democratic party and not pursuant to a state statute, the Court reasoned that it did not amount to state action. Thus, it did not violate either the Fourteenth or the Fifteenth Amendments. The Supreme Court, however, eventually rejected its decision in *Grovey v. Townsend* and struck down this mechanism to preserve the white primary in its 1944 opinion in *Smith v. Allwright*.[64]

The Supreme Court also struck down various governmental schemes aimed at fostering housing segregation. In 1910 Baltimore adopted the first housing segregation ordinance in the country.[65] Between 1911 and 1916 additional laws to establish legal segregation in housing were adopted in several cities including Ashland, Norfolk, Portsmouth, Richmond and Roanoke, Virginia; Winston-Salem and Greenville, North Carolina; Atlanta, Georgia; Louisville, Kentucky; St. Louis, Missouri; Oklahoma City, Oklahoma; and New Orleans.[66] In the 1917 decision in *Buchanan v. Warley*,[67] the Supreme Court addressed the constitutionality of the Louisville, Kentucky housing segregation ordinance. The Louisville ordinance made it unlawful for any colored person to move into and occupy as a residence a house on a block where the majority of residents were white. It also prohibited white persons from moving into and occupying a house on a block where the majority of the residents were black. In *Buchanan*, a white person sought to sell a piece of property on a block where the majority of residents were also white to a black person. The purchaser intended to erect a house on the property that would be his residence. The Court did not strike the ordinance on equal protection grounds. Rather, it concluded that the ordinance infringed upon the ability of the owner to alienate his property in violation of the due process clause of the Fourteenth Amendment.

Proponents of housing segregation quickly formulated a way to circumvent the Court's decision in *Buchanan.* The Court struck down the Louisville housing segregation ordinance under the Fourteenth Amendment because it involved state action. State action mandating segregation implicated civil rights. But if someone who happened to be white sold their property to another on the condition that any subsequent resale by the buyer would only be to another white person, then arguably the matter was a private one without government involvement. The use of these racially restrictive covenants thus implicated social, and not civil, rights. Racially restrictive covenants were employed to circumvent the Supreme Court's decision in *Buchanan* until 1948 when the Court delivered its opinion in *Shelley v. Kraemer.*[68] In that case, the Supreme Court did not strike down the racially restrictive covenants, but concluded that the enforcement of these covenants required government action. Thus, government enforcement of racially restrictive covenants converted the assertion of a social right into a civil one. The enforcement by government, therefore, constituted unconstitutional racial discrimination.

Many of the cases which made their way to the Supreme Court were brought by lawyers working for the National Association for the Advancement of Colored People (NAACP). In 1939, the NAACP established the NAACP Legal Defense and Educational Fund, Inc., known also as the Legal Defense Fund (LDF)or the Inc. Fund. After its establishment, the LDF became responsible for the NAACP's legal work.[69] The history of the NAACP is therefore relevant in discussing the legal history of Colorblind Individualism.

Along with the spread of Jim Crow laws in the 1890s were lynchings and race riots intended to assure that blacks were maintained in a subordinate position. In the early part of the twentieth century, armed whites attacked blacks in places as diverse as New York; Atlanta, Georgia; Brownsville, Texas; Greensburg, Indiana; and Springfield, Ohio. The worst riot actually occurred in 1908 in Springfield, Illinois, Abraham Lincoln's home town. Journalist William English Walling, a wealthy southerner whose family had owned slaves, investigated the Springfield riot and published a number of newspaper articles about it. Mary White Ovington, a descendant of abolitionists, was so shocked by the description of the rioting that she contacted Walling to see if there was something that could be done about it. Over the next few months, Walling, Ovington and Dr. Henry Moskowitz met in New York and made plans to call a meeting for a national conference to address the rights of blacks in honor of Lincoln's one-hundredth birthday.

Oswald Garrison Villard, the grandson of William Lloyd Garrison, took the lead in drafting a call to believers in democracy to join in a national conference for the renewal of the struggle for civil and political liberty. Among the approximately fifty people who signed the call were noted educator John Dewey, Mary E. Woolley—the president of Mount Holyoke College—and W. E. B. Du Bois.[70] From the 300 people who attended this meeting, the NAACP was created as an interracial organization. The NAACP has proved to be the most important civil rights organization in American history. Control of the NAACP was primarily in the hands of an interracial board of directors who appointed and paid an administrative staff. Walling was elected chair of the Executive Committee, Moorfield Storey, past President of the American Bar Association,[71] was elected National President and John Milholland was elected Treasurer. Du Bois was assigned the position of the Director of Publications and Research.

From the very beginning, absolute political and social equality was the basic policy objective of the NAACP. The NAACP conducted numerous programs in pursuit of these objectives. The NAACP was active in attacks on lynchings, disenfranchisement, educational inequality, crime and discrimination in public accommodations and employment. While the organization did not want to compel both races to mix socially, its objective always included a belief that no law should prohibit persons who mutually desire to associate together from doing so. Segregation was thus considered wrong and full integration was the right and ultimate goal to be obtained.[72]

One way for the NAACP to pursue its objectives was through the creation and publication of a magazine. Du Bois, in his capacity as the Director of Publicity and Research, was given control over the NAACP's magazine entitled the *Crisis*. The objective of the *Crisis* was to "set forth...facts and arguments which show[ed] the danger of race prejudice, particularly as manifested" towards those who were colored.[73] The *Crisis* championed the triumphs of blacks and publicized the most flagrant examples of racial discrimination.

A number of Supreme Court cases that dealt with disenfranchisement and housing segregation discussed above were brought in front of the Supreme Court by lawyers for the NAACP or the LDF. The NAACP did more than just fight disenfranchisement in the courts. It conducted an intensive study of the 1920 election and published a report noting that of the 5,522,475 voting age blacks, some 4,500,000 lived in states where they were disenfranchised.[74] The NAACP conducted voter registration and voter education projects. The NAACP also maintained a very successful legal campaign attacking segregation of colored people.

They won legal victories attacking segregation including in housing, as mentioned above, in graduate and professional schools[75] and in transportation and interstate commerce.[76] The NAACP also litigated against discrimination in employment.[77]

Conclusion

This Chapter has discussed Colorblind Individualism, a discourse that is structured around the conception of society as a collection of Knowing Individuals. Colorblind Individualism is the dominant discourse which controls much of the public perceptions and discussions about race in American society today. This discourse values the ability of free-willed, rational, and autonomous individuals to pursue their self-determined goals and objectives. Within this discourse, to treat a person as a member of a racial or ethnic group without their consent denies that person their individuality. Though the Supreme Court has not formally adopted a colorblind approach to the equal protection clause, by basing the determination of unconstitutional discrimination on discriminatory motives and limiting the use of racial classifications by government to those applications that survive strict scrutiny, much of the discussions regarding equal protection rights are based upon the underlying assumptions of Colorblind Individualism's view of society as a collection of Knowing Individuals.

This chapter has also presented a version of the historical treatment of African-Americans as conceptualized by this pattern of understanding. This version of history emphasizes efforts to recognize and expand the treatment of blacks as self-determined, free-willed individuals in American society.

Chapter Four

The Discourse of American Collectivism

The motivating idea of American Collectivism is advancing the best interest of the collective American people. This utilitarian pattern of understanding views all Americans as united into one people, *E Pluribus Unum*. When racial phenomena are conceptualized, racial issues are discussed and resolutions of racial conflicts proposed, the general interest of the American collective is paramount. The collective interest of American society can be advanced either by increasing the aggregate happiness or reducing the aggregate suffering of the nation.

When attempting to determine what advances the best interest of American society, it is necessary to refer to what Americans value. Certain values have been at the core of American society from the founding of the nation. America has always valued liberty, equality, democracy and the pursuit of happiness. But the meanings of these fundamental American values change over time. Each generation of Americans, therefore, has to define the meaning of these fundamental values to fit their current times. Thus, the meanings of fundamental American values and what is considered as advancing the best interest of American society is not necessarily the same from one generation of Americans to the next.

Section I of this Chapter will describe the general structure of this cognitive framework. Section II will present a version of the historical treatment of African-Americans as conceptualized by this pattern of understanding. This version of history will emphasize how the treatment of blacks was consistent with a desire to advance the best interest of American society. At times the best interest of American society dictated favorable treatment of African-Americans. At other times the interest of blacks was sacrificed at the altar of the greater good for the country. Section II begins by discussing colonial times and how slavery advanced the aspirations of the British Empire. Then it will discuss the acceptance of slavery by the drafters of the Constitution and its acceptance during the Antebellum Period. Next the discussion will turn to the abolition of slavery which occurred as a direct result of the efforts of the Union to win the Civil War. The discussion of the Civil War will be followed by a discussion about Reconstruction. During this period of time, three Amendments were added to the Constitution which abolished slavery and granted significant civil and political rights to blacks. Section II will conclude with a discussion of how disenfranchisement and legally enforced segregation advanced the interest of American society.

I. The Conceptual Structure

This section will describe the basic conceptual features of this discourse. American Collectivism views the social world primarily in terms of the collective American people. A discussion of the epistemology of this system of meaning will follow the discussion of the basic conceptual features. The desire to advance the interest of the American people also generates its own principles for determining moral and ethical behavior. Within this system of meaning the ideal moral person is someone who willingly sacrifices his or her personal interests and desires for the best interest of the country. The discussion about moral and ethical beliefs will be followed by a discussion of the role of government. The guiding principal of government decisions and actions should be the promotion of the common good. Finally, the relationship of this discourse with the other three—Traditional Americanism, African-American Centralism and Colorblind Individualism—will be discussed.

A. Conception of the Social World

This utilitarian pattern of understanding views all Americans as united into one people. As Justice Scalia put it "we are all just one race here. It is American."[1] The motivating idea within this system of meaning is the best interest of the American people. The collective interest of American society can be advanced either by increasing the aggregate happiness or reducing the aggregate suffering of the nation. Whether a given decision should be arrived at, a given act engaged in, a given law enacted, a given regulation promulgated, a given rule adopted, a given ordinance ordained or a given social practice instituted, perpetuated or terminated depends upon whether it promotes the overall interest of the American collective.

This pattern of understanding has long dealt with issues and conflicts that arise from a society that is formulated with so many people from diverse countries, religions and ethnic and racial backgrounds. A significant historical fact about the United States is that it is a land of immigrants and expatriates. Except for the small percentage of Native Americans and indigenous inhabitants of the far and south west, the rest of the population of the United States are either people or descendants of people who came from other lands. Immigration to the United States has been the largest single voluntary migration in human history. Between 1820 and 1996, total immigration to the United States exceeded 63 million people.[2] From the beginning of the colonial period until after the Civil War, European immigrants to the United States were primarily protestant and from northern and western Europe. The character of American immigration changed drastically around 1880 with the nation receiving large numbers of Catholic and Jewish immigrants and immigrants from southern and eastern Europe. Between 1900 and 1930 the Catholic population in the United States doubled to 24 million.[3] The population of Jews increased from 229,000 in 1887 to over 4,228,000 forty years later. This represented an increase from .5% of the nation's population to 3%.[4] Immigration into the U.S. continues up to the present, with new immigrants coming from China, Cuba, El Salvador, Haiti, Honduras, India, Japan, Korea, Mexico, Nicaragua, Nigeria, Philippines, Vietnam and many other countries. These recent immigrants have added the religions of Buddhism, Shintoism, Islam, Hinduism and Sikhism to those of the Anglican, the Baptist, the Puritan, the Calvinist, the Catholic, the Episcopalian, the Lutheran, the Jew, the Methodist, the Seventy Day Adventist and the Russian Orthodox. In addition, to the massive voluntary immigration to the United States, almost 500,000 sons and daughters from the soil of Africa were forcibly brought to this country. Even though a significant number of Africans have immigrated to the United States in recent years, the overwhelming majority of the current 39 million black population of today are descendants from people forced into slavery in the Americas.[5]

Judgements about what advances the best interest of American society are bound up in the current meanings attached to fundamental values that Americans cherish. Certain values like liberty, equality, democracy and the pursuit of happiness have been basic values of the nation since the beginning. The meanings of these values, however, change over time in response to internal and international developments. Historically the dominant meanings about liberty and equality in American society were not the individualist, liberal attitudes that began to emerge in the 1950s and 1960s. In the past, American society took for granted the exploitation of blacks from Africa, the conquest and extermination of the Native Americans, the oppression of women and the working class and the closeting of homosexuals. Throughout most of American history blacks were not accorded the same respect regarding their well-being as whites.[6] Thus, the calculation of the best interest of the American collective openly recognized that blacks were non-citizens and then second-class citizens. As a result, their enslavement and, following Reconstruction, their disenfranchisement and segregation were easily justified in terms of advancing the common good for the American collective and consistent with fundamental values of liberty and equality.

As Harvard Professor Samuel Huntington stated, U.S. identity is now centered around a "set of universal ideas and principles articulated in the founding documents by American leaders: liberty, equality, democracy, constitutionalism, liberalism, limited government and private enterprise."[7] At present, in the Land of the Free, concern about advancing the best interest of American society does not lose sight of the current interpretation of liberty and equality in terms of individual liberty, freedom and self-determination for all, regardless of race or ethnicity. Yet, while this pattern of understanding views individual liberty and freedom as fundamental values, there are times when the individual's interest must be sacrificed for the benefit of the collective good.

Many Americans also cherish and celebrate various group connections including those derived from religious beliefs, racial or ethnic heritages, gender or sexual orientation. Within the conceptual boundaries of this cognitive framework, the importance of these attachments are not ignored. Rather the concerns of religious, ethnic, racial, gender or sexual orientation groups are subsumed in the larger analysis that focuses on the best interest of American society. Discussions that seek to assert the interest of a particular group when they are in conflict with the interest of the American collective are understood as parochial attempts of one group to gain an advantage, possibly at the sacrifice of the collective interest. In order for arguments that seek to advance the concerns of any given religious, racial, ethnic, gender or sexual orientation group to be persuasive within this discourse, those arguments must be cast in a form that does not so much stress the benefits for that particular group, but illuminates the benefits for all Americans.

B. Epistemology and the Meaning of Words Related to Racial Issues

When this system of meaning is used to discuss racial issues, concepts like racism, racial oppression, racial discrimination and racial equality draw their meaning from an understanding that what is important is the advancement of the collective interest of American society. Thus, the suffering of a particular racial or ethnic group can be justified if it produces enough of a benefit to the entire community to outweigh the suffering. This suffering could be inflicted on African-Americans as it was during slavery, on Japanese-Americans as it was during their internment during World War II or white Americans as it was, and is, during the implementation of affirmative action policies. These decisions are not understood as racist or racially oppressive. Rather they reflect the recognition of the interest of the American collective over the parochial interest of various groups.

Since the focus of this cognitive framework is on the collective good, it discounts the problems and sufferings of any particular racial or ethnic group. For example, African-Americans have certainly suffered discrimination while in the United States. But within this discourse a discussion about the discrimination against blacks cannot be confined to harms inflicted on that group alone. While it is true that blacks have been victims of discrimination, so have Native Americans and, to a lesser extent, Latinos and Asian Americans. If, as Justice Powell wrote in his opinion in *Bakke,* the facade of a monolithic white group is pierced, it becomes obvious that some white ethnic groups were also exploited and victimized when they came to America. These white ethnics had to struggle—and to some extent struggle still—to overcome the prejudices not of a monolithic majority, but of a majority composed of various minority groups.[8] In addition, a discussion about instituting ameliorative measures to attack the suffering of a particular racial or ethnic group will not be limited to the beneficial impact on that particular group. Rather, such beneficial impact must be balanced against the detriment inflicted on the collective good by such measures. Thus, efforts to discuss measures to attenuate the current effect of racial practices in the past on blacks, will quickly turn into a discussion about how other groups have suffered and the potential detriment such beneficial measures could have on the interest of the American collective.

C. Moral and Ethical Beliefs

Moral and ethical beliefs within this discourse are a function of the solicitude about advancing the best interest of the American collective. Within this system of meaning being an American carries with it an obligation to protect the vital interest of the country. America, love it or leave it! Thus, the individual may be called upon to sacrifice his or her personal interest for the benefit of the collective. For example, during times of prolonged military conflict individuals may be subjected to compulsory military service if not enough enlistments can be obtained through voluntary measures. Despite objections that many individuals may have about their tax dollars being used to fund the military, provide transfer payments to the elderly or the poor, provide funds for the operations of national parks or provide financial assistance to foreign countries, because of the advantages to the collective these objections are outweighed by the benefits to the collective interest that such funding provides.

Unselfish service to the country is the highest moral good. The ideal moral person is one who is willing to sacrifice his or her personal interests and desires for the benefit of the country. A special place of reverence goes to those who have paid the ultimate price and sacrificed their lives for the betterment of the country. War heroes, soldiers and dedicated government servants are the best examples of the kinds of people held in highest regard by the morality within this cognitive framework. African-American heroes who stood side by side with others in defense of the country or to make real the creed of liberty, freedom and justice to which this society is dedicated are also honored. This cognitive framework celebrates the sacrifices for and contributions to the American collective of African-Americans like Crispus Attucks, Salem Poor, Peter Salem, Harriet Tubman, the 54th Massachusetts Volunteers, the Hell Fighters[9] and the Tuskegee Airmen.

Conversely, individuals or countries that seek to harm America are considered morally depraved by this discourse. When America is in a state of war with another country, that country and its people or leaders will be conceptualized as irrational, insane, fanatical or morally corrupt. Japan and her people were derided during World War II. President Ronald Reagan called the Soviet Union an evil empire during the Cold War. And today radical Islamic fundamentalist are portrayed as insane religious zealots in the war on terrorism.

The most immoral individuals, however, are Americans who betray the country like Benedict Arnold and Aldrich Ames. In addition to their acts of betrayal being harmful to American interest, as Americans they are also violating their obligation to protect the vital interest of American society. Thus, they have sinned twice.

D. The Role of Government and Society

The principal function for government is the advancement of the collective interest. Government must "ensure domestic tranquility, provide for the common defense, promote the general welfare, and secure the blessings of liberty."[10] In advancing or protecting the common good, government should also regulate certain personal liberties and economic activities for the benefit of the public good, ban certain drugs and other products that are too dangerous for public consumption, prohibit the performance of certain injurious practices to society and disseminate useful information that will benefit Americans.

It is also a function of government to foster patriotism and positive sentiments toward the country through a number of social practices. One such practice is declaring certain days to be holidays. Many government declared holidays are intended to promote patriotism and respect and admiration for self-sacrificing Americans including the following: July 4th, which celebrates the birth of the nation; President's Day, which honors political leaders; Veterans Day, which honors the valor displayed by men and women who have served in the armed forces and thereby protected the freedoms of this country; and Memorial Day, which honors those who have paid the ultimate price by giving their lives in service of the country. Organizing and implementing celebrations of those holidays helps to venerate those days and increase patriotic feelings for the country. Government buildings, cities, counties and even states are also named in honor of individuals who are venerated for the contributions they made to the betterment of American society.

E. Contrasted with Other Systems of Meaning

Traditional Americanism always conceptualizes blacks in a negative way. For much of America's history the dominant beliefs about Africa and the descendants of her soil were that they were demonstrably inferior to whites. Even though equality has always been a fundamental American value, as the discussion of history contained in the next section will demonstrate, the calculation of the interest of the American collective throughout much of the nation's history was openly based upon the notion of black inferiority. Within this cognitive framework the justifications for the oppressive treatment of blacks was based on advancing the perceived interest of the country. But, the interest of black people was severely discounted in the calculations of the collective interest. One of the most significant changes over the past fifty years is that mainstream American beliefs reject the conscious and explicit racism of the past. As dominant American values have come to reject the conscious racism of the past, there is much less overlap with American Collectivism and Traditional Americanism today than in the past.

Sometimes the liberation of African-Americans, which forms the basic idea of African-American Centralism, can be advanced in this discourse. There have been times in the past and the present when the interest of the nation has coincided with promoting the interest of blacks, such as emancipation from slavery, granting blacks the right to vote after the Civil War or affirmative action at selective colleges, universities or graduate programs. When advancing the interest of blacks coincides with advancing the collective interest, arguments can be generated within this pattern of understanding to assist black people. But support for measures that advance the interest of African-Americans within this discourse is always tentative. It is not the interest of blacks, but the interest of the American collective that is important to advance. Thus, at other times advancing the interest of the American collective will justifiably sacrifice the interest of blacks.

Concern about advancing the best interest of American collective cannot lose sight of the fact that today individual liberty, freedom and self-determination for all are among the most cherished values. As a consequence, Color-blind Individualism's dogged belief in the desire to advance the rights associated with individual self-determination will be similar to what is perceived to be in the best interest of the American collective. But individual liberty and self-determination are not ends in themselves within American Collectivism. Thus, there will be times where the rights of individuals must give way for the sake of the prosperity of the nation.

II. History of Blacks in America

This section will present a version of the historical experience of African-Americans up to the Supreme Court's opinion in *Brown v. Board of Education* as conceptualized by this pattern of understanding. This version of history will emphasize how the treatment of blacks was consistent with a desire to advance the best interest of American society. At times the best interest of American society dictated favorable treatment of African-Americans. At other times the interest of blacks was sacrificed at the altar to the greater good for the country.

This section will start with the colonial period and how slavery fit into the British view of its colonies in North America. Next, this section will discuss acceptance of the institution of slavery in the establishment of the nation and the Antebellum Period. At the Constitutional Convention there was no serious discussion about abolishing slavery. Without founding a nation in which slavery was legal, the United States could not have united all of the colonies that joined in the revolt against Great Britain. After the discussion of the Antebellum period, this section will discuss the Civil War and the abolition of slavery. The original motivation of the North for waging war with its southern neighbor was the preservation of the Union. But the war effort eventually compelled the North to also fight for the abolition of slavery. This section then turns to a discussion of Reconstruction. During this period of time three Amendments were added to the Constitution which abolished slavery and granted significant civil and political rights to blacks. This section will conclude with an interpretation of how disenfranchisement and legally enforced segregation advanced the interest of American society.

A. The Colonial Period: How Slavery in America Advanced the Collective Interest of the British Empire

The principal reasons for black slavery in North America were not moral, but economical circumstances; they relate not to vice and virtue, but to production.[11] While the first Africans landed in the English colony of Jamestown, Virginia in 1619, during the Seventeenth century the British were generally able to meet their labor demands with white indentured servants.[12] In the first century of colonization some 400,000 English left for the New World.[13] By the beginning of the 18th century, however, the British discovered that given their limited population, the demand for labor in their colonies came to outstrip the available supply of people they could send. In addition, it made economical sense for an enterprising entrepreneur to buy black slaves. For what it cost to purchase a white indentured servant for a period of ten years, a person could buy a black slave for life.[14]

The British realized the importance of slavery to the maintenance and development of their empire during the colonial period. As one of the contemporary English economist said, "[t]he daily bread of the most-considerable part of our British manufacturers, are owning primarily to the labor of the Negroes."[15] Slave labor was used for the cultivation of a large portion of the British agricultural exports for world trade such as sugar, tobacco, rice and rum. There were also indirect benefits for the British Empire derived from slavery. The need to protect the slave trade led to improvements in British shipping and the navy. Britannia came to rule the waves, in part, out of the necessity to protect its slave trade. Slavery helped develop other important sectors of the economy of Great Britain, such as the banking and insurance industries. Barclays Bank, for example, was founded with profits derived from the slave trade and Lloyds of London prospered by insuring slaving ventures.[16]

The British were primarily interested in their colonies throughout the world as sources of income. At the time of the Revolutionary War, the economic jewel of the British Empire was not North America, but the West Indies. The sugar plantations of the West Indies were a major source of revenue. At the time of the Revolutionary War there were 800,000 slaves in the West Indies compared to 650,000 in the colonies that would comprise the United States.[17] Prime Minister William Pitt estimated that British income from the West Indies was four times that produced by the rest of their colonies throughout the world.[18] One of the realities that the British faced during the Revolutionary

War was a limit on the amount of money they were prepared to commit in order to hold onto one of their less valuable economic assets.

B. Founding of the Republic and the Antebellum Period: How Slavery Advanced the Interest of America

The waging of the Revolutionary War highlighted the issue of how to treat the interest of the black race in the context of the collective interest of the United States for the first time. The armed forces of the colonies contained both local militias and the Continental Army. Since the Continental Congress had no power to conscript troops, it assigned quotas of soldiers for each state to provide for the Continental Army.

Blacks were involved in the first armed confrontations with the British. One of the first persons to die for American independence was a runaway slave named Crispus Attucks who was killed in the Boston Massacre on March 5, 1770. Colored soldiers also took part in the first military engagements of the Revolutionary War, including the Battles of Lexington, Concord and Bunker Hill. The first British soldiers captured during the war at Monotomy in 1775 were captured by a group led by an African-American, David Lamson.[19] The heroism of Salem Poor was instrumental in the success of colonial forces at the Battle of Bunker Hill and the black, Peter Salem, is reported to have shot and killed British Major John Pitcairn.[20]

After the early participation of black soldiers in the War, the concern about arming slaves and freed blacks came to outweigh the benefit of their use as soldiers. Many of the colonies depended on the institution of slavery for their very livelihood. They strenuously objected to the use of black troops. In order to maintain the unity of the various colonies, the high command officials of the Continental Army decided to exclude blacks from the Continental Army at a meeting in Cambridge on October 8, 1775. Blacks who were enlisted in the state militias were allowed to stay. The state militias, however, soon followed the lead of the Continental Army and by the summer of 1776 every state that had allowed black soldiers to enlist agreed to ban them.[21] In practice, though, there were many violations of this exclusion policy.

Almost as soon as the policy to exclude blacks from military service in the Continental Army was agreed upon in Cambridge, necessity began to dictate its reversal. Lord Dunmore, the British governor of Virginia, issued a proclamation on November 7, 1775 in which he declared the freedom of all slaves who were able and willing to bear arms for the British.[22] The concern that blacks would enlist and fight for the British caused General George Washington to rethink the policy of exclusion of blacks from the Continental Army.

On December 31, 1775, General Washington declared a partial reversal of the policy of the high command and announced that he was permitting the enlistment of free blacks in the Continental Army. The Continental Congress, however, largely rejected Washington's decision two and a half weeks later.[23]

The initial exclusion of blacks from the Continental Army was based, in part, on the belief that the war would not last long. As the war dragged on, the patriotic fervor of the colonist began to subside and many white men began to shun enlistment. The difficulty of getting enough white men into the armed forces made it necessary to reconsider arming black men. In 1776 New York passed a law that permitted the substitution of blacks for whites who had been drafted. By the summer of 1777, a reversal of policy of excluding blacks from colonial forces was well in the works. In 1777 the Continental Congress began to fix quotas of black soldiers for each of the states. Only South Carolina and Georgia refused to permit any enlistment of blacks, slave or free. By the summer of 1778, however, there were plenty of blacks in the Continental Army. Despite its small black population, New England probably furnished more black soldiers than any other section of the country.

Alexander Hamilton in a letter to the President of the Continental Congress in March, 1779 in support of enlistment of blacks stated:

> [I]t should be considered, that if we do not make use of them in this way, the enemy probably will; and that the best way to counteract the temptations they will hold out will be to offer them ourselves. An essential part of the plan is to give them their freedom with their muskets. This will secure their fidelity, animate their courage, and I believe will have a good influence on those that remain, by opening a door to their emancipation.[24]

In the Spring of 1779, the Continental Congress went so far as to recommend the enlistment of slaves. Owners were to be paid $1,000 for each able-bodied black man under the age of 35. No payment would go to the slave. But in order to motivate the slave to fight, he was told that he would receive his freedom and $50 if he fought well.[25]

By the end of the Revolutionary War 5,000 blacks served as soldiers or seamen in the Continental Army or Navy.[26] Another 5,000 blacks participated in the war effort in other indispensable ways. They were used as guides, messengers and spies. They were also used as military laborers forging munitions, driving wagons, erecting fortifications, destroying bridges and repairing roads.

With independence for the new Republic secured, America turned to the difficult job of forming a new nation. This began with establishing an effective and workable government in which to unite the different states. At the time of the

Constitutional Convention 675,000 slaves represented almost one in five Americans. Six of the thirteen original states permitted slavery, with over 93% of the slaves residing in the five southernmost states of Virginia, North Carolina, South Carolina, Georgia and Maryland.[27] Blacks would, in fact, remain primarily in slaveholding states during the entire antebellum period. On the eve of the Civil War, over 90% of blacks resided in the states that legalized slavery.[28]

There was no serious talk at the Constitutional Convention about equality of women, universal suffrage, free public education nor the rights of homosexuals.[29] Nor was there any serious discussion about abolishing slavery. There had been voices during the colonial period who argued that it was best for the country to supply its labor needs with white indentured servants instead of black slaves because the existence of blacks in the country degraded the nation.[30] Many felt that slavery tended to deprive the whites of the will to work and the industry necessary to improve their own conditions. Slavery also taints the very moral fiber of the country because it created too many temptations for abuse by the masters. The Founders, however, started the discussion about the Constitution with what they already knew as British colonists. Although the black race had been brought to America against its will, this inherited historical reality could not be undone. As Gourverneur Morris of Pennsylvania stated on the day the Convention voted to adopt the Constitution, "[t]he great questions will be, shall there be a national Government or not? And this must take place or a general anarchy will be the alternative."[31]

The sacrifice of the freedom of black slaves to the expediency of creating a nation benefitted the collective interest in a number of ways. It was thought that America, especially in the South, could not be developed without slave labor. Charles Pinckney, an unsuccessful federalist presidential candidate in 1804 and 1808 summarized the sentiment during the Constitutional Convention. "This country is not capable of being cultivated by white men.... Negroes are to this country what raw materials are to another country.... No planter can cultivate his land without slaves."[32] Pinckney noted that the United States was in good historical company, because the Roman and Greek Empires had been sustained through slavery.[33]

John Rutledge also remarked about the role of the slaves in the emerging nation during the discussions about a proposal to tax the importation of slaves.

> Religion and humanity have nothing to do with this question. Interest alone is the governing principle of nations. The true question at present is whether the Southern states shall or shall not be parties to the Union. If the Northen states consult their interest, they will not

> oppose the increase of slaves which will increase the commodities of which they will be carriers.[34]

Beyond the need for slaves to supply the labor for the new nation, there were other reasons to accept slavery. Under slavery, slave owners were responsible for providing bondsmen with food, shelter and clothing. They provided them with medical care when they were ill and a system was in place to take care of those too young to work and too old to be of any continued useful benefit. There were few white Americans who believed that if unshackled from their chains, the slaves could help develop the country. They simply, were not equipped to function as free and responsible citizens. If the slaves were freed, then American society would have to cope with the enormous social consequences of so many people suddenly being emancipated who did not possess the marketable and other skills necessary to be self-sufficient.

Freedom would also increase the access of the former slaves to weapons and their ability to organize for armed rebellion. As Alexis de Tocqueville noted in his monumental book on the American situation *Democracy in America,* everywhere that blacks and whites have lived without the restraint of slavery one group has destroyed the other.[35] During the colonial period there were plenty of attempts by slaves to revolt. One of the main reasons which prompted Jefferson to include a provision critical of King George's sanction of the slave trade in an earlier draft of the Declaration of Independence, is because Virginia had long complained of the potential for revolt which existed with a large number of slaves.[36] Hugh Thomas in his book *The Slave Trade: The Story of the Atlantic Slave Trade 1440–1870* noted that the fear of too many slaves creating the condition for slave rebellions had as much influence over the abolition movement after 1770 as did philanthropy.[37] Even after the Revolutionary War, the possibility of a race war continued to be a real concern. Attempted slave rebellions led by Nat Turner, Denmark Vessey and Gabriel Prosser were thwarted in large part because of the obstacles slavery placed in the way of the ability of black people to organize for armed revolution. Records indicate that there were over 250 slave revolts and conspiracies.[38] If blacks were freed they would no doubt find themselves struggling for bare existence. The general dissatisfaction among impoverished blacks could be expected to grow. This could create conditions where many of the blacks were willing to turn to armed revolutionary struggle for salvation. Freed from the shackles of their slave chains, their ability to arm themselves and organize for rebellion would greatly increase. Thus, freed blacks could constitute a more serious threat to the nation than enslaved blacks.

Though not prepared to abolish slavery there were a number of matters necessitated by the institution that were addressed by the Founders at the Constitutional Convention.[39] At least seven provisions in the Constitution focused directly or indirectly on slavery.[40] One main source of conflict was how to count blacks for purposes of representation in the lower house of Congress. The delegates came to a compromise that slaves would count as three-fifths of a person for purposes of determining representation in the House of Representatives. James Wilson from Pennsylvania pointed out the lack of logic of the compromise.

> On what principle the admission of blacks in the proportion of three-fifths could be explained. Are they admitted as Citizens? Then why are they not admitted on an equality with White Citizens? Are they admitted as property? Then why is not other property admitted into the computation.[41]

The answer that Wilson sought was simple. The three-fifths clause represented what was needed to resolve a divisive issue that threatened the interest of the American collective. Enslaved blacks were counted as human beings, to the extent that the interest of the country required it. Beyond that they were property.[42]

The delegates also took up the issue of eliminating the Trans-Atlantic Slave Trade. Even before the Revolutionary War, many of the colonies sought to discourage the importation of slaves. A common method used was to impose prohibitive duties on imported slaves. In 1750 Pennsylvania imposed a prohibitive duty on each slave imported into the state. New Jersey followed suit with a duty of 15 pounds per head and in 1771 Maryland imposed a duty of 8 to 9 pounds per head.[43] By 1772 all the Southern colonies, except Georgia had already passed a law outlawing or suspending the Trans-Atlantic Slave Trade.

One reason to abolish the slave trade was because the colonies, except Georgia, were complaining that they were overstocked with bondsmen. The slave trade was also draining money out of America for the sole benefit of English merchants. In addition, without a source of resupply, the bondsmen that were already in the colonies would become more valuable. The abolition of the slave trade also provided an incentive for "home growing" slaves. Slaves coming from Africa had much stronger memories and desires for freedom than blacks who had been born into and reared in a slave society. Thus, the Trans-Atlantic Slave Trade also increased the peril of black insurrection. In the northern colonies the desire to prohibit the importation of slaves was primarily the result of the opposition of white immigrants to slave labor. Experience demonstrated that slave labor negatively impacted on the desire of whites to move to regions of the country where slavery thrived. Slave labor tended to depress wages and thus made it difficult for white immigrants to earn a decent living.

The delegates ended their discussion on the Trans-Atlantic Slave Trade by adding a provision that prevented Congress from eliminating the trade before 1808.[44] Congress, however, abolished the trade at the earliest opportunity. It enacted a law in 1807 which became effective on January 1, 1808.

As slavery had proved its benefit for the British, it also proved helpful to the new nation. Labor was the most important factor in the development of America and slaves continued to provide that labor. At the time of the adoption of the Constitution, slaves were primarily involved in the cultivation of indigo, rice and tobacco. But in 1794 Eli Whitney developed the cotton gin which separated out the cotton seeds from the lint. By separating the seeds from the lint, the machine could do the work of 50 pairs of hands. This reduction in the cost of production turned cotton into the major cash crop in the South. In 1791 only 9,000 bales of cotton were produced in the South, by 1800 it increased to over 79,000 bales. From there, cotton production skyrocketed, with the South producing over 500,000 bales in 1822, over 1,000,000 in 1831 and over 2,000,000 bales in 1840. Cotton production reached 3,000,000 bales in 1852 and on the eve of the Civil War the South generated over 5,000,000 bales.[45] The need to cultivate cotton required a substantial expansion in the number of black slaves. Cotton also encouraged the development of the inland southern states, eventually producing a Cotton Belt that covered almost 300 million acres running in a huge arc 1,600 miles in length and 300 miles in width from eastern North Carolina to western Texas.

Since 80% of the cotton grown in the South was exported to Britain and the European continent, it accounted for about half of all U.S. exports. Much of the cotton exported was transported by Northern shipping interest. New York became the center for U.S. exports and the financial center for the cotton trade. Northern merchants and industrialists processed enough slave grown cotton in New England mills to create the first major U.S. manufacturing industry.[46] The cotton textile industry employed the second largest number of people in the United States. Thus, slave grown cotton also helped the United States to develop the shipping, financial and textile industries in the North.

C. The Civil War: How Abolition of Slavery Advanced the Collective Interest of the Union

While there were abolitionist movements and those who sought to restrict the spread of slavery, the institution was firmly rooted on American soil during the Antebellum Period. It took a national crisis that threatened to dissolve the Union to provide enough motivation to end slavery. Such a crisis developed in 1860 with the election of Abraham Lincoln to the Presidency.

The rebels fired the shots that started the Civil War when they bombarded Fort Sumter on April 12, 1861. As soon as the call for volunteers went out, blacks offered their services as soldiers willing to fight to preserve the Union. Once again the use of black troops in time of war was resolved primarily with reference to the collective interest of the nation. Lincoln and Congress were clear that the initial aims and objectives for the war was the restoration of the Union as it was—that is one that protected the institution of slavery. The position that the war was not being fought to eliminate slavery was also consistent with the initial theory which the Union government used to justify the war. Since secession was seen as illegal, the Confederate states were still legally in the Union, though under the temporary control of insurrectionists. As a result Lincoln and the Union government were still bound by the constitutional guarantee that protected the institution of slavery.[47]

On July 4, 1861, Lincoln delivered a message to the special session of Congress called to address the succession of the southern states from the Union and other war related issues. In that message he reiterated his inaugural pledge that he had no purpose, directly or indirectly to interfere with slavery in the states where it existed. Three weeks later, Congress demonstrated its solidarity with Lincoln's July 4th address by passing—almost unanimously—a resolution affirming that the war was being fought not for the purpose of "overthrowing or interfering with the rights or established institutions of those states, but only to defend and maintain the supremacy of the Constitution and to preserve the Union."[48]

There were good reasons not to make abolition of slavery an objective at the beginning of the war. A war of abolition entailed the risk that the slaveholding border states of Delaware, Maryland, Missouri and Kentucky which remained in the Union would choose to join the rebel cause. In addition, many of the whites in the North were willing to fight a war to preserve the Union, but they were not eager to fight a war where the primary beneficiaries would be black slaves. Also, as long as the abolition of slavery was not an object of the war, an incentive existed for southerners to rejoin the Union. Fighting a war for abolition would create a permanent rift between the states that joined the Confederacy and the Union. Thus, the best way to win the war and preserve the Union was to agree with the rebels that this conflict would be a "white man's war." The desire of blacks to join the Union Army was consistently rejected until the summer of 1862.[49]

At the beginning of the war Generals Burnside, Buell, Hooker, Thomas, Williams and McClellan all warned their soldiers against receiving slaves and most of them permitted masters to come and remove slaves found within Union lines.[50] Newspapers, orators and preachers that advocated for the war, stringently disclaimed any desire to interfere with slavery. As Frederick Douglass accurately said in Boston in 1865, the Civil War began with the interests of slavery on both sides. The South was fighting to take slavery out of the Union, and the North was fighting to keep it in.[51]

Early in the war a Confederate officer came to General Benjamin Butler to retrieve three fugitive slaves who had escaped and took up refuge in Fortress Monroe, Virginia. Butler refused to return the slaves stating, "I shall hold these Negroes as contraband of war, since they are engaged in the construction of your battery and are claimed as your property. The question is simply whether they shall be used for or against the government of the United States."[52] Thus, even though there was reluctance in the beginning by the Union to use blacks as soldiers, they were employed by the Union in non-military capacities. By the end of the war about 200,000 blacks had worked for the Union in such capacities as laborers, teamsters, cooks, carpenters, nurses and scouts.[53] They helped to build forts, loaded and discharged cargo and built bridges. Blacks also proved to be some of the best spies in the Union Army. They knew the southern country better than northerners and could move in and out of the rebels encampment often without arousing suspicion.[54]

As the war dragged on, the benefits of abolition began to outweigh the costs. Casualties from the war were far greater than had been anticipated in the beginning. The first major battle of the Civil War was the Battle of Bull Run on July 21, 1861. This battle ended with the Union forces in full retreat back to Washington D.C. Over 5,000 men were wounded or died as a result of the battle. The Battle of Shiloh, which was fought on April 6–7, 1862, was to that point the worst blood bath in American history. More than 1,700 Union soldiers were killed, 8,000 wounded (of which 2,000 would soon die) and almost 4,000 were captured.[55] In March of 1862 the Union Army of the Potomac moved to Yorktown, Virginia. After arriving, it began a slow march towards Richmond. On May 31st and June 1st Union forces collide with Confederate troops in the Battle of Fair Oaks. While the Union forces inflicted almost 6,600 casualties on the South, it suffered over 4,500 dead or wounded.[56] At this battle the Confederate commander was wounded and Robert E. Lee took control of the main Confederate Army. Lee immediately went on the offensive. After seven days of continuous fighting, he had inflicted over 16,000 casualties on the Union Army.[57] And in May and June of 1862, Stonewall Jackson's Confederates inflicted over 7,000 casualties on the Union Army in the Shenandoah Valley.

The casualties inflicted in the early battles of the Civil War were staggering in comparison to other U.S. wars. For example, total American casualties in the

Revolutionary War were only 4,400 killed and 6,200 wounded.[58] The War of 1812 claimed a total of 2,260 American lives with 4,505 non-fatal wounds. The Mexican American War fought a dozen years before the Civil War only cost 1,733 battle deaths and 4,152 non-fatal wounds. An additional 11,550 deaths were attributed to other causes, including diseases.[59] Even in comparison to modern conflicts, the American casualties in the early part of the Civil War were extremely high. There were only 114 combat deaths inflicted on American forces up to May 1, 2003 when President Bush declared major hostilities over in the second Iraq war. In the 1991 Desert Storm operation total casualties were only 299 killed and 467 wounded.[60] During the over eight year Vietnam conflict when the population of America was six times what it was in 1860,[61] American causality figures were 58,000 dead and another 153,000 wounded.[62]

In May of 1862, General David Hunter sent out a call for ex-black slaves to join the army. He also went so far as to declare that persons still held as slaves in Georgia, Florida and South Carolina were henceforth free. Lincoln quickly disclaimed this action, stating that neither Hunter nor any other Union commander had the authority to issue such proclamations.[63] Nevertheless, that next month Lincoln announced to his cabinet his decision to issue the Emancipation Proclamation.[64] Lincoln's cabinet convinced him, however, to wait until a Union military victory before announcing his intention. They felt that to announce his decision to free the slaves before then would seem like an act of desperation. President Lincoln, thus, delayed his public announcement until after the Union victory at the Battle of Antietam in September of 1862.[65] Lincoln announced that he would sign the Proclamation on January 1, 1863, in order to provide the states of the Confederacy with a final chance to rejoin the Union.

Before Lincoln announced his intention to issue the Emancipation Proclamation, abolitionist felt that Lincoln had not moved quickly or forcibly enough to eliminate slavery. In mid-August of 1862 Horace Greeley, the editor of the New York Times, published a letter in the Times in which he gave voice to this dissatisfaction.[66] Lincoln spelled out his justification for issuing the Emancipation Proclamation in response to Greeley's letter. Though Lincoln's response was before he publicly announced his intention to issue the Emancipation Proclamation, it was after the time he had decided such a measure was necessary. In that letter Lincoln stated:

> My paramount object is to save the Union, and not anywhere to save or destroy slavery. If I could save the Union without freeing any slave, I would do it: if I could save it by freeing all the slaves, I would do it; and if I could do it by freeing some and leaving others alone, I would also do that. What I do about slavery and the colored race, I do be-

> cause I believe it helps to save this Union; and what I forbear, I forbear because I do not believe it would help to save the Union. I shall do less whenever I shall believe what I am doing hurts the cause, and I shall do more whenever I believe doing more will help the cause.... I have here stated my purpose according to my view of official duty....[67]

No state in rebellion rejoined the Union during the waiting period. As announced, Lincoln signed the Proclamation on January 1, 1863. The Emancipation Proclamation, however, only sought to free slaves that were in the areas in rebellion. Excluded from its provisions were slaves in Delaware, Kentucky, Maryland and Missouri, the areas of Tennessee occupied by the Union and portions of Louisiana and Virginia.[68] As a result the Emancipation Proclamation left over one million bondsmen in the hands of masters who were considered loyal to the Union.[69]

Considering the best interest of the American collective there were three very good tactical reasons to issue the Emancipation Proclamation regardless of any beliefs about the morality of slavery or any desire to benefit blacks.[70] At the commencement of the war there were approximately nine million people in the Confederacy, but three and a half million of those were slaves.[71] African servitude allowed the South to put a much higher percentage of white men on the battle field than the North. As Jefferson Davis put it "the white men go into the army and leave the cultivation of their fields and the care of their flocks, as well as their wives and children"[72] to the bondsmen. Blacks also constituted a significant percentage of the workforce in a number of services that supported the southern war effort. They were half of the workers in the Confederate lead and iron mines and constituted a majority of the nurses in Confederate military hospitals. In addition slaves were cooks, servants and construction laborers in the Confederate armies. Thus, the institution of slavery was a tower of strength for the South. Depriving the rebellious states of their slaves would cripple the Confederacy's ability to wage war.[73] Second, there were indications that foreign powers such as France and Great Britain might be willing to recognize the Confederacy and provide it with financial support.[74] Both of these countries, however, had strong abolitionist movements. It was less likely that these foreign governments would be willing to intervene on the side of the Confederacy if their assistance would be understood as supporting slavery rather than the self-determination of the southern people desiring to establish their own nation. Third, war casualties suffered by the Union had been mounting as the war dragged on. Eliminating slavery would provide the catalyst for enlisting thousands of blacks in the Union Army. The Proclamation was necessary as a measure to win and end the war as soon as possible. Thus, even though the Emancipation Proclamation would help the plight of blacks, it was clearly justifiable on grounds of advancing the collective interest of the Union.

The Proclamation served its useful purposes. None of the European powers intervened in the Civil War. Black troops were also a very significant factor in the ultimate defeat of the Confederate Army. They volunteered and served in huge numbers. By the end of the war, blacks comprised over 10% of the Union's armed forces. Official statistics show that almost 179,000 black soldiers served in the Union army with 7,122 being officers.[75] An additional 29,000 served as sailors comprising 25% of the Union sailors.[76] Approximately 37,300 black soldiers were killed during the war, which amounted to over 10% of the Union soldiers killed.[77]

D. Reconstruction: How Granting Blacks Civil and Political Rights Advanced the Collective Interest

With the Civil War won and slavery abolished, the country had to turn to the issues of reconstruction and lasting peace. One of the most significant needs for the freedmen after the Civil War was education. In March 1865 the Bureau of Refugees, Freedmen and Abandoned Lands, better known as the Freedmen's Bureau, was established by Congress. While the Freedmen's Bureau provided rations to blacks and whites and operated forty-six hospitals staffed with physicians, surgeons and nurses, the Bureau excelled at educational work.[78] It set up and supervised all kinds of schools including day, night, Sunday and industrial schools. The Freedmen's Bureau provided financial assistance to colleges and universities including Howard University, Hampton Institute, Atlanta University and Fisk University. In 1869 there were over 9,500 teachers in Freedmen's schools. By 1870, when the educational work of the Bureau ceased there were almost 250,000 students enrolled in the 4,329 schools operated.

Like the abolition of slavery, black men received the franchise because at the time it advanced the interest of the American collective. It was essential that the Union victory in the Civil War and the principals upon which it was fought be secured. Most Republicans, the party that came to dominate national politics during the Civil War, felt that their election in 1860 and the Union's victory on the battlefield preserved the Union. It also prevented the South's way of life from destroying the freedoms and liberties on which the nation was founded and depended.[79] Since the Democratic party was the party of the rebels, the readmission of a solidly Democratic South would jeopardize the fruits of the Civil War. Those who had led the rebellion and those who followed had done so with the purpose of destroying the Union. There was little question that many of the men overcome by force of arms were as hostile to the Union as ever. To allow them to return to their positions of power in state and federal government ran the risk that they would continue to seek the destruction of the Union clothed with the power that comes from political office.

The best interest of the American collective required that a reconstructed South needed to be led by men who accepted the outcome of the Civil War.[80] There were two potential ways to guarantee that the states which seceded were governed by loyal men when readmitted to the Union. One path lay in enfranchising southern black males. The other way, was to deny political rights to some or all of those who participated in the rebellion in hopes that white men loyal to the Union would seize control of the reconstituted southern governments. Since 75% of the South's white men between the ages of 18 and 45 had served in the Confederate armies there were few white men who could say that they did not take any part in the rebellion.[81] Nevertheless, the latter solution was initially preferred to the former.

Granting blacks the franchise also lacked widespread support in the North. At the end of the Civil War, only in the five New England states were blacks granted the right to vote on par with whites. In the Fall of 1865 referenda in three different northern states, Connecticut, Minnesota and Wisconsin, rejected granting black males the right to vote.[82] Votes in later referenda in Kansas, Ohio, New York and the Nebraska Territory also rejected black enfranchisement.[83] Many in the North, including President Johnson, still strongly felt that blacks were a degraded population. The freedmen had just emerged from slavery. Degradation and ignorance were their lot. Blacks were inculcated with all servile habits and instincts of the most inveterate slavery. Residing in states that prohibited teaching slaves to read, 95% of them were illiterate. The freedmen, it was believed, were simply not fit to be members of the political community. In addition, there was no principle on which the right to vote could be extended to blacks that would not require it to be extended to other races who at the time were also considered degraded like the Chinese and Native Americans. Thus, allowing the freedmen the right to vote would bring into the political process a large mass of ignorant voters who would be susceptible to demagoguery, pecuniary and social influences and thereby corrupt and demean the entire election process to the detriment of all.

As noted in Chapter One, as southern governments were reconstituted in the Fall of 1865, they enacted a series of measures known as the "Black Codes." The goal of the Black Codes was to introduce a new system to ensure that the whites could continue to extract the labor of blacks as was done during slavery. Many in the North saw the Black Codes as evidence that the South did not accept the military outcome of the war.

The 39th Congress assembled in January of 1866 against the backdrop of the adoption of the Black Codes and recalcitrance from the reconstituted southern governments. This Congress faced a lot of pressing matters in the aftermath of the end of the Civil War and abolition. Congress began to debate a civil rights bill (the Civil Rights Act of 1866) that would give meaning to the Thirteenth Amendment's implicit abolition of the badges and incidents of slavery by assuring that blacks possessed basic civil rights. In addition, the ratification of the Thirteenth Amendment also created a huge political anomaly that Congress was compelled to address. Once blacks were free, apportionment of representatives in the lower house of Congress and determination of votes in the Electoral College would be effected. Blacks would count as a full person, instead of three-fifths of a person. Without adjustment, the ratification of the Thirteenth Amendment would increase the voting power of the states that had the most slaves before the Civil War. Thus, political power at the national level would be redistributed in favor of the very states that had rebelled.

Congress debated the Fourteenth Amendment during the first months of its term. This amendment passed out of Congress and was sent to the states in June of 1866. Section 1 of the Amendment[84] bestowed upon blacks the status of citizenship of the United States and the state where they resided; prohibited states from abridging their privileges or immunities as citizens of the United States; prohibited states from depriving them of life, liberty or property without due process; and granted them the equal protection of the laws. The Amendment did not grant black males political equality, but Section 2 dealt with the anomaly created by the abolition of slavery and was also intended to be an inducement to encourage the states to grant blacks the franchise. Under this provision if a state enfranchised the freedmen, then the former slaves would count in determining its representation in Congress and the Electoral College. But if a state refused to grant the right to vote to the freedmen over the age of 21, then the states representation would be reduced in proportion to the number such freedmen bore to the whole number of the male population over the age of 21.[85] Section 3 of the Fourteenth Amendment[86] barred from any civil or military office at both the state and federal levels those who previously took an oath as a member of federal or state office to support the Constitution of the United States and then engaged in the rebellion. A vote of two-thirds of those in Congress could remove this disability. Thus, Section 3 made virtually the entire political leadership of the former Confederate states before the war ineligible for public office. In so doing, Section 3 sought to institute a sweeping change in southern politics without granting blacks the right to vote.

By the Fall elections of 1866, the split between Congress and President Johnson was complete. Johnson took to the campaign trail speaking against leading Republicans in Congress, but this backfired. Those he campaigned for were resoundingly defeated at the polls. Republicans won every northern state legislature, every gubernatorial contest and more than two-thirds of the seats in both houses of Congress. In both Arkansas and Maryland, however, Democrats ousted wartime Unionists. In addition, urged on by Johnson, between October 1866 and the following January all of the states of the former Confederacy—with the exception of Tennessee—rejected the Fourteenth Amendment.[87] Tennessee was thus the only state that was readmitted into the Union at this time. None of the former eleven states of the Confederacy granted black males the right to vote.

By December of 1866, it was apparent that the strategy of ensuring that loyal white unionists exercised political control in the states of the former Confederacy had not worked. As Congress came back into session, it passed the First Reconstruction Act. The ten southern state governments that failed to ratify the Fourteenth Amendment were ordered disbanded and those states were divided into five military districts under commanders who were authorized to use the army to protect life and property. Congress went on to specify the steps necessary for readmittance into the Union. These included the ratification of the Fourteenth Amendment and the holding of a convention that would draft a new constitution for the state which required universal manhood suffrage.

After the election of 1868, Congress then adopted the Fifteenth Amendment which provided that "[t]he right of citizens of the United States to vote shall not be denied or abridged by the United States or by any state on account of race, color, or previous condition of servitude."[88] This Amendment was ratified in 1870. Thus, blacks could no longer be excluded from voting because of race throughout the country.

The need to allow blacks the right to vote was motivated by many reasons that advanced the interest of the American collective. It was thought that enfranchising blacks would assure that the new state governments would not fall into the hands of the rebellious elements in the South. Also, by the end of the Civil War it was generally understood that one of the causes of the war was the difference in treatment of blacks. The southern governments constituted under Presidential Reconstruction sought to reimpose a pseudo-slavery upon the colored race. But, unless justice was done for the blacks, there would never be a lasting peace between the two regions of the country. Resolving the rights of blacks once and for all and placing them on a stable footing would eliminate a source of constant agitation for the country. Finally, granting blacks the franchise would allow them to look after their own interest by electing representatives to government who would be beholden to their vote. This would be a less expensive way to protect the interest of the blacks than continuing to station federal troops on southern soil to prevent the reintroduction of slavery.

E. Segregation and Disenfranchisement: How Segregation and Blacks' Loss of the Right to Vote Advanced the Collective Interest

Although the desire to grant the right to vote to the freedmen appeared to advance the interest of the American collective at the time, enfranchisement was always a source of controversy. The inclusion of black males in the political process of the South was always problematic. The white southerners never truly yielded to the enfranchisement of black males. They corrupted the electoral process by intimidating black and Republican voters, stuffed ballot boxes and changed polling stations without notice. These acts brought shame and ignominy to the entire electoral process in the South.

As time passed, the justifications for enfranchising blacks weakened. The reconstitution of the Union became an accomplished reality. As southerners accepted the outcome of the Civil War and no longer threatened to destabilize the Union, a principal reason for the country to protect the right of blacks to vote diminished. Another problem with preventing former southern political leaders from fully participating in the political process was that it took the best and brightest out of government. Good government for all Americans required that the political power be in the hands of intelligent men.[89] In 1872, Congress enacted a general amnesty restoring full political rights to all but a few hundred former Confederate officials. Many also came to believe that the only way to eliminate fraud and violence, which occurred so often at the polls, and restore confidence in the democratic process was to exclude black male voters. The reason that whites should be the ones to make the laws of the country was ably summarized by Governor Thomas Bickett of North Carolina when he indicated that it was necessary for the protection, the progress and the happiness of both races for the government to be run by white people.[90]

The legal disenfranchisement of black men began in 1890 in Mississippi. Mississippi amended its constitution to include several provisions to disenfranchise blacks. South Carolina followed Mississippi's lead amending its constitution in 1895; Louisiana did so in 1898; North Carolina in 1900; Alabama in 1901; Virginia in 1901 and 1902; Georgia in 1908; and Oklahoma in 1910. Four other southern states, Arkansas, Florida, Tennessee and Texas, accomplished effective disenfranchisement of the black men without the necessity of amending their constitutions.[91] By the early part of the Twentieth Century, blacks were effectively removed from the political process in the Deep South.

Regardless of the outcome of the Civil War, abolition and enfranchisement of black males, dominant attitudes regarding the inferiority of blacks were not significantly altered. As mentioned in Chapter One discussing Traditional Americanism, for centuries scientists, philosophers, religious authorities and politicians continued to be convinced of the innate inferiority of the descendants of the soil of Africa.[92] Thus, abolition of slavery also meant that for the benefit of the American collective new ways in which to manage the generally regarded inferiority of blacks were needed.

Most northern and western states instituted segregation during the Antebellum Period. Segregation, however, was not adaptable to a slave holding society where intimate contact between master and slave was often necessary. The effective disenfranchisement of blacks allowed the South to institute legal segregation as the successive system to slavery to control the black population. During the latter part of the Nineteenth Century—in part as a response to the acceptance of the doctrine of "separate but equal" by the Supreme Court in *Plessy v. Ferguson*—the adoption of segregation statutes accelerated. Eventually the system of segregation in the South became total.

Segregation was justified because amalgamation of the races would result in the degeneracy of both races, but particularly the white race. Both scientists and the general public long believed that close association of blacks with whites would weaken the white race and thereby the country.[93] This was clear from a letter written before the end of the Civil War by Louis Agassiz to S. G. Howe, a member of Lincoln's Inquiry Commission. Agassiz wrote that although legal equality must be granted to all, blacks should be denied social equality, lest the white race be compromised and diluted. "Social equality I deem at all time impracticable. It is a natural impossibility flowing from the very character of the negro race." Agassiz asserted that blacks were:

> [I]ndolent, playful, sensuous, imitative, subservient, good natured, versatile, unsteady in their purposes, devoted, affectionate, in everything unlike other races, they may be compared to children, grown in stature of adults while retaining a childlike mind.... Therefore I hold that they are incapable of living on a footing of social equality with the whites, in one and the same community, without being an element of social disorder.[94]

The potential for miscegenation was another problem in the post Civil War America. Before the Civil War the social costs attributed to miscegenation were viewed to be so high that few people actually seriously considered allowing miscegenation to occur outside the bounds of master-slave relations.[95] With the end of slavery, race mixing and miscegenation, became a particular concern in the South.[96] From social amalgamation, there is but a small step to illicit intercourse and, but, another to interbreeding.

As noted in Chapter One, even before the Civil War, French aristocrat Count Arthur de Gobineau had published a revealing book which was highly regarded in the United States.[97] Among the issues that Gobineau dealt with in his book were the laws that explain the rise and fall of civilizations.[98] Gobineau claimed to have discovered the dangers miscegenation represented to a given civilization. Despite the existence of the civilizations in China, Ancient Egypt, India, Central and South America and Western Africa, Gobineau asserted that all high civilizations derive from the white race. The peculiar racial characteristics of the white race produced a people with reflective energy, energetic intelligence, feeling for utility, unusual perseverance, great physical power, extraordinary instinct for order, lovers of liberty and life and haters of despotism. Gobineau also claimed to have discovered that a society is great and brilliant only so far as it preserves the blood of the noble group that created it. He asserted that nations and civilizations degenerate only in consequences of the various admixtures of blood which they undergo. Their degeneration corresponds exactly to the quantity and quality of the new blood. The logical conclusion from Gobineau's work for the United States was that miscegenation between whites and blacks could destroy the nation.

Before the turn of the century a number of scientific research studies also stressed the dangers of miscegenation. Mulatto offspring were believed to be inferior to blacks. The work of Sanford Hunt was often cited to demonstrate this. Hunt studied the results of 405 autopsies of white and black soldiers during the Civil War. His research revealed not only that the average brain of a black person was smaller than that of a white person, but that the average brain of mulattoes was actually smaller than that of the blacks.[99] Given that brain size was believed to correspond with intelligence, Hunt concluded that interbreeding of the races would produce offspring inferior to even pure-blooded blacks. Benjamin Gould, who had been hired by the United States Sanitary Commission, also performed several anthropometric studies of autopsy reports on black and white soldiers. He discovered that the lung capacity of the black soldier was less than that of the white. But the lung capacity of the black soldier was greater than that of the mulatto.[100] Nathanial Shaler, a prominent Harvard professor wrote that the mulatto was less healthy, died earlier and was less likely to reproduce than members of either the black or white race. Shaler argued that mulattoes grew up with disharmonic features. Their body frames were too large for their small hearts and kidneys and their large teeth were tightly crowded into an undersized mouth. In addition, Shaler contended that mulattoes inherit from their white parent a refinement unfitting them for all the arduous work which is all that they are capable of performing.[101] Frederick Hoffman also argued that all mulattoes were inferior to members of either the black or white race.[102]

The belief that social amalgamation was detrimental to the interest of the American collective was also built into the public education system. In order to reduce the possibility of miscegenation, it was important to keep young people separate in education because this was a principal place where their values were formed. Both scientists and the general public also believed that blacks learned far more slowly than whites. Thus, race mixing in education would be detrimental to the entire society. It would weaken the education of white children by placing an inferior element in their schools.[103] It would be injurious to the educational interest of black children, because they would be placed in schools where the difficulty and complexity of the material covered would be beyond their intellectual abilities. From the standpoint of the nation's collective interest, since the black child could not benefit from education as much as the white child, the education of white children was more important than that of black children.[104] Thus, the public schools that white students attended were better funded, with longer school terms, more highly paid teachers and better physical facilities than black public schools.

This did not mean that the education of blacks was of no concern. Many white philanthropists were interested in the betterment of the interest of the nation. They agreed with the 1895 address delivered by Booker T. Washington at the opening of the Atlanta Industrial Exposition. Washington had noted that since one-third of the people in the South were black, "[n]o enterprise seeking the material, civil, or moral welfare of this section can disregard this element" of the American people. Blacks would "constitute one-third and more of the ignorance and crime of the South, or one-third of its intelligence and progress," they would contribute "one-third to the business and industrial prosperity of the South" or they would "prove a veritable body of death, stagnating, depressing [and] retarding every effort to advance the body politic."[105] Washington also went on to state that the masses of blacks will earn their living through common labor, for it is at the bottom of life that blacks must begin.

Educating blacks for positions and occupations not open to them was a waste of societal resources. Vocational training and industrial education helped to provide an able-bodied, simple-minded black workforce that would stay in the South and labor at modest wages. In this way blacks could further the economic interest of the country. By educating the black for the menial positions, it freed whites to be educated to handle the more complex work and the supply of skilled labor the South needed. The entire work force of the South would become more efficient and productive if blacks received vocational training and industrial education.

Conclusion

The discourse of American Collectivism is motivated by a desire to advance the best interest of the collective American people. This utilitarian pattern of understanding views all Americans as united as one people. The interest of American society can be advanced either by increasing the aggregate happiness or reducing the aggregate suffering of the nation. Whether a given decision should be arrived at, a given act engaged in, a given law enacted, a given regulation promulgated, a given rule adopted, a given ordinance ordained or a given social practice instituted, perpetuated or terminated depends upon whether it promotes the overall interest of the American collective.

In order to determine which actions advance the best interest of the country it is necessary to refer to the values that Americans hold dear. Certain values such as liberty, equality, democracy and the pursuit of happiness have been at the core of American society from the beginning of the republic. But the meanings of these fundamental American values change over time. Each generation of Americans defines the meaning of these fundamental values for their generation. One of the major changes in American society over the past fifty years has been the change in the meaning of liberty and equality. Historically, the dominant meanings about blacks have not been the egalitarian attitudes that began to emerge in the 1950s and 1960s. Throughout most of American history blacks were not accorded the degree of concern regarding their well-being as whites. Notions of advancing the interest of the nation were based upon a conscious perception of blacks as possessing an inferior nature to whites. For a long time the calculation of the best interest of the American collective openly recognized that blacks were non-citizens and then second-class citizens.

The version of the historical experience of African-Americans as conceptualized by this pattern of understanding emphasized how the treatment of blacks was consistent with a desire to advance the best interest of American society. At times the best interest of American society dictated favorable treatment of the African-Americans. At other times the interest of blacks was sacrificed at the altar of the greater good for the country.

Part II

Brown v. Board of Education and the Rise of School Desegregation as Conceptualized within Each of the Four Discourses

The desegregation of public schools was largely created, directed and ultimately restricted and terminated by federal court interpretations of the equal protection clause. There are two chapters in this part. Chapter Five discusses the Supreme Court's school desegregation jurisprudence that encouraged the desegregation of public schools. This Chapter begins by discussing four graduate and professional school desegregation decisions handed down by the Supreme Court between 1938 and 1950 that preceded the Court's opinion in *Brown v. Board of Education.* In granting the African-Americans plaintiffs relief in these cases, the Supreme Court did not have to overturn the "separate but equal" doctrine announced in *Plessy v. Ferguson.* The notion of "separate" in the graduate and professional school context provided by the southern states did not approach measurable equality. As a result, the Court did not need to consider whether segregation *per se* had a negative impact on African-Americans or on the educational process of black educational institutions.

Chapter Five will then discuss the Supreme Court's opinion in *Brown v. Board of Education* striking down statutes that required segregation of public schoolchildren. While many states complied with the obligation to desegregate their public schools, the Court's opinion in *Brown* was met with massive resistance in many states of the former Confederacy. As a result, ten years after the *Brown* decision only 2.14% of black students attended desegregated schools in the Deep South. Chapter Five will recount some of the resistance to the obligation to desegregate public schools. In its 1968 decision in *Green v. New Kent County School board* the Supreme Court placed an obligation on school districts that had formerly operated a dual school system to desegregate and do it now. In discharging this duty, the Court demanded that school systems treat their students, teachers and administrators as members of racial groups in order to promote desegregation.

Three years later the Court clarified the extent of the desegregation obligation it placed on school districts. In *Swann v. Charlotte Mecklenburg Board of Education,* the Court commanded school boards to achieve the greatest possible degree of actual desegregation. In setting out guidelines for integrating schools, the Court also approved school busing as an appropriate tool. *Green* and *Swann* quickened the pace of school desegregation. The amount of desegregation in public schools increased significantly between 1968 and 1972. After the Court's opinion in Swann, however, the Court began a steady march away from its commitment to desegregate America's public schools. These decisions will be discussed in Chapter Seven of Part III.

One of the two overlapping objectives of this book is to advance the discussion about racial issues, particularly those that involve African-American schoolchildren, by discussing those issues with a Post-Desegregation Awareness. Chapter Six will review the Supreme Court's school desegregation jurisprudence that encouraged the use of racial classifications in order to promote the desegregation of public schools through each of the four different cognitive frameworks—Traditional Americanism, African-American Centralism, Colorblind Individualism and American Collectivism—that were discussed more fully in Part I. As stated earlier, these discourses structure and limit the perception of given phenomena and thus the discussion of racial issues. However, these cognitive frameworks do not provide a definitive answer to a given racial conflict. Thus, arguments can be generated within these cognitive frameworks that support the desegregation of public schools or reject it. Since America celebrated, as opposed to lamented, the Golden Anniversary of *Brown v. Board of Education,* Chapter Six will present only the type of arguments that would be generated within each of the four discourses which would argue for the use of racial classifications in order to promote desegregated education.

Chapter Five

The Rise of School Desegregation

The litigation that resulted in the Supreme Court's *Brown v. Board of Education* (*Brown I*) decision was the result of a long term legal strategy to attack segregation initiated by the NAACP and later carried on by the NAACP Legal Defense and Educational Fund, Inc. ("LDF").[1] Between 1938 and 1950, the Supreme Court addressed four cases dealing with segregation in graduate and professional schools.[2] Section I of this Chapter discusses the four graduate and professional school decisions that preceded the Supreme Court's decision in *Brown*. Despite the equal protection doctrine of "separate but equal" announced in *Plessy v. Ferguson*,[3] prior to the NAACP's legal campaign, African-Americans experienced numerous disadvantages in seeking higher educational opportunities. In the 1930s, a white student desiring to enroll in higher education had five times as many colleges to choose from as did his African-American counterpart.[4] Black public colleges also were unequal to white public colleges in terms of facilities, faculty training and the breadth and depth of curriculum. This inequality was most apparent at the graduate and professional school level.

In *Brown I* the Supreme Court struck down the segregation statutes of twenty-one states. The Court followed this decision with its implementation decision, *Brown II*, the following year. Section II revisits the Court's opinion in *Brown I* and focuses on the Court's articulated rationale for striking down segregation statutes. That section highlights the fact that Chief Justice Earl Warren's opinion for the Court justified striking down segregation statutes because segregation psychologically damaged black schoolchildren.

While many states sought to comply with the Court's *Brown* rulings, the decision was met with massive resistance in the eleven states that formerly constituted the Confederacy. These states employed various methods to minimally comply or avoid compliance with their constitutional obligation to desegregate public schools. Resistance was so effective that ten years after the Court's decision in *Brown I*, only 2.14% of the black students in the eleven states in the Deep South attended desegregated schools.[5] Section III discusses some of the varied ways in which resistance to school desegregation occurred.

In the 1968 opinion of *Green v. New Kent County School Board,*[6] the Supreme Court declared that the duty placed on school boards by *Brown I* and *II* required compulsory integration. The Court announced that school boards which had operated a dual school system had an affirmative duty to take whatever steps were necessary to convert to a unitary system in which racial discrimination would be eliminated root and branch and they were to do it "now."[7] Three years after the Court's opinion in *Green,* the Supreme Court finally articulated the appropriate limit of the duty to desegregate a school system. In *Swann v. Charlotte-Mecklenburg Board of Education*[8] the Court placed the obligation on school boards to achieve the greatest possible degree of actual desegregation. The impact of the these decisions on racial mixing in public schools was dramatic and almost immediate. Section IV of this Chapter will discuss these Supreme Court decisions which led to significant desegregation of public schools.

I. Graduate School Cases that Preceded *Brown v. Board of Education*

Between 1938 and 1950, the Supreme Court addressed four cases dealing with segregation in graduate and professional schools. Prior to the NAACP's legal campaign, African-Americans experienced numerous disadvantages in seeking higher educational opportunities, especially at the graduate and professional school level. In 1940 only three of the seventeen segregationist states[9]—Virginia, Texas and North Carolina—carried on any graduate instruction at their black public colleges. In addition, none of the approximately thirty black public colleges in the segregationist states offered any programs leading to a Ph.D., and only two had professional schools. There were two black professional schools at North Carolina College for Negroes, a law school and a library science school. The other professional school was the recently created law school at Lincoln University in Missouri. In contrast all seventeen segregationist states had white public colleges with extensive graduate and professional school programs. The number of different professional curricula at white public colleges were as follows: graduate engineering-17, law-16, medicine-15, graduate commerce and business-15, pharmacy-14, library science-11, social service-9 and dentistry-4.[10]

Lincoln University's recently created law school was the result of the NAACP's litigation success in *Gaines v. Canada.*[11] The all-white University of Missouri Law School had refused to admit Lloyd Lionel Gaines because he was black. The State of Missouri, however, offered to pay Gaines' extra expenses for a legal education in an out-of-state law school or, alternatively, to build a law school for African-Americans at Lincoln University, the black public college. The Missouri Supreme Court rejected Gaines equal protection challenge to the denial of his admissions to the University of Missouri Law School. The Missouri Supreme court held that the scholarship program was substantially equal to the opportunity offered white students at the University of Missouri.[12]

In reversing the Missouri Supreme Court, the U.S. Supreme Court noted that the validity of segregation laws "rest[ed] wholly upon the equality of the privileges which the laws give to the separated groups within the State."[13] While law schools in other states might have been every bit as good as that of the University of Missouri, the relevant question was what kind of opportunity the state of Missouri provided for the two racial groups. Missouri had given whites a privilege of attending a law school in the state that it had not given to African-Americans. The Supreme Court ruled that Gaines was entitled to be admitted to the University of Missouri Law School in the absence of other and proper provision for his legal training within the State.

After the U.S. Supreme Court's decision, the Missouri legislature established a law school for African-Americans at Lincoln University. Gaines again challenged the refusal to admit him to the white law school. The Missouri Supreme Court ruled that as long as the facilities at Lincoln University were "substantially equivalent" to those at the University of Missouri, the absence of other and proper provision for Gaines had been redressed.[14] Thus, he had no right to attend the University of Missouri Law School.

While the United States Supreme Court had ruled that Gaines was "entitled to be admitted to the State University in the absence of other and proper provision for his training," it remained unclear if the Court would have agreed with the Missouri Supreme Court's conclusion that the creation of a separate law school satisfied Missouri's constitutional obligation. The NAACP, however, was unable to locate Gaines to challenge Missouri's establishment of a separate black law school. It is reported that Gaines mysteriously disappeared from a train that was headed back to Missouri from Chicago and was never heard from again.[15]

Ten years later, in *Sipuel v. Oklahoma State Board of Regents*,[16] the Court found itself addressing a situation similar to that presented in *Gaines*. Ada Louis Sipuel had applied for and been denied admission into the University of Oklahoma Law School. Her application for admission was rejected solely because a separate law school for blacks with "substantially equal" facilities would open soon. The Supreme Court handed down a *per curiam* opinion just four days after oral argument. The Court ruled that Oklahoma had to provide Sipuel with a legal education in the same time frame as it did for applicants of other groups.

Both *Sipuel* and *Gaines* involved the complete denial of any opportunity for professional training within the state which the African-American plaintiffs resided. In the 1950 companion cases of *Sweatt v. Painter*[17] and *McLaurin v. Oklahoma State Regents*,[18] the states provided professional or graduate training for African-Americans, albeit on a segregated basis. These cases forced the Court to address more substantive demands of equality within the context of graduate and professional education.

Heman Marion Sweatt had applied for admission to the University of Texas Law School in Austin, Texas. Sweatt's application was rejected solely because he was an African-American. At the time he applied, there was no law school in the state of Texas for African-Americans. While Sweatt's appeal was pending, however, the Texas legislature appropriated enough money to establish a law school for blacks. As the case reached the Supreme Court, the issue involved whether the newly created law school provided equal educational opportunities—in a constitutional sense—with those of the University of Texas Law School. The Supreme Court in comparing the law schools noted that the University of Texas Law School had a student body of 850 students, over 65,000 volumes in its library and a faculty of sixteen full-time and three part-time professors. Also available at the University of Texas Law School were a law review, moot court facilities and the Order of the Coif affiliation. In contrast, the law school set up for blacks enrolled only twenty-three students. The teaching was to be carried on by five full-time professors and the library consisted of approximately 16,500 volumes. In addition to the tangible inequalities between the two schools, the Court also noted that the University of Texas Law School possessed to a far greater degree those qualities which are incapable of objective measurement but which make for greatness in a Law School. These qualities included reputation of the faculty, experience of the administration, position and influence of the alumni, standing in the community, traditions and prestige.

The Supreme Court noted that "few students and no one who has practiced law would choose to study in an academic vacuum, removed from the interplay of ideas and the exchange of views with which the law is concerned."[19] The physical facilities of the all-black law school were no match for those of the University of Texas Law School. Even if the physical facilities could equal those provided by the University of Texas Law School, a newly-created segregated law school could not match the intangible educational benefits available at the University of Texas Law School. The Court concluded that the education offered Sweatt was not equal to the education he would receive at the University of Texas Law School.

In *McLaurin v. Oklahoma State Regents,* the Court addressed segregation in graduate education in a different context. When George McLaurin, a 67-year-old man, originally applied for admission to the University of Oklahoma to pursue a Doctorate in Education his application was denied solely because of his race. McLaurin filed a complaint requesting injunctive relief. He alleged that the actions of the school authorities and the statutes upon which their actions were based were unconstitutional and deprived him of equal protection of the laws. A three-judge District Court panel held that the State had a constitutional duty to provide McLaurin with the education he sought just as it provided education for applicants of any other group.[20]

While McLaurin was eventually admitted to the University of Oklahoma Graduate School, his admission was on a segregated basis. He was, therefore, subjected to the segregation rules and regulations that the President of the University considered necessary. McLaurin was originally required to sit apart from the rest of his classmates at a designated area during class. While he was allowed on the main floor of the library, McLaurin was restricted to his own table. Although he could eat in the cafeteria at the same time as the white students, he was confined to his own segregated table. In striking down the segregation regulations, the Court noted that the regulations resulted in McLaurin being handicapped in his pursuit of effective graduate instruction. The Court noted that such restrictions impaired and inhibited his ability to study, to engage in discussions and exchange views with other students, and in general, to learn his profession.

In granting the African-American plaintiffs relief in the graduate and professional school cases the Supreme Court did not need to overturn the "separate but equal" doctrine announced in *Plessy v. Ferguson.*[21] The harm from segregation in these cases was the denial to African-Americans of opportunities for professional training equal to those provided to Caucasian students. The "separate" provided by the Southern states in the graduate and professional context did not approach equality. Thus, in none of the graduate and professional school cases did the Court need to consider whether segregation *per se* produced a negative impact on African-Americans or on the educational process of segregated black institutions.

II. *Brown v. Board of Education:* Striking Down Statutes that Segregate Public Schools

In *Brown v. Board of Education* and its companion cases, the Supreme Court addressed equal protection challenges to segregation in elementary and secondary education from four different states: Kansas, South Carolina, Delaware and Virginia. A fifth decision, *Bolling v. Sharpe,*[22] involved a due process challenge under the Fifth Amendment to segregation in the schools of the District of Columbia. In the Topeka, Kansas case, the Court addressed a situation where a lower court had found that separate black and white schools were equal in terms of physical facilities and other tangible resources. In two of the companion cases—*Briggs v. Elliot*[23] from South Carolina and *Davis v. County School Board of Prince Edward County*[24] from Virginia—the lower federal courts sustained the validity of segregation. Both lower courts, however, found that the black schools were inferior to white schools in terms of resources and ordered the defendants to immediately begin to equalize the facilities. In *Gebhart v. Belton,*[25] the Delaware case, black plaintiffs were admitted to white schools upon a determination that the schools they attend were inferior in terms of resources to those of white students. But the Supreme Court of Delaware intimated that the school officials might be able to obtain a modification of the decree after equalization of the black and white schools was accomplished.[26]

In the unanimous Supreme Court opinion in *Brown,* Chief Justice Earl Warren noted that black children sought admission to the public schools of their community on a non-segregated basis. Addressing their equal protection challenge, the Court started its opinion with the declaration that:

> Education is perhaps the most important function of state and local governments. Compulsory school attendance laws and the great expenditures for education both demonstrate our recognition of the importance of education to our democratic society. It is required in the performance of our most basic public responsibilities, even service in the armed forces. It is the very foundation of good citizenship. Today it is a principal instrument in awakening the child to cultural values, in preparing him for later professional training, and in helping him to adjust normally to his environment. In these days, it is doubtful that any child may reasonably be expected to succeed in life if he is denied the opportunity of an education.[27]

The Court's analysis then turned to the harm generated by segregation. Since Warren's opinion was addressing the Kansas case, he assumed that the physical facilities and other tangible factors of the public schools attended by black and white students were equal. Given the objectively measurable equality of segregation in this context, for the first time the Court was forced to identify the harm resulting from segregation *per se.* In one of the most quoted phrases from *Brown I,* the Court stated: "[t]o separate [African-American youth] from others of similar age and qualifications solely because of their race generates a feeling of inferiority as to their status in the community that may affect their hearts and minds in a way unlikely ever to be undone." Warren's opinion went on to quote approvingly from the district court in Kansas:

> Segregation of white and colored children in public schools has a detrimental effect upon the colored children. The impact is greater when it has the sanction of law; [f]or the policy of separating the races is usually interpreted as denoting the inferiority of the negro group. A sense of inferiority affects the motivation of a child to learn. Segregation with the sanction of law, therefore, has a tendency to [retard] the educational and mental development of negro children and to deprive them of some of the benefits they would receive in a racial[ly] integrated school.[28]

Chief Justice Warren buttressed his conclusion in *Brown* that segregation in public schools inflicted psychological harm on African-Americans by citing to studies by social scientist in its now (in)famous footnote 11.[29] Prominent social scientists also filed an amicus brief with the Court[30] pointing to the effect of segregation on blacks. But the brief also discussed the psychological harm of segregation on the majority group. With regard to the harm suffered by whites from segregation the brief stated:

> With reference to the impact of segregation and its concomitants on children of the majority group, the report indicates that the effects are somewhat more obscure. Those children who learn the prejudices of our society are also being taught to gain personal status in an unrealistic and non-adaptive way. When comparing themselves to members of the minority group, they are not required to evaluate themselves in terms of the more basic standards of actual personal ability and achievement. The culture permits and, at times, encourages them to direct their feelings of hostility and aggression against whole groups of people the members of which are perceived as weaker than themselves. *They often develop patterns of guilt feelings, rationalizations and other mechanisms which they must use in an attempt to protect themselves from recognizing the essential injustice . . . .*[31] (emphasis added).

From the very beginning scholars argued that the Court's opinion in *Brown* did not rest on the social science evidence.[32] I cite to the social science evidence, because that evidence presented the Court with a road that it choose not to pursue, that segregation generated a dual harm. If segregation created a false sense of inferiority within blacks then it must have also generated the psychological harm of a false sense of superiority in whites. If blacks were being harmed by a false doctrine that preached their inferiority, then *a fortiori* whites were being psychological harmed by being subjected to false doctrine that preached their superiority. The dual psychological harm of segregation means that the entire society was suffering from two different aspects of the same delusion. In other words, the coin of segregation had two sides. On the one side there was the myth that blacks were inferior, but on the other side there was the myth that whites were superior. If the Court had rested its opinion on the recognition of the dual nature of the psychological harm of segregation then the justification for striking down segregation statutes in public schools would have been different. The Court would have noted that segregation harmed blacks because it taught the false doctrine of their inferiority. But segregation also harmed whites because it taught the false doctrine of their superiority.

If the Court had specifically recognized the dual nature of the educational and mental harm of segregation in *Brown,* then it would have made a firm break with its past interpretation of the equal protection rights of blacks as based upon some notion that blacks are inferior. The Court would have proclaimed that desegregation and all other remedies for the operation of a dual school system were for the benefit of all schoolchildren. There would have been a symmetry in the remedies and the explanation for the need for those remedies that did not come to exist in the Court's subsequent school desegregation jurisprudence. For example, integration of classrooms would have been pursued because it benefitted all schoolchildren, not just the black ones. Educational components that were ordered as part of desegregation decrees would have addressed the need to attack the falsely created psychological feelings of superiority of whites and the falsely created psychological feelings of inferiority in blacks. But the reality was that in 1954 the Supreme Court could not be expected to publicly pronounce that whites were psychologically damaged by the experience of slavery and segregation. Nor could the Court base its opinion for striking down segregation statutes on the statement that whites would also be advantaged by interracial contact. There were certainly good reasons that the Court did not focus on segregation as creating a dual harm and desegregation a dual benefit. The Court needed to reach a unanimous opinion in order to minimize the anticipated resistance to its opinion in the Deep South. Even with Warren's opinion, resistance to school desegregation in the South was massive. In 1954, a statement by the Supreme Court that whites were psychologically damaged would have seemed patently ridiculous to the overwhelming majority of whites in the North and the South. Nevertheless, the Court's view of segregation as producing a one way harm set it and lower federal courts on a certain path with regard to remedies for *de jure* segregation. According to the Court's opinion, remedies for *de jure* segregation were needed, not in spite of, but because African-Americans were made inferior to whites through the psychological damage inflicted during segregation.

After concluding that segregation statutes denied black students the constitutional guarantee of equal protection, the Court rejected their request for immediate relief. Chief Justice Warren noted that due to the wide applicability of the decision and the great variety of local conditions, the formulation of decrees in these cases presented problems of considerable complexity. The Court redocketed the cases for the next term to address the question of the appropriate remedy.

A year later, the Court issued its decision on implementing the *Brown I* ruling in *Brown II.*[33] The Court required public schools to effectuate a transition to a "racially nondiscriminatory school system." The Court noted that the full implementation of the constitutional principles require varied solutions to local school problems. The precise parameters of what was meant by a racially nondiscriminatory school system was left originally to the discretion of school authorities who had the primary responsibility for elucidating, assessing and solving this problem. Chief Justice Warren went on to note that orders and decrees should be entered to admit the plaintiffs to public schools on a racially nondiscriminatory basis "with all deliberate speed."

III. Resistance to School Desegregation

The Court's opinion in *Brown* struck down segregation statutes in twenty-one states. The segregation statutes in Arizona, Kansas, New Mexico and Wyoming did not mandate segregation, only permitted local school districts the option of adopting racial segregation. These states generally complied with the Supreme Court's decision that state mandated segregated schools were unconstitutional without much difficulty.[34] Six other states, Delaware, Kentucky, Maryland, Missouri, Oklahoma and West Virginia, along with the District of Columbia, also complied with the Court's ruling without much opposition. But the eleven states that had formerly been part of the Confederacy employed various methods to minimally comply or avoid complying with their constitutional obligation.[35]

Resistance to school desegregation actually began before the Court's opinion in *Brown* was delivered. As the 1950s unfolded, southern circles thought it increasingly clear that the Supreme Court might soon move to require integration of public elementary and secondary schools. In September 1950 prominent black Atlanta attorney Austin T. Walden and Thurgood Marshall filed a claim in federal district court on behalf of two hundred black schoolchildren and their parents in Atlanta. The suit sought either the equalization of educational resources for the black children or the admission of black children to white schools.[36] In response to this lawsuit Roy Harris predicted, in the Augusta Courier, that if the courts ordered the desegregation of public schools, white Georgians would stop taxing themselves to support public education and eventually place their children in private schools.[37] Harris argued that if the public school system would mean destroying segregation, which was so predominant in the South, then the state of Georgia should do away with the public school system. Harris went on to suggest a publicly funded private school plan.[38]

Within months of Harris' article, the Georgia General Assembly considered legislation that would cut off funds and thus close all public schools if black children were allowed to integrate the former all-white schools. The General Assembly had the power to turn state-owned educational property over to private individuals, and indicated a willingness to do so. The General Assembly also set up a program that would provide grants for educational purposes to individuals. These grants could be used at private schools chosen by the recipient.[39]

In November 1952, South Carolina followed the actions of the Georgia legislature. Voters there approved a constitutional amendment that eliminated the state's duty to educate all children. This meant that education could be handled as a private matter. Governors of two other states, Mississippi and Virginia, considered similar proposals.[40]

One month after the Court's decision in *Brown*, eight Governors of states that were part of the Confederacy and three representatives sent by the governors of Arkansas, Tennessee and Texas met in Virginia. They unanimously vowed not to comply voluntarily with the Supreme Court's decision.[41] And on March 12, 1956, a group of southern Senators and Congressmen presented the Southern Manifesto in which they asserted their intention to use every legal tactic possible to resist desegregation.[42]

The Deep South states implemented measures to resist desegregation including: closing public schools instead of integrating them; delegating control of the public schools to the governor or the state legislature in hopes of frustrating federal court orders directed at local school officials; providing tuition grants to pay for segregated private schools for those who did not wish to attend integrated schools; denying state funds to schools attended by pupils of different races; abolishing compulsory schooling; criminalizing teaching in or attending an integrated school; and firing teachers who advocated desegregation.[43] Little Rock, Arkansas presents a good example of both massive resistance and how public funding of private education was used to avoid the obligation to desegregate public schools. Little Rock was one of the first communities below the Potomac to make preparations for compliance with *Brown's* requirement to desegregate schools. It was considered a moderate southern city without a record of political extremism on racial issues. The city had already desegregated the city buses without resistance and assumed that school desegregation would proceed without much opposition either.[44]

Three days after the first *Brown* opinion, the Little Rock District School Board adopted a policy stating that it was the Board's responsibility to comply with the Federal Constitution. The Board further stated that it intended to do so when the Supreme Court of the United States outlined the methods to be followed. On May 24, 1955, seven days before the Supreme Court's *Brown II* decision, the School Board approved a gradual desegregation plan. Desegregation was to start in September, 1957 at the high school level and involve grades 10 through 12. A total of 9 black students were assigned to the all-white Central High School, which had over 2,000 students. The School Board also announced that it would proceed to the junior high and elementary level with complete desegregation of the school system to be accomplished by 1963.

The day before school started, Governor Orval Faubus ordered units of the Arkansas National Guard to Central High School to prevent attendance by the black students.[45] When the black students arrived at Central High School on September 4, 1957, they were greeted by mobs of angry whites. The Arkansas National Guard forcibly prevented them from entering the school building. Public hostility to the integration of Central High School increased. The black students were unable to enter Central High School until President Eisenhower ordered federal troops to Little Rock on September 24th.[46] While Eisenhower withdrew the federal troops on November 27th, federalized National Guardsmen remained in Central High School throughout the remainder of the school year to protect the "Little Rock Nine."

Due to the hostility generated by the Governor's resistance to school desegregation, the Little Rock School Board went back to the federal district court in February of 1958 and requested a two and one-half year delay in its duty to desegregate schools. The School Board argued that the Governor's actions hardened the core of opposition to the desegregation plan. It caused many persons who reluctantly accepted the plan to believe that the State of Arkansas had the power to nullify federal law. Shortly before the start of the school year in September of 1958, the Supreme Court in *Cooper v. Aaron*[47] rejected the request. The Supreme Court stated that preventing race conflicts, as desirable as it may be and as important as it is in the preservation of the peace, could not be accomplished by means which denied rights created or protected under the Constitution.

The Supreme Court's decision in *Cooper v. Aaron* did not end the Little Rock controversy. On the day of the Court's decision Governor Faubus signed into law two measures that had been passed earlier by the Arkansas General Assembly.[48] These measures allowed him to close the schools in Little Rock. In addition, the Governor was also empowered to withhold state educational funds and money from the County General School Fund of any school district that he closed. The monies withheld could then be made available, on a per capita basis, to any other public school or any non-profit private school accredited by the State Board of Education (of which the Governor was a member), which could be attended by students of a closed school.[49]

Pursuant to these new statutes, the Governor ordered the senior high schools closed in Little Rock. The schools remained closed during the entire 1958–59 school year. During that school year approximately $500,000 was withheld from the Little Rock school district. A significant portion of the funds were used to pay for white students who enrolled in a private school, Raney High School.[50]

One of the companion cases to *Brown* came from Prince Edwards County, Virginia.[51] In *Brown II*'s implementation decision a year later, Prince Edwards County was placed under a duty to convert to a "racially non-discriminatory school system with all deliberate speed."[52] As early as 1956, however, the Board of Supervisors of Prince Edward County determined that they would not operate public schools where black and white children were taught together. The Board of Supervisors were aided in their desire to resist integrated education by actions of the State of Virginia. The Virginia Constitution was amended in 1956 to authorize the General Assembly and local governing bodies to appropriate funds to assist students who would rather go to nonsectarian private schools than public schools.[53] The General Assembly also met in special session and enacted legislation to close any public schools where white and colored children were enrolled together, to cut off state funds to such schools, to pay tuition grants to children in nonsectarian private schools and to extend state retirement benefits to teachers in newly created private schools.[54] Governor Almond of Virginia used the powers from the new legislation to close schools in three counties to prevent them from being integrated. The Virginia Supreme Court, however, ruled in 1959 that the legislation closing racially mixed schools and cutting off funds to such schools violated Virginia's Constitution.[55]

In June 1959, the United States Court of Appeals for the Fourth Circuit directed the Federal District Court (1) to enjoin discriminatory practices in Prince Edward County schools; (2) to require the County School Board of Prince Edwards County to take immediate steps toward admitting students without regard to race to the white high school in the school term beginning September 1959; and (3) to require the County School Board to make plans for admissions to elementary schools without regard to race.[56] The Board of Supervisors—as opposed to the County School Board—of Prince Edwards County, however, refused to levy school taxes for the 1959–60 school year. As a result the schools of the County did not open in the Fall of 1959. They remained closed until the Supreme Court addressed the situation in its 1964 opinion in *Griffin v. County School Board*.[57]

In order to provide education for white children the Prince Edward School Foundation was formed. The Foundation built its own school and started operating when the public schools were closed. While an offer was made to set up private schools for black schoolchildren, the African-American community rejected the offer, preferring litigation instead. As a result, black schoolchildren were without education from 1959 to 1963 until federal, state and county authorities cooperated to have classes for blacks and whites in school buildings owned by the county.

During the 1959–60 academic school year, schools set up for the white children by the Foundation were completely supported by private funds. In 1960 the Virginia General Assembly, however, adopted a new tuition grant program. Every child in the state, regardless of race, was eligible for tuition assistance of $125 or $150 to attend a nonsectarian private school or a public school outside his locality. The legislation also authorized localities to provide their own education grants to students attending private schools or public schools outside the district. After this legislation was passed, the Board of Supervisors of Prince Edward County adopted an ordinance providing tuition grants of $100 per student. Thus, each child in Prince Edward County attending the Foundation's schools received a total of $225 if in elementary school or $250 if in high school. These grants constituted the major source of funding for the Foundation schools in the 1960–61 academic school year. The Board of Supervisors also passed an ordinance allowing property tax credits up to 25% for contributions to any nonprofit, nonsectarian private school in the county.

In 1961 the black petitioners filed a supplemental complaint with the District Court adding new parties and seeking to enjoin both the refusal by County officials to operate the public schools and the use of public funds to support private schools which excluded students on account of race. The District Court concluded that the end result of every action taken by the Board of Supervisors of Prince Edwards County was designed to preserve separation of the races in the schools. The Court enjoined the county from paying tuition grants or giving tax credits so long as public schools remained closed.[58] The District Court, however, did not address the issue of whether the public schools of the County could be closed. Rather the District Court abstained from addressing this issue pending determination by the Virginia courts on whether the Constitution and Laws of Virginia required the public schools be kept open. Eleven months later, however, the District Court issued a ruling in which it held that "the public schools of Prince Edward County may not be closed to avoid the effect of the law of the land as interpreted by the Supreme Court, while the Commonwealth of Virginia permits other public schools to remain open at the expense of the taxpayers."[59]

Not long after the District Court's ruling, the Board of Supervisors and the County School Board filed for a declaratory judgment in a Virginia Circuit Court. The Board of Supervisors and the County School Board also asked the Federal District Court to abstain from further proceedings until the state court ruled on the pending declaratory judgment. The District Court declined and the parties appealed. The Fourth Circuit reversed, with Judge Bell dissenting. The Fourth Circuit concluded that the District Court should have waited for the state court to rule on the validity of the tuition grants, the tax credits and the validity of the closing of the public schools.[60]

By the time the United States Supreme Court rendered its opinion the Supreme Court of Appeals of Virginia had ruled in the case.[61] The Virginia high court upheld the state law used to close the Prince Edward County public schools, the state and county tuition grants for children who attend private schools and the County's tax concessions for those who make contributions to private schools.[62] The Supreme Court of Appeals of Virginia concluded that each county had the option to operate or not to operate public schools.

In its opinion, the United States Supreme Court concluded that it could not be clearer that Prince Edward's public schools were closed and private schools operated in their place with state and county assistance, for one reason—to ensure that white and colored children in Prince Edward County would not go to the same school. The Supreme Court further stated that "whatever nonracial grounds might support a State allowing a county to abandon public schools, the object must be a constitutional one, and grounds of race and opposition to desegregation do not qualify as constitutional."[63]

The State of Louisiana provides another example of resistance to school desegregation. On May 25, 1960, the Federal District Court in Louisiana entered an order restraining and enjoining the St. Helena Parish School Board and its superintendent from continuing racial segregation in the public schools under their supervision. The District Court order required the School Board, with all deliberate speed, to make necessary arrangements for the admission of children to schools on a racially non-discriminatory basis. The Fifth Circuit affirmed this judgment on February 9, 1961.[64] It also delivered decisions affirming desegregation rulings related to Baton Rouge public schools and five state trade schools later in that month.[65]

On the same day that the Fifth Circuit affirmed the District Court order regarding St. Helena Parish schools, the Governor of Louisiana called an Extraordinary Session of the Louisiana Legislature to act regarding the education of the schoolchildren of the State. He proposed emergency legislation designed to continue racial segregation in the public schools despite the orders of the federal courts. The legislation allowed public schools under desegregation orders to be changed to private schools. These schools would be operated in the same way, in the same buildings, with the same furnishings, with the same money and under the same supervision as they had been when they were public schools. The legislation also required school boards of the parish with closed public schools to furnish free lunches, transportation and grants-in-aid to the children attending the private schools. When this authorizing legislation was challenged in federal court, however, the District Court struck it down.[66]

In addition to the outright resistance to *Brown I* and *Brown II,* many southern federal judges and school officials in implementing the *Brown* decisions relied on the language from the District Court opinion in *Briggs v. Elliot.*[67] *Briggs* was the South Carolina companion case to *Brown.* On remand from the Court's decisions in *Brown I* and *Brown II* the three-judge federal District Court panel interpreted the constitutional obligation that the *Brown* decisions pronounced.

> [The Supreme Court] has not decided that the states must mix persons of different races in the schools or must require them to attend schools or must deprive them of the right of choosing the schools they attend. What it has decided, and all that it has decided, is that a state may not deny to any person on account of race the right to attend any school that it maintains. . . . The Constitution, in other words, does not require integration. It merely forbids discrimination. It does not forbid such segregation as occurs as the result of voluntary action. It merely forbids the use of governmental power to enforce segregation.[68]

Since integration of public schools was not popular, many southern federal judges and school officials stopped far short of requiring mandatory massive integration of public schools. Jackson County, Tennessee provides an example of this willingness to delay the implementation of desegregation. The school system had 7,650 children enrolled with about 40% of whom were black. In 1954, by law, Tennessee required racial segregation in its public schools. Accordingly, five elementary schools, two junior high schools and one senior high school were operated as white schools. There were an additional three elementary schools, one junior high school and one senior high school operated as black schools. Racial segregation extended to all aspects of school life, including faculty and staff. After the *Brown* decisions, Tennessee enacted a pupil placement law that continued previously enrolled pupils in their assigned schools and vested local school boards with the exclusive authority to approve assignment and transfer requests. No white children enrolled in any of the black schools in Jackson County. The Jackson County School Board granted only seven applications of black children to enroll in 'white' schools. The first did not occur until 1961, when three such applications were approved. Four additional applications were approved in 1962.[69]

IV. The Obligation to Achieve the Greatest Possible Degree of Actual Desegregation

Resistance effectively blocked school desegregation in the Deep South for the first ten years. By 1964, only 2.14% of the black students in the eleven states of the former confederacy attended desegregated schools.[70] The passage of the Civil Rights Act of 1964, however, had an important impact on school desegregation. One provision of the Civil Rights Act of 1964 authorized the Attorney General to intervene in or to initiate school desegregation suits. With the enormous resources of the federal government being brought to bear on local school districts throughout the country, the pace of school desegregation litigation quickened. Another provision of the Civil Rights Act of 1964, Title VI, banned discrimination in all federally-aided programs. The Secretary of Health, Education and Welfare (HEW) was empowered to deny federal funds to any school district found in violation of this provision. At the time the Act was passed, however, federal aid to public education was insignificant. Education and its funding were considered primarily obligations of state and local government.

A year later Congress passed the Elementary and Secondary Education Act of 1965. This Act provided funds for remedial assistance in reading and math to schools with a disproportionate number of economically disadvantaged children. Because of the poverty that existed in the Deep South, a large portion of these funds were ear marked for the states that had resisted school desegregation the most. In order to be eligible to receive these funds, however, school systems had to comply with HEW guidelines as to what constituted a non-discriminatory school system. This pot of money provided an additional incentive for school systems to desegregate.

In the 1968 *Green v. New Kent County School Board*[71] opinion, the Supreme Court declared that the duty placed on school boards by *Brown I and II* required compulsory integration. New Kent County had only two schools in the entire district. New Kent School was on the east side of the County and the George W. Watkins School was on the west side of the County. Watkins was considered the school for blacks and New Kent the school for whites. Segregation in the schools had been maintained under Virginia law until the Supreme Court struck these laws down in *Brown I.* Even after the Court's opinion in *Brown,* segregation was maintained in New Kent County. As late as September, 1964, no black student attended the white school and no white student the black school. In order to remain eligible for federal financial assistance, the New Kent County School Board adopted a freedom of choice plan for desegregating the schools in August 1965. Under the plan each pupil, except those entering the first and eighth grades, may annually choose between the two schools. Pupils who did not choose a school were assigned to the school previously attended. The students entering the first and eighth grades were required to choose a school. During the three years the desegregation plan was in effect, no white student enrolled in the Watkins School and only 15% of the black students in the County attended New Kent School.

The federal District Court approved the freedom of choice plan. The Court of Appeals for the Fourth Circuit, *en banc,* approved the freedom of choice provisions of the plan, but remanded the case to the District Court to enter an order regarding faculty.[72] Before the Supreme Court, the School Board argued that its freedom of choice plan could only be faulted by reading the Fourteenth Amendment as requiring compulsory integration. The Fourteenth Amendment, the School Board asserted, could not support such a reading. The Supreme Court, however, held that such an argument ignored the thrust of *Brown II.* The Court noted that the issue was whether the Board had achieved the racially nondiscriminatory school system that *Brown I* required in order to remedy the established unconstitutional deficiencies of its segregated system. The Court noted that against the background of long standing state-imposed segregated schools the freedom of choice plan did not end, but merely began the process. *Brown II* was a call for the dismantling of well-entrenched dual systems tempered by an awareness that complex and multifaceted problems would arise which would require time and flexibility to resolve. As a result school boards like the New Kent County School Board were charged with an affirmative duty to take whatever steps might be necessary to convert to a unitary system in which racial discrimination would be eliminated, root and branch.[73] The duty imposed on school boards was to obtain racial balance in every facet of school operations including existing policies and practices with regard to students, faculty, staff, transportation, extra-curricular activities and facilities.

The Court further stated that the governing constitutional principles were no longer newly enunciated. A plan, which at this late date failed to provide meaningful assurance of prompt and effective elimination of a dual school system, was intolerable. The time for deliberate speed had run out. According to the Court, the burden on the School Board was to come forward with a plan that promised realistically to work and to work now. Thus, the Court rejected New Kent County's freedom of choice school attendance plan because it failed to produce integrated schools.

Green v. New Kent County School Board represented a fundamental change in the Supreme Court's school desegregation jurisprudence. The Court's jurisprudence before *Green* could have been read to be consistent with the language from *Briggs v. Elliot,* which limited the scope of the *Brown* opinions to non-discriminatory student assignment policies, not compulsory integration. In *Green* the Court announced that in order to remedy the harm created by the operation of a segregated school system, it was necessary to treat students, teachers, staff and administrators as members of racial and ethnic groups in order to bring them together in integrated schools.[74]

Three years after the decision in *Green,* the Supreme Court articulated with particularity the responsibilities of school authorities in desegregating a state enforced dual school system. Chief Justice Burger's unanimous opinion for the Court in *Swann v. Charlotte-Mecklenburg Board of Education*[75] provided guidelines to pursue in formulating desegregation plans. He noted that school authorities were to eliminate invidious racial distinctions with respect to such matters as transportation, supporting personnel and extracurricular activities. Corrective action is also required with regard to the maintenance of buildings and the distribution of equipment. Normal administrative practices should produce schools of like quality, facilities and staff. With regard to student assignment, the Court stated that the district judge or school authorities should make every effort to achieve the greatest possible degree of actual desegregation. In pursuing that objective, the Court approved busing students beyond their neighborhood schools.

Conclusion

After the Court's initial opinions in *Brown I* and *Brown II,* many school districts and states resisted the obligation to desegregate their schools. A full ten years after the Court's opinion in *Brown I* little actual integration had occurred, especially in the Deep South where resistance was the greatest. In 1964, only 2.14% of the black students in the eleven states of the former Confederacy attended desegregated schools. But the Court's opinions in *Green v. New Kent County School Board* and *Swann v. Charlotte-Mecklenburg Board of Education* along with the passage of the Civil Rights Act of 1964, helped to spur the desegregation of public schools. The impact of the these developments was dramatic and immediate. In the 1968–69 school year 23.4% of black students attended majority white schools nationwide. By the 1972–3 school year this percentage had increased to 36.4%. While in 1968–9 school year 64.3% of black students were in schools that were 90% or more minority, that percentage had decreased to 38.7% four years later.[76] Desegregation was even more rapid and sizable in the South. In 1967, only 13.9% of blacks students attended majority white schools, but by 1972 that figure had jumped to 36.4%.[77] This percentage continued to climb reaching its zenith of 43.5% in 1988.[78]

Chapter Six

The Rise of School Desegregation Comprehended within Each of the Four Different Discourses

In *Brown I,* the Supreme Court rested its decision to strike down segregation on the negative psychological impact that it had only on African-Americans. What stands out in reading the justifications of the Court for striking down segregation with the cold reflection that occurs more than fifty years removed from the opinion is the reality that the Court did not reject the fundamental belief in the inferiority of black people. Segregation in public schools was struck down not because of, but in spite of, the fact that blacks were not equal to whites. In a way, the Supreme Court's explanation for the harm derived from *de jure* segregation on black schoolchildren was a continuation of its use of the Traditional Framework applied to segregation to comprehend the legal rights of African-Americans. Remedies for *de jure* segregation embodied the same basic belief about the second rate nature of blacks that at earlier times justified slavery ("[blacks] were regarded as beings...so far inferior, that they had no rights which the white man was bound to respect"[1]) and separate but equal ("[i]f one race be inferior to the other socially, the Constitution of the United States cannot put them upon the same plane"[2]). What made *Brown* such an historic break from the dominant racial attitudes about African-Americans was not its acceptance of blacks as equal to whites, but the Court attributing black inferiority to differences in the respective social environments of blacks and whites, as opposed to ontological distinctions. This change in the cause of the "less than" nature of blacks was comparatively optimistic and hopeful when placed against the background of the historical dominant beliefs about blacks. If the problem of blacks was in a deficit social environment, then it was not necessary to abandon all hope about the race problem. It was possible to improve black people by improving their social environment.

The Court never abandoned the view of the harm of segregation articulated in *Brown I.* As noted in Chapter Five, it was not until fourteen years after *Brown,* in *Green v. New Kent County School Board,* that the Supreme Court placed upon school boards an affirmative obligation to mix the races in public schools in order to remedy the harm derived from operating a dual school system. The Court's explanation for the duty to treat students, teachers, staff and administrators as members of racial groups in order to desegregate public schools was simply that the constitutional rights of African-American schoolchildren recognized in *Brown I and II* required it.

The assumption that segregation produced negative psychological harms upon black schoolchildren was the basis of the Court's rationale for approving educational remedies to combat the effects of the operation of *de jure* segregated schools twenty-three years after *Brown I,* in *Milliken v. Bradley*[3] (*Milliken II*). In *Milliken II,* the District Court ordered certain educational components to be included in the remedy for the operation of a dual school system. The District Court determined that the State of Michigan was just as responsible for the segregation of Detroit's public schools as the local school officials. As a result, the District Court assigned responsibility for half of the cost of the educational components of the desegregation plan to the Detroit Public School System and the other half to the State of Michigan. This case reached the Supreme Court because the State of Michigan objected to being made partially responsible for funding the educational components. In explaining its approval of *the Milliken II* educational remedies, the Supreme Court once again focused on the presumed negative impact of *de jure* segregation only on African-American children. In reference to the African-American schoolchildren who would continue to attend segregated schools, the Court stated that "[c]hildren who have been... educationally and culturally set apart from the larger community will inevitably acquire habits of speech, conduct, and attitudes reflecting their cultural isolation.... Pupil assignment alone does not automatically remedy the impact of previous, unlawful educational isolation; the consequences linger...."[4] While the Court goes on to note that the problems of African-American children were not peculiar to their race, the Court's reasoning clearly implied that distortion in the speech, conduct and attitudes of African-American children were the result of their racial isolation. There was no indication from the Court that racial isolation of white students from blacks generated any kind of corresponding harm to the white students. Thus, consistent with its rationale for striking down segregation statutes in *Brown,* the Court's reasoning in *Milliken II* also rested upon the belief that racial isolation psychologically damaged African-American children alone.

Finally, in 1992 the Supreme Court again articulated its statement that the harm generated by segregation was the psychological damage to black schoolchildren in its second school desegregation termination opinion, *Freeman v. Pitts*.[5] The opinion written by Justice Kennedy addressed a situation in which a school system under federal court supervision had not eradicated the vestiges of its prior *de jure* conduct in all aspects of the system, but had done so in some aspects. In this opinion, the Court agreed that active federal court supervision could be terminated over the portion of the school system in which the vestiges of the prior *de jure* conduct were eliminated, with supervision remaining over the other aspects. In articulating what a school district must prove in order to obtain partial release from federal court supervision, Justice Kennedy wrote:

> [t]he duty and responsibility of a school district once segregated by law is to take all steps necessary to eliminate the vestiges of the unconstitutional *de jure* system. This is required in order to ensure that the principal wrong of the *de jure* system, the injuries and stigma inflicted upon the race disfavored by the violation, is no longer present. This was the rationale and the objective of *Brown I* and *Brown II*.[6]

Kennedy went on to state:

> In *Brown I* we said: '[t]o separate [black students] from others of similar age and qualifications solely because of their race generates a feeling of inferiority as to their status in the community that may affect their hearts and minds in a way unlikely ever to be undone.' We quoted a finding of the three-judge District Court in the underlying Kansas case that bears repeating here: 'Segregation of white and colored children in public schools has a detrimental effect upon the colored children...; for the policy of separating the races is usually interpreted as denoting the inferiority of the negro group. A sense of inferiority affects the motivation of a child to learn. Segregation with the sanction of law, therefore, has a tendency to [retard] the educational and mental development of negro children and to deprive them of some of the benefits they would receive in a racially integrated school system.'[7]

Thus, the Supreme Court always asserted that the primary justification for remedies for *de jure* segregation was the psychological damage inflicted by segregation upon African-Americans.[8]

Despite the rationale advanced by the Supreme Court to justify its *de jure* school segregation jurisprudence, judges and scholars have offered other interpretations of the meaning behind the Court's jurisprudence. Some have argued that *Brown* should be understood as an anti-subordination opinion. Recently, Justice Ginsburg, in her dissenting opinion in *Gratz,* adopted this point of view. She argued that in implementing the equal protection clause, "government decision-makers may properly distinguish between policies of exclusion and inclusion."[9] Thus, actions designed to burden groups (like African-Americans) long denied full citizenship stature are not sensibly ranked with measures taken to hasten the day when entrenched discrimination and its effects have been extirpated.[10] Another common interpretation of the Court's opinion in *Brown* and the school desegregation that it fostered, views *Brown* as declaring the simple proposition that it is wrong for government to classify and treat individuals as members of racial and ethnic groups. "Distinctions between citizens solely because of their ancestry are by their very nature odious to a free people."[11] As a result, segregation was wrong not because it psychologically harmed African-Americans, but because government was wrong to classify and treat people based on an involuntary characteristic like race. Still other commentators, particularly Professor Derrick Bell, have asserted that *Brown* should be understood as a utilitarian opinion seeking to advance the collective interest of American society. Bell has long argued that the Court's opinion in *Brown I* and the school desegregation it spawned were particularly helpful in assisting America in its struggle against the Soviet Union during the Cold War.[12] There are, however, other reasons that can also be put forth to explain why *Brown I* advanced the interest of the American collective.

One of the central features of the Post-Desegregation Era is that discussions of important social phenomena, like the Supreme Court's school desegregation jurisprudence, are more enlightening when discussed within different discourses.[13] The Supreme Court's interpretations of the equal protection clause represent American society's final resolution of racial issues or conflicts. Even though the Court's opinions are decisive for the purpose of determining legal rights and obligations, they do not represent the only valid understanding of a particular racial issue, like school desegregation.

One of the two overlapping objectives of this book is to advance the discussion about racial issues, particularly those that involve African-American schoolchildren, by discussing those issues with the Post-Desegregation Awareness. This Chapter reviews the Supreme Court's jurisprudence which led to the rise of school desegregation through each of the four different cognitive frameworks—Traditional Americanism, African-American Centralism, Colorblind Individualism and American Collectivism. There are two different aspects of the Supreme Court's jurisprudence that led to the rise of school desegregation. In *Brown v. Board of Education* the Court struck down school segregation statutes. But in *Green v. New Kent County* and *Swann v. Charlotte-Mecklenburg Board of Education* the Supreme Court required public schools to use racial classifications in order to achieve the greatest possible degree of actual desegregation. Traditional Americanism, African-American Centralism and American Collectivism generally view the difference between striking down segregation statutes and compelling the use of racial classifications in order to promote desegregated education as differing in degree of actual integration, but not in kind. Within the conceptual boundaries of Colorblind Individualism there is a difference not in degree, but in kind between prohibiting government from treating people as members of racial and ethnic groups as the Court did in *Brown,* and mandating that government use racial classifications even for such laudable purposes as promoting integrated education which the Court did in *Green* and *Swann.* Within Colorblind Individualism, government should generally not treat people as members of racial and ethnic groups. Thus, striking down segregation statutes in *Brown* was consistent with the basic view of advancing individual self-determination that Colorblind Individualism is based upon. But using racial classifications to promote integrated education requires government to treat people as members of involuntary racial and ethnic groups. This is much harder to justify.

As stated earlier, the various perceptions of a given racial phenomena, such as the Supreme Court's jurisprudence that gave rise to school desegregation, are structured and limited by these diverse patterns of understandings. These cognitive frameworks do not provide a definitive answer to a given racial conflict, such as whether school desegregation is positive or negative. They do, however, structure and limit both the arguments that are persuasive when discussing a particular racial issue and the possible range of solutions that can be advanced to resolve a given racial conflict. Thus, arguments could be generated within each of these cognitive frameworks that would oppose desegregated education (some of these arguments will be made in Chapter Ten which discusses the benefits of the current educational reform movement based upon an expansion of school choice in each of these cognitive frameworks). This Chapter, however, will only discuss the arguments derived from each of the discourses that find favor with the Supreme Court's decisions to take account of race in order to obtain the greatest possible degree of actual desegregation.

I. Traditional Americanism

The central feature of Traditional Americanism is the belief that black people in some way do not measure up to the relevant norm. The cause of this inferiority has been explained in different ways throughout history. Up until the twentieth century, this cognitive framework based the inferiority of blacks on either the divine will of God, their defective physical environment while in Africa or their defective biology. When the substandard nature of blacks was attributed to causes that were essentially immutable, it was difficult to advance reasons for desegregated education. During the 1930s and onward, the argument that black inferiority could be traced to black cultural and socio-environmental factors became the dominant explanation for the apparent inadequacies of blacks among social scientists. Blacks suffered from both an impoverished social environment and a pathological culture that retarded their psychological and intellectual development. It was the acceptance of these twin environmental factors as the source of the inferiority of blacks, that gave rise to the hope that the black race could be elevated through changing its social environment. This would occur by increasing their contact with whites and by assisting them in shedding a pathological culture that resulted from their experience of slavery and segregation. The rationale articulated by the Supreme Court in *Brown I* for remedies for *de jure* segregation embodied this optimistic view of the cause of the less than nature of blacks. Thus, school desegregation was needed, not in spite of, but precisely because African-Americans were not the equals of Caucasians.

The beneficial aspects of desegregating public schools involved more than just the physical integration of students. The Supreme Court's statement in Brown that "separate educational facilities are inherently unequal"[14] justifies closing schools where black students attended in order to reassign them to the former white schools. Given the Court's pronouncement that segregation affected the hearts and minds of black children in ways unlikely ever to be undone, black adults—who had obviously attended segregated schools, including public school educators—must also suffer from psychological damage.[15] Many scholars have pointed to the disproportionately high price that African-American educators paid for desegregation.[16] Samuel Etheridge, for example, reported that between 1954 and 1972 over 70,000 black teachers lost their jobs in the Southern and border states.[17] In addition, testimony before the United States Senate revealed that 96% of the African-American principals lost their jobs in North Carolina, 90% in Kentucky and Arkansas, 80% in Alabama, 78% in Virginia and 77% in South Carolina and Tennessee.[18] Within Traditional Americanism, however, closing black schools, terminating African-

American teachers and demoting black principals were reasonable efforts to increase the quality of education for all students, especially black students.[19]

The Supreme Court's opinion in *Brown v. Board of Education* also ignited an educational reform movement directed at assisting African-American schoolchildren. Educational reforms incorporated the assumptions about African-Americans that formed the basis of the *Brown I* opinion. Accepting the Court's view as gospel, educational reforms of the 1960s and 1970s for African-Americans were dominated by a "cultural deprivation paradigm."[20] The popular notion of "cultural deprivation" viewed black children as imprisoned in a pathological culture.[21] One review of the studies on the need to make changes to address the educational problems of the disadvantaged and minority children, up until the end of the 1960s, found that 82% of studies stressed the need to make changes in the children. Only 8% of the studies saw a need to make changes in the schools.[22] As a result the premise and structure of public education remained intact and were not seriously questioned during the early period of school desegregation.[23]

As Professor Banks—a leading advocate for multi-cultural education—pointed out, the two major goals of educators during the early period of desegregation were to raise the self-concepts of ethnic minority youths and to increase their racial pride.[24] Educators assumed that students with healthy self-concepts were better learners and, thus, would fare better in school.[25] The movement embodied the notion that the self-concept of black children would improve if they were portrayed as being essentially colored whites. The changes made by commercial textbook publishers, for instance, were not substantive but cosmetic. Dick and Jane retained all of their usual white middle-class social and behavioral traits, but had black and brown faces.[26] Traditional instructional programs underwent revision to recognize previously neglected contributions of individual ethnic minorities. To be acknowledged, however, the individuals had to satisfy mainstream norms of what was considered acceptable. Thus, attempts to include African-Americans in curricular materials resulted in racial content grafted onto white instruction typified by the standard educational programs.[27] Professor Banks noted that even the later focus on multi-cultural education did not eliminate the Anglo-American cultural bias of the traditional educational program.[28]

The establishment of a number of cultural enrichment programs followed these changes in the curriculum. Trips to concerts, art galleries, scientific laboratories and museums became part of the educational system. The purpose of these programs was to expose minority children to the artifacts and traditions of America's mainstream. No corresponding programs exposed white children to important social institutions in the African-American community.[29] The underlying message of this one-way exposure was that racial minorities would improve by simply dropping their deviant cultural traits and attitudes and adopting the requisite mainstream characteristics.[30]

Within Traditional Americanism, the primary purpose of furthering the desegregation of public schools was to improve black schoolchildren. Bringing black children into predominately white schools and would enrich their social environment by increasing their exposure to more intelligent and better behaved white children and better qualified white teachers. The white teachers and students that black children came into contact with would be role models and demonstrate to the black child the appropriate attitudes and forms of behavior they should emulate. The black children could listen to the white children's and teachers' manner of speaking and hopefully learn proper use of the English language. Integrated education could help black children repudiate their pathological culture and its associated ideas. Integrated education would also reduce the time that black children spent in their normal deficient social environment. In other words, it would reduce the time that black children were confined to situations where there were only other blacks.

II. African-American Centralism

Against the background of 335 years of racial domination that preceded the 1954 decision, the descendants of the sons and daughters of the soil of Africa formulated a discourse counter to Traditional Americanism's notion of blacks as the paradigmatic inferior group in the United States. This pattern of understanding provides a counter interpretation of the behaviors, attitudes and experiences of African-Americans to that derived from Traditional Americanism. Within this pattern of understanding, African-Americans are not conceptualized as inferior, but as oppressed. The desire to eradicate the racial oppression of blacks is the driving force of African-American Centralism.

African-American Centralism views every black person, regardless of religious creed, social or economic status, level of education, gender, the region of the country from which they hail, sexual orientation or associational or political affiliations as having an obligation to assist in the liberation struggle of the black community. As noted earlier in the discussion of Traditional Americanism, black educators paid a disproportionately high price for the integration of public schools. African-American schoolchildren also suffered during the integration of America's schools. In Prince Edward County, Virginia, for example, many black schoolchildren went without education for five years, as part of the effort to compel the integration of the county's public schools. When integration did occur, black schoolchildren desegregating white schools often encountered hostile educational environments. Rather than being embraced as an integral part of the student body, they were often treated as unwelcome visitors at what were now their own schools. The rude reception which met the brave black children who integrated Little Rock's Central High School was repeated in public schools all over the country, albeit generally to a lesser extent. Because of the extra distance they traveled, black schoolchildren suffered in other ways to integrate public schools. Since white parents often refused to send their children to formerly black schools, African-American children often were the ones being bused over long distances to white schools. Black students disproportionately started their school days earlier and ended them later than their white counterparts.

The benefit to be derived by the black community through the end of segregation justified the sacrifice of so many African-Americans involved in the process of integrating public schools. Those benefits were substantial. In the long struggle against racial subordination, African-Americans have often addressed the issue of the benefits of integrated education, as opposed to racially separate education. The long history of dealing with this issue has revealed an abiding lesson—if black children are racially segregated in public schools they are vulnerable to systematic under-funding of their educational needs.[31] Separate schools tends to mean underfunded black schools.[32] Throughout much of the twentieth century, segregation was entrenched in American public schools in the North and the South. Blacks were segregated by explicit law in the South and by custom and racially discriminatory decision-making in the North. Blacks rarely received adequate resources for the schools that they attended throughout the first half of the twentieth century. White southern legislators during the segregation period were not averse to reducing educational expenditures for both black and white students. Even so, they went as far as possible in cutting the funds for the black schools before trimming the budgets of the white schools.[33] As long as blacks attend integrated educational facilities they are not vulnerable to the systematic under-funding of their schools.[34]

In addition to making it harder to systematically deprive black schoolchildren of the resources necessary for their education, integrated education assists in the eradication of racial subordination in a number of other ways. Past and present day realities are such that to succeed in mainstream employment and take advantage of mainstream business opportunities, a black person must be able to exist in a predominately white corporate world. Integrated public education provides black students with an excellent opportunity to learn how to interact with whites. Black children are given the opportunity to better understand and learn the culture of whites. This should help the black students when they become adults to feel more comfortable being in surroundings where whites are in the majority. Being able to operate effectively in majority white environments will improve the black student's future economic opportunities. As these students translate the experience of being in an integrated environment into increased earning potential, it benefits the entire black community.

Caucasians generally come from wealthier households than do African-Americans. As a result, whites have better access to financial resources and sources of useful information than African-Americans. If black children attend integrated schools, they could develop contacts and friendships with more affluent white students. These contacts could provide them with more access to employment and business opportunities and political and social contacts which they can use their entire lives. In the long run this will also increase the material and economic well-being, as well as political and social power, of the black community.

African-Americans were negatively impacted by racial stereotypes before the rise of desegregation. By fostering integration, the Supreme Court's school desegregation jurisprudence provided black children with the opportunity to demonstrate to whites that the negative stereotypes about blacks, and thus the rationalizations of the continued oppression of blacks, were untrue. By learning with white students, black youths could demonstrate their intelligence, diligence, hard work and leadership capabilities. Integrated education also allows black children to realize that they are just as intelligent and diligent about their studies and motivated to be successful in life as white children. From their exposure to white children, black children also learn that the supposed enduring truths of presumed inferiority of blacks are false.

Integrated education can also assist in the eradication of racial oppression by reducing the importance that whites attach to racial distinctiveness. Integrated education helps teach whites to treat blacks as individuals and not members of a substandard group. As white students come to know black students as individuals instead of as members of a deficient racial group, they come to look at blacks less in terms of being members of an inferior race and more in non-racial terms of being individuals. Integrated education can also reduce a white person's focus on racial distinctiveness by promoting a sense of commonality among the different racial and ethnic groups. Whites can come to see that what the races have in common as Americans is greater than what distinguishes the races. We are all one race here and it is American.[35] Racial differences are less important when all Americans are seen as one people.

III. Colorblind Individualism

The defining idea of Colorblind Individualism is the belief in the view of society as a collection of Knowing Individuals. This system of meaning is built upon the ontological presupposition that all individuals possess within themselves a true self which originates as a separate, unique and distinct entity. Knowing Individuals are free-willed, rational, autonomous and self-determined people who are capable of pursuing their self-formulated goals and objectives. This pattern of understanding celebrates the ability of the Knowing Individual to discover his or her true self and then follow its internally generated desires as long as those pursuits do not unduly effect the ability of others to do the same. According to this cognitive framework, government comes into existence in order to protect the rights of Knowing Individuals to pursue their constrained self-determined goals and objectives. Government must both respect the individuality of its citizens and mediate their conduct so as to allow them to purse their own desires and to prevent them from unjustly interfering with the rights of their fellow persons to do likewise. Government should thus be neutral on the question of the type of goals and objectives individuals should pursue or what constitutes a good society. By doing this, government allows individuals to choose their own goals and ends for themselves consistent with a similar liberty for others.

Minors are not Knowing Individuals. The difference "between the minor and adult—however much we may be baffled by borderline problems, . . . demands for adequate criteria, [and] administrative difficulties—is fundamental and inescapable."[36] Minors lack the experience, cognitive development, maturity and judgment of adults. Children cannot critically evaluate what is being presented to them. Children must go through a maturation process during which they will develop perspectives that will indelibly effect their view of themselves, their fellow citizens and their world.[37] At the end of this maturation process, children will be accorded the rights of adults. No matter how misguided their beliefs turn out, as adults they will be entitled to act on their own ideas. Thus, in contrast to adults, children are viewed within this discourse as learners, not constrained choosers.

Public schools are institutions that acculturate America's youth. It is the one place where government is suppose to be actively involved in the socialization of the next generation of adult citizens. In the institution of public education, government exerts a tremendous influence on learners in order to produce the kind of choosers that possess the values necessary for the maintenance of a democratic society dedicated to self-determination. But public education, like other governmental functions, must maintain the neutrality that flows from the conception of society as a collection of Knowing Individuals.[38] In order for government to maintain its neutrality with respect to children, government should provide an educational environment where minors can be acculturated to become constrained choosers.

Public schools seek to broaden the sensibilities of children, kindle their imagination and foster a spirit of free inquiry. Public schools also foster the self-determination of students by providing children the opportunity to equip themselves with the vocational knowledge and skills necessary for them to become self-sufficient and self-reliant adults. But public schools have to teach students to constrain their choices so that their fellow citizens are also afforded the same rights to self-determination. Public schools need to teach students to respect the rights of others, tolerance for political and religious diversity, belief in racial equality and a commitment to faithfully discharge the duties imposed upon them by citizenship.

Public schools pursue their mission by disseminating useful information and teaching academic skills, such as reading, writing and math. But, the process of educating youth is not confined to books and curricular materials; schools also teach shared values through administrative rules and regulations governing the operation of the schools, including policies governing discipline and determining admission to various schools in the district.[39] For example, rules prohibiting fighting on school premises attempt to inculcate a belief that violence is not a legitimate means to resolve a dispute. Rules requiring all students to start school at the same time also inculcates habits of dependability and punctuality.

Statutes that provided for racial segregation in public schools were the antithesis of the primary goal that animates this pattern of understanding. Within this cognitive framework, striking down segregation statutes in *Brown v. Board of Education* was justified because segregation statutes violated respect for individuality in three different ways. First, public schools were not treating students, teachers or administrators as individuals, but as members of racial groups. Hence, the individuals, especially if they happen to be black, were being confined and segregated not based upon individual characteristics, qualifications or results of their choices, but upon accidents of birth. Through segregation statutes applied to public education, the government was imprisoning individuals within racial traditions and not providing protection to allow them to be self-determining. Second, despite the Supreme Court's assertion of equality regarding physical facilities and other tangible factors in *Brown,* students who happened to be white were generally provided with better equipped and funded schools and a superior education than what was provided to students who happened to be black. Finally, segregation was stigmatizing to those who happened to be black because the government was conveying the message that these individuals were not the equals of those who happened to be white. The dissemination of this stigmatic message was also a violation of the constraint of governmental neutrality.

Within this pattern of understanding striking down segregation statutes differs not in degree, but in kind from using race conscious measures to determine school composition. Striking down segregation statutes obviously advances individual self-determination. But when government treats people as members of racial and ethnic groups, even for such laudable purposes as promoting integrated education, government is infringing upon their individuality. The only way such an infringement of individuality could be justified is by creating more capacity for individual self-determination than what is lost by treating people as members of racial and ethnic groups. In other words, the use by government of an involuntary trait, like race, to determine which students, teachers and administrators are assigned to which schools is contrary to the self-determination that is the driving force of this cognitive framework. This system of meaning can only justify the use of racial classifications to foster integrated education if their use promotes individual self-determination more than it deters it. All arguments for the use of racial classifications to foster integrated education must start with the assumption that race matters. As Justice Blackmun stated so well in *Regents of California v. Bakke,* "[i]n order to get beyond racism, we must first take account of race."[40]

In 1968 when the Supreme Court rendered its opinion in *Green v. New Kent County School Board,* the use of racial classifications to promote integrated education sent the message to public school students that involuntary characteristics such as race and ethnicity matter. But, at that time, it also promoted individuality and self-determination more than it harmed it. It could be argued that in a period of transition from a racially conscious society to a colorblind society there were many justifications within this cognitive framework for using racial classifications to promote integrated education among the young.[41] When the Court rendered its opinions in *Green* and *Swann* many people judged others, especially those who happened to be black, with reference to stereotypes attached to their skin color. When people act towards others based upon stereotypes, they deny that person their individuality and interfere with that person's ability to be self-determining. Under the right conditions, integrated education could help the young overcome racial stereotyping of those who happen to be black. Integrated education exposed children to the diversity of people within a racial group. Students gained first-hand experience of the reality that the various general rules and stereotypes attached to different racial groups do not apply to all individuals of that particular group. Children who happen to be white or black could realize that some people who happen to be white or black will be intelligent, diligent, hard working, law abiding, honest and others will not. Children could learn that some people who happen to be white or black are ignorant, careless, lazy, prone to aggressive and criminal behavior, untrustworthy and others are not. In other words, students in integrated schools can come to understand that what matters is the content of an individual's character not the color of their skin.

Integrated education can also help to further the conversion of racial affiliations into mere voluntary associations in a number of different ways. Some Knowing Individuals who happen to be black or white will choose to celebrate their racial or ethnic heritage, make it a salient part of their individual identity or choose to associate primarily with others who share their racial or ethnic backgrounds. Others, however, will find none of this individually appealing. Integrated education allows students to see that members of their own racial group, as well as members of other racial groups, can choose to primarily associate with racial or ethnic group members or non-group members. Thus, all students will see students who happen to be black who choose either to associate primarily with other students of the same color or with students who do not happen to be black. All students will also see students who happen to be white who choose to associate primarily with other white students as well as those who choose to associate primarily with non-white students. This experience provides all students with an understanding that they have control over whether they celebrate their racial or ethnic heritage as well as whether they associate primarily with members of their own racial or ethnic group.

Integrated student bodies provide students with a better opportunity to learn tolerance for racial differences. For those who choose to make their race a significant part of their individuality, they need to be able to make such choices without having their desires unduly infringed upon by others. Thus, integrated education exposes students to people from different racial backgrounds who choose to celebrate their racial heritage or make their race a salient part of their identity. Through this exposure in the controlled disciplinary environment of public education all students can learn to tolerate these choices of others, even if they do not agree with them.[42]

IV. American Collectivism

This system of meaning is structured around the goal of maximizing the best interest of the collective American people. Even though the presumption of this utilitarian system of meaning presupposes the existence of an accurate yardstick in which to measure the utility of given actions, decisions, policies, regulations or rules, it recognizes that these judgments are bound up in the very values that Americans hold dear. Certain values in America such as liberty, equality, pursuit of happiness, democracy and capitalism have always been fundamental to the nation. But the meanings of these core American values have changed over time. Each generation defines the meaning of these basic values to fit its current times. In order to determine what is considered to be in the best interest of the country, it is necessary to refer to the interpretations of these fundamental values at a given time.

Universal and free public education provides many different advantages for American society. As the Founding Fathers recognized over 200 years ago, schools are the "most vital civic institution for the preservation of a democratic system of government."[43] Thomas Jefferson, for example, wrote "I know no safe depository of the ultimate powers of the society but the people themselves; and if we think them not enlightened enough to exercise their control with a wholesome discretion, the remedy is not to take it from them, but to inform their discretion by education."[44] John Adams, James Madison and others also expressed their desire for a strengthened commitment to learning in order to safeguard the republic.[45]

In a country like the United States with such wide-spread racial, ethnic and religious diversity, it is necessary to focus on generating and maintaining cultural cohesion. A society can survive only if there exists among its members a sufficient degree of homogeneity. Public schools promote social cohesion in America. A common language, English, is taught to all. Students develop a sense of nationhood by learning about U.S. history, observing patriotic holidays, and being involved in patriotic rituals such as the pledge of allegiance and singing the *Star Spangled Banner.* Public schools provide a mechanism in which to ensure that the overwhelming majority of children receive a uniform moral and social education regardless of their family background. This sense of cultural commonality also helps to reduce the danger of conflict between different racial, ethnic and religious groups that has flared up so often in other places of the world.

The development of the importance of public education for promoting social cohesion in American society was, in part, the result of the tremendous immigration that America experienced in the latter part of the nineteenth century and the early part of the twentieth century. As America moved into the latter part of the nineteenth century it experienced the industrial revolution. The rapid industrialization of American urban areas created an economic need for labor from immigrating white European ethnics. The character of American immigration changed drastically around 1880.

A principally protestant nation with immigrants from northern and western Europe began to receive large numbers of Catholic and Jewish immigrants and immigrants from southern and eastern Europe. The expressed desire of educators to "Americanize" the immigrants proved to be a potent force in augmenting support for public and compulsory education. Public education functioned as a tool to promote common American cultural values.[46] Public schools and compulsory attendance laws spread most rapidly in states having the greatest influx of non-Anglo immigrants. During the early part of the twentieth century, several changes in the educational program of public schools reflected this "Americanizing" agenda. Fifteen states forbade the teaching of foreign languages in public schools.[47] Many state legislatures enacted statutes mandating courses in United States history and citizenship and requiring all instruction in public schools to be conducted in English.[48]

With the Supreme Court's opinion in *Brown v. Board of Education,* public schools were being called upon to carry out the same assimilating mission on blacks that it had performed a generation or two earlier in response to the immigration of large numbers of non-Anglo Europeans. Just as schools were supposed to repress the native culture of the immigrants and foster their assimilation into American society, they were to do the same with African-Americans.

Separating children along racial lines usually means virtual separation throughout much of their lives. The result is misunderstanding, friction and racial hatred. Integrated education can reduce racial intolerance and racial prejudice. It helps to break down barriers between different racial groups in American society. Children who attend integrated public education will have experiences with students from different racial backgrounds than their own. By fostering these types of interactions, the knowledge that people from different racial groups have about each other will increase. A greater sense of understanding can reduce potentially destructive racial and ethnic tensions which are a product of fear and ignorance. Children attending integrated schools can also come to learn to see the commonalities in people from diverse racial groups and thereby help to appreciate the fact that all Americans constitute one people.

Integrated education also helped to advance the commitment of American society to social justice. After the Supreme Court declared segregation unconstitutional, it became increasingly clear to Americans that segregation stood in sharp contrast to the notions of individual liberty and freedom upon which the nation was founded. Integrated education advanced the interest of the American collective by trying to eliminate the injustice that had historically been inflicted upon black people.

The impact of school desegregation on the academic performance of public school students has been studied quite often. In general, integration seems to improve the overall educational performance of America's schoolchildren. The research indicates that integrated education is of some benefit to the minority child and does not harm the educational interest of the white child.[49]

In addition to the above advantages of integrated education for the American collective, Professor Derrick Bell has also pointed out how attacking segregation advanced the American cause in the Cold War with the Soviet Union.[50] With the end of World War II, the importance of the status and condition of blacks became a major concern for the country. In fighting the Germans, America had fought a war with racially segregated armed forces against an enemy whose national policy was based on the dogma of racial superiority. Shortly after the end of World War II, the United States found itself engaged in a struggle against the Soviet Union. As American foreign policy came to view the matter, the world was bipolar: communist or capitalist. The Soviet Union was "animated by a... fanatic faith... [that was] antithetical to our own" and sought the ultimate elimination of any effective opposition to it.[51] The differences between the two super powers were deep, significant and enduring. The Soviets championed the cause of the collective, America the cause of the individual. The Soviets were tightly centralized with an army of ant-like bureaucrats. America was decentralized with states enjoying considerable freedoms. The Soviets decried the evils of private property, America worshiped it.

The fight against the spread of Communism was the major force in determining American foreign policy. The Cold War cost Americans $8 trillion dollars and took the lives of nearly 100,000 young men and women.[52] A quick perusal of America's foreign policy initiatives after the end of World War II to the collapse of the Berlin wall demonstrates this. The United State's Cold War efforts started in March 1947 when President Harry S. Truman indicated U.S. willingness to aid Greece and Turkey in their efforts to prevent a Communist takeover. This commitment turned into a general commitment to assist any nation that faced a Communist threat. The economic arm of this effort was the Marshall Plan that was announced three months later.

In 1948, the Soviets stopped all surface traffic into the western zones of Berlin that were controlled by the British, French and Americans. Truman's response to the Berlin Blockade was to airlift supplies to the western zones of the City. The Berlin air lift lasted 324 days and reached 13,000 tons of supplies per day.

Most American deployment and use of military forces from the end of World War II to the fall of the Berlin wall were motivated by the desire to prevent Communist ascendency in other parts of the world. The national interest dictated that the U.S. station troops in western Europe, Japan and the Philippines and send Americans to fight and die against communist forces in Korea and Vietnam. Even as late as 1996, six years after the collapse of the Berlin wall, a majority of the American military forces were still deployed in foreign lands due to Cold War concerns. Of the approximately 240,000 troops stationed outside the United States, almost 85,000 were stationed in western Europe as part of America's commitment to NATO and 36,000 were quartered in Korea.[53] The Cold War also set off an unprecedented arms race in which both sides built and stockpiled weapons of mass destruction at considerable financial expense.

In October 1957, the Soviets placed Sputnik in orbit for three months. This was followed by another eight launches. The Sputnik launches demonstrated that Soviet rocket power was the best in the world. In response, America developed its own space program, which—under President Kennedy—was committed to placing a man on the moon by the end of the 1960s. Thus, the space program was a product of the U.S. effort to prevent the Soviets from dominating the exploration of space and being able to turn it into a tremendous military advantage.

During the 1960s, 1970s and 1980s, America supported repressive regimes in foreign countries, including South Africa, Zaire, Iran, the Philippines, El Salvador and Nicaragua because of their support for America's Cold War efforts. The U.S. also intervened in internal disputes in many countries including Chile, Angola and Mozambique. In response to the Soviet invasion of Afghanistan in 1980, for the first time in American history, America boycotted the Summer Olympics held in Moscow. The Soviets returned the favor in 1984 when it boycotted the Summer Olympics held in Los Angeles.

Desegregation of American society could also be viewed as a part of the strategy to win the Cold War. The ability of the United States to advance democracy abroad was compromised by internal racial policies and practices of segregation at home. In the late 1940s and early 1950s, America's Cold War rhetoric of commitment to democracy, freedom and equality stood in sharp contradiction to its disenfranchisement and segregation of African-Americans. International perceptions of American democracy affected the nation's ability to maintain its international leadership, particularly among newly independent nations in Asia, Africa and Latin America.[54] Soviet propaganda focused the world's attention on America's internal racial practices. The Soviets made effective arguments about the exploitation inherent in the American form of society by pointing to the racial failings of the United States. Newspapers throughout the world also carried stories about the discrimination faced by non-white visiting foreigners and black Americans.

During an address to the NAACP annual conference in June 1947, President Truman asserted that because democratic nations must convince the world of their superiority to Communist dictatorships, America could "no longer afford the luxury of a leisurely attack upon prejudice and discrimination."[55] Truman backed up these bold words with concrete initiatives. On July 26, 1948, Truman issued Executive Order 9981 to desegregate the military. This was a monumental and historic step on the road to desegregation. The Justice Department of the Truman Administration also joined the legal battle to end segregation. In the 1948 case of *Shelley v. Kraemer*,[56] the federal government filed a brief repudiating racially restrictive covenants. The Justice Department's brief specifically pointed to the fact that "the United States has been embarrassed in the conduct of foreign relations by acts of discrimination taking place in this country."[57]

The Justice Department also filed a brief with the Supreme Court in *Brown v. Board of Education* calling for an end to segregation and citing the difficulties it created for American foreign policy. Proof that the Supreme Court's opinion striking down segregation was important in the Cold War is evidenced by the State Department's use of the decision. An hour after the decision was handed down, the Voice of America was broadcasting it to Eastern Europe. Newspapers in Africa also provided extensive favorable coverage of the Supreme Court's decision.

Conclusion

This chapter has reviewed the Supreme Court's school desegregation jurisprudence that led to the rise of desegregation through each of the four different discourses—Traditional Americanism, African-American Centralism, Colorblind Individualism and American Collectivism. As indicated before, these discourses only structure and limit the perception of a given racial phenomena and thus structure and limit the type of arguments that are deemed persuasive for resolving a given racial conflict. Thus, while arguments could be made that would place *Brown* and the desegregation of public schools it generated in a negative light within each of these systems of meaning, this section only presented the arguments in favor of the Supreme Court's decision to strike down segregation statutes in *Brown* and later decisions compelling mandatory desegregation. The primary point to this presentation is to demonstrate that the perception of racial phenomena, like the desegregation of public schools, does not have one true meaning. The understanding and interpretation of racial phenomena, like the school desegregation, is more a function of particular discourses used to comprehend the phenomena than something inherent in the understanding of the phenomena.

Part III

The Post-Desegregation Era: Resegregation and Increasing School Choice

There are four chapters in Part III. Part III will sketch out how American society moved from the desegregation of public schools discussed in Part II to the current educational situation where one of the most significant educational reform movements is increasing school choice. The major premise of this Part is that the Supreme Court—and lower federal courts following its lead—changed the background assumptions for interpreting the equal protection clause to determine the rights of black schoolchildren. These changes have made increasing school choice, both public and private, one of the few strategies available for responding to the poor educational performance of black schoolchildren.

In explaining why the Supreme Court struck down the segregation statutes presented in *Brown v. Board of Education,* Chief Justice Warren noted that segregation had psychologically damaged black schoolchildren. In a way, Warren's opinion was consistent with a long line of Supreme Court cases interpreting the rights of African-Americans based upon the built-in assumption of Traditional Americanism, that in some way blacks were less than the relevant norm. What made *Brown* a break with the Supreme Court's past interpretations of the rights of blacks (or lack thereof), however, was that it attributed the inferiority of blacks to environmental causes instead of ontological causes. When situated in a historical context, *Brown* was a very sanguine opinion because it suggested that there was a cure for—or at least a way to improve—black people. Blacks could be made better by enriching their social environment, particularly the educational environment of the young. Born out of this belief was a special concern for the educational interest of black schoolchildren. If their educational environment could be ameliorated, they could be improved as a people. But beginning with its 1973 decision in *Keyes v. School District No. 1,* the Court backed away from this interpretation of the equal protection clause and moved increasingly towards interpreting the equal protection rights of black schoolchildren in terms of treating all as individuals. Generally speaking, the current underlying assumption for applying the equal protection clause is the notion that forms the core value and belief of Colorblind Individualism—society is a collection of Knowing Individuals.

The effect of this shift in the background assumptions for interpreting the equal protection rights of black students on the current educational situation regarding African-Americans can not be overstated. This shift produces two significant consequences. First, unconstitutional discrimination is defined as racially motivated decision making which fails to treat a person as an individual, not negative disparate effects on African-American schoolchildren generated by various educational policies and practices. But because the decision to institute various educational policies and practices can almost always be justified based on legitimate educational concerns, it is difficult to prove that they were primarily motivated by racial considerations. Thus, the continued gaps in academic achievement between black and non-Hispanic white children derived from legitimate educational policies and practices are generally viewed, for equal protection purposes, as unfortunate byproducts of racially neutral educational decisions that do not raise constitutional concerns. Second, this shift severely limits the programs and policies that public school authorities can implement to attack racial achievement gaps in educational performance. Educational strategies that employ racial and ethnic classifications must survive strict scrutiny. Though strict scrutiny is no longer viewed to be strict in appearance and fatal in fact, outside of the need to remedy an existing equal protection violation or obtain the benefits derived from diversity in education, the use or racial classifications will seldom survive an equal protection challenge. Thus, legislators and educators interested in reducing the racial achievement gap are increasingly forced to advocate for the adoption of race-neutral educational policies and practices.

Chapter Seven will discuss three trends over the last thirty years in the interpretation of the equal protection clause that, first constrained, then halted and now is reversing the desegregation of public schools. The three trends are the waning of the Supreme Court's commitment to aggressively pursue integration starting in the early 1970s; the impact of the Supreme Court's opinions regarding the termination of school desegregation decrees beginning in the 1990s; and lower federal court decisions starting in the mid 1990s that addressed challenges to the use of racial classifications to promote integrated education when it could not be constitutionally justified by the need to remedy the prior operation of a dual school system. These three trends all reflect a shift in the cognitive framework against which the equal protection rights of black schoolchildren are interpreted. Thus, the effect of the change from viewing the equal protection clause with the view of blacks as psychologically harmed through racial isolation, to viewing it in terms of protecting the rights of individuals, has meant that public schools for the past fifteen years have been resegregating. What is more, this resegregation is likely to continue for the foreseeable future.

Chapter Eight extends the analysis of legal decisions interpreting the equal protection clause that was discussed in Chapter Seven to educational issues affecting black schoolchildren other than student school assignments in the context of school desegregation. Outside the area of student school assignments, the change in background assumptions for determining the legal rights of black schoolchildren has also had dramatic effects on their educational opportunities. These effects can be noted regardless of whether particular educational policies or practices are being challenged in the context of a school system under federal court supervision in order to remedy the vestiges of its prior operation of a dual school system or not. In other words, the change in background assumptions can be noted even in litigation that arises during the process to eliminate the vestiges of *de jure* segregation.

In *Wygant v. Jackson Board of Education* the Supreme Court rejected the argument that providing role models for minority public school students was a compelling state interest. Although the Supreme Court has not done so, lower federal courts have also addressed equal protection challenges to educational policies and practices, including tracking or ability skills grouping, high school graduation examinations and challenges to curriculum content. During the 1960s and 1970s, lower federal courts also viewed the equal protection rights of black schoolchildren against the background belief that segregation had psychologically damaged them. Based on this assumption, many lower federal courts struck down a number of legitimate educational policies and practices because of their adverse impact on the educational opportunities of black schoolchildren. Over the past thirty years, however, the same change in background assumptions by federal courts noted with regard to student assignments can also be observed in decisions dealing with other educational policies and practices. Generally speaking, federal courts addressing equal protection challenges to educational policies and practices outside of school assignments, whether in the context of school desegregation litigation or not, have shifted from viewing black schoolchildren as suffering from psychological damage as a result of their racial isolation, to embracing the idea that all students should be treated as individuals. Chapter Eight goes on to note that the same twin consequences of this shift discussed in Chapter Seven apply to those other educational issues.

Chapter Nine discusses why the expansion of school choice, both public and private, is one of the primary educational reform movements today. There are three major considerations that are influencing the direction of public education reform for black schoolchildren, the latter two are the result of changes in the interpretation of the Equal Protection Clause. First, three "achievement gaps" among American schoolchildren have proved especially persistent. Low-income children on average score lower on standardized tests than their middle- and upper-income counterparts. Black, Latino and Native American children on average score lower than white and Asian children. Children attending urban public schools on average score lower than children attending schools in the suburbs. Children with all three of these characteristics score on average lowest of all. Given the disproportionate number of African-American schoolchildren attending predominantly minority low-income urban schools, black students—as a racial group—congregate at the losing end of America's educational performance spectrum. The second consideration influencing educational reform is that racial separation in public schools has been on the increase the past fifteen years. Third, the shift in the interpretation of the equal protection clause involving the educational interest of black schoolchildren produces two significant consequences already discussed above that are relevant to current school reform efforts. To begin with, the determination of unconstitutional discrimination is based upon the motives that generate given educational policies and practices, not their discriminatory effect. Educational policies and practices motivated by legitimate educational considerations that have a disparate negative effect on the educational opportunities of black schoolchildren are not unconstitutionally discriminatory. The second consequence of the shift in the background assumptions of the equal protection clause is to limit the programs and policies that legislators and public school authorities can implement to attack the racial achievement gaps. Legislators and educators must generally seek to adopt racially neutral policies and practices to attack the continuing racial achievement gap.

Given the above three considerations, politicians and educational strategist desiring to improve the performance of black schoolchildren are increasingly compelled to argue for race-neutral policies and programs. The most obvious direction of responding to the educational situation of black schoolchildren in the Post-Desegregation Era will be to increase school choice. Under increased choice proposals all parents in a given school district, a given school, a given area in a given school district or below a particular income level are provided with an increased opportunity to choose the school their child attends. Increased parental choice is thus based upon a qualification unrelated to the race or ethnicity of the child. But since low-income parents of minority schoolchildren in urban areas are the ones who have the least capability to choose the good schools for their children either through residential choices or paying for private education, the increase in choice should disproportionately advantage these parents and their children. Increased choice can be done primarily through the expansion of public school choice—including through the creation and establishment of charter schools—or through increasing public funding for private education. There are significant differences between public school choice and pubic funding of private education. But both are born out of the same concerns, that in order to respond to the educational crisis facing low-income minority students in urban public schools, what is needed is a race-neutral way to increase innovation and competition in education.

Chapter Ten concludes this part of the book by discussing the contemporary legal and educational situation of African-American schoolchildren in the Post-Desegregation Era. This contemporary situation is characterized by increasing public and private school choice against a background of resegregation of public schools. Consistent with the Post-Desegregation Awareness, however, this current situation will be discussed in each of the four different cognitive frameworks—Traditional Americanism, African-American Centralism, Colorblind Individualism and American Collectivism.

Chapter Seven

Equal Protection Clause Interpretations that Led to Resegregation

The scope and extent of school desegregation was principally the product of the Supreme Court's interpretations of the equal protection rights of black schoolchildren. After opinions that embraced the use of race to bring about the greatest possible degree of actual desegregation, the Court began to back away from its commitment to desegregate American education in the early 1970s. This Chapter is divided into three sections. Each section discusses one of three trends over the last thirty years in the interpretation of the equal protection clause that constrained school desegregation. Section I discusses the Supreme Court's decisions backing away from its commitment to aggressively pursue desegregation in the 1970s. In the 1990s, the Supreme Court's school desegregation jurisprudence entered a new phase. The Court began to address what a school district that had previously operated a dual school system had to accomplish in order to terminate federal court supervision. Section II discusses the impact of the three Supreme Court school desegregation termination opinions rendered in the 1990s. Finally, the Supreme Court has never directly addressed the issue of the power of state and local school officials to take account of race and ethnicity to further integrated public education in a context that did not involve the need to remedy the operation of a *de jure* segregated school system. This issue, however, was always in the background of the Supreme Court's school desegregation jurisprudence. That jurisprudence assumed that state and local school officials could go further in terms of desegregating their public schools than federal courts could order in response to the need to remedy an equal protection violation. Until the mid to late 1990s, lower federal courts accepted that public school authorities possessed broad powers to take steps to promote integrated public education even in the absence of a need to remedy a constitutional violation. Since 1998 the First, Second, Fourth and Ninth Circuits, however, have addressed equal protection challenges to the use of racial classifications by school systems not employing them to remedy a constitutional violation. Only the Second Circuit opinion, reluctantly, endorsed the earlier position that school districts maintain a broad power to use racial classifications in order to prevent racial isolation. Section III discusses these lower federal court decisions which have generally restricted the use of racial and ethnic classifications to promote integrated education when not justified by the need to remedy the prior operation of a dual school system.

The practical impact of the three trends noted above has produced the current situation of increasing racial segregation in public schools. Figures from the Harvard Civil Rights Project show that the percentage of African-American students attending majority-minority schools has decreased from its all-time high of 37.1% in 1980–81, to 31.2% in the 1996–97 school year, to 28.4% in 2000. The percentage of African-Americans in hypersegregated schools, schools where 90% or more of the students are minorities, has also increased from its low point of 32.5% in the 1986–87 school year, to 35% in 1996–97, to 37.4% in 2000.[1] The result is that "we have already seen the maximum amount of racial mixing in public schools that will exist in our lifetime."[2]

One of the most significant developments that helps to explain the decisions to back away from the commitment to desegregate American public schools is the Supreme Court's change in its decisions regarding the background assumptions that equal protection rights of black schoolchildren were interpreted against. In explaining why the Supreme Court struck down the segregation statutes presented in *Brown v. Board of Education,* Chief Justice Warren noted that segregation had psychologically damaged black schoolchildren. In a way, Warren's opinion was consistent with a long line of Supreme Court cases interpreting the rights of African-Americans based upon the built-in assumption of Traditional Americanism—that in some way blacks were less than the relevant norm. What made *Brown* a break with the past interpretation of the rights of blacks, however, was that it attributed this inferiority of blacks not to ontological causes, but to social or environmental ones. Born out of this belief was a special concern for the educational interest of black schoolchildren. If their educational environment could be ameliorated, they could be improved as a people. The current underlying assumption for determining rights under the equal protection clause is the notion that forms the core value and belief of Colorblind Individualism—society is a collection of Knowing Individuals. Each of the trends discussed in the following three sections of this Chapter that limited the desegregation of American public schools reflects this clear change in the background assumptions.

I. Supreme Court Decisions of the 1970s Backing Away from the Commitment to Pursue Desegregation

Through the early 1970s, the Supreme Court's support for school desegregation was unquestioned. But as the 1970s progressed, the Supreme Court's commitment to integrating American public schools waned. This section deals with Supreme Court decisions that limited the expanse of school desegregation remedies. This section will start by discussing the Supreme Court's 1973 decision in *Keyes v. School District No. 1.*[3] In decisions rendered by the Supreme Court before *Keyes* the operation of a dual school system was the result of a state statute that existed in 1954 which either required or permitted school segregation. But, in *Keyes* the Supreme Court, for the first time, addressed a desegregation case from a state that did not segregate students in 1954 pursuant to a state statute.[4] Thus, the Court had to decide when segregation in public schools violates the equal protection clause in the absence of state statutory authority. The Supreme Court opined that de *jure,* and not *de facto* segregation, violated the Constitution. Unlike *de facto* segregation which could be established by showing racial concentrations of students in the public schools, *de jure* segregation was a "current condition of segregation resulting from intentional state action directed specifically to [segregate schools]."[5] *Keyes* is significant for two reasons. It is the first case where the Supreme Court begins to back away from the commitment to further the desegregation of public schools based on the special concern about improving the educational environment of black schoolchildren. The *de jure/de facto* distinction meant that some racially segregated schools were never part of the desegregation process. In some school districts school desegregation proponents could not establish that the segregation which existed was the result of intentional governmental conduct directed at segregating the schools. The second significant aspect of this decision is that it represents the Court's first decision in which the equal protection rights of black schoolchildren are being interpreted against the pattern of understanding of Colorblind Individualism. This is a trend that is furthered through subsequent Supreme Court opinions in the 1970s, 1980s and 1990s.[6]

A year after its *Keyes* decision, the Supreme Court rendered its opinion in the Detroit school desegregation case, *Milliken v. Bradley* (*Milliken I*).[7] In *Milliken I,* the Court for the first time addressed an interdistrict school desegregation remedy. The District Court concluded that both agencies of the State of Michigan and Detroit public school officials were responsible for operating a *de jure* segregated school system. The District Court then concluded that there were not enough white students in Detroit public schools to effectively desegregate the schools. Thus, the District Court imposed a desegregation remedy that included the predominately white suburban school districts. In addressing the scope of this remedy, the Supreme Court concluded that, absent a showing that a constitutional violation within one school district produced a significant segregating effect in another, there was no justification for cross-district remedies. The *Milliken I* decision was a dramatic retreat from the efforts to integrate public schools. Since the overwhelming majority of suburban school districts were of relatively recent origins, few of these school systems would have been around long enough to have contributed to the segregation in an urban school district. Thus, the general rule became that desegregation remedies stopped at the boundary of the offending school district. The result was that many urban school districts throughout the country were never successfully integrated because not enough white students remained in the school districts.

Finally, this section will discuss the Supreme Court's 1976 decision in *Pasadena v. Spangler.*[8] In that decision the Court addressed the issue of periodic adjustments of student school assignments in a school system undergoing the desgregation process to take account of changes in residential segregation. The Court held that such subsequent resegregation of students was not part of the original constitutional violation. Thus, a district court cannot require annual adjustments in order to maintain a certain amount of desegregation.

A. *Keyes v. School District No. 1*—The *De Jure/De Facto* Segregation Distinction

Prior to 1954, twenty-one states had enacted laws that either required or permitted local school districts the option of operating segregated schools. *Brown II* charged school districts segregated pursuant to state statute with an affirmative duty to effectuate a transfer to a racially nondiscriminatory school system. Thus, the questions that the Supreme Court dealt with from these states related to the scope of the remedy for a constitutional violation, not its existence. In *Keyes,* the Court for the first time addressed a desegregation case that came from a state that did not segregate students pursuant to state statute in 1954. At the time, approximately 40% of the nation's public schoolchildren were enrolled in segregated schools in those states.[9] The issue presented to the Court in *Keyes* required the Court to formulate a method for determining when segregation in school districts in states like Colorado—where the cause of the segregation could not be traced to the existence of a state statute—violated the equal protection clause.

The Supreme Court decided that the difference between an unconstitutionally segregated school and a constitutionally segregated school necessarily depends on the facts of each particular case. Whether the racial and ethnic separation in public schools violates the Constitution depended on the cause of the separation. *De jure,* not *de facto,* segregation violated the Constitution. Unlike *de facto* segregation, which could be established by showing a racial concentration of students in the various public schools of a given school district, *de jure* segregation was defined as a "current condition of segregation resulting from intentional state action directed specifically to [segregated schools]."[10]

Keyes is the Supreme Court's first major decision in its school desegregation jurisprudence that articulates the intent standard as the way to determine when facially neutral government practices and policies violate the equal protection clause. In subsequent decisions, including *Washington v. Davis*[11] and *Arlington Heights v. Metropolitan Housing Development Corporation,*[12] the Court reaffirms its conclusion that facially neutral government practices and policies violate the equal protection clause only when they were motivated by discriminatory intent.

The Court's adoption of the intent test in *Keyes* represents the Court's first major decision in which it failed to analyze the equal protection rights of black schoolchildren with regard to the special concern about their educational environment. The Court touched upon the question of *de jure,* as opposed to *de facto,* segregation in its opinion in *Brown v. Board of Education.* When the Court rendered its *Brown* opinion, it stated: "*Segregation of white and colored children in public schools has a detrimental effect upon the colored children. The impact is greater when it has the sanction of law....*" (emphasis added).[13] Thus, according to the Court's opinion in *Brown,* the physical separation of black schoolchildren from white schoolchildren—alone—was damaging to the black schoolchildren. The Court only noted that this effect was greater when it was sanctioned by law. In *Keyes,* however, the Court drew a distinction between segregation as a factual matter and segregation caused by discriminatory governmental intent. While the former presumably was still harmful, only the latter triggered an equal protection violation.

By looking at the intent to discriminate instead of looking at the mere presence of segregation, the Court shifted the pattern of understanding used to determine equal protection violations of the educational rights of black schoolchildren from Traditional Americanism to Colorblind Individualism. Colorblind Individualism dictates that a distinction be drawn between racial separation that is the result of voluntary choices by private individuals and entities and racial separation that is the product of governmental conduct motivated by discriminatory intent. If parents of schoolchildren choose to separate themselves, even along racial lines, they follow their own desires and therefore are self-determining. If segregation, however, results from governmental influence, it violates governmental neutrality. This kind of segregation is not the product of the voluntary choices of private individuals and entities, but of government's denial of individuality. Employing the intent test to determine equal protection violations is also consistent with Colorblind Individualism in another significant way. It analogizes governmental actions to those of Knowing Individuals. Thus, government, like Knowing Individuals, is presumed capable of acting for many different reasons. Government actions motivated by racially neutral reasons may adversely affect African-Americans. But these adverse impacts do not meet the definition of discrimination in Colorblind Individualism because they are not motivated by discriminatory intent. Governmental actions only constitute discrimination when they are motivated by justifications that violate the constraints of neutrality, i.e., when motivated by discriminatory intent. Any negative impact on the educational interests of black schoolchildren resulting from government actions motivated by legitimate nondiscriminatory educational considerations is only an unfortunate byproduct of racially neutral actions.

The *Keyes* decision also constrained the desegregation of public schools in two different ways. First, the adoption of the intent standard significantly increased the difficulty of establishing a constitutional violation over the use of *de facto* segregation.[14] Often trials could last up to six weeks and produce thousands of pages of testimony and exhibits.[15] The added cost of obtaining and introducing such evidence was enough to discourage potential plaintiffs from going to court at all. Second, even though courts almost always found *de jure* segregation whenever litigation was seriously pursued,[16] there were exceptions. The adoption of an intent standard meant that some school districts with *de facto* segregated student bodies were adjudicated as not unconstitutionally segregated. A federal judge in Grand Rapids, Michigan, for instance, ruled that optional attendance zones, construction of schools in segregated neighborhoods and assignments of black teachers to black schools all had permissible explanations.[17] A federal judge in nearby Kalamazoo, Michigan, held similar practices to be unconstitutional.[18] On appeal, the Sixth Circuit affirmed both lower court decisions.[19]

B. *Milliken v. Bradley* (*Milliken I*)—Limitation on Cross-District Desegregation Remedies

A year following its decision in *Keyes*, the Supreme Court delivered the deathblow to the ability to successfully integrate the nation's public schools. In a five to four opinion in the Detroit school segregation case of *Milliken v. Bradley* (*Milliken I*)[20] the Court rejected an interdistrict school desegregation remedy. The District Court concluded that the Detroit public schools were unconstitutionally segregated. It also determined that agencies of the State of Michigan were also responsible for the segregated schools in Detroit. White students comprised only 36.2% of Detroit's 1970 public school enrollment.[21] The District Court felt that there were not enough white students in the Detroit public schools to successfully integrate the student body. In order for meaningful integration to occur, it was necessary to include the predominantly white suburban school systems in the desegregation decree. Thus, the District Court imposed an inter-district desegregation remedy that included the city of Detroit and fifty-three of its surrounding suburban school districts. The District Court felt justified in including the suburban school systems because it viewed local school districts as creations of the State of Michigan. It seemed logical to include state-created school districts since the State of Michigan was also responsible for the segregation in Detroit public schools.

The Supreme Court, however, rejected the inclusion of the suburban schools in the desegregation remedy. The Court noted that there was no showing that the suburban school districts had contributed to the segregation of students in Detroit in any way. Since the scope of a desegregation remedy is determined by the extent of the constitutional violation, the Court concluded that, absent a showing that a constitutional violation within one district produced a significant segregating effect in another, there was no justification for cross-district remedies.

The *Milliken I* decision was a dramatic blow to the ability to ever integrate a large percentage of American public schools. Since the overwhelming majority of suburban school districts had only recently been created, few of these school systems would be included in desegregation orders. Thus, the general rule was that a desegregation remedy would stop at the boundary of the offending school district. In addition, by allowing suburban school districts to be safe harbors for parents who did not want their children to be part of a school desegregation remedy, *Milliken I* helped to contribute to "white flight" from urban to suburban school districts.

The issue dealt with in *Milliken I* regarding the limits of the remedial duty does not necessarily implicate the cognitive framework used to determine the equal protection rights of black schoolchildren in *Keyes*. But it seems likely that if the Court had considered the equal protection rights of black children in terms of the special concern about improving the educational environment of black schoolchildren, it would have approved cross-district desegregation remedies. The Sixth Circuit, for example, stated as much when it upheld the District Court opinion in *Milliken* ordering the cross-district remedies. "This record reflects a present and expanding pattern of all black schools in Detroit (resulting in part from State action) separated only by school district boundaries from nearby all white schools. We cannot see how such segregation can be any less harmful to the minority students than if the same result were accomplished within one school district."[22]

C. *Pasadena City Board of Education v. Spangler*—The Impact of Subsequent Resegregation of Students

Two years after the Supreme Court's decision in *Milliken I,* the Court reviewed a district court order in *Pasadena v. Spangler*[23] requiring periodic adjustments of student assignments in order to maintain the approximate amount of desegregation among students originally achieved. When the District Court addressed the issue of periodic adjustments of student school assignments, the unified Pasadena school district was not unitary with respect to other aspects of its school system, such as hiring and promotion of teachers and administrators. The Supreme Court, however, held that once a school district has implemented a racially neutral attendance plan for students, a district court cannot require continued adjustments in order to maintain a certain amount of desegregation. The subsequent resegregation of students is not part of the original constitutional violation, which the district court had the authority to remedy. Accordingly, the Supreme Court concluded that because the resegregation was not caused by government conduct, the public school officials were not required to make periodic adjustments in student school assignments.

The Court's conclusion that the subsequent resegregation was not a part of the original constitutional violation was not inevitable. If the Court were still concerned about improving the educational environment of black schoolchildren, the Court could have used an analysis similar to that employed in *Green* and concluded that the subsequent resegregation was traceable to the original constitutional violation. Thus, school districts had an obligation to make periodic adjustments in order to maintain the greatest possible degree of actual desegregation. But in addressing the issue of resegregation in the context of a school district undergoing the desegregation process, the Court relied on the same distinction it drew in *Keyes*—distinguishing resegregation between that derived from conduct of private individuals and entities as opposed to resegregation resulting from intentional governmental action directed specifically to resegregate students. In the context of school systems undergoing desegregation, lower federal courts had to decide if any resegregation that occurred was the result of governmental conduct or that of private actors. If the resegregation was the result of decisions by private actors—i.e., parents deciding to change their place of residence—then the resegregation was not the result of governmental action. Thus, there was no reason to order periodic adjustments of student assignments to take account of it.

D. Conclusion

The consequences of the Supreme Court's decisions in *Milliken I, Keyes, Pasadena* and other Court decisions[24] limited the potential for America to desegregate its public schools. The practical effect of these decisions by the Supreme Court was to significantly slow and then halt the progress of school desegregation throughout the country. As noted in Chapter Five, school desegregation increased dramatically in the four years following the Court's 1968 decision in *Green v. New Kent County School District.* In the 1968–69 school year, 23.4% of black students attended majority white schools nationwide, but in 1972–73 this percentage had increased to 36.4%. In the 1968–69 school year, 64.3% of black students were in schools that were hypersegregated. That percentage decreased sharply to 38.7% four years later.[25] Over the next 14 years, however, school integration only increased marginally. The percentage of black students nationwide attending majority-minority schools increased slightly to its all time high of 37.1% in the 1980–81 school year, but by the 1986–87 school year it had slipped to 36.7%.[26] The percentage of black schoolchildren attending hypersegregated schools only dropped during this period from 38.7% to its all time low of 32.5% in 1986–87.[27]

II. School Desegregation Termination Cases

This section discusses the Supreme Court's school desegregation termination jurisprudence. Beginning with its 1991 decision in *Board of Education v. Dowell,*[28] the Supreme Court's school desegregation jurisprudence entered a new stage. The Court began to address issues related to the termination of school desegregation decrees. In addition to *Dowell,* the Court rendered two other school desegregation termination opinions over the next four years, *Freeman v. Pitts*[29] and *Missouri v. Jenkins.*[30] In these three cases, the Court clarified a number of issues related to the termination of school desegregation litigation. In *Dowell,* the Court made it clear that a desegregation decree should be dissolved after the local authorities have operated in good faith compliance with it for a reasonable period of time if the vestiges of past discrimination have been eliminated to the extent practicable.[31] Once the effects of the prior *de jure* conduct have been eradicated, new equal protection violations are to be determined based on the existence of discriminatory intent. Thus, new student assignment plans that might significantly increase racial segregation can be adopted, as long as their adoption is not motivated by discriminatory intent.

In *Freeman v. Pitts* the Court held that, in a proper case, a federal court could conclude that a school system subject to a court-supervised desegregation plan was in compliance in some areas of operation but not all areas. A federal court could return control to the school system in those areas where compliance had been achieved, limiting further judicial supervision to operations that are not yet in full compliance with the court decree. In particular, a federal court could determine that it would not order further remedies in the area of student assignments where racial imbalance is not traceable in a proximate way to constitutional violations, but maintain control over other aspects of the school system.

In *Missouri v. Jenkins,* the Court addressed a situation where massive educational improvements had been ordered by the supervising District Court in the Kansas City School District desegregation case. Since the District Court found the State of Missouri was also responsible for the discriminatory conditions of the Kansas City public schools, the majority of the funds to finance the educational improvements came from the State. The State of Missouri challenged its continuing obligation to fund the educational remedies. The District Court offered two justifications for the continuing obligation to fund educational improvements. One was to increase the desegregation attractiveness of Kansas City public schools in the hopes of luring white children from suburban school districts to the Kansas City public schools. In this way, the District Court sought to obtain the greatest possible degree of actual desegregation. In addition, the District Court justified the continuing expenditures for educational improvements by the fact that student achievement levels in Kansas City public schools were at or below the national norms at many grade levels. The Supreme Court rejected these justifications for the continuing obligation of the State of Missouri to fund educational improvements. The Supreme Court concluded that since there was no finding of an interdistrict violation, a remedy that sought to attract white students from suburban school districts to Kansas City public schools was beyond the scope of a remedy for the intradistrict violation found. In addition, the Court concluded that even if achievement gaps in the performance of minority and majority students were a result of the prior operation of a dual school system, the proper inquiry for whether this vestige had been remedied was not the obtainment of some level of academic performance by the Kansas City schoolchildren. The Court noted that numerous external factors beyond the control of school officials could affect minority student achievement. These external factors were not the result of segregation and should not factor into the remedial duty imposed. The basic task of the District Court was to decide whether reduced achievement by minority students attributable to the prior *de jure* segregation had been remedied to the extent practicable. In so doing, the District Court focus should be on the educational opportunities provided students in the Kansas City public schools, not their educational performance.

A. *Board of Education v. Dowell*—The Supreme Court's First School Desegregation Termination Opinion

With its 1991 opinion in *Board of Education v. Dowell,* the Supreme Court's school desegregation jurisprudence moved into a new phase. *Dowell* provided the Court with its first opportunity to address issues related to the termination of school desegregation decrees. The Oklahoma City school desegregation case commenced in 1961 with the filing of a complaint by African-American students and their parents against the Board of Education of Oklahoma City.[32] In the ensuing years after the complaint was filed, the parties struggled through the difficult task of formulating a desegregation plan. This process culminated in 1972 with the District Court imposing a desegregation plan, known as the Finger Plan. Under the Finger Plan, kindergartners would be assigned to neighborhood schools unless their parents chose otherwise; children in grades 1 through 4 would attend formerly all-white schools. Children in grade 5 would attend formerly all-black schools. Students in the upper grades who lived in integrated neighborhoods would attend stand-alone schools. The other students would be bused to various schools in order to achieve and maintain integrated schools.[33]

In 1977, the District Court, pursuant to a motion by the Board, terminated supervision of the case. The District Court found that the Finger Plan achieved the court's objectives, and the school system was, therefore, "unitary." Although the motion was contested, the District Court's order was not appealed. The Board, however, did not seek to change the Finger Plan until 1984.

In 1984, the Board of Education adopted a student reassignment plan (SRP) for the 1985–86 school year. Unlike the Finger Plan, the SRP relied on neighborhood school assignments for students in grades K through 4. The Board argued that changes in demographics increased the distance which young black children were bused under the Finger Plan. The Finger Plan was, therefore, too burdensome. The Board also asserted its desire to increase parental involvement in the schools, which it felt was necessary for quality education. Neighborhood school assignments would accomplish this goal. The SRP, however, significantly increased the racial segregation of students in the school system's elementary schools.

In February 1985, the plaintiffs sought to reopen the case. The District Court found that demographic changes made the Finger Plan unworkable and that the school district had bused students for more than a decade in good-faith compliance with its orders. The District Court also found that the Board did not promote residential segregation, which it deemed the result of private decision making and economics. It was, therefore, too attenuated to be a vestige of the former school segregation. The District Court further held that the previous injunctive decree be vacated and the school district returned completely to local control.

The Tenth Circuit approached the case primarily as one dealing with the proper application of the federal law on injunctive remedies. The Tenth Circuit reversed the District Court decision holding that "an injunction takes on a life of its own and becomes an edict quite independent of the law it is meant to effectuate."[34] Relying on *United States v. Swift & Co.*,[35] the Tenth Circuit held that a desegregation decree remains in effect until a school district can show grievous wrong evoked by new and unforeseen conditions and dramatic changes in conditions unforeseen at the time of the decree that impose extreme and unexpectedly oppressive hardships on the obligor. The Tenth Circuit held that the Board of Education failed to meet this burden and the desegregation decree was to remain in effect.

In the majority opinion written by Chief Justice Rehnquist, the Supreme Court held that the Tenth Circuit's reliance on *Swift* was wrong. The Court noted that the Tenth Circuit's test would subject a school district to judicial supervision for an indefinite future. Such a draconian result could not be justified by the principles governing the entry and dissolution of injunctive decrees nor the commands of the equal protection clause. The Court emphasized that a school desegregation decree is warranted only as a temporary measure. The decree is intended to displace local decision-making authority until transition to a unitary nonracial system of public education is achieved. A desegregation decree is dissolved after local authorities have operated in compliance with it for a reasonable period of time.

The Court went on to stress that, in considering terminating supervision, the District Court should address whether the Board had complied in good faith with the desegregation decree and whether the vestiges of past discrimination had been eliminated to the extent practicable. The Court went on to note that once a school system had eliminated the vestiges of its prior *de jure* segregation, the school system no longer needed court authorization to promulgate policies and rules regulating matters such as the assignment of students. Challenges to subsequent actions by school boards, including those related to student reassignments, should be evaluated by the equal protection principles articulated in *Washington v.*

Davis[36] and *Arlington Heights v. Metropolitan Housing Development Corp*,[37] that is, by the determination of discriminatory intent.

B. *Freeman v. Pitts*—Approval of Partial Release of a School District from Federal Court Supervision

The Court returned to school desegregation termination issues the following year in *Freeman v. Pitts*.[38] This case came to the Court from Dekalb County, a suburb of Atlanta, Georgia. After *Brown I*, Dekalb County School System (DCSS) did nothing to desegregate its schools until the 1966–67 school year when it adopted a freedom of choice transfer plan. Some African-American students chose to attend the formerly all-white schools, but no whites attended the formerly all-black schools. In the 1969–70 school year, DCSS implemented a comprehensive school desegregation plan. Under the plan, all former *de jure* black schools were closed and their students reassigned to the remaining neighborhood schools. The plan was also accepted by the Department of Health, Education and Welfare (HEW).

In 1969, African-Americans made up only 5.6% of the student body of Dekalb County schools, but by 1986 they comprised 47% of the students. As the Dekalb County population increased during the 1970s and 1980s, whites generally migrated to the northern part of the county and African-Americans to the southern part. By the 1986–87 school year, there was a considerable amount of segregation among the student population of DCSS. Over 50% of African-American students attended schools that were over 90% black, and 62% of them attended schools that were at least 67% black. In other words, 62% of the black students were in schools where the black student population exceeded the county average of black students by 20% or more. White students were also concentrated in racially identifiable schools. Twenty-seven percent of the white students were in schools that were 90% or more white, and 59% of them attended schools where the white student population exceeded the county average of white students by 20% or more.

Despite the existence of substantial school segregation, DCSS filed a motion for final dismissal of the school desegregation decree. The District Court examined the interaction between DCSS policies and the demographic changes in Dekalb County. Of the 170 changes made by DCSS, only three were found to have had a partial segregative effect—and the impact was minor. The District Court found that DCSS policies had not contributed to the demographic shifts in Dekalb County. The District Court held that DCSS was unitary with regard to student assignments, transportation, physical facilities and extracurricular activities. The District Court went on to rule that it would order no further relief in those areas. It found, however, that while there had not been any intentional segregation, the teachers in the white schools were better educated and more experienced than their counterparts in schools with higher percentages of African-American students. Furthermore, the per pupil expenditure rates in majority white schools exceeded those in majority black schools. The District Court concluded that vestiges of the dual system remained in the areas of teacher and principal assignments, resource allocation and quality of education. It ordered further relief in those areas.

The Eleventh Circuit rejected the District Court's incremental approach to eliminating vestiges of prior *de jure* conduct. It held that, in order for a school system to achieve unitary status, it must completely eradicate the vestiges of its prior *de jure* conduct. Since DCSS had not done so, it was responsible for the current racial imbalance regarding its student population. The Eleventh Circuit held that DCSS could not shirk its constitutional duties by pointing to demographic shifts that occurred prior to eradicating all of the vestiges of its prior *de jure* conduct. DCSS had to correct the racial imbalance in its public schools.[39] In order to correct this imbalance, the School Board would have to take actions that may be administratively awkward, inconvenient and even bizarre in some situations.

Justice Kennedy[40] wrote the opinion for the Court. He agreed with the District Court's conclusion that a federal court has the discretion to order an incremental or partial withdrawal of its supervision and control. The Court specifically held that:

> in the course of supervising desegregation plans, federal courts have the authority to relinquish supervision and control of school districts in incremental stages, before full compliance has been achieved in every area of school operations. While retaining jurisdiction over the case, the court may determine that it will not order further remedies in areas where the school district is in compliance with the decrees. That is to say, upon a finding that a school system subject to a court-supervised desegregation plan is in compliance in some but not all areas, the court in appropriate cases may return control to the school system in those areas where compliance has been achieved, limiting further judicial supervision to operations that are not yet in full compliance with the court decree. In particular, the district court may determine that it will not order further remedies in the area of student assignments where racial imbalance is not traceable, in a proximate way, to constitutional violations.[41]

Kennedy's opinion notes that there are three factors which should be considered in determining whether partial withdrawal is warranted. The first is whether there has been full and satisfactory compliance with the decree in those aspects of the system where supervision is being withdrawn. Second, whether retention of judicial control is necessary or practicable to achieve compliance with the decree in other facets of the school system. The third factor is whether the school district has demonstrated, to the public and to the parents and students of the once disfavored race, its good faith commitment to the whole of the court's decree and to those provisions of the law and the Constitution that were the predicate for judicial intervention in the first place.

After accepting the ability of a federal court to grant partial release, Kennedy addressed whether the District Court, in this case, was correct in releasing its control over student assignments. With respect to students assignments, Kennedy noted that racial balance is not to be achieved for its own sake. Rather, it should be pursed when a constitutional violation has caused racial imbalance. Once such imbalance is remedied, the school district is under no duty to remedy imbalance caused by private demographic factors. Absent a showing that either school authorities or some other state agency deliberately attempted to fix or alter demographic patterns to affect the racial composition of the schools, further intervention by a district court was unnecessary.

Much of the remaining discussion in the Court's opinion focused on whether existing student segregation could be attributed either to private decision making or to the original constitutional violation and subsequent state action. The Court's analysis turned on the realization that existing student segregation came about because of residential segregation. If residential segregation could be traced to factors other than the state's attempt to fix or alter demographic patterns, then the residential segregation was not caused by state action. Thus, the existing student segregation was not a vestige of prior *de jure* conduct and did not have to be remedied.

Kennedy noted that our society is very mobile. "In one year (from 1987 to 1988) over 40 million Americans, or 17.6% of the total population, moved households. Over a third of those people moved to a different county and over six million migrated between States."[42] Kennedy went on to note that the District Court heard evidence stating that since blacks prefer neighborhoods with a racial mix of 50–50 and whites prefer neighborhoods with a racial mix of 80% white and 20% black, racially stable neighborhoods are unlikely to emerge. Where resegregation is the product of private choices, the Court concludes, it does not have constitutional implications. It is beyond the authority and the practical ability of federal courts to try to counteract these kinds of continuous and massive demographic shifts. To attempt such results would require ongoing and never-ending court supervision of school districts simply because they were once segregated by law. As time passes between the original violation and the present, demographic changes intervene and a new justification emerges for the continued separation of blacks and whites in public schools.[43]

C. *Missouri v. Jenkins*—Limitations on Educational Remedies

The Court's final school desegregation termination opinion came in the 1995 case of *Missouri v. Jenkins.*[44] The case had been before the same District Court judge since 1977. In June 1985, the District Court issued its first remedial order and established as its goal the elimination of all vestiges of state-imposed segregation.[45] The District Court determined that segregation had caused a systemwide reduction in student achievement in the schools of the Kansas City Metropolitan School District (KCMSD). The District Court made no particular findings regarding the extent to which student achievement had been reduced or what portion of that reduction was attributable to segregation. The District Court also found that KCMSD and the State of Missouri were both responsible for the constitutional violations.

The District Court, pursuant to plans submitted by KCMSD and the State, ordered a wide range of quality education programs for all students attending KCMSD. The District Court's desegregation plan has been described as the most "expensive remedial program in the history of school desegregation."[46] The programs included reduction of the student-teacher ratio, implementation of an effective schools program, comprehensive magnet school and capital improvement plan and salary assistance for all but three employees in the school system. The following were among the physical improvements in KCMSD schools financed by the District Court's remedy: high schools in which every classroom had air conditioning; alarm systems; 15 microcomputers; a 2,000-square-foot planetarium; greenhouses and vivariums; a 25-acre farm with an air-conditioned meeting room for 104 people; a Model United Nations facility wired for language translation; broadcast capable radio and television studios with an editing and animation lab; a temperature controlled art gallery; movie editing and screening rooms; a 3,500-square-foot dust-free diesel mechanics room; 1,875 square foot elementary school animal room for use in a zoo project; and swimming pools.[47] Since both KCMSD and the State of Missouri were responsible for the constitutional violation, they were held jointly and severally liable for the cost of the educational improvements. The result, however, was that the State bore the brunt of the financial burden.

The State of Missouri challenged the District Court's requirement that it fund salary increases and continue to fund the remedial quality education programs for the 1992–93 school year. The State contended that under *Freeman v. Pitts,* it had achieved partial unitary status with respect to the quality education programs already in place. It argued that, as a result of partial unitary status, it should be relieved of the responsibility for funding these programs.

The District Court rejected the State's arguments. The District Court grounded its ruling for the State's continued funding of such extensive academic improvements in the fact that remedying the vestiges of segregation would improve the desegregative attractiveness of KCMSD. The District Court's reasoning for making KCMSD an attractive school district was the desire to attract white students from suburban areas in order to obtain the maximum actual desegregation possible. The District Court believed that some of the white suburban students would be willing to voluntarily enroll in KCMSD schools in order to take advantage of its incredible educational opportunities. In addition, the District Court found that such remedies were also necessary because student achievement levels in KCMSD were at or below the national norms at many grade levels.

The Eighth Circuit affirmed the District Court's decision.[48] It rejected the State's argument that the salary increases did not directly address or relate to the State's constitutional violation or that teachers' low salaries did not flow from any earlier constitutional violations by the State. The Eighth Circuit observed that in addition to compensating victims, the remedy in this case was designed to reverse white flight by offering superior educational opportunities.

Justice Kennedy wrote the opinion for the five person Supreme Court majority. Kennedy repeated the Court's often stated language that the nature and scope of the remedies for *de jure* segregation are to be determined by the violation. In this case, the District Court sought to create a school district equal or superior to the surrounding suburban school districts in order to attract white students from those surrounding school districts to KCMSD. But attracting students from surrounding school districts suggested that the remedy was for an interdistrict violation. However, since the violation was confined to the KCMSD, attracting nonminority students from surrounding school districts was beyond the scope of a remedy for the intradistrict violation found.

Kennedy also concluded that the District Court's requirement that the State continue to fund the quality education programs, because student achievement at many grade levels was at or below national norms, could not be sustained. Kennedy noted that on remand, the basic task of the District Court was to decide whether reduced achievement by minority students attributable to prior *de jure* segregation had been remedied to the extent practicable. Numerous external factors beyond the control of school officials or the State affect minority student achievement. So long as these external factors were not the result of government conduct, they should not figure into the remedial calculus. Kennedy went on to state that all parties conceded the fact that improved achievement on test scores was not necessarily required for the State to achieve partial unitary status as to the quality education program. Kennedy's opinion stated that the District Court should sharply limit, if not dispense with, its reliance on this factor. Finally, Kennedy advised the District Court that it should consider that many goals of its quality education plan already have been attained. KCMSD now is equipped with facilities and opportunities not available anywhere else in the country. The minority students in kindergarten through grade seven in the KCMSD have always attended well funded schools and minority students in the KCMSD that previously attended schools before the educational remedies were instituted have since received remedial education programs for a period of up to seven years.

The Court's opinion in *Jenkins* allows public schools to terminate federal court supervision, even if there are large achievement gaps in the performances of their minority and majority students. The Court's treatment of continuing achievement gaps by racial minorities is consistent with Colorblind Individualism's conclusion that minorities are only victims of racial discrimination when it is motivated by discriminatory intent. In effect, the Supreme Court concludes that such continuing achievement gaps in the school districts that are coming out from under federal court supervision may simply be the unfortunate results of racially-neutral educational policies and practices.

D. Conclusion

Over the past two decades, many school systems received a judicial determination that they had remedied the effects of their prior discriminatory conduct. By the beginning of 2000, about forty-five school districts had been released from court supervision.[49] Among the districts were Buffalo, New York; Broward County (Fort Lauderdale), Florida; Clark County (Las Vegas), Nevada; Nashville-Davidson County, Tennessee; Duval County (Jacksonville), Florida; Mobile, Alabama; Minneapolis, Minnesota; Cleveland, Ohio; San Jose, California; and Wilmington, Delaware.[50]

The Court's termination cases show the same drift towards interpreting the equal protection rights of black schoolchildren through the assumptions embedded in Colorblind Individualism, first noted in the Court's *Keyes* opinion. In *Dowell*, the Court rejected the idea that a school desegregation decree takes on a life of its own and therefore lasts a very long time. Once a school system eradicates the vestiges of its prior *de jure* conduct, the existing desegregation decree is dissolved. Complete control over the school system is returned to local educational authorities. New equal protection violations are determined based on the application of the discriminatory intent test first articulated by the Court in *Keyes* and reaffirmed in *Washington v. Davis* and *Arlington Heights v. Metropolitan Housing Development Corp.* Thus, the Court concluded that the rights of black schoolchildren in school systems that complete the desegregation process will be determined against the conceptual background of Colorblind Individualism, as opposed to Traditional Americanism.

In *Freeman,* the Court decided that even for a school system which had not eradicated the vestiges of its prior *de jure* conduct in all areas, federal court supervision could be released over student assignments. This partial release could occur even if at the time the schools were substantially racially segregated. As long as the racial segregation in the schools could be traced to private decision making and not governmental conduct, no obligation exists on the part of a school system under federal court supervision to remedy such segregation. This is the case even if the school district has not eradicated the vestiges of its prior *de jure* conduct in other areas. Kennedy's opinion carried over into the context of partial termination of federal court supervision the requirement dictated by Colorblind Individualism for distinguishing between racial separation that is the result of voluntary choices by private individuals and entities and racial separation that is the product of governmental conduct motivated by discriminatory intent that was first articulated in *Keyes.*

Finally, the Court's opinion in *Missouri v. Jenkins* makes it clear that a school system does not have to obtain substantial improvement in academic achievement of black students in order to obtain release from federal court supervision. It is not equalization of educational achievement between black and white students that school systems must pursue, but rather equalization in the quality of educational opportunities. The continued poor educational performance of black students when equal educational opportunities exist is viewed as simply the unfortunate result of racially-neutral educational polices and practices.

In all three school desegregation termination opinions, the Court noted that as a prerequisite to the termination of all or part of court supervision, school districts and state defendants should demonstrate that they complied in good faith with the court decree for a reasonable period of time.[51] The Court also noted the importance of determining if a school system would return to intentionally discriminatory practices.[52] Good faith compliance and assurances that the school system would not return to its former discriminatory ways are examinations directed towards determining whether the school district's and state defendants' attitudes toward black students have changed. The Court asks the school district and state defendants seeking partial or complete termination of federal court supervision to prove that they view African-American students as individuals and will no longer engage in racially motivated discriminatory conduct.

III. Equal Protection Challenges to the Use of Racial Classifications to Promote Integrated Education

In addition to decisions by the Supreme Court limiting school desegregation remedies and terminating school desegregation decrees, a third equal protection trend has developed in the lower federal courts. During the 1970s, a number of opinions by different justices on the Court endorsed the position that the equal protection clause was not a bar to school authorities taking account of race in order to further integrate education.[53] The Court's most supportive statement of this broad power was in its 1971 landmark opinion of *Swann v. Charlotte-Mecklenburg Board of Education.* Chief Justice Burger, writing for a unanimous Court, endorsed the power of school authorities to use racial classifications to foster integrated education:

> School authorities are traditionally charged with broad power to formulate and implement educational policy and might well conclude, for example, that in order to prepare students to live in a pluralistic society each school should have a prescribed ratio of Negro to white students reflecting the proportion for the district as a whole. To do this as an educational policy is within the broad discretionary powers of school authorities.[54]

Driven by political beliefs that an integrated society is a better society, legislators and educators adopted policies and practices aimed at fostering integrated public education, even if they were not required to remedy an equal protection violation. Until the mid 1990s, federal and state courts that addressed the issue of using racial classifications to foster integrated public education in the absence of a need to remedy an equal protection violation took their lead from the Supreme Court's school desegregation jurisprudence. These courts recognized that school districts possessed broad powers to implement measures to integrate their student bodies and faculties.[55] They viewed the desire to end *de facto* segregation as an adequate justification for integration.

The Supreme Court has not directly addressed the use of racial classifications by public schools to foster integrated education in the absence of a need to remedy a constitutional violation. Since 1995, however, a number of federal courts have addressed equal protection challenges to the use of racial classifications to foster integrated education where the compelling state interest of the need to remedy a constitutional violation did not exist. Rather than relying upon the Supreme Court's apparent endorsement of the broad power of public school authorities to promote integrated education noted in *Swann*, these lower federal courts took their lead from the Supreme Court's statement in its 1995 opinion in *Adarand Constructors Inc. v. Pena*. In *Adarand* the Court stated that "all racial classifications, imposed by whatever federal, state, or local governmental actor, must be analyzed by a reviewing court under strict scrutiny."[56] As a result, lower federal courts have analyzed the constitutionality of using racial classifications as a means to promote voluntary integration by examining whether they were justified by a compelling state interest and whether the means used to advance that interest were narrowly tailored. Many of these lower court decisions concluded that either the state or local school officials failed to articulate a compelling state interest for the use of racial classifications in their admissions policies or that the policies were not narrowly tailored. The First, Second, Fourth and Ninth circuits have rendered opinions addressing the issue. The First and Fourth circuits rejected the integration plans presented to them. The first subsection will address these decisions. The second subsection will discuss the decisions of the federal circuit courts that have upheld the use of racial classifications to promote integrated student bodies without the compelling justification of the need to remedy the prior operation of a dual school system. Even the decisions that upheld the integration plans, however, contained serious reservations about the ability of public schools to use racial classifications to promote integrated student bodies without a remedial justification.

A. First and Fourth Circuit Cases Rejecting the Use of Racial Classifications to Promote Voluntary Integration

1. First Circuit Case of *Wessmann v. Gittens*

In 1998, the First Circuit became the first federal appellate court to uphold an equal protection challenge to the use of racial classifications in admissions policies of a public school in the absence of a need to remedy the effects of a prior equal protection violation. Over the dissent of Judge Lipez, the First Circuit struck down a plan adopted by the Boston School Committee, which governed its three examination high schools in *Wessmann v. Gittens*.[57] Prior to litigation, admissions to Boston Latin School (BLS), Boston Latin Academy and O'Bryant were generally determined based upon performance by applicants on a standardized examination. These three examination high schools were considered to be Boston's elite public high schools. Although blacks and Latinos made up over 70% of Boston's public school students, they would constitute only 15–20% of the student population[58] at these schools if admissions were based purely on student test scores. The plan adopted by the Boston School Committee took account of race and ethnicity in order to increase the percentage of black, Latino and Native American students that would be admitted to the examination schools. It was expected under the plan that nearly 35% of the students at the examination schools would be black, Latino or Native American.

Under the plan, all students interested in entering an examination school took a standardized test. The students were ranked based on a composite score that combined their test score with their grade point average. Half of the available seats were awarded based on strict application of the rankings from the composite scores. The other seats were allocated to students based on their composite score and their racial or ethnic classification. In order to determine which students would constitute the other 50% of admitted students, the plan required the calculation of the percentage of five different racial/ethnic groups—non-Hispanic white, black, Latino, Asian and Native American—in the remaining qualified applicant pool (RQAP). The RQAP comprised the top 50% of applicants based on their composite score, excluding those already admitted. The school district would calculate the relative proportion of the five different racial/ethnic groups in the RQAP. This calculation determined the percentage of the remaining students to be admitted from each racial/ethnic group to an examination school. Once percentages for each racial/ethnic group were determined, students would be admitted based upon their relative ranking within their particular racial/ethnic group until the relevant proportion of enrolling students from their racial/ethnic group was achieved. The result of this process was that individuals in certain racial/ethnic group who had higher average composite scores would be passed over in favor of students from a different racial/ethnic group with lower composite scores.

The plan went into effect for the 1997–98 school year. There were ninety available seats in the Boston Latin School (BLS) for that year. The first forty-five were awarded based solely on composite scores. The percentages for each of the five racial/ethnic groups in the RQAP were as follows: African-Americans-27.83%; non-Hispanic whites-40.41%; Asians-19.21%; Latinos-11.64%; and Native Americans-0.31%. Thus, of the remaining 45 students to be enrolled, there were thirteen blacks, eighteen non-Hispanic whites, nine Asians and five Latinos. Since two students who were admitted decided not to attend, in order to reach the remaining forty-five students, forty-seven were admitted.

Sarah Wessmann's composite score ranked her ninety-first on the list. Thus, if admission was determined solely on composite scores, she would have been admitted. Acting on Sarah's behalf, her father sued the School Committee, challenging the constitutionality of the plan. The District Court entered judgment for the school officials, which was reversed by the First Circuit. Agreeing that the admissions policy did not constitute a quota, the First Circuit nevertheless noted that at a certain point in the application process the policy relied on race and ethnicity, and nothing else, to select a subset of entrants. The First Circuit applied strict scrutiny to the plan.

The School Committee argued that the plan was justified by two compelling interests: (1) the need to remedy the effects of identified discrimination; and (2) the need to obtain the educational benefits of a diverse student body. Starting in the early 1970s, Boston had been subject to a federal desegregation decree. In 1987, the federal district court released supervision over student assignment policies of the Boston public schools. The School Committee argued that a provision in a decree issued in its desegregation litigation required it to remedy any racial imbalance occurring in the school system. Judge Garrity issued the provision in question in a 1994 decree. The provision enjoined the School Committee from discriminating on the basis of race in the operation of the public schools of the city of Boston and from creating, promoting or maintaining racial segregation in any school or other facility in the Boston public school system. The School Committee argued that this provision mandates it to remedy any racial imbalance occurring in the school system. The First Circuit rejected this argument. It noted that over ten years ago there had been a finding that Boston public schools obtained unitariness with regard to student assignments. Once there was such a finding of unitariness and the affirmative duty to desegregate had been accomplished, school authorities were not expected to make year-by-year adjustments of the racial composition of student bodies absent a showing that either the school authorities or some other agency of the State has deliberately attempted to fix or alter demographic patterns to affect the racial composition of the schools. Thus, the provision contained in the 1994 decree did not require the school officials to take affirmative action. It was a negative injunction. As long as school officials did not engage in intentional discrimination against minorities, they would not violate this negative injunction.

The School Committee went on to argue that the achievement gap between black and Latino students, on the one hand, and non-Hispanic white and Asian students, on the other, was rooted in the discriminatory regime of the 1970s and before. The School Committee pointed to statistical evidence demonstrating persistent achievement gaps in the relative performance on standardized tests at the primary school level by non-Hispanic white and Asian students, on one hand, and black and Latino students on the other. The First Circuit accepted arguendo that a documented achievement gap may be a vestige of past discrimination. It asserted, however, that there must be satisfactory evidence of a causal connection between the achievement gap and discriminatory state conduct. The First Circuit noted that achievement gap statistics, by themselves, did not eliminate the possibility that the gaps were caused by factors outside the school district's control. The fact that an institution once discriminated against minority students was insufficient, in and of itself, to satisfy a state actor's burden of producing reliable evidence linking achievement gaps to discriminatory state conduct.

To satisfy the causal connection requirement, the School Committee argued that the chief reason for the achievement gap was lower teacher expectations for black and Latino students. The First Circuit, however, rejected the testimony provided by the School Committee to establish a causal connection as inadequate. The expert who testified about the link between low teacher expectation and low student achievement had not conducted a systematic study of Boston school teachers. Rather, he analogized his work in the Kansas City public schools to the Boston public schools. The First Circuit concluded that other evidence introduced by the School Committee to support the connection between lower teacher expectations and achievement gaps on standardized tests was anecdotal, and, therefore, not persuasive in light of the absence of a systematic pattern of discrimination.

Although the First Circuit concluded that the School Committee failed to establish a remedial purpose as a compelling state interest, it still went on to address the narrowly tailored aspect of this interest. Even if there was a systemwide achievement gap due to lower teacher expectations, the First Circuit noted that the plan did not address lower teacher expectations. The First Circuit indicated that it could be argued that the plan is intended to be partial compensation for injustices done at the elementary school level. But, given the minority students who benefit from the plan, this argument did not logically follow. The plan was not limited to black and Latino students attending Boston's public elementary schools. Many of the black and Latino students who would be admitted under the plan would come from private or parochial elementary schools. Since they had not been harmed by lower teacher expectations in Boston's public elementary schools, the plan was not narrowly tailored toward curing the harm done to the class of actual victims. The First Circuit also noted that the inclusion of Asians who were admitted over Sarah Wessmann was particularly problematic. Since there was no evidence of lower teacher expectations regarding Asian students, their inclusion in the plan could not be justified. Finally, the First Circuit noted that the policy could lead to the exclusion of Latino students in favor of whites or Asians in certain anomalous situations. This in fact happened in 1997 when two Latinos were excluded in favor of a non-Hispanic white student.

The First Circuit also addressed the argument that diversity was a compelling state interest which justified the plan. The First Circuit agreed that diversity recognized by Justice Powell in his opinion in *Regents of the University of California v. Bakke*[59] could be a compelling state interest to justify the use of racial classifications, but concluded that the plan was not narrowly tailored to advance the interest of diversity. The School Committee asserted different aspects of diversity to justify its admissions policy. First, it argued that a diverse student body helped to prepare students for living in a pluralistic society. Drawing on testimony from school administrators, experts and alumni, the School Committee argued that because American society is racially and ethnically heterogeneous, future leaders must learn to converse with those who do not share their outlook or experience. This is even more imperative in light of technological advances which now require more communication and cooperation with those from previously estranged nations and cultures. Given these developments, diversity is essential to the modern learning experience. Second, the School Committee asserted that diversity improved the academic environment by creating an atmosphere for the robust exchange of ideas. Unless adequate numbers of a given racial or ethnic group exist, it is difficult, if not impossible, for the few minority members to express themselves. As a result, the robust exchange of ideas, which is the goal of diversity, does not occur.

The First Circuit rejected the School Committee's argument that a threshold level of black and Latino students was necessary to produce a robust exchange of ideas. The School Committee had not provided the strong evidentiary showing of necessity for the requirement of a minimum number of minorities in order to create such an atmosphere. More importantly, the First Circuit noted that the diversity which Justice Powell alluded to was one that encompassed a far broader array of qualifications and characteristics than just racial or ethnic origin. Powell's concept of diversity, therefore, focused on individuals and not on racial and ethnic groups. To the extent the Boston policy promoted racial and ethnic diversity over individual diversity, it was at variance with Justice Powell's opinion in *Bakke*. When this point was raised at oral argument, counsel for the School Committee responded that BLS had historically been diverse with respect to everything, except race and ethnicity. The School Committee pointed to the work of a consultant it hired to study various options for determining admissions to the examination schools. The consultant stated that all admissions options under consideration would result in substantial gender, neighborhood and socioeconomic diversity, but that, unless race and ethnicity were explicitly factored into the admissions calculus, attainment of racial and ethnic diversity might be jeopardized. The First Circuit rejected this argument. It reasoned that strict merit-selection would produce a combined percentage of black and Latino students between 15% and 20%. Even assuming that the need for racial and ethnic diversity alone sometimes constituted a compelling interest sufficient to warrant some type of corrective governmental action, it was perfectly clear that the need would have to be much more acute than what existed in this instant case.

The First Circuit concluded that the plan was a mechanism for racial balancing. Placing its imprimatur on racial balancing risks setting a precedent that is both dangerous to democratic ideals and almost always constitutionally forbidden. The First Circuit concluded that racial balancing was neither a legitimate nor necessary means for advancing the lofty principles of the plan.[60]

2. Fourth Circuit Opinions in *Tuttle v. Arlington County School Board* and *Eisenberg v. Montgomery County Public Schools*

Two cases from the Fourth Circuit rejected the use of racial classifications to determine public school admissions. They were *Tuttle v. Arlington County School Board*[61] and *Eisenberg v. Montgomery County Public Schools.*[62] In *Tuttle,* the Fourth Circuit addressed a challenge to the use of racial classifications in the kindergarten admissions policy (Policy) of Arlington Traditional School (ATS). ATS accepted applications for kindergarten throughout the school district. It sought to obtain a student body in proportions that approximated the distribution of students from three different groups in the district's overall student population. Thus, the Policy focused on three different characteristics of applicants: (1) whether the applicant was from a low-income or special family background, (2) whether English was the applicant's first or second language and (3) whether the applicant belonged to a minority racial or ethnic group. In 1998, the year the Policy went into effect, there were 185 applications for sixty-nine available seats. ATS first offered admissions to twenty-three kindergartners who were the siblings of students already attending ATS. For the remaining forty-six spaces, ATS conducted a weighted random lottery. The probability that a given applicant would be selected in the lottery was weighted so that applicants from underrepresented groups had an increased chance of being selected.

The District Court struck down the Policy. Although the Policy included three different characteristics of applicants, on appeal, the Fourth Circuit focused only on the aspect of race and ethnicity. Like the First Circuit in *Wessmann,* the Fourth Circuit agreed that diversity was a compelling state interest, but found the Policy was not narrowly tailored to advance that interest. The Fourth Circuit noted a number of problems with the Policy's use of racial classifications. First, alternative race-neutral methods could be used to promote diversity. Second, the Policy lacked a terminating point. The third criticism was the most fundamental. The Fourth Circuit noted that the Policy did not consider each applicant to kindergarten on an individual basis to determine if his or her inclusion promoted diversity. What the Policy sought to achieve was racial and ethnic diversity in its classes in approximate proportions to the distribution of the district's overall student population. As a result, the Policy sought to advance the impermissible objective of racial balancing. Finally, the Fourth Circuit stated that the innocent third parties in this case were young kindergarten-age children. The Fourth Circuit noted the irony of a policy intended to teach young children to regard people as individuals which classified children as members of racial and ethnic groups.

Two weeks after issuing its *Tuttle* opinion, the Fourth Circuit followed it with its decision in *Eisenberg v. Montgomery County Public Schools.*[63] The Fourth Circuit found *Eisenberg* to be practically indistinguishable from *Tuttle.* Montgomery County is a large school district with over 125,000 students and over 180 schools. The County was never subject to a school desegregation order, but adopted a number of steps voluntarily to dismantle its former segregated school system. Part of its desegregation effort was to implement magnet school programs. These programs sought to attract and retain a diverse student enrollment on a voluntary basis. School stability and utilization were the first factors considered in determining whether to grant a request to attend a magnet school. Since the purpose of the magnet school program was to promote integration, transfers which negatively affected diversity were usually denied.[64]

Jacob Eisenberg applied as a first grader for a transfer to the Rosemary Hills Elementary School, a math and science magnet school, for the 1998–99 school year. Montgomery County school officials denied his request due to the negative impact it would have on diversity. Jacob was assigned to Glen Haven Elementary School, where the enrollment of white students was below the 53.4% of whites for the entire school district. The percentage of white students at Glen Haven had declined in the past three years from 38.9% to 24.1%.

In addressing Jacob's equal protection challenge, the District Court opined that Montgomery County's asserted interest in avoiding the creation of segregative enrollment through racial isolation and in promoting a diverse student population were each sufficiently compelling to justify the transfer policy's race-based classifications under strict scrutiny. The Fourth Circuit reversed. It concluded that despite the different nomenclature, the two asserted compelling interests were one and the same. As it did in *Tuttle,* the Fourth Circuit assumed that diversity was a compelling state interest. It then analyzed the transfer policy to determine if it was narrowly tailored. The Fourth Circuit concluded that the use of racial classifications by the school authorities in their transfer decisions was not narrowly tailored to its diversity interest. The plan was one of pure racial balancing and such nonremedial racial balancing is unconstitutional.

B. Federal Court of Appeals Opinions Upholding Integration Plans

1. Ninth Circuit Opinion in *Hunter v. Regents of University of California*

Over the dissent of Judge Beezer,[65] the Ninth Circuit in *Hunter v. Regents of University of California*,[66] upheld the use of racial classifications to determine the student make up at Corinne A. Seeds University Elementary School (UES). UCLA's graduate schools of Education and Information Studies operated UES as a research laboratory. UES's research and training mission was to help the State of California meet the needs of a dramatically changing public school population. To this end, UES identified issues relevant to the education and social development of children in multicultural urban communities, conducted research on these issues and developed teaching innovations based on this research. UES shared its research results with public school teachers throughout the State of California through seminars, workshops, teacher training programs and published articles.

Under the direction of the Dean of the Graduate School of Education and Information Studies and the Director of UES, UES's Admissions Committee decided what characteristics are needed in its 460-student body to fulfill its research and training agenda. Gender, race/ethnicity and family income are specifically considered in the admissions process. Other factors that might affect the suitability of a given student as a research subject, such as dominant language, permanence of residence and parents' willingness to comply with UES's mandatory involvement requirement were also considered.

Keeley Hunter was denied admission to UES and her parents brought suit challenging the constitutionality of the admissions process. The district court upheld the admissions process and the Ninth Circuit affirmed. In applying strict scrutiny to the challenge to UES's use of race/ethnicity as a factor in its admissions process, the Ninth Circuit concluded that California's interest in the operation of a research-oriented elementary school dedicated to improving the quality of education in urban public schools is a compelling state interest.[67] The Ninth Circuit acknowledged the challenges posed by California's increasingly diverse population. Cultural and economic differences in the classroom posed special problems for public school teachers. Among these challenges were limited language proficiency, different learning styles, involvement of parents from diverse cultures with different expectations and racial and ethnic conflict among families and children.

In its opinion, the Ninth Circuit relied heavily on the fact that UES was a laboratory school with a research mission. This research mission made it an exceptional school and a valuable resource to California's public education system. In determining that the use of racial classifications in the admissions process was narrowly tailored, the Ninth Circuit pointed to the importance of the judgment of the academic researchers. The Ninth Circuit noted that the Supreme Court had stressed the importance of avoiding second-guessing legitimate academic judgments.

2. Second Circuit Opinion in *Brewer v. West Irondequoit Central School District*

The only recent decision by a Court of Appeals upholding the broad power of public elementary and secondary schools to use racial classifications for the purpose of integrating schools is the Second Circuit's opinion in *Brewer v. West Irondequoit Central School District.*[68] Justice Straub wrote the opinion for the divided Second Circuit. Justice Parker who signed on to Straub's opinion, also wrote a separate concurring opinion.[69] Judge Miner wrote a dissenting opinion.[70]

The Second Circuit addressed a challenge to the operation of the Urban-Suburban Interdistrict Transfer Program (Program) from parents of a white fourth grader residing in the Rochester City School District (RCSD). The Program was one of the oldest interdistrict voluntary desegregation efforts in the nation, the only one of its kind in New York and one of only two or three such voluntary programs in the United States. The Program provided for voluntary student transfers between participating school districts to reduce, prevent and eliminate minority group isolation in their schools. Funding came from the State of New York. The effect of such funding was to allow a student to transfer to another school district without any financial consequences to the student.

As of July 1997, RCSD had 37,153 pupils, of whom roughly 29,700 were minorities. Under the Program, only minority pupils from RCSD were allowed to transfer from the city schools to suburban schools. The Program was very popular and the number of applicants far exceeded the spaces available in the six suburban districts. White students could transfer from suburban schools to the city, so long as the transfer did not negatively affect the racial balance of the receiving school. RCSD reported that 591 minority pupils transferred to suburban schools during the 1996–97 school year and 29 white students were accepted into RCSD.

The district court granted the plaintiff's motion for a preliminary injunction. The Second Circuit reversed. The Second Circuit in *Brewer* concluded that it was bound by an earlier opinion, its 1979 decision in *Parent Association of Andrew Jackson High School v. Ambach*[71] (*Andrew Jackson Case*). In the Andrew Jackson case, Second Circuit rejected a challenge to a desegregation plan for Andrew Jackson High School in Queens, New York. Applying strict scrutiny to the challenge, the Second Circuit concluded that the aim of promoting a more lasting integration was sufficiently compelling to justify the use of racial classifications. The implication drawn from that holding was that a compelling state interest existed in a program with an objective to reduce racial isolation and *de facto* segregation.

After agreeing that the plan in *Brewer* was justified by a compelling state interest, the Second Circuit addressed the aspect of narrowly tailored. In its narrowly tailored analysis the Second Circuit concluded that if reducing racial isolation, standing alone, was a constitutionally permissible goal, then there was no more effective means of achieving that goal than to base decisions on race.

Justice Parker's concurring opinion, however, included a major reservation to approving the Program. Parker agreed with the opinion, but noted that the Program had been in existence for thirty-five years. In that time, the percentage of minorities in RCSD increased from 25.6% to 80%, and the current percentage of white students in the suburban schools ranged from 85% to 92%. While there were 36,000 students in Rochester, only 580 participated in the program during the 1998–99 school year. Parker stated that if those statistics were accurate, it was extremely difficult to see how this Program had any meaningful impact on the existence of schools or school districts with a predominant number or percentage of students of particular racial/ethnic groups. Parker opined that although the defendants may have had a sufficiently compelling interest to justify the Program at its inception, given the Program's limited impact, that interest may no longer exist. Parker noted that the district court did not explore this because the plaintiffs made no facial challenge to the Program as a whole. Given the very limited development of this issue on the record, Parker suggested that further consideration of this issue on remand was the appropriate disposition.

C. Conclusion

The Supreme Court has not directly addressed the use of racial classifications by public schools to foster integrated education in the absence of a need to remedy a constitutional violation. Lower federal courts, however, have rejected their earlier position of accepting the broad power of school officials to use racial classifications in order to promote integrated education. Since the Court's 1995 decision in *Adarand Constructors Inc. v. Pena*, lower federal court's have applied *Adarand's* requirement that the use of racial classifications by any governmental entity be analyzed under strict scrutiny to equal protection challenges to the use of racial classifications to promote integrated public schools. With the exception of the Second Circuit's opinion in *Brewer*, the federal circuits that have addressed this issue have significantly restricted the use of racial classifications to promote integrated student bodies.

Restricting the use of racial classifications to promote integrated student bodies by legislators and school officials reflects the ascendency of interpreting the equal protection rights of black students against the background assumptions of Colorblind Individualism. Because the use of racial classifications involves government treating people as members of racial and ethnic groups instead of as individuals, their use is severely limited. In the Summer of 2003, the Supreme Court handed down its long awaited opinions in two companion cases dealing with affirmative action plans at the University of Michigan. It is too early to tell how the Supreme Court's decision upholding the University of Michigan Law School's affirmative action program in *Grutter v. Bollinger*[72] will apply to the use of racial classifications to promote voluntary integration by public elementary and secondary schools. The Court's holding in *Grutter* was that racial classifications could be used in an individualized admissions process as a means to pursue a critical mass of under represented minority students from groups with a history of discrimination. Applying that holding to the First Circuit and Fourth Circuit opinion would probably not have changed their results. It is possible that *Grutter's* holding would reject the decisions by the Ninth Circuit in *Hunter v. Regents of University of California* and the Second Circuit decision in *Brewer v. West Irondequoit Central School District* that upheld the use of racial classifications in those cases. *Brewer's* holding is particularly vulnerable because the compelling state interest was not related to the academic freedom First Amendment right of colleges, universities and graduate programs upon which *Grutter* and, arguably, *Hunter* were based. Thus, unless the *Grutter* holding is significantly broadened when it is applied to elementary and secondary public education,[73] it may provide little room for elementary and secondary schools to use racial classifications to promote integrated education.

Conclusion

In explaining why the Supreme Court struck down the segregation statutes presented in *Brown v. Board of Education,* Chief Justice Warren noted that segregation had psychologically damaged black schoolchildren. Warren's opinion was thus based on the embedded assumptions about blacks that is the basis of Traditional Americanism. *Brown* was, however, a break with the past interpretation of the rights of blacks regarding segregation in the past because it attributed the inferiority of blacks to environmental causes. When situated in a historical context, *Brown* was a very sanguine opinion because it suggested that there was a cure for—or at least a way to improve—black people. African-Americans could be made better by enriching their social environment, particularly the educational environment of the young. Born out of this belief was a special concern for the educational interest of black schoolchildren. If their educational environment could be ameliorated, they should improve.

Much of the integration of public schools that occurred in the United States was the result of the Supreme Court's school desegregation jurisprudence. After a slow start, desegregation in public schools increased sharply from the mid 1960s to the early 1970s. Racial and ethnic mixing among student bodies held fairly consistent from the early 1970s until the late 1980s. But racial resegregation has been on the increase over the past fifteen years and it is clear that the amount of racial and ethnic segregation in public elementary and secondary schools will continue to increase in the twenty-first century.

Three trends over the last thirty years in the interpretation of the Equal Protection Clause have constrained school desegregation. They are the waning of the Supreme Court's commitment to aggressively pursue integration starting with *Keyes* in 1973, the impact of the Court's school desegregation termination opinions of the 1990s and decisions by lower federal courts that have limited the use of racial classifications to promote integrated student bodies in the absence of the need to remedy an existing equal protection violation. These trends all reflect a shift in the cognitive framework against which the equal protection rights of black schoolchildren are interpreted. In general, there was a change from interpreting the equal protection clause within the discourse of Traditional Americanism, which generated a special concern to improve the educational environment of black schoolchildren, to Colorblind Individualism. The effect of this change was to slow down, stop and eventually reverse public school integration.

Chapter Eight

Equal Protection Clause Trends that Limit the Ability to Attack the Racial Academic Achievement Gaps

One of the two overlapping objectives of this book is to present the educational situation of African-American schoolchildren in the Post-Desegregation Era. Many changes have occurred in the educational situation of African-American schoolchildren over the past fifty years. One of the most significant developments is the change in the background assumptions against which rights of black schoolchildren derived from the equal protection clause are interpreted. Chapter Seven discussed how the Supreme Court's initial school desegregation jurisprudence was based upon the notion that segregation had inflicted psychological damage upon black schoolchildren. But as time wore on, federal courts began to embrace the background assumptions of Colorblind Individualism for interpreting the equal protection rights of black schoolchildren with regard to student assignments. The result of this shift was to slow down, stop and eventually reverse public school desegregation.

Outside the area of student assignments, the shift in background assumptions for determining the legal rights of black schoolchildren has also had a dramatic effect on the educational opportunities of black schoolchildren. This effect can be noted in legal challenges raised against school systems under federal court supervision in order to remedy the vestiges of their prior operation of a dual school system, as well as school systems not undergoing the remedial process for a prior *de jure* segregation violation. The effect of this shift can not be overstated. This shift in the interpretation of the equal protection clause produces two significant consequences that are relevant to the current legal situation facing black schoolchildren.

The first significant consequence is that programs and policies which legislatures and public educational officials can employ to attack the continuing racial gaps in educational performance are generally limited to those that do not employ racial or ethnic classifications. According to the Supreme Court's equal protection jurisprudence "all racial classifications, imposed by whatever federal, state, or local governmental actor, must be analyzed by a reviewing court under strict scrutiny. In other words, such classifications are constitutional only if they are narrowly tailored measures that further compelling governmental interests."[1] While this is not a true colorblind standard for interpreting the equal protection clause, it generally proscribes the use in public schools of educational policies and practices that employ racial and ethnic classifications outside the context of the need to remedy vestiges of the former operation of a dual school system or to provide the benefits of diversity based on individual characteristics. Chapter Seven pointed to the impact of this consequence during the discussion about decisions by lower federal courts that have severely restricted the use of racial classifications to promote integrated public schools absent the need to remedy a prior constitutional violation. Section I of this Chapter will extend that discussion to the Supreme Court's opinion in *Wygant v. Jackson Board of Education.*[2] In that case, the Court rejected the argument that using racial classifications to limit layoffs of minority teachers in order to ensure adequate role models for minority students was a compelling state interest. Since the use of racial classifications must survive strict scrutiny, strategies to advance the educational interest of black schoolchildren today must rely heavily upon racially neutral policies and programs that are not specifically targeted to their educational problems.

The second significant consequence of the shift in background assumptions is that for educational policies and practices to be deemed unconstitutionally discriminatory they must result from racially discriminatory motives. The Supreme Court has not addressed equal protection challenges involving educational polices and practices such as tracking or ability skills grouping, high-stakes testing or curricular disputes. During the 1960s and 1970s, lower federal courts also viewed the equal protection rights of black schoolchildren against the background belief that segregation had psychologically damaged black schoolchildren. As a result, these lower federal courts struck down a number of legitimate educational policies and practices because of their adverse impact on the educational opportunities of black schoolchildren. But, over the past thirty years the same general change in background assumptions noted with regard to student assignments can also be observed in decisions dealing with other educational policies and practices. This change prevents African-American students from making cogent legal arguments against a number of educational policies and practices such as tracking or achievement skills grouping, high-stakes testing or curricular decisions that have a discriminatory effect. These educational policies and practices can almost always be justified based on legitimate educational concerns. Thus, it is difficult to prove that they were primarily motivated by discriminatory intent. As a result, many equal protection legal strategies for attacking the academic achievement gaps that existed between black and non-Hispanic white schoolchildren which were promising from the perspective of black schoolchildren after the Supreme Court's opinion in *Brown* have run their inevitable course. The effect of this shift has led federal courts from upholding equal protection challenges to racially neutral educational policies and practices that had a disparate impact on the educational opportunities of African-American schoolchildren, to rejecting those challenges. From an equal protection standpoint the discriminatory effect of educational policies and practices motivated by legitimate educational concerns is now understood as an unfortunate side effect of racially-neutral educational decision making. Thus, equal protection lawsuits calling into question racially neutral educational policies and procedures which have a disparate racial impact generally do not succeed.[3] Section III of this Chapter will discuss the impact of the change in the concept of discrimination for equal protection purposes by focusing on a number of educational policies and practices of public schools other than those related to student assignments.

Before discussing various discriminatory challenges to educational policies and practices under the equal protection clause, Section II will discuss developments interpreting discrimination under Title VI of the Civil Rights Act of 1964. This is necessary to demonstrate that the Supreme Court has recently foreclosed the possibility that private rights of actions could be pursued under Title VI disparate impact regulations. Many equal protection challenges filed against educational policies and practices like tracking, high stakes testing and curricular decisions included a challenge or challenges under either or both Section 601 and Section 602 of the Civil Rights Act of

1964. Section 601 bans discrimination from any program receiving federal funds. Section 602 authorizes federal agencies to effectuate the provisions of Section 601 through appropriate regulations. The Supreme Court has conclude that the test for discrimination under Section 601 is the same as under the equal protection clause, i.e., intentional discrimination. But, the Court has also concluded that the regulations promulgated under Section 602 may validly proscribe activities that have a disparate impact on racial groups. The Court has held that private rights of action exist to enforce the prohibition against intentional discrimination under Section 601. The Supreme Court concluded in its 2001 decision in *Alexander v. Sandoval,*[4] however, that no private right of action exists to enforce the disparate impact regulations adopted pursuant to Section 602.

I. Limitations on the Use of Educational Policies and Procedures Employing Racial Classifications

Generally speaking, the solutions that can be pursued to address the continuing racial gap in educational achievement of African-American students are going to have to be those that do not use racial classifications. Chapter Seven pointed out how lower federal courts have restricted the ability of school officials to use racial classifications in order to promote integrated schools when not justified to remedy the effects of the operation of a dual school system or obtain the benefits of a diverse student body based on individual diversity. The same limitation on the use of racial classifications will apply to other educational policies and programs. This section will look at one other circumstance where educational officials were prevented from using racial classifications in order to pursue educational policies that might assist black schoolchildren. In *Wygant v. Jackson Board of Education,*[5] school administrators sought to protect some of their black school teachers when it was necessary to lay teachers off. The school officials felt it was important to maintain their African-American teachers because they served as role models for black students. Despite the potential benefits that black teachers might provide for black students, the Supreme Court rejected the argument that public schools had a compelling interest in retaining black school teachers over more senior white school teachers in deciding which teachers to lay off.

In 1972, because of racial tension in the community, the Jackson Board of Education considered adding a layoff provision to the Collective Bargaining

Agreement between it and the Jackson Education Association (Union). The provision would protect certain minority teachers against layoffs. The Board and the Union eventually agreed on a new provision for its collective bargaining agreement which provided that "in the event of layoffs teachers with the most seniority in the district shall be retained, except that at no time will there be a greater percentage of minority personnel laid off than the current percentage of minority personnel employed at the time of the layoff."[6] Pursuant to this provision, during the 1976–77 and 1981–82 school years, nonminority teachers were laid off, while minority teachers with less seniority were retained.[7]

Nonminority teachers filed suit claiming that the operation of the layoff provision violated the equal protection clause. Both the District Court and the Sixth Circuit agreed that the Board's interest in providing minority role models for its minority students, as an attempt to alleviate the effects of societal discrimination, was sufficiently important to justify the racial classification embodied in the layoff provision.[8] The plurality opinion for the Supreme Court rejected the argument that the role model theory represented a compelling state interest. The Court noted that since the role model theory was not intended to be remedial, it did not bear any relationship to the harm caused by prior discriminatory hiring practices.[9] Instead, the Court found the provision to violate the equal protection rights of the white teachers who would have been effected by the provision.

II. Recent Developments Interpreting Title VI

When Congress passed the 1964 Civil Rights Act, Section 601 stated that no person shall, "on the ground of race, color, or national origin, be excluded from participation in, be denied the benefits of, or be subjected to discrimination under any program or activity."[10] In the Supreme Court's 1974 opinion in *Lau v. Nichols*,[11] the Court held that a school system's failure to provide English language instruction to Chinese-speaking students denied them a meaningful opportunity to participate in the educational programs offered by the school district in violation of Title VI. In the opinion, the Court noted that HEW guidelines declared that "discrimination is barred which has that effect even though no purposeful design is present."[12] Thus, the court adopted the position that Title VI regulations prohibit discrimination based on disparate impact. But the Court's opinion in *Regents of the University of California v. Bakke*[13] raised serious questions about the discriminatory-effects holding in *Lau*. In *Bakke*, five members of the Court concluded that the standard for a Title VI violation ought to be the same as for an equal protection violation. In the Court's 1983 decision in *Guardians Association v. Civil Service Commission of New York City,*[14] the Court made clear that under *Bakke* only intentional discrimination was forbidden by Section 601.[15] Recently, the Supreme Court reiterated this position in *Alexander v. Sandoval,* stating "Title VI itself directly reaches only instances of intentional discrimination."[16] The Court has also made it clear that there exists a private right of action under Section 601 that allows private individuals to challenge actions of recipients of federal funds.[17] Thus, if there is an equal protection clause violation by a public school due to its engaging in intentional discriminatory conduct, then there is also a Section 601 violation as well. A discussion of the equal protection clause could therefore also double as a discussion of Section 601.

Section 602 of Title VI authorizes federal agencies to effectuate the provisions of Section 601 by issuing rules, regulations or orders of general applicability. The Department of Justice, in an exercise of this authority, promulgated a regulation forbidding funding recipients to utilize criteria or methods of administration which have the *effect* of subjecting individuals to discrimination because of their race, color or national origin. The Supreme Court has held that "regulations promulgated under § 602 of Title VI may validly proscribe activities that have a disparate impact on racial groups, even though such activities are permissible under § 601."[18] However, the conclusion that the regulations promulgated under Title VI can proscribe activities with a disparate impact is in considerable tension with the Court's conclusion that Section 601 forbids only intentional discrimination.[19]

A law that employs a disparate impact framework is kinder to plaintiffs challenging discriminatory practices than one requiring the proof of discriminatory intent. This point was noted in Chapter Seven which discussed the Supreme Court's distinction between *de jure* segregation and *de facto* segregation. But in a five to four 2001 decision in *Alexander v. Sandoval,*[20] the Supreme Court held that there is no private right of action to enforce disparate impact regulations promulgated under Section 602. In his dissenting opinion for the four justices in *Sandoval,* Justice Stevens wrote

> Litigants who in the future wish to enforce the Title VI regulations against state actors in all likelihood must only reference § 1983 to obtain relief; indeed, the plaintiffs in this case (or other similarly situated individuals) presumably retain the option of re-challenging [the state's] ...policy in a complaint that invokes § 1983 even after today's decision.[21]

Thus, Justice Stevens's opinion concluded that the Supreme Court's implied right of action cases are separate and distinct from their 42 U.S.C. § 1983 cases.[22] As a result, a litigant might be able to enforce under § 1983 a benefit or interest that could not be enforced under the statute that, arguably, created it.

The prospects of using Justice Stevens's alternative suggestion of enforcing Title VI regulations through a 42 U.S.C § 1983 action to circumvent the Court's decision in *Alexander v. Sandoval* was dealt a fatal blow by the Supreme Court's 2002 opinion in *Gonzaga University v. Doe.*[23] In that opinion the Supreme Court stated,

> We now reject the notion that our cases permit anything short of an unambiguously conferred right to support a cause of action brought under § 1983. Section 1983 provides a remedy only for the deprivation of "rights, privileges, or immunities secured by the Constitution and laws" of the United States. Accordingly, it is *rights,* not the broader or vaguer "benefits" or "interests," that may be enforced under the authority of that section. This being so, we further reject the notion that our implied right of action cases are separate and distinct from our § 1983 cases. To the contrary, our implied right of action cases should guide the determination of whether a statute confers rights enforceable under § 1983.[24]

The initial inquiry in a Section 1983 action, regarding whether a private right of action exists, is "whether or not a statute 'confers rights on a particular class of persons.'"[25] Since the Supreme Court in *Alexander v. Sandoval* rejected the argument that Congress intended to create a private right of action under the disparate impact regulations of Section 602, it is now doubtful that a private right of action to enforce those regulations exists under 42 U.S.C. § 1983.[26] Thus, it is doubtful that private litigants can now maintain a cause of action under the disparate impact regulations under Title VI or under 42 U.S.C. § 1983 to enforce the disparate impact regulations of Title VI.

Many of the tracking, high stakes testing and curricular decision cases discussed in this Chapter not only involved an equal protection challenge, but also an assertion of a private right of action challenge under the Title VI discriminatory impact regulations. The disparate impact regulation claims brought by private entities, however, are now barred. The Department of Education's Office for Civil Rights (OCR) continues to have the duty to ensure that recipients of federal financial assistance do not discriminate against students, or other individuals, on the basis of race, color, national origin, sex, disability or age. OCR can investigate a claim and generate the necessary evidence for a disparate impact challenge to given educational policies or procedures of recipients of federal funds. If OCR finds a violation of the Title VI regulations and fails to secure voluntary compliance, it can then issue a finding of a violation and seek to withdraw federal funds. But the cases that OCR pursues, as well as its willingness to cut off federal funds to an offending school district, will also be governed by political considerations regarding what types of discrimination cases appear to be most important, as well as financial constraints on their budget.

III. Challenging Certain Educational Policies and Practices as Discriminatory Under the Equal Protection Clause

This section will discuss a number of educational policies and practices other than those related to student school assignments, including tracking or ability skills groupings, high stakes testings and curricular decisions. This discussion will point out that the same shift over the past thirty years in interpreting the equal protection rights of black schoolchildren noted in the discussions of student assignments in Chapter Seven can also be seen in the lower federal courts' treatment of other educational policies and practices. Viewing the equal protection rights of black schoolchildren against a background that saw them as suffering from psychological damage as a result of their racial isolation led lower federal courts to uphold challenges to various educational policies and practices, even though they could be motivated by legitimate pedagogical concerns. The federal courts often focused on the discriminatory impact of the policies on the educational opportunities of black schoolchildren as the reason to invalidate their use. Federal courts addressing equal protection challenges to educational policies and practices other than student assignments—whether in the context of school desegregation litigation or not—have now, generally, shifted to interpreting the equal protection rights of black schoolchildren within the conceptual boundaries of Colorblind Individualism. Thus, whether educational policies and practices instituted by school officials violates the equal protection clause is determined by focusing on the motivations of the school officials, not the impact on the educational opportunities of black schoolchildren. Actions of school officials, like those of Knowing Individuals, are motivated by many different considerations. Often times school officials will adopt policies and procedures motivated by legitimate race-neutral pedagogical reasons, but those policies or procedures may produce a discriminatory effect on educational opportunities of African-American schoolchildren. The individuals whose interests are harmed by actions motivated by race-neutral considerations, however, are not considered to be victims of racial discrimination. It is not the consequences of government actions that determine whether they are unconstitutionally discriminatory, but the intent that motivates the actions. The discriminatory effect of educational policies and practices motivated by legitimate educational concerns is now generally understood as just an unfortunate side effect of racially-neutral educational decision making.

A. Tracking or Ability Skills Grouping

One common educational practice that tends to negatively impact the educational opportunities of African-Americans is tracking or ability skills grouping. A significant number of challenges to these practices have been brought by or on behalf of black students in lower federal courts since the late 1960s. This section will first define tracking or ability skills grouping. This practice was largely abandoned by schools in the 1930s, before making a comeback with school desegregation in the 1960s. This subsection will conclude with a review of some significant tracking cases. The review of the cases demonstrates the general movement by lower federal courts from rejecting tracking or ability skills grouping because it harmed the educational opportunities of black schoolchildren in the 1960s and 1970s, to accepting tracking as a legitimate educational practice despite the fact that blacks are still disproportionately confined to the lower ability skills groups.

1. Defining Tracking or Ability Skills Grouping

Tracking or ability skills grouping can be defined as the sequencing of academic classes that range from slow-paced remedial courses, to general academic courses.[27] While some tracking systems will encompass a student's entire educational program, it is more common for schools to limit their tracking or ability skills groupings to skill mastery courses such as mathematics, language arts and science courses. Skill mastery courses are those that are viewed by educators as requiring the mastery of a certain skill before a student is ready to go on to study and master more advanced or complex skills. In math, for example, a student must master addition and subtraction before being ready to go on to multiplication and division. Similarly, in English a student must have mastered simple "Jack and Jill" texts before tackling Shakespeare. Mastery in reading and math are also thought to be necessary for the mastery of other academic subjects such as social studies and health.

At the upper end of the tracking spectrum are courses for gifted, talented or honors students. The next lower level would be students who are assigned to a more general educational or comprehensive track. Below the general or comprehensive ability skills grouping are students placed in a low-track, though not a special education track. At the lowest end of the spectrum would be students assigned to special education placement. Placement of a student in special education is based on the belief that the student suffers from some form of disability, including a physical disability, mental retardation, emotional disturbance or specific learning disability that impairs academic performance.

The Individuals with Disabilities Education Act (IDEA), a federal law, governs many aspects of the educational opportunities of students with disabilities. This law requires that an individual education program be developed for each such student. The school system must meet special education needs of students with disabilities in the least restrictive environment necessary to serve the child's needs. Therefore, some special education students do not leave the regular classroom at all, but others might receive some special instruction in separate classrooms. One advantage in being placed in special education over being placed in a low-ability skills grouping is that special education students are entitled to receive support services specifically tailored to their educational needs. Since students placed in low ability skills groups are not covered by the IDEA these services do not have to be provided to them.

Students are normally assigned to their various tracks based upon their presumed academic abilities. Schools that use tracking or ability skills groupings typically assign students to academic tracks based on grade point averages and teacher recommendations. Standardized tests are also a very important factor in determining educational placement, especially for highly selective gifted and talented programs. IQ tests play an important role, especially in the special education evaluation process. Parents can also influence the academic placement of their children. Middle class parents tend to intervene to obtain a more advantageous placement for their child more often than poor parents.[28] At the high school level, student and parental choices play important roles in determining the rigorousness of a particular student's courses. A student's choice of courses in high school, however, often reflects earlier academic judgements about the student's abilities.

Proponents of tracking argue that there are several reasons why the comprehensive schools need to be systematically organized and structured to provide differing levels of education for students with differing levels of ability.[29] First, tracking is educationally logical because it seeks to classify students according to their ability—whether present or potential—and to provide the education best suited to the needs of each individual child. Academically prepared students can be separated and placed in advanced courses that challenge them without, at the same time, being beyond the abilities of students who are more academically challenged. This keeps the academically prepared students from wasting their educational time with material they already know and becoming bored with lessons that are too easy. Ability skills grouping allows less-prepared students to learn at their own rate and, as a result, prevents them from becoming frustrated with trying to cover educational material that is too difficult for them. Secondly, for some low-track students their placement in lower tracks should be temporary. During this temporary placement, those students identified with special problems can be remedied. Once remedied they can be moved to a higher level of education. Finally, tracking is also supported by the realization that a crucial function of schools is to prepare students for an economy that requires workers with very different knowledge and skills. Demanding academic classes prepare students heading for jobs that require college degrees, whereas more basic academic classes and vocational programs prepare students who lack high academic abilities for low-skilled jobs or post-high school technical training.

Opponents of tracking note that while the theory may be sound, the practices reveal a different reality. In theory, the process of tracking is supposed to facilitate learning by grouping students with similar abilities together. Some researchers have noted that students with extraordinarily wide ranges of ability, as measured by standardized tests, are placed together in different tracks.[30] Thus, despite the claims of homogenous ability skills grouping, the various tracks encompass a wide range of abilities. Opponents also note that there is no clear evidence that ability skills grouping helps students at the higher levels and it appears to harm students at the lower levels.[31] While ability skills grouping is supposed to make students feel comfortable with their educational environment, in practice, this only happens with students in higher tracks. Students in the lower tracks are perceived as placed in remedial or lower academic groups.[32] They are stigmatized as being academically sluggish. Students quickly realize this and tend to respond to this labeling by lowering their assessment of their own academic abilities. In addition, teachers in the lower tracks are also likely to be less experienced in the classroom than those in the upper tracks. Teachers tend to view moving from low ability skills grouping classes to high ability skills grouping classes as a promotion to a more challenging class. The result is that in lower academic tracks students and their teachers reduce their expectations for academic achievement. This reduces their educational opportunities and drops them further behind their higher tracked counterparts. Thus, the academic tracks tend to become largely self-contained educational worlds with little movement by students once they are assigned.[33] Since the education provided in the lower tracks is watered-down, the students placed in there receive a less challenging education that may not prepare them for the academic rigors demanded by many colleges and universities.

Despite the legitimate educational justifications for it, tracking has long been identified as a major source of racial inequality in educational opportunities.[34] Separating black students in different classes within a given school is a carry-over of educational policies and practices which justified segregation of blacks in different schools for over 100 years before the Court's opinion in *Brown v. Board of Education.* One of the principal justifications for separating black students from white students in different schools was the presumed educational inadequacies of black children. For example, in the 1849 case of *Roberts v. Boston,*[35] the Massachusetts Supreme Judicial Court upheld the operation of segregated public schools in Boston. The General School Committee of Boston asserted that the operation of separate schools for the black children was best adapted to promote the instruction of that class of the population. The Massachusetts Supreme Judicial Court agreed that the School Committee had the authority to make such a decision. It also agreed that the decision to separate public school students by race was a reasonable exercise of that authority, based on just grounds of reason and experience. According to the Court the decision to place black students in separate schools was the result of a discriminating and honest judgment.[36]

Tracking came into vogue within schools attended by whites in the 1920s. At this time, the concept of hereditary intelligence was being expounded by Lewis Terman and others.[37] By the 1930s, however, ability skills grouping had begun to fade from schools because research suggested that grouping by ability had little or no effect on achievement gains.[38]

Tracking made a huge rebound in the wake of the Supreme Court's opinion in *Brown v. Board of Education.*[39] After school desegregation began in earnest in the late 1960s and early 1970s, public schools, especially in the South, resorted to ability skills grouping to determine academic placement. The effect of such assignment policies tended to produce racially identifiable schools or classrooms within the same school. Tracking could certainly be viewed as a means of circumventing court required desegregation. But, arguably, the selection was done based on the nonracial factor of academic ability.[40]

2. Legal Challenges to Tracking or Ability Skills Grouping

Many early desegregation opinions that addressed the issue of tracking in schools undergoing desegregation generally struck down the practice. Even though there were demonstrated academic ability gaps between black students and white students, these courts generally concluded that the equal protection rights of the black students were violated by grouping students on such a basis.[41] Later school desegregation cases, however, began to uphold tracking practices. These policies were upheld for one of two reasons. Some courts expressed the view that tracking or ability skills grouping was actually helpful to the minority schoolchildren who were disproportionately tracked into lower ability skills groups. For these courts tracking was another way to address the presumed inadequacies of black students. Thus, tracking became justified as a means to respond to the continued inadequacies of blacks school students. Other courts tended to view the decisions about where to place students as racially neutral. Thus, tracking was not remedial in nature. The fact that black and other minority students were disproportionately confined to the lower ability skills groupings was simply the unfortunate result of racially neutral academic decision making.

(a) *Hobson v. Hansen*

The first major legal attack on tracking was the 1967 decision in *Hobson v. Hansen*,[42] addressing the tracking system employed in the District of Columbia public schools. Soon after the Supreme Court's decision in *Bolling v. Sharpe*,[43] one of the companion cases to *Brown*, Assistant Superintendent Dr. Hansen devised and instituted a tracking system in D.C. public schools. Hansen realized that there were large academic ability gaps between black and white students now attending integrated schools. He sought to design a system that would assign students to academic programs adjusted to their differing levels of academic ability. This would permit the school district to challenge its academically advanced students without presenting less-prepared students with material beyond their ability. The educational benefits derived from providing every student with the maximum opportunity for self-development was the motivation for instituting the tracking system.

The tracking system divided students into separate, self-contained curricula or tracks, ranging from "Basic" for the academically challenged learners, to "General" for the average to above-average students, to "Honors" for the academically gifted students. At the high school level, a fourth track existed for college preparatory students.

The decision regarding the placement of particular students was left up to teachers. The teachers, however, relied in part on the students' performance on standardized aptitude tests. The aptitude tests were designed to predict the students' ability in future academic settings. The aptitude tests measured verbal skills, including a student's command of standard English and grammar. The tests emphasized these skills because of the belief that, without high verbal skills, students could not be academically successful. Under the tracking system, African-American and poor children were disproportionately assigned to the lower tracks.

Circuit Court Judge Skelly Wright, sitting as designated judge, found that the tracking system as a whole denied black schoolchildren equal educational opportunities, when compared to those provided to the more affluent white schoolchildren. Wright ordered that the tracking system in operation be abolished and barred any tracking system that failed to bring the great majority of children into the mainstream of public education.[44]

Wright noted that the law has a special concern for minority groups because the judicial branch of government is often the only hope for redressing their legitimate grievances. Wright noted that the disadvantaged poor and minority students are handicapped because they compete in an ethnocentric academic environment in public schools. Public schools mirror American society, which is strongly influenced by white and middle class experiences and values. Nothing is necessarily wrong with this, but it creates barriers apparent in most aptitude tests for lower class and black children. Wright went on, however, to state that:

> Apart from factors related to socio-economic status, there is striking evidence that Negro children undergo a special kind of psychological stress that can have a debilitating effect on academic and test performance. Because of their race and the ever present reminders of being "different," Negro children generally are subject to very serious problems of self-identification. By the time the Negro child is about to enter school he has become very much racially self-conscious, which causes considerable psychological turmoil as he attempts to come to terms with his status as a Negro. He tends to be imbued with a sense of worthlessness, of inferiority, of fear and despair which is transmitted to him primarily through his parents.
>
> In this state of turmoil, many Negro children approach school with the feeling they are entering a strange and alien place that is the property of a white school system or of white society, even though the school may be all-Negro. And when the school *is* all-Negro or predominantly so, this simply reinforces the impressions implanted in the child's mind by his parents, for the school experience is then but

a perpetuation of the segregation he has come to expect in life generally.[45]

From Judge Wright's opinion, one can see that part of his justification for striking down the tracking system employed in the District of Columbia was the desire to improve the educational environment of black schoolchildren. Wright echoed the Supreme Court's conclusion in *Brown* that the black schoolchildren suffered from psychological problems associated with being black. He viewed the schools as their only hope of overcoming these problems. The influence of the school is not confined to how well it can teach the disadvantaged child, but is also significant in shaping the student's emotional and psychological makeup. If the school fails, the disadvantaged child is handicapped both in class and in test taking.[46] The tracking system instituted by the District of Columbia would have deprived the black students of the enriched educational environment they needed in order to elevate themselves beyond the limited horizons of their disadvantaged backgrounds.

(b) *Fifth and later Eleventh Circuits*

Until 1981 the Fifth circuit covered the following former states of the Old Confederacy: Alabama; Florida; Georgia; Louisiana; Mississippi; and Texas. In 1981 the states of Alabama, Florida and Georgia were placed in the newly created Eleventh Circuit. Through the early 1980s the Fifth and Eleventh Circuits were the most active with regard to school desegregation litigation.[47] Thus, they were also the most active circuits in addressing tracking issues.

Two years after *Hobson,* the Fifth Circuit, sitting *en banc* in *Singleton v. Jackson Municipal Separate School District,*[48] rejected a plan to desegregate two school districts, where the district court approved plans to assign students to schools on the basis of achievement test scores. "We pretermit a discussion of the validity per se of a plan based on testing except to hold that testing cannot be employed in any event until unitary school systems have been established."[49] In this context, what the Fifth Circuit meant by "unitary" was the operation pursuant to a desegregation order that was sufficient enough to begin the process of eradicating the vestiges of the prior operation of a dual school system. Unitary was the intermediate state between the operation of a dual school system and the elimination of the vestiges of the prior *de jure* conduct. The Fifth Circuit decision rejecting student assignment based on testing was no doubt motivated by the fact that such an assignment policy would go a long way to perpetuating racially identifiable schools.

Two years later, the Fifth Circuit addressed an appeal from an order of a district court approving a school board plan to desegregate its schools by assigning students to one of two schools based on their scores on the California

Achievement Test. Again, rejecting a plan to assign students to different schools based on their academic abilities, the Fifth Circuit stated that "regardless of the innate validity of testing, it could not be used until a school district had been established as a unitary system. We think at a minimum this means that the district in question must have for several years operated as a unitary system."[50]

In the 1975 case of *McNeal v. Tate,*[51] the Fifth Circuit addressed the issue of tracking within schools, as opposed to using academic abilities to determine school assignments. The Tate County School District replaced its freedom of choice school attendance policies in August 1970 with a system that made pupil assignments to schools based upon residence in attendance zones. However, the School District retained a ten-year-old classroom assignment plan for elementary and junior high school students that was based on faculty-predicted ability skills grouping. Under this system, teachers evaluated the pupil's past performance and recommended the next year's assignment to the principal, who made the final decision. Entering first grade students were placed into sections (classrooms) based on whether they had attended the public preschool program. These student assignments could be adjusted during the school year if the student's performance demonstrated abilities that were better or worse than initially predicted. The result of this student assignment program, however, produced one to four all-black sections in every elementary (1–6) grade, and a few all-white sections in the advanced grades.

The Fifth Circuit rejected the district court's decision to uphold the student assignment procedure. The Fifth Circuit noted that "notwithstanding the fact that tracking assignments are made without regard to race, children who have been the victims of educational discrimination in the dual systems of the past may find themselves resegregated in any school in the district solely because they still wear a badge of their old deprivation—underachievement."[52] The Fifth Circuit went on to hold that, if ability grouping causes segregation in an otherwise unitary system, whether in classrooms or in schools, it is only permitted "if the school district can demonstrate that its assignment method is not based on the present results of past segregation, or will remedy such results through better educational opportunities."[53]

By the mid 1980s, the Fifth and Eleventh Circuits had picked up on the language in *McNeal* that invalidated tracking only when the results were based on past segregation, and followed them through to their logical conclusion. The opinion that best epitomizes the movement of these circuit courts from being suspicious about discriminatory impact of tracking on black schoolchildren to accepting their confinement in lower tracks as the result of legitimate educational decisions is the Eleventh Circuit's 1985 opinion in the case of *Georgia State Conference of Branches of NAACP v. Georgia.*[54] The plaintiffs at the trial court level were thirty-five black schoolchildren who sued state school officials and local school officials in Burke, Coweta, Crisp, Evans, Lee, Liberty, Miller and Vidalia City school districts.[55] The plaintiffs claimed that black students were disproportionately assigned to lower-tracked regular classes and programs for the educable mentally retarded (EMR) in Georgia public schools in a discriminatory manner. The plaintiffs alleged that the use of ability skills grouping in Georgia public schools is intended to achieve, or results in, intra-school racial segregation in violation of the Fourteenth Amendment, among other provisions.

It was undisputed that there were more blacks in the lower ability skills groups and EMR classes in the school districts examined than would be expected from a random distribution given the percentage of black students in each school system. The District Court, however, found in favor of the defendants on all counts. Applying the test articulated by the Fifth Circuit in *McNeal v. Tate,* the District Court concluded that (1) the plaintiffs failed to prove that the disparity in the lower ability skills groups is the result of the present effects of past discrimination; and (2) the local defendants' ability skills classification schemes serve to remedy the past results of prior segregation through better educational opportunities for black students.

The plaintiffs representing the Vidalia City and Burke, Coweta and Lee County school systems appealed to the Eleventh Circuit. The Eleventh Circuit reaffirmed the position taken by the Fifth Circuit in *McNeal v. Tate.* It drew a distinction in how legal challenges to ability skills grouping operates, with regard to two different types of school districts undergoing desegregation. The Eleventh Circuit noted the importance of examining the school district's history of segregation. Ability skills grouping "may perpetuate the effects of past discrimination by resegregating, on the basis of ability, students who were previously segregated in inferior schools on the basis of race or national origin." In addition, ability skills grouping, when coupled with a relatively recent history of discrimination, could be probative evidence of a discriminatory motive. If a school district has recently instituted a school desegregation plan and seeks to use ability skills grouping, then it has just embarked on its unitary phase. These school districts would be like the ones that were discussed above, when the Fifth Circuit first addressed tracking. For these districts, ability skills grouping that would produce a disparate impact on minority students is clearly traceable to the operation of the previous dual school system. To recognize the poor academic performance of these black students would simply be to lock them into the cycle of poor social environment that they had always experienced. The school systems involved in this litigation, however, fell into a different category. They ceased operating dual school systems in 1970–71 and, therefore, had been unitary for a long enough period of time that none of the current students in these school districts would have attended a dual school system. Because of the passage of time, the Eleventh Circuit concluded that the ability skills grouping was not based on past segregation.

The Eleventh Circuit's holding meant that, under the *McNeal* test, a school system that had operated under a valid desegregation decree for twelve years (the time it takes for a student to go from first enrolling in school to graduation from high school) could institute ability skills grouping. This could be done despite the tendency of such groupings to disproportionately assign black students to the lower ability skills groups. It could also be done even if the school district had not yet eradicated all of the vestiges of its prior *de jure* conduct. Thus, the disparate negative effect of tracking on black students is not understood as traced to the present effects of the past operation of a dual school system, but the unfortunate result of the institution of racially-neutral, legitimate, educational practices and procedures.[56]

Another example where the Fifth Circuit upheld tracking by a public school system still under a desegregation order was in the 1989 case of *Quarles v. Oxford Municipal Separate School District.*[57] The ability skills grouping system used in Oxford, Mississippi public schools placed students in grades three through eight into high, middle and low groups for instruction in language arts and mathematics, based on their performance on the Stanford Achievement Test scores in those areas. With the exception of those courses, the students were grouped heterogeneously in other classes. It was undisputed that white students were highly concentrated in the upper level groups and black students in the lower groups. The Fifth Circuit, however, agreed with the district court's finding that Oxford's ability grouping plan provided several opportunities for movement among ability levels during the school year and students could be moved on the basis of their performance on the Stanford Achievement Test, which was given once a year. According to the court, there was an impressive degree of movement among ability skills levels by black, as well as, white students. Thus, the ability skills grouping in grades three through eight did not violate the equal protection clause.

At the high school level, the schools operated advanced placement or accelerated courses which were racially identifiable as white. But Oxford allowed students to choose whether to enroll in the accelerated classes. The Fifth Circuit concluded that under these circumstances the fact that there are more white students than black students enrolled in the accelerated classes cannot be attributed to racial discrimination.[58] The Fifth Circuit appeared to be resting this conclusion on the notion that the black children were choosing not to enroll in the more rigorous academic classes. The Fifth Circuit also rejected testimony of anti-tracking educational authority, Jeanne Oakes, and concluded that tracking was an issue that was best left to educators than to courts.

The Fifth and Eleventh Circuit's treatment of the issue of tracking mirrored the same change in background assumptions for interpreting the equal protection clause that was apparent in the Supreme Court's school desegregation jurisprudence. The Fifth Circuit, during its opinions in the late 1960s and early 1970s, rejected ability skills grouping because acceptance of this educational practice would simply freeze black students into the same educational environment that needed to be enriched if they were to overcome their handicaps related to being black. But by the time the Fifth and the Eleventh Circuits had reached the mid to late 1980s, a shift had occurred. The Fifth and Eleventh Circuits begin to uphold tracking systems, despite their disparate impact of confining black students to the lower tracks. These educational results were viewed as the effects of racially-neutral academic judgments.

(c) *Other Tracking Cases*

Not all courts have provided deference to tracking systems during the latter stages of this nation's desegregation process. For example, in *Simmons v. Hooks,*[59] the District Court struck down a tracking system. The District Court found that the system of ability skills grouping was adopted in 1970, shortly after termination of its dual school system.[60] The District Court assumed that the tracking system was not the product of intentional discrimination. Since the Eighth Circuit did not have a tracking case precedent, it applied the Fifth Circuit's *McNeal v. Tate* test. But it did not apply the test in the way the Fifth and Eleventh Circuits did. The District Court concluded that, since the ability skills grouping system was not instituted by the school district until blacks and whites started attending the same schools, the students in the low-ability group's parents had attended racially segregated schools. As a result, the racial segregation that occurred in the tracking system constituted the present effect of past discrimination. Thus, according to the District Court, even though the present case focused on the tracking that occurred in the 1992–93 academic year, some twenty years after the school system had ended its operation of a dual school system, the disproportionate placement of black students in the lower tracks was traceable to the operation of the former dual school system.

While the District Court in Arkansas struck down the tracking system it examined, the Seventh Circuit, in its 1997 decision in *People Who Care v. Rockford Board of Education School District,*[61] upheld the tracking system it considered in a school desegregation case. The District Court judge found that the Rockford School District had intentionally discriminated against black and Latino students in violation of the equal protection clause.[62] The inference of intentional discrimination was drawn primarily from disparities in educational achievement between non-Hispanic white students on the one hand and minority students on the other. The District Court judge concluded that the cause of the achievement gap derived from the school district's failure to take effective steps to prevent its schools from becoming all-white or all-minority. The school district accepted the determination of liability. The parties consented to have a magistrate judge preside over the remedial phase of the litigation with power to enter judgment.

The evidence in front of the magistrate demonstrated that there were significant and long-lasting disparities as measured by standardized test scores between the achievement level of minority students compared to majority students in the district.[63] The magistrate acknowledged that the achievement gaps between minority and non-minority students can be caused by a number of factors. But some of the achievement gaps were the result of the school district's intentional discriminatory conduct. The magistrate found that the cause of the achievement disparities attributable to the school district were the school district's student assignment practices that led to racial isolation of minority students in different schools, discriminatory tracking practices where minority students were often placed in lower achieving tracks because of their race and disparities in facilities of schools where the minority students were assigned. The magistrate noted, however, that segregation within schools was the most pervasive student enrollment problem in the school district. African-American and Latino students were consistently enrolled in disproportionate numbers in the lower tracks, while non-Hispanic white students, at all grade levels, were disproportionately assigned to the high ability skills groupings. The magistrate also noted that, once placed in a lower track, it was often difficult, if not impossible, to change into a higher track. But the most troubling aspect was that many minority students who scored well above the national mean on standardized tests were intentionally put in racially-identifiable, low ability skills tracks, while low or average scoring non-Hispanic white students were often placed in disproportionately non-Hispanic white higher tracks.

In 1996 the magistrate judge issued the comprehensive remedial order. Part of the comprehensive remedial order required that student school assignments in each school in the district be within 15 percent of the district wide percentage of minority students at a particular grade configuration. In addition, numerous provisions in the comprehensive remedial order addressed student assignments within schools. In order to prevent the reoccurrence of in-school segregation, the magistrate ordered that most of the classes and programs be within 5 percent of the percentage of minority students at a given grade level within each school. This percentage limitation also applied to the core courses and honors courses at the district's high schools, but not the elective courses. Even though black students constituted 51 percent of the students placed in special education (compared to constituting only 25 percent of the student body districtwide), the magistrate excluded special education placement from its anti-tracking provisions. While the gifted and talented program was exempted from the in-school segregation requirement, the magistrate ordered the gifted and talented program to have an overall student enrollment within 15 percent of the districtwide minority ratio for each grade configuration. The magistrate also ordered that, for the grade level years in which students entered the various gifted and talented programs, the percentage of minority students admitted had to at least equal their districtwide percentage. Another provision in the order limited minority enrollment in compensatory (that is remedial) education to within 5 percent of the percentage of minority students as well. In adopting this particular provision, the magistrate stated that any remedial program that is all or mostly minority reinforces the culture of this school district that negatively stereotypes the minority student.

In its opinion addressing the appeal of the comprehensive remedial order, the Seventh Circuit strenuously objected to the anti-tracking requirements. The Seventh Circuit noted that tracking is a controversial educational policy and lawyers and judges are not competent to resolve the controversy. The Seventh Circuit chastised the lower court, stating that the myth of the legal profession's omnicompetence was exploded long ago. According to the Seventh Circuit,

> [t]o abolish tracking is to say to bright kids, whether white or black, that they have to go at a slower pace than they're capable of; it is to say to the parents of the brighter kids that their children don't really belong in the public school system; and it is to say to the slower kids, of whatever race, that they may have difficulty keeping up, because the brighter kids may force the pace of the class.[64]

The Seventh Circuit struck down the provision in the comprehensive remedial order that limited the percentage of minority students who could be enrolled in compensatory (that is remedial) education programs. These programs are designed largely, although not entirely, for minority students, because they have, on average, more educational deficits. The Seventh Circuit rejected the district court's conclusion that the limit was justified because disproportionate assignment of minority students to these programs would foster unfavorable stereotypes.

The Seventh Circuit stated that rather than prohibit tracking, the district court should forbid the school district—on pain of contempt if the prohibition is flouted—to track students in any way other than based upon criteria that have been validated as objective and nonracist. According to the Seventh Circuit, this form of remedy is proportioned to the violation and duly respectful of the autonomy of educators. The Seventh Circuit did not shy away from the reality that tracking would segregate classrooms in otherwise desegregated schools. It noted that the well-known correlation between race and academic performance makes tracking, even when implemented in accordance with strictly objective criteria, a pretty effective segregator.

The Seventh Circuit's treatment of tracking for a school system undergoing desegregation conforms with the general drift of courts regarding the issue of ability skills grouping by public schools. Rather than rejecting a tracking system which disproportionately placed blacks in lower tracks as was done by many federal courts in the late 1960s and early 1970s, the Seventh Circuit accepted tracking as a legitimate educational strategy even in the beginning of the process to remedy the school district's prior unconstitutional conduct. The disparate confinement of black and Latino students in the lower ability skills tracks is presumed to simply be the unfortunate result of the application of race-neutral academic judgments that do not raise any equal protection violations.[65]

B. High-Stakes Testing

This subsection will first start with a general discussion about high-stakes testing. High-stakes testing uses standardized examinations to measure whether students are competent in given areas, usually reading and math. The difference between high-stakes testing and the use of other standardized exams by public school officials is that these tests are used to make crucial decisions concerning whether students will advance to the next grade level or receive their high school diploma. These tests may also be used to measure the performance of schools and, thereby, determine whether a given school will receive an academic award or be subject to negative sanctions including state takeover. Next, this subsection will discuss the implications of high-stakes testing for the educational opportunities of African-American schoolchildren. Standardized tests, including high stakes testings, have long been attacked for their negative impact on black schoolchildren. Black schoolchildren typically do not perform as well as their non-Hispanic white counterparts on standardized tests. This subsection will conclude with a look at legal challenges that have been raised to the impact of high-stakes testing on students. Because of the importance of the interest involved, legal challenges to high stakes testing have generally centered on attacks on high school exit examinations.

1. General Discussion about High-Stakes Testing

While standardized tests should not be the only criteria used to determine whether students are learning in public schools, the importance of these tests in determining academic success is undeniable. Despite objections to their use, standardized tests have become the measure for much of our determination of academic success and ability.

High-stakes testing is growing in importance with the passage, in 2001, of the No Child Left Behind Act (NCLB), supported by President Bush.[66] NCLB requires states, through the 2004–05 school year, to administer assessments at least once during grades 3 through 5, 6 through 9 and 10 through 12. But, beginning no later than the 2005–06 school year, tests must be given in each grade from 3 through 8, and at least once between grades 10 and 12. NCLB requires schools to send reports of individual student performance to parents. NCLB also requires states to report the results of their assessment tests publicly. States must arrange the results by race, gender, English language proficiency, disability and socioeconomic status. Under NCLB, schools and school districts must demonstrate adequate yearly progress in improving the test scores of disadvantaged students. A system of sanctions and rewards must be developed in order to hold schools and school districts accountable.

Proponents of high-stakes tests assert that these tests are designed to assess the skills important to understanding a student's comprehension of various subject materials or to a student's success in school. It is argued by proponents of the tests that this can not always accurately be done by focusing solely on grades because of the wide variations that exist in different courses taught in different schools by different teachers. Proponents also argue that these tests motivate students to learn and teachers to teach. The tests provide a definitive standard for schools and students that can be used to monitor student and school performance. Sanctions placed on students who fail the test provides them with the incentive to take their studies seriously. Sanctions or rewards for schools and teachers will motivate them to provide the best educational environment possible for the students in their charge. The motivation and the accountability that such tests provide are viewed as essential tools to increase academic performance. Increased academic performance ensures that the students are better prepared for higher education or future employment. In addition, proponents also argue that testing helps to standardize educational materials by assuring that the test measure the content of what students are taught. High-stakes testing is thus the best way to assure fairness to all students, including minority students, in a given state across different educational settings.[67]

There is another argument advanced for requiring students to pass a high school exit exam as a condition of receiving a high school diploma. A high school diploma is an educational credential by which the conferring institution certifies that the recipient possesses all of the knowledge and skills expected of individuals who have been exposed to a rigorous academic discipline. Thus, the state has a legitimate interest in attempting to ensure the value of its high school diplomas. High-stakes testing can be used to effectuate this objective.

Opponents of these examinations argue that high-stakes testing places too much emphasis on a single test and that student achievement cannot be accurately determined with such a narrow measure. In addition, testing leads to teachers spending too much time teaching material covered on the exam, rather than teaching students problem solving skills. Teachers teach the students how to choose the correct item on the exam without teaching the larger concepts, which the test is supposed to encourage students to learn. This has a detrimental impact on the education process because it restricts the type of learning to which students are exposed. A report released by the National Academy of Science/National Research Council stated that "schooling that too closely resembles training, as in preparation for testing, *cannot* accomplish the task the nation has set for itself, namely, the development of adaptive and educated citizens for this new millennium."[68] Tests are especially detrimental to school districts serving large numbers of poor and minority children, because they are apt to score poorly on standardized tests. Thus, their educational opportunities are restricted, not expanded, by a regime of high-stakes testing.

2. Implications of High-Stakes Testing for African-American Schoolchildren

High-stakes testing, including the requirement that students pass a high school exit exam as a prerequisite to obtaining a high school diploma, could have serious adverse consequences for black schoolchildren. Proponents of the test assert that by creating a competitive environment for public schools, this will improve education, particularly for urban-minority children. But three factors combine to produce lower stardarized test scores for black students. Test scores will often depend upon socioeconomic factors that will clearly work to disadvantage African-American students as a group because of the lower income and wealth of black families when compared to non-Hispanic whites. In addition, African-Americans have been victimized in the past, if not in the present, by reduced educational opportunities. The result of which continues to negatively impact their performance on standardized tests. Finally, a built-in cultural bias that favors middle-class non-Hispanic whites in the standardized tests will contribute to lower test scores and passage rates by African-American students.

When these tests are used to determine who is to be promoted to the next grade, they could also further increase the dropout rates of black and other minority students.[69] "[R]etention in grade is the single most reliable predictor of a student eventually dropping out of school."[70] Because most high-stakes testing regimes are of recent origin, it is still too early to tell if high-stakes tests will produce enough improvement in academic performance by black schoolchildren to offset the expected higher failure rates than non-Hispanic whites.

3. Equal Protection Challenges to High-Stakes Testing

Because of the importance of a high school diploma, high school exit exams have generated a significant amount of litigation.[71] The following states currently use high-school graduation exit exams to grant or withhold diplomas: Alabama, Florida, Georgia, Indiana, Louisiana, Maryland, Minnesota, Mississippi, Nevada, New Jersey, New Mexico, New York, North Carolina, Ohio, South Carolina, Tennessee, Texas and Virginia. There are currently nine states that are in the process of developing high school graduation exams: Alaska, Arizona, California, Delaware, Hawaii, Massachusetts, Utah, Washington and Wisconsin.[72]

Debra P. v. Turlington[73] was the first case to address Fourteenth Amendment challenges to high-stakes testing. This decision dealt with the requirement in Florida that students pass a high school exit exam as a prerequisite to receiving their high school diploma. The Florida Legislature enacted the Educational Accountability Act of 1976. The purpose of the legislation was to provide a system of accountability for education in the state and to ensure that each student was afforded similar educational opportunities regardless of geographic location. The legislature established three standards for graduation from Florida public schools. First, students were required to complete a minimum number of credits for graduation. Second, students were to master certain basic skills. Finally, in order to receive a high school diploma, students must perform satisfactorily in functional literacy as determined by the State Board of Education. In 1978, the Act was amended to require passage of a functional literacy examination prior to receipt of a state high school diploma.

During the Summer of 1977, the Florida Department of Education distributed to all Florida public schools the basic skill and functional literacy objectives that students had to meet. Public school teachers were aware of the objectives of the functional literacy examination four months in advance of the first administration of the test, but only two months were available for instruction in the application of the skills. In the Fall, 1977 administration of the exam, 78 percent of the black students, in contrast with only 25 percent of the white students, failed one or more sections of the exam. Almost 75 percent of the 4,480 black students, in contrast to only 25 percent of the white students, taking the test for the second time in the Fall of 1978, failed one or both sections. The results of the third administration in Spring, 1979, were released during trial. Those results showed that 60 percent of the blacks taking the mathematics exam for the third time failed, as compared with only 36 percent of the whites. By May, 1979, when students were to have passed the test in order to receive their high school diploma, 3,466, or 20% of the black students still had not passed the test, compared with 1,342, or 2% of the white students.

Litigation was brought on behalf of the black students who failed the test. They challenged the right of the state to impose the passing of the examination as a condition to the receipt of a high school diploma. Among the claims raised by the plaintiffs were due process and equal protection challenges. The District Court found that the test violated both the due process clause[74] and the equal protection clause and enjoined its use until the 1982–83 school year. On the equal protection challenge, the District Court noted that until 1967 Florida had operated a dual school system, segregating students on the basis of race. From 1967 to 1971, segregation persisted in Florida schools, and predominantly black schools remained inferior in physical facilities, course offerings, instructional materials and equipment. The Florida Commissioner of Education, Ralph D. Turlington, admitted during the litigation that the failures of the black students taking the high school graduation exam could be attributed, in part, to the unequal education they received during the "dual schools" period. The record clearly indicated that appellants were aware of the possibility that more blacks than whites would fail the test.

The Fifth Circuit upheld the trial court's injunction not to use the test before the 1982–83 school year. The students in the high school class of 1983 would be the first to have attended schools operating under desegregation remedies for all twelve years of their educational careers. But the Fifth Circuit remanded the case back to the trial court to reexamine the issue of the vestiges of past discrimination on twelfth grade black students. On remand, the District Court reviewed the issue of vestiges of the past discrimination. The District Court noted that more than 90 percent of black students in the Class of 1983 passed the test, including 99.5 percent passing the communications portion of the test and 91 percent passing the mathematics portion. However, while black students constituted only 20 percent of the Class of 1983, 57 percent of the students who failed the test were black. Nevertheless, the District Court lifted the injunction preventing the diploma sanction for the Class of 1983.

The District Court concluded that the diploma sanction was needed to remedy the present effects of past segregation in Florida's schools. Although the sanction is to deny the student the diploma, according to the District Court the diploma denial reflects adversely on the teachers and administrators of the school system responsible for the student's education. Thus, the diploma sanction will motivate teachers and administrators, as well as students, to perform better.

The case was appealed. Since Florida was one of the state's in the Fifth Circuit that was placed in the newly created Eleventh Circuit in 1981, the Eleventh Circuit heard the appeal. In its 1984 decision, the Eleventh Circuit[75] noted that it believed it was clear that teachers and administrators would work to avoid the stigma attached to their students failing the exam. As a result, the high school examination graduation requirement would tend to remedy any lingering lower expectations on the part of teachers. The remarkable improvement in the high school graduation examination pass rate among black students over the previous six years was offered as proof that use of the test as a diploma sanction would be effective in overcoming the effects of past segregation. The Eleventh Circuit, therefore, affirmed the finding that the use of the high school examination requirement as a diploma sanction would help remedy vestiges of past discrimination. The Eleventh Circuit acknowledged "a heavy sense of discomfort over the unfairness *if* discriminatory vestiges (albeit much attenuated) had in fact caused a student to fail the test. However, that apparent unfairness would be outweighed by the demonstrated effect of the diploma sanction in remedying the greater unfairness of functional illiteracy."[76]

In *GI Forum v. Texas Education Agency*,[77] a federal District Court addressed a challenge to another high school examination graduation requirement. Texas required students to pass the Texas' Assessment of Academic Skills (TAAS) test in order to receive their high school diplomas. A disproportionately high number of black and Latino students failed the tests. But in challenging the test, they did not even raise an equal protection challenge based on intentional discrimination. Instead they challenged the validity of the test under the disparate impact regulations of Title VI (a challenge that has been foreclosed by Supreme Court decisions in *Alexander v. Sandoval*[78] and *Gonzaga University v. Doe*[79]). The District Court concluded that under the Title VI regulations, a prima facie case of discrimination can be made by demonstrating a disparate impact on minority students from the use of the TAAS. When so done, the burden of production switches to the educational authorities to produce evidence that the use of the test to determine receipt of high school diplomas was justified by an educational necessity. If that is done, the plaintiff may still ultimately prevail, if they can demonstrate that an equally effective alternative practice could result in less racial disproportionality while still serving the articulated need.

The District Court agreed that the plaintiffs challenging the graduation requirement made out a *prima facie* case of disparate impact discrimination. The Texas educational authorities then responded that the articulated goals of the implementation of the TAAS requirement are to hold schools, students and teachers accountable for education and to ensure that all Texas students receive the same adequate learning opportunities. The District Court concluded that the TAAS test bears a manifest relationship to these legitimate goals. In response, the plaintiffs sought to discharge their obligation to provide an equally effective alternative with a smaller disparate impact. Among the approaches suggested by the plaintiffs was to employ a sliding-scale system. This system would allow educators to use high academic grades to compensate for a student's low test performance and to use outstanding test scores to compensate for lower grades. The District Court concluded, however, that the

> [p]laintiffs failed to present evidence that this, or other alternatives, could sufficiently motivate students to perform to their highest ability. In addition, and perhaps more importantly, the present use of the TAAS test motivates schools and teachers to provide an adequate and fair education, at least of the minimum skills required by the State, to all students.[80]

Thus, the District Court concluded that the plaintiffs produced no alternative that adequately addressed the goal of systemic accountability. As a result, the use of TASS survived a discrimination challenge brought under the much tougher disparate impact test.

4. Conclusion to High-Stakes Testing

There have not been many reported cases by African-American students raising equal protection challenges to high-stakes testing. However, the same shift that occurred regarding tracking or achievement skills grouping that was noted earlier can be seen in the few cases addressing high-stakes testing. When the Florida high school exit exam was first addressed in the late 1970s, the federal courts rejected its use to deny high school diplomas to blacks students, in part, because of the presumption that black schoolchildren could not be expected to achieve. Even though black students continue to fail high school exit exams at a larger rate than white students, later court decisions have upheld the use of these exams. When the Eleventh Circuit upheld the Florida graduation examination in its 1984 opinion, it did not do so through changing the background assumptions for interpreting the equal protection rights of black schoolchildren to those consistent with Colorblind Individualism. Rather the Eleventh Circuit upheld the use of the Florida graduation examination requirement consistent with the background assumptions of Traditional Americanism which viewed black children as having suffered through segregation. According to the Eleventh Circuit, the examination requirement could be justified because it improved the educational opportunities of black students despite the disproportionate failure rates. In other words, despite the disparate failure rates, black students were better off with the graduation requirements than they were without them.

The equal protection justifications of the Eleventh Circuit can be contrasted with those accepted sixteen years later by the federal District Court in *GI Forum* in addressing discrimination under the Title VI disparate impact regulations. The District Court in *GI Forum* reached the same conclusion as the Eleventh Circuit did in its 1984 decision but it employed a different rationale to reach that decision. The District Court in *GI Forum* did not rest its judgement not on the benefit for black schoolchildren to be derived from the high school graduation requirement. Rather it rested its opinion on the fact that the use of the TAAS test motivates schools and teachers to provide an adequate and fair education to all students in Texas, not just minority students. Further, the *GI Forum* court was applying the disparate impact regulation of Title VI, not the equal protection clause. The plaintiffs in *GI Forum* viewed their ability to establish discriminatory intent—and thereby succeed in an equal protection challenge—as so small that they did not even pursue it.

C. Equal Protection Challenges to the Educational Curriculum

Challenges to decisions regarding curricular material to present to students is another area where African-American schoolchildren have generally failed to establish violations of their equal protection rights. In *Grimes v. Sobol,*[81] African-American plaintiffs brought an action alleging that the New York City public schools used a culturally biased curriculum in violation of the equal protection clause.[82] The plaintiffs argued that the curriculum systematically distorted and demeaned the role of African-Americans and excluded the existence, contributions and participation of blacks in various aspects of the world, American culture, sciences, history, arts and other areas of human endeavor. The plaintiffs apparently styled their allegation of the harm generated by the curricular bias to mimic the harm that the Supreme Court stated was produced by segregation in *Brown v. Board of Education.* According to the plaintiffs the use of such a curriculum resulted in emotional and psychological harm to black children and, thereby, negatively affected their self-esteem and ability to learn.

The District Court seemed willing to concede that the curriculum in New York City's public schools was culturally biased and, hence, harmful to minorities, including African-Americans. The District Court noted, however, that in analyzing this issue for the purpose of an equal protection violation, it is not the effect of the curriculum that is determinative. Rather, the plaintiffs must allege that the adoption of the curriculum was motivated because of, and not in spite of, its detrimental effect on African-American students. Discriminatory purpose cannot be inferred from the state's awareness of the detrimental effects or consequences of its culturally biased curriculum content, nor from its conscious refusal to adopt Afro-centric educational initiatives.

The District Court went on to note that the curriculum employed in the New York City public schools was adopted because of legitimate pedagogical considerations. Thus, its adoption was not motivated by discriminatory intent. As a result, the negative impact of such a curriculum on black students is an unfortunate consequence of racially neutral governmental action.

Another case that rejected an equal protection challenge to a curricular decision was the Ninth Circuit opinion in *Monteiro v. Tempe Union High School District.*[83] In this case, the parent of a black schoolchild challenged the requirement that her daughter be compelled to read two classic literary works-the novel *The Adventures of Huckleberry Finn,* by Mark Twain and the short story *A Rose for Emily,* by William Faulkner. The complaint, brought by Kathy Monteiro on behalf of her daughter, Jane Doe, alleged that each of these literary works contains repeated use of the profane, insulting and racially derogatory term "nigger." The complaint alleged that Doe and similarly situated African-American students suffered psychological injuries and lost educational opportunities due to the required reading of the literary works. It further alleged that the assignment of the literary works created and contributed to a racially hostile educational environment, including increased racial harassment by other students. Finally, the complaint alleged that, by its conduct, the school district intentionally discriminated against Doe. The complaint requested a temporary and permanent injunction that would prohibit the defendants from committing similar unlawful acts in the future. It did not, however, seek the exclusion of the literary works from a voluntary reading list or from classroom discussions where Doe, or similarly situated African American students, were not held as a captive student audience or consigned to a separate and unequal educational environment.

The District Court dismissed the complaint, concluding that it did not state a claim under the equal protection clause because the complaint did not contain specific allegations of facts necessary to sustain a claim of discriminatory intent. The plaintiff then sought to submit an amended complaint which contained additional allegations regarding the hostile racial environment at the school. The amended complaint alleged that Doe and other African-American students were subjected to oral racial harassment by being called "nigger" by their white classmates and by the use of graffiti. This type of harassment existed prior to the discussion of the literary works, but increased as a result of their assignments as required readings. Finally, the amended complaint alleged that the school district, when notified of incidents of racial harassment, refused to accept the complaints or take any appropriate remedial measures regarding them. The District Court, however, rejected the effort to file the amended complaint. The District Court concluded that it failed to state a claim as well.

Monteiro appealed to the Ninth Circuit. The Ninth Circuit analyzed the request to prevent the use of the literary works separate from the argument regarding the existence of a racially hostile learning environment. With regard to the effort to prohibit the use of the books, the Ninth Circuit noted in its opinion that, according to the American Library Association, Twain's book is the most frequently banned book in the United States. The reason is because the book contains the word "nigger" some 215 times.[84] After expressing concern about the use of the word "nigger" in the book, however, the Ninth Circuit also rejected the challenge to its use. The Court expressed sympathy with the plaintiff's position. It recognized that books and words, are powerful tools that can convey extremely injurious messages. Nevertheless, the Ninth Circuit concluded that the allegations that a school required a book to be read and then refused to remove it from the curriculum was not enough to establish an equal protection violation. "[A]ssignment of a literary work determined to have intrinsic educational value by the duly authorized school authorities cannot constitute the type of discriminatory conduct prohibited by the Fourteenth Amendment. . . , regardless of the fact that the work may be deemed to contain racist ideas or language."[85]

These two cases demonstrate the difficulty of challenging curricular material which African-American schoolchildren might find objectionable. Both courts were willing to accept that the curricular decisions would negatively impact black schoolchildren. However, the motivation for the curricular decisions was not discriminatory, but based on legitimate educational justifications. As a result, despite the potential harm to the educational opportunities of black schoolchildren, there was not an equal protection violation.

Conclusion

This Chapter has extended the analysis of legal decisions interpreting the equal protection clause that was discussed in Chapter Seven to issues other than student school assignments. The same change in the background assumptions for interpreting the equal protection rights of black schoolchildren noted in Chapter Seven can also be seen with regard to the legal treatment of other educational policies and practices. With regard to other educational policies and practices, this shift generated two significant consequences that are relevant to the current legal situation facing black schoolchildren. First, programs and policies, which state and public educational officials can employ to attack the continuing racial academic gaps in educational performance, are generally limited to those that do not employ racial or ethnic classifications. The Supreme Court has held that when government seeks to use racial classifications, their use must survive strict scrutiny. While this is not a true colorblind approach to the Constitution, it is a near approximation that in many educational circumstances will function the same way. Chapter Seven pointed to decisions by lower federal courts that have severely restricted the use of racial classifications to promote integrated public schools. This Chapter extended that discussion by focusing on the Supreme Court's opinion in *Wygant v. Jackson Board of Education.* In that case, the Court rejected the argument that using racial classifications to limit layoffs of minority teachers in order to ensure adequate role models for minority students was a compelling state interest. Since the use of racial classifications must survive strict scrutiny, strategies to advance the educational interest of black schoolchildren today must rely heavily upon racially neutral policies and programs.

The second consequence of this shift in background assumptions is that from an equal protection standpoint unconstitutional discrimination exists only when governmental actions are motivated by discriminatory intent. Since it is the motives that determine whether the institution of various educational policies and practices are unconstitutionally discriminatory, the discriminatory effect of educational policies and practices motivated by legitimate educational concerns do not create an equal protection violation. The negative disparate impact on black schoolchildren from policies and practices motivated by legitimate educational concerns are now understood as an unfortunate side effect of racially-neutral educational decision making. Equal protection lawsuits calling into question racially neutral educational policies and procedures, which have a disparate racial impact, generally will no longer succeed. Thus, many legal strategies for attacking racially neutral educational policies and practices, which had a disparate negative impact on the educational opportunities of black schoolchildren that were promising after the Supreme Court's opinion in *Brown,* have run their course.

Chapter Nine

Why Increased School Choice is a Growing Educational Reform Movement in the Post-Desegregation Era

There are three major considerations influencing the direction of public educational reform directed towards increasing the educational opportunities for black schoolchildren. First, three "achievement gaps" among American schoolchildren have proved especially persistent. Low-income children, on average, score lower on standardized tests than their middle- and upper-income counterparts. Black, Latino and Native American children, on average, score lower than non-Hispanic white and Asian children. Children attending urban public schools, on average, score lower than children attending schools in the suburbs. Children with all three of these characteristics score on average lowest of all. Given the disproportionate number of African-American schoolchildren attending predominantly minority, low-income, urban schools—as a racial group—they congregate at the losing end of America's educational performance spectrum not only in regards to performance on standardized tests, but also other measures of academic achievement. Section I will discuss the racial achievement gaps on standardized tests, high school dropout rates, grade retention rates and tracking or ability skills grouping practices. In addition, it will also point out the underrepresentation of black public school teachers when compared to the percentage of black public school students.

The last two considerations are tied to federal court interpretations of the equal protection clause. The second consideration involves increasing levels of racial separation in public schools over the past fifteen years. The scope and extent of school desegregation was principally the product of the Supreme Court's interpretations of the equal protection clause. As discussed in detail in

Chapter Seven, federal court decisions interpreting the equal protection clause are the predominant factor in the resegregation of public schools. Figures from the Harvard Civil Rights Project show that the percentage of African-American students attending majority-white schools has decreased from its all time high of 37.1% in 1980–81 to 31.2% in 1996–97 school year to the 28.4% in 2000. Increasing segregation is also apparent in the percentage of black students in hyper-segregated schools (schools where the student population is 90% or more minority). Their percentage in these schools has increased from its low point of 32.5% in 1986–87 school year, to 35% in 1996–97, to 37.4% in 2000.[1]

Third, over the past thirty years federal courts have shifted the background assumptions for interpreting the equal protection rights of black schoolchildren. This shift in the background pattern of understanding of equal protection challenges was discussed in both Chapter Seven—which addressed student school assignments—and Chapter Eight—which focused on educational policies and practices other than student school assignments. There are two significant consequences derived from this shift. First, the determination of unconstitutional discrimination is based upon the motives that generate given educational policies and practices, not their discriminatory effect. Educational policies and practices motivated by legitimate educational considerations that have a disparate negative effect on the educational opportunities of black schoolchildren are not unconstitutionally discriminatory. The second consequence of this shift is to limit the programs and policies that legislators and public school authorities can implement to attack the racial achievement gaps. Legislators and educators must generally seek to adopt racially neutral policies and practices to attack the continuing racial achievement gap.

Given the above considerations, politicians and educational strategists who want to reduce the existing racial achievement gaps are increasingly forced to argue for policies and programs that are race-neutral and, therefore, not specifically targeted to the problems of black schoolchildren. One of the most significant racially neutral educational reform movements sweeping the country is increasing the educational choices of parents. By choosing where to reside, parents exercise a tremendous amount of choice over what school their child attends. One of the major considerations in choosing where to live is the quality of the available schools. Families with financial means are not only able to place their children in private schools, but they are also able to leave a given public school district by moving to another school district. Due to this mobility, maintaining excellent public schools is central to most affluent communities' appeal to those who can afford to live there and central to moderate-income communities' strategies to attract new tax-paying residents. In districts where people have the means to choose whether to leave or stay (i.e. the more affluent districts), the public schools are predictably among the best. Thus, in terms of residential choice, the affluent parents of schoolchildren reap tremendous educational benefits for their children that come from their considerable capacity to choose the school their children attend. As Professors James Ryan and Michael Heise recently pointed out, "suburbanites are generally satisfied with the public schools their children attend and thus are not supportive of school choice."[2]

Section II of this Chapter discusses the movement to increase school choice. Under increased choice proposals all parents in a given school district, given school or schools in a given district, a given area of a given school district or below a particular income level are provided the limited opportunity to choose the school their child attends. Choice is thus granted to parents with reference to a qualification unrelated to the race or ethnicity of the child. But low-income parents of minority schoolchildren in urban areas are the ones who have the least capacity to exercise the primary forms of school choice by moving into neighborhoods with good schools or by paying for private education. Increasing racially neutral forms of school choice, therefore, should disproportionately advantage these parents and their children.

Although significant differences exist between public school choice and public funding of private education, also called school vouchers, both are born out of the same concerns. Advocates for increased choice generally assert that it will improve educational achievement, particularly of low-income, urban, minority students in a number of ways. Increased choice creates a competitive environment that forces schools to compete for students. Thus, increased school choice should produce new and innovative schools, including those that are particularly effective at responding to the educational needs of low-income, urban, minority students. In a competitive environment the schools that cannot adequately educate the students in their charge will not survive. In addition, the programs and policies of schools that are effective will be copied by other schools. Thus, establishing a competitive environment for schools should increase the educational performance of the students currently attending the worse performing schools.

I. Current Academic Performance of African-American Students and Condition of Black School Teachers

In almost all important indicia of academic success, African-American schoolchildren lag behind their non-Hispanic white counterparts. African-American schoolchildren tend to underperform their non-Hispanic white counterparts on standardized tests. African-American schoolchildren are more likely to drop out of school before obtaining their high school diploma than their non-Hispanic white counterparts. During their academic careers, black schoolchildren are also twice as likely to be retained in a grade. In addition, black students are overrepresented in the lower academic tracks or achievement skills groups and underrepresented in the higher academic tracks or achievement skills groups. Finally, before the Supreme Court's opinion fifty years ago, black students were typically taught by black public school teachers. These teachers could serve as important role models of academic success for the students. Now, there is a severe shortage of African-American school teachers in comparison to the percentage of black students. In the wake of the waning of school desegregation, it is clear that fifty years after the Court's opinion in *Brown* this society is far from achieving the promised land of racial parity in academic achievement. Unfortunately, the realization of this dream is not even visible on the educational horizon.

A. Performance on Standardized Tests

Standardized tests have long been attacked for their negative impact on educational opportunities of African-Americans. As early as 1969, the Association of Black Psychologists called for a complete moratorium on all testing of black people until more equitable tests could be developed.[3] The NAACP was a signatory of a "Statement to Urge a Ban on Standardized Testing of Young Children" in 1980.[4] In 1991, the NAACP also joined with a coalition of anti-testing organizations to protest federal achievement testing proposed by President George Bush.[5] Elaine Jones, the former Director-Counsel of the NAACP Legal Defense and Educational Fund, has compared high-stakes testing to the literacy tests that were used to prevent blacks from voting during the era of segregation.[6] The National Urban League also criticized proponents of high-stakes testing for "using low-achievers as cannon fodder in the education accountability wars."[7]

The performance of black schoolchildren on standardized tests lags far behind that of their non-Hispanic white counterparts. For instance, according to the College Board's 2003 National Report profiling SAT test takers,[8] the gap between the SAT scores of African-Americans and that of non-Hispanic whites is 206 points (857 and 1063, respectively).[9] Through the 1970s and 1980s,[10] the racial performance gap lessened. However, the gap between the average scores of African-Americans and non-Hispanic whites has widened by almost twenty points over the past twelve years.[11] Significant racial gaps between the performance of blacks and non-Hispanic whites on the ACT also exist. The average composite score of African-Americans on the ACT is 16.9 compared to the non-Hispanic white score of 21.7.[12] This gap has been fairly consistent over the past seven years.[13]

More than half of all states have enacted measures that require students to pass a standardized exit exam in order to qualify for a high school diploma.[14] Black and other minority students and low-income students fail these exams at disproportionately high rates. A recent report showed that in Florida, for example, nine percent of the prospective graduating class, approximately 12,800 students, will not receive their high school diploma because they failed the Florida Comprehensive Assessment Test. While only two percent of non-Hispanic whites failed the exit exam, sixteen percent of African-Americans and thirteen percent of Latinos failed.[15] In 1999, ninety-seven percent of African-Americans, Latinos and Native Americans were reported to have failed the math portion of Arizona's high school graduation test.[16] In 1997 only one out of every two African-American, Mexican-American and economically disadvantaged sophomores passed each section of Texas' high-stakes test—Texas' Assessment of Academic Skills. In contrast, however, four out of every five non-Hispanic white students passed the test.[17] Similar disturbing results were seen in Georgia where two out of every three low-income students failed the math, English and reading sections compared with no students from the state's well-to-do counties.[18]

To get a view of the existence of racial gaps for a broader section of elementary and secondary students, it is necessary to focus on other standardized tests. The National Assessment of Educational Progress exams were created by Congress in 1969 to assess trends in progress of elementary and secondary students in certain academic areas, including reading, math and science. Since 1971, three age groups of school students—ages nine, thirteen and seventeen—have been tested. In reading from 1971 to 1988, blacks in all three age groups showed progress in closing the gap with white students.[19] The test scores of black students increased while those of white students remained essentially the same. The average scores of 9-year old black students increased from 170 to 189, for 13-year olds from 222 to 243 and for 17-year olds from 239 to 274. The corresponding scores of whites were 214 to 218 (the racial gap was reduced from 44 to 29), 261 to 261 (the racial gap reduced from 39 to 18) and 291 to 295 (the racial gap was reduced from 52 to 21). Thereafter, these gaps began to widen as the scores of all black age groups fell while those of whites showed a modest rise. From 1988 to 1999 the racial gaps of 9-year olds increased from 29 to 35 points, for 13-year olds from 18 to 29 points and for 17-year olds from 21 to 31 points.[20] The racial gaps in the performance on science tests also fell for all three age groups from 1970 to 1986, but it began to rise during the 1990s. From 1970 to 1986, the racial gap in the scores of black 9-year olds decreased from 57 points to 36, 13-year olds from 49 points to 38 and 17-year olds from 54 points to 45. From 1986 to 1999, however, the racial gaps increased for all three age groups from 36 points to 41, 38 points to 39 and 45 points to 52, respectively.[21] With respect to math scores, they fell during the 1970s and 1980s, but showed more stabilization in the 1990s.[22]

B. High School Graduation Rates

Another criteria to examine in determining the academic performance of African-American students in public schools is high school graduation rates. But, the racial disparity between high school graduation rates of blacks and that of non-Hispanic whites cannot be completely separated from the gaps in standardized tests because many states now require students to pass a standardized test before they receive their high school diploma.

According to the Census Bureau in 2001, 13.8% of African-Americans between the ages of 18 and 24 had not completed nor were enrolled in high school, compared to 13.4% of non-Hispanic whites.[23] However, official reports of dropout rates and high school graduation rates may significantly understate the problem. "Graduation rates based on reported enrollment suggest strongly that there are large numbers of 'missing' students that go completely unaccounted for in either official dropout or graduation rate reports."[24] High school dropout rate figures also include those who left school and later received GED credentials.[25]

A recent report on high school graduation rates released by the Civil Rights Project at Harvard University, the Urban Institute, Advocates for Children of New York and the Civil Society Institute also note that "official dropout statistics neither count nor report the vast numbers of students who do not graduate from high school."[26] The Report determined graduation rates by developing a more accurate measure called the "Cumulative Promotion Index (CPI)."[27] Each school district provides its actual enrollment data to the nation's Common Core of Data. The CPI uses this actual enrollment data to develop a more accurate measure of high school graduation rates. The CPI examines changes in enrollment and the likelihood of graduating with a high school diploma by combining the average success of groups of students moving from ninth grade to tenth grade, from tenth grade to eleventh grade, from junior year to senior year and from senior year to graduation. According to the Report only 68% of those who enter 9th grade graduate with a regular diploma in the 12th grade, but there are vast differences between various racial/ethnic groups. The graduation rate for non-Hispanic whites is 74.9% and Asian/Pacific Islanders at 76.8%. In contrast, the graduation rates for African-Americans, Native Americans and Latinos are 50.2%, 51.1% and 53.2%, respectively.[28] According to the Report only 39 states and the District of Columbia reported their graduation rates for black students separately. Only Rhode Island (84.1%) reported the black graduation rate at higher than 70%. In contrast, 31 of the states reported the graduation rates for non-Hispanic whites at over 70%. There were eight states where the percentage of non-Hispanic whites who graduated exceeded that of blacks by more than 30% (Wisconsin 41.3% (82.4–41.1); New York 40.2% (75.3–35.1); Nebraska 36.5% (81.7–45.2); Ohio 36.3% (75.0–39.6); Illinois 35.1% (82.9–47.8); Iowa 31.3% (79.3–48); and Minnesota 30.4% (81.4–51)).[29]

C. Grade Retention

Students are retained in a grade if it is believed that they do not have the academic and social skills necessary to advance to the next grade level. Retention in a grade, however, is the single most reliable predictor of a student eventually dropping out of school.[30] African-American students are more likely to be retained in one grade during their educational career than any other racial/ethnic group, with the exception of Native-Americans. In 1999, 18% of black school students had been retained at least one time between kindergarten and 12th grade, which is double the rate of non-Hispanic whites.[31]

D. Tracking or Achievement Skills Grouping

As discussed in Chapter Eight, tracking or achievement skills grouping has been a major source of racial inequality in educational opportunities since the 1960s.[32] Figures from 1998 reveal that non-Hispanic white high school graduates were almost 50% more likely to be in the highest academic placement in math, in comparison to African-American high school graduates (45.1% to 30.4%, respectively). Blacks were 50% more likely than non-Hispanic whites to be in the two lowest math tracks (11.9% to 7.8%, respectively).[33] Black high school graduates were also less likely to be in advanced academic placements in science and English courses. Approximately 64% of non-Hispanic white high school graduating students took at least one chemistry or physics course in high school with 33.8% having taken at least two of these courses. In contrast, only 55% of African-Americans took at least one physics or chemistry course, with only 22.3% having taken at least two of these courses.[34] Black high school graduates were also 50% more likely than their non-Hispanic white counterparts to be in the least challenging English course.[35] Because these statistics are limited to high school graduates, however, they understate the racial gaps that exist in achievement skills groupings. These statistics do not adjust for the fact that blacks have higher high school dropouts rates than non-Hispanic whites.

In terms of disability, African-American schoolchildren are under represented in the group of students with physical disability, but over represented in special education placements due to a mental disability. Black students constitute only 17% of public schoolchildren, but they represent 21% of those enrolled in special education and 25.1% of those classified as having emotional and behavioral disorders.[36] African-American schoolchildren are three times as likely as non-Hispanic white students to be labeled mentally retarded and in five states the disparity is as high as four to one.[37] Almost 15% of African-American students compared to only 10.9% of non-Hispanic white students between the ages of 3 and 21 were served under the Individuals with Disabilities Education Act during the 1999–2000 school year.[38]

E. Underrepresentation of African-American School Teachers

The role and position of the black educator in public schools has changed drastically over the past fifty years. Prior to the desegregation litigation, black teachers typically taught black schoolchildren. They were generally thought to be too poorly trained to teach white children. But in the days before the end of segregation, there were few occupational options for college-educated blacks other than the ministry and public education. In the 1950s, half of all black professionals were public school teachers.[39]

Because of the increased opportunities in American society today, equally talented blacks have far more options. The teachers of the 1950s are the black lawyers, doctors, accountants, engineers and business professionals of today. The number of black educators has been affected, however, by more than the opening of other occupational options for talented blacks. As discussed in Chapter Six, the black educator paid a very high price for the desegregation of public schools. School boards and judges that crafted desegregation plans often closed black schools, fired African-American teachers and demoted black principals. More recently, however, the black school teacher has suffered as a result of educational reform movements beginning in the 1980s.

In 1983, the National Commission on Excellence in Education published its influential report "A Nation At Risk." In the Report, the Commission stated that public schools were failing in their mission to educate students and were creating "a rising tide of mediocrity that threatens our very future as a Nation and a people."[40] This Report, and the educational reform movements it helped to spawn, placed a good portion of the blame for the problem of public education on school teachers.[41] The typical criticism of teaching was that it did not attract high-caliber people. The Report argued for higher academic standards and more rigorous training of teachers.

The call for higher teaching standards has frequently been answered through enforced teacher testing. Yet, using standardized tests to determine prospective teachers has a devastating impact on African-Americans interested in the teaching profession. The Praxis Series of tests is the only national teacher-testing program.[42] The Praxis I test assesses reading, writing and math ability. Passing this test is a prerequisite for acceptance into many degree-granting college programs in education. The Praxis II tests focus on content and pedagogical knowledge in specific subject areas. These tests are often used by states to determine qualifications for the initial teaching certificate.[43] A study by the Educational Testing Service, conducted between the years of 1994 and 1997, of over 300,000 people who took one, or both, of the Praxis tests reveals the negative effects of standardized testing for minorities interested in teaching.[44] All minority groups, African-Americans, Latino, Asian American/Asian, Native American and Other, scored lower on both Praxis tests than non-Hispanic whites.[45] Only 53.5 percent of the African-Americans who took the Praxis I test passed, compared to 83.7 percent of all test takers, and 86.7 percent of non-Hispanic white test takers.[46] Thus, while blacks constituted 7.3 percent of those who took the test, they only constituted 4.6 percent of those who actually passed.[47] The same results were revealed for the Praxis II tests as well. Of the blacks who took the Praxis II test, 65.2 percent passed, compared to 88.3 percent of test takers overall and 91.8 percent of non-Hispanic whites.[48]

These developments have helped to create a situation where there is significant underrepresentation of minorities and overrepresentation of non-Hispanic whites teaching in public schools. In 1999–2000 academic year only 7.7 percent of public school teachers were black,[49] despite the fact that black children constitute 17.2 percent of public school students in 2001–02.[50] In fact, while non-Hispanic whites make up only 60.3 percent of public school students,[51] they constitute 86.4 percent of public school teachers.[52]

II. Increasing Parental Choice Through Providing Charter Schools and Tuition Vouchers

The persistence of achievement gaps for low income minority students in urban school systems is a major force in educational reform. One of the most important approaches to educational reform is increasing school choice, particularly through an expansion of charter schools and, possibly in the future, an expansion of publicly funded private education. The enactment of President Bush's No Child Left Behind Act (NCLB), signed into law on January 8, 2002,[53] will spur the school choice movement.

The quality of the neighborhood schools is normally an important consideration in choosing where to live. Thus, the primary form of school choice is through selection of residential neighborhoods. Families with financial means are not only able to pay to put their child in a private school, but they are also able to leave a given school district by moving to another district. Since good schools are necessary to appeal to home buyers who have a number of residential options, schools in districts where people have the means to choose whether to leave or stay are among the best. As a form of school choice, selection of residential neighborhoods tends to advantage non-Hispanic white and middle class students the most. They are the ones with the greatest capacity to choose where to live.

Racially neutral school choice proposals seek to give all parents in a given school district, given school or schools in a given district, a given area of a given school district or below a particular income level the limited opportunity to choose the school their child attends. Since the criteria used to determine choice is not based on race or ethnicity, for purposes of an equal protection challenge these choice plans do not have to satisfy strict scrutiny. Thus, these programs seldom generate equal protection issues. But, low-income parents of minority schoolchildren in urban areas are the ones who have the least capability to exercise school choice either through moving into neighborhoods with good schools or by paying for private education. As a result, increasing choice is a racially neutral educational policy that should disproportionately advantage these parents and their children.

Advocates for increased choice generally assert that it will improve educational achievement in a number of ways. Increasing choice requires increasing the number and types of public or private schools. Increased choice also creates a competitive environment that forces schools to compete for students. As a result, increased school choice has the potential to produce new and innovative schools, including those that are particularly effective at responding to the educational needs of minority low-income urban school students. In a Darwinian competitive environment, schools that cannot demonstrate their ability to provide a good education should not survive. Increased choice also reduces administrative burdens on educators. Educational decisions are driven increasingly down to the level of the individual school. This should allow educators to respond more effectively to the educational needs of students enrolled in their particular school. These justifications explain why charter schools are one of the fastest growing forms of public school choice. Charter schools are public schools which are freed from many of the oversight procedures of normal public schools. Charter schools are intended to encourage experimentation, innovation and the development of alternative forms of education.

It is too early to determine whether increased choice in the form of charter schools and school vouchers will lead to significant improvement in academic achievement.[54] In order for diverse educational opportunities and a competitive atmosphere to occur, a sufficient market for school choice must first be generated. Furthermore, the effects of increased choice may not be noticeable for a number of years after competitive market forces are in place. While charter schools currently exist, the charter school movement is only a dozen years old and considerably younger in many states. Although private schools have existed since the foundation of this country, one cannot easily compare the academic performance of private school students using school vouchers with their public school student counterparts. The issue of bias in the determination of which former public school students either use school vouchers to attend private schools or public schools of choice, like charter schools, has always been a problem in assessing the impact of choice on educational performance. Even if differences in income, parental education, neighborhood, hours spent studying and other relevant factors could be controlled for, selection bias would make comparisons between the academic performance of students in schools of choice as opposed to traditional public schools difficult. The students whose parents select charter schools or private schools funded with public funds are generally different from the ones whose parents do not. Families who are informed enough to select the school their child will attend have made a special effort that evinces their concern about their child's education and, more importantly, the wherewithal to advance that concern. A second form of selection bias is that operators of charter schools or private schools that accept school vouchers are likely to try to recruit the type of students that should do well in their educational programs. Thus, even if admission to the school is open to all, there is still likely to be biases in which students are recruited to attend a given charter school or private school accepting school vouchers. The existence of these biases makes it difficult to draw general conclusions about whether the academic performance of students in charter schools or private schools is the result of the competitive environment created for the schools as a result of choice or the result of selection bias in the students who attend.

This section first discusses the increases in school choice represented by the charter school movement. It then examines recent efforts to provide public funding for private education. It concludes with a look at the NCLB. While the driving thrust of NCLB is the desire to create accountability measures for public schools, its provisions consider public school choice as one of the principal solutions for students stuck in failing public schools. The NCLB's emphasis on school choice will certainly foster an expansion of school choice.

A. Public School Choice in the Form of Charter Schools

Beyond residential choices, the concept of school choice is a varied one. It can broadly be defined as educational policies and practices that allow a student to attend a school other than his or her neighborhood school. With this definition there are a number of methods to increase choice within the public school system.

Since the 1960s, most school choice options have been largely the result of a desire to promote integration. There are some public school districts that participate in interdistrict school choice programs, but the numbers are limited. These choice programs tend to be expensive because transportation must be provided. In addition, suburban school districts may resist taking students from urban school districts for fear that these students would significantly disrupt their educational system without a corresponding educational value for the suburban school students. Suburbanites also want to protect both their financial resources and physical safety of their children. Interdistrict choice might adversely effect property values in suburban neighborhoods and bring into their neighborhoods what these residents consider to be undesirable individuals.

Intradistrict public choice often began as part of the remedy for actions by school officials that led to a segregated school system. Many school desegregation plans encouraged students to seek voluntary transfers that would improve the racial and ethnic mix of the sending and receiving schools. Magnet schools are a well known and popular intradistrict school choice program. Magnet programs target specific schools and spend significant amounts of money upgrading the physical quality of the school, as well as, their curricular offerings. Magnet schools usually concentrate their academic focus on a given subject area. The educational programs in magnet schools ordinarily focus on foreign languages, reading, science, math or the arts. The unique focus of the magnet school helps to attract students of diverse racial and ethnic backgrounds from the entire school district. In order to promote integration, racial and ethnic limits are often used to determine the appropriate mix of the student body. The 1,736 magnet schools in the country enrolled some 3.0% of American students in 2001.[55]

School choice options, including magnet schools, initiated for the purpose of promoting integrated schools, however, are being scaled back. The principal reason is the equal protection concerns related to the use of racial classifications by public school officials that were discussed in detail in Chapter Seven. As school districts terminate their school desegregation decrees, they are also eliminating the compelling justifications needed that allowed them to employ racial classifications to further school choice directed at promoting integrated schools. As a result school choice motivated by a desire to promote integrated public education is increasingly seen as constitutionally suspect.

Charter schools are another type of intradistrict choice option. Charter schools differ from magnet schools in that they focus on educational reform, not integration.[56] Minnesota was the first state in the nation to pass charter school legislation in 1991.[57] As of January, 2003, there were nearly 2,700 charter schools operating in thirty-seven states with over 684,000 students enrolled.[58] Charter legislation will vary from state to state,[59] but it generally allows for private persons and institutions, including so called educational management companies like the Edison Schools, Inc. or Nobel Learning Communities, Inc.,[60] to develop and implement plans for a given school. Charter schools are considered public schools. They are, however, under less supervisory control by public educational officials and can often operate somewhat independently of public school authorities. Charter schools are intended to foster new approaches to education with innovative curriculum and instruction. The unique focus of charter schools forms the primary means of attracting parents and children to the school. While charter schools are not allowed to discriminate on the basis of race or ethnicity in their admissions criteria, enrollment numbers suggest that these schools also tend to be segregated. One survey showed that over 43% of charter schools report that over 60% of their students are minorities.[61] A survey of 1,010 charter schools started in 1998–99 and still open a year later showed that 27.3% of the students were black, with another 20.8% being Latino (this contrasted with 16.9 and 14.9 of students in traditional pubic schools being black or Latino, respectively).[62]

Encouraging the establishment of charter schools is one viable race-neutral alternative to pursue in efforts to improve the educational situation of African-American schoolchildren. Most charter schools are concentrated in urban areas.[63] Charter schools can provide black parents with the opportunity to become more involved in the design of their children's educational program. Charter schools encourage experimentation and the adoption of alternative educational programs, which can be structured to be more effective at educating certain black youths. Plus, charter schools vest ultimate authority for the school decision in the hands of the parents. If children in a charter school are not learning, their parents can send them to a different school. But, as noted earlier, a consensus regarding the ability of charter schools to significantly improve educational achievement has yet to develop.

B. Public Funding of Private School Choice or School Vouchers

Public funding of private school choice or school vouchers presents another potential racially neutral way to address the educational problems of African-Americans.[64] Contemporary discussions of the issue of school vouchers normally start their historical analysis of this issue with Milton Friedman's 1955 essay.[65] But, for the African-American community, school vouchers have a history that predates and overshadows the economic professor and Nobel Laureate's proposal. As noted in Chapter Five, after the Supreme Court rendered its opinion in *Brown v. Board of Education*, resistance to school desegregation, particularly in the Deep South, was massive. Privatizing education was one of the principal ways that segregationists resisted the integration of public schools.

School vouchers are currently a relatively minor, but growing, aspect of school choice. The recently enacted voucher programs are generally targeted to assist low-income students or student in schools that are substandard. The effect, however, is to disproportionately provide vouchers for low-income, minority students in urban school settings. The Supreme Court's 2002 decision in *Zelman v. Harris*[66] significantly increased the attraction of public funding of private education. In a five to four decision, the Supreme Court upheld a voucher program operated by Cleveland, Ohio against an establishment clause challenge. Only three recent publicly-funded voucher programs, in Cleveland, Milwaukee and the State of Florida, were in operation at the time of the Court's opinion in *Zelman*.[67] The voucher programs in Cleveland and Milwaukee were targeted to assist low-income parents with children in urban school districts that have large numbers of low-income and minority students. The Florida program was targeted to help students in the worse performing schools in Florida.

The origins of the Cleveland voucher program can be traced to its school desegregation litigation. In 1995 the federal district court supervising the school desegregation process in Cleveland public schools declared a "crisis of magnitude" existed within the school district and placed the entire Cleveland school district under state control.[68] Not long after the Court acted, the state auditor found that Cleveland's public schools were in the midst of a "crisis... perhaps unprecedented in the history of American education."[69] The Cleveland school district had failed to meet any of the eighteen state standards for minimal acceptable performance. The conditions in the schools were so bad that only 10% of the ninth graders could pass a basic proficiency examination. Students at all levels performed dismally when compared to students in other Ohio school districts. The graduation rates in Cleveland were also horrific. More than two-thirds of high school students failed to graduate. And a full 25% of the students who reached their senior year still failed to graduate. Few of the graduates of Cleveland public schools could read, write or compute at levels comparable to their counterparts in other cities.

The State of Ohio responded by enacting a law that created a program to provide financial assistance to families in any Ohio school district that was or had been under federal court order. Cleveland was the only Ohio school district to fall within that category. A tuition aid component was one of the provisions of the Cleveland plan. The law provided that low income students attending private schools could receive up to $2,250. The maximum tuition voucher for other students was capped at $1,875. The Cleveland program also provided for the use of the vouchers in consenting suburban public schools. A minimum of $7,000 would be paid to the suburban public schools for each student they accepted.[70] At the time of the Supreme Court's opinion in *Zelman,* however, no suburban school had volunteered to accept students from Cleveland who had the vouchers.[71]

In the 1999–2000 school year, fifty-six private schools participated in the program. Forty-six (or 82%) of them were religiously affiliated. A General Accounting Office ("GAO") report of the program filed for the 1998–99 school year revealed that 70% of families with children participating in the program were headed by single mothers, with average family incomes of $18,750. A majority of the students who participated in the program, 73.4%, were minorities and 26.6% were white.[72] The GAO Report noted that approximately 3,400 voucher students were enrolled in fifty-two private schools. These schools received approximately $5.2 million in publicly funded payments for the 1999–2000 academic year. In contrast, the cost of educating the remaining 76,000 students in Cleveland's 121 public schools was $712 million, or about $9,368 per student.

When *Zelman* was decided Milwaukee also had a school voucher program. The Parental Choice Program in Milwaukee provided for school vouchers to students in the Milwaukee school district with family incomes below 175% of the poverty level. The vouchers are tied to the per pupil state aid or private school tuition, whichever was less. The value of the vouchers was $5,553 for the 2001–02 school year.[73] As of January 2002, there were 10,789 students participating in the program.[74]

Florida was operating two voucher programs at the time of the Court's opinion in *Zelman.* The Opportunity Scholarships voucher program was passed by the Florida legislature in 1998. It allowed students who attended the lowest rated pubic schools in Florida to use state money to attend another public or private school. The amount of the voucher was tied to the state's share in the expenses of eligible students. For 2001–02, the average amount of the award was $3,500 to $3,900. Transportation was provided only if students choose a public school within their home districts. As of the Fall 2001, only about 45 students attended private schools.[75] The second program, the McKay Scholarship program, was serving only a few students in 2000–01 school year.[76] The McKay Scholarships program provides vouchers to special education students, with challenges ranging from learning disabilities to profound handicaps, to pay for private schooling. The amount of the vouchers varied from $4,500 to $21,000 depending upon the student and the disability.[77]

President Bush praised *Zelman* as "a great victory to parents and schoolchildren throughout the nation."[78] In the 2002 elections, voters in Colorado, New Hampshire, Texas and South Carolina elected governors and state legislative leaders who favored school choice.[79] In April 2003, Colorado became the first state to initiate a voucher program since the Court's decision on *Zelman.*[80] The Colorado voucher program sought to provide up to $5,000 to students in kindergarten through 12th grade in districts with academic performance ratings of "low" or "unsatisfactory" on the Colorado School Accountability Report. To be eligible, however, the students must qualify for free or reduced-cost lunches. Initially about 3,500 students would be eligible under the program, with as many as 20,000 eligible by the 2007–08 school year.[81] A voucher program has also recently been adopted for public school students in Washington D.C.[82] The plan provides for up to $7,500 for 2,000 low income students to fund private school education. Students attending schools identified as needing improvement or correction have priority. Since *Zelman,* Florida's McKay Scholarship program has expanded dramatically. This program went from serving only a few students in 2000–01 school year to an estimated 12,000 McKay Scholarships in the Fall of 2003.[83] Florida has also instituted a third voucher program that began in 2002.[84] This program is funded by state tax credits given to companies that donate money to nonprofit groups for scholarships for parents who meet income and other eligibility requirements. Under this program, companies can donate up to three-quarters of their state corporate-income taxes to nonprofit groups that give scholarship money for students to attend private schools. About 20,000 students have applied for these tax-credit scholarships. The tax-credit scholarships provide the lesser of $3,500 or the total of the school's tuition, book and transportation costs.[85]

Zelman may not be the last word on the federal constitutionality of public funding of private school choice. But, for now, a well-crafted school voucher proposal can survive an establishment clause challenge brought under the First Amendment.[86] With regard to vouchers, *Zelman* is merely permissive. Thus, it removes a potential establishment clause objection to states that desire to provide school vouchers. But voucher programs may still be vulnerable to state constitutional challenges. Both the Cleveland and Milwaukee programs in operations at the time of the Court's decision in *Zelman* had to survive legal challenges brought under provisions of their respective state constitutions.[87] The Florida Opportunity Scholarship program initially survived a state constitutional challenge before the Supreme Court's opinion in *Zelman.* But on remand from the Florida Appeals Court and just six weeks after the Supreme Court's decision in *Zelman,* a Florida Circuit Court struck down this plan in August 2002 as violating the Florida Constitution.[88] Article I, Section 3 of the Florida Constitution states that "No revenue of the state or any political subdivision or agency thereof shall ever be taken from the public treasury directly or indirectly in aid of any church, sect, or religious denomination or in aid of any sectarian institution." The Circuit Court on remand empathized with the salutary purpose of the legislation creating the vouchers. But, the Circuit Court concluded that the clear mandate of the people enunciated in the Florida Constitution did not grant Florida authority to use the funds to provide money for religious education. The state has appealed the ruling. The Circuit Court has allowed the program to operate until the appeal is resolved.[89] On June 28, 2004, the Colorado Supreme Court upheld a lower court ruling that struck down the Colorado voucher program. The high court concluded the program requires school districts to turn over a portion of locally raised funds to private schools, over which local school boards have no control. This violates the local-control provisions of the Colorado Constitution. Voucher supporters, however, are likely to introduce a new version of the legislation in the 2005 Legislature to conform to the ruling.[90]

The primary state constitutional challenges are likely to come from state constitutional provisions that in some way prohibit public funding of religious education. About three dozen states have these provisions which supporters of vouchers refer to as "Blaine amendments" in their state constitutions.[91] These provisions get their name from the 19th-century congressman James G.

Blaine, who led an unsuccessful effort to amend the U.S. Constitution to add an amendment that would specifically make the religion clauses of the First Amendment applicable to the states. Blaine was motivated by a desire to prevent control of lands or funds raised for use in public schools falling into the control of any religious sect. His resolution stated "no State shall make any law respecting an establishment of religion or prohibiting the free exercise thereof." The resolution actually was adopted by the House of Representatives in 1875 and 1876 but was defeated by the Senate. Though unsuccessful in adding such a provision to the federal constitution, a number of states added such provisions to their state constitutions.[92]

It is likely that many voucher programs that are enacted by state legislators will have to also survive an attack under state constitutional provisions.[93] Even though voucher programs are likely to face state constitutional challenges, they are still likely to be a major potential method of educational reform in the coming years.

C. Private School Choice Provides for More Educational Diversity than Public School Choice

An advantage of school vouchers over charter schools is that privatizing a significant portion of public education affords educators more flexibility in designing their academic programs. Experimentation and flexibility of charter schools are limited by constitutional rights. As the Supreme Court stated in *Tinker v. Des Moines*, "students do not leave their constitutional rights at the schoolhouse gate."[94] Public schools, including charter schools, must abide by constitutional limits derived from the equal protection clause and the establishment clause, as well as ensure students' constitutional liberties, including their rights to due process,[95] privacy[96] and free speech.[97] These constitutional restrictions, however, do not apply to private schools.[98]

1. Involvement of Black Churches in Education

Constitutional requirements about the separation of Church and State limit the ability of churches to be involved in public schools, including charter schools.[99] This may prove to be a significant concern for black schoolchildren because of the historic role the Black Church has played in the African-American community. Major social protest movements by African-Americans generally start in the church. Many of the most significant African-American community leaders such as Reverend Jesse Jackson, Reverend Martin Luther King, Jr. and Malcolm X are or were religious leaders. Many African-Americans would be happy with the opportunity to send their children to schools operated by, and in, their local churches. Such schools could provide a safe and protective learning environment for students in institutions where their parents are already involved. While charter schools can not be religiously affiliated, most private schools have a religious affiliation. Thus, vouchers could be a potent weapon in allowing black churches to get more actively involved in the education of black children.

2. Gender Segregated Education for African-American Males and Females

Another potential educational reform movement of the late 1980s and early 1990s, the establishment of African-American Male Academies, was thwarted by equal protection considerations. A special issue of *Ebony* magazine published in August 1983 introduced the African-American community to Walter Leavy's provocative question: Is the black male an endangered species?[100] To emphasize the deteriorating condition of the African-American male, Leavy pointed to the high homicide rates, high rates of incarceration, an increase in the rate of suicide, the infant mortality rate and a decrease in life expectancy. The crisis of the African-American male was brought to the attention of mainstream America with proposals by a few public school systems in the late 1980s and early 1990s to establish African-American male classrooms or academies. These proposals raised one of the most controversial educational issues of the early 1990s. Proposals for such education surfaced in a number of cities, including Baltimore, Detroit, Miami, Milwaukee and New York.

The legality of race- and gender-segregated public schools limited to African-American males, however, was open to serious legal questions from the start. The Milwaukee school system, on advice of counsel, abandoned its original proposal to establish all-black male schools, with black male school teachers.[101] In order to comply with legal concerns raised, Milwaukee eventually established two African-American immersion schools that were open to both males and females. In one school, half the student population was composed of neighborhood girls, the faculty was two-thirds white and there were only two African-American male teachers.[102] Miami abandoned its plan to establish experimental separate schools for African-American males after receiving a letter from the Department of Education indicating that it was the Department's position that such schools were illegal.[103]

The Detroit School Board sought to go ahead with its plans to open up African-American Male Academies but its decision was challenged in federal court. Almost all of Detroit's public school students were black. Thus, gender segregated education in Detroit public schools meant, for the boys, African-American Male Academies.

The Detroit School Board argued that the need for male academies was due, in part, to the failure of the traditional coeducational program.[104] The School Board pointed to statistics which showed the poor academic performance of black males and their high dropout rates. The plaintiffs who challenged the efforts of the Detroit school officials were represented by the American Civil Liberties Union of Michigan and the National Organization of Women Legal Defense and Education Fund. The plaintiffs ignored the race-based decision-making that motivated the adoption of proposals for these schools and only challenged the gender based exclusion of female students.

In *Garrett v. Board of Education,*[105] a federal District Court in August 1991 granted a preliminary injunction against the Detroit School Board's proposal for male academies. The District Court concluded that the Detroit plan violated state law, the equal protection clause's prohibition against discrimination based on gender and Title IX—the federal law that prohibits gender discrimination in public education.

Regardless of the legal issues involved, the logic supporting black male academies also supports separate schools for African-American females. Many supporters and opponents of proposals for African-American male academies also argued that a similar crisis faced African-American females. During discussion about African-American male Academics in Milwaukee, for example, it was noted that the dropout rate of black females was 45%, only slightly better than the 55% rate for black males.[106] In the brief filed by the National Organization for Women and the ACLU of Michigan attacking Detroit's male-only academies, the plaintiffs argued that urban girls (African-American females) suffer loss of self-esteem, become parents at an early age and get involved in criminal activities just like the males.[107] In *Garrett,* the District Court pointed to a resolution by the Board of Education of Detroit which noted that in addition to the crisis facing African-American male students in public schools, there is an "equally urgent and unique crisis facing . . . female students."[108] In its opinion striking down the male academies, the District Court wrote that "[u]rban girls drop out of school, suffer loss of self-esteem and become involved in criminal activity. Ignoring the plight of urban females institutionalizes inequality and perpetuates the myth that females are doing well in the current system."[109]

Neither public nor private schools can use race as a condition for admissions.[110] But, assuming gender segregated education does not violate state law, as it might have in Michigan, it is possible that gender segregated public schools could be established in such a way that they do not violate the equal protection clause or Title IX. The Supreme Court has twice issued decisions in cases involving gender segregated education, *Mississippi Univer-*

sity for Women v. Hogan[111] and *United States v. Virginia.*[112] In both of those cases, as well as the District Court decision in *Garrett,* the courts addressed equal protection challenges where gender segregated educational opportunities provided to males and females were demonstrably unequal. As Professor Rosemary Salome has noted, under the equal protection clause separate is not inherently unequal in the context of gender. Thus all single-sex programs are not *per se* unconstitutional. The opposite, however, is also true.[113] In order to survive equal protection and Title IX challenges, a school district seeking to provide gender segregated public education must—at a minimum—provide girls and boys with equal educational opportunities. The question that a federal court would have to address relates to whether separate educational opportunities provide to males and females could, in a constitutional sense, be equal.

Whether gender segregated public education could be established is still an open question under the equal protection clause and Title IX. In addition, gender segregated education may be proscribed under state law. There is no doubt, however, that gender segregated private schools are legal. Providing parents with increased school choice options through school vouchers could remove these legal concerns to the establishment of African-American Male Academies and corresponding separate educational schools for black females.

3. African-American Immersion Schools

While the effort to establish African-American Male Academies was largely contained in the 1990s, many public school districts modified their educational curriculum to make them more Afrocentric. An Afrocentric curriculum is an emerging educational concept which calls generally for the structuring of an educational program centered around the experiences of African-Americans. An Afrocentric curriculum provides black students with the opportunity to study concepts, history and the world, from a perspective that places their cultural group at the center of the discussion.[114] An Afrocentric curriculum teaches courses using Africa and the socio-historical experience of Africans and African-Americans as its reference points.[115] An Afrocentric perspective is not a celebration of black pigmentation or a glorification of everything blacks have done. Rather, it evaluates, explains and analyzes the actions of individuals and groups from a common yardstick—the liberation and enhancement of the lives of Africans and African-Americans.[116]

An Afrocentric curriculum infuses Afrocentric educational materials into the content of various subjects, including language arts, mathematics, science, social studies, art and music.[117] Students are provided with both instruction as well as a holistic and thematic awareness of the history, culture and contributions of people of African descent. From an Afrocentric perspective, for instance, the focal point of the beginnings of human civilization is the ancient Egyptian civilization on the continent of Africa ("Kemet" or "Sais"), and not the civilization of Ancient Greece.[118] Therefore, Egypt, not Greece, is the origin of the basic concepts of math and science. A reason for tracing the origins of math and science to Kemet instead of Ancient Greece is to combat the idea that academics, including science and math, are not matters in which black people excel. The discussion of American history within the discourse of African-American Centralism included in Chapter Two provides an example of how American history would be presented from an Afrocentric viewpoint. Afrocentric education, thus, helps to combat the undervaluing of African-American accomplishments which often occurs in the standard public school curriculum.

Charter schools open to all students regardless of race or ethnicity have been established with an Afrocentric curriculum.[119] As of yet, no equal protection challenges to Afrocentric education have been raised. Some scholars argue that such education is potentially vulnerable to constitutional challenges.[120] One commentator has already speculated that in certain circumstances culturally-centric charter schools, including Afrocentric ones, may be unconstitutional.[121] Others have raised questions about the legality of teaching to public school students certain claims made in some of the Afrocentric materials.[122] However, Professor Kenneth Karst has stated, "surely there is no constitutional objection based on the curriculum, provided that the school population is not officially segregated and attendance remains voluntary."[123] While it may be that Afrocentric charter schools do not generate any equal protection objections, private Afrocentric education certainly would not run afoul of the equal protection clause.

D. The No Child Left Behind Act

NCLB is subtitled "Improving the Academic Achievement of the Disadvantaged." The first words of the Act are, "an Act to close the achievement gap with accountability, flexibility and choice, so that no child is left behind."[124] Among the NCLB's purposes is meeting the educational needs of low-achieving children in the country's highest poverty schools. The Act also desires to close the achievement gap between high and low performing children, especially the achievement gaps between minority and non-minority students and between disadvantaged students and their more advantaged peers.

NCLB requires all states to implement statewide accountability mechanisms at both school and district levels. States must develop challenging academic content and student achievement standards. The standards are to be uniform throughout the state and should apply to all public schools and students. "Content" standards must specify what all students are expected to know and be able to do. The standards currently cover reading/language, arts and mathematics. Beginning in the 2005–06 school year, they are to be expanded to include science.

NCLB requires states, through the 2004–05 school year, to administer assessments at least once during grades 3 through 5, 6 through 9 and 10 through 12. But, beginning no later than the 2005–06 school year, tests must be given in each grade from 3 through 8 and at least once between grades 10 and 12. The test results are to be published in a clear and easy-to-understand manner by the beginning of the following school year. A key aspect of the testing requirements is that scores must be monitored and recorded so that they are accessible by itemized student categories including: each major racial and ethnic group, English proficiency status and economic disadvantage. In addition, states must produce individual student performance reports for every student's parent or guardian.

The core of NCLB is its requirement for adequate yearly progress. NCLB requires states, school districts and individual schools demonstrate adequate yearly progress toward enabling all public school students to meet the state's academic achievement standards, while working toward the goal of narrowing the achievement gaps in the state. Thus, states must first establish a starting point from which improvement can be assessed (i.e. the current percentage of students meeting or exceeding the state's "proficient" level of achievement). Thereafter, states must identify for *each* subsequent school year (beginning no later than the 2004–05 school year), a minimum percentage of students who must meet or exceed the proficient level of academic achievement. To achieve the required adequate yearly progress, the percentage of students meeting the state's minimum proficient level of academic achievement must increase by a predetermined rate. The rate is calculated to achieve the long-term requirement that *all* students meet or exceed the state's "proficient" level of academic achievement no later than the 2013–14 school year. Since a major goal of NCLB is to narrow achievement gaps, states, school districts and schools must separately account for and achieve adequate yearly progress with respect to specific subgroups of students. The subgroups include, but are not limited to, economically disadvantaged students, racial and ethnic minority students, students with disabilities and students with limited English proficiency. For a school to make adequate yearly progress, all subgroups must make progress. Thus, for example, if non-Hispanic whites, Asians and Latino students make adequate yearly progress, but black students do not, the school fails to make adequate yearly progress.

NCLB triggers sanctions for schools that fail to make adequate yearly progress. States are required to identify for "improvement" any school that fails, for two consecutive years, to make adequate yearly progress. A school identified for improvement is required to develop an improvement plan grounded in scientifically based research. The plan must be enacted in consultation with parents, school and district personnel and outside experts. It must seek to strengthen instruction in the core academic subjects and address the specific academic needs which rendered it a school in need of improvement. Schools must implement this improvement plan.

Schools that fail to make adequate yearly progress after two years of operating under their improvement plan are designated for "corrective action" administered by the district. Corrective action includes one or more of the following options: replacing the school staff identified to be the cause of the school's failure, instituting and fully implementing a new curriculum, providing professional development for staff, significantly decreasing management authority at the school level, appointing outside experts to advise the school, extending either the school year or school day and restructuring the internal organization of the school.

While corrective action appears to be severe intervention into the operation of a public school, it is only a midpoint sanction. If after one year of corrective action a school still fails to make adequate yearly progress, it becomes subject to "restructuring." Restructuring involves a major reorganization of a school's governance arrangement and entails one or more of the following: reopening the school as a public charter school, replacing all or most of the staff responsible for the school's failure to make adequate yearly progress, entering into a contract with a private management company or turning the operation of the school over to the state.

NCLB mandates similar accountability structures for states and districts. Districts are also required to achieve adequate yearly progress for all schools. If districts fail to make adequate yearly progress for two consecutive years, they, like schools, are identified for improvement, and thereafter, for corrective action. Corrective action ranges from mild (imposing new curricula or replacing district personnel), to moderate (reducing or deferring state education funds), to severe (removing failing schools from the district), to terminal (abolishing the district). States are also held accountable. States failing to make adequate yearly progress (measured by statewide test scores) face reductions in federal education funding.

At all three levels—school, district and state—success in achieving adequate yearly progress for two consecutive years results in imposed corrective accountability measures being lifted. However, until the measures have been lifted, districts must make tutoring available to disadvantaged students at failing schools. Finally, common to all NCLB's accountability mechanisms, and perhaps its most stark departure from traditional approaches to public education, is its mandated public school choice option. Private school vouchers were not included in NCLB. But, where a school has been identified for "improvement," "corrective action" or "restructuring," NCLB mandates that the district provide all students enrolled in the school with the option to transfer to another public school in the district, which has not also been identified for improvement.

In July 2002, the U.S. Department of Education announced that the first round of NCLB mandated evaluations had identified 8,600 public schools in the United States for improvement.[125] This number can be expected to increase in the near future because schools that fail to make adequate yearly progress in even *one* category of students in a *single* grade level will be designated as failing. Sandy Kress, an attorney who helped the Bush Administration draft the NCLB and who currently advises states on complying with it, predicted that "50 to 90 percent of the schools in some states" could soon be identified as failing.[126] Michael Winerip, education writer for *The New York Times,* estimates that NCLB is "likely to result in 85 percent of public schools in America being labeled as failing."[127]

School choice, in light of NCLB's public school choice option, is set to explode. A recent study of the impact of high stakes testing covering 18 states noted that in "all but one analysis, student learning is indeterminate, remains at the same level it was before the policy was implemented, or actually goes down when high-stakes testing policies are instituted."[128] Thus, it may be that NCLB's testing regime will simply create a requirement to provide school choice for a tremendous number of students in failing schools. For example, in Baltimore, 30,000 students were eligible for transfer under NCLB. However, there were only 194 available slots in non-failing schools in the district.[129] In Chicago, 19,000 students applied for 1,100 available slots.[130] In 2002, Los Angeles had 223,000 children in 120 failing schools, and no available openings in non-failing schools.[131]

A number of problems exist that may significantly affect NCLB's implementation. NCLB allows states to define their own proficiency levels. Thus, a way school officials could avoid significant and systemic failures of schools in the state would be to set low standards for student performance. The State of Ohio followed this path. It originally identified 760 failing schools, but later reduced the number to 212 by lowering the proficiency standards, which state officials decided had been set unrealistically high.[132] Another provision in the

NCLB states that nothing in the Act shall require the states to spend any funds or incur any costs not paid for under the Act. It is obvious that measures like, replacing the school staff, instituting and fully implementing a new curriculum, providing professional development for staff, appointing outside experts to advise the school, extending either the school year or school day, transferring students to different schools and closing failing schools will require expenditures of significant amounts of money. Congress allotted an initial $18.5 billion for NCLB, but budget constraints have resulted in NCLB's funding being lower than promised. In October 2003, the Bush Administration withheld more than $6 billion dollars from the funding of the NCLB.[133]

Conclusion

Three major considerations are influencing the direction of public education reform involving black schoolchildren. First, racial separation in public schools has been on the increase for the past fifteen years and will continue to rise. Second, fifty years after the Supreme Court's opinion in *Brown v. Board of Education,* African-American schoolchildren continue to lag far behind their non-Hispanic white counterparts in important indicia of academic success. Third, current interpretations of the equal protection clause make it difficult for federal courts to get involved in attacking continuing racial achievement gaps and limits the programs and policies that legislators or public school authorities can use to improve the educational performance of black schoolchildren. Given these three factors, increasing school choice has become one of the most important racially neutral approaches to educational reform.

Chapter Ten

Increased School Choice as Comprehended in the Four Discourses

There are two interwoven objectives of this book. One is to advance the discussion of racial issues, particularly those involving African-American schoolchildren, through the Post-Desegregation Awareness. The Post-Desegregation Awareness is the conscious awareness that important social phenomena, including racial phenomena, are more enlightening when they are comprehended by different systems of meaning. The principal means to accomplish this objective is through tracing and discussing the developments of the educational situation of African-Americans schoolchildren from the Supreme Court's opinion in *Brown v. Board of Education,* which propelled American society into the Desegregation Era, through to the present situation, in this the Post-Desegregation Era, with its emphasis on expanding school choice against the background of increasing racial segregation in public schools.

Many of the developments impacting on the educational situation of African-American schoolchildren over the past fifty years can be traced to Supreme Court decisions interpreting the equal protection clause. The scope and extent of school desegregation was principally the product of the Court's interpretations of the equal protection clause. When the Supreme Court struck down segregation statutes and required schools that operated dual school systems to take account of race and ethnicity of their students in order to desegregate public schools, the Court also set off an educational reform movement outside of the legal system based on the Court's justifications for striking down segregation statutes in public schools. There should also be little doubt that the attractiveness of increasing school choice as a major educational reform movement to respond to the continued racial academic achievement gaps between African-American (and other minority students) and non-Hispanic whites is also due in large part to the Supreme

Court's current interpretations of the equal protection clause. The Court has severely limited the use by school officials of racial classifications in the pursuit of educational policies and practices. Because legislators and school officials still face significant racial and ethnic achievement gaps in the performance of black (red and brown) students on the one hand and non-Hispanic white (and yellow) students on the other, they are forced to respond to these gaps with programs and policies that are not structured around race or ethnicity. In the Post-Desegregation Era, expanding school choice, against a background of already increasing racial segregation in the public schools, has become an important racially neutral means by which to respond to the continuing educational problems of African-American schoolchildren, particularly in urban areas.

Supreme Court opinions represent the final resolution of constitutional conflicts in American society. While interpretations of the equal protection clause are based upon a point of view centered around treating all people—regardless of race or ethnicity—as individuals, this is not the only valid understanding of racial phenomena. This reality is especially significant when addressing major educational reform movements. Since society precedes schooling, major educational reforms pass in and out of favor depending on social conditions and how prevailing patterns of understanding interpret those conditions.[1] This Chapter reviews the justifications for the growing movement in favor of increasing school choice. Consistent with Post-Desegregation Awareness, increasing school choice against the background of increasing racial segregation in public schools will be discussed through each of the four cognitive frameworks: Traditional Americanism, African-American Centralism, Colorblind Individualism and American Collectivism.

As stated earlier, the various perceptions of a given racial phenomena are structured and limited by diverse patterns of understandings. These cognitive frameworks do not provide a definitive answer to a given racial issue, such as whether expanding school choice is positive or negative. They do, however, structure and limit both the arguments that are persuasive when discussing a particular racial issue and the possible range of solutions that can be advanced to resolve a given racial conflict. Thus, arguments could be generated within each of these cognitive frameworks that would oppose expanding school choice. This Chapter, however, will only discuss the arguments derived from each of the discourses that find favor with the educational reform movement directed towards expanding school choice. Increasing school choice, is being discussed against the background of increasing racial segregation in public school schools. Choice, when constrained by the desire to promote integrated public schools, was one of the means used to pursue desegregation. But, one of the ways in which southern school districts sought to contain or avoid desegregation during the late 1950s and 1960s was through increasing school choice—public, as well as private. Thus, many of the arguments that would be proposed against school choice, especially with the current background of increasing racial segregation in public schools, would be similar to those discussed in Chapter Six which presented the arguments in favor of the efforts to desegregate public schools. Many of those same arguments could be advance in opposition to increasing school choice today.

Except where necessary, this Chapter will not distinguish increased public school choice from increasing school choice through the provision of school vouchers. While there are important and significant differences, public and private school choice are born out of same set of beliefs. Increased choice creates a competitive environment that forces schools to compete for students. Thus, increased school choice should produce new and innovative schools, including those that are particularly effective at responding to the educational needs of low-income, urban, minority students. In a competitive environment, the schools that cannot adequately educate the students in their charge will not survive. In addition, the programs and policies of schools that are effective will be copied by other schools. Thus, establishing a competitive environment for schools should increase the educational performance of the students currently attending the worse performing schools. Also, each of the discourses would cite to the expected improved performance in academic achievement that, at least in theory, can be expected from increased choice. Despite the theoretical justifications that lead many to suspect that increasing choice will improve academic performance, as of yet, a consensus has not developed that increased school choice will lead to significant improvement in academic achievement of black schoolchildren.[2] Therefore, this chapter will highlight justifications for increasing school choice that are not based upon proof that increasing school choice will lead to significant improvement in educational achievement.

I. Traditional Americanism

The salient feature of this cognitive framework when perceiving racial phenomena involving African-Americans is the perception of blacks as the paradigmatic inferior racial group. Non-Hispanic whites can be conceptualized as individuals or as members of a superior racial group. But in some relevant way, blacks are always understood as not measuring up to the applicable norm. Until the 20th century, this discourse on the second rate nature of blacks was premised on causes that were more or less immutable to social engineering. The defective nature of blacks was attributed to the Divine will of God, the evolutionary fact of the consequences of living for so long in the hostile climate of Africa or their defective biology. From the 1930s and onward, the idea that the cause of the inferiority of blacks was primarily the result of cultural and social environmental deficits became the dominant explanation. As the social environmental argument was accepted, it generated a belief that blacks could be significantly improved if their social environment could be ameliorated. The cure for the disease afflicting blacks was enriching their cultural environment through increased contact with whites.

Discussions about increasing school choice against a background of increasing racial segregation in the public schools, within this cognitive framework would recognize what was learned during the experience of desegregation. Research on the benefits of school desegregation has failed to document consistently that school desegregation generated significant improvements in educational achievement of black students.[3] Now that more than fifty years have elapsed since the Court's opinion in *Brown,* it is clear that black students seldom demonstrate the same academic abilities as non-Hispanic white students. Significant racial gaps still exist between black schoolchildren and their non-Hispanic white counterparts in virtually every measure of academic achievement. Black students continue to lag far behind their non-Hispanic white counterparts in their performance on standardized tests. Even more, over the last ten to fifteen years the racial gaps on a number of standardized tests have either remained the same or actually widened. Black students are less likely to finish high school than non-Hispanic white students. African-American students are also twice as likely to be retained in the same grade during their educational career than non-Hispanic white schoolchildren. Black students are overrepresented in the lower academic tracks in schools and underrepresented in the more challenging academic skills groupings.

Having now experienced integrated education for over fifty years, it is obvious that black children in integrated schools are exposed to the reality that the non-Hispanic white students are academically superior to them. Black students in racially integrated schools experience the reality that they are seldom on the honor roll, seldom participate in programs that honor high academic achievement, seldom graduate with academic honors and are seldom the class valedictorian or salutatorian. The exposure to academically superior white students may attenuate the black students' willingness to put forth their best effort in their school work. In his dissenting opinion in *Grutter,* Justice Clarence Thomas pointed to studies which, at least for blacks that attend colleges, demonstrate that racial heterogeneity actually impairs the learning of black students.[4] A substantial amount of diversity may moderate the cognitive development of black students.[5] By exposing black students to the more academically gifted non-Hispanic white students, integrated education may actually retard the educational motivation of black children. Thus, desegregation could produce the very psychological harm that the Supreme Court attributed to segregation in its opinion in *Brown.*

The possibility that integrated education could actually serve to reinforce the view that blacks are not as intelligence as whites was actually noted by the Massachusetts Supreme Judicial Court over 150 years ago in its opinion in *Roberts v. Boston.* In responding to a challenge by a black father brought on behalf of his school age child to the racial segregation in Boston public schools, Chief Justice Shaw's opinion stated:

> It is urged, that this maintenance of separate schools tends to deepen and perpetuate the odious distinction of caste, founded in a deep-rooted prejudice in public opinion. This prejudice, if it exists, is not created by law, and probably cannot be changed by law. Whether this distinction and prejudice, existing in the opinion and feelings of the community, would not be as effectually fostered by compelling colored and white children to associate together in the same schools, may well be doubted. . . .[6]

The Supreme Court in its opinion in *Plessy v. Ferguson* also specifically rejected the notion that social prejudices against blacks could be overcome by legislation that would seek integration of the races. If the races are to meet on terms of social equality it must be the result of natural affinities, mutual appreciation and voluntary consent.[7] Thus, the attempt to bring it about through enforcing integration was ultimately bound to fail.

Increasing school choice should also decrease the sense of blacks to blame others for their lack of adequate educational performance. If competitive free markets are established with regard to education, then poor black parents would be able to exercise choices in determining where their child attends schools. The ability to exercise this choice also carries with it the responsibility for the successes, as well as the failures, of the choices. The establishment of a competitive environment would mean that the blacks themselves would be the ones who would choose which schools survived and which schools failed. If choice increases the performance of African-American schoolchildren, then everyone wins. But if they do not perform any better, the responsibility for the failure should lie with those making the "wrong" choice. Thus, increasing school choice could lead African-Americans to be more willing to accept the fact that their place at the bottom of the social order is the result of the natural order of things.

Finally, increasing school choice may also work to save limited public resources by reducing the amounts spent on education, particularly of low-income, urban, minority students. Charter schools and the provision of public funds for private education may prove to be a less expensive way to fund education. The Supreme Court noted this in its opinion addressing a challenge to the school voucher program established in Cleveland in *Zellman v. Harris.*[8] Cleveland had a charter school program, which it called a community school program, funded under state law. For each child enrolled, the charter schools received state funding of $4,518. The private schools that participated in the Cleveland voucher program received a voucher that provided a maximum benefit of $2,250 to low income students and $1,875 to other participants in the program. In contrast, the cost of educating the remaining 76,000 students in Cleveland's 121 public schools was $712 million, or about $9,368 per student.[9] Private schools, particularly religiously affiliated private schools can draw on donations and other financial support from their congregations. This could allow them to provide an adequate education to the students that attend their schools at a cost well below that of public schools. The funding levels for the vouchers in Milwaukee and Florida's Opportunity Scholarship voucher program, for example, also suggest that vouchers may be a less expensive way to provide for education. Typically money for public education comes from both the state and local property tax revenues. The vouchers provided to parents in Milwaukee, however, were only tied to the per pupil state aid or private school tuition, whichever was less. The value of the vouchers was $5,553 for the 2001–02 school year.[10] In Florida, the voucher amounts were also tied only to the state's share in the expenses of eligible students. For 2001–02, the average amount of the award was $3,500 to $3,900.

II. African-American Centralism

The driving idea of African-American Centralism that organizes its view of the social world is the desire to liberate black people from racial domination. As a result African-American Centralism views the social world as a collection of racial and ethnic groups struggling for scarce societal resources. Non-Hispanic whites, as a group, have a disproportionately large share of beneficial social resources. Anyone, regardless of race or ethnicity, can perceive racial phenomena within this system of meaning and assist blacks in eradicating racial oppression. But, since this system of meaning is focused on the liberation of the black community, it ascribes special moral obligations to black individuals who—by definition—are members of that community. Regardless of personal predilections, every black individual is viewed as always linked to the struggle against racial oppression. Every black person is under a never ceasing obligation to fight for the liberation of African-American people.

For African-American Centralism, a component of the discussion about current moves to increase school choice is the benefits of racially separate education as opposed to integrated education. The first reality to recognize in this portion of the discussion is a lesson that has been well learned as a result of the past fifty years. Integrated education is often beyond the power of blacks to bring about. Non-Hispanic whites, motivated by rational self-interest, as well as, discriminatory beliefs, often refuse to send their children to schools where there are a significant number of African-Americans. When non-Hispanic whites were ordered to attend schools in black areas during the Desegregation Era, they often refused to go. The terms "tipping point" and "white flight" were coined to describe the phenomena of the resistance and abandonment of whites to the desegregation process in urban school districts. Despite all the struggle and angst to desegregate America's public schools, at the height of the integration of public schools 62.9% of black students still attended majority-minority schools and 32.5% were in schools where at least 90% of the students were minorities.[11] Statistics during the Desegregation Era also indicated that non-Hispanic white enrollment in private schools tended to be largest in those school districts with large percentages of minorities students in the public schools. For example in the 1989–90 school year 67% of white students were enrolled in private schools in Washington D.C.; 65% in New Orleans; 55% in Philadelphia; 54% in Chicago; 49% in San Francisco; 48% in Boston; 47% in Cleveland; and 45% in New York City.[12]

The resistance of non-Hispanic whites to integrated education seen over the last fifty years was not historically unique. During the drafting of the state constitutional conventions in the former Confederate states that were called to pave the way for readmission to the Union in 1867 and 1868, the issue of integrated public education was brought up. Except in North Carolina, prior to the Civil War there was no general system of public education in the South. The first massive effort in the South at constructing a public education system was the result of reconstruction after the Civil War. Because of white resistance to integrated schools, the heated debates that occurred in nearly every state convention regarding the issue of public school integration were—to a large degree—only theoretical. As during discussions about integrated education after the Civil War, discussions about integrated education during the Desegregation Era proved to be purely theoretical for a large number of black schoolchildren. The reality for the African-American community is that for a large segment of black schoolchildren, school desegregation has never and will never occur.

While it is true that most black students will attend majority-minority schools, some black schoolchildren could be in integrated educational settings. Increased parental choice for these students is likely to have a segregating effect. But when integrated education does occur, black students often feel that the school environment in integrated schools is racially hostile to them. This too is nothing new. Black students that attended the first integrated urban public educational systems established in the U.S. over two hundred years ago experienced this. At a town meeting in Boston, Massachusetts in 1789, three writing schools and three reading schools were established for the instruction of children between the ages of seven and fourteen.[13] The early Boston school law did not exclude blacks from attendance at these community schools. Within a year, however, "vex and insult" had driven all but three or four black students from Boston's community schools.[14] Hosea Easton, a black who had been enrolled in the Boston community schools, recalled that his former school teachers sent bad youngsters, white and black, to the so-called "nigger seat," telling them such things as they would be as poor or ignorant as a nigger, or have no more credit than a nigger.[15] It was in Boston, within the context of discrimination in integrated schools, that blacks made their first request for publicly funded separate education. The parents of Boston's black schoolchildren wanted to be certain that their children would receive a quality education, but also shield them from the prejudice they were being subjected to in integrated schools.[16]

A hostile learning environment also met many African-American schoolchildren when desegregation of their respective school districts began. Many whites in places as diverse as Little Rock, Arkansas; Prince Edwards County, Virginia; and Boston, Massachusetts made no secret of their desire to prevent blacks from attending schools with whites. Black students in integrated schools still can face hostile learning environments, though they are far more subtle than the openly racist environments that black students of early times experienced. In a number of different ways, the education in integrated schools may assume that there is something wrong with black students that needs to be fixed. Professor Banks, for example, pointed out that the two major goals of educators during the desegregation movement were to raise the self-concepts of ethnic minority youths and to increase their racial pride.[17] However, the movement embodied the notion that the self-concept of ethnic minorities would improve by a portrayal of blacks as essentially colored whites. The changes made by commercial textbook publishers during this period were not substantive, but cosmetic. Dick and Jane retained all of their usual middle-class social and behavioral traits, but were given black and brown faces.[18] Traditional instructional programs in public schools underwent revisions to recognize previously neglected contributions of individual ethnic minorities. However, to be acknowledged, the individuals had to satisfy the Anglocentric norms of acceptability and excellence. Thus, attempts to include African-Americans resulted in ethnic content grafted onto the white instruction typified by traditional educational programs.[19] The establishment of a number of cultural enrichment programs followed these changes in the curriculum. Trips to concerts, art galleries, scientific laboratories and museums became part of the educational system. The purpose of these programs was to expose minority children to the artifacts and traditions of America's mainstream. However, no corresponding programs exposed non-Hispanic white children to important social institutions in the African-American community.[20] The underlying message of this one-way exposure reinforced the changes in curricular material which were structured around the view that blacks would be improved by simply dropping their deviant cultural traits and attitudes and adopting the requisite mainstream characteristics.

Another problem with integrated education is that such education is normally geared to the interest of the non-Hispanic white students. In schools engaged in integration, faculty and administrators were often integrated first. Often times many of the best African-American teachers were siphoned off and placed in predominately non-Hispanic white schools. The non-Hispanic white teachers sent to the predominately black schools tended to be less qualified and less experienced than the other non-Hispanic white teachers that remained in the largely white schools. Thus, the black students remaining in segregated schools suffered both the loss of the best black teachers, who could motivate them to learn and act as positive role models, and received the least effective white teachers. The same often held true for the best black students. Often it was the best black students that were integrated into classes with whites. The more academically gifted black students could provide good role models for the less academically inclined black students and also assist their black brothers and sisters with their academic work.

Another justification for increasing school choices is that it should allow for the creation and development of more schools structured around the social-cultural environment of blacks. The benefit of any education is measured by how well it prepares students to deal with the situations that they will encounter throughout their lives. To the extent that education is standardized, it tends to be standardized on the experiences of non-Hispanic whites. But, the basic educational needs of African-American schoolchildren should take account of their general social-cultural environment. This environment is different for blacks. For as Justice O'Connor candidly noted in her opinion in *Grutter v. Bollinger*, "being a racial minority in a society like our own, in which race unfortunately still matters" will effect a person's experiences growing up.[21] When educating black youth for life in American society, black students must be taught to deal with the twin aspects of this reality. Black children have to be taught to accept the duties imposed upon them by the need to engage in the collective struggle to eradicate racial subordination. They must come to understand that the collective interest of the black community in this struggle is paramount. Black children should be socialized to believe that sometimes their individual interest may have to yield to the best interest of the black community. The second aspect that must be taken into account in the education of black children is the ever present reality that African-Americans will encounter the persistent belief at the core of Traditional Americanism, that in some relevant way they do not measure up. Black students need to be taught techniques and skills to cope with racism and to overcome the obstacles that it will inevitably place in their path to success. These are extremely important aspects of the education of black children, which is seldom adequately stressed in integrated schools. Increasing parental school choice should lead to experimentation in education and increase the types of schools and the kinds of educational programs that are employed to educate schoolchildren. Thus, experimentation and multiplication of the types of schools should allow for the development of schools that will take account of the socio-cultural environment of African-Americans. Increased parental choice should therefore assist in the struggle by the black community to overcome racial oppression through encouraging the development of schools whose education is more relevant to black students because it is drawn from the experiences of African-Americans.

Increased school choice should also help black schoolchildren because they are being inadequately served by the current public school system. As Justice Thomas noted in his concurring opinion in *Zellman v. Simmons-Harris*,[22]

> Although one of the purposes of public schools was to promote democracy and a more egalitarian culture, failing urban public schools disproportionately affect minority children most in need of educational opportunity. At the time of Reconstruction, blacks considered public education a matter of personal liberation and a necessary func-

> tion of a free society. Today, however, the promise of public school education has failed poor inner-city blacks. While in theory providing education to everyone, the quality of public schools varies significantly across districts. Just as blacks supported public education during Reconstruction, many blacks and other minorities now support school choice programs because they provide the greatest educational opportunities for their children in struggling communities.[23]

As could be expected, minority and low-income parents express the greatest support for parental choice and are most interested in placing their children in private schools. "[T]he appeal of private schools is especially strong among parents who are low income, minority, and live in low-performing districts: precisely the parents who are the most disadvantaged under the current system."[24] Almost seventy-five percent of all public school parents with an annual income less than $20,000 support vouchers, compared to fifty-seven percent of with an annual income of over $60,000. In addition, seventy-five percent of black public school parents support vouchers.[25]

Beyond increasing racial segregation in the public schools, increasing parental options, even on a racially neutral basis, for choosing the school that their child attends should disproportionately advantage the black community. One of the major considerations in choosing where to live is the quality of the available schools. By choosing where to reside, parents exercise a tremendous amount of choice over what school their child attends. The average non-Hispanic white family has more housing options because they have more financial means and are less constrained by discrimination endemic in housing choices than the average African-American family. Increasing racially neutral forms of school choice, therefore, should disproportionately advantage African-American parents and their children. Thus, increasing racially neutral forms of school choice helps to further the struggle against racial oppression by working to level the playing field regarding the ability of the black community to choose the best schools for their children.

Increased choice in education should increase the possibility that parents will be able to assure that their school age black child has an African-American teacher. Non-Hispanic white teachers often do not seem to be as concerned about the educational interest of the black students as they are the white students. This reality may help to explain the fact that blacks students tend to be underrepresented in the academically challenging classes and overrepresented in the lower academic classes. Scholars have identified several important reasons why students of color stay in school longer and achieve more when they have teachers that look like themselves.[26] Teachers of color provide students of color with invaluable role models. This is especially true in education, where they function as examples of academic success in an area where blacks are often expected not to succeed.[27] Black teachers also share their black students' cultural and life experiences and, thus, may be better able to respond to the particular difficulties that these students face, both in school and in American society in general. Black teachers may be able to reach out and work successfully with parents of students of color who are more likely to trust their judgment and evaluation of their children.[28] It may also be that teachers of color will hold higher expectations for students of color. Many studies have demonstrated that teacher expectations have a significant impact on how well students learn.[29]

Schools of choice might also come to function as important community centers for the dissemination of an array of useful information to the black community. Catering to the interests of the black parents who will make the selection about where to send their children to school, school operators might develop and implement educational programs that are useful for the parents of their students. In order to attract and maintain students, the operators of choice schools, whether public or private, may also provide medical services such as a place for flu vaccinations or health care checkups for blood pressure or cholesterol screening. Choice schools could also become community resources for organizing and conducting seminars about legal rights of tenants, federal and state income tax information or employment opportunities. Thus, in an effort to attract and maintain students, choice schools might help the black community by being a provider of important information on a variety of topics to the parents of the students who attend their schools.

Giving parents of black schoolchildren the power to select their child's school may work to empower these parents in other ways. To choose the best school for their child, parents will need to become more actively involved in the educational options available in their community. The same skills employed in researching educational options for their child could be applied to other significant areas of a person's life. For example, these parents may use their investigative skills to discover better employment or economic opportunities or increase their knowledge about nutritional information and health risks that they may face. Thus, the personal empowerment of parents of black children that is the result of exercising school choice may have a spillover effect into other areas and thereby advance the interest of the black community in other ways.

Giving parents of black students a choice of where to send their children to school also increases the power of the black community to influence the education of black children. Rather than have educational placement in the hands of public school authorities, the power is in the hands of black parents. This shift in where the educational placement power is located could increase the ability of the black community to determine the best educational environment for black children.

Increasing public funding for private schools, as opposed to increasing public school choice, could also provide for the Black Church to get actively involved in the education of black children. There are a number of reasons to believe that the involvement of Black Churches in the education of black schoolchildren could be beneficial to the black community. First, the religiously oriented education could provide an important counterbalance to the negative influences in the broader community that encourage young children to experiment with pre-marital sex and drugs and become involved in gangs and criminal activities. Schools run by Black Churches are also likely to provide a safe learning environment for the students. The problems of the prevalence of school violence and drugs will be somewhat attenuated by the respect normally accorded to sacred religious places. Simply put, students are more likely to be on their best behavior at religious schools run by their churches than in public schools. Many black parents will be active members of the church that would open the school. Having black children attend schools at their churches means that they are attending schools at places where their parents are already actively involved.

III. Colorblind Individualism

Colorblind Individualism views society as a collection of Knowing Individuals. Knowing Individuals are free-willed, rational, autonomous and self-determined people who are capable of pursuing their self formulated goals and objectives. According to this cognitive framework, government comes into existence in order to protect the rights of Knowing Individuals to pursue their self-determined goals and objectives. Thus, government should be neutral on the question of the type of goals and objectives individuals should pursue or what constitutes a good society. Government must both respect the individuality of its citizens and mediate their conduct so as to allow them to purse their own desires and to prevent them from unjustly interfering with the rights of their fellow persons to do likewise. By doing this, government allows individuals to choose their own goals and ends for themselves consistent with a similar liberty for others.

Minors are not Knowing Individuals because they lack the experience, cognitive development, maturity and judgment of adults. They must go through a maturation process. Thus, in contrast to adults, children are viewed within this discourse as learners, not constrained choosers. Public schools participate in the maturation process of minors through educating students. Since public schools are government institutions, however, the socialization of the next generation of adult citizens must respect the limits of neutrality placed upon government within this cognitive framework. Public education should produce learners who are the kinds of choosers that are necessary for a society committed to individual self-determination.[30] Public schools should seek to broaden the sensibilities of children, kindle their imagination and foster a spirit of free inquiry. But equally important is the need for public schools to produce learners who constrain their choices in order to allow others the same right of self-determination. Thus, schools must strive to further the values of independence and toleration.

The discussion about increasing school choice taking place against the background of increasing racial segregation in public schools is about the benefits of respecting individual choices of parents, guardians and students. The increase in racial segregation is primarily the result of eliminating the ability of public school officials and federal courts from taking account of race in order to promote integrated education. Within this discourse there was always an important distinction between striking down statutes that segregated students by race and using racial classifications to further integrated education. The objection to segregation statutes was that they required government to use racial classifications to determine public school attendance and teacher and administrator assignments. By treating public school students, teachers and staff as members of racial groups, government denied them their individuality. Government commits the same sin when public school officials use racial classifications to further the laudable purpose of integrated education. Even though the purpose is commendable, it still denies the individuality of those treated as members of racial groups. When government classifies students by their race and ethnicity, it is also teaching impressionable young people that race and ethnicity matters. The only way, arguably, such an infringement of self-determination could be justified is by generating more capacity for individual self-determination than what is lost by treating people as members of racial and ethnic groups.

Initiated by the Supreme Court's opinion in *Brown v. Board of Education* and *Green v. New Kent County,* the widespread use of racial classifications to promote the desegregation of public schools began in earnest in the late 1960s. At that time the assumption that race and ethnicity were significant in determining the life experiences of individuals in America could be taken for granted. Many people in America consciously judged others, especially minorities, with reference to stereotypes attached to their skin color. But the America that existed in the 1960s is not the America of today. Americans live in a society that has been fundamentally altered by the Desegregation Era sparked by *Brown v. Board of Education.* It is clear to all but the most obstinate observers of race relations that race is currently less of a factor in limiting the opportunities of those who happen to be black than at any other time in this country's collective past. The success of many individual African-Americans testifies to this change. As a result, the use of racial classifications to promote integrated public education is far less effective in advancing respect for individuality than it was thirty-five years ago.

School choice, whether public or private, increases the ability of parents to choose the best educational situation for their children. What the Supreme Court stated in *Brown* is more true today. "It is doubtful that any child may reasonably be expected to succeed in life if he is denied the opportunity of an education."[31] One of the primary purposes of education is to turn learners into choosers and provide them with the maximum number of options to pursue as adults for their own self-fulfillment that is consistent with a similar liberty for others. The better a person's education the higher their cognitive skills and abilities will become. Improved intellectual awareness increases a person's capacity to choose more productive lifestyles that better allows them to obtain their self-formulated goals and objectives. Increased school choice should produce new and innovative schools and thereby, multiply the types of educational situations that parents can choose for their child. While there is certainly a huge concern that parents will attempt to bias the education of their child and thereby restrict potential choices that the child can make, most parents are also in the best position to determine the best educational setting for their child. No one knows a given child better than the child's parent. Thus, increased parental choice should improve the chances of placing each individual child in the best educational environment possible.

Increased school choice is also more likely to be employed in urban, low income, predominately minority areas. These are the parents who have less capacity to choose the best education for their children. A lack of income affects the ability of these parents to choose neighborhoods with good public schools for their children, as well as prevents them from being able to afford tuition at private schools. Thus, increasing parental choice of financially disadvantaged children is also justified from a moral point of view. It helps to offset the built-in advantage that accrues to the children of middle class parents who are able to exercise a tremendous amount of educational choice by selecting the appropriate neighborhood where their child will attend schools. Increasing the ability of parents of low-income students who do not possess the capacity to make such a choice helps to offset an advantage that children of wealthier parents have over those of poorer parents.

IV. American Collectivism

The goal of this cognitive framework is to maximize the interest of the one American community. This interest is improved either by increasing happiness or reducing suffering of the entire American community. In order to determine what is in the best interest of the American people, it is necessary to refer to the values they hold dear. Certain values in America such as democracy, liberty, equality and the pursuit of happiness have always been fundamental to the nation. But the meanings of these basic values change over time. Thus, each generation defines the meaning of these core values to fit their current times. In order to determine what is considered to be in the best interest of the country, it is necessary to refer to the interpretations of these timeless values at a given time.

For American Collectivism, the discussion about increasing school choice taking place against the background of increasing racial segregation in public schools is about the benefits to the country derived from the elimination of forced desegregation and increasing school choice. When school desegregation began in earnest in the 1960s, many Americans believed that segregated education harmed the education and academic achievement of black and minority children. This belief was based in part on the fact that the schools that black and other minority children attended were inadequately supplied and staffed. Minority students were also thought to suffer from damaged self-esteems, which deprived them of the motivation to do well in school. School integration was, therefore, expected to generate significant educational and psychological benefits for minority schoolchildren. The research on the benefits of school desegregation, however, has failed to document either of these expected benefits.[32] For example, in 1991 a group of social scientist submitted a statement to the Supreme Court as part of the NAACP brief in the second school desegregation termination case of *Freeman v. Pitts*.[33] The social scientist stated that "[d]esegregation is generally associated with moderate gains in the achievement of black students and the achievement of white students is unaffected."[34] In addition, there is no consensus that African-American schoolchildren that attend desegregated schools possess a higher self-esteem than those who do not. The research concerning the effects of desegregation on personality development is simply inadequate to determine the impact of segregated schooling on personality development.[35] Plus, since the late 1960s the evidence has clearly suggested that the self-esteem of blacks is about the same as that of whites.[36] It may very well have been that blacks never suffered from low self-esteem during the Segregation Era, despite the Supreme Court's pronouncement in *Brown.*

When the Supreme Court rendered its opinion in *Brown,* segregation and disenfranchisement of blacks stood in sharp contrast to America's fundamental values of liberty, equality and democracy. During the Desegregation Era it became accepted that

> [W]hen the architects of our American republic wrote the magnificent words of the Constitution and the Declaration of Independence, they were signing a promissory note to which every American was to fall heir. This note was a promise that all men would be guaranteed the inalienable rights of life, liberty, and the pursuit of happiness.[37]

In addition, during the Cold War Soviet propaganda focused the world's attention on America's internal racial practices. Newspapers throughout the world carried stories about the discrimination faced by non-white visiting foreigners and black Americans. The Soviets made effective arguments about the exploitation inherent in the American form of society by pointing to the racial failings of the United States. But, America has now bleached out a significant portion of the stain of segregation and disenfranchisement of blacks that was on the American soul. America is a far more just nation than it was fifty years ago. America has also prevailed in the Cold War. Thus, desegregation is less important in advancing the collective good of American society today.

The use of racial classifications to promote integration of American society, including the public schools, always had a potential downside in terms of the commitment to social justice. One of the lessons of the use of race in American society to determine governmental benefits and obligations is that distinctions between citizens solely because of their ancestry are by their very nature odious to a free people whose institutions are founded upon the doctrine of equality.[38] Due to the importance many people in American society place on individuality, treating children as members of racial or ethnic groups, even to promote integrated student bodies, appears to be unjust because it fails to treat them as individuals. This represents one of the fundamental changes in dominant American values regarding race that his occurred over the past fifty years. Admittedly, Americans continue to live with the impact of its past racism, but many do not believe that the way to cure racism is to practice reverse racism. The way to overcome the effects of the past and advance American society along its path of increasing social justice is not to tolerate any retreat from the principle that government must treat people as individuals. Reducing the use of racial classifications by public schools is an important step in increasing the commitment of American society to social justice despite an increase in racial segregation in the public schools.

Beyond the elimination of court ordered school desegregation, increasing the ability of parents to select the school that their children will attend provides parents and children with a greater sense of ownership in the child's education. Students and parents given a voice in where their children go to school feel better about their education. Research suggests that parents who choose the schools their children attend are more pleased with the results.[39] Thus, choice seems to improve parental contentment with their children's education.

School choice can advance the notion of increased social justice in American society. In a society like the U.S., there is a strong belief that positions of social advantage should be earned through individual efforts as oppose to ascribed based on the good fortunes of birth. Economically disadvantaged minority students in urban school districts, however, do not have the same educational opportunities as non-Hispanic white, suburban students. Increasing school choice for economically disadvantaged minority schoolchildren provides them with more educational opportunities. In so doing it should improve their ability to find the right educational setting. This will improve the chances that their future success will be based upon their individual abilities and efforts as opposed to the inauspicious fact of being born to less fortunate parents and, thereby, confined to schools of poor quality.

In the long run, increasing the number of charter schools and school vouchers may also be a less expensive way of funding education. As noted in the discussions about Cleveland, charter schools were provided with less funds than regular public schools. In addition, amounts for vouchers for private schools have normally been considerably less than corresponding per pupil expenditures on public schools. Private schools, especially those affiliated with religious institutions, tend to charge less in tuition than what public schools spend per pupil to educate students. If schoolchildren obtain the same educational achievement with less money spent, that is a benefit for all in American society.

Providing low-income, urban, minority parents with a greater ability to control the education of their children could have additional benefits in terms of empowering them in other aspects of their lives. In order to make the right decision for their child, parents will need to become actively involved in coming to understand the educational options available in their community. Some parents who may feel powerless to change their desperate circumstances may be able to gain new found confidence in their abilities after going through the process of selecting the right school for their child. This personal empowerment could carry over into other areas of their lives and thereby make them more effective people generally which would benefit all Americans.

Within this system of meaning, public school choice may differ from private school choice in kind as opposed to in degree. Since public schools are still government schools, the community is still involved in assuring the existence of a strong public school. A widespread program of public funding of private education could lead to the promotion of self-interest over social commitment. Self-interested individuals inevitably view their human interactions as essentially contractual exchanges. In this cult of individualism, relationships established with fellow persons are done so primarily in order to advance one's self-interest. This self-interested ideology ultimately runs counter to notions of sacrificing that interest for the good of the American collective. Thus, this cognitive framework will tend to support public school choice more so than private school choice.

Conclusion

This Chapter has reviewed educational reform efforts to increase school choice against the background of resegegretation in each of the four different discourses. As indicated before, these discourses only structure and limit the perception of a given racial phenomena and thus structure and limit the type of arguments that are deemed persuasive to resolve a given racial conflict. Thus, while arguments could be made that would place the expansion of school choice against the background of increasing segregation in public schools in a negative light within each of these systems of meaning, this section only presented the arguments in favor of increased school choice. The primary point to this presentation is to demonstrate that the perception of racial phenomena, like increasing school choice against a background of increasing racial segregation in public schools, does not have one true meaning. The understanding and interpretation of racial phenomena, like increasing school choice, is more a function of particular discourses used to comprehend the phenomena than something inherent in the understanding of the phenomena.

Conclusion

There are two interwoven objectives of this book. One is to discuss the developments of the current educational situation of African-American schoolchildren fifty years after the Supreme Court's opinion in *Brown v. Board of Education*. There are three major factors that shape the current educational situation of African-American schoolchildren in the Post-Desegregation Era. First, significant gaps between African-American schoolchildren and their non-Hispanic white counterparts can be seen in measures of academic achievement including scores on standardized tests, high school graduation/dropout rates, percentage of students retained in a given grade and achievement skills grouping. The second and third factors can be traced to changes in the Supreme Court's interpretations of the equal protection clause. Over the past fifteen years racial segregation in American public schools has been on the increase. Given decisions by federal courts addressing school desegregation, this trend is likely to continue into the foreseeable future. Third, changes in the Supreme Court's interpretation over the past thirty years of the equal protection clause generally prevent successful constitutional challenges to legitimate educational policies and practices that disproportionately impact the educational opportunities of black schoolchildren in a negative way. These changes also significantly limit the ability of legislators and educators to adopt and implement educational policies and procedures that take account of race in order to counteract the continuing racial achievement gaps.

The result of these three factors—continuing gaps in academic achievement, increasing levels of racial segregation in public schools and limits on the adoption or implementation of racially neutral educational policies or practices—is that politicians and educational reformist are increasingly forced to argue for policies and programs that are race-neutral. One of the most significant racially neutral educational reform movements sweeping the country is the expansion of school choice, both public and private. By choosing where to reside, parents exercise a tremendous amount of choice over what school their child attends. One of the major considerations in choosing where to live is the quality of the available schools. Families with financial means can not only pay for private education, but are also able to leave a given school district by moving to another district. Due to this mobility, maintaining excellent public schools is central to most affluent communities' appeal to those who can afford to live there and central to moderate-income communities' strategies to attract new tax-paying residents. In districts where people have the means to choose whether to leave or stay (i.e. the more affluent districts), the public schools are predictably among the best. Thus, in terms of residential choice, the affluent parents of schoolchildren reap tremendous educational benefits for their children that come from their considerable capacity to choose the school their children attend.

Under increased choice proposals all parents in a given school district, given school or schools in a given district, a given area of a given school district or below a particular income level are provided the limited opportunity to choose the school their child attends. Choice is thus granted to parents with reference to a qualification unrelated to the race or ethnicity of the child. But low-income parents of minority schoolchildren in urban areas are the ones who have the least capability to exercise the primary forms of school choice by moving into neighborhoods with good schools or by paying for private education. Increasing racially neutral forms of school choice, therefore, should disproportionately advantage these parents and their children.

Although significant differences exist between public school choice and public funding of private education, also called school vouchers, both are born out of the same concerns. Advocates for increased choice generally assert that it will improve educational achievement, particularly of low-income, urban, minority students in a number of ways. Increased choice creates a competitive environment that forces schools to compete for students. Thus, increased school choice should produce new and innovative schools, including those that are particularly effective at responding to the educational needs of low-income, urban, minority students. In a competitive environment the schools that cannot adequately educate the students in their charge will not survive. In addition, the programs and policies of schools that are effective will be copied by other schools. Thus, establishing a competitive environment for schools should increase the educational performance of the students currently attending the worse performing schools. Despite the theoretical justifications that lead many to suspect that increasing choice will improve academic performance, as of yet, a consensus has not developed that increased school choice will lead to significant improvement in academic achievement of black schoolchildren. Thus, additional rationales that justify increasing school choice beyond improved educational achievement must be important in explaining the increase in school choice.

The other interwoven objective of this book is to advance the discussion of racial issues, particularly those involving African-American schoolchildren, through the Post-Desegregation Awareness. The Post-Desegregation Awareness is the conscious awareness that important social phenomena—including racial phenomena such as the development of the educational situation of black schoolchildren over the past fifty years—are more enlightening when they are comprehended from multiple perspectives or points of view. The Post-Desegregation Awareness is, thus, a conscious awareness that racial or ethnic phenomena are not understood as separate, isolated and unconnected incidents. The comprehension of any particular racial phenomena is always done against a *sub silentio* background of a much larger set of ideas about race and ethnicity, and there are always many different implicit backgrounds. These larger sets of ideas both structure and limit the perception of a given racial phenomena, dictate the kinds of arguments that are persuasive in discussing various racial issues and limit the potential solutions that can be implemented to resolve racial conflicts. This book refers to these larger diverse sets of ideas as the following: "discourses"; "patterns of understanding"; "systems of meaning"; or "cognitive frameworks".

The principal means to accomplish the second objective was by discussing both the desegregation of public education initiated by the Court's opinion in *Brown* and the current educational situation of African-Americans that has spawned educational reform movements focusing on increased school choice. Current increases in school choice are taking place against a background of increasing racial segregation in public schools. These developments in the education of black schoolchildren are discussed within the conceptual boundaries of each of the four different discourses—Traditional Americanism; African-American Centralism; Colorblind Individualism; and American Collectivism.

Each of the four patterns of understanding is based on a different fundamental view of the social world. They produce alternative and incommensurable understandings of a given racial phenomena, such as the desegregation of public schools caused by the Supreme Court's school desegregation decisions in the 1950s, 1960s and 1970s or the current educational reform movement directed at expanding school choice against a background of increasing racial segregation in public schools.

America's traditional culture (Traditional Americanism)—traditional in the sense that its roots are deep in the history of American society—views people of African descent as members of a substandard racial group. Blacks were classified first as non-citizens, and then as second-class citizens for 300 years before the Court's opinion in *Brown*. The salient feature of perceiving racial phenomena involving African-Americans within Traditional Americanism is the perception of blacks as in some way "less than" the relevant norm. During the long struggle against racial oppression, blacks—and those whites and others sympathetic to their cause—created a counter discourse to Traditional Americanism. African-American Centralism sees the social world in terms of one major purpose, goal and objective—the liberation of black people from racial domination. Within this discourse, blacks are viewed as victims of racial oppression, not inferior. Colorblind Individualism views the social world as a collection of Knowing Individuals. Knowing Individuals are viewed as autonomous, self-directed and free-willed people who know what they want in life and are capable of pursuing their self-determined goals and objectives. The primary objective of this pattern of understanding is the advancement of individual self-determination. The fourth and final cognitive framework, American Collectivism, views all Americans as constituting one people and seeks to further their collective interest. Within this utilitarian discourse, the suffering of a portion of the American community is justified if it produces enough of a benefit for the entire community to outweigh that suffering.

There is nothing intrinsic nor inevitable about these four systems of meaning. These four discourses were selected because they capture the general cultural sense of the ways in which Americans think about racial issues. Thus, the ways in which each of these cognitive frameworks perceives racial phenomena should be familiar to most Americans. While there is nothing intrinsic or inevitable about any of these discourses, I stressed throughout this book that Traditional Americanism for a long time dominated discussions regarding the determination of the legal rights (or lack thereof) of blacks throughout much of American history. Over the past thirty years, however, the Supreme Court's equal protection jurisprudence has come to increasingly embrace Colorblind Individualism. This change in the interpretation of the equal protection clause is largely responsible for the popularity of expanding school choice as a principal method of educational reform.

The Supreme Court's decision in *Brown v Board of Education* led to desegregation as the principal educational reform movement of the 1960s, 1970s and 1980s. This book examined the Supreme Court's jurisprudence which led to the rise of school desegregation through each of the four different cognitive frameworks—Traditional Americanism, African-American Centralism, Colorblind Individualism and American Collectivism. The various perceptions of a given racial phenomena, such as the Supreme Court's jurisprudence that gave rise to school desegregation, are structured and limited by these diverse patterns of understandings. These cognitive frameworks do not provide a definitive answer to a given racial conflict, such as whether school desegregation is positive or negative. They do, however, structure and limit the arguments that are persuasive when discussing a particular racial issue. Thus, arguments could be generated within each of these cognitive frameworks that would oppose desegregated education; however, in Chapter Six only arguments derived from each of the discourses in favor of the Supreme Court's decisions to take account of race in order to obtain the greatest possible degree of actual desegregation were discussed.

The explanations provided for in the Supreme Court's school desegregation jurisprudence that justified remedies for *de jure* segregation were based upon the belief that segregation inflicted psychological harm upon blacks. Segregation, with the sanction of law, had a tendency to retard the mental and educational development of black schoolchildren in ways unlikely ever to be undone. This explanation most closely resembles justifications for school desegregation remedies that would be generated within Traditional Americanism, which views blacks as in some relevant way less than whites. Within this system of meaning the primary reasons to desegregate public schools were based upon the belief that improving the educational environment of black children through interracial contact with whites would make them better people. Thus, desegregation was needed not because of, but in spite of, the fact that blacks were inferior to whites. African-American Centralism would downplay the explanation for remedies for *de jure* segregation contained in the language of the Court's opinion in *Brown.* Instead, this discourse would find favor with school desegregation because it aided African-Americans in their struggle to overcome their racial oppression. School desegregation provided a number of benefits to African-Americans in terms of breaking down the oppressive structures of segregation. Colorblind Individualism would approve of the Court's jurisprudence that led to the rise of school desegregation because it helped to advance individual self-determination. As a general rule within this cognitive framework, government should not treat people as members of racial and ethnic groups. But in the context of American society that existed at the time school desegregation was implemented, using racial classifications to integrate public schools helped children to overcome entrenched stereotypes and assisted in advancing the view that all should be treated as individuals in American society. Finally, American Collectivism viewed the increase in school desegregation as beneficial because it advanced the best interest of American society in a number of different ways. By eliminating segregation, school desegregation more closely aligned the actual practices of

American society with the basic values of liberty and equality that are among the fundamental values of this country. School desegregation was also of aid to the country in the struggle against communism. Thus, while school desegregation could be justified by each discourse, the perception of school desegregation, and thus the rationales for supporting it, were very different within each cognitive framework.

This book has also presented the justifications for the current growing movement of increasing school choice, both public and private, against a background of increasing racial segregation in the public schools within each of the four discourses. Only the arguments in favor of increasing school choice were presented. Traditional Americanism views increasing school choice as favorable because it largely viewed school desegregation as having failed to substantially improve African-Americans. Having now experienced integrated education for over fifty years, it is obvious that black students in racially integrated schools are seldom on the honor roll, seldom participate in programs that honor high academic achievement, seldom graduate with academic honors and are seldom the class valedictorian or salutatorian. Resegregating public schools through increased school choice would advance the educational interest of the academically superior white students and the academically inferior black students, because it would allow for education to be more tailored to their respective capacities. African-American Centralism could embrace increasing school choice against a background of increasing segregation because it would increase the black communities control over the education of its children. In addition, increased choice could assure that education in schools that black students attend is less hostile and more responsive to their educational needs. Colorblind Individualism was always somewhat troubled by the notion of government treating people as members of racial and ethnic groups in order to promote desegregated schools. Treating students as members of racial and ethnic groups sent the message to impressionable youngsters that race and ethnicity do and should matter. Eliminating conscious considerations of race and fostering individual choices of parents and their children is more in line with fostering the self-determination that is at the core of this pattern of understanding. American Collectivism can also support school choice because it could be viewed as advancing the best interest of the American collective in a number of important ways.

Endnotes

Introduction

1. 347 U.S. 483 (1954). There have been a number of recent books examining *Brown v Board of Education* in its Golden Anniversary. *See, e.g.*, DERRICK BELL, SILENT COVENANTS: BROWN V BOARD OF EDUCATION AND THE UNFULFILLED HOPES FOR RACIAL REFORM (2004); MICHAEL J. KLARMAN, FROM JIM CROW TO CIVIL RIGHTS: THE SUPREME COURT AND THE STRUGGLE FOR RACIAL EQUALITY; CHARLES OGLETREE, ALL DELIBERATE SPEED: REFLECTIONS ON THE FIRST HALF CENTURY OF BROWN V BOARD OF EDUCATION (2004); BROWN V BOARD OF EDUCATION: CASTE, CULTURE, AND THE CONSTITUTION (Robert J. Cottrol, Leland Ware, and Raymond Diamond eds. 2003).
2. Swann v. Charlotte-Mecklenburg Bd. of Educ., 402 U.S. 1, 13 (1971).
3. For example, in September 1999, Ford reached an agreement with the EEOC expected to cost it approximately ten million dollars to resolve claims by females alleging sexual and racial harassment. *See* EEOC press release, *EEOC and Ford Sign Multi-Million Dollar Settlement of Sexual Harassment Case* (Sept. 7, 1999) *available at* http://www.eeoc.gov/press/9–7–99.html.
4. *See* BARI-ELLEN ROBERTS WITH JACK E. WHITE, ROBERTS VS. TEXACO: A TRUE STORY OF RACE AND CORPORATE AMERICA 276 (1998).
5. *See* Lieff, Cabraser, Heimann & Bernstein, LLP, *Employment Discrimination Lawsuits, available at* http://lieffcabraser.com/practice_employment_rd.htm (last visited Jan. 12, 2004). *See also Cracker Barrel Settles Discrimination Suits*, CNN, Sept. 9, 2004, *available at* http://www.cnn.com/2004/LAW/09/09/cracker.barrel.ap/index.html (noting the Cracker Barrel restaurant chain has agreed to pay $8.7 million to settle lawsuits accusing the chain of mistreating and segregating black customers and discriminating against black employees.
6. *See* Yale University (Fall 2002) *available at* http://www.yale.edu/oir/factsheet.html (last visited Jan. 12, 2004); Harvard College (Fall 2002) *available at* http://vpf-web.harvard.edu/factbook/current_facts/enroll_ethnicity_7.html (last visited Jan. 12, 2004).
7. *See* Joint Center for Political and Economic Studies, *Number of Black Elected Officials in the United States, by State and Office, available at* http://jointcenter.org/DB/table/graphs/BEO_00.pdf.

8. U.S. Bureau of the Census, *2002 Statistical Abstract of the United States, Table 382: Members of Congress-Selected Characteristics 1983-2002* (2002), *available at* http://www.census.gov/prod/2003pubs/02statab/election.pdf. The number reported is thirty-nine, but that includes delegates from the District of Columbia and the Virgin Islands.

9. *See* The National Coalition on Black Civic Participation, *Table 1: The Black National Electorate by Demographic Group 1996 v. 2000, available at* http://www.bigvote.org/stats.htm (citing Voter News Service (NY Times, 11/12/00); compiled by David A. Bositis, Ph.D., JCPES).

10. The following individuals were severely criticized for racial insensitive statements. Professional baseball player John Rocker commented: "Imagine having to take the [number] 7 train to the ballpark, looking like you're [riding through] Beirut next to some kid with purple hair next to some queer with AIDS right next to some dude who just got out of jail for the fourth time right next to some 20-year-old mom with four kids. It's depressing." "The biggest thing I don't like about New York are the foreigners. I'm not a very big fan of foreigners." In the article, Rocker "calls an overweight black teammate 'a fat monkey,'" and "I'm not a racist or prejudiced person, but certain people bother me." Jeff Pearlman, *At Full Blast,* SPORTS ILLUSTRATED, Dec. 27, 1999, *available at* http://sportsillustrated.cnn.com/features/cover/news/1999/12/22/rocker.

    Jimmy "The Greek" Snyder "says the black athlete is 'bred to be the better athlete because, this goes all the way to the Civil War when...the slave owner would breed his big woman so that he would have a big black kid.'" *Jimmy "The Greek" Snyder canned for 'racist' remarks,* SPORTS ILLUSTRATED, Jan. 16, 1988, *available at* http://sportsillustrated.cnn.com/ almanac/video/1988/#2.

    Golfer Fuzzy Zoeller commenting on Tiger Woods after Tiger's Masters win (the winner of the Masters chooses the menu for the Champions Dinner the following year) "You pat him [Woods] on the back and say congratulations and enjoy it and tell him not to serve fried chicken...or collard greens or whatever the hell they serve." Associated Press, Atlanta, Georgia, (Apr. 21, 1997), also *available at* http://www.cnn.com/US/9704/21/fuzzy/.

11. *See* U.S. Bureau of the Census, *Historical Income Table P-1b (historical income table for African-Americans), available at* http://www.census.gov/hhes/income/histinc/p01b.html (last modified Sept. 30, 2002); U.S. Census Bureau, *Historical Incomes Table P-1a (historical income table for whites), available at* http://www.census.gov/hhes/income/histinc/p01a.html (last modified Sept. 30, 2002).

12. *See* U.S. Bureau of the Census, *Historical Poverty Tables: 2002, Table 2: Poverty Status of People by Family Relationship, Race, and Hispanic Origin: 1959 to 2002 available at* http://www .census.gov/hhes/poverty/histpov/hstpov2.html (revised Oct. 6, 2003).

13. For those under the age of 18 and over the age of 65 *see* U.S. Bureau of the Census, *Historical Poverty Tables: 2002, Table 3: Poverty Status of People, by Age, Race, and Hispanic Origin: 1959 to 2002 available at* http://www.census.gov/hhes/poverty/histpov/hstpov3.html (revised Oct. 6, 2003).

14. *See* U.S. Bureau of the Census, *supra* note 12.

15. For those under the age of 18 and over the age of 65 *see* U.S. Bureau of the Census, *supra* note 13.

16. *See* U.S. Bureau of the Census, *supra, note 12.*

17. For those under the age of 18 and over the age of 65 *see* U.S. Bureau of the Census, *supra* note 13.

18. *See* National Center for Educational Statistics, *Digest of Education Statistics 2002, Table 186: Enrollment rates of 18- to 24-year-olds in degree-granting institutions by sex, and race/ethnicity: 1967 to 2001, available at* http://www.nces.ed.gov/programs/digest/d02/tables/PDF/table186.pdf (last visited Jan. 13, 2004).

19. *Id.*

20. For 1970 figures, *see* BLACK AMERICANS: A STATISTICAL SOURCEBOOK 128 (Louise L. Hornor ed. 2000). For the 2000 figures, *see* The U.S. Bureau of the Census, Racial Statistics Branch, Population Division, *Current Population Survey, Table 7: Education Attainment of the Population 25 Years and Over by Sex, and Race and Hispanic Origin: March 2000* (Feb. 22, 2001), *available at* www.census.gov/population/socdemo/race/black/ppl-142/tab07.txt.

21. For 1970 figures, *see* BLACK AMERICANS: A STATISTICAL SOURCEBOOK *supra* note 20, at 128. For the 2000 figures, *see* The U.S. Bureau of the Census, *supra* note 20.

22. *See* U.S. Bureau of the Census, *2002 Statistical Abstract, Table 211: Mean Earnings by Highest Degree Earned: 1999, available at* http://www.census.gov/prod/2003pubs/02statab/educ.pdf. African-Americans with high school degrees only, with bachelor's degrees and with professional degrees earn $20,991, $37,422, and $75,509, respectively. Their non-Hispanic white counterparts earn $25,270, $46,894, and $103,450.

23. WILLIAM BOWEN & DERRICK BOK, THE SHAPE OF THE RIVER: LONG-TERM CONSEQUENCES OF CONSIDERING RACE IN COLLEGE AND UNIVERSITY ADMISSIONS 5 (1998) *citing* Robert O'Neil, *Preferential Admissions: Equalizing Access to Legal Education,* U. TOL. L. REV. Spring/Summer 1970, at 300.

24. BLACK AMERICANS: A STATISTICAL SOURCEBOOK *supra* note 20, at 202.

25. Number of Inmates in State or Federal prisons and local jails, by race, June 30, 2002.
Total inmate population: 1,848,700
Black inmate population: 884,500 (47.8%)
White inmate population: 699,500 (37.8%)

U.S. Department of Justice, Office of Justice Programs, Bureau of Justice Statistics, *Prison and Jail Inmates at Midyear 2002, Table 13: Number of inmates in State or Federal prisons and local jails, by gender, race, Hispanic origin, and age, June 30, 2002* (Apr. 2003), *available at* http://www.ojp.usdoj.gov/bjs/pub/pdf/pjim02.pdf.

26. Statistics indicate that African-Americans have a one-in-six chance of going to prison in their lifetime. *See* BLACK AMERICANS: A STATISTICAL SOURCEBOOK 160 (Louise L. Hornor ed. 2000). For every 100,000 people in the United States, 2,489 blacks were locked up, compared with only 378 whites and 922 Hispanics. *See* Human Rights Watch, *Race and Incarceration in the United States, Backgrounder Table 1: Rates of Incarceration Per 100,000 State Residents by Race* (Feb. 27, 2002), *available at* http://www.hrw.org/backgrounder/usa/race/pdf/table1.pdf. But if the focus is on males, almost 8% of black males between the ages of 18 and 64 are incarcerated in comparison to only 1.1% of white men and 2.7% of Hispanic men. In twelve states over 10% of black males are behind bars. The twelve states are Colorado (10.7%), Iowa (11%), Kansas (11%), Kentucky (10.3%), Oklahoma (12.2%), Oregon (10.1%), Pennsylvania (10.5%), South Dakota (13.9%), Texas (11%), West Virginia (15.2%),

Wisconsin (13%) and Wyoming (14%). *See* Human Rights Watch, *Race and Incarceration in the United States, Backgrounder Table 3: Percentage of Adult Men (Age 18–64) Incarcerated, by Race* (Feb. 27, 2002), *available at* http://www.hrw.org/ backgrounder/usa/race/pdf/table3.pdf.

27. Centers for Disease Control and Prevention, Table 23. Infant mortality rates, fetal mortality rates, and perinatal mortality rates, according to race: United States, selected years 1950–99, http://www.cdc.gov/nchs/data/hus/tables/2001/01hus023.pdf.

28. *See* Centers for Disease Control and Prevention, *National Vital Statistics Report,* Vol. 49, No. 12, at 24 (Oct. 9, 2001), *available at* http://www.cdc.gov/nchs/data/nvsr/ nvsr49/nvsr49_12.pdf.

29. Stephan Thernstrom, The Demography of Racial and Ethnic Groups 12–13, (2001), *available at* http://www.hoover.stanford.edu/publications/books/fulltext/colorline/13.pdf.

30. *See* U.S. Bureau of the Census, *Table 1: Population by Race, for Hispanic or Latino Origin for all Ages and for 18 years and older for the United States 2000* (Apr. 2, 2001), *available at* http://www.census.gov/population/cen2000/phc-t1/tab01.pdf.

31. *See* Beth Aronstamm Young, *Public School Student, Staff, and Graduate Counts by State, School Year 2001–02, Table 5: Percentage of public school membership by race/ethnicity and state: school year 2001–02, available at* http://nces.ed.gov/pubs2003/2003358.pdf.

32. 60 U.S. 393 (1857).

33. 163 U.S. 537 (1896).

34. 438 U.S. 265 (1978) (Powell J. concurring in part, dissenting in part).

35. Legal thought can be viewed as a language for discussing the circumstances of the social world. *See* Gary Peller, *The Metaphysics of American Law,* 73 Cal. L. Rev. 1151, 1154 (1985). Law is also knowledge in the sense that it is "vernacular characterizations of what happens connected to vernacular imaging of what can happen." Clifford Geertz, Local Knowledge: Further Essays in Interpretative Anthropology 215 (1983).

36. *See* Harry P. Stumpf, American Judicial Politics 42 (1988).

37. *See* Jan G. Deutsch, *Neutrality, Legitimacy, and the Supreme Court: Some Intersections Between Law and Political Science,* 20 Stan. L. Rev. 169 (1968).

38. Stephen L. Wasby, The Supreme Court in The Federal Judicial System 31 (3d ed. 1988).

39. *See* Martha Minow, *The Supreme Court, 1986 Term: Foreword: Justice Engendered,* 101 Harv. L. Rev. 10, 33 (1987); *see also* Gerald Torres, *Local Knowledge, Local Color: Critical Legal Studies and The Law of Race Relations,* 25 San Diego L. Rev. 1043, 1050 (1988).

40. Christopher E. Smith, *The Supreme Court and Ethnicity,* 69 Or. L. Rev. 797, 810 (1990).

41. 539 US 306 (2003).

42. Gary Orfield & John T. Yun, *Resegregation in American Schools* 14 (June 1999), *available at* http://www.civilrightsproject.harvard.edu/research/deseg/Resegregation_American_Schools99.pdf.

43. *Id.*

44. *See* Erica Frankenberg et al., *A Multiracial Society with Segregated Schools: Are We Losing the Dream?* 31 (Jan. 2003), *available at* http://www.civilrightsproject.harvard.edu/research/reseg03/AreWeLosingtheDream.pdf.

45. 515 U.S. 200 (1995).

46. *See, e.g.,* Eisenberg v. Montgomery County Pub. Sch., 197 F.3d 123 (4th Cir. 1999); Tuttle v. Arlington County Sch. Bd., 195 F.3d 698 (4th Cir. 1999); Wessmann v. Gittens, 160 F.3d 790 (1st Cir. 1998). *But see* Brewer v. West Irondequoit Cent. Sch. Dist., 212 F.3d 738 (2d Cir. 2000) (upholding a voluntary school integration plan); Hunter v. Regents of the Univ. of Calif., 190 F.3d 1061 (9th Cir. 1999) (upholding a voluntary school integration plan on very narrow grounds).

47. *See* Erica Frankenberg et al., *supra* note 44, at 31.

48. *Id.* at 33.

49. 539 U.S. 306 (2003).

50. 539 U.S. 244 (2003).

51. Grutter, 539 U.S. at 333.

52. *Id.* But O'Connor also notes that "The Law School does not premise its need for critical mass on 'any belief that minority students always (or even consistently) express some characteristic minority viewpoint on any issue.'" *Id.* at 335.

53. *See e.g.,* Dred Scott v. Sandford 60 U.S. 393 (1857) (Chief Justice Taney's opinion drew a distinction between the situation with Native Americans on the one hand and descendants from Africa on the other). *See also* Gong Lum v. Rice 275 U.S. 78 (1927). This was one of the Court's major education opinions of the segregation era. Martha Lum, a nine-year-old girl, was denied admission into the local school for whites because of her Chinese ancestry. When the Supreme Court of Mississippi heard this case it directed its attention towards the proper construction of a provision in the state's constitution which provided that "[s]eparate schools shall be maintained for the children of the white and colored races." Rice v. Gong Lum, 104 So. 105, 107 (Miss. 1925). The Mississippi Supreme Court concluded that this provision had divided educable children into those of pure white or Caucasian race and those of colored races of brown, yellow and black. Therefore, Martha Lum could not insist on being classified as white. *Id.* Since the Legislature was not compelled to provide separate schools for each of the colored races, all were given the benefit of a unified colored school. *Id.* The Mississippi Supreme Court, therefore, denied Martha Lum admission to the white school. *Id.* The Supreme Court noted that the ability of the state to segregate had been decided many times. Gong Lum, 275 U.S. at 86. Though the issue had generally arisen in the establishment of separate schools between white and black pupils, the Court did not think that the question was any different between white and yellow pupils. *Id.* at 87. Accordingly, the Court upheld the decision to prevent Martha Lum from being admitted to the white school. In Keyes v. School District No. 1, 413 U.S. 189, 195–98 (1973), the Supreme Court noted that, in the Southwest, Hispanics and African-Americans have a great many things in common, including economic and cultural deprivation and discrimination. *See also* "When I say 'black' I also mean 'brown' and 'yellow' and 'red' and all other people who suffer discrimination because of their color...." Lyndon B. Johnson, "Running Against the Twelfth Man of History", New York Times, Dec. 26, 1972, at 33.

54. For scores for 1975–76 *see* BLACK AMERICANS: A STATISTICAL SOURCEBOOK *supra* note 20, at 106. *See* http://www.collegeboard.com/press/senior01/html/pdf/table9.pdf (SAT averages rose for almost all racial/ethnic groups between 1991 and 2001). For 2001–02 scores *see*, Nat'l Ctr. for Educ. Statistics, Digest of Educ. Statistics 2002, *Table 133—Scholastic Assessment Test (SAT) averages, by race/ethnicity:* 1986–87 to 2001–02, page 154, *available at* http://nces.ed.gov/pubs2003/2003060b.pdf.

55. African-Americans constitute about 11.2% (120,506 of the 1,074,016) of those who take the SAT. *See* The College Board, *2001 College-Bound Seniors: A Profile of SAT Program Test Takers* 6 (2001).

56. The College Board, *2003 College-Bound Seniors: A Profile of SAT Program Test Takers, available at* http://www.collegeboard.com/prod_downloads/about/news_info/cbsenior/yr2003/ pdf/2003_TOTALGRP_PRD.pdf.

57. In 1975–76 the gap between the average SAT scores of African-Americans and whites was 258 (686 in comparison to 944).

58. For the 1990–91 assessment year the gap was only 187 points (1031 as opposed to 846). In the 1996–97 assessment year the gap had increased to 195 points (1052 as opposed to 857); in 1998–99 it was 199 (1055–856); and in 2000–01 it was 201 (1060–859). Nat'l Ctr. for Educ. Statistics, *supra* note 54.

59. ACT High School Profile, *ACT Nat'l and State Scores, available at* http:/ /www.act.org/news/data/03/pdf/t1-2.pdf (last visited October 18, 2003).

60. For students graduating in 1997 for example, the average ACT score for blacks was 16.4 compared to 21.2 for whites. All racial/ethnic groups: American Indian, Mexican-American, Asian-American and Other Hispanics all scored lower on the ACT than Caucasians (18.0, 17.8, 20.4 and 18.1, respectively). *See* ACT Nat'l and State Scores, *The 1997 ACT High School Profile Report—Nat'l Normative Data, available at* http://www.act.org/ news/data/97/t5-6-7.html (1997).

61. The average scores of black nine-year-olds increased from 170 to 189, thirteen-year-olds from 222 to 243, and seventeen-year-olds from 239 to 274. The corresponding scores of whites were 214 to 218, 261 to 261 (no change) and 291 to 295, respectively. *See* Nat'l Ctr. for Educ. Statistics, *Trends in Average Reading Scale Scores, by Race, Age and Score Quartile* 1971–99, *available at* http://nces.ed.gov/programs/coe/2002/section2/tables/t08There is_2.asp (2000).

62. From 1988 to 1999 the scores of black nine-year-olds decreased from 189 to 186, thirteen-year-olds from 243 to 238 and for seventeen-year-olds from 274 to 264. The corresponding scores of whites went from 218 to 221, 261 to 267 and 295 to 295 (no change). As a result, the racial gaps for black nine-year-olds increased by six points; for thirteen-year-olds by eleven points; and for seventeen-year-olds by ten points. *See id.*

63. From 1970 to 1986 the gap in the scores of black nine-year-olds decreased from fifty-seven points to thirty-six points, thirteen-year-olds from forty-nine points to thirty-eight points and for seventeen-year-olds from fifty-four points to forty-five points, respectively. From 1986 to 1999 the gaps increased thirty-six points to forty-one points, thirty-eight points to thirty-nine points and forty-five points to fifty-two points, respectively. *See id.* at Table 13–2, *available at* http://nces.ed.gov/programs/coe/2002/section2/tables/t13_2.asp.

64. *See* Nat'l Ctr. for Educ. Statistics, *The Nation's Report Card, NAEP 1999 Long-Term Trend Mathematics Summary Data Tables for Age 9–13 Student Data, available at* http://nces.ed.gov/nationsreportcard/tables/Ltt1999/NTM11011.asp (last visited Jan. 13, 2004); Nat'l Ctr. for Educ. Statistics, *The Nation's Report Card, NAEP 1999 Long-Term Trend Mathematics Summary Data Tables for Age 13 Student Data, at* http://nces.ed.gov/nationsreportcard/tables/Ltt1999/NTM21011. asp (last visited Jan. 13, 2004); Nat'l Ctr. for Educ. Statistics, *The Nation's Report Card, NAEP 1999 Long-Term Trend Mathematics Summary Data Tables for Age 17 Student Data, available at* http://nces.ed.gov/nationsreportcard/tables/ Ltt1999/NTM31011.asp (last visited Jan. 13, 2004).

65. Jennifer Mueller, *Facing the Unhappy Day: Three Aspects of the High Stakes Testing Movement,* 11 KAN. J.L. & PUB. POL'Y 201, 206 (2002).

66. U.S. Bureau of the Census, *2003 Statistical Abstract of the United States, 177, Table 270: High School Dropouts Race and Hispanic Origins* (2003). The rate for Hispanics is an alarming 31.7%.

67. For an extended discussion of the inaccuracies and misleading estimates of high school graduates and school dropouts *see* LOSING OUR FUTURE: HOW MINORITY YOUTHS ARE BEING LEFT BEHIND BY THE GRADUATION RATE CRISIS, GARY ORFIELD, DANIEL LOSEN, JOHANNA WALD AND CHRISTOPHER B. SWANSON 7–14 (April 2004).

68. *Id.*

69. *Id.* at 2.

70. *See* U.S. Dept. Of Educ. Institute of Educ. Services, Nat'l Ctr. for Educ. Statistics, *Status and Trends in Education of Blacks, available at* http://nces.edgov/pubs2003/ 2003034.pdf 38 (Sept. 2003).

71. *See* Daniel J. Losen & Kevin G. Welner, *Disabling Discrimination in Our Public Schools: Comprehensive Legal Challenges to Inappropriate and Inadequate Special Education Services for Minority Children,* 36 HARV. C.R.-C.L. L. REV. 407, 422 (2001).

72. *See* Nat'l Ctr. for Educ. Statistics, *supra* note 70, at 57.

73. *See* Nat'l Ctr. for Educ. Statistics, *supra* note 70, at 59.

74. *See* Nat'l Ctr. for Educ. Statistics, *supra* note 70, at 57.

75. *See* Nat'l Ctr. for Educ. Statistics, *supra* note 70, at 143.

76. Grutter, 539 U.S. at 327

77. For a brief primer about charter schools *see* Wendy Parker, *The Color of Choice: Race and Charter Schools,* 75 TUL. L. REV. 563, 574–77 (2001).

78. U.S. Charter Schools, *available at* http://www.uscharterschools.org/pub/ uscs_docs/o/ index .htm#national, (*citing* CENTER FOR EDUCATION REFORM, THE NATIONAL CHARTER SCHOOL DIRECTORY 2003).

79. A charter school movement pioneer has offered "nine essentials" that make up the core underlying what a charter school is:
(1) The school may be organized, owned, and run by any of several parties; (2) the organizers may approach more than one public body for their charter; (3) the school is a legal entity; (4) the school is public and may not charge tuition, discriminate or engage in selective admissions, must follow health and safety laws, and is not affiliated with a religious group; (5) the school is accountable for the students' academic

performance and the school loses its charter if it fails to achieve its goals; (6) the school gets real freedom to change instructional and management practices; (7) the school is a school of choice: no student is required to attend; (8) the state transfers a fair share of school funding from each student's home district to the charter school; and (9) the schools' teachers are protected and given the opportunity to participate in the design of schools.

Gerard Toussaint Robinson, *Can the Spirit of Brown Survive in the Era of School Choice? A Legal and Policy Perspective,* 45 How. L.J. 281, 295–96 (2002) (*citing* BRIAN HASSEL, CHARTER SCHOOLS: THE PROMISE AND THE PITFALLS, FULFILLING THE PROMISE 5 (1999) (*paraphrasing* Ted Kolderie)).

80. 536 U.S. 639 (2002).

81. United States General Accounting Office, School Vouchers: Publicly Funded Programs in Cleveland and Milwaukee, GAO-01- 914, at 14 (Aug. 2001) (Table 1: Characteristics of Cleveland Families with Students in the Voucher Program or Public Schools and Table 4: Racial and Ethnic Composition of Cleveland Public School Voucher School Students, School Year 1998–99).

82. Vermont adopted a school choice program in 1869 limited to communities that did not build their own public schools. Maine adopted a similar program in 1873. The Vermont program serves approximately 6,500 students today and Maine's about 5,600. CLINT BOLICK, VOUCHER WARS: WAGING THE LEGAL BATTLE OVER SCHOOL CHOICE 2 (2003).

83. Milwaukee Parental Choice Program Frequently Asked Questions for 2001–02, *available at* http://www.dpi.state.wi.us/dpi/dfm/sms/doc/mpc01fnf.doc.

84. *Id.*

85. *See* Myra DeGrow, *Educational Vouchers and Tax Credits: A State-by-State Summary of Current Programs* (December 18, 2002) *available at* http://i2i.org/Publications/IB/Education/2002f.htm.

86. Caroline Hendrie, *The Florida* Experiment, EDUC. WK., January 4, 2004, *available at* http://www.edweek.org.

87. Alan Richard, *Florida Sees Surge in Use of Vouchers,* EDUC. WK., September 4, 2002, *available at* http://www.edweek.org.

88. Associated Press, *Growth of Vouchers Slow Year After Court Decision,* June 28, 2003, *available at* http://www.cnn.com/2003/EDUCATION/06/28/school.vouchers.ap/ index.html.

89. *See* John Gehring, *Gov. Owens Signs Colorado Voucher Bill,* EDUC. WK., April 23, 2003, *available at* http://www.edweek.org.

90. The Washington D.C. voucher program will be available to 1,700 children and will award them vouchers of up to $7,500 to attend private schools. Spencer S. Hsu & Justin Blum, *D.C. School Vouchers Win Final Approval,* WASH. POST, Jan. 23, 2004, at A1.

91. Hendrie, *supra* note 86.

92. *Id.*

93. *Id.*

94. *See, e.g.,* Charles Fried, *Five to Four: Reflections on the School Voucher Case,* 116 HARV. L. REV. 1 (2002); Kathleen M. Sullivan, The New Religion and the Constitution, 116

HARV. L. REV. 1397, 1398–89 (2003); John Gehring, Voucher Battles Head to State Capitals, EDUC. WK., July 10, 2002, *available at* http://www.edweek.org.

95. *See* Jackson v. Benson 578 N.W. 2d 602 (Wis. 1998); and Simmons-Harris v. Goff 711 N.E. 2d 203 (Ohio 1999).

96. Holmes v. Bush, 767 So.2d 668 (Fla. Dist. Ct. App. 2000), *rev. den.*, 790 So.2d 1104 (Fla. 2001). On remand the plaintiff was granted summary judgement which was upheld on appeal. *See* Holmes, 2002 WL 1809079 (Fla. Cir. Ct. 2002).

97. Nancy Mitchell, Court Hears Vouchers Case, ROCKY MOUNTAIN NEWS, May 26, 2004, http://www.rockymountainnews.com/drmn/education/article/0,1299,DRMN_957_2914560,00.html.

98. On December 3, 2003 Denver District Judge Joseph Meyer III issued an injunction barring implementation of the voucher plan because it violated a state constitutional provision that gives local school boards control of schools in Colorado, not the state. *See* Alan Richard, EDUC. WK., December 10, 2003, *available at* http://www.edweek.org.

99. PRIVATE SCHOOL RACIAL ENROLLMENT & SEGREGATION, SEAN REARDON AND JOHN T. YIN 3 (foreword by Gary Orfield stating "there is no systematic research showing that charter schools perform better than public schools.") (June 2002). *See, e.g.*, Jeffrey R. Henig, *School Choice Outcomes* in SCHOOL CHOICE AND SOCIAL CONTROVERSY: POLITICS, POLICY, AND LAW 89–101 (STEPHEN D. SUGARMAN & FRANK R. KEMERER eds. 1999) (noting the difficulties with the ability of empirical data to answer the question about educational achievement resulting from increased choice). Dan D. Goldhaber & Eric R. Eide, *What Do We Know (and Need to Know) About the Impact of School Choice Reforms on Disadvantaged Students?*, 72 HARVARD EDUCATIONAL REVIEW 157, 158 (2002) (although the empirical evidence on the academic effects of school choice reforms is mixed, those studies that do find positive effects of choice tend also to find that minorities living in urban areas disproportionately benefit from enhanced schooling options). *See also* Peter Cookson, SCHOOL CHOICE: THE STRUGGLE FOR THE SOUL OF AMERICAN EDUCATION 98 (1994) (in terms of student achievement, choice makes little difference).

100. For most purposes this system of meaning reflects the traditional practice of liberal justification. David Boaz's book LIBERTARIANISM: A PRIMER (1997) is a good introduction to many of the concepts that are presented in Colorblind Individualism. For a critique of the practice of liberal justifications that reveals the common conceptual structures of a number of disparate liberal thinkers like John Rawls, Ronald Dworkin, Frank Michelman and Bruce Ackerman *see* Pierre Schlag, *The Empty Circles of Liberal Justification,* 96 MICH. L. REV. 1 (1997) (arguing that these diverse liberal thinkers actually employ a similar structure of justifications for their versions of liberal values).

101. Martin Luther King, Jr., (Aug. 28, 1963), *I Have a Dream, in* A TESTAMENT OF HOPE: THE ESSENTIAL WRITINGS OF MARTIN LUTHER KING, JR. 217, 219 (James Melvin Washington ed., 1986). ("I have a dream my four little children will one day live in a nation where they will not be judged by the color of their skin but by content of their character.").

102. ROBERT N. BELLAH ET AL., HABITS OF THE HEART: INDIVIDUALISM AND COMMITMENT IN AMERICAN LIFE 143 (1985).

103. *See, e.g.*, Pierre Schlag, *Normative and Nowhere to Go*, 43 STAN. L. REV. 167, 181 (1990); Seyla Benhabib, *Critical Theory and Postmodernism: On the Interplay of Ethics, Aesthetics, and Utopia in Critical Theory*, 11 CARDOZO L. REV. 1435 (1990).
104. Michael J. Sandel, *Religious Liberty—Freedom of Conscience or Freedom of Choice?*, 1989 UTAH L. REV. 597, 598 (1989).
105. 413 U.S. 189 (1973).
106. 426 U.S. 229 (1976).
107. 438 U.S. 265 (1978) (Powell, J., concurring in part dissenting in part).
108. 476 U.S. 267 (1986).
109. 488 U.S. 469 (1989) (O'Connor, J.).
110. 515 U.S. 900 (1995).
111. 515 U.S. 200 (1995).
112. 539 U.S. 244 (2003).
113. 539 U.S. 306 (2003).
114. *See* Paul Glastris and Jeannye Thornton, "A New Civil Rights Frontier," *U. S. News and World Report*, Jan. 17, 1994.
115. 539 U.S. at 301 (Ginsburg, J., dissenting).
116. *Id.* at 301 (quoting Stephen Carter, *When Victims Happen To Be Black*, 97 YALE L.J. 420, 433–34 (1988)).
117. 391 U.S. 430 (1968).
118. 402 U.S. 1 (1971).
119. 413 U.S. 189 (1973).

Chapter One

1. Professor Lawrence has made the point that we are all products of a society where racism was one of its core values. Charles R. Lawrence III, *The Id, The Ego, and Equal Protection: Reckoning with Unconscious Racism*, 39 STAN. L. REV. 317, (1987).
2. Paul Glastris and Jeannye Thornton, *A New Civil Rights Frontier*, U. S. NEWS AND WORLD REPORT, Jan. 17, 1994, at 38–39.
3. *See generally* John A. Powell, *Race and Space: What Really Drives Metropolitan Growth* 16 BROOKINGS REVIEW, 20 (1998).
4. *See* Rudyard Kipling, *The White Man's Burden, in* RUDYARD KIPLING'S VERSE: INCLUSIVE EDITION 1885–1926, at 373–74 (1931).
5. The Slaughter-House Cases, 83 U.S. 36 (1873).
6. 163 U.S. 537, 552 (1896).
7. Abolitionists felt that Lincoln had not moved quickly or forcibly enough to attack slavery. In mid-August of 1862 Horace Greeley published a letter in the New York Times in which he gave voice to this dissatisfaction. *See* Horace Greeley, *To Abraham Lincoln, President of the United States, reprinted in* CIVIL RIGHTS AND AFRICAN-AMERICANS: A

DOCUMENTARY HISTORY, 192–95 (Albert P. Blaustein & Robert L. Zangrando eds., 1968). Though Lincoln's response was before he publicly announced his intention to issue the Emancipation Proclamation, it was after the time he had decided such a measure was necessary.

8. HUGH THOMAS, THE SLAVE TRADE: THE STORY OF THE ATLANTIC SLAVE TRADE: 1440–1870, at 21–23 (1997).

9. *Id.* at 174.

10. CAPTAINE JOHN SMITH, THE GENERALL HISTORIE OF VIRGINIA, NEW ENGLAND, AND THE SUMMER ISLES, VOL 1, at 246–47 (Glasgow: James MacLehose & Sons, 1907). This account can also be found printed in CIVIL RIGHTS AND AFRICAN-AMERICANS *supra* note 7, at 4.

11. 1 VIRGINIA BERNHARD ET AL., FIRSTHAND AMERICA: A HISTORY OF THE UNITED STATES 16 (2d ed. 1992).

12. *See* THOMAS, supra *note 8, at 453.*

13. In one 1671 Virginia declaration, slaves were put in the same categories as sheep, horses and cattle. *See* JOE R. FEAGIN, RACIST AMERICA: ROOTS, CURRENT REALITIES, AND FUTURE REPARATIONS 41 (2000).

14. *Id.* at 12.

15. Article 1, Section 2, which counts slaves as three-fifths of a person; (2) Article 1, Sections 2 and 9, which apportion taxes on the states using the three-fifths formula; (3) Article 1, Section 8, which gives Congress the authority to suppress slave and other insurrections; (4) Article 1, Section 9, which prevents the slave trade from being abolished before 1808; (5) Article 1, Section 9 and 10, which exempts goods made by slaves from export duties; (6) Article 4, Section 2, which requires the return of fugitive slaves; and (7) Article 4, Section 4, which stipulates that the federal government must help state governments put down domestic violence, including slave uprisings. DONALD E. LIVELY, THE CONSTITUTION AND RACE 4–5 (1992).

16. RICHARD KLUGER, SIMPLE JUSTICE: THE HISTORY OF *BROWN V. BOARD OF EDUCATION* AND BLACK AMERICA'S STRUGGLE FOR EQUALITY 31–33 (1976).

17. BUREAU OF THE CENSUS, U.S. DEP'T OF COMMERCE, SER. P–23, NO. 80, THE SOCIAL AND ECONOMIC STATUS OF THE BLACK POPULATION IN THE UNITED STATES: AN HISTORICAL VIEW, 1790–1978, at 254 (1979) [hereinafter HISTORICAL VIEW]. While blacks began to spread throughout the country in the twentieth century, the 1910 census showed that 89% of African-Americans resided in the South. Even as late 1940, fourteen years before Brown I, the South was home to over three quarters of the African-American population. *Id* at 13.

18. DAILY INTELLIGENCER (Atlanta), January 9, 1860 *reprinted in* W. E. B. DuBois, BLACK RECONSTRUCTION IN AMERICA 1860–1880, at 39–40 (Macmillan 1992) (1935).

19. James H. Dorman & Robert R. Jones, THE AFRO-AMERICAN EXPERIENCE: A CULTURAL HISTORY THROUGH EMANCIPATION 145 (1974).

20. *Id.* at 118.

21. 60 U.S. 393 (1857).

22. *Id.* at 407.

23. *Id.* at 416.

24. *See generally* LEON F. LITWACK, NORTH OF SLAVERY: THE NEGRO IN THE FREE STATES (1961) (presenting an authoritative account of the treatment of African-Americans north of the Mason-Dixon Line).

25. C. VAN WOODWARD, THE STRANGE CAREER OF JIM CROW 20 (3d rev. ed. 1974). *See also* BERNARD GROFMAN ET AL., MINORITY REPRESENTATION AND THE QUEST FOR VOTING EQUALITY 4, n1 (1992).

26. *See, e.g.*, 1 RACIAL THOUGHT IN AMERICA: FROM THE PURITANS TO ABRAHAM LINCOLN 263–68 (Louis Ruchames ed., 1969) (reprinting a statement by John Quincy Adams).

27. JUDGE SAMUEL SEWALL, THE SELLING OF JOSEPH *reprinted in* CIVIL RIGHTS AND AFRICAN-AMERICANS, *supra* note 7, at 192–95 (Albert P. Blaustein & Robert L. Zangrando eds., 1968).

28. CIVIL RIGHTS AND AFRICAN-AMERICANS, *supra* note 7, at 171–72 (printing a portion of Lincoln's speech made on September 18, 1858 at Charleston, Illinois).

29. *See* ALEXIS DE TOCQUEVILLE, DEMOCRACY IN AMERICA 344 (George Lawrence trans., 1966).

30. *See* THOMAS, *supra* note 8, at 459.

31. *See, e.g.*, DANIEL RAYMOND, THE MISSOURI QUESTION *reprinted in* 1 RACIAL THOUGHT IN AMERICA, *supra* note 26 at 274 (Louis Ruchames ed., 1969).

32. TOCQUEVILLE, *supra* note 29, at 345–46.

33. JOHN HOPE FRANKLIN & ALFRED A. MOSS, JR., FROM SLAVERY TO FREEDOM: A HISTORY OF NEGRO AMERICANS 154–57 (6th ed. 1988).

34. *Id.* at 189.

35. ERIC FONER, RECONSTRUCTION: AMERICA'S UNFINISHED REVOLUTION 1863–1877, at 6 (1988).

36. *See* FEAGIN, *supra* note 13, at 57.

37. *See* JAMES M. MCPHERSON, ORDEAL BY FIRE: THE CIVIL WAR AND RECONSTRUCTION 265–66 (1982).

38. W. E. B. DuBois, *supra* note 18, at 56.

39. 5 ABRAHAM LINCOLN *in* THE COLLECTED WORKS OF ABRAHAM LINCOLN 357–423 (Roy P. Basler ed., 1955).

40. FONER, *supra* note 35, at 425.

41. *Id.* at 119.

42. *Id.*

43. *Id.* at 428.

44. FEAGIN, *supra* note 13, at 58.

45. *See* Herbert Hovenkamp, *Social Science and Segregation Before Brown*, 1985 DUKE L.J. 624, 648–49 (1985).

46. *See, e.g.*, William E. Nelson, The Fourteenth Amendment: From Political Principal to Judicial Document 66–68 (1988).

47. Hovenkamp, *supra* note 45, at 648.

48. KLUGER, supra note 16, at 635.

49. U.S. CONST. amend. XIV, § 2. The section states in full: "Representatives shall be apportioned among the several States in according to their respective numbers, counting the whole number of persons in each State, excluding Indians not taxed. But when the right to vote at any election for the choice of electors for President and Vice President of the United States, Representatives in Congress, the Executive and Judicial officers of a State, or the members of the Legislature thereof, is denied to any of the male inhabitants of such State, being twenty-one years of age, and citizens of the United States, or in any way abridged, except for participation in rebellion, or other crime, the basis of representation therein shall be reduced in the proportion which the number of such male citizens shall bear to the whole number of male citizens twenty-one years of age in such State."

50. *See* FONER, supra note 35, at 259.

51. *Id.* at 269.

52. U.S. CONST. amend. XV, § 1.

53. Charles L. Black, *The Lawfulness of the Segregation Decisions*, 69 YALE L.J. 421, 424–25 (1960).

54. Black Population in the South after the Civil War: Statistics for the year 1870 (numbers in thousands)

    Alabama Total pop: 997,000 Black pop: 476,000 (47.7%)
    Delaware Total pop: 125,000 Black pop: 23,000 (18.4%)
    Florida Total pop: 188,000 Black pop: 92,000 (48.9%)
    Georgia Total pop: 1,184,000 Black pop: 545,000 (46.0%)
    Kentucky Total pop: 1,321,000 Black pop: 222,000 (16.8%)
    Louisiana Total pop: 727,000 Black pop: 364,000 (50.1%)
    Maryland Total pop: 781,000 Black pop: 175,000 (22.4%)
    Mississippi Total pop: 828,000 Black pop: 444,000 (53.6%)
    Missouri Total pop: 1,721,000 Black pop: 118,000 (6.9%)
    North Carolina Total pop: 1,071,000 Black pop: 392,000 (36.6%)
    South Carolina Total pop: 706,000 Black pop: 416,000 (58.9%)
    Tennessee Total pop: 1,259,000 Black pop: 322,000 (25.6%)
    Texas Total pop: 819,000 Black pop: 253,000 (30.9%)
    Virginia Total pop: 1,225,000 Black pop: 513,000 (41.9%)

    BUREAU OF THE CENSUS, U.S. DEPARTMENT OF COMMERCE, HISTORICAL STATISTICS OF THE UNITED STATES: COLONIAL TIMES TO 1970 PART 1, Series A-195-209 (1975).

55. Paraphrasing Senator Ben Tillman of South Carolina's boast on the floor of the Senate in 1900, stating: "We have done our best. We have scratched our heads to find out how we could eliminate the last one of them. We stuffed ballot boxes. We shot them. We are not ashamed of it." SEAN DENNIS CASHMAN, AFRICAN-AMERICANS AND THE QUEST FOR CIVIL RIGHTS, at 8 (1991).

56. FONER, *supra* note 35, at 342–43.

57. *Id.* at 426.

58. *Id.* at 427.

59. *Id.* at 427–28.

60. *Id.* at 431.

61. 92 U.S. 542 (1876).

62. A. LEON HIGGINBOTHAM, JR., SHADES OF FREEDOM: RACIAL POLITICS AND PRESUMPTIONS OF THE AMERICAN LEGAL PROCESS 175 (1996). The "Red Shirts" were southern white men, clad in red shirts, who advocated for white supremacy and the Democratic Party. They attempted, usually through violence or the threat of violence, to stop African-Americans from exercising their voting rights during the elections of 1898 and 1900.

63. BURKE MARSHALL, FEDERALISM AND CIVIL RIGHTS 13–14 (1964) (quoting Judge Chrisman speaking at the 1890 Mississippi constitutional convention).

64. *See* CASHMAN, *supra* note 55, at 7.

65. *See* FONER, *supra* note 35, at 422.

66. *See* Williams v. Mississippi, 170 U.S. 213 (1898).

67. 189 U.S. 475 (1903).

68. *Id.* at 488.

69. 238 U.S. 347 (1915).

70. *See* Smith v. Allwright 321 U.S. 649 (1944).

71. VAN WOODWARD, *supra* note 25, at 97.

72. 163 U.S. 537 (1896).

73. VAN WOODWARD, *supra* note 25, at 69–74 (discussing the weakening of the North's resistance against racism); *see also* Stephen J. Riegel, *The Persistent Career of Jim Crow: Lower Federal Courts and the "Separate but Equal" Doctrine, 1865–1896,* 28 AM. J. LEGAL HIST. 17 (1984) (examining federal lower courts' treatment of the issue of separate but equal before Plessy and concluding from the lower cases that the Court's opinion in Plessy was very predictable and obvious).

74. Riegel, *supra* 73, at 17.

75. 175 U.S. 528 (1899).

76. 211 U.S. 45 (1908).

77. 275 U.S. 78 (1927). The Supreme Court noted that the ability of the state to segregate had been decided many times. Gong Lum, 275 U.S. at 86. Though the issue had generally arisen in the establishment of separate schools between white and black pupils, the Court did not think that the question was any different between white and yellow pupils. *Id.* at 87.

78. Rice v. Gong Lum, 104 So. 105, 110 (Miss. 1925).

79. In 1917 the U.S. Bureau of Education published *Negro Education: A Study of Private and Higher Schools for Colored People in the United States.* The report was written by Thomas Jesse Jones and in two volumes it chronicled the conditions of the nation's black schools. His report was "the most comprehensive survey of segregated schools for its time." ROBERT A. MARGO, RACE AND SCHOOLING IN THE SOUTH 1880–1950: AN ECONOMIC HISTORY 21–23 (1990).

80. *Id.* at 21–22.
81. *Id.* at 18–19.
82. Diane Ravitch, The Troubled Crusade: American Education 1945–1980, 121 (1983).
83. *Id.*
84. Hovenkamp, *supra* note 45, at 634; *See also* Thomas F. Gossett, Race: The History of an Idea in America 4–16 (1968).
85. Anthony E. Cook, *Beyond Critical Legal Studies: The Reconstructive Theology of Dr. Martin Luther King, Jr.*, 103 Harv. L. Rev. 985, 1016 (1990).
86. Daniel Mannix in collaboration with Malcolm Cowley, Black Cargoes: A History of the Atlantic Slave Trade 1518–1865, 59 (1965).
87. *See, e.g.*, 1 Corinthians 12:13; Titus 2:9–10; Philemon; Colossians 3:22; and Ephesians 6:5–6.
88. Cook, *supra* note 85, at 1016.
89. *See* Gossett, *supra* note 84, at 5; *see also* Winthrop Jordan, White Over Black 18–19 (1968).
90. Feagin, *supra* note 13, at 74.
91. Dinesh D'Souza, The End of Racism 113 (1995).
92. Thomas, *supra* note 8, at 561–62.
93. Mannix in collaboration with Malcom Cowley, *supra* note 86, at XI.
94. Thomas, *supra* note 8, at 550.
95. *Id.* at 562.
96. *Id.* at 712–13.
97. William Hannibal Thomas, The American Negro: What He Was, What He Is, And What He May Become 21 (1901).
98. London Magazine VII, 129 (March 1738) *reprinted in* Thomas, *supra* note 8, at 468–69.
99. Thomas, *supra* note 8, at 403.
100. 1 Racial Thought in America, *supra* note 26, at 388 (reprinting a letter written by John C. Calhoun to Richard Pakenham, the British envoy to the United States).
101. *Id.*
102. *See generally* William Stanton, The Leopard's Spots: Scientific Attitudes Toward Race in America 1815–1859 (1960) (describing the attempts made by nineteenth century American scientists to study race).
103. For a discussion of the views of segregationists regarding the inferiority of African-Americans, *see, e.g.*, James J. Kilpatrick, The Southern Case for School Segregation (1962); I. A. Newby, Challenge to the Court: Social Scientists and the Defense of Segregation, 1954–1966, at 36–41 (rev. ed. 1969).
104. Nott, J.C., *Types of Mankind*, Philadelphia: Lippincott, Grambo (1854).
105. Leonard Lieberman et al., *The Debate Over Race: Thirty Years and Two Centuries Later in* Race and IQ Expanded Edition 56 (Ashley Montagu ed, 1999).
106. *Id.*

107. *See, e.g.*, Jordan, *supra* note 89, at 220–21.

108. Feagin, *supra* note 13, at 81.

109. Paul G. Lauren, Power and Prejudice: The Politics and Diplomacy of Racial Discrimination 21 (1988) (quoting an article on Negroes from the 1798 edition of the Encyclopedia Britannica).

110. *See, e.g.*, Benjamin Rush, *Observations Intended to Favor a Supposition that the Black Color (as it is Called) of the Negroes is Derived from Leprosy reprinted in* 1 Racial Thought in America, *supra* note 26, at 218–25.

111. Cornel West, Prophesy Deliverance! 56–57 (1982).

112. Stephen J. Gould, Mismeasure of Man 79 (1981).

113. For a critique of the work by Morton *see id.* at 82–101.

114. West, *supra* note 111, at 57–58.

115. William H. Tucker, The Science and Politics of Racial Research 23–24 (1994).

116. Feagin, *supra* note 13, at 82.

117. Gould, *supra* note 112, at 381.

118. Charles Darwin, The Descent of Man, and Selection in Relation to Sex 201 (1871).

119. Hovenkamp, *supra* note 45, at 654.

120. Tucker, supra note 115, at 35 (1994).

121. Hovenkamp, *supra* note 45, at 653–54.

122. *Id.* at 632.

123. Kluger, *supra* note 16, at 306.

124. *See* Hovenkamp, *supra* note 45, at 633–34.

125. Thomas Jefferson, Notes on the State of Virginia 145 (Frank Shuffelton ed., Penguin 1999) (1785).

126. Ronald Takaki, Iron Cages: Race and Culture in 19th Century America 50 (Oxford Univ. Press 1990) (1979) (quoting Benjamin Franklin).

127. A. Leon Higginbotham, Jr., Shades of Freedom: Racial Politics and Presumptions of the American Legal Process 41 (1996).

128. L. Eiseley, Darwin's Century 51–52 (1958). Jean Baptiste Lamarck (1744–1829), was an early evolutionist who believed in alteration of species rather than extinction. He believed that physical characteristics of organisms, caused by their bodies' responses to physical needs, and developed due to changed habits during a particular organism's lifetime, could be passed down to their offspring.

129. *Id.* at 119–25.

130. Feagin, *supra* note 13, at 60.

131. Gould, *supra* note 112, at 181.

132. *Id.* at 188.

133. Lewis M. Terman, The Measurement of Intelligence (Riverside Press 1916).

134. Gould, *supra* note 112, at 227.

Chapter Two

1. Joseph E. Holloway, *The Origins of African-American Culture, in* AFRICANISM IN AMERICAN CULTURE 1 (Joseph E. Holloway ed. 1991).
2. Alex M. Johnson Jr., *Destabilizing Racial Classifications Based on Insights Gleaned from Trademark Law,* 84 CAL. L. REV. 887, 889 (1996).
3. K. ANTHONY APPIAH & AMY GUTMANN, COLOR CONSCIOUS: THE POLITICAL MORALITY OF RACE 171–4 (1996).
4. ELLIS COSE, COLOR-BLIND: SEEING BEYOND RACE IN A RACE-OBSESSED WORLD xii (1997).
5. HOLLOWAY, *supra* note 1, at 1–10. This area covers the modern day west coastal African nations of Senegal, Gambia, Guinea-Bissau, Guinea, Sierra Leone, Liberia, Ivory Coast, Ghana, Togo, Benin, Nigeria, Cameron, Equatorial Guinea, Gabon, the Republic of the Congo and Angola.
6. *See, e.g.,* LAURENTI MAGESA, AFRICAN RELIGION: THE MORAL TRADITIONS OF ABUNDANT LIFE (1997); JACQUES MAQUET, AFRICANITY: THE CULTURAL UNITY OF BLACK AFRICA 16 (1972); JOHN V. TAYLOR, THE PRIMAL VISION: CHRISTIAN PRESENCES AMID AFRICAN RELIGION 19 (1963); JOHN MBITI, AFRICAN RELIGIONS AND PHILOSOPHY 5–10 (1969) (Mbiti posits that there are many different African religions because there are many different systems of beliefs, ceremonies, rituals with their own religious leaders. But on the issue of African philosophy underlying these religious expression there is but one.) *See also* JAMES H. DORMAN & ROBERT R. JONES, THE AFRO-AMERICAN EXPERIENCE: A CULTURAL HISTORY THROUGH EMANCIPATION 46–53 (1974) (noting the basic belief system discussed above existed before European contact).
7. Segun Gbadegesin, *Individuality, Community and the Moral Order, in* PHILOSOPHY FROM AFRICA: A TEXT WITH READINGS 294 (P.H. Coetzee & A.P. J. Roux eds. 1998).
8. SAMUEL YEBOAH, THE IDEOLOGY OF RACISM: THE ORIGIN OF RACISM 41 (1988).
9. DORMAN & JONES, *supra* note 6, at 46–48.
10. GBADEGESIN, *supra* note 7, at 295.
11. C. NYAMITI, THE SCOPE OF AFRICAN THEOLOGY 20 (1973).
12. MAGESA, *supra* note 6, at 47.
13. African-Americans have retained many cultural traits from their African past. *See, e.g.,* JAMES H. DORMAN & JONES, *supra* note 6, at 86–92 (1974).
14. *See, e.g.,* VINCENT HARDING, THERE IS A RIVER 3 (1981).
15. An extract from Dr. Thomas Trotter, a surgeon in the Royal Navy discussed this in an answer to questions posed to him. *Reprinted in* YEBOAH, *supra* note 8, at 39.
16. *Reprinted in* YEBOAH, *supra* note 8, at 39–40.
17. YEBOAH, *supra* note 8, at 41.
18. Normal losses attendant to the crossing was 18–20% of the cargo. DORMAN & JONES, *supra* note 6, at 81.
19. U.S. BUREAU OF THE CENSUS, Ser. P–23, No. 80, THE SOCIAL AND ECONOMIC STATUS OF THE BLACK POPULATION IN THE UNITED STATES: AN HISTORICAL VIEW, 1790–1978, 13 (1979). For most northern and western states, there was very little historical

African-American presence. As late as 1910, 89% of African-Americans still resided in the South. Even as late as 1940, fourteen years before Brown I, 77% of African-Americans still resided in the states of the Old Confederacy or the border states.

20. Hugh Thomas, The Slave Trade: The Story of the Atlantic Slave Trade 1440–1870, 462 (1997).

21. Harding, *supra* note 14, at 35.

22. Phillip T. Drotning, Black Heroes In Our Nation's History: A Tribute To Those Who Helped Shape America 74 (1969).

23. Herbert Aptheker, American Negro Slave Revolts 162 (1983).

24. Harding, *supra* note 14.

25. *Id.* at 49.

26. The safety valve of running away from slavery kept down the chance of insurrection. W. E. B. DuBois, Black Reconstruction In America: 1860–1880 62 (1934).

27. John Hope Franklin and Alfred A. Moss, Jr., From Slavery To Freedom: A History Of Negro Americans 70 (6th ed. 1988).

28. Benjamin Quarles, The Negro In The Making Of America 53–56 (1969).

29. Kenneth M. Stampp, The Peculiar Institution: Slavery In The Ante-Bellum South 330–33 (1956).

30. DuBois, *supra* note 26, at 40. *See also* Stampp, *supra* note 29, at 334–36, 126–27.

31. Anthony E. Cook, *Beyond Critical Legal Studies: The Reconstructive Theology of Dr. Martin Luther King, Jr.*, 103 Harv. L. Rev. 985, 1020 (1990) (quoting Galatians 3:26–28).

32. Drotning, *supra* note 22, at 77.

33. James M. McPherson, The Negro's Civil War: How American Blacks Felt & Acted During the War for the Union 166–7 (1991).

34. Michael L. Levine, African-Americans And Civil Rights: From 1619 To The Present 88 (1996).

35. McPherson, *supra* note 33, at 145.

36. The Emancipation Proclamation, *reprinted in* Civil Rights and African-Americans 200–1 (eds. Albert P. Blaustein and Robert L. Zangrando 1990).

37. Harding, supra *note* 14, at 232.

38. 6 Roy Basler, The Collected Works Of Abraham Lincoln, 149–50 (1953) (emphasis in original).

39. The militia act of July 17, 1862 provided that blacks would be paid $10 per month of which $3 would be deducted for clothing. White privates were paid $13 per month with an additional $3.50 per month for clothing allowance. At the time the law was enacted, the government planned to use the blacks primarily as laborers and not soldiers. It was not until June 15, 1864 that Congress finally enacted a bill to grant the black soldiers equal pay. The law was retroactive to January 1, 1864 for all black soldiers, and retroactive to the date of enlistment for those blacks who had been free on April 19, 1861. McPherson, *supra* note 33, at 200.

40. *Id.* at 173.

41. *Id.* at 145.

42. *Id.* at 241.

43. Maulana Karenga, Introduction to Black Studies 144 (2d ed. 1993).

44. McPherson, supra *note 33, at 241.*

45. Franklin & Moss, *supra* note 27, at 198.

46. Harding, *supra* note 14, at 304–6.

47. Eric Foner, Reconstruction: America's Unfinished Revolution 1863–1877, 239–40 (1988).

48. *Id.*

49. The Civil Rights Act of 1866 (most important provisions were those that declared blacks citizens and granted equal rights to enter into contracts; to buy, sell, lease or rent property; to sue and be sued in court; and to give testimony in court); the Enforcement Act of May 31, 1870 (outlawed state actions intended to deprive blacks of the right to vote); the Enforcement Act of February 28, 1871 (amended the Enforcement Act of 1870 and was designed to eliminate fraudulent registration practices and establish a complex system of federal machinery to supervise elections in the states if the circuit court was petitioned); the Enforcement Act of April 20, 1871 (also known as the Ku Klux Klan Act, was designed primarily to prevent intimidation of blacks by illegal action where states were unwilling or unable to provide such protection. It also gave the President the right to employ the militia and to suspend the right of habeas corpus when public safety was endangered by unlawful combinations); and the Civil Rights Act of 1875 (guaranteed to all persons, regardless of race or color, the full and equal enjoyment of inns, public conveyances, and public places of amusement. It also gave the right to sue for personal damages, gave federal courts exclusive jurisdiction over cases arising under the act and made it a misdemeanor to bar any qualified person from serving as a grand or petit juror).

50. For a list of major black state officials during Reconstruction, *see* Foner, *supra* note 47, at 353.

51. Levine, *supra* note 34, at 102.

52. For a brief biography of the blacks elected to Congress during the nineteenth century, *see* Bruce A. Ragsdale & Joel D. Treese, Black Americans in Congress, 1870–1989 (Office of the Historian, U.S. House of Representatives, Raymond W. Smock, Historian & Director, 1990).

53. Robert Norrell, Reaping the Whirlwind: The Civil Rights Movement in Tuskegee 112 (1985).

54. 170 U.S. 213 (1898).

55. C. Eric Lincoln, Race, Religion, and the Continuing American Dilemma 72 (1999).

56. *Id.* at 69.

57. James M. McPherson, Ordeal by Fire: The Civil War and Reconstruction 537, 575–76 (1982).

58. *Id.*

59. Quarles, *supra* note 28, at 162–63.

60. Louis R. Harlan, Booker T. Washington: The Wizard of Tuskegee 1901–1915, 134 (1983).
61. August Meier, Negro Thought in America, 1880–1915, 110–18 (1969).
62. Karenga, *supra* note 43, at 150.
63. Manning Marable, W.E.B. Du Bois: Black Radical Democrat 32 (1986).
64. Quarles, *supra* note 28, at 168–70.
65. Levine, *supra* note 34, at 130.
66. *Id.* at 152–54.
67. *Id.* at 175.
68. *Id.* at 176.
69. Nancy J. Weiss, The National Urban League 1910–1940, 64 (1974).
70. Marable, *supra* note 63, at 56–57.
71. Warren D. St. James, NAACP: Triumphs of a Pressure Group 1909–1980, 113 (2d ed. 1980).
72. Levine, *supra* note 34, at 136.
73. Marable, *supra* note 63, at 75.
74. *Id.* at 76.
75. *Id.* at 78, 97.
76. Richard Kluger, Simple Justice: The History of *Brown v. Board of Education* and Black America's Struggle for Equality 143 (1975).
77. In 1939 the NAACP established the NAACP Legal Defense and Educational Fund, Inc., known later as the Legal Defense Fund or the Inc. Fund. After that time the LDF became responsible for the legal work. For a book discussing the history of the legal efforts of the NAACP and the Legal Defense Fund, *see id.; see* Mark v. Tushnet, Making Civil Rights Law: Thurgood Marshall and the Supreme Court, 1936–1961 (1994).
78. 245 U.S. 60 (1917).
79. 334 U.S. 1 (1948).
80. 238 U.S. 347 (1915).
81. 321 U.S. 649 (1944).

Chapter Three

1. 413 U.S. 189 (1973).
2. 426 U.S. 229 (1976).
3. 429 U.S. 252 (1977).
4. *See* Adarand Constructors, Inc. v. Pena, 515 U.S. 200, 227 (1995).
5. *See, e.g.*, Wygant v. Jackson Bd. of Educ., 476 U.S. 267, 280–81 (1986); Miller v. Johnson, 515 U.S. 900, 921–22 (1995); City of Richmond v. J.A. Croson Co., 488 U.S. 469, 489 (1989).
6. 539 U.S. 306 (2003).

7. *See, e.g.*, Pierre Schlag, *Normative and Nowhere to Go*, 43 STAN. L. REV. 167, 181 (1990); Seyla Benhabib, *Critical Theory and Postmodernism: On the Interplay of Ethics, Aesthetics, and Utopia in Critical Theory (Deconstruction of the Possibility of Justice)*, 11 CARDOZO L. REV. 1435 (1990).
8. *See* ROBERT N. BELLAH ET AL., HABITS OF THE HEART: INDIVIDUALISM AND COMMITMENT IN AMERICAN LIFE 76 (1985); *see also* MICHAEL J. SANDEL, LIBERALISM AND THE LIMITS OF JUSTICE 1–11 (1982).
9. HUBERT L. DREYFUS & PAUL RABINOW, MICHEL FOUCAULT: BEYOND STRUCTURALISM AND HERMENEUTICS 245 (2d ed. 1983).
10. In his book, Michael Sandel articulates three conceptions of community. One is what he calls an "instrumental conception" based upon the conventional individualist assumptions which take for granted the self-interested motivations of agents. This "account conceives [of] community...in wholly instrumental terms and evokes...image[s] of a 'private society', where individuals regard social arrangements as a necessary burden." An example of this kind of community is an individual joining a food co-op in order to reduce the amount of money that they individually pay for food. The person is part of a community that is bound by its individual interest in reducing the cost paid for food. The second conception is one where the "participants have certain 'shared final ends' and regard the scheme of cooperation as a good in itself. Their interests are not uniformly antagonistic but in some cases complementary and overlapping." An example of this kind of community is where the individual agrees to join a group in a food co-op because they do not believe that anyone should make a profit off of selling food. The difference here is that it is not the individual interest, but rather the shared final ends that motivates the desire to come together. This "sentimental conception" of community is also individualistic since it assumes "the antecedent individuation of subjects of co-operation, whose actual motivations may include benevolent aims as well as selfish ones." And finally, Sandel notes a third conception of community which he calls "constitutive conception." This occurs when members of a society conceive that their identity is defined to some extent by the community of which they are a part. For them, "community describes not just what they *have* as fellow citizens but also what they *are*, not a relationship they choose (as in a voluntary association) but an attachment they discover, not merely an attribute but a constituent of their identity." SANDEL, *supra* note 8, at 147–54. If racial and ethnic groups were sentimental communities, instead of constitutive communities, then they would be consistent with the Colorblind Individualism commitment to self-determination.
11. *See, e.g.*, OLIVER C. COX, RACE RELATIONS: ELEMENTS AND SOCIAL DYNAMICS 21–40, 226–41 (1976); THEODORE CROSS, THE BLACK POWER IMPERATIVE: RACIAL INEQUALITY AND THE POLITICS OF NONVIOLENCE 81–130 (1984). *See generally* GORDON W. ALLPORT, THE NATURE OF PREJUDICE (1954); GUNNAR MYRDAL, AN AMERICAN DILEMMA: THE NEGRO PROBLEM AND MODERN DEMOCRACY (1944).
12. Martin Luther King, Jr. (Aug. 28, 1963), *I Have a Dream*, *in* A TESTAMENT OF HOPE: THE ESSENTIAL WRITINGS OF MARTIN LUTHER KING, JR. 217, 219 (James Melvin Washington ed., 1986).
13. For the Dalit struggle in India *see, e.g.*, Vijay Prashad, *Afro-Dalits of the Earth, Unite!* 43 AFR. STUD. REV. 189 (2000); LATA MURUGKAR, DALIT PANTHER MOVEMENT IN MAHARASHTRA: A SOCIOLOGICAL APPRAISAL (1991); Janet A. Contursi, *Political Theology: Text and Practice in a Dalit Panther Community*, 52 J. ASIAN STUD. 320 (1993).

For South Africa *see, e.g.*, GEORGE M. FREDRICKSON, BLACK LIBERATION: A COMPARATIVE HISTORY OF BLACK IDEOLOGIES IN THE UNITED STATES AND SOUTH AFRICA 325–26 n.4 (1995) (for a bibliography of works on the connection between blacks in the United States and South Africa); THEMBA SONO, REFLECTIONS ON THE ORIGINS OF BLACK CONSCIOUSNESS IN SOUTH AFRICA 34 (1993) ("Black Consciousness as it is known and articulated in South Africa [the doctrine, style, language and rhetoric], is lock, stock and barrel Black American invention, exported to the South African black radical almost *verbatim*.").

14. Justice Samuel Sewall wrote this in his pamphlet attacking slavery entitled *The Selling of Joseph. See* 1 RACIAL THOUGHT IN AMERICA: FROM THE PURITANS TO ABRAHAM LINCOLN, A DOCUMENTARY HISTORY 47–52 (Louis Ruchames ed., 1969).

15. Individualism was embedded in the civic and religious structures of colonial life. The term, however, was not given a name until Tocqueville used "individualism" to describe the "restless [American] quest for material betterment." BELLAH ET AL., *supra* note 8, at 147.

16. KENNETH L. KARST, BELONGING TO AMERICA: EQUAL CITIZENSHIP AND THE CONSTITUTION 45(1989).

17. *Id.*

18. HUGH THOMAS, THE SLAVE TRADE: A STORY OF THE ATLANTIC SLAVE TRADE: 1440–1870, 458 (1997).

19. *Reprinted in* CIVIL RIGHTS AND AFRICAN AMERICANS: A DOCUMENTARY HISTORY 10–12 (Albert P. Blaustein & Robert L. Zangrando eds., 1968).

20. *See* portions of Samuel Sewall, *The Selling of Joseph, reprinted in* Civil Rights and African Americans, *supra* note 19, at 13–17.

21. THOMAS, *supra* note 18, at 460.

22. DANIEL P. MANNIX IN COLLABORATION WITH MALCOLM COWLEY, BLACK CARGOES: A HISTORY OF THE ATLANTIC SLAVE TRADE 1518–1865, 171 (1965) (1962).

23. *See* CIVIL RIGHTS AND AFRICAN AMERICANS, *supra* note 19, at 21.

24. 1 WILLIAM BLACKSTONE, COMMENTARIES ON THE LAWS OF ENGLAND 424 (Wayne Morrison ed., 2001).

25. ROBERT M. COVER, JUSTICE ACCUSED: ANTISLAVERY AND THE JUDICIAL PROCESS 16 (1975).

26. DAVID BOAZ, LIBERTARIANISM: A PRIMER 36 (1997).

27. *See* JOHN LOCKE, THE SECOND TREATISE OF GOVERNMENT (J.W. Gough ed., 3d ed. 1966) (1690). The founding fathers were inspired by Locke's writings and Locke's positions are evident in the Declaration of Independence. *See, e.g.*, RICHARD KLUGER, SIMPLE JUSTICE: THE HISTORY OF *BROWN V. BOARD OF EDUCATION* AND BLACK AMERICA'S STRUGGLE FOR EQUALITY 29 (1975).

28. Thomas Hobbes was the first contract theorist to promote an emancipator concept of the individual. In *Leviathan*, first published in 1651, Hobbes explicated his political truths. He viewed each individual as an atomistic entity that was self-sufficient in his ability to care for his needs. Hobbes' view of human nature, however, led him to believe that in the state of nature every man was the enemy to every other

man. Thus in the state of nature what prevailed was a continual war of all against all and life was nasty, brutish and short. THOMAS HOBBES, LEVIATHAN 186 (C.B. Macpherson ed., Penguin Classics 1968). Given that this was the state of affairs of men in the state of nature, Hobbes posits a type of social contract where a Leviathan, which may be a King or a legislature, rules the state with an iron fist. On a philosophical level, the state for Hobbes becomes both a source of all power and at the same time an emancipatory force because it frees men from the nasty, brutish and short life that he would live in the state of nature. On the political level, Hobbes in *Leviathan* argues "forcefully... that the only... legitimacy of government is,... the ruler's capacity to offer protection" and against some subjective religious standard. DEREK HIRST, AUTHORITY AND CONFLICT: ENGLAND, 1603–1658, 297–98 (1986). Hence in *Leviathan,* Hobbes is also undermining religious domination of the political arena.

Locke offered a different application of the concept of the state of nature. For Locke men in a state of nature were in "a state of perfect freedom to order their actions and dispose of their possessions and persons as they think fit, within the bounds of the law of nature, without asking leave, or dependency upon the will of any other man." JOHN LOCKE, THE SECOND TREATISE OF GOVERNMENT 4(J.W. Gough ed., 3d ed. 1966) (1690). By seeing humans as individuated selves with their own free will to determine and dispose of their possessions and their persons, Locke is implicitly suggesting that they should not be subservient to religious or feudal obligations that had come to the individual from the past.

29. BELLAH ET AL., *supra* note 8, at 143.

30. Locke was a devout Christian and even produced an important work to justify the faith. *See* JOHN LOCKE, THE REASONABLENESS OF CHRISTIANITY: AS DELIVERED IN THE SCRIPTURES (George W. Ewing ed., Gateway edition 1965). Nevertheless, his political philosophy made it possible to begin to think about individuals as individuals, rather than as subjects of a divine being.

31. DECLARATION OF INDEPENDENCE para. 2 (U.S. 1776).

32. *Reprinted in* CIVIL RIGHTS AND AFRICAN AMERICANS, *supra* note 19, at 43–44.

33. Bernard Bailyn concluded from a study of the pre-revolutionary pamphlet literature that attacks on slavery coupled with the growing demand for freedom from the slavery of the British rule had become commonplace by 1774 in the northern and middle colonies. Bernard Bailyn, *Introduction* to PAMPHLETS OF THE AMERICAN REVOLUTION, 1750–1776, 74–75 (Bernard Bailyn with assistance from Jane N. Garrett eds., 1965).

34. JOHN HOPE FRANKLIN & ALFRED A. MOSS, JR., FROM SLAVERY TO FREEDOM: A HISTORY OF NEGRO AMERICANS 66 (6th ed. 1988).

35. COVER, *supra* note 25, at 20.

36. MANNIX IN COLLABORATION WITH MALCOLM COWLEY, *supra* note 22, at 174.

37. JAMES H. DORMAN & ROBERT R. JONES, THE AFRO-AMERICAN EXPERIENCE: A CULTURAL HISTORY THROUGH EMANCIPATION 121 (1974).

38. COVER, *supra* note 25, at 8.

39. Portion *reprinted in* CIVIL RIGHTS AND AFRICAN AMERICANS, *supra* note 19, at 44–46. Shortly after the American Revolution, Massachusetts adopted the notion of equality

before the law and wrote it into its state constitution. *See also* ANDREW KULL, THE COLOR-BLIND CONSTITUTION 2 (1992).

40. U.S. CONST. art. I, § 9, cl. 1.
41. Letter Written by Benjamin Franklin to Congress *reprinted in* 1 RACIAL THOUGHT IN AMERICA, *supra* note 14, at 206.
42. A. LEON HIGGINBOTHAM, JR., SHADES OF FREEDOM: RACIAL POLITICS AND PRESUMPTIONS OF THE AMERICAN LEGAL PROCESS 57 (1996).
43. 1 PHILIP S. FONER, THE LIFE AND WRITINGS OF FREDERICK DOUGLASS: EARLY YEARS, 1817–1849, 40 (1950).
44. U.S. Bureau of the Census, *Historical Statistics of the United States, Colonial Times to 1970, Bicentennial Edition* 14 (1975).
45. The five major civil rights bills include The Civil Rights Act of 1866; the Enforcement Act of 1870; the Enforcement Act of February 28, 1871; the Enforcement Act of April 20, 1871 and the Civil Rights Act of 1875.
46. *See* Herbert Hovenkamp, *Social Science and Segregation Before Brown,* 1985 DUKE L. J. 624, 648 (1985)
47. KLUGER, *supra* note 27, at 635.
48. BENJAMIN QUARLES, THE NEGRO IN THE MAKING OF AMERICA 162–63 (1969).
49. *See also* McCabe v. Atchinson, Topeka & Santa Fe Railroad Co., 235 U.S. 151 (1914) (striking down an Oklahoma law permitting railroads to provide first class accommodations only to white (or only to black) passengers).
50. 100 U.S. 303 (1879).
51. 109 U.S. 3 (1883).
52. 163 U.S. 537 (1896).
53. Justice Harlan makes this point in his dissent. *Id.* at 559 (Harlan, J. dissenting).
54. *Id.* at 544.
55. *Id.* at 551–52.
56. *Id.* at 552 (Harlan, J. dissenting). Professor Krull has noted that colorblindness rhetoric about the Constitution has existed since the 1850s, but it did not become a real constitutional alternative until the passage of the Fourteenth Amendment. KULL, *supra* note 39, at 1–6.
57. Plessy, 163 U.S. at 559 (Harlan, J. dissenting).
58. *Id.* at 557 (Harlan, J. dissenting).
59. 170 U.S. 213 (1898).
60. 238 U.S. 347 (1915).
61. 273 U.S. 536 (1927).
62. 286 U.S. 73 (1932).
63. 295 U.S. 45 (1935).
64. 321 U.S. 649 (1944).
65. Michael J. Klarman, *Race and the Court in the Progressive Era* 51 VAND. L. REV. 881, 935 (1998).

66. Douglas S. Massey & Nancy A. Denton, American Apartheid: Segregation and the Making of the Underclass 41 (1993).
67. 245 U.S. 60 (1917).
68. 334 U.S. 1 (1948).
69. *See* Mark v. Tushnet, Making Civil Rights Law: Thurgood Marshall and the Supreme Court, 1936–1961, 27 (1994).
70. *The Call* is *reprinted in* Warren D. St. James, NAACP: Triumphs of A Pressure Group 1909–1980, 239–41 (2d ed. 1980).
71. Nancy J. Weiss, The National Urban League 1910–1940, 57 (1974).
72. St. James, *supra* note 70, at 25–28.
73. W. E. B. Du Bois, *Editorial, The Crisis,* Crisis 1, Nov. 1910, at 10.
74. St. James, *supra* note 70, at 34.
75. *See* McLaurin v. Okla. State Regents for Higher Educ., 339 U.S. 637 (1950); Sweatt v. Painter, 339 U.S. 629 (1950); Sipuel v. Board of Regents of the Univ. Of Okla., 332 U.S. 631 (1948); Missouri ex rel. Gaines v. Canada, 305 U.S. 337 (1938).
76. *See* Bob-Lo Excursion Co. v. Michigan 333 U.S. 28 (1948); Mitchell v. United States 313 U.S. 80 (1941); Morgan v. Virginia, 328 U.S. 373 (1946).
77. Steele v. Louisville & Nashville R. R. Co., 323 U.S. 192 (1944); James v. Marinship Corp., 155 P.2d 329 (Cal. 1944).

Chapter Four

1. Adarand Constructors, Inc. v. Pena, 515 U.S. 200, 229 (1995) (Scalia, J., concurring).
2. The New York Times 1999 Almanac 294 (ed. John W. Wright 1998).
3. Michael J. Klarman, *Rethinking the Civil Rights and Civil Liberties Revolutions,* 82 Va. L. Rev. 1, 49 (1996). Between 1850 and 1900 the number of Catholics increased from 1.7 million to 12 million. The number doubled again between 1900 and 1930.
4. *Id.*
5. The percent of blacks who were foreign born had increased from 3.1% in 1980 to 4.1% in 1990. Throughout the latter half of the 19th century this percentage was less than .5%. It did not reach 1% until 1970. *See* Table 8, *Race and Hispanic Origin by Nativity from 1850–1990, available at* http://www.census.gov/population/www/documentation/twps0029/ tab08.html.
6. American society has also had a very long political and judicial history of treating blacks as means to advancing the national interest. Professor Derrick Bell has advanced a version of the American Collectivism's understanding of the role of African-Americans in American history. *See, e.g.,* Derrick Bell, *Brown v. Board of Education and the Interest-Convergence Dilemma,* 93 Harv. L. Rev. 518 (1980) reprinted in Derrick Bell, Shades Of Brown: New Perspectives On School Desegregation (1980) and Derrick Bell, Race, Racism and American Law 27 (4th ed. 2000). He suggests that only when the interest of African-Americans corresponds with those of white elites does racial progress for African-Americans occur.

7. Samuel P. Huntington, "The Erosion of American National Interest," FOREIGN AFFAIRS 28 (Sept./Oct. 1997).
8. Regents of Univ. of Cal. v. Bakke, 438 U.S. 265, 292 (1978).
9. This is what the Germans called the 369th Infantry which was the first black U.S. combat unit overseas in World War I. This regiment did not loose a man or an inch of ground in 191 days of action. *See* SHARON HARLEY, TIMETABLE OF AFRICAN-AMERICAN HISTORY: A CHRONOLOGY OF THE MOST IMPORTANT PEOPLE AND EVENTS IN AFRICAN-AMERICAN HISTORY 218 (1995).
10. U.S. CONST. pmbl.
11. *See* ERIC WILLIAMS, *Origin of Negro Slavery* in THE AFRICAN PHILOSOPHY: AN ANTHOLOGY BOOK 383 (1998).
12. HUGH THOMAS, THE SLAVE TRADE: THE STORY OF THE ATLANTIC SLAVE TRADE 1440–1870, 453 (1997).
13. 1 VIRGINIA BERNHARD ET AL., FIRSTHAND AMERICA: A HISTORY OF THE UNITED STATES 16 (2d ed. 1992).
14. V. T. HARLOW, A HISTORY OF BARBADOS, 1625–1685, 295 (1926).
15. VINCENT HARDING, THERE IS A RIVER 8 (1985).
16. S. E. ANDERSON, THE BLACK HOLOCAUST FOR BEGINNERS 9 (1995).
17. THOMAS, *supra* note 12, at 481–82.
18. *Id.* at 516.
19. PHILLIP T. DROTNING, BLACK HEROES IN OUR NATION'S HISTORY: A TRIBUTE TO THOSE WHO HELPED SHAPE AMERICA 23–25 (1968).
20. *Id.* at 28.
21. BENJAMIN QUARLES, THE NEGRO IN THE MAKING OF AMERICA 46 (1965).
22. *See, e.g.*, JOHN HOPE FRANKLIN & ALFRED A. MOSS, JR., FROM SLAVERY TO FREEDOM 69 (6th ed. 1988).
23. *See, e.g., id.* at 70.
24. DROTNING, *supra* note 19, at 28.
25. QUARLES, *supra* note 21, at 48–49.
26. *See* HARLEY, *supra* note 9, at 52.
27. RICHARD KLUGER, SIMPLE JUSTICE: THE HISTORY OF *BROWN V. BOARD OF EDUCATION* AND BLACK AMERICA'S STRUGGLE FOR EQUALITY 31–33 (1976).
28. Bureau of the Census, Ser. P–23, No. 80, THE SOCIAL AND ECONOMIC STATUS OF THE BLACK POPULATION IN THE UNITED STATES: AN HISTORICAL VIEW, 1790–1978, 254 (1979).
29. KLUGER, *supra* note 27, at 30–31. It has been estimated that no more than 160,000 out of 4,000,000 people living in America at the time (4% of the population) were connected in any way with the process of drafting and ratifying the Constitution. *Id.* at 30.
30. Justice Samuel Sewall wrote this in his pamphlet attacking slavery entitled the "The Selling of Joseph" *see* 1 RACIAL THOUGHT IN AMERICA: FROM THE PURITANS TO ABRAHAM LINCOLN, A DOCUMENTARY HISTORY 47–52, 48 (ed. Louis Ruchames 1969).

31. 2 The Records Of The Federal Convention Of 1787, 645 (Max Farrand ed., rev. ed. 1966).
32. Thomas, *supra* note 12, at 502.
33. Kluger, *supra* note 27, at 34.
34. *Id.* at 33.
35. Alexis De Tocqueville, Democracy In America 342 (George Lawrence trans., 1966).
36. Bell, Race, Racism And American Law, *supra* note 6, at 45.
37. Thomas, *supra* note 12, at 461.
38. Herbert Aptheker, American Negro Slave Revolts 162 (1983).
39. *See* Paul Johnson, A History Of The American People 188 (1997).
40. Article 1, Section 2 which counts slaves as three-fifths of a person; (2) Article 1, Sections 2 and 9, which apportions taxes on the states using the three-fifths formula; (3) Article 1, Section 8, which gives Congress the authority to suppress slave and other insurrections; (4) Article 1, Section 9, which prevents the slave trade from being abolished before 1808; (5) Article 1, Section 9 and 10, which exempts goods made by slaves from export duties; (6) Article 4, Section 2, which requires the return of fugitive slaves; and (7) Article 4, Section 4, which stipulates that the federal government must help state governments put down domestic violence, including slave uprisings. Donald E. Lively, The Constitution And Race 4–5 (1992).
41. Joe R. Feagin, Racist America: Roots, Current Realities, And Future Reparations 11 (2000).
42. *Id.* Feagin actually talks about the interest of whites and not of the country. I treat those interests as the same.
43. Thomas, *supra* note 12, at 462–63.
44. Article 1, Section 9, prevents the slave trade from being abolished before 1808.
45. Kluger, *supra* note 27, at 35.
46. Feagin, *supra* note 41, at 53.
47. *See* James M. McPherson, Ordeal By Fire: The Civil War And Reconstruction 265–66 (1982).
48. Cong. Globe, 37th Cong., 1st Sess. 222 (1861).
49. For reprints of documents by blacks to enlist in the war effort *see*, 1 A Documentary History Of The Negro People In The United States 459–71 (ed. Herbert Aptheker 1951).
50. W. E. B. Dubois, Black Reconstruction In America 1860–1880, 60 (1935).
51. *Id.* at 61.
52. Drotning, *supra* note 19, at 73–74.
53. Michael L. Levine, African Americans And Civil Rights: From 1619 To The Present 88 (1996).
54. James M. McPherson, The Negro's Civil War: How American Blacks Felt & Acted During the War for the Union 145 (1965).

55. Benson J. Lossing, Matthew Brady's Illustrated History Of The Civil War 96 (1996).

56. *Id.* at 128.

57. *Id.*

58. 1999 New York Times Almanac 151 (John W. Wright ed. 1998).

59. *Id.*

60. *Id.*

61. *Id.* at 266–67.

62. *Id.* at 151.

63. Drotning, *supra* note 19, at 79.

64. McPherson, *supra* note 47, at 293.

65. *Id.*

66. For a reprint of Greeley's letter *see* Horace Greeley, "To Abraham Lincoln, President of the United States" *reprinted in* Civil Rights And African-Americans 192–95 (eds. Albert P. Blaustein & Robert L. Zangrando 1990).

67. For a reprint of Lincoln's response to Horace Greeley's letter *see* "Lincoln's Reply to Greeley", (August 22, 1863) *reprinted in* Civil Rights And African-Americans, *supra* note 66, at195–96.

68. Eric Foner, Reconstruction: America's Unfinished Revolution 1863–1877, 1 (1988).

69. Their freedom was not legally secured until the ratification of the Thirteenth Amendment in late 1865.

70. Despite the utilitarian justifications for the Emancipation Proclamation articulated by Lincoln, it is clear that he personally abhorred slavery. He is on record as having called slavery "an unqualified evil to the negro, the white man and to the State. . . . The monstrous injustice of slavery...deprives our republican example of its just influence in the world—enables the enemies of free institutions, with plausibility to taut us as hypocrites." The Collected Works Of Abraham Lincoln, Vol. II 255, Vol. III 92 (Roy P. Basler ed. 1953–55).

71. According to the 1860 Census, the population of the eleven states that joined the Confederacy in 1860 was 8,991,000, with a slave population of 3,521,000. *See* McPherson, *supra* note 54, Appendix A.

72. 1 Jefferson Davis, The Rise And Fall Of The Confederate Government 262 (1990).

73. McPherson, *supra* note 47, at 267.

74. Bell, Race, Racism and American Law, *supra* note 6, at 29.

75. McPherson, *supra* note 54, at 241.

76. Maulana Karenga, Introduction To Black Studies 144 (2d ed. 1993).

77. *Id.*

78. Franklin and Moss, *supra* note 22, at 209.

79. William E. Nelson, The Fourteenth Amendment: From Political Principal To Judicial Document 46 (1988).

80. *Id.* at 40.

81. Foner, *supra* note 68, at 185.

82. *Id.* at 223.

83. *Id.*

84. "All persons born or naturalized in the United States and subject to the jurisdiction thereof, are citizens of the United States and of the State wherein they reside. No State shall make or enforce any law which shall abridge the privileges or immunities of citizens of the United States; nor shall any State deprive any person of life, liberty or property, without due process of law; nor deny to any person within its jurisdiction the equal protection of the laws." U.S. Const. amend. XIV, § 1.

85. "Representatives shall be apportioned among the several States in according to their respective numbers, counting the whole number of persons in each State, excluding Indians, not taxed. But when the right to vote at any election for the choice of electors for president and Vice President of the United States, Representatives in Congress, the Executive and Judicial officers of a State, or the members of the Legislature, thereof, is denied to any of the male inhabitants of such State, being twenty-one years of age, and citizens of the United States, or in any way abridged, except for participation in rebellion, or other crime, the basis of representation therein shall be reduced in the proportion which the number of such male citizens shall bear to the whole number of male citizens twenty-one years of age in such state." U.S. Const. amend. XIV, § 2.

86. "No person shall be a Senator or Representative in Congress or elector of President and Vice President, or hold any office, civil or military, under the United States, or under any State, who, having previously taken an oath, as a member of Congress, or as an officer of the United States, or as a member of any State legislature, or as an executive or judicial officer of any State, to support the Constitution of the United States, shall have engaged in insurrection or rebellion against the same, or given aid or comfort to the enemies thereof. But Congress may be a vote of two-thirds of each House remove such disability." U.S. Const. amend. XIV, § 3.

87. Foner, *supra* note 68, at 269.

88. U.S. Const. amend. XV.

89. Foner, *supra* note 68, at 424–25.

90. Thomas W. Bickett, Public Letters And Papers Of Thomas Walter Bickett, Governor Of North Carolina, 1917–1921, 292 (R.B. House ed. 1923) (telegram to the Chicago Herald & Examiner).

91. Sean Dennis Cashman, African-Americans And The Quest For Civil Rights 1900–1990, 7 (1991).

92. I.A. Newby, Challenge To The Court: Social Scientists And The Defense Of Segregation, 1954–1966, 8–9 (1967).

93. This argument was also an accepted legal argument as well. *See, e.g.*, Berea Coll. v. Commonwealth, 123 Ky. 209, 221, 94 S.W. 623, 626 (1906), *aff'd*, 211 U.S. 45 (1908).

Kentucky's stated public purpose in passing the statute, as well as other segregation laws, was to preserve race identity, to maintain the purity of blood, and to prevent amalgamation of races. Berea Coll. v. Kentucky, 211 U.S. 45, 51 (1908).

94. STEPHEN J. GOULD, MISMEASURE OF MAN 47–48 (1981).

95. *See, e.g.*, Herbert Hovenkamp, *Social Science and Segregation Before Brown*, 1985 DUKE L. J. 624, 657 (1985).

96. James Bryce, *Thoughts on the Negro Problem*, 153 N. AM. REV. 641, 649–51 (1891).

97. NEWBY, *supra* note 92, at 9.

98. *Id.*

99. J. HALLER, OUTCASTS FROM EVOLUTION: SCIENTIFIC ATTITUDES OF RACIAL INFERIORITY, 1859–1900, 33 (1971).

100. B. GOULD, INVESTIGATIONS IN THE MILITARY AND ANTHROPOLOGICAL STATISTICS OF AMERICAN SOLDIERS 471 (1869).

101. Nathaniel Shaler, *Our Negro Types*, 29 CURRENT LIT. 45, 47 (1900) (mulattoes are "general[ly] of feeble vitality, rarely surviving beyond middle age"); *see* NATHANIEL SHALER, THE NEIGHBOR: THE NATURAL HISTORY OF HUMAN CONTACTS 59–64 (1904) (arguing that miscegenation is undesirable); Nathaniel Shaler, *Science and the African Problem*, 66 ATL. MONTHLY 36, 37 (1890) (same). For further discussion of the Gilded Age's perception of mulattoes, *see generally* J. MECKE, MULLATTOES AND RACE MIXTURE: AMERICAN ATTITUDES AND IMAGES, 1865–1918 (1979); NEWBY, *supra* note 92, at 132–35; J. WILLIAMSON, NEW PEOPLE: MISCEGENATION AND MULATTOES IN THE UNITED STATES (1980).

102. Hoffman, *Race Traits and Tendencies of the American Negro*, 11 PUBLICATIONS AM. ECON. A. 1, 310–29 (1896).

103. GOULD, *supra* note 94, at 20–145 (discussing and criticizing Nineteenth century studies on race).

104. The inequality in school funding has been extensively documented. *See, e.g.*, HORACE M. BOND, NEGRO EDUCATION IN ALABAMA (1939); HORACE M. BOND, THE EDUCATION OF THE NEGRO IN THE AMERICAN SOCIAL ORDER (1934); LOUIS R. HARLAN, SEPARATE AND UNEQUAL (1958); ROBERT A. MARGO, RACE AND SCHOOLING IN THE SOUTH 1880–1950: AN ECONOMIC HISTORY 21–22 (1990); J. Morgan Kousser, *Progressivism-For Middle-Class Whites Only: North Carolina Education*, 1880–1910, 46 J. SOC. HIST. 169 (1980).

105. BOOKER T. WASHINGTON, UP FROM SLAVERY 157–62.

Chapter Five

1. In 1939 the NAACP established the NAACP Legal Defense and Educational Fund, Inc. ("LDF"), known later as the Legal Defense Fund or the Inc. Fund. After that time the LDF became responsible for the legal work. *See* MARK V. TUSHNET, MAKING CIVIL RIGHTS LAW: THURGOOD MARSHALL AND THE SUPREME COURT, 1936-1961, 27 (1994).

2. *See* Gaines v. Canada, 305 U.S. 337 (1938); Sipuel v. Board of Regents, 332 U.S. 631 (1948); Sweatt v. Painter, 339 U.S. 629 (1950); McLaurin v. Oklahoma State Regents,

339 U.S. 637 (1950). The Supreme Court cases addressing segregation in graduate and professional schools were actually preceded by Pearson v. Murray, 169 Md. 478, 182 A. 590 (Md. 1936). Donald Murray, an African-American graduate of Amherst College, applied to the University of Maryland Law School, which denied him admission because of his race. *Id.* at 590. While Maryland did not provide any legal training for African-Americans, it quickly appropriated $10,000 to fund an out-of-state scholarship program. *Id.* at 593. The Maryland Court of Appeals ruled that the program was insufficient to provide Murray with equal educational opportunities. *Id.*

3. 163 U.S. 537 (1896).
4. *See* Diane Ravitch, The Troubled Crusade: American Education 1945–1980, 121 (1983). In 1956, the Supreme Court confirmed that Brown I applied to colleges and universities. Board of Trustees v. Frasier 350 U.S. 979 (1956) (per curiam) *aff'g* 134 F. Supp. 589 (M.D.N.C. 1955). Professor Kujovich, in an insightful article, discusses the history of the systematic underfunding of African-American institutions of higher education. *See* Gil Kujovich, *Equal Opportunity in Higher Education and the Black Public College: The Era of Separate But Equal,* 72 Minn. L. Rev. 29 (1987).
5. *See* U.S. Commission on Civil Rights, Twenty Years After Brown: Equality of Educational Opportunity 46 (1975).
6. 391 U.S. 430 (1968).
7. Id. at 437–38 (1968).
8. 402 U.S. 1, 13 (1971).
9. The states referred to as the segregationist states are the 17 states and the District of Columbia that maintained a rigid system of segregation in public education during the separate but equal era. These states are Alabama, Arkansas, Delaware, Florida, Georgia, Kentucky, Louisiana, Maryland, Mississippi, Missouri, North Carolina, Oklahoma, South Carolina, Tennessee, Texas, Virginia and West Virginia.
10. Gil Kujovich, *supra* note 4, at 113 n.303.
11. 305 U.S. 337 (1938).
12. State ex rel. Gaines v. Canada, 113 S.W.2d 783 (Mo. 1937), *rev'd,* 305 U.S. 337 (1938).
13. Gaines, 305 U.S. at 349.
14. Gaines, 131 S.W.2d 217, 218–19 (Mo. 1939).
15. *See* Lucile H. Bluford, *The Lloyd Gaines Story,* 1958 J. Legal Educ. Soc. 242–46 (1959).
16. 332 U.S. 631 (1948).
17. 339 U.S. 629 (1950).
18. 339 U.S. 637 (1950).
19. Sweatt, 339 U.S. at 634.
20. McLaurin v. Oklahoma State Regents for Higher Educ., 87 F. Supp. 528 (W.D. Ok. 1949).
21. 163 U.S. 537 (1896).
22. 347 U.S. 497 (1954).
23. 103 F. Supp. 920, 922 (E.D.S.C. 1952), *rev'd sub nom.* Brown v. Bd. of Educ., 347 U.S. 483 (1954).

24. 103 F. Supp. 337 (E.D. Va. 1952), *rev'd sub nom.* Brown v. Bd. of Educ., 347 U.S. 483 (1954).

25. 91 A.2d 137 (Del. 1952), *aff'd sub nom.* Brown v. Bd. of Educ., 347 U.S. 483 (1954).

26. *Id* at 152.

27. Brown, 347 U.S. at 493.

28. Brown, 347 U.S. at 494 (quoting Brown v. Bd. of Educ., 98 F. Supp. 797 (D. Kan. 1951)).

29. K. B. Clark, Effect of Prejudice and Discrimination on Personality Development (Mid Century White House Conference on Children and Youth, 1950); E. Frazier, The Negro in the United States 674–81 (1949); G. Myrdal, An American Dilemna (1944); H. Witmer & R. Kotinsky, Personality in the Making: The Fact-finding Report of the Midcentury White House Conference on Children and Youth (1952); Chein, What Are the Psychological Effects of Segregation Under Conditions of Equal Facilities? 3 Int'l J. Opinion and Attitude Res. 229 (1949); Brameld, Educational Costs, in Discrimination and National Welfare 44 (R. MacIver ed. 1949); Deutscher & Chein, The Psychological Effects of Enforced Segregation: A Survey of Social Science Opinion, 26 J. Psychol. 259 (1948); *see* Brown I, 347 U.S. at 494 n.11.

30. *See, The Effects of Segregation and the Consequence of Desegregation: A Social Science Statement* reprinted at 37 Minn. L. Rev. 427 (1953).

31. *Id.* at 431.

32. *See, e.g.,* Edmond Cahn, Jurisprudence, 30 N.Y.U. L. Rev. 150, 157–58 & n.16 (1955); Ralph Ross & Ernest Van Den Haag, Prejudice About Prejudice, *in* The Fabric of Society (1957).

33. 349 U.S. 294 (1955).

34. Civil Rights And African-Americans: A Documentary History 453 (eds. Albert P. Blaustein and Robert L. Zangrando 1968).

35. *Id.*

36. *See* Thomas V. O'Brien, *Aron v. Cook and the NAACP in Georgia Before Brown,* 23 J. Midwest Hist. Educ. Soc'y 129, 129–32 (1996).

37. "Roy v. Harris, Strictly Personal", *Augusta Courier,* Oct. 9, 1950, at 1.

38. For a discussion of Roy Harris as the original proponent of publicly funded private education, *see* Molly Townes O'Brien, *Private School Tuition Vouchers and the Realities of Racial Politics,* 64 Tenn. L. Rev. 359, 374–85 (1997).

39. *Id.* at 385.

40. *Id.*

41. *See* Numan V. Bartley, The Rise Of Massive Resistance: Race And Politics In The South During The 1950s, 77 (1969) (citing *Richmond News Leader,* June 11, 1954).

42. Mary Frances Berry, Black Resistance White Law: A History Of Constitutional Racism In America 139 (1994).

43. Ravitch, *supra* note 4, at 133. The history of resistance by southern schools has been chronicled by a number of authors. *See, e.g.,* Earl Black, Southern Gover-

NORS AND CIVIL RIGHTS: RACIAL SEGREGATION AS A CAMPAIGN ISSUE IN THE SECOND RECONSTRUCTION (1976); C. VANN WOODWARD, THE STRANGE CAREER OF JIM CROW (3d ed. 1974); Frank T. Read, *Judicial Evolution of the Law of School Integration Since Brown v. Board of Education,* 39 LAW & CONTEMP. PROBS. 7, 13–28 (1975).

44. *See* Judith A. Hagley, *Massive Resistance—The Rhetoric and the Reality* 27 N. M. L. REV. 167, 190–93 (1997).

45. *See* Cooper v. Aaron, 358 U.S. 1, 9 (1958).

46. *See* Executive Order 10730 issued September 24, 1957.

47. 358 U.S. 1 (1958).

48. Aaron v. McKinley, 173 F. Supp. 944, 947 (D. Ark. 1959). For a discussion of several statutes the Arkansas legislature adopted to maintain school segregation, *see* Raymond T. Diamond, *Confrontation as Rejoinder to the Compromise: Reflections of the Little Rock Desegregation Crisis,* 11 NAT'L BLACK L.J. 151, 155 (1989).

49. *See* Aaron, 173 F. Supp. at 947.

50. According to the District Court $350,586 in funds allocable to the Little Rock School District had been withheld up to May 4, 1959. The total amount to be withheld by the end of the 1958–59 school year, if these Acts remained in effect, would be slightly in excess of $510,000. Of the funds withheld, $187,768 were paid to other schools, public and private. Of this amount, $71,907.50 was paid to the private Raney High School. *Id.* at 952.

    After the Arkansas Supreme Court upheld the statutes upon which Faubus acted, Garrett v. Faubus, 323 S.W.2d 877, 884, (Ark. 1959), his actions were challenged in federal District Court by a class action brought by school age black children and their parents and guardians. In June of 1959 the Federal District Court declared the state statutes which Governor Faubus relied upon unconstitutional. The Supreme Court affirmed the decision per curiam without a hearing. Aaron v. McKinley, 173 F. Supp. at 944 *aff'd sub nom.* Faubus v. Aaron, 361 U.S. 197 (1959).

51. This case was actually argued in front of the Supreme Court by Governor Almond when he was attorney general for the State of Virginia.

52. 349 U.S. 294, 301 (1955).

53. Virginia tuition grants originated in 1930 as aid to children who had lost their fathers in World War I. The program was expanded until the Supreme Court of Appeals of Virginia held that giving grants to children attending private schools violated the Virginia Constitution. Almond v. Day, 197 Va. 419, 89 S.E.2d 851 (1955). It was then that the Constitution was amended.

54. *See* Griffin v. County Sch. Bd., 377 U.S. 218, 221–22 (1964).

55. *See* Harrison v. Day, 106 S.E.2d 636 (Va. 1959).

56. Allen v. County Sch. Bd. of Prince Edward County, 266 F.2d 507, 511 (4th Cir. 1959).

57. 377 U.S. 218, 222–23 (1964). The public schools in every other county in Virginia remained open.

58. Allen v. County Sch. Bd. of Prince Edward County, 198 F. Supp. 497, 503 (E.D. Va. 1961).

59. Allen v. County Sch. Bd. of Prince Edward County, 207 F. Supp. 349, 355 (E.D. Va. 1962).

60. Griffin v. Bd. of Supervisors, 322 F.2d 332 (4th Cir. 1963).

61. Sch. Bd. of Prince Edward County v. Griffin, 133 S.E.2d 565 (Va. 1963).

62. Griffin, 377 U.S. at 229–30.

63. *Id.* at 231 (citing Brown v. Bd. of Educ., 349 U.S. 294, 300 (1955)).

64. St. Helena Parish Sch. Bd. v. Hall, 287 F.2d 376 (5th Cir. 1961).

65. *See* Easton Baton Rouge Parish Sch. Bd. v. Davis 287F 2d 380 (5th Cir. 1961).

66. Hall, v. St. Helena Parish Sch. Bd., 197 F. Supp. 649 (D. La. 1961), *aff'd* Helena Parish Sch. Bd. v. Hall, 368 U.S. 515 (1962).

67. 132 F. Supp. 776 (E.D.S.C. 1955).

68. 132 F. Supp at 777.

69. Monroe v. Bd. of Commissioners, 391 U.S. 450 (1968).

70. *See* U.S. Commission on Civil Rights, *supra* note 5 at 46.

71. 391 U.S. 430 (1968).

72. 382 F.2d 338 (4th Cir. 1967).

73. Green v. New Kent County 391 U.S. 430, 437–38 (1968).

74. In a companion case to Green, Monroe v. Bd. of Commissioners, 391 U.S. 450 (1968), the Court struck down another variant of the freedom of choice scheme commonly known as "free transfer." Under the free transfer system struck down in Monroe, students were originally assigned to schools based on geographic zones, but could voluntarily transfer to other schools if there was no room in the school assigned to them. The Court struck this plan down because it failed to produce integrated schools as well.

75. 402 U.S. 1 (1971).

76. Gary Orfield and John T. Yin, *Resegregation in American Schools* 14 (June 1999) *available at* www.law.harvard.edu/civilrights/publications/resegregation99.html.

77. *Id.* at 13.

78. *Id.*

Chapter Six

1. Dred Scott v. Sandford, 60 U.S. 393, 407 (1857).

2. Plessy v. Ferguson, 163 U.S. 537, 552 (1896).

3. 433 U.S. 267 (1977).

4. *Id.* at 287.

5. 503 U.S. 467 (1992).

6. *Id.* at 485.

7. *Id.* at 485–86 (quoting Brown I, 347 U.S. at 494 (quoting Brown v. Board of Educ., 98 F. Supp. 797 (D. Kan. 1951))).

8. Justice Clarence Thomas noted in his concurring opinion in Missouri v. Jenkins, 515 U.S. 70, 120–21 (1995) (Thomas, J. concurring) that the Court's opinion in Brown v. Board of Education has been misread. According to Thomas, "Brown I did not need to rely upon any psychological or social-science research in order to announce the simple, yet fundamental, truth that the government cannot discriminate among its citizens on the basis of race...Segregation was not unconstitutional because it might have caused psychological feelings of inferiority... Psychological injury or benefit is irrelevant" to the harm generated by the state's treatment of individuals as members or racial or ethnic groups. *Id.*

   Justice Kennedy, in the Court's 1995 redistricting opinion in Miller v. Johnson, intimated that the problem with segregation struck down by the Court in Brown was that government should treat people as individuals not as members of racial or ethnic groups. Since segregation required government to treat both white and black students as members of racial groups, segregation could be viewed as violating the equal protection rights of both white and black school children. *See* 515 U.S. 900, 911 (1995).

   The studies cited in Brown I received severe criticism from the very beginning. *See, e.g.*, Edmond Cahn, *Jurisprudence,* 30 N.Y.U. L. Rev. 150, 157–58, n.16 (1955); Ralph Ross & Ernest Van Den Haag, *Prejudice About Prejudice, in* The Fabric of Society 165–66 (1957). *See also* Mark A. Yudof, *School Desegregation: Legal Realism, Reasoned Elaboration, and Social Science Research in the Supreme Court,* 42 Law & Contemp. Prob. 57, 70 (Autumn 1978); Lino O. Graglia, Disaster by Decree: The Supreme Court Decisions on Race and the Schools 27–28 (1976).

9. Gratz v. Bollinger, 539 U.S. 244, 301 (2003) (Ginsburg, J., dissenting). *See also* Wygant v. Jackson Bd. of Ed., *476 U.S. 267, 316* (1986) (Stevens, J., dissenting) ("There is, however, a critical difference between a decision to *exclude* a member of a minority race because of his or her skin color and a decision to *include* more members of the minority...for that reason. The exclusionary decision rests on the false premise that differences in race, or in the color of a person's skin, reflect real differences that are relevant to a person's right to share in the blessings of a free society. The inclusion... inevitably tends to dispel that illusion whereas their exclusion could only tend to foster it. The inclusionary decision is consistent with the principle that all men are created equal; the exclusionary decision is at war with that principle. One decision accords with the Equal Protection Clause of the Fourteenth Amendment; the other does not.").

10. *See also* Stephen L. Carter, *When Victims Happen To Be Black,* 97 Yale L.J. 420, 433–34 (1988) ("[T]o say that two centuries of struggle for the most basic of civil rights have been mostly about freedom from racial categorization rather than freedom from racial oppression, is to trivialize the lives and deaths of those who have suffered under racism. To pretend ... that the issue presented in *Bakke* was the same as the issue in *Brown* is to pretend that history never happened and that the present doesn't exist.").

11. Hirabayashi v. United States, 320 U.S. 81, 100 (1943). *See also* Graglia, *supra* note 8. *De jure* segregation is a public symbol of the inferior position of African-Americans. Charles R. Lawrence III, *Segregation "Misunderstood": The Milliken Decision Revisited,*

12 U.S.F. L. Rev. 15, 26 (1977). As such a symbol, racial segregation in public schools violates the Constitution because such segregation is an "invidious labeling device." *Id.* at 24. Through segregation, government insults or offends the dignity of the minority against whom the prejudice is directed. *See* Larry G. Simon, *Racially Prejudiced Governmental Actions: A Motivation Theory of the Constitutional Ban Against Racial Discrimination,* 15 San Diego L. Rev. 1041, 1047 (1978). There is no need for evidence to support the proposition that segregation is an insult to African-Americans, "[s]egregation does involve stigma; the community knows it does." Cahn, *supra* note 8, at 158.

12. *See, e.g.,* Derrick A. Bell, Jr., *Brown v. Board of Education and the Interest-Convergence Dilemma,* 93 Harv. L. Rev. 518, 524 (1980) *reprinted in* Shades of brown: New Perspectives on School Desegregation 90–106 (Derrick A. Bell ed., 1980). *See also* Mary L. Dudziak, Cold War Civil Rights: Race and the Image of American Democracy (2000).

13. Grutter, 539 U.S. 306, at 333. But O'Connor also notes that "The Law School does not premise its need for critical mass on 'any belief that minority students always (or even consistently) express some characteristic minority viewpoint on any issue.'" *Id.* at 335 (quoting Brief for Resp't Bollinger et al. at 30).

14. Brown, 347 U.S. at 495.

15. In an early article, I criticized the implicit racism on which the Supreme Court's school desegregation jurisprudence was based upon. *See* Kevin Brown, *Has the Supreme Court Allowed the Cure for De Jure Segregation to Replicate the Disease?,* 78 Cornell L. Rev. 1 (1992).

16. *See, e.g.,* Alvis v. Adair, Desegregation: The Illusion of Black Progress (1984); Harrell R. Rodgers, Jr. & Charles S. Bullock, III, Law and Social Change: Civil Rights Laws and their Consequences 94–97 (1972); David G. Carter, *Second-Generation School Integration Problems for Blacks,* 13 J. Black Stud. 175, 175–88 (1982). *See also* Derrick A. Bell, *Neither Separate Schools Nor Mixed Schools: The Chronicle of the Sacrificed Black Schoolchildren, in* And we are not Saved: The Elusive Quest for Racial Justice 102, 109 (1987) (citing Brief of Amicus Curiae Nat'l Educ. Assoc., *United States v. Georgia,* 445 F.2d 303 (5th Cir. 1971) (No. 30–338) (for empirical data on burden borne by black teachers, administrators, and students because of school integration)); James E. Blackwell, The Black community: Diversity and Unity 158–60 (2d ed. 1985); Harold Cruse, Plural but Equal: A Critical Study of Blacks and Minorities and America's Plural society 22 (1987).

Not all courts were oblivious to this situation. The Fifth Circuit, for example, in Singleton v. Jackson Mun. Separate Sch. Dist., 419 F.2d 1211 (5th Cir. 1969), *cert. denied,* 396 U.S. 1032 (1970), specified criteria to use in the event it was necessary to reduce the number of principals, teachers, teachers aides, or other professional staff employed by a school district. The Fifth Circuit stated that any dismissal or demotion must be based upon objective and reasonable nondiscriminatory standards.

"In addition if there is any such dismissal or demotion, no staff vacancy may be filled through recruitment of a person of a race, color, or national origin different from that of the individual dismissed or demoted, until each displaced staff member who is qualified has had an opportunity to fill the vacancy and has failed to accept an offer to do so." *Id.* at 1218.

17. *See* Samuel B. Etheridge, *Impact of the 1954 Brown v. Topeka Board of Education Decision on Black Educators,* 30 The Negro Educ. Rev. 213, 223–24 (1979). Another source put the number at more than 31,000 in southern and border states. Smith & Smith, *Desegregation in the South and the Demise of the Black Educator,* 20 J. Soc. & Behav. Sci. 28–40 (1974).

18. *Displacement and Present Status of Black School Principals in Desegregated School Districts: Hearings Before the U.S. Senate Select Committee on Equal Educational Opportunity,* 92d Cong., 1st Sess. (1971) (statement of Benjamin Epstein). In addition, Epstein also testified that 50% of the African-American principals lost their jobs in Georgia and 30% did so in Maryland. *Id.*

19. In some ways what happened to African-American schools was a repeat of the events of one-hundred years earlier when the Massachusetts state legislature attempted to desegregate the Boston public schools. In 1850 in Roberts v. City of Boston, 59 Mass. (5 Cush.) 198 (1850), the Massachusetts Supreme Judicial Court upheld the authority of the Boston School Committee to segregate the schools in Boston. However, proponents of integrated schools prevailed in the Massachusetts General Legislature which passed a law in 1855 making segregation illegal. But because whites would not allow their children to be educated by blacks, black school teachers and assistants were fired. For a discussion of the desegregation of the Boston schools in the 1850s, *see* Arthur O. White, *The Black Leadership Class and Education in Antebellum Boston,* 42 J. Negro Educ. 504, 513 (1973).

20. *See* Carl Bereiter & Seigfried Engelmann, Teaching Disadvantaged Children in the Preschool (1966); *see also* James A. Banks, Multiethnic Education: Theory and Practice 99–100 (2d ed. 1988).

21. James M. Jones, *The Concept of Racism and its Changing Reality, in* Impacts of Racism on White Americans 27, 40 (Benjamin P. Bowser & Raymond G. Hunt eds., 1981). This view was also reflected in the influential book published during the late 1960s by two African-American psychiatrists, William Grier and Price Cobbs. They, among others, pointed to the existence of a pathological consciousness in black people. William H. Grier & Price M. Cobbs, Black Rage 23–38 (1968).

22. Doxey A. Wilkerson, *Prevailing and Needed Emphases in Research on the Education of Disadvantaged Children and Youth, in* The Disadvantaged Child: Issues and Innovation 275, 278 (Joe L. Frost & Glenn R. Hawkes eds., 1966).

23. *See* James A. Banks, *Race, Ethnicity and Schooling in the United States: Past, Present and Future, in* Multicultural Education in Western Societies 30–50 (James A. Banks & James Lynch eds., 1986).

24. *Id.* at 46.

25. *Id.* at 46–7; Donald H. Bouma & James Hoffman, The Dynamics of School Integration: Problems and Approaches in a Northern City 72–81 (1968).

26. Geneva Gay, *Achieving Educational Equality Through Curriculum Desegregation,* 72 Phi Delta Kappan 56, 59 (1990).

27. Larry Cuban, *Ethnic Content and "White" Instruction, in* Teaching Ethnic Studies: Concepts and Strategies 103, 104 (James A. Banks ed., 1973).

28. *See,* Banks, *supra* note 20, at 12.

29. White students attending desegregated schools are seldom exposed to the histories and cultures of their minority classmates. *See* Carl A. Grant & Christine E. Sleeter, After the School Bell Rings 130–31 (1986).

30. Mildred Dickeman, *Teaching Cultural Pluralism, in* Teaching Ethnic Studies: Concepts and Strategies 5, 19 (James A. Banks ed., 1973).

31. *See* Peter M. Shane, *School Desegregation Remedies and the Fair Governance of Schools,* 132 U. Pa. L. Rev. 1041, 1043 (1984).

32. *See generally id.*

33. John Hope Franklin, *Jim Crow Goes to School: The Genesis of Legal Segregation in Southern Schools,* S. Atlantic Q., Spring 1959, at 234–35.

34. The expenditures per student for white schools even during the Reconstruction years of the 1870s was reported to be 30% to 40% higher than those at the black schools. James M. McPherson, Ordeal by Fire: The Civil War and Reconstruction 577 (1982).

35. Adarand Constructors, Inc. v. Pena, 515 U.S. 200, 239 (1995) (Scalia, J., concurring in part, concurring in the judgment).

36. Joseph Tussman, Government and the Mind 53 (1977).

37. Some commentators have challenged the notion that schools have an enduring effect on attitudes, values, and even intellectual development. *See* Randall Collins, The Credential Society: An Historical Sociology of Education Stratification 1–21 (1979); Christopher Jencks, Inequality: A Reassessment of the Effect of Family and Schooling in America 135 (1972). Collins stresses that what is learned in school is rapidly forgotten and makes little contribution to the effectiveness of adult role job performance. The importance of schooling for Collins lies in the general acceptance of the principle that educational credentials are a fair and rational method of allocating occupational positions in American society. Collins, *supra* at 20–21.

38. The equal protection clause's acceptance of society as a collection of Knowing Individuals provides an implicit model of public education. This implicit model recognizes the constraint of governmental neutrality. For a discussion of that implicit model of education *see* Kevin Brown, *Do African-Americans Need Immersion Schools?: The Paradoxes Created by Legal Conceptualization of Race and Public Education,* 78 Iowa L. Rev. 813, 858–67 (1993).

39. *Cf.* Mary Harter Mitchell, *Secularism in Public Education: The Constitutional Issues,* 67 B.U. L. Rev. 603, 684 (1987).

40. Regents of the Univ. of California v. Bakke, 438 U.S. 265, 407 (Blackmun, J., concurring) (1978).

41. *See, e.g.,* Paul Gewirtz, *Choice in the Transition: School Desegregation and the Corrective Ideal,* 86 Colum. L. Rev. 728 (1986).

42. There are additional advantages to integrated education that would be recognized within Colorblind Individualism today that would not have been viewed as important in the late 1960s and early 1970s. The recognition that exposure of students to more diverse points of view was not generally understood as beneficial thirty-five years ago as it is today. Exposing students to people from diverse racial and ethnic backgrounds

could be viewed as providing all of the students with a broader and richer educational experience. Through interactions with students from different racial and ethnic backgrounds, all students are more likely to be exposed to different types of music, different kinds of movies and television programs, different styles of dress, different forms of entertainment and different foods. A racially and ethnically diverse student body contributes to the atmosphere of speculation, experiment and creation. This broader and richer educational experience provides all students with more diverse experiences which in the future they can draw upon in order to determine what is best for themselves. In addition, American business is far more connected to the global marketplace than it was thirty-five years ago. American society is also far more racially and ethnically diverse now. The percentage of minorities in this country continues to grow. Projections are that by the year 2040, only one-half of the U.S. population will be composed of non-Hispanic whites. *See* U.S. Bureau of the Census, *Projections of the Population by Age, Sex, Race, and Hispanic Origin for the U.S.: 1999 to 2100 (Middle Series), available at* http://www.census.gov/population/projections/nation/detail/d2031_40.pdf. The American business person is more and more likely to have to deal with employees, consumers, suppliers and investors from diverse racial or ethnic cultural backgrounds. Individuals who will be successful business employees, managers or entrepreneurs are going to increasingly be the ones who can understand the different desires of culturally distinct consumers and investors and motivate a diverse workforce. The ability to do so starts with understanding and knowing more about people from different racial and ethnic backgrounds. Thus, integrated education can further the future career and employment opportunities of those individuals exposed to a diverse educational environment.

43. Plyler v. Doe, 457 U.S. 202, 221 (1982) (quoting Abington Sch. Dist. v. Schempp, 374 U.S. 203, 230 (1963) (Brennan, J., concurring)).

44. David Tyack et al., Law and the Shaping of Public Education, 1785–1954, 23 (1987).

45. *Id.*

46. *See, e.g.*, Banks, *supra* note 23, at 31; Philip Gleason, *American Identity and Americanization, in* Concepts of Ethnicity 57, 79–96 (William Petersen et al. eds., 1982) (discussing the role ethnicity played in American identity in the late nineteenth and early twentieth centuries); Milton M. Gordon, Assimilation in American Life: The Role of Race, Religion, and National Origins 85, 89 (1964) (discussing the contribution of education in "Anglo-Conformity"); William M. Newman, American Pluralism: A Study of Minority Groups and Social Theory 53–62 (1973) (examining the role of education as a factor in cultural assimilation). *See also* Pierre Bourdieu, *Cultural Reproduction and Social Reproduction, in* Knowledge, Education and Cultural Change 71, 81 (Richard Brown ed., 1973) (claiming that one of the main functions of any educational system is the production of the culture and social values of the dominant group in the society which it serves).

47. *See* Kenneth L. Karst, *Paths to Belonging: The Constitution and Cultural Identity*, 64 N.C. L. Rev. 303, 314 (1986).

48. *See generally* Tyack et al., *supra* note 44. The number and percent of states proscribing patriotic instruction or rituals in 1903 and 1923 were:

	1903	1923
History of U.S.	30 (67%)	43 (90%)
Citizenship	1 (2%)	39 (81%)
Flag Displays	17 (38%)	39 (81%)
All Instruction in English	14 (31%)	35 (73%)

Id. at 171.

In 1885, only eleven states mandated American history by law and only nine states required instruction be conducted in English. *Id.* at 170. "The campaign to mandate patriotism by law gained momentum in the 1890s and accelerated after World War I." *Id.*

49. *School Desegregation: A Social Science Statement,* Brief of Amicus Curiae NAACP et al. in support of Resp't at 7a, Freeman v. Pitts, 503 U.S. 467 (1992), *on writ of cert.* to 11th Cir. (June 21, 1991).

50. *See, e.g.,* BELL, *supra* note 12, at 524; DERRICK BELL, RACE, RACISM AND AMERICAN LAW 201–14 (4th ed. 2000).

51. NATIONAL SECURITY COUNCIL, U.S. OBJECTIVES AND PROGRAMS FOR NATIONAL SECURITY, NSC–68 (Apr. 14, 1950), *available at* http://www.fas.org/irp/offdocs/nsc-hst/nsc-68-1.htm. In early 1950, President Truman instructed the National Security Council to reappraise the U.S. Cold War position. The document produced, NSC–68, was not declassified until the 1970s. It had a formative influence on the way America waged the Cold War. *See* MARTIN MCCAULEY, RUSSIA, AMERICA, AND THE COLD WAR, 1949–1991, 15–16 (1998).

52. WALTER LAFEBER, AMERICA, RUSSIA, AND THE COLD WAR 1945–1996, 1 (8th ed. 1997).

53. THE NEW YORK TIMES 1999 ALMANAC 150 (John W. Wright ed., 1998).

54. *See* DUDZIAK, *supra* note 12 for a discussion about the impact of the Cold War on America's civil rights agenda.

55. MICHAEL L. LEVINE, AFRICAN AMERICANS AND CIVIL RIGHTS: FROM 1619 TO THE PRESENT 174 (1996).

56. 334 U.S. 1 (1948) (determining that the enforcement of racially restrictive covenants placed on real estate was state action and, therefore, striking their enforcement as a violation of the Fourteenth Amendment.). With the filing by the Truman Administration of its brief, the federal government began to place in front of the United States Supreme Court the damage done in the international arena by America's internal racial situation.

57. Brief of Amicus Curiae United States at 19, Shelley v. Kraemer, 334 U.S. 1 (1948) (quoting letter from Ernest A. Gross, Legal Adviser to the Secretary of State, to the Attorney General (Nov. 4, 1947)).

Chapter Seven

1. ERICA FRANKENBERG ET AL., A MULTIRACIAL SOCIETY WITH SEGREGATED SCHOOLS: ARE WE LOSING THE DREAM? 31 (Jan. 2003), *available at* http://www.civilrightsproject.harvard.edu/research/reseg03/AreWeLosingtheDream.pdf.

2. James S. Kunen, *The End of Integration*, Time, Apr. 29, 1996, at 38, 40 (quoting Kevin Brown, Professor, Indiana University School of Law—Bloomington).
3. 413 U.S. 189 (1973).
4. In 1954 there were 17 states and the District of Columbia that required segregation by statute. The 17 states were Alabama, Arkansas, Delaware, Florida, Georgia, Kentucky, Louisiana, Maryland, Mississippi, Missouri, North Carolina, Oklahoma, South Carolina, Tennessee, Texas, Virginia and West Virginia. Four other states permitted local school boards to make this choice. These states were Arizona, Kansas, New Mexico and Wyoming.
5. Keyes, 413 U.S. at 205–6.
6. *See, e.g.*, Washington v. Davis, 426 U.S. 229, 232, 239 (1976) (analyzing police application tests); Vill. of Arlington Heights v. Metropolitan Hous. Dev. Corp., 429 U.S. 252, 254 (1977) (analyzing rezoning); Regents of the Univ. of California v. Bakke, 438 U.S. 265, 269–70 (1978) (analyzing use of race and ethnicity in a medical school's admission plan); Wygant v. Jackson Bd. of Educ., 476 U.S. 267 (1986) (analyzing layoff provision in collective bargaining agreement that protected minority teachers); City of Richmond v. J.A. Croson Co., 488 U.S. 469, 476–77 (1989) (analyzing a city government provision requiring the use of racial and ethnic classifications in awarding local government contracts); Adarand Constructors, Inc. v. Pena, 515 U.S. 200 (1995) (analyzing federal provision requiring the use of racial and ethnic classifications in awarding government contracts); Miller v. Johnson, 515 U.S. 900, 903–4 (1995) (analyzing consideration of race of voters in drawing legislative boundaries in a state's congressional redistricting plan).
7. 418 U.S. 717 (1974).
8. 427 U.S. 424 (1976).
9. Diane Ravitch, The Troubled Crusade: American Education, 1945–1980, at 127 (1983).
10. Keyes, 413 U.S. at 205–6.
11. 426 U.S. 229 (1976).
12. 429 U.S. 252 (1977).
13. Brown I, 347 U.S. at 494 (quoting Brown v. Board of Educ., 98 F. Supp. 797 (D. Kan. 1951)) (emphasis added).
14. While the *Keyes* Court rejected *de facto* segregation as the basis of the constitutional harm, it also adopted a procedural rule that made proving *de jure* segregation easier. If plaintiffs establish intentional segregation in a substantial portion of the school system, the Court will presume that unlawful segregation exists throughout the school system. 413 U.S. at 208–9. This presumption removed the enormous burden that could have been placed on plaintiffs of establishing unlawful segregation for each school in the system in order to justify a system-wide remedy.
15. J. Harvie Wilkinson, From Brown to Bakke: The Supreme Court and School Integration, 1954–1978, at 199 (1979). *See School Busing: Hearing on Proposed Amendments to the Constitution and Legislation Relating to Transportation and Assignment of Public School Pupils Before Subcomm. No. 5 of the House Comm. on the Judiciary*, 92d Cong., 2d Sess. 1311 (1972) (statement of Julia Maulden).
16. Gary Orfield, Must We Bus? 24 (1978).

17. Higgins v. Bd. of Educ., 395 F. Supp. 444, 462–78 (W.D. Mich. 1973), *aff'd,* 508 F.2d 779 (6th Cir. 1974).
18. Oliver v. Kalamazoo Bd. of Educ., 368 F. Supp. 143, 194–201 (W.D. Mich. 1973), *aff'd,* 508 F.2d 178 (6th Cir. 1974).
19. Higgins, 508 F.2d 779 (Grand Rapids); *Oliver,* 508 F.2d 178, (Kalamazoo).
20. 418 U.S. 717 (1974).
21. Bradley v. Milliken, 338 F. Supp. 582, 585–86 (E.D. Mich. 1971), *aff'd in part and vacated in part,* 484 F.2d 215 (6th Cir. 1973), *rev'd,* 418 U.S. 717 (1974).
22. Bradley v. Milliken, 484 F.2d 215, 245 (6th Cir. 1973).
23. 427 U.S. 424 (1976).
24. *See, e.g.,* Crawford v. Board of Education, 458 U.S. 527 (1982).
25. Gary Orfield & John T. Yun, Resegregation in American Schools 13–14 (June 1999), *available at* http://www.civilrightsproject.harvard.edu/research/deseg/Resegregation_American_Schools99.pdf.
26. *Id.*
27. *Id.*
28. 498 U.S. 237 (1991).
29. 503 U.S. 467 (1992).
30. 515 U.S. 70 (1995).
31. *See id.* at 89; Freeman, 503 U.S. at 498; Dowell, 498 U.S. at 249–50.
32. In 1963, the District Court found that Oklahoma City was operating a dual school system and had intentionally segregated schools in the past. Dowell v. Sch. Bd. of Oklahoma City, 219 F. Supp. 427 (W.D. Okla. 1963).
33. Dowell, 498 U.S. at 241.
34. 890 F.2d 1483, 1490 (10th. Cir. 1989) (citation omitted).
35. 286 U.S. 106 (1932).
36. 426 U.S. 229 (1976).
37. 429 U.S. 252 (1977).
38. 503 U.S. 467 (1992).
39. 887 F.2d 1438, 1446 (11th Cir. 1989).
40. Kennedy's opinion was joined by Rehnquist, White, Souter and Scalia. Both Souter and Scalia, however, wrote separate concurrences. Scalia in his concurrence argued that residential segregation is a result of public and private action. That it is impossible to separate out what part is public from what part is private and the attempt to do so is only guesswork. He argues for a standard with respect to residential segregation that would say if school boards adopt plans that allow for neighborhood schools and for free choice of other schools (transportation paid), then the constitutional violation with respect to students is cured. He sees the constitutional right as equal racial access to schools, not access to racially equal schools; whatever racial imbalances such a free-choice system might produce would be the product of private forces.

    Justice Souter notes that the opinion of the Court indicated that judicial control of student and faculty assignments may still be necessary to remedy the persisting vestiges of a dual system. He writes separately, however, to note two additional situations in which continued judicial control may be necessary. The first situation is when the demographic change toward segregated residential patterns is itself caused by past school segregation and the patterns of thinking that segregation creates. This kind of demographic change is not an independent, supervening cause of racial imbalance in the student body. And when demographic change is not independent of efforts to segregate, the causal relationship may be considered in fashioning a school desegregation remedy. The second situation occurs after the district relinquishes supervision over a remedied aspect and future imbalance in that remedied aspect is caused by the remaining vestiges of the dual system. In other words, the vestige of discrimination in one aspect becomes the incubator for resegregation in others. Justice Souter discusses the potential that segregated faculties could send whites and blacks into schools based on faculty race and, as a result, increase segregation along those lines. Therefore, even though the student assignment problem has been remedied, it is possible that resegregation of students could be the result of people being moved to the schools where the faculties were segregated. Consequently, before a District Court ends its supervision of student assignments, it should make a finding that there is no immediate threat of unremedied Green-type factors causing population or student enrollment changes that, in turn, may imbalance student composition. Freeman, 503 U.S. at 507–9 (Souter, J., concurring).

41. 503 U.S. at 490–91.
42. *Id.* at 494–95 (citing U.S. Dept. Of Commerce, Bureau of the Census, Statistical Abstract of the United States 19, table 25 (111th ed. 1991)).
43. Kennedy's opinion also considered whether judicial control over student attendance was necessary to achieve compliance with other facets of the school system. Racial balancing of student assignments may be a "legitimate remedial device to correct other fundamental inequities that were themselves caused by the constitutional violation." Kennedy noted that there was no showing that racial balancing was an appropriate mechanism to cure those aspects of the school system—teacher and principal assignments, resource allocation, and quality of education—not in compliance at the time the district court released supervision of student assignments. The case was remanded so that the district court could make specific findings on whether it was necessary to retain control over student assignments in order to accomplish compliance in these areas. Kennedy also noted that the district court did not address the *Dowell* issue regarding the good faith compliance by the school district with court order over a reasonable period of time. *Id.* at 497–99.
44. 515 U.S. 70 (1995).
45. Jenkins v. Missouri, 639 F. Supp. 19, 22 (W.D. Mo. 1985).
46. Jenkins *ex rel.* Agyei v. Missouri, 19 F.3d 393, 397 (8th Cir. 1994) (Beam, J., dissenting).
47. Missouri v. Jenkins, 495 U.S. 33, 77 (1990) (Kennedy, J., concurring in part and concurring in judgment).
48. 11 F.3d 755 (8th Cir. 1993).
49. *See* Sue Anne Pressley, *New Ways to Assign Students Sought After Order to End Busing,* Washington Post, Nov. 8, 1999, at A3; *See also* Bradley W. Joondeph, *Review Essay: A Second Redemption?,* 56 Wash. & Lee L. Rev. 169, 169 (1999).

50. Orfield, *supra* note 25, at 6.

51. Jenkins, 515 U.S. at 89; Freeman, 503 U.S. at 498; Dowell, 498 U.S. at 249–50.

52. *See* Jenkins, 515 U.S. at 101; Freeman, 503 U.S. at 491–92; Dowell, 498 U.S. at 249–53.

53. *See* Swann v. Charlotte-Mecklenburg Bd. of Educ., 402 U.S. 1, 16 (1971) (stating that "School authorities are traditionally charged with broad power to formulate and implement educational policy and might well conclude, for example, that in order to prepare students to live in a pluralistic society each school should have a prescribed ratio of Negro to white students reflecting the proportion for the district as a whole. To do this as an educational policy is within the broad discretionary powers of school authorities."); Washington v. Seattle Sch. Dist. No. 1, 458 U.S. 457 (1982) (rendering an opinion that allowed the school authorities in Seattle public schools to implement a school desegregation program in the absence of an equal protection violation, even though the plan exceeded the remedy which could have been imposed by federal district courts if there had been an equal protection violation. *See also* Justice Powell's dissenting opinion in Columbus Bd. of Educ. v. Penick, 443 U.S. 449, 488 n.7 (1979) (Powell, J., dissenting) (praising a voluntary majority to minority integration plan adopted by the State of Wisconsin); Bustop, Inc. v. Bd. of Educ., 439 U.S. 1380 (1978) (Justice Rehnquist denied an application for a stay of an order issued by the California Supreme Court pursuant to an interpretation that it was necessary to engage in massive school desegregation in Los Angeles under the California state constitution. The order required the reassignment of over 60,000 students in Los Angeles public schools. In rejecting the stay, Rehnquist pointed out that the novel aspect of the plaintiff's request for the stay rested on the contention that "[E]ach citizen of a State who is either a parent or a schoolchild has a federal right to be free from racial quotas and to be free from extensive pupil transportation that destroys fundamental rights of liberty and privacy. While I have the gravest doubts that the Supreme Court of California was required by the United States Constitution to take the action that it has taken in this case, I have very little doubt that it was permitted by that Constitution to take such action." *Id.* at 1383.

54. 402 U.S. 1 at 16.

55. *See, e.g.*, Vaughns v. Bd. of Educ., 742 F. Supp. 1275, 1301 (D. Md. 1990) (justifying the efforts to maintain integrated faculty assignments); Willan v. Menomonee Falls Sch. Bd., 658 F. Supp. 1416, 1422 (E.D. Wis. 1987) (stating "[i]t is well-settled in federal law that state and local school authorities may voluntarily adopt plans to promote integration even in the absence of a specific finding of past discrimination."); *See also* Lee v. Nyquist, 318 F. Supp. 710, 714 (W.D.N.Y. 1970) (noting that it is well recognized that children that attend ethnically isolated schools do not enjoy the opportunity to know or embrace those of other races, and the elimination of such educational isolation may well be the key—or at least a large step—to racial harmony in this country), *aff'd*, 402 U.S. 935 (1971); Jenkins v. Township of Morris Sch. Dist., 279 A.2d 619, 633 (N.J. 1971) (granting power to the Commissioner to merge Morris Township and Morristown school systems if he finds it necessary to fulfill the state's educational and desegregation policies); Parent Ass'n of Andrew Jackson High School v. Ambach, 598 F.2d 705 (2d Cir. 1979) (applying strict scrutiny test and concluding that the aim of a plan to promote a more lasting integration was sufficiently compelling to justify limiting some minority students from schools of their choice); and Martin ex rel. Lauren v. Sch. Dist. of Philadelphia,

1995 U.S. Dist. LEXIS 13861 (E.D. Pa. 1995). For cases recognizing that school officials could use racial classifications to promote integrated faculties absent a finding of *de jure* segregation, *see* Jacobson v. Cincinnati Board of Education, 961 F.2d 100, 103 (6th Cir. 1992) and Kromnick v. School District, 739 F.2d 894, 903 (3d Cir. 1984).

56. 515 U.S. 200, 227 (1995).

57. 160 F.3d 790 (1st Cir. 1998).

58. *See id.* at 798 n.4. "Over the past decade, the relevant proportions have been more or less as follows: 48% black, 25% Latino, 8% Asian, and 17% white."

59. 438 U.S. 265 (1978) (Powell J. concurring in part, dissenting in part).

60. In the aftermath of this decision striking down the plan, the number of black students in the examination schools in Boston predictably dropped. *See* Darrell S. Pressley, *Fewer Minorities Invited to Boston Latin,* Boston Herald, March 23, 1999, at 10; Beth Daley, *Troubling Admission Statistics at Latin: Chances for Blacks Attending Remain Poor,* Boston Globe, March 23, 1999, at B1. This same effect has occurred from highly talented students at other school districts that operate similar programs when race has been eliminated as a factor. *See, e.g.,* Melanie Markley, Magnet Schools See Dip in Minority Enrollment, Houston Chron., May 14, 1998, at A25.

61. 195 F.3d 698 (4th Cir. 1999), *cert. denied,* 529 U.S. 1050 (2000).

62. 197 F.3d 123 (4th Cir. 1999), *cert. denied,* 529 U.S. 1019 (2000).

63. *Id.*

64. *Id.* at 126. Students are classified by their racial/ethnic group as African-American, Asian, Latino, or white. *Id.*

65. Judge Beezer asserted that the only compelling state interest that should justify the use of racial classifications was remedial. *See* Hunter *ex rel.* Brandt v. Regents of Univ. of Cal., 190 F.3d 1061, 1071 (9th Cir. 1999) (Beezer, J., dissenting). Beezer also found that the consideration of race was not narrowly tailored. *See id.* at 1076 (Beezer, J., dissenting). Beezer argued that the University based its use of race and ethnicity on the belief "that 'children with different ethnic backgrounds often have different learning styles.'" *Id.* at 1077 (Beezer, J., dissenting) (quoting testimony of Professor Deborah Stipek). The University had not, however, established that these particular children, from their particular racial or ethnic backgrounds, had different learning styles. *See id.* at 1078 (Beezer, J., dissenting). In addition, the University had failed to consider race-neutral ways of accomplishing its objective, specifically, "the establishment of one or more additional laboratory elementary schools in areas of California where the demographic diversity would naturally produce applicant pools with any desired racial/ethnic mix." *Id.* (Beezer, J., dissenting). Finally, he criticized the inclusion of a category for mixed-race children. *See id.* at 1080 (Beezer, J., dissenting). Noting that if what the University was trying to define were the learning styles of different racial and ethnic groups, the inclusion of a mixed-race group of students was "incomprehensible." *See id.* (Beezer, J., dissenting).

66. 190 F.3d 1061 (9th Cir. 1999), *cert. denied,* 531 U.S. 877 (2000).

67. *Id.* at 1063.

68. 212 F.3d 738 (2d Cir. 2000).

69. *See id.* at 740, 753 (Parker, J., concurring).

70. *See id.* at 740, 754 (Miner, J., dissenting). Judge Miner agreed that the court was bound by its decisions in the Andrew Jackson cases. *See id.* at 756 (Miner, J., dissenting). Thus, he accepted that promoting more lasting integration in the face of *de facto* segregation, promoting racial diversity, or reducing racial isolation were all similarly compelling state interests. *Id.* (Miner, J., dissenting). Miner, however, did not believe that the narrowly tailored prong was satisfied. *See id.* at 757 (Miner, J., dissenting). He noted that:

    The Supreme Court has enumerated the factors to be considered in assessing the appropriateness of race-conscious remedies: 'the necessity for the relief and the efficacy of alternative remedies; the flexibility and duration of the relief, including the availability of waiver provisions; the relationship of the numerical goals to the relevant [student population]; and the impact of the relief on the rights of third parties.' *Id.* at 756–57 (Miner, J., dissenting) (quoting United States v. Paradise, 480 U.S. 149, 171 (1987) (plurality opinion) (alteration in original)). In considering those factors, Judge Miner noted that "[t]here was absolutely no effort of any kind to assess any of these factors in establishing the Program." *Id.* at 757 (Miner, J., dissenting). In applying the Paradise factors, he noted that there was no consideration given to the length of time the Program had been in effect without any apparent success in reducing racial isolation. *Id.* (Miner, J., dissenting). There was no showing that any alternate remedies, such as magnet schools, vouchers, open enrollment, or redrawing boundaries, were examined. *Id.* (Miner, J., dissenting). The relationship of the numerical goals to the total student population were not examined. *Id.* (Miner, J., dissenting). The impact on the rights of third parties was not considered. *See id.* (Miner, J., dissenting).

71. 598 F.2d 705 (2d Cir. 1979).

72. 539 U.S. 306 (2003).

73. I have previously made the argument that the use of racial classifications to foster integrated education in public education should be viewed from the perspective of the Supreme Court's education jurisprudence as opposed to its equal protection jurisprudence. Such a view might allow public school authorities far more discretion in using race and ethnicity to promote integrated education than what appears to be allowed under Grutter. *See* Kevin Brown, *The Constitutionality of Racial Classifications in Public School Admissions*, 29 Hofstra L. Rev. 1 (2000).

Chapter Eight

1. Adarand Constructors, Inc. v. Pena, 515 U.S. 200, 227 (1995).

2. 476 U.S. 267 (1986). This opinion was a plurality opinion written by Justice Powell and joined by Burger and Rehnquist. Justice O'Connor joined all but Section IV of the opinion and wrote a separate concurrence. Justice White was the fifth person in the majority. His separate opinion concurring in judgment simply stated that the layoff policy was no different than discharging whites and hiring blacks until the suitable percentage of blacks in the work force was achieved.

3. *See, e.g.*, Bryant v. Independent School District, 334 F.3d 928 (10th Cir. 2003) (recognizing as intentional discrimination a claim of racial harassment and adopting the test

articulated by the Department of Education for what constitutes the establishment of a racially hostile learning environment. According to the Department of Education, a school district violates Title VI when (1) there is a racially hostile environment; (2) the district had notice of the problem; and (3) it "failed to respond adequately to redress the racially hostile environment. A racially hostile environment is one where the racial harassment is severe, pervasive or persistent so as to interfere with or limit the ability of an individual to participate in or benefit from the services, activities or privileges provided by the recipient. *See also* Monteiro v. Tempe Union High School District, 158 F.3d 1022 (9th Cir. 1998), recognizing a deliberate indifference test as intentional discrimination under Title VI. *See also* Gant v. Wallingford Bd. of Educ., 195 F.3d 134 (2d Cir. 1999).

4. 532 U.S. 275 (2001).
5. 476 U.S. 267 (1986).
6. *Id.* at 270.
7. When layoffs became necessary in 1974, it was obvious that adherence to this provision meant that some majority teachers with more seniority would be laid off in order to keep minority teachers with less seniority. Rather than comply with the provision, the Board of Education retained tenured teachers and laid off probationary minority teachers, thus failing to maintain the percentage of minority personnel that existed at the time of the layoff. The Union, together with two minority teachers who had been laid off, brought suit in federal court. They claimed that the Board's failure to adhere to the layoff provision violated the equal protection clause of the Fourteenth Amendment and Title VII of the Civil Rights Act of 1964. Eventually, the plaintiffs prevailed in their litigation. After the litigation, the Jackson School Board adhered to the provision when it became necessary to lay teachers off in 1976–77 and 1981–82 school years. *Id.* at 271–72.
8. 546 F. Supp. 1145 (E.D. Mich. 1982); *aff'd* 746 F.2d 1156 (6th Cir. 1984); *rev'd* 476 U.S. 267 (1986).
9. Wygant, 476 U.S. at 276.
10. 42 U.S.C § 2000(d) (2003).
11. 414 U.S. 563 (1974).
12. *Id.* at 568.
13. 438 U.S. 265 (1978).
14. 463 U.S. 582 (1983).
15. 463 U.S. at 610–11 (Powell, J., joined by Burger, C. J., and Rehnquist, J., concurring in judgment); *id.* at 612 (O'Connor, J., concurring in judgment); *id.* at 642 (Stevens, J., joined by Brennan and Blackmun, JJ., dissenting).
16. 532 U.S. 275, 281 (2001) (quoting Alexander v. Choate, 469 U.S. 287, 293 (1985)).
17. *See* Alexander, 532 U.S. at 279 ("Private individuals may sue to enforce § 601 of Title VI and obtain both injunctive relief and damages").
18. *See* Alexander, 532 U.S. at 281–82 ("Though no opinion of this Court has held that, five Justices in *Guardians* voiced that view of the law at least as alternative grounds for their decisions").
19. *Id.* at 282.

20. 532 U.S. 275 (2001).

21. *Id.* at 299–300.

22. Prior Supreme Court cases had led to this conclusion. *See, e.g.,* Blessing v. Freestone, 520 U.S. 329, 340 (1997) ("[T]o seek redress through § 1983,...a plaintiff must assert the violation of a federal *right,* not merely a violation of federal *law*").

23. 536 U.S. 273 (2002).

24. *Id.* at 283.

25. *Id.* at 284–85 (quoting California v. Sierra Club, 451 U.S. 287, 294 (1981)).

26. *See* Save Our Valley v. Sound Transit, 335 F.3d 932 (9th Cir. 2003), for a recent decision applying the Court's decisions in Alexander v. Sandoval and Gonzaga University v. Doe to conclude that there is no private right of action to enforce the disparate impact regulations under Title VI or under 42 U.S.C. § 1983.

27. *See* ANNE WHEELOCK, CROSSING THE TRACKS: HOW "UNTRACKING" CAN SAVE AMERICA'S SCHOOLS ix (1992).

28. For a good discussion of the racially disparate effects of tracking *see* Pamela J. Smith, *Our Children's Burden: The Many-Headed Hydra of the Educational Disenfranchisement of Black Children,* 42 How. L.J. 133, 197–203 (1999).

29. One study from the National Education Association found that 63 percent of teachers in the United States believed tracking was useful. *See* Academic Tracking, Report of the NEA Subcommittee on Academic Tracking (1990).

30. *See, e.g.,* KEVIN G. WELNER, LEGAL RIGHTS, LOCAL WRONGS: WHEN COMMUNITY CONTROL COLLIDES WITH EDUCATIONAL EQUITY (2001) (the author studied tracking in four school districts (San Jose, California; Wilmington, Delaware; Woodland Hills, Pennsylvania; and Rockford, Illinois) and found a clear pattern of discrimination. All four districts were also operating under court-ordered desegregation plans.).

31. *See* Rena F. Subotnik & Karen D. Arnold, *Longitudinal Study of Giftedness and Talent, in* BEYOND TERMAN: CONTEMPORARY LONGITUDINAL STUDIES OF GIFTEDNESS AND TALENT 1 (Rena F. Subotnik & Karen D. Arnold eds., 1994); Jack W. Londen, *School Desegregation and Tracking: A Dual System Within Schools,* 29 U.S.F. L. REV. 705, 710 (1995) ("[S]ubstantial educational research show[s] that tracking is harmful, particularly to students placed in low-track classrooms."); and Robert Slavin, *Achievement Effects of Ability Grouping in Secondary Schools: A Best-Evidence Synthesis,* 60 Review of Educational Research 471 (1990). *See also* Simmons v. Hooks, 843 F. Supp 1296, 1299 (E.D. Ark. 1994) (mentioning testimony of Dr. Robert Slavin in a tracking case).

32. *See generally* JEANNIE OAKES, KEEPING TRACK: HOW SCHOOLS STRUCTURE INEQUALITY (1985); JEANNIE OAKES, MULTIPLYING INEQUALITIES: THE EFFECTS OF RACE, SOCIAL CLASS, AND TRACKING ON OPPORTUNITIES TO LEARN MATHEMATICS AND SCIENCE (1990).

33. *See, e.g.,* WELNER, *supra* note 30.

34. "The general view is that tracking does not benefit minority students." People Who Care v. Rockford Bd. of Educ. Sch. Dist., 111 F.3d 528, 536 (7th Cir. 1997) (citing DANIEL U. LEVINE & RAYNA F. LEVINE, SOCIETY AND EDUCATION 38–41 (9th ed. 1996). *See* also OAKES, KEEPING TRACK, *supra* note 32 and WELNER, *supra* note 30.

35. 59 Mass. 198 (1849).

36. *Id.* at 209–10.

37. *See, e.g.*, LEWIS M. TERMAN, THE MEASUREMENT OF INTELLIGENCE (Riverside Press 1916).

38. Daniel J. Losen, *Silent Segregation in Our Nation's Schools*, 34 Harv. C.R.–C.L. L. Rev. 517, 520–21 (1999).

39. *See, e.g.*, Kevin G. Welner & Jeannie Oakes, *(Li)Ability Grouping: The New Susceptibility of School Tracking Systems to Legal Challenges*, 66 HARVARD EDUCATIONAL REVIEW 451, 452 (1996).

40. *See, e.g.*, KENNETH J. MEIER ET AL., RACE, CLASS, AND EDUCATION: THE POLITICS OF SECOND-GENERATION DISCRIMINATION (1989); MARTHA MINOW, MAKING ALL THE DIFFERENCE: INCLUSION, EXCLUSION, AND AMERICAN LAW (1990).

41. *See, e.g.*, Hobson v. Hansen, 269 F. Supp. 401 (D.D.C. 1967) (upheld as Smuck v. Hobson, 408 F.2d 175 (D.C. Cir. 1969)); Singleton v. Jackson Mun. Separate Sch. Dist., 419 F.2d 1211 (5th Cir. 1969), *rev'd*, 396 U.S. 290 (1970); McNeal v. Tate, 508 F.2d 1017 (5th Cir. 1975). *See also* Larry P. v. Riles, 793 F.2d 969 (9th Cir. 1984) (as amended on denial of rehearing and rehearing *en banc* 1986) (holding under Title VI regulations use of IQ test to determine placement in educable mentally retarded classes to constitute illegal discrimination against black students).

42. 269 F. Supp. 401 (D.D.C. 1967).

43. 347 U.S. 497 (1954).

44. The Board of Education decided not to appeal the decision. After Dr. Hansen resigned from the post of Superintendent and a new D. C. Board of Education was elected to replace the prior appointed Board, an appeal by Hansen, an individual board member, (Smuck) and a group of parents sought to intervene and bring the case before the Court of Appeals for the District of Columbia. The Court concluded that only the parents whose asserted interest in preserving the freedom of the Board of Education to exercise the broadest discretion constitutionally permissible had standing to appeal. The Court of Appeals concluded that the parents could not appeal the order abolishing the tracking system in existence at the time of the district court order which was operated contrary to its own stated goals. The Court of Appeals concluded that the district court's decree must be taken to refer to the tracking system as it existed at the time of the decree, but the opinion did not prohibit ability grouping that did not suffer from the infirmities of the system which was struck down. *See* Smuck v. Hobson 408 F.2d. 189 (D.C. Cir 1969).

45. 269 F. Supp at 482.

46. *Id.* at 483.

47. *See, e.g.*, Singleton v. Jackson Mun. Separate Sch. Dist., 419 F.2d 1211 (5th Cir. 1969); United States v. Tunica County Sch. Dist., 421 F.2d 1236 (5th Cir. 1970); United States v. Sunflower County Sch. Dist., 430 F.2d 839 (5th Cir. 1970); Lemon v. Bossier Parish Sch. Bd., 444 F.2d 1400 (5th Cir. 1971); Moses v. Washington Parish Sch. Bd., 456 F.2d 1285 (5th Cir. 1972); United States v. Gadsden County School District, 572 F.2d 1049 (5th Cir. 1978).

48. 419 F.2d 1211 (5th Cir. 1969).

49. *Id.* at 1219.

50. Lemon v Bossier, 444 F.2d 1400, 1401 (5th Cir. 1971).

51. 508 F.2d 1017 (5th Cir. 1975).
52. *Id.* at 1019.
53. *Id.* at 1020.
54. 775 F.2d 1403 (11th Cir. 1985).
55. The named defendants were the State of Georgia, the State Superintendent of Schools, the State Board of Education (the State defendants), and the Americus, Bleckley, Burke, Coweta, Crisp, Evans, Jefferson, Lee, Liberty, Miller, Thomaston, Pelham and Vidalia school districts (the local defendants). The claims against the Americus, Bleckley, Jefferson, Thomaston, and Pelham school systems were settled prior to the trial.
56. The Eleventh Circuit also found that the district court's conclusion that the ability grouping system provided for better educational opportunities for minority children was not clearly erroneous.
57. 868 F.2d 750 (5th Cir. 1989).
58. *See also* Montgomery v. Starkville Mun. Separate Sch. Dist., 665 F. Supp. 487 (N.D. Miss. 1987), *aff'd,* 854 F.2d 127 (5th Cir. 1988).
59. 843 F. Supp. 1296 (E.D. Ark. 1994).
60. As alternative ground of liability, the District Court concluded that the plaintiff established by a preponderance of evidence that the school district intended to discriminate against black students when it adopted the ability grouping policy which became effective at the same time that it ended its operation of a dual school system. Thus, the implementation of the ability skills grouping plan was a continuation of racial segregation. As a result, the school district never operated in a unitary manner. *Id.* at 1302.
61. 851 F. Supp. 905 (N.D. Ill. 1993). The court broke the liability findings up from the remedial stage. For comprehensive remedial order, *see* People Who Care v. Rockford Bd. of Educ. Sch. Dist., 1996 WL 364802 (N.D. Ill. 1996), *aff'd in part, rev'd in part,* 111 F.3d 528 (7th Cir. 1997).
62. 851 F. Supp. 905. The current lawsuit is "only" eight years old, but litigation over racial segregation in the Rockford public schools began a quarter of a century ago. *See* Quality Educ. for All Children, Inc. v. Sch. Bd., 362 F. Supp. 985 (N.D. Ill. 1973).
63. 1996 WL 364802 at *67–68. In 1991 and 1992, the achievement scores of white students were more than twice that of the black students. White students scored at the 58th percentile on national tests, while the black students in comparison scored at the 27th percentile. At the various high schools in the district in 1992, the achievement gap ranged from a low of 17 percent to a high of 44 percent in reading comprehension, and a low of 18 percent to a high of 49 percent in math. The magistrate also included a chart of reading and math scores from 1995 for grades three through eight, and ten. The chart broke down students into African-American and non-minority. In an effort to control for family income, the chart also categorized these students in terms of the ones who were receiving subsidized lunch from those that were not. This chart revealed for all grades included that the achievement gaps between black kids who were not on subsidized lunch when compared to the white kids who were not on subsidized lunch were significantly greater than the gaps between the black and the white kids that received subsidized lunch.

64. 111 F.3d at 536.

65. *See also* United States v. Yonkers Bd. of Educ., 123 F. Supp. 2d 694 (S.D.N.Y. 2000), addressing the tracking used in Yonkers public schools as a potential vestige of the prior *de jure* conduct of a school system under a federal desegregation order.

66. *See* No Child Left Behind Act of 2001, Pub. L. No. 107–110, 115 Stat. 1425 (2002) (codified in 20 U.S.C.A. § 6301 *et. seq.*) (enacting plan).

67. *See, e.g.,* United States v. Yonkers Bd. of Educ., 984 F. Supp. 687 (S.D. N.Y. 1997) (concluding *inter alia* that one of the ways to attack the continuing achievement gap between minority and non-minority students in a school system undergoing desegregation was a unitary set of standards for what all students, regardless of race or ethnicity, at each grade level should learn).

68. Audrey L. Amrein & David C. Berliner, *High-Stakes Testing, Uncertainty, and Student Learning,* Education Policy Analysis Archives, Mar. 2002, at 55 n.28, *available at* http://epaa.asu.edu/epaa/v10n18.

69. Jim Ysseldyke, *Reflections on a Research Career: Generalizations from 25 Years of Research on Assessment and Instructional Decision Making,* 67 Exceptional Child 304 (2001); *See also* GI Forum v. Texas Educ. Agency, 87 F. Supp. 2d 667, 676 (W.D. Tex. 2000).

70. Daniel J. Losen & Kevin G. Welner, *Disabling Discrimination in Our Public Schools: Comprehensive Legal Challenges to Inappropriate and Inadequate Special Education Services for Minority Children,* 36 Harv. C.R.-C.L. L. Rev. 407, 421 (2001).

71. A number of procedural due process challenges have reached the courts regarding high-stakes testing. Students who fail to pass the test typically argue that they were not provided with adequate notice of the fact that the awarding of their high school diploma depended upon a new requirement, passage of a high school exit examination. Courts have generally rejected procedural due process challenges if the students are provided with adequate notice. For example, in Debra P. v. Turlington, 644 F.2d 397 (5th Cir. 1981), the Fifth Circuit held that four years of notice to the students was adequate. In 1983, the New York Court of Appeals in Board of Education v. Ambach, 60 N.Y.2d 758 (N.Y. 1983) addressed an appeal dealing with the failure of two handicapped students to pass a graduation exam that was required for receipt of their high school diploma. The Court of Appeals held that (1) a requirement of basic competency tests as a prerequisite to obtaining a high school diploma, after three-years notice of such requirement, did not violate the Due Process Clause; and (2) the three-years notice given was not of such brief duration as to prevent school districts from programming individualized education programs of remedially handicapped children to enable them to pass basic competency tests required for diploma graduation. *See also* Rene v. Reed, 751 N.E.2d 736 (Ind. App. 2001) (upholding trial court's rejection of a due process challenge brought by handicapped students to the state's requirement of successful completion of a graduation exam in order to receive a high school diploma, where the students and their parents had at least three years notice); *see also* Brookhart v. Illinois State Bd. of Educ., 697 F.2d 179 (7th Cir. 1983) (holding that handicapped students' procedural due process rights were violated when they were given no more than one and one-half years notice that a graduation test requirement would be imposed on them as a condition to the receipt of their diploma).

72. Amrein & Berliner, *supra* note 68, at 15.

73. 474 F. Supp. 244 (M.D. Fla. 1979), *aff'd in part,* 644 F.2d 397 (5th Cir. 1981), *remanded to* 564 F. Supp. 177 (M.D. Fla. 1983), *aff'd,* 730 F.2d. 1405 (11th Cir. 1984).

74. In addition to procedural due process challenges discussed above, *see supra* note *71,* there was also a substantive due process and a rational relationship equal protection challenge raised. During the course of pre-trial litigation in Debra P. v. Turlington, the Florida Department of Education stipulated that no effort was made to ascertain whether or not all of the minimum student performance standards built into the high school exit exam were in fact being taught in Florida public schools. Florida thus failed to establish the curricular validity of its test. While the trial court rejected a substantive due process challenge, the Fifth Circuit noted that this failure could create a substantive due process or an equal protection problem. If the examination tests matters outside the curriculum, its continued use would violate the equal protection clause, because the test would not be rationally related to the purpose for which it was designed. The Fifth Circuit remanded the issue of the curricular validity of the test to the trial court for further consideration. On remand, the trial court concluded that the defendants carried their burden of proving by a preponderance of the evidence that the test was instructionally valid and therefore constitutional.

    The Due Process Clause should not be much of an impediment to instituting high-stakes testing. School authorities can overcome a procedural due process objection by providing students with adequate notice (probably three years) that they will need to pass the test. As long as school authorities prove that the test is a valid measure of what is being taught in its schools, then the test should withstand a substantive due process challenge as well.

75. Debra P. v. Turlington, 730 F. 2d 1405 (11th Cir. 1984).

76. *See also* Anderson v. Banks, 520 F. Supp. 472 (S.D. Ga. 1981). The Court addressed a challenge to the requirement that students pass a high school exit examination in order to receive their high school diploma. In the first use of the exam, ten of the twelve students who failed the exam were black. In the second year, all six of the students who failed the exam were black. The District Court concluded that the graduation requirement was adopted without racial animus. The District Court, however, determined that the high school exit examination requirement could not be applied to a school system that had not yet eliminated the vestiges of the operation of its prior dual school system.

77. 87 F. Supp. 2d 667 (W.D. Tex. 2000).

78. 532 U.S. 275 (2001).

79. 536 U.S. 273 (2002).

80. 87 F. Supp. 2d at 681.

81. 832 F. Supp. 704 (S.D. N.Y. 1993), *aff'd,* 37 F.3d 857 (2d Cir. 1994).

82. They also challenged the curriculum as a violation of Title VI implementing regulations.

83. 158 F.3d 1022 (9th Cir. 1998).

84. *See* Dan Cryer, *Why Is Huck So Controversial?,* Newsday, Oct. 15, 1996, at A33.

85. The Ninth Circuit, however, concluded that the complaint did set forth as an allegation of a violation of Title VI based upon the creation of a hostile racial environment.

The Ninth Circuit adopted the test articulated by the Department of Education for what constitutes the establishment of a racially hostile learning environment. According to the Department of Education, a school district violates Title VI when (1) there is a racially hostile environment; (2) the district had notice of the problem; and (3) it "failed to respond adequately to redress the racially hostile environment. A racially hostile environment is one where the racial harassment is severe, pervasive or persistent so as to interfere with or limit the ability of an individual to participate in or benefit from the services, activities or privileges provided by the recipient. The existence of a hostile educational environment is a question of fact which is determined with reference to the totality of the circumstances, including the victim's race and age. Racial harassment creates a hostile environment if it is sufficiently severe that it would interfere with the educational program of a reasonable person of the same age and race as the victim. *See also* Gant v. Wallingford Bd. of Educ., 195 F.3d 134 (2d Cir. 1999). *See also* Bryant v. Independent School District, 334 F.3d 928 (10th Cir. 2003).

Chapter Nine

1. ERICA FRANKENBERG, ET AL., A MULTIRACIAL SOCIETY WITH SEGREGATED SCHOOLS: ARE WE LOSING THE DREAM? 31 (2003).
2. James E. Ryan & Michael Heise, *The Political Economy of School Choice,* 111 YALE L.J. 2043, 2045 (2002).
3. *See* GREGORY CAMILLI & LORRIE A. SHEPARD, METHODS FOR IDENTIFYING BIASED TEST ITEMS 6 (1994)(mentioning the Association of Black Psychologist's resolution).
4. STEPHAN THERNSTROM & ABIGAIL THERNSTROM, AMERICA IN BLACK AND WHITE: ONE NATION, INDIVISIBLE 363 (1997) (discussing the resolution).
5. Kenneth J. Cooper, *Exams Opposed over Potential Harm to Minorities,* WASHINGTON POST, June 12, 1991, at A21.
6. *Critics Target Wrong Culprit as Minorities' Test Scores Lag,* USA TODAY, May 30, 2000, at 16A.
7. Gail Russell Chaddock, *Adverse Impact?,* CHRISTIAN SCIENCE MONITOR, November 30, 1999, at 14.
8. African-Americans constitute about 11.2% (120,506 of the 1,074,016) of those who take the SAT. *See* THE COLLEGE BOARD, 2001 COLLEGE-BOUND SENIORS: A PROFILE OF SAT PROGRAM TEST TAKERS 6 (2001).
9. THE COLLEGE BOARD, 2003 COLLEGE-BOUND SENIORS: A PROFILE OF SAT PROGRAM TEST TAKERS, *available at* http://www.collegeboard.com/prod_downloads/about/news_info/cbsenior/yr2003/pdf/2003_TOTALGRP_PRD.pdf.
10. In 1975-76 the gap between the average SAT scores of African-Americans and whites was 257 (687 in comparison to 944). BLACK AMERICANS: A STATISTICAL SOURCEBOOK 106 (Louise L. Hornor ed., 2000).
11. For the 1990-91 assessment year the gap was only 187 points (1031 as opposed to 846). In the 1996-97 assessment year the gap had increased to 195 points (1052 as opposed to 857) and in 1999-2000, it was 198 (1058-860). *See* NAT'L CTR. FOR

Educ. Statistics, Scholastic Assessment Test (SAT) Score Averages by Race/Ethnicity, *available at* http://nces.ed.gov/pubs2002/digest2001/tables/dt134.asp.

12. ACT National and State Scores, *available at* http://www.act.org/news/data/03/pdf/t1-2.pdf. (last visited October 18, 2003).

13. For students graduating in 1997 the average ACT score for blacks was 16.4 compared to 21.2 for whites. This gap of 4.8 points is the same as was reported in 2003. *See* ACT National and State Scores, The 1997 ACT High School Profile Report— National Normative Data, *available at* http://www.act.org/news/data/97/t5-6-7.html.

14. *See* Jennifer Mueller, *Facing the Unhappy Day: Three Aspects of the High Stakes Testing Movement* 11 Kan. J.L. & Pub. Pol'y 201, 209 (2002).

15. *See* Fredreka Schouten (Gannett News Service), Make-or-Break Graduation Tests Spur Protests, A-14, col. 3 Indianapolis Star, May 25, 2003.

16. Audrey L. Amrein & David C. Berliner, *High-Stakes Testing, Uncertainty, and Student Learning,* Education Policy Analysis Archives, Mar. 2002, at 12 n.28, *available at* http://epaa.asu.edu/epaa/v10n18.

17. *Id.*

18. *Id.*

19. Test scores for Latinos were not separately listed in 1971.

20. *See* Nat'l Ctr. for Educ. Statistics, Average NAEP Reading Scale Scores, by age and race/ethnicity: selected years 1975 to 1998, *available at* http://nces.gov/Pubs2003/Hispanics/figures.asp?FigureNumber=4_2a.

21. *See* Nat'l Ctr. For Educ. Statistics, Trends in the science performance of 9-, 13-, and 17-Year-Olds, Table 13-2 Average white-black and white-Hispanic score gaps in science achievement 1970-99, *available at* http://nces.ed.gov//programs/coe/2001/section2/tables/t13_2.asp (visited on February 7, 2002).

22. *See* Nat'l Ctr. For Educ. Statistics, The Nation's Report Card, NAEP 1999 Long-Term Trend Mathematics Summary Data Tables for Age 9 Student Data, *available at* http://nces.ed.gov/nationsreportcard/tables/Ltt1999/NTM21011.asp (last visited June 19, 2003); Nat'l Ctr. For Educ. Statistics, The Nation's Report Card, NAEP 1999 Long-Term Trend Mathematics Summary Data Tables for Age 13 Student Data, *at* http://nces.ed.gov/nationsreportcard/tables/Ltt1999/ NTM21011.asp (last visited June 19, 2003); Nat'l Ctr. For Educ. Statistics, The Nation's Report Card, NAEP 1999 Long-Term Trend Mathematics Summary Data Tables for Age 17 Student Data, *available at* http://nces.ed.gov/nationsreportcard/tables/Ltt1999/NTM31011.asp (last visited June 19, 2003).

23. U.S. Bureau of the Census, 2003 Statistical Abstract of the United States 177 (2003) (Table 270: High School Dropouts Race and Hispanic Origins). The rate for Hispanics is an alarming 31.7%.

24. For an extended discussion of the inaccuracies and misleading estimates of high school graduates and school dropouts *see* Gary Orfield, Daniel Losen, Johanna

WALD AND CHRISTOPHER B. SWANSON, LOSING OUR FUTURE: HOW MINORITY YOUTHS ARE BEING LEFT BEHIND BY THE GRADUATION RATE CRISIS, 7-14 (April 2004).

25. A study of high school graduation rates prepared for the Black Alliance for Educational Options was recently revised. *See* JAY P. GREENE, HIGH SCHOOL GRADUATION RATES IN THE UNITED STATES(2002). In the foreword to the study Kaleem Caire notes that current measures of high school dropouts which calculates those who receive GEDs as graduates understates the dropout rate. *Id.* at page 5. The author of the study calculates high school dropout rates by taking the 8th grade public school enrollment for each jurisdiction and sub-group from the fall of 1993 and the number of graduates from the Spring of 1998. To adjust for the possibility that students moving into or out of a school district would distort the graduation rate, he adjusted the 1993 figures to account for population change. The formula used to calculate the graduation rate was:

    graduation rate = regular diplomas from 1998/adjusted 8th grade enrollment from 1993, adjusted 8th grade enrollment = actual 8th grade enrollment = (actual 8th grade enrollment x percentage change in total or ethnic sub-group enrollment in the jurisdiction between 1993-4 and 1997-8).

    According to the study, of the eighth graders who entered high school in 1994-95 school year only 56% of African-Americans graduated compared to 71% of all students and 76% of Caucasian students graduated four years later. No state in the nation had an African-American graduation rate that exceeded the state average. The lowest graduation rates for African-Americans were reported to be Wisconsin (40%), the same state which had the Milwaukee school voucher program. Wisconsin also had the third highest overall graduation rate (85%, for whites 92%). Thus, the disparity between the graduation rates for blacks and whites in Wisconsin was the largest in any state. The next lowest graduation rate for blacks was Minnesota at 43% (compared to 82% overall, for whites 87%); Tennessee and Georgia both at 44% (compared to overall of 60% and 54% respectively and for whites of 64% and 61% respectively). In Ohio, the location of the Cleveland voucher program, the gap between high school graduation was also large. The graduation rate for African-Americans was only 49% compared to a state wide average of 77% and an average for whites of 82%.

    The study also reported graduation rates for selected cities. Milwaukee's was reported as 34% for blacks compared to 43% overall and 73% for whites. Cleveland's was 28% overall compared with 29% for blacks and 23% for whites. The graduation rates for blacks in several cities was below 50% including Chicago School District 299 (45%); Clark County (49%); Cobb County (47%); Columbus City (45%); DeKalb County, Georgia (46%); Memphis City (39%); New York City (42%); Indianapolis, Indiana (44%); Newark, New Jersey (48%); Oakland (39%). *Id.* at Table 6.

26. ORFIELD, LOSEN, WALD AND SWANSON, *supra* note 24, at 7.

27. The Cumulative Promotion Index bases graduation rates on the actual enrollment data that each district provides annually to the nation's Common Core of Data. The index examines changes in enrollment and the likelihood of graduating with a high school diploma by combining the average success of groups of students moving from ninth grade to tenth grade, from tenth grade to eleventh grade, from junior year to senior year and from senior year to graduation. For a full discussion *see Id.* at 9-10.

28. *Id.* at 2.
29. *Id.* at Appendix 4, 83–92.
30. *See* Daniel J. Losen & Kevin G. Welner, *Disabling Discrimination in Our Public Schools: Comprehensive Legal Challenges to Inappropriate and Inadequate Special Education Services for Minority Children,* 36 Harv. CR.-C.L. L. Rev. 407, 421 (2001).
31. *See* Nat'l Ctr. for Educ. Statistics, Status and Trends in the Education of Blacks 38 (2003).
32. *See* Jeannie Oakes, Keeping Track (1985). *See also* Kevin Welner, Legal Rights, Local Wrongs: When Community Control Collides With Educational Equity (2001) (the author studied tracking in four school districts (San Jose, California; Wilmington, Delaware; Woodland Hills, Pennsylvania; and Rockford, Illinois) and found a clear pattern of discrimination. All four districts were operating under court-ordered desegregation plans).
33. *See* Nat'l Ctr. for Educ. Statistics, *supra* note 31, at 57.
34. *See id.*
35. *See id.* at 59.
36. *See* David Osher, et. al., *Exploring the Relationships Between Inappropriate and Ineffective Special Education Services for African American Children and Youth and their Overrepresentation in the Juvenile Justice System* 1, in Minority Issues in Special Education. *See, e.g.,* Linda Darling-Hammond, *Inequality and Access to Knowledge,* in Handbook of Research on Multicultural Education 465, 474 (James A. Banks & Cherry A. McGee Banks eds., 1995); Dan French & Sheldon Rothman, Massachusetts Board of Education, Structuring School for Student Success: A Focus on Ability Grouping 7 (1990) (stating that minority students are overrepresented in the lowest ability tracks).
37. *See* Losen & Welner, *supra* note 30, at 412.
38. *See* Nat'l Ctr. for Educ. Statistics, *supra* note 31, at 143.
39. *See* Sabrina Hope King, *The Limited Presence of African-American Teachers,* 63 Rev. Educ. Res. 115, 124 (1993).
40. David P. Gardner, et. al., A Nation at Risk: The Imperative for Educational Reform 7 (1983), *available at* http://www.mat.uc.pt/~emsa/PMEnsino/ANationatRisk .pdf.
41. *See, e.g.,* Carnegie Forum on Education and the Economy, *A Nation Prepared: Teachers for the 21st Century* (1986).
42. The report looked at a three-year window from 1994 to 1997 of those who took the Praxis test. There were almost 600,000 tests takers during that period. The report created two parallel data sets: one for candidates who took the SAT and one for candidates who took the ACT. They searched both SAT and ACT data sets from 1977 to 1995 and matched the most recent SAT/ACT scores with the Praxis scores and background information that came from the Praxis questionnaire and the SAT and ACT background questionnaire. Individuals who took both Praxis I and Praxis II during the 1994 to 1997 period were counted in both data sets. The report thus dealt with at least 300,000 people who were in the teaching pipeline between 1994-1997. The authors of the report concluded that there was "no compelling reason to believe that the

sample's overall profile was skewed substantially with respect to that of the overall prospective teaching population." *See* Educational Testing Service, *The Academic Quality of Prospective Teachers: The Impact of Admissions and Licensure Testing* 13 (1999), *available at* http://ftp.ets.org/pub/res/researcher/RR-03-35.pdf

43. There have been a number of legal challenges to teacher testing requirements. *See* Groves v. Alabama State Bd. of Educ., 776 F. Supp. 1518 (M.D. Ala. 1991); Massachusetts Fed'n of Teachers v. Bd. of Educ., 436 Mass. 763 (Mass. 2002); Richardson v. Lamar County Bd. of Educ., 729 F. Supp. 806 (M.D. Ala. 1989); State v. Project Principle, Inc., 724 S.W.2d 387 (Tex. 1987).
44. *See* Educational Testing Service, *supra* note 42, at 18, Table 4, and 21, Table 7.
45. *Id.*
46. *Id.* at 18, Table 4. The table actually breaks test takers down into those who took the SAT and those who took the ACT. There was a total of 33,770 people who took the SAT and Praxis I, of which 3,603 were black and 27,506 were white, and 54,797 people who took the ACT and Praxis I, of which 2,829 were black and 49,548 were white. There was a total of 26,115 who took the SAT and Praxis I who passed, of which 1,650 were black and 22,537 were white. There was a total of 48,036 who took the ACT and Praxis I who passed, of which 1,790 were black and 44,293 were white. The total number of those who passed the test was 74,151 (26,115 + 48,036) out of a total of 88,567 (33,770 + 54,797) for a pass rate of 83.7 percent. The total number of blacks who passed Praxis I exam was 3440 (1650 + 1790) out of a total of 6432 (3603 + 2829) for a pass rate of only 53.5 percent. The total number of whites who passed Praxis I was 66,830 (22,537 + 44,293) out of a total of 77,054 (27,506 + 49,548) who took the exam for a pass rate of 86.7 percent.
47. *Id.* The table actually breaks test takers down into those who took the SAT and those that took the ACT. There was a total of 33,770 people who took the SAT and Praxis I, of which 3,603 were black, and 54,797 who took the ACT and Praxis I, of which 2,829 were black. Of the test takers, there was a total of 26,115 of those who took the SAT and Praxis I who passed, of which 1,650 were black, and 48,036 who took ACT and Praxis I who passed, of which 1,790 were black. Thus, the total number of blacks who took the test were 6,432 (3,603 + 2,829) out of a total of 88,567 (33,770 + 54,797) or 7.3 percent. There was a total of 3,440 (1,650 + 1,790) blacks who passed Praxis I out of 74,151 (26,115 + 48,036) or 4.6 percent.
48. *Id.* at 21, Table 7. The table actually breaks test takers down into those who took the SAT and those that took the ACT. There was a total of 159,270 people who took the SAT and Praxis II, of which 11,510 were black and 135,035 were white, and 111,591 who took the ACT and Praxis II, of which 11,111 were black and 94,846 were white. Of the test takers, there was a total of 139,245 who took the SAT and Praxis II who passed, of which 7,984 were black and 122,534 were white. There was a total of 99,804 who took ACT and Praxis II who passed, of which 6,757 were black and 88,583 were white. The total number of those who passed the test was 239,049 (139,245 +99,804) out of a total of 270,861 (159,270 + 111,591) for a pass rate for all Praxis II test takers of 88.3 percent. The total number of blacks who passed the Praxis II exam was 14,741 (7,984 + 6,757) out of a total of 22,621 (11,510 + 11,111) for a pass rate of only 65.2 percent. The total number of whites who passed Praxis II was 211,117 (122,534 + 88,583) out of a total of 229,881 (135,035 + 94,846) who took the exam for a pass rate of 91.8 percent.

49. Bureau of the Census, *supra* note 22 (Table 249: Public Elementary and Secondary School Teachers Selected Characteristics: 1999-2000).

50. *See* Beth Aronstamm Young, *Public School Student, Staff, and Graduate Counts by State, School Year 2001-02, Table 5: Percentage of public school membership by race/ethnicity and state: school year 2001-02, available at* http://nces.ed.gov/pubs2003/2003358 .pdf.

51. *Id.*

52. U.S. Bureau of the Census, *supra* note 23 (Table 249: Public Elementary and Secondary School Teachers Selected Characteristics: 1999-2000).

53. P.L. 107-110, 115 Stat. 1425, 107th Cong., January 8, 2002. NCLB is a reauthorization of the Elementary and Secondary Education Act of 1965 (ESEA), which provided federal oversight and funding to state education initiatives to improve the educational performance of low-income children. NCLB's provisions are limited to states receiving ESEA funds.

54. Private School Racial Enrollment & Segregation, Sean Readon and John T. Yin 3 (foreword by Gary Orfield stating, "there is no systematic research showing that charter schools perform better than public schools.") (June 2002). *See, e.g.,* Jeffrey R. Henig, *School Choice Outcomes* in School Choice and Social Controversy: Politics, Policy, and Law 89-101 (Stephen D. Subarman & Frank R. Kemerer eds. 1999) (noting the difficulties with ability of empirical data to answer the question about educational achievement resulting from increased choice). Dan D. Goldhaber & Eric R. Eide, *What Do We Know (and Need to Know) About the Impact of School Choice Reforms on Disadvantaged Students?,* 72 Harvard Educational Review 157, 158 (2002) (although the empirical evidence on the academic effects of school choice reforms is mixed, those studies that do find positive effects of choice tend also to find that minorities living in urban areas disproportionately benefit from enhanced schooling options). *See also* Peter Cookson, School Choice: The Sturggle for the Soul of American Education 98 (1994) (in terms of student achievement, choice makes little difference).

55. Erica Frankenberg & Chungmei Lee, Charter Schools and Race: A Lost Opportunity for Integrated Education 12 (June 2002).

56. Robin Barnes, *Black America and School Choice: Charting a New Course,* 106 Yale L.J. 2375, 2404 (1997).

57. For a brief basic primer about charter schools *see* Wendy Parker, *The Color of Choice: Race and Charter Schools,* 75 Tul. L. Rev. 563, 574-77 (2001).

58. U.S. Charter Schools, *available at* http://www.uscharterschools.org/pub/uscs_docs/o/index.htm# national, (*citing* Center for Education Reform, The National Charter School Directory 2003).

59. A charter school movement pioneer has offered "nine essentials" that make up the core underlying what a charter school is:

(1) The school may be organized, owned, and run by any of several parties; (2) the organizers may approach more than one public body for their charter; (3) the school is a legal entity; (4) the school is public and may not charge tuition, discriminate or engage in selective admissions, must follow health and safety laws, and is not affiliated with a religious group; (5) the school is accountable for the students' academic per-

formance and the school loses its charter if it fails to achieve its goals; (6) the school gets real freedom to change instructional and management practices; (7) the school is a school of choice: no student is required to attend; (8) the state transfers a fair share of school funding from each student's home district to the charter school; and (9) the schools' teachers are protected and given the opportunity to participate in the design of schools.

Gerard Toussaint Robinson, *Can the Spirit of Brown Survive in the Era of School Choice? A Legal and Policy Perspective,* 45 How. L.J. 281, 295-296 (2002) (*citing* Brian Hassel, Charter Schools: The Promise and the Pitfalls, Fulfilling the Promise 5 (1999) (*paraphrasing* Ted Kolderie)).

60. William C. Symonds, *Edison: How Big a Blow for School Choice?,* Bus. Wk., June 3, 2002, at 44 (detailing how Nobel currently operates 174 schools serving 25,000 students).

61. The Ctr. For Educ. Reform, Charter Schools 2002: Results from CER's Annual Survey of Americas Charter Schools, *available at* http://207.201.191.212/charter_schools/ survey2002.pdf.

62. U.S. Bureau of the Census, *supra* note 23, at 159 (*Table 239: Public Charter and Traditional Schools-Selected Characteristics: 1999-2000).*

63. Frankenberg & Lee, *supra* note 55 at 11.

64. Contemporary discussions of the issue of school vouchers normally start their historical analysis of this issue with Milton Friedman's 1955 essay. Milton Friedman, *The Role of Government in Education, in* Economics and the Public Interest (Robert A. Solo ed., 1955). Long range historians note that Adam Smith seems to have been the first social theorist to propose that the government finance education by giving money to parents to hire teachers. *See, e.g.,* The Center for the Study of Public Policy, Education Vouchers: A Report on Financing Elementary Education by Grants to Parents vii (1970).

For the African-American community, school vouchers have a history that predates and overshadows the economic professor and Nobel Laureate's proposal. After the Supreme Court rendered its opinion in Brown v. Board of Education, resistance to school desegregation, particularly in the Deep South was massive. For a recent discussion of the use of public funding of private education to avoid desegregation *see* Kevin Brown, *Reexamination of the Benefit of Publicly Funded Private Education for African-American Students in a Post-desegregation Era,* 36 Ind. L. Rev. 477 (490–97 2003).

65. Milton Friedman, *The Role of Government in Education, in* Economics and the Public Interest (Robert A. Solo ed., 1955).

66. 536 U.S. 639 (2002). For an indepth discussion of this litigation *see* Clint Bollick, voucher Wars: Waging the Legal Battle Over School Choice (2003).

67. Dan D. Goldhaber & Eric R. Eide, *What Do We Know (and Need to Know) about the Impact of School Choice Reforms on Disadvantaged Students?,* 72 Harv. Educ. Rev. 157, 158 (2002). Vermont adopted a school choice program in 1869 limited to communities that did not build their own public schools. Maine adopted a similar program in 1873. The Vermont program serves approximately 6,500 students today and Maine's about 5,600. Bolick, *supra* note 66, at 2 (2003).

68. *See* Reed v. Rhodes, 1 F. Supp. 2d 705 (N.D. Ohio 1995).

69. *See* Zelman, 536 U.S. at 644 (quoting Cleveland City School District Performance Audit 2-1 (Mar. 1996)).

70. Although the parties disputed the precise amount of state funding available to suburban school districts adjacent to the Cleveland City School District, there was no dispute that any suburban district agreeing to participate in the program would receive a $2,250 tuition grant *plus* the ordinary allotment of per-pupil state funding for each program student enrolled in a suburban public school which was at least $4,750 and could have been as high as $6,544. Zelman, 536 U.S. at 646 n.1 (2002).

71. James E. Ryan & Michael Heise, *supra* note 2 at 2047.

72. United States General Accounting Office, School Vouchers: Publicly Funded Programs in Cleveland and Milwaukee, GAO-01- 914, at 14 (Aug. 2001) (Table 1: Characteristics of Cleveland Families with Students in the Voucher Program or Public Schools and Table 4: Racial and Ethnic Composition of Cleveland Public School Voucher School Students, School Year 1998-99).

73. Milwaukee Parental Choice Program Frequently Asked Questions for 2001-2002, *available at* http://www.dpi.state.wi.us/dpi/dfm/sms/doc/mpc01fnf.doc.

74. *Id.*

75. *See* Myra DeGrow, *Educational Vouchers and Tax Credits: A State-by-State Summary of Current Programs* (December 18, 2002), *available at* http://i2i.org/Publications/IB/Education/ 2002f.htm.

76. Caroline Hendrie, *The Florida Experiment,* Educ. Wk., January 4, 2004, *available at* http://www.edweek.org.

77. Alan Richard, *Florida Sees Surge in Use of Vouchers,* Educ. Wk., September 4, 2002, *available at* http://www.edweek.org.

78. President George W. Bush, Speech in Cleveland, Ohio (July 1, 2002), *available at* http://www.whitehouse.gov/news/releases/2002/07/20020701-7.html.

79. Mary Leonard, *Proponents of Vouchers See Opening: Planning Suits in Six States, Including Massachusetts,* Boston Globe, Nov. 18, 2002, at A1.

80. Associated Press, *Growth of Vouchers Slow Year After Court Decision,* June 28, 2003, *available at* http://www.cnn.com/2003/EDUCATION/06/28/school.vouchers.ap/index.html.

81. *See* John Gehring, *Gov. Owens Signs Colorado Voucher Bill,* Educ. Wk., April 23, 2003, *available at* http://www.edweek.org.

82. The Washington D.C. voucher program will be available to 1,700 children and will award them vouchers of up to $7,500 to attend private schools. Spencer S. Hsu & Justin Blum, *D.C. School Vouchers Win Final Approval,* Wash. Post, Jan. 23, 2004, at A01.

83. Hendrie, *supra* note 76.

84. *Id.*

85. *Id.*

86. *See, e.g.,* Charles Fried, *Five to Four: Reflections on the School Voucher Case,* 116 Harv. L. Rev. 1 (2002); Kathleen M. Sullivan, *The New Religion and the Constitution,* 116 Harv. L. Rev. 1397, 1398-89 (2003); John Gehring, *Voucher Battles Head to State Capitals,* Educ. Wk., July 10, 2002, *available at* http://www.edweek.org.

87. *See* Jackson v. Benson, 578 N.W.2d 602 (Wis. 1998); and Simmons-Harris v. Goff, 711 N.E.2d 203 (Ohio 1999).

88. Holmes v. Bush, 767 So.2d 668 (Fla. Dist. Ct. App. 2000), review denied, 790 So.2d 1104 (Fla. 2001). On remand the plaintiff was granted summary judgement which was upheld on appeal. *See* Holmes, 2002 WL 1809079 (Fla. Cir. Ct. 2002).

89. Richard, *supra* note 77.

90. Nancy Mitchell, *Court Hears Vouchers Case,* ROCKY MOUNTAIN NEWS, May 26, 2004, http://www.rockymountainnews.com/drmn/education/article/0,1299, DRMN_957_2914560,00.html.

91. *See* Caroline Hendrie, *High Court Upholds State's Bar on Aid to Theology Majors,* EDUC. WK., March 3, 2004, *available at* http://www.edweek.org.

92. For a more complete discussion of the history of state Blaine amendments, *see* Steven K. Green, *The Blaine Amendment Reconsidered,* 36 AM. J. LEGAL HIST. 38 (1992).

93. A recent Supreme Court opinion failed to resolve the constitutionality of these Blaine Amendments, but may provide some indications of how the Supreme Court would treat a constitutional attack on these provisions. In Locke v. Davey 124 S.Ct. 1307 (2004) the Court addressed a free exercise challenge to the Promise Scholarship Program established by the State of Washington to assist academically gifted students with postsecondary education expenses. The Washington Constitution stated that "[n]o public money or property shall be appropriated for or applied to any religious worship, exercise or instruction, or the support of any religious establishment." *Id.* at 1312 n2. This was not the Blaine Amendment provision contained in the Washington Constitution. Washington's Blaine Amendment provision was included in Article IX, § 4, of the Washington Constitution ("All schools maintained and supported wholly or in part by the public funds shall be forever free from sectarian control or influence"), and was not at issue in this case.

The statute authorizing the Promise Scholarship Program codified the State's constitutional prohibition on providing funds to students to pursue degrees that are "devotional in nature or designed to induce religious faith." Religiously affiliated private institutions qualify as eligible postsecondary institutions as long as they are recognized by a nationally recognized accrediting body. It is only the pursuit of devotional studies that is proscribed.

The Respondent in the case, Joshua Davey, was awarded a Promise Scholarship. He chose to attend Northwest College which is a private, Christian college affiliated with the Assemblies of God denomination. Northwest is an eligible postsecondary institution under the Promise Scholarship Program. But Davey planned to pursue a double major in pastoral ministries and business management/administration. The pastoral ministries degree was clearly devotional and, thus, Promise Scholarship funds could not be used in pursuit of that degree. Davey challenged the refusal to award him the Promise Scholarship arguing several constitutional violations including free exercise of religion and establishment clause. While the District Court denied Davey's request for a preliminary injunction, a divided panel of the United States Court of Appeals for the Ninth Circuit reversed on free exercise grounds.

Chief Justice Rehnquist, writing for the seven person majority of the Court, upheld the argument by the State of Washington that it was entitled to prohibit students from using these scholarships to pursue theology degrees under its own constitution's ban on the financing of religious instruction. Rehnquist noted that the Court had long taken the position that there is some play between the Establishment Clause and the Free Exercise Clause. "In other words, there are some state actions permitted by the Establishment Clause but not required by the Free Exercise Clause." *Id.* at 1311. Rehnquist went on to write that "Training someone to lead a congregation is an essentially religious endeavor. Indeed, majoring in devotional theology is akin to a religious calling as well as an academic pursuit.... That a state would deal differently with religious education for the ministry than with education for other callings is...not evidence of hostility toward religion." *Id.* at 1313.

Michael D. Simpson, a lawyer with the National Education Association, which is fighting voucher programs in Florida and Colorado, stated that "[w]hat was encouraging about Chief Justice Rehnquist's opinion was that it said it was all right to fund a secular education and to refuse to fund a religious education." Though the Court in Locke was not addressing the Washington Constitution's Blaine Amendment, opponents of vouchers cite to Locke for the proposition that Blaine Amendments must be respected. Thus, if state constitutions prohibit the use of state funds at private religious institutions, such prohibitions do not violate the religion clauses of the First Amendment. This would mean that voucher programs would be subject to state constitutional challenges and would have to be resolved on a state by state basis. In contrast to Simpson's opinion, Mr. Neily of the Institute for Justice said that anyone who claimed that the Supreme Court had resolved the question of whether voucher programs must include religious schools if they offer aid for secular ones is woefully mistaken. Niely points to the fact that Rehnquist's opinion stressed the limitations of the majority ruling only to the state's interest in not funding the religious training of clergy. *See* Hendrie, *supra* note 91.

If the narrower reading of Locke v. Davey favored by proponents of vouchers holds, then there is still a possibility that excluding religious schools from voucher programs could violate one of the religion clauses of the First Amendment. Thus, the Supreme Court in one decision could eliminate Blaine Amendment obstacles to school vouchers used at religious schools. But if the broader reading favored by opponents holds, then whether religious schools could be included in voucher programs will be decided on a state by state basis. Either way this is an issue that the Supreme Court will likely have to decide.

94. Tinker v. Des Moines Indep. Cmty. Sch. Dist., 393 U.S. 503, 506 (1969).

95. *See* Goss v. Lopez, 419 U.S. 565 (1975).

96. *See* Board of Educ. Pottawatomie County v. Earle, 536 U.S. 822 (2002); Vernonia Sch. Dist. 47J v. Acton, 515 U.S. 646, 656 (1995); New Jersey v. T.L.O., 469 U.S. 325, 341 (1985).

97. *See* Hazelwood Sch. Dist. v. Kuhlmeier, 484 U.S. 260, 272-73 (1988); Bethel Sch. Dist. No. 403 v. Fraser, 478 U.S. 675, 681 (1986); Tinker v. Des Moines Indep. Cmty. Sch. Dist., 393 U.S. 503, 511 (1969).

98. *See* Rendell-Barker v. Kohn, 457 U.S. 830 (1982) (holding that a private school whose income is derived primarily from public sources and which is regulated by public authorities could not be considered as engaging in state action).

99. *See, e.g.,* Edwards v. Aguillard, 482 U.S. 578, 581, 583, 585, 612 (1987) (striking down a statute requiring teachers to teach creation science whenever they taught the theory of evolution); Wallace v. Jaffree, 472 U.S. 38, 55-56 (1985) (striking down an Alabama

statute authorizing a one minute period of silence for meditation or prayer); Stone v. Graham, 449 U.S. 39, 40-41 (1980) (per curiam) (striking down a statute providing for posting of the Ten Commandments, paid for by private funds, on the walls of each public classroom in Kentucky).

100. Walter Leavy, *Is the Black Male an Endangered Species?*, EBONY, Aug. 1983, at 41. There have been debates and discussions about the survivability and viability of the African-American male. *See, e.g.*, BLACK MEN (Lawrence E. Gary ed., 1981); YOUNG, BLACK, AND MALE IN AMERICA: AN ENDANGERED SPECIES (Jewelle Gibbs et al. eds., 1988).

101. *See* Kevin Brown, *Do African-Americans Need Immersion Schools?: The Paradoxes Created by Legal Conceptualization of Race and Public Education*, 78 IOWA L. REV. 813, 850 (1993) (citing letter from David S. Tatel et al., to Robert S. Peterkin, Superintendent of Schools, Milwaukee Public Schools).

102. Rogers Worthington, Milwaukee Idea Shapes a New School, Chi. Trib., Dec. 1, 1991, at C25.

103. *See* Brown, *supra* note 101, at 850 (citing letter from Jesse L. High, Regional Civil Rights Director, Office of Civil Rights, U.S. Department of Education, to Dr. Joseph A. Fernandez, Superintendent of Schools, Dade County Public Schools (Aug. 31, 1988)).

104. Memorandum of Law in Opposition to Plaintiffs' Motion for Temporary Restraining Order and Preliminary Injunction at 15, Garrett v. Board of Educ., 775 F. Supp. 1004 (E.D. Mich. 1991).

105. 775 F. Supp. 1004 (E.D. Mich. 1991).

106. Worthington, *supra* note 102, at C25.

107. Memorandum of Law, *supra* note 104, at 14.

108. Garrett, 775 F. Supp. at 1007 n.5.

109. Garrett, 775 F. Supp. at 1007.

110. *See,* Runyon v. McCrary, 427 U.S. 160 (1976) (holding that 42 U.S.C. § 1981 proscribes private schools from racial discrimination with regard to student admissions).

111. 458 U.S. 718 (1982).

112. 518 U.S. 515 (1996). The Court also addressed this issue in Vorchheimer v. School Dist., 430 U.S. 703 (1977) (per curiam). The city of Philadelphia operated a number of coeducational academically high-tracked high schools. Vorchheimer v. School Dist., 532 F.2d 880, 881 (3d Cir. 1976). But, Philadelphia segregated the boys from the girls in its best academic high schools. *Id.* An evenly divided Court upheld this separate but equal gender segregated educational practice. 430 U.S. at 703.

113. Rosemary Salomone, *Rich Kids, Poor Kids and the Single Sex Education Debate* 34 AKRON L. REV. 209, 222 (2000).

114. *See* ROBERT K. LANDERS, CONFLICT OVER MULTICULTURAL EDUCATION, in EDITORIAL RESEARCH REPORTS 682, 691 (Cong. Q. Inc. 1990). *See generally* MOLEFI K. ASANTE, THE AFROCENTRIC IDEA (1987); MOLEFI K. ASANTE, AFROCENTRICITY: THE THEORY OF SOCIAL CHANGE (1980); C. TSEHLOANE KETO, THE AFRICA CENTERED PERSPECTIVE OF HISTORY AND SOCIAL SCIENCES IN THE TWENTY-FIRST CENTURY (1989).

115. Sonia R. Jarvis, *Brown and the Afrocentric Curriculum*, 101 YALE L.J. 1285, 1294 (1992).

116. KETO, *supra* note 114, at 31.

117. Portland, Oregon, for example, began using African-American baseline essays which were first developed in 1982 as part of a multicultural program. Portland has developed similar materials on the history, culture and contributions of five other geo-cultural groups: Asian-Americans, European- Americans, Hispanic-Americans, Indian-Americans and Pacific Island-Americans. The Portland essays have been the inspiration for Afrocentric curriculum in Milwaukee, Indianapolis, Pittsburgh, Washington D.C., Richmond, Atlanta, Philadelphia, Detroit, Baltimore and other cities. *See* Steven Siegel, *Ethnocentric Public School Curriculum in a Multicultural Nation: Proposed Standards for Judicial Review* 40 N.Y.L. SCH. L. REV. 311, 319 (1996).

118. A number of scholars have argued that Egypt was a black African nation whose culture influenced the development of the philosophy, science, math, religion, and culture of the ancient Greeks. *See generally* 1 MARTIN BERNAL, BLACK ATHENA: THE AFROASIATIC ROOTS OF CLASSICAL CIVILIZATION (1987); 2 MARTIN BERNAL, BLACK ATHENA: THE AFROASIATIC ROOTS OF CLASSICAL CIVILIZATION (1991); CHEIKH A. DIOP, THE AFRICAN ORIGIN OF CIVILIZATION: MYTH OR REALITY (Mercer Cook ed. & trans., 1974); GEORGE M. JAMES, STOLEN LEGACY (1954); YOSEF A. BEN-JOCHANNAN, AFRICA: MOTHER OF "WESTERN CIVILIZATION," (1971); WILLIAM N. HUGGINS, AN INTRODUCTION TO AFRICAN CIVILIZATIONS (1969).

119. For example, Harvest Preparatory School is a charter school in Minneapolis. It uses an Afrocentric curriculum with an emphasis on basic skills. *See* Rob Hotakainen, *Minnesota's Charter School Concept Wins a Crucial Vote,* STAR TRIBUNE (Minneapolis), July 8, 1998.

120. *But see* Brown, *supra* note 101 (arguing that public African-American Immersion schools should survive an equal protection challenge).

121. Parker, *supra* note 57, at 615.

122. *See* Siegel, *supra* note 117, at 319-321 noting that some Afrocentric scholars and educators have propounded the theory that blacks are a genetically superior race because the high concentration of melanin in the skin makes possible superior mental cognitive abilities. The author concludes by arguing that there is a legitimate and limited role for the judiciary in addressing claims in ethnocentric curriculum. These would include the constitutional power to strike down the establishment of schoolwide ethnocentric curriculum that promotes segregation.

123. Kenneth Karst, *Law, Cultural Conflict, and the Socialization of Children* 91 CAL. L. REV. 967, 999 (2003).

124. P.L. 107-110, Preamble (January 8, 2002).

125. Diana Jean Schemo, *New Federal Rule Tightens Demands on Failing Schools,* N.Y. TIMES, November 27, 2002, at A1.

126. *Id.*

127. Michael Winerip, *On Education: A Pervasive Dismay on Bush School Law,* N.Y. TIMES, March 19, 2003, at B7.

128. AMREIN & BERLINER, *supra* note 16, in abstract.

129. Diana Jean Schemo, *Few Exercise Right to leave Failing Schools,* N.Y. TIMES, August 28, 2002, at A1.

130. Winerip, *supra* note 127, at B8.

131. Schemo, *supra* note 129.

132. *Id.*

133. Editorial, *Bait-and-Switch on Public Education,* N.Y. TIMES, October 21, 2003, at A26.

Chapter Ten

1. *See* PETER COOKSON, SCHOOL CHOICE: THE STRUGGLE FOR THE SOUL OF AMERICAN EDUCATION 9 (1994).

2. PRIVATE SCHOOL RACIAL ENROLLMENT & SEGREGATION, SEAN REARDON AND JOHN T. YIN 3 (foreword by Gary Orfield stating "there is no systematic research showing that charter schools perform better than public schools.") (June 2002). *See, e.g.,* Jeffrey R. Henig, *School Choice Outcomes* in SCHOOL CHOICE AND SOCIAL CONTROVERSY: POLITICS, POLICY, AND LAW 89–101 (Stephen D. Sugarman & Frank R. Kemerer eds., 1999) (noting the difficulties with ability of empirical data to answer the question about educational achievement resulting from increased choice). Dan D. Goldhaber & Eric R. Eide, *What Do We Know (and Need to Know) About the Impact of School Choice Reforms on Disadvantaged Students?,* 72 HARVARD EDUCATIONAL REVIEW 157, 158 (2002) (although the empirical evidence on the academic effects of school choice reforms is mixed, those studies that do find positive effects of choice tend also to find that minorities living in urban areas disproportionately benefit from enhanced schooling options). *See also* Cookson, *supra* note 1 at 98 (in terms of student achievement, choice makes little difference).

3. ROBERT L. CRAIN, MAKING DESEGREGATION WORK 70 (1982); Mahard and Crain, *Research on Minority Achievements in Desegregated Schools,* in THE CONSEQUENCES OF SCHOOL DESEGREGATION 103–25 (C. Russell & W. Hawley eds. 1983); *See* Green, *Thinking Realistically About Integration,* 16 NEW PERSPECTIVES 35 (Fall 1984); Mahard, Narot & Stephan, *School Desegregation: An Evaluation of Predictions Made in Brown v. Board of Education,* 85 PSYCHOL. BULL. 217 (1978); School Desegregation: Lessons of the First Twenty-Five Years, LAW & CONTEMP. PROBS. 1, 1–133 (Summer 1978).

4. Grutter v. Bollinger, 539 U.S. 306, at 364 (Thomas J., dissenting) (citing to Flowers & Pascarella, *Cognitive Effects of College Racial Composition on African American Students After 3 Years of College,* 40 J. OF COLLEGE STUDENT DEVELOPMENT 669, 674 (1999) (concluding that black students experience superior cognitive development at Historically Black Colleges (HBCs) and that, even among blacks, "a substantial diversity moderates the cognitive effects of attending an HBC")).

5. *Id.* (citing Allen, *The Color of Success: African-American College Student Outcomes at Predominantly White and Historically Black Public Colleges and Universities,* 62 HARV. EDUC. REV. 26, 35 (1992) (finding that black students attending HBCs report higher academic achievement than those attending predominantly white colleges)).

6. 59 Mass. (5 Cush.) 198, 209–10 (1850).

7. Plessy v. Ferguson, 163 U.S. 537, 551–52 (1896).
8. 536 U.S. 639 (2002).
9. *See* General Accounting Office Report which noted that the cost for educating the remaining 76,000 students in Cleveland's 121 public schools was $712 million or about $9,368 per student. United States General Accounting Office, School Vouchers: Publicly Funded Programs in Cleveland and Milwaukee, GAO-01- 914, at 25 (Aug. 2001) (Table 1: Characteristics of Cleveland Families with Students in the Voucher Program or Public Schools and Table 4: Racial and Ethnic Composition of Cleveland Public School Voucher School Students, School Year 1998–99).
10. Milwaukee Parental Choice Program Frequently Asked Questions for 2001–02, *available at* http://www.dpi.state.wi.us/dpi/dfm/sms/doc/mpc01fnf.doc.
11. Erica Frankenberg, et al., A Multiracial Society With Segregated Schools: Are We Losing The Dream? 31 (2003).
12. Sean Reardon and John T. Yin, Private School Racial Enrollment & Segregation 3–7 (June 2002).
13. *See* Ellwood P. Cubberley, Public Education in the United States: A Study and Interpretation of American Educational History 304–5 (Houghton Mifflin 1947) (1919).
14. Arthur O. White, *The Black Leadership Class and Education in Antebellum Boston,* 42 J. Negro Educ. 504, 505 (1973).
15. Hosea Easton, A Treatise on the Intellectual Character and Civil and Political Conditions of the Colored People of the United States and the Prejudice Exercised Toward Them 40–43 (Boston, Knapp 1837); *see also* Stanley K. Schultz, The Culture Factory: Boston Public Schools, 1789–1860, at 160 (1973) (pointing to the fact that the lack of attendance at Boston schools by blacks was also a result of the deplorable economic condition of the black community in Boston).
16. Prince Hall et al., *Petition to the Honorable Senate and House of Representatives of the Commonwealth of Massachusetts Bay in General Court Assembled (Oct. 17, 1787),* in 1 A Documentary History of the Negro People in the United States 19 (Herbert Aptheker ed., 1969).
17. *See* James A. Banks, *Race, Ethnicity and Schooling in the United States: Past, Present and Future, in* Multicultural Education in Western Societies 46–47 (James A. Banks & James Lynch eds., 1986). The self-esteem theory was also advanced by psychologists both before and after the Court's opinion in Brown I. *See gen.* Mark of Oppression (Abram Kardiner & Lionel Ovesey eds., 1951).
18. Geneva Gay, *Achieving Educational Equality Through Curriculum Desegregation,* 72 Phi Delta Kappan 56, 59 (1990).
19. Larry Cuban, *Ethnic Content and "White" Instruction, in* Teaching Ethnic Studies: Concepts and Strategies 103, 104 (James A. Banks ed., 1973).
20. White students attending desegregated schools are seldom exposed to the histories and cultures of their minority classmates. *See* Carl A. Grant & Christine E. Sleeter, After the School Bell Rings 130–31 (1986).
21. 539 U.S. 306, 333 (2003).

22. 536 U.S. 639 (2002).
23. Zellman 536 U.S. at 681–82 (Thomas J. concurring) (quoting J. ANDERSON, EDUCATION OF BLACKS IN THE SOUTH, 1860–1935, 18 (1988)).
24. T. Moe, Schools, Vouchers, and the American Public 164 (2001).
25. *See id.,* at 214 (Table 7–3).
26. REBECCA GORDON ET AL., FACING THE CONSEQUENCES: AN EXAMINATION OF RACIAL DISCRIMINATION IN U.S. PUBLIC SCHOOLS 20 (2000). Teachers of color also provide important benefits for white children as well.
27. *See* J. Stewart et al., *In Quest of Role Models: Change in Black Teacher Representation in Urban School Districts 1968–86,* 58 J. NEGRO EDUC. 140 (1989).
28. *See generally* John U. Ogbu, *Immigrant and Involuntary Minorities in Comparative Perspectives, in* MINORITY STATUS AND SCHOOLING: A COMPARATIVE STUDY OF IMMIGRANT AND INVOLUNTARY MINORITIES 3–33 (Margaret A. Gibson & John Ogbu eds., 1991) (discussing the general distrust that involuntary minorities have about public education).
29. *See, e.g.,* Robert T. Tauber, *Good or Bad, What Teachers Expect from Students They Generally Get!,* ERIC DIGEST 97–7, *available at* http://www.ericsp.org/pages/digests/Good_or_bad.html; L. Jussim & J. Eccles, *Teacher Expectations II: Construction and Reflection of Student Achievement,* 63 J. PERSONALITY & SOC. PSYCHOL. 947 (1992); T.L. Good, *Two Decades of Research on Teacher Expectations: Findings and Future Directions,* 38 J. TEACHER EDUC. 32 (1987).
30. The equal protection clause's acceptance of society as a collection of Knowing Individuals provides an implicit model of public education. This implicit model recognizes the constraint of governmental neutrality. For a discussion of that implicit model of education *see* Kevin Brown, *Do African-Americans Need Immersion Schools?: The Paradoxes Created by Legal Conceptualization of Race and Public Education,* 78 IOWA L. REV. 813, 858–67 (1993).
31. 347 U.S. at 493.
32. *See, e.g.,* DAVID ARMOR, FORCED JUSTICE: SCHOOL DESEGREGATION AND THE LAW 221 (1995); *See generally* BEYOND DESEGREGATION: THE POLITICS OF QUALITY IN AFRICAN-AMERICAN SCHOOLING (Mwalimu J. Shugjaa ed. 1996) (providing examples of majority black schools that successfully educate students and critiquing the claims that blacks learn best in racially desegregated settings).
33. *School Desegregation: A Social Science Statement,* Brief of Amicus Curiae NAACP et al. in support of Resp't at 7a, Freeman v. Pitts, 503 U.S. 467 (1992), *on writ of cert.* to 11th Cir. (June 21, 1991).
34. *Id.* at 7a.
35. *See, e.g.,* Epps, *Minority Children: Desegregation, Self-Evaluation, and Achievement Orientation,* in EFFECTIVE SCHOOL DESEGREGATION 85, 95 (W. Hawley ed. 1981); St. John, *The Effects of School Desegregation on Children: A New Look at the Research Evidence,* in RACE AND SCHOOLING IN THE CITY 84, 90–92 (1981); Cook, *Social Science and School Desegregation: Did We Mislead the Supreme Court?,* 5 PERSONALITY & SOC. PSYCHOLOGY BULL. 420, 423–26 (1979); Stephan, *School Desegregation: An Evaluation of Predictions Made in Brown v. Board of Education,* 85 PSYCHOLOGICAL BULL. 217, 226–28 (1978).

36. ARMOR, *supra* note 32, at 100.

37. Martin Luther King, Jr. (Aug. 28, 1963), *I Have a Dream, in* A TESTAMENT OF HOPE: THE ESSENTIAL WRITINGS OF MARTIN LUTHER KING, JR. 217, 219 (James Melvin Washington ed., 1986).

38. Adarand v. Pena, 515 U.S. 200, 214 (1995) (quoting Hirabayashi v. United States, 320 U.S. 81, 100 (1943).

39. *See, e.g.*, Henig, *supra* note 2, at 80–83. *See* NAT'L CTR. FOR EDUC. STATISTICS, STATUS AND TRENDS IN THE EDUCATION OF BLACKS 159 (2003).

Bibliography

Books

Adair, Alvis v., Desegregation: The Illusion of Black Progress (1984).

Allport, Gordon W., The Nature of Prejudice (1954).

Anderson, S. E., The Black Holocaust for Beginners (1995).

Appiah, K. Anthony & Amy Gutmann, Color Conscious: The Political Morality of Race (1996).

Aptheker, Herbert, A Documentary History of the Negro People in the United States (ed. Herbert Aptheker 1951).

Aptheker, Herbert, American Negro Slave Revolts (1983).

Armor, David, Forced Justice: School Desegregation and the Law (1995).

Asante, Molefi K., Afrocentricity: The Theory of Social Change (1980).

Asante, Molefi K., The Afrocentric Idea (1987).

Banks, James A., Multiethnic Education: Theory and Practice (2d ed. 1988).

Bartley, Numan V., The Rise of Massive Resistance: Race and Politics in the South During the 1950s (1969).

Basler, Roy, The Collected Works of Abraham Lincoln (Roy P. Basler ed. 1953-55).

Bell, Derrick, Race, Racism and American Law (4th ed. 2000).

Bell, Derrick, Shades of Brown: New Perspectives on School Desegregation (1980).

Bell, Derrick, Silent Covenants: Brown v. Board of Education and the Unfulfilled Hopes for Racial Reform (2004).

Bellah, Robert N., et al., Habits of the Heart: Individualism and commitment in American Life (1985).

Ben-Jochannan, Yosef A., Africa: Mother of "Western Civilization" (1971).

Bereiter, Carl, & Seigfried Engelmann, Teaching Disadvantaged Children in the Preschool (1966).

Bernal, Martin, Black Athena: The Afroasiatic Roots of Classical Civilization (1987).

Bernal, Martin, Black Athena: The Afroasiatic Roots of Classical Civilization (1991).

Bernhard, Virginia, et al., Firsthand America: A History of the United States (2d ed. 1992).

Berry, Mary Frances, Black Resistance White Law: A History of Constitutional Racism in America (1994).

Bickett, Thomas W., Public Letters and Papers of Thomas Walter Bickett, Governor of North Carolina, 1917-1921 (R.B. House ed. 1923).

Black, Earl, Southern Governors and Civil Rights: Racial Segregation as a Campaign Issue in the Second Reconstruction (1976).

Blackstone, William, Commentaries on the Laws of England (Wayne Morrison ed., 2001).

Blackwell, James E., The Black community: Diversity and Unity (2d ed. 1985).

Blaustein, Albert P., Civil Rights and African-Americans: A Documentary History (eds. Albert P. Blaustein and Robert L. Zangrando 1968).

Boaz, David, Libertarianism: A Primer (1997).

Bollick, Clint, voucher Wars: Waging the Legal Battle Over School Choice (2003).

Bond, Horace M., Negro Education in Alabama (1939).

Bond, Horace M., The Education of The Negro in the American Social Order (1934).

Bowen, William, & Derrick Bok, The Shape of the River: Long-Term Consequences of Considering Race in College and University Admissions (1998).

Bouma, Donald H., & James Hoffman, The Dynamics of School Integration: Problems and Approaches in a Northern City (1968).

Camilli, Gregory, & Lorrie A. Shepard, Methods for Identifying Biased Test Items (1994).

Cashman, Sean Dennis, African-Americans and the Quest for Civil Rights (1991).

The Center for the Study of Public Policy, Education Vouchers: A Report on Financing Elementary Education by Grants to Parents (1970).

Clark, Kenneth. B., Effect of Prejudice and Discrimination on Personality Development (Mid Century White House Conference on Children and Youth, 1950).

Collins, Randall, The Credential Society: An Historical Sociology of Education Stratification (1979).

Cong. Globe, 37th Cong., 1st Sess. (1861).

Cookson, Peter, School choice: The Struggle for The Soul of American Education (1994).

Cose, Ellis, Color-Blind: Seeing Beyond Race in a Race-Obsessed World (1997).

Cottrol, Robert J., Brown v Board of Education: Caste, Culture, and the Constitution (Robert J. Cottrol, Leland Ware, and Raymond Diamond eds. 2003).

Cover, Robert M., Justice Accused: Antislavery and the Judicial Process (1975).

Cox, Oliver C., Race Relations: Elements and Social Dynamics (1976).

Crain, Robert L., Making Desegregation Work 70 (1982).

Cross, Theodore, The Black Power Imperative: Racial Inequality and the Politics of Nonviolence (1984).

Cruse, Harold, Plural but Equal: A Critical Study of Blacks and Minorities and America's Plural society (1987).

Cubberley, Ellwood P., Public Education in the United States: A Study and Interpretation of American Educational History (Houghton Mifflin 1947) (1919).

D'Souza, Dinesh, The End of Racism (1995).

Darwin, Charles, The Descent of Man, and Selection in Relation to Sex (1871).

Davis, Jefferson, The Rise and Fall of the Confederate Government (1990).

Diop, Cheikh A., The African Origin of Civilization: Myth or Reality (Mercer Cook ed. & trans., 1974).

Dorman, James H. & Robert R. Jones, The Afro-American Experience: A Cultural History Through Emancipation (1974).

Dreyfus, Hubert L. & Paul Rabinow, Michel Foucault: Beyond Structuralism and Hermeneutics (2d ed. 1983).

Drotning, Phillip T., Black Heroes in our Nation's History: A Tribute to Those Who Helped Shape America (1969).

Dubois, W. E. B., Black Reconstruction In America 1860-1880 (1935).

Dudziak, Mary L., Cold War Civil Rights: Race and the Image of American Democracy (2000).

Easton, Hosea, A Treatise on the Intellectual Character and Civil and Political Conditions of the Colored People of the United States and the Prejudice Exercised Toward Them (Boston, Knapp 1837).

Eiseley, Loren, Darwin's Century (1958).

Farrand, Max, The Records of the Federal Convention of 1787 (Max Farrand ed., rev. ed. 1966).

Feagin, Joe R., Racist America: Roots, Current Realities, and Future Reparations (2000).

Foner, Eric, Reconstruction: America's Unfinished Revolution 1863-1877 (1988).

Frankenberg, Erica, et al., A Multiracial Society with Segregated Schools: Are We Losing the Dream? (2003).

Frankenberg, Erica & Chungmei Lee, Charter Schools and Race: A Lost Opportunity for Integrated Education (June 2002).

Franklin, John Hope & Alfred A. Moss, Jr., From Slavery to Freedom: A History of Negro Americans (6th ed. 1988).

Frazier, Franklin E., The Negro in the United States (1949).

Fredrickson, George M., Black Liberation: A Comparative History of Black Ideologies in the United States and South Africa (1995).

French, Dan & Sheldon Rothman, Massachusetts Board of Education, Structuring School for Student Success: A Focus on Ability Grouping (1990).

Foner, Philip S., The Life and Writings of Frederick Douglass: Early Years, 1817-1849 (1950).

Geertz, Clifford, Local Knowledge: Further Essays in Interpretative Anthropology (1983).

Gordon, Milton M., Assimilation in American Life: The Role of Race, Religion, and National Origins (1964).

Gordon, Rebecca, et al., Facing the Consequences: An Examination of Racial Discrimination in U.S. Public Schools (2000).

Gossett, Thomas F., Race: The History of an Idea in America (1968).

Gould, Benjamin, Investigations in the Military and Anthropological Statistics of American Soldiers (1869).

Gould, Stephen J., Mismeasure of Man (1981).

Graglia, Lino O., Disaster by Decree: The Supreme Court Decisions on Race and the Schools (1976).

Grant, Carl A. & Christine E. Sleeter, After the School Bell Rings (1986).

Gray, Lawrence E., Black Men (Lawrence E. Gary ed., 1981).

Greene, Jay P., High School Graduation Rates in the United States (2002).

Grier, William H. & Price M. Cobbs, Black Rage (1968).

Grofman, Bernard, et al., Minority Representation and the Quest for Voting Equality (1992).

Haller, John S., Outcasts From Evolution: Scientific Attitudes Of Racial Inferiority, 1859-1900 (1971).

Harding, Vincent, There is a River (1981).

Harlan, Louis R., Booker T. Washington: The Wizard of Tuskegee 1901-1915 (1983).

Harlan, Louis R., Separate And Unequal (1958).

Harley, Sharon, Timetable of African-American History: A Chronology of the Most Important People and Events in African-American History (1995).

Harlow, Vincent T., A History of Barbados, 1625-1685 (1926).

Hassel, Brian, Charter Schools: The Promise and the Pitfalls, Fulfilling the Promise (1999).

Higginbotham, A. Leon, Jr., Shades of Freedom: Racial Politics and Presumptions of the American Legal Process (1996).

Hirst, Derek, Authority and Conflict: England, 1603-1658 (1986).

Hobbes, Thomas, Leviathan (C.B. Macpherson ed., Penguin Classics 1968).

Hornor, Louise L., Black Americans: A Statistical Sourcebook (Louise L. Hornor ed., 2000).

Huggins, William N., An Introduction to African Civilizations (1969).

James, George M., Stolen Legacy (1954).

Jefferson, Thomas, Notes on the State of Virginia (Frank Shuffelton ed., Penguin 1999) (1785).

Jencks, Christopher, Inequality: A Reassessment of the Effect of Family and Schooling in America (1972).

Johnson, Paul, A History of the American People (1997).

Jordan, Winthrop, White Over Black (1968).

Karenga, Maulana, Introduction to Black Studies (2d ed. 1993).

Kardiner, Abram, Mark of Oppression (Abram Kardiner & Lionel Ovesey eds., 1951).

Karst, Kenneth L., Belonging to America: Equal Citizenship and the Constitution (1989).

Keto, C. Tsehloane, The Africa Centered Perspective of History and Social Sciences in the Twenty-first Century (1989).

Kilpatrick, James J., The Southern Case for School Segregation (1962).

Klarman, Michael J., From Jim Crow to Civil Rights: The Supreme Court and the Struggle for Racial Equality (2004).

Kluger, Richard, Simple Justice: The History of Brown v. Board of Education and Black America's Struggle for Equality (1976)

Kull, Andrew, The Color-Blind Constitution (1992).

LaFeber, Walter, America, Russia, and the Cold War 1945-1996 (8th ed. 1997).

Landers, Robert K., Conflict Over Multicultural Education, in Editorial Research Reports (Cong. Q. Inc. 1990).

Lauren, Paul G., Power and Prejudice: The Politics and Diplomacy of Racial Discrimination (1988)

Levine, Daniel U. & Rayna F. Levine, Society and Education (9th ed. 1996).

Levine, Michael L., African-Americans and Civil Rights: From 1619 to the Present (1996).

Lincoln, C. Eric, Race, Religion, and the Continuing American Dilemma (1999).

Litwack, Leon F., North of Slavery: The Negro in the Free States (1961).

Lively, Donald E., The Constitution and Race (1992)

LOCKE, JOHN, THE REASONABLENESS OF CHRISTIANITY: AS DELIVERED IN THE SCRIPTURES (George W. Ewing ed., Gateway edition 1965).

LOCKE, JOHN, THE SECOND TREATISE OF GOVERNMENT (J.W. Gough ed., 3d ed. 1966) (1690).

LOSSING, BENSON J., MATTHEW BRADY'S ILLUSTRATED HISTORY OF THE CIVIL WAR (1996).

MAGESA, LAURENTI, AFRICAN RELIGION: THE MORAL TRADITIONS OF ABUNDANT LIFE (1997).

MANNIX, DANIEL P., IN COLLABORATION WITH MALCOLM COWLEY, BLACK CARGOES: A HISTORY OF THE ATLANTIC SLAVE TRADE 1518-1865 (1965) (1962).

MAQUET, JACQUES, AFRICANITY: THE CULTURAL UNITY OF BLACK AFRICA (1972).

MARABLE, MANNING, W.E.B. DU BOIS: BLACK RADICAL DEMOCRAT (1986).

MARGO, ROBERT A., RACE AND SCHOOLING IN THE SOUTH 1880-1950: AN ECONOMIC HISTORY (1990).

MARSHALL, BURKE, FEDERALISM AND CIVIL RIGHTS (1964).

MASSEY, DOUGLAS S. & NANCY A. DENTON, AMERICAN APARTHEID: SEGREGATION AND THE MAKING OF THE UNDERCLASS (1993).

MBITI, JOHN, AFRICAN RELIGIONS AND PHILOSOPHY (1969).

MCCAULEY, MARTIN, RUSSIA, AMERICA, AND THE COLD WAR, 1949-1991 (1998).

MCPHERSON, JAMES M., ORDEAL BY FIRE: THE CIVIL WAR AND RECONSTRUCTION (1982).

MCPHERSON, JAMES M., THE NEGRO'S CIVIL WAR: HOW AMERICAN BLACKS FELT & ACTED DURING THE WAR FOR THE UNION (1965).

MENCKE, JOHN G., MULLATTOES AND RACE MIXTURE: AMERICAN ATTITUDES AND IMAGES, 1865-1918 (1979).

MEIER, AUGUST, NEGRO THOUGHT IN AMERICA, 1880-1915 (1969).

MEIER, KENNETH J., ET AL., RACE, CLASS, AND EDUCATION: THE POLITICS OF SECOND-GENERATION DISCRIMINATION (1989).

MINOW, MARTHA, MAKING ALL THE DIFFERENCE: INCLUSION, EXCLUSION, AND AMERICAN LAW (1990).

MOE, TERRY, SCHOOLS, VOUCHERS, AND THE AMERICAN PUBLIC (2001).

MURUGKAR, LATA, DALIT PANTHER MOVEMENT IN MAHARASHTRA: A SOCIOLOGICAL APPRAISAL (1991).

Myrdal, Gunnar, An American Dilemma: The Negro Problem and Modern Democracy (1944).

National Center for Education Statistics, Status and Trends in the Education of Blacks (2003).

Nelson, William E., The Fourteenth Amendment: From Political Principal to Judicial Document (1988).

The New York Times 1999 Almanac (John W. Wright ed. 1998).

Newby, Idus A., Challenge to the Court: Social Scientists and the Defense of Segregation (rev. ed. 1969).

Newman, William, American Pluralism: A Study of Minority Groups and Social Theory (1973).

Norrell, Robert, Reaping the Whirlwind: The Civil Rights Movement in Tuskegee (1985).

Nyamiti, Charles, The Scope of African Theology (1973).

Oakes, Jeannie, Keeping Track: How Schools Structure Inequality (1985). Jeannie Oakes, Multiplying Inequalities: The Effects of Race, Social Class, and Tracking on Opportunities to Learn Mathematics and Science (1990).

Ogletree, Charles, All Deliberate Speed: Reflections on the First Half Century of Brown v. Board of Education (2004).

Orfield, Gary, Daniel Losen, Johanna Wald and Christopher B. Swanson, Losing our Future: How Minority Youths are Being Left Behind by the Graduation Rate Crisis (April 2004).

Orfield, Gary, Must We Bus? (1978).

Quarles, Benjamin, The Negro in the Making of America (1969).

Ragsdale, Bruce A. & Joel D. Treese, Black Americans in Congress, 1870-1989 (Office of the Historian, U.S. House of Representatives, Raymond W. Smock, Historian & Director, 1990).

Ravitch, Diane, The Troubled Crusade: American Education 1945-1980 (1983).

Reardon, Sean and John T. Yin, Private School Racial Enrollment & Segregation (June 2002).

Roberts, Bari-Ellen with Jack E. White, Roberts vs. Texaco: A True Story of Race and Corporate America (1998).

Rodgers, Harrell R., Jr. & Charles S. Bullock, III, Law and Social Change: Civil Rights Laws and their Consequences (1972).

Ruchames, Louis, Racial Thought in America: From the Puritans to Abraham Lincoln, A Documentary History (Louis Ruchames ed., 1969).

Sandel, Michael J., Liberalism and the Limits of Justice (1982).

Schultz, Stanley K., The Culture Factory: Boston Public Schools, 1789-1860 (1973).

Shaler, Nathaniel, The Neighbor: The Natural History of Human Contacts (1904).

Shugjaa, Mwalimu J., Beyond Desegregation: The Politics of Quality in African-American Schooling (Mwalimu J. Shugjaa ed. 1996).

Smith, John, The Generall Historie of Virginia, New England.

Sono, Themba, Reflections on the Origins of Black Consciousness in South Africa (1993).

St. James, Warren D., NAACP: Triumphs of a Pressure Group 1909-1980 (2d ed. 1980).

Stampp, Kenneth M., The Peculiar Institution: Slavery in the Ante-Bellum South (1956).

Summer Isles, Vol 1 (Glasgow: James MacLehose & Sons, 1907).

Stanton, William, The Leopard's Spots: Scientific Attitudes Toward Race in America 1815-1859 (1960).

Stumpf, Harry P., American Judicial Politics (1988).

Takaki, Ronald, Iron Cages: Race and Culture in 19th Century America (Oxford Univ. Press 1990) (1979).

Taylor, John V., The Primal Vision: Christian Presences Amid African Religion (1963).

Terman, Lewis M., The Measurement of Intelligence (Riverside Press 1916).

Thernstrom, Stephan & Abigail Thernstrom, America in Black and White: One Nation, Indivisible (1997).

Thomas, Hugh, The Slave Trade: A Story of the Atlantic Slave Trade: 1440-1870 (1997).

Thomas, William Hannibal, The American Negro: What He Was, What He Is, And What He May Become (1901).

De Tocqueville, Alexis, Democracy in America (George Lawrence trans., 1966).

Tucker, William H., The Science and Politics of Racial Research 23-24 (1994).

Tushnet, Mark V., Making Civil Rights Law: Thurgood Marshall and the Supreme Court, 1936-1961 (1994).

Tussman, Joseph, Government and the Mind (1977).

Tyack, David, et al., Law and the Shaping of Public Education, 1785-1954 (1987).

U.S. Bureau of the Census, 2003 Statistical Abstract of the United States (2003).

U.S. Bureau of the Census, Ser. P-23, No. 80, The Social and Economic Status of the Black Population in the United States: An Historical View, 1790-1978 (1979).

U.S. Bureau of the Census, U.S. Department of Commerce, Historical Statistics of the United States: Colonial Times to 1970 Part 1, Series A-195-209 (1975).

U.S. Commission on Civil Rights, Twenty Years After Brown: Equality of Educational Opportunity (1975).

U.S. Dept. Of Commerce, Bureau of the Census, Statistical Abstract of the United States (111th ed. 1991).

Wasby, Stephen L., The Supreme Court in the Federal Judicial System (3d ed. 1988).

Washington, Booker T., Up From Slavery (1901).

Weiss, Nancy J., The National Urban League 1910-1940 (1974).

West, Cornel, Prophesy Deliverance! (1982).

Wheelock, Ann, Crossing the Tracks: How "Untracking" can Save America's Schools (1992).

Weiss, Nancy J., The National Urban League 1910-1940 (1974).

Welner, Kevin G., Legal Rights, Local Wrongs: When Community Control Collides With Educational Equity (2001).

Wilkinson, J. Harvie, III, From Brown to Bakke: The Supreme Court and School Integration, 1954-1978 (1979).

Williamson, Joel, New People: Miscegenation and Mulattoes in the United States (1980).

Witmer, Helen & Ruth Kotinsky, Personality in the Making: The Fact-finding Report of the Midcentury White House Conference on Children and Youth (1952).

Woodward, C. Vann, The Strange Career Of Jim Crow (3d ed. 1974).

Yeboah, Samuel, The Ideology of Racism: The Origin of Racism (1988).

Gibbs, Jewelle T., Young, Black, and Male in America: An Endangered Species (Jewelle Gibbs et al. eds., 1988).

Articles, Book Chapters, and Other Publications

Academic Tracking, Report of the NEA Subcommittee on Academic Tracking (1990).

Allen, Walter R., *The Color of Success: African-American College Student Outcomes at Predominantly White and Historically Black Public Colleges and Universities,* 62 Harv. Educ. Rev. 26 (1992).

Bailyn, Bernard, *Introduction* to Pamphlets of the American Revolution, 1750-1776 (Bernard Bailyn with assistance from Jane N. Garrett eds., 1965).

Banks, James A., *Race, Ethnicity and Schooling in the United States: Past, Present and Future, in* Multicultural Education in Western Societies (James A. Banks & James Lynch eds., 1986).

Barnes, Robin, *Black America and School Choice: Charting a New Course,* 106 Yale L.J. 2375 (1997).

Bell, Derrick A., Jr., *Brown v. Board of Education and the Interest-Convergence Dilemma,* 93 Harv. L. Rev. 518 (1980), *reprinted in* Shades of *brown:* New Perspectives on School Desegregation (Derrick A. Bell ed., 1980).

Benhabib, Seyla, *Critical Theory and Postmodernism: On the Interplay of Ethics, Aesthetics, and Utopia in Critical Theory (Deconstruction of the Possibility of Justice),* 11 Cardozo L. Rev. 1435 (1990).

Black, Charles L., *The Lawfulness of the Segregation Decisions,* 69 Yale L.J. 421 (1960).

Bluford, Lucile H., *The Lloyd Gaines Story,* 1958 J. Legal Educ. Soc. 242 (1959).

Bourdieu, Pierre, *Cultural Reproduction and Social Reproduction, in* Knowledge, Education and Cultural Change (Richard Brown ed., 1973).

Brameld, Theodore, Educational Costs, *in* Discrimination and National Welfare (R. MacIver ed. 1949).

Brief of Amicus Curiae United States, Shelley v. Kraemer, 334 U.S. 1 (1948).

Brown, Kevin, *Do African-Americans Need Immersion Schools?: The Paradoxes Created by Legal Conceptualization of Race and Public Education,* 78 Iowa L. Rev. 813 (1993).

Brown, Kevin, *Has the Supreme Court Allowed the Cure for De Jure Segregation to Replicate the Disease?,* 78 Cornell L. Rev. 1 (1992).

Brown, Kevin, *The Constitutionality of Racial Classifications in Public School Admissions*, 29 HOFSTRA L. REV. 1 (2000).

Bryce, James, *Thoughts on the Negro Problem*, 153 N. AM. REV. 641 (1891).

Carnegie Forum on Education and the Economy, *A Nation Prepared: Teachers for the 21st Century* (1986).

Carter, Stephen, *When Victims Happen To Be Black*, 97 YALE L.J. 420 (1988).

Chaddock, Gail Russell, *Adverse Impact?*, CHRISTIAN SCIENCE MONITOR, November 30, 1999.

Chein, Isidor, *What Are the Psychological Effects of Segregation Under Conditions of Equal Facilities?* 3 INT'L J. OPINION AND ATTITUDE RES. 229 (1949).

The College Board, *2001 College-Bound Seniors: A Profile of SAT Program Test Takers* (2001).

Cook, Anthony E., *Beyond Critical Legal Studies: The Reconstructive Theology of Dr. Martin Luther King, Jr.*, 103 HARV. L. REV. 985 (1990).

Cook, Stuart W., *Social Science and School Desegregation: Did We Mislead the Supreme Court?*, 5 PERSONALITY & SOC. PSYCHOLOGY BULL. 420 (1979).

Cooper, Kenneth J., *Exams Opposed over Potential Harm to Minorities*, WASHINGTON POST, June 12, 1991.

Critics Target Wrong Culprit as Minorities' Test Scores Lag, USA TODAY, May 30, 2000.

Contursi, Janet A., *Political Theology: Text and Practice in a Dalit Panther Community*, 52 J. ASIAN STUD. 320 (1993).

Cuban, Larry, *Ethnic Content and "White" Instruction*, *in* TEACHING ETHNIC STUDIES: CONCEPTS AND STRATEGIES (James A. Banks ed., 1973).

Cryer, Dan, *Why Is Huck So Controversial?*, NEWSDAY, Oct. 15, 1996.

DAILY INTELLIGENCER (Atlanta), January 9, 1860 *reprinted in* W. E. B. DuBois, BLACK RECONSTRUCTION IN AMERICA 1860-1880 (Macmillan 1992) (1935).

Daley, Beth, *Troubling Admission Statistics at Latin: Chances for Blacks Attending Remain Poor*, BOSTON GLOBE, March 23, 1999.

Darling-Hammond, Linda, *Inequality and Access to Knowledge*, *in* HANDBOOK OF RESEARCH ON MULTICULTURAL EDUCATION (James A. Banks & Cherry A. McGee Banks eds., 1995).

Deutsch, Jan G., *Neutrality, Legitimacy, and the Supreme Court: Some Intersections Between Law and Political Science*, 20 STAN. L. REV. 169 (1968)

Deutscher, Max & Isidor Chein, *The Psychological Effects of Enforced Segregation: A Survey of Social Science Opinion*, 26 J. PSYCHOL. 259 (1948).

Diamond, Raymond T., *Confrontation as Rejoinder to the Compromise: Reflections of the Little Rock Desegregation Crisis,* 11 NAT'L BLACK L.J. 151 (1989).

Dickeman, Mildred, *Teaching Cultural Pluralism, in* TEACHING ETHNIC STUDIES: CONCEPTS AND STRATEGIES (James A. Banks ed., 1973).

Displacement and Present Status of Black School Principals in Desegregated School Districts: Hearings Before the U.S. Senate Select Committee on Equal Educational Opportunity, 92d Cong., 1st Sess. (1971)

Du Bois, W. E. B., *Editorial, The Crisis,* CRISIS 1, Nov. 1910.

The Emancipation Proclamation, reprinted in CIVIL RIGHTS AND AFRICAN-AMERICANS 200-1 (eds. Albert P. Blaustein and Robert L. Zangrando 1990).

Epps, Edgar G., *Minority Children: Desegregation, Self-Evaluation, and Achievement Orientation, in* EFFECTIVE SCHOOL DESEGREGATION (W. Hawley ed. 1981).

Flowers, Lamont A. & Ernest T. Pascarella, *Cognitive Effects of College Racial Composition on African American Students After 3 Years of College,* 40 J. OF COLLEGE STUDENT DEVELOPMENT (1999).

Franklin, John Hope, *Jim Crow Goes to School: The Genesis of Legal Segregation in Southern Schools,* S. ATLANTIC Q., Spring 1959.

Fried, Charles, *Five to Four: Reflections on the School Voucher Case,* 116 HARV. L. REV. 1 (2002).

Friedman, Milton, *The Role of Government in Education, in* ECONOMICS AND THE PUBLIC INTEREST (Robert A. Solo ed., 1955).

Gay, Geneva, *Achieving Educational Equality Through Curriculum Desegregation,* 72 PHI DELTA KAPPAN 56 (1990).

Gbadegesin, Segun, *Individuality, Community and the Moral Order, in* PHILOSOPHY FROM AFRICA: A TEXT WITH READINGS (P.H. Coetzee & A.P. J. Roux eds. 1998).

Gewirtz, Paul, *Choice in the Transition: School Desegregation and the Corrective Ideal,* 86 Colum. L. Rev. 728 (1986).

Glastris, Paul and Jeannye Thornton, *A New Civil Rights Frontier,* U. S. NEWS AND WORLD REPORT, Jan. 17, 1994.

Gleason, Philip, *American Identity and Americanization, in* CONCEPTS OF ETHNICITY (William Petersen et al. eds., 1982) .

Goldhader, Dan D. & Eric R. Eide, *What Do We Know (and Need to Know) about the Impact of School Choice Reforms on Disadvantaged Students?,* 72 HARV. EDUC. REV. 157 (2002).

Good, T.L., *Two Decades of Research on Teacher Expectations: Findings and Future Directions*, 38 J. Teacher Educ. 32 (1987).

Greeley, Horace, *To Abraham Lincoln, President of the United States, reprinted in* Civil Rights and African-Americans (eds. Albert P. Blaustein & Robert L. Zangrando 1990).

Green, Max, *Thinking Realistically About Integration,* 16 New Perspectives 35 (Fall 1984).

Green, Steven K., *The Blaine Amendment Reconsidered,* 36 Am. J. Legal Hist. 38 (1992).

Hagley, Judith A., *Massive Resistance—The Rhetoric and the Reality* 27 N. M. L. Rev. 167 (1997).

Hall, Prince et al., *Petition to the Honorable Senate and House of Representatives of the Commonwealth of Massachusetts Bay in General Court Assembled (Oct. 17, 1787), in* 1 A Documentary History of the Negro People in the United States (Herbert Aptheker ed., 1969).

Henig, Jeffrey R., *School Choice Outcomes, in* School Choice and Social Controversy: Politics, Policy, and Law (Stephen D. Sugarman & Frank R. Kemerer eds., 1999).

Hoffman, Frederick L., *Race Traits and Tendencies of the American Negro,* 11 Publications Am. Econ. A. 1 (1896).

Holloway, Joseph E., *The Origins of African-American Culture in* Africanism in American Culture (Joseph E. Holloway ed. 1991).

Hotakainen, Rob, *Minnesota's Charter School Concept Wins a Crucial Vote,* Star Tribune (Minneapolis), July 8, 1998.

Hovenkamp, Herbert, *Social Science and Segregation Before Brown,* 1985 Duke L. J. 624 (1985).

Hsu, Spencer S. & Justin Blum, *D.C. School Vouchers Win Final Approval,* Wash. Post, Jan. 23, 2004.

Huntington, Samuel P., *The Erosion of American National Interest,* Foreign Affairs 28 (Sept./Oct. 1997).

Jarvis, Sonia R., *Brown and the Afrocentric Curriculum,* 101 Yale L.J. 1285 (1992).

Johnson, Lyndon B., *Running Against the Twelfth Man of History,* New York Times, Dec. 26, 1972.

Jones, James M., *The Concept of Racism and its Changing Reality, in* Impacts of Racism on White Americans (Benjamin P. Bowser & Raymond G. Hunt eds., 1981).

Joondeph, Bradley W., *Review Essay: A Second Redemption?*, 56 WASH. & LEE L. REV. 169 (1999).

Jussim, Lee & Jacquelynne Eccles, *Teacher Expectations II: Construction and Reflection of Student Achievement*, 63 J. PERSONALITY & SOC. PSYCHOL. 947 (1992).

Karst, Kenneth, *Law, Cultural Conflict, and the Socialization of Children* 91 CAL. L. REV. 967 (2003).

Karst, Kenneth L., *Paths to Belonging: The Constitution and Cultural Identity*, 64 N.C. L. REV. 303 (1986).

King, Martin Luther, Jr., (Aug. 28, 1963), *I Have a Dream*, *in* A TESTAMENT OF HOPE: THE ESSENTIAL WRITINGS OF MARTIN LUTHER KING, JR. (James Melvin Washington ed., 1986).

King, Sabrina Hope, *The Limited Presence of African-American Teachers*, 63 REV. EDUC. RES. 115 (1993).

Kipling, Rudyard, *The White Man's Burden*, *in* RUDYARD KIPLING'S VERSE: INCLUSIVE EDITION 1885-1926 (1931).

Klarman, Michael J., *Race and the Court in the Progressive Era* 51 VAND. L. REV. 881 (1998).

Klarman, Michael J., *Rethinking the Civil Rights and Civil Liberties Revolutions*, 82 VA. L. REV. 1 (1996).

Kousser, J. Morgan, *Progressivism-For Middle-Class Whites Only: North Carolina Education*, 1880-1910, 46 J. SOC. HIST. 169 (1980).

Kujovich, Gil, *Equal Opportunity in Higher Education and the Black Public College: The Era of Separate But Equal*, 72 MINN. L. REV. 29 (1987).

Kunen, James S., *The End of Integration*, TIME, Apr. 29, 1996.

Lawrence, Charles R., III, *Segregation "Misunderstood": The Milliken Decision Revisited*, 12 U.S.F. L. REV. 15 (1977).

Lawrence, Charles R., III, *The Id, The Ego, and Equal Protection: Reckoning with Unconscious Racism*, 39 STAN. L. REV. 317 (1987).

Leavy, Walter *Is the Black Male an Endangered Species?*, EBONY, Aug. 1983.

Leonard, Mary, *Proponents of Vouchers See Opening: Planning Suits in Six States, Including Massachusetts*, BOSTON GLOBE, Nov. 18, 2002.

Lieberman, Leonard, et al., *The Debate Over Race: Thirty Years and Two Centuries Later*, *in* RACE AND IQ EXPANDED EDITION (Ashley Montagu ed, 1999).

Lincoln, Abraham, *"Lincoln's Reply to Greeley"*, (August 22, 1863) *reprinted in* CIVIL RIGHTS AND AFRICAN-AMERICANS (eds. Albert P. Blaustein & Robert L. Zangrando 1968).

Londen, Jack W., *School Desegregation and Tracking: A Dual System Within Schools,* 29 U.S.F. L. Rev. 705 (1995).

Losen, Daniel J. & Kevin G. Welner, *Disabling Discrimination in Our Public Schools: Comprehensive Legal Challenges to Inappropriate and Inadequate Special Education Services for Minority Children,* 36 Harv. CR.-C.L. L. Rev. 407 (2001).

Losen, Daniel J., *Silent Segregation in Our Nation's Schools,* 34 Harv. C.R.-C.L. L. Rev. 517 (1999).

Mahard, Rita E. and Robert L. Crain, *Research on Minority Achievements in Desegregated Schools, in* The Consequences of School Desegregation (C. Russell & W. Hawley eds. 1983).

Mahard, Rita E., Ruth E. Narot & Walter G. Stephan, *School Desegregation: An Evaluation of Predictions Made in Brown v. Board of Education,* 85 psychol. bull. 217 (1978).

Markley, Melanie, *Magnet Schools See Dip in Minority Enrollment,* Houston Chron., May 14, 1998.

Minow, Martha, *The Supreme Court, 1986 Term: Foreword: Justice Engendered,* 101 Harv. L. Rev. 10 (1987).

Mitchell, Mary Harter, *Secularism in Public Education: The Constitutional Issues,* 67 B.U.L. Rev. 603 (1987).

Mueller, Jennifer, *Facing the Unhappy Day: Three Aspects of the High Stakes Testing Movement,* 11 Kan. J.L. & Pub. Pol'y 201 (2002).

New York Times Editorial, *Bait-and-Switch on Public Education,* N.Y. Times, October 21, 2003.

O'Brien, Molly Townes, *Private School Tuition Vouchers and the Realities of Racial Politics,* 64 Tenn. L. Rev. 359 (1997).

O'Brien, Thomas V., *Aron v. Cook and the NAACP in Georgia Before Brown,* 23 J. Midwest Hist. Educ. Soc'y 129 (1996).

Ogbu, John U., *Immigrant and Involuntary Minorities in Comparative Perspectives, in* Minority Status and Schooling: A Comparative Study of Immigrant and Involuntary Minorities (Margaret A. Gibson & John Ogbu eds., 1991).

O'Neil, Robert, *Preferential Admissions: Equalizing Access to Legal Education,* U. Tol. L. Rev. Spring/Summer 1970.

Osher, David, et. al., *Exploring the Relationships Between Inappropriate and Ineffective Special Education Services for African American Children and*

Youth and their Overrepresentation in the Juvenile Justice System, in MINORITY ISSUES IN SPECIAL EDUCATION.

Parker, Wendy, *The Color of Choice: Race and Charter Schools,* 75 TUL. L. REV. 563 (2001).

Peller, Gary, *The Metaphysics of American Law,* 73 CAL. L. REV. 1151 (1985).

Powell, john A., *Race and Space: What Really Drives Metropolitan Growth* 16 BROOKINGS REVIEW 20 (1998).

Prashad, Vijay, *Afro-Dalits of the Earth, Unite!* 43 AFR. STUD. REV. 189 (2000).

Pressley, Darrell S., *Fewer Minorities Invited to Boston Latin,* BOSTON HERALD, March 23, 1999.

Pressley, Sue Anne, *New Ways to Assign Students Sought After Order to End Busing,* WASHINGTON POST, Nov. 8, 1999.

Read, Frank T., *Judicial Evolution of the Law of School Integration Since Brown v. Board of Education,* 39 LAW & CONTEMP. PROBS. 7 (1975).

Riegel, Stephen J., *The Persistent Career of Jim Crow: Lower Federal Courts and the "Separate but Equal" Doctrine, 1865-1896,* 28 AM. J. LEGAL HIST. 17 (1984)

Robinson, Gerard Toussaint, *Can the Spirit of Brown Survive in the Era of School Choice? A Legal and Policy Perspective,* 45 HOW. L.J. 281 (2002).

Ross, Ralph & Ernest Van Den Haag, *Prejudice About Prejudice, in* THE FABRIC OF SOCIETY (1957).

Harris, Roy V., *Strictly Personal,* AUGUSTA COURIER, Oct. 9, 1950.

Ryan, James E. & Michael Heise, *The Political Economy of School Choice,* 111 YALE L.J. 2043 (2002).

Salomone, Rosemary, *Rich Kids, Poor Kids and the Single Sex Education Debate* 34 Akron L. Rev. 209 (2000).

Sandel, Michael J., *Religious Liberty—Freedom of Conscience or Freedom of Choice?,* 1989 UTAH L. REV. 597 (1989).

Schemo, Diana Jean, *Few Exercise Right to leave Failing Schools,* N.Y. TIMES, August 28, 2002.

Schemo, Diana Jean, *New Federal Rule Tightens Demands on Failing Schools,* N.Y. TIMES, November 27, 2002.

Schlag, Pierre, *Normative and Nowhere to Go,* 43 STAN. L. REV. 167 (1990).

Schlag, Pierre, *The Empty Circles of Liberal Justification,* 96 MICH. L. REV. 1 (1997).

School Busing: Hearing on Proposed Amendments to the Constitution and Legislation Relating to Transportation and Assignment of Public School Pupils

Before Subcomm. No. 5 of the House Comm. on the Judiciary, 92d Cong., 2d Sess. 1311 (1972).

School Desegregation: A Social Science Statement, Brief of Amicus Curiae NAACP et al. in support of Resp't at 7a, Freeman v. Pitts, 503 U.S. 467 (1992), *on writ of cert.* to 11th Cir. (June 21, 1991).

Schouten, Fredreka(Gannett News Service), *Make-or-Break Graduation Tests Spur Protests,* INDIANAPOLIS STAR, May 25, 2003.

SEWALL, SAMUEL, *The Selling of Joseph, reprinted in* CIVIL RIGHTS AND AFRICAN-AMERICANS (Albert P. Blaustein & Robert L. Zangrando eds., 1968).

Simon, Larry G., *Racially Prejudiced Governmental Actions: A Motivation Theory of the Constitutional Ban Against Racial Discrimination,* 15 SAN DIEGO L. REV. 1041 (1978).

Shaler, Nathaniel, *Our Negro Types,* 29 CURRENT LIT. 45 (1900).

Shane, Peter M, *School Desegregation Remedies and the Fair Governance of Schools,* 132 U. PA. L. REV. 1041 (1984).

Siegel, Steven, *Ethnocentric Public School Curriculum in a Multicultural Nation: Proposed Standards for Judicial Review* 40 N.Y.L. SCH. L. REV. 311 (1996).

Slavin, Robert, *Achievement Effects of Ability Grouping in Secondary Schools: A Best-Evidence Synthesis,* 60 Review of Educational Research (1990).

Smith, Christopher E, *The Supreme Court and Ethnicity,* 69 OR. L. REV. 797 (1990).

Smith, Pamela J., *Our Children's Burden: The Many-Headed Hydra of the Educational Disenfranchisement of Black Children,* 42 HOW. L.J. 133 (1999).

Smith, John & Bette M. Smith, *Desegregation in the South and the Demise of the Black Educator,* 20 J. SOC. & BEHAV. SCI. (1974).

St. John, Nancy H., *The Effects of School Desegregation on Children: A New Look at the Research Evidence, in* RACE AND SCHOOLING IN THE CITY (1981).

Stephan, Walter G., *School Desegregation: An Evaluation of Predictions Made in Brown v. Board of Education,* 85 PSYCHOLOGICAL BULL. (1978).

Stewart, Joseph, Jr., et al., *In Quest of Role Models: Change in Black Teacher Representation in Urban School Districts 1968-86,* 58 J. NEGRO EDUC. 140 (1989).

Subotnik, Rena F. & Karen D. Arnold, *Longitudinal Study of Giftedness and Talent, in* BEYOND TERMAN: CONTEMPORARY LONGITUDINAL STUDIES OF GIFTEDNESS AND TALENT (Rena F. Subotnik & Karen D. Arnold eds., 1994).

Sullivan, Kathleen M., *The New Religion and the Constitution,* 116 HARV. L. REV. 1397 (2003).

Torres, Gerald, *Local Knowledge, Local Color: Critical Legal Studies and The Law of Race Relations,* 25 San Diego L. Rev. 1043, 1050 (1988).

U.S. Bureau of the Census, *2003 Statistical Abstract of the United States, 177, Table 270: High School Dropouts Race and Hispanic Origins* (2003).

United States General Accounting Office, *School Vouchers: Publicly Funded Programs in Cleveland and Milwaukee,* GAO-01- 914 (Aug. 2001).

Welner, Kevin G. & Jeannie Oakes, *(Li)Ability Grouping: The New Susceptibility of School Tracking Systems to Legal Challenges,* 66 Harvard Educational Review 451 (1996).

White, Arthur O., *The Black Leadership Class and Education in Antebellum Boston,* 42 J. Negro Educ. (1973).

Wilkerson, Doxey A., *Prevailing and Needed Emphases in Research on the Education of Disadvantaged Children and Youth, in* The Disadvantaged Child: Issues and Innovation (Joe L. Frost & Glenn R. Hawkes eds., 1966).

Williams, Eric, *Origin of Negro Slavery* in the African Philosophy: An Anthology Book (1998).

Winerip, Michael, *On Education: A Pervasive Dismay on Bush School Law,* N.Y. Times, March 19, 2003.

Worthington, *Milwaukee Idea Shapes a New School,* Chi. Trib., Dec. 1, 1991.

Ysseldyke, Jim, *Reflections on a Research Career: Generalizations from 25 Years of Research on Assessment and Instructional Decision Making,* 67 Exceptional Child 304 (2001).

Yudof, Mark A., *School Desegregation: Legal Realism, Reasoned Elaboration, and Social Science Research in the Supreme Court,* 42 Law & Contemp. Prob. 57, 70 (Autumn 1978).

The Effects of Segregation and the Consequence of Desegregation: A Social Science Statement reprinted at 37 Minn. L. Rev. 427 (1953).

Websites and Materials Available on the Internet

ACT High School Profile, *ACT Nat'l and State Scores, available at* http:/ /www.act.org/ news/data/03/pdf/t1-2.pdf.

ACT National and State Scores, *available at* http://www.act.org/news/data/ 03/pdf/t1-2.pdf.

ACT National and State Scores, The 1997 ACT High School Profile Report—National Normative Data, *available at* http://www.act.org/news/ data/97/t5-6-7.html.

AMREIN, AUDREY L. & DAVID C. BERLINER, *High-Stakes Testing, Uncertainty, and Student Learning*, EDUCATION POLICY ANALYSIS ARCHIVES, Mar. 2002, *available at* http://epaa.asu.edu/epaa/v10n18.

Associated Press, *Golfer Says Comments about Woods 'Misconstrued,'* Atlanta, Georgia, (Apr. 21, 1997), *available at* http://www.cnn .com/US/9704/21/fuzzy/.

Associated Press, *Growth of Vouchers Slow Year After Court Decision*, June 28, 2003, *available at* http://www.cnn.com/2003/EDUCATION/06/28/school.vouchers.ap/ index.html.

Bush, George W., Speech in Cleveland, Ohio (July 1, 2002), *available at* http://www.whitehouse.gov/news/releases/2002/07/20020701-7.html.

Centers for Disease Control and Prevention, *National Vital Statistics Report*, Vol. 49, No. 12, at 24 (Oct. 9, 2001), *available at* http://www.cdc.gov/nchs/data/nvsr/ nvsr49/nvsr49_12.pdf.

Centers for Disease Control and Prevention, *Table 23. Infant mortality rates, fetal mortality rates, and perinatal mortality rates, according to race: United States, selected years 1950-99*, http://www.cdc.gov/nchs/data/hus/tables/2001/01hus023.pdf.

The Center for Education Reform, *Charter Schools 2002: Results from CER's Annual Survey of Americas Charter Schools, available at* http://207.201.191.212/charter_schools/ survey2002.pdf.

The College Board, *2003 College-Bound Seniors: A Profile of SAT Program Test Takers, available at* http://www.collegeboard.com/prod_downloads/about/ news_info/ cbsenior/yr2003/pdf/2003_TOTALGRP_PRD.pdf.

Cable News Network, *Cracker Barrel Settles Discrimination Suits*, CNN, Sept. 9, 2004, *available at* http:// www.cnn.com/2004/LAW/09/09/cracker.barrel.ap/index.html.

DeGrow, Myra, *Educational Vouchers and Tax Credits: A State-by-State Summary of Current Programs* (December 18, 2002), *available at* http://i2i.org/Publications/ IB/Education/ 2002f.htm.

Educational Testing Service, *The Academic Quality of Prospective Teachers: The Impact of Admissions and Licensure Testing* (1999), *available at* http://ftp.ets.org/pub/res/researcher/RR-03-35.pdf.

EEOC press release, *EEOC and Ford Sign Multi-Million Dollar Settlement of Sexual Harassment Case* (Sept. 7, 1999) *available at* http://www.eeoc.gov/press/9-7-99.html.

Frankenberg, Erica, et al., *A Multiracial Society with Segregated Schools: Are We Losing the Dream?* (Jan. 2003), *available at* http://www.civilrightsproject.harvard .edu/research/reseg03/ AreWeLosingtheDream.pdf

Gardner, David P., et. al., *A Nation at Risk: The Imperative for Educational Reform* (1983), *available at* http://www.mat.uc.pt/~emsa/PMEnsino/ANationatRisk .pdf.

Gehring, John, *Gov. Owens Signs Colorado Voucher Bill,* Educ. Wk., April 23, 2003, *available at* http://www.edweek.org.

Gehring, John, *Voucher Battles Head to State Capitals,* Educ. Wk., July 10, 2002, *available at* http://www.edweek.org.

Harvard College *Racial Statistics (Fall 2002) available at* http://vpfweb.harvard.edu/factbook/current_facts/enroll_ethnicity_7.html.

Hendrie, Caroline, *High Court Upholds State's Bar on Aid to Theology Majors,* Educ. Wk., March 3, 2004, *available at* http://www.edweek.org.

Hendrie, Caroline, *The Florida Experiment,* Educ. Wk., January 4, 2004, *available at* http://www.edweek.org.

Human Rights Watch, *Race and Incarceration in the United States, Backgrounder Table 1: Rates of Incarceration Per 100,000 State Residents by Race* (Feb. 27, 2002), *available at* http://www.hrw.org/backgrounder/usa/race/pdf/table1.pdf.

Human Rights Watch, *Race and Incarceration in the United States, Backgrounder Table 3: Percentage of Adult Men (Age 18-64) Incarcerated, by Race* (Feb. 27, 2002), *available at* http://www.hrw.org/ backgrounder/usa/race/pdf/table3.pdf.

Joint Center for Political and Economic Studies, *Number of Black Elected Officials in the United States, by State and Office, available at* http://jointcenter.org/DB/table/ graphs/BEO_00.pdf.

Lieff, Cabraser, Heimann & Bernstein, LLP, *Employment Discrimination Lawsuits, available at* http://lieffcabraser.com/practice_employment_rd.htm.

Milwaukee Parental Choice Program Frequently Asked Questions for 2001-02, *available at* http://www.dpi.state.wi.us/dpi/dfm/sms/doc/mpc01fnf.doc.

Mitchell, Nancy, *Court Hears Vouchers Case,* Rocky Mountain News, May 26, 2004, *available at* *http:*//www.rockymountainnews.com/drmn/education/article/0,1299,DRMN_ 957_2914560,00.html.

National Center for Educational Statistics, *Average NAEP Reading Scale Scores, by age and race/ethnicity: selected years 1975 to 1998, available at* http://nces.gov/Pubs2003/Hispanics/figures.asp?FigureNumber=4_2a.

National Center for Educational Statistics, Digest of Educ. Statistics 2002, *Table 133—Scholastic Assessment Test (SAT) averages, by race/ethnicity:* 1986-87 to 2001-02, *available at* http://nces.ed.gov/pubs2003/2003060b.pdf.

National Center for Educational Statistics, *Digest of Education Statistics 2002, Table 186: Enrollment rates of 18- to 24-year-olds in degree-granting institutions by sex, and race/ethnicity: 1967 to 2001, available at* http://www.nces.ed.gov/programs/digest/d02/ tables/PDF/table186.pdf.

National Center for Educational Statistics, *Scholastic Assessment Test (SAT) Score Averages by Race/Ethnicity, available at* http://nces.ed.gov/pubs2002/digest2001/tables/dt134.asp.

National Center for Educational Statistics,, *The Nation's Report Card, NAEP 1999 Long-Term Trend Mathematics Summary Data Tables for Age 17 Student Data, available at* http://nces.ed.gov/nationsreportcard/tables/ Ltt1999/NTM31011.asp.

National Center for Educational Statistics, *The Nation's Report Card, NAEP 1999 Long-Term Trend Mathematics Summary Data Tables for Age 13 Student Data, at* http://nces.ed.gov/nationsreportcard/tables/Ltt1999/ NTM21011.asp .

National Center for Educational Statistics,, *The Nation's Report Card, NAEP 1999 Long-Term Trend Mathematics Summary Data Tables for Age 9 Student Data, available at* http://nces.ed.gov/nationsreportcard/tables/Ltt1999/NTM21011.asp.

National Center for Educational Statistics, *The Nation's Report Card, NAEP 1999 Long-Term Trend Mathematics Summary Data Tables for Age 17 Student Data, available at* http://nces.ed.gov/nationsreportcard/tables/ Ltt1999/NTM31011.asp.

National Center for Educational Statistics,, *The Nation's Report Card, NAEP 1999 Long-Term Trend Mathematics Summary Data Tables for Age 13 Student Data, at* http://nces.ed.gov/nationsreportcard/tables/Ltt1999/NTM21011. asp.

National Center for Educational Statistics, *The Nation's Report Card, NAEP 1999 Long-Term Trend Mathematics Summary Data Tables for Age 9-13 Student Data, available at* http://nces.ed.gov/nationsreportcard/tables/Ltt1999/NTM11011.asp

National Center for Educational Statistics, *Trends in Average Reading Scale Scores, by Race, Age and Score Quartile* 1971-99, *available at* http://nces.ed.gov/programs/coe/2002/section2/ tables/t08There is_2.asp (2000).

National Center for Educational Statistics, *Trends in the science performance of 9-, 13-, and 17-Year-Olds, Table 13-2 Average white-black and white-Hispanic score gaps in science achievement* 1970-99,*available at* http://nces.ed.gov//programs/coe/2001/section2/tables/t13_2.asp.

The National Coalition on Black Civic Participation, *Table 1: The Black National Electorate by Demographic Group 1996 v. 2000, available at* http://www.bigvote.org/ stats.htm (citing Voter News Service (NY Times, 11/12/00); compiled by David A. Bositis, Ph.D., JCPES).

National Security Council, *U.S. Objectives and Programs for National Security, NSC*-68 (Apr. 14, 1950), *available at* http://www.fas.org/irp/offdocs/nsc-hst/nsc-68-1.htm.

Orfield, Gary and John T. Yin, *Resegregation in American Schools* (June 1999) *available at* www.law.harvard.edu/civilrights/publications/resegregation99.html.

Pearlman, Jeff, *At Full Blast,* Sports Illustrated, Dec. 27, 1999, *available at* http://sportsillustrated.cnn.com/features/cover/news/1999/12/22/rocker.

Richard, Alan, Educ. Wk., December 10, 2003, *available at* http://www.edweek.org.

Richard, Alan, *Florida Sees Surge in Use of Vouchers,* Educ. Wk., September 4, 2002, *available at* http://www.edweek.org.

Sports Illustrated, *Jimmy "The Greek" Snyder canned for 'racist' remarks,* Sports Illustrated, Jan. 16, 1988, *available at* http://sportsillustrated.cnn.com/ almanac/video/1988/#2.

Thernstrom, Stephan, *The Demography of Racial and Ethnic Groups* (2001), *available at* http://www.hoover.stanford.edu/publications/books/fulltext/color-line/13.pdf.

U.S. Bureau of the Census, Racial Statistics Branch, Population Division, *Current Population Survey, Table 7: Education Attainment of the Population 25 Years and Over by Sex, and Race and Hispanic Origin: March 2000* (Feb. 22, 2001), *available at* www.census.gov/population/socdemo/race/ black/ppl-142/tab07.txt.

U.S. Bureau of the Census, *2002 Statistical Abstract of the United States, Table 382: Members of Congress-Selected Characteristics 1983-2002* (2002), *available at* http://www.census.gov/prod/2003pubs/02statab/election.pdf.

U.S. Bureau of the Census, *2002 Statistical Abstract, Table 211: Mean Earnings by Highest Degree Earned: 1999, available at* http://www.census.gov/prod/2003pubs/ 02statab/educ.pdf.

U.S. Bureau of the Census, *Historical Income Table P-1b (historical income table for African-Americans), available at* http://www.census.gov/hhes/income/histinc/p01b.html

U.S. Bureau of the Census, *Historical Poverty Tables: 2002, Table 2: Poverty Status of People by Family Relationship, Race, and Hispanic Origin: 1959 to 2002 available at* http://www.census.gov/hhes/poverty/histpov/hstpov2.html.

U.S. Bureau of the Census, *Historical Poverty Tables: 2002, Table 3: Poverty Status of People, by Age, Race, and Hispanic Origin: 1959 to 2002 available at* http://www.census.gov/hhes/poverty/histpov/hstpov3.html.

U.S. Bureau of the Census, *Projections of the Population by Age, Sex, Race, and Hispanic Origin for the U.S.: 1999 to 2100 (Middle Series), available at* http://www.census.gov/population/projections/nation/detail/ d2031_40.pdf.

U.S. Bureau of the Census, *Table 1: Population by Race, for Hispanic or Latino Origin for all Ages and for 18 years and older for the United States 2000* (Apr. 2, 2001), *available at* http://www.census.gov/population/cen2000/phc-t1/tab01.pdf.

U.S. Census Bureau, *Historical Incomes Table P-1a (historical income table for whites), available at* http://www.census.gov/hhes/income/histinc/ p01a.html.

U.S. Charter Schools, *available at* http://www.uscharterschools.org/pub/ uscs_docs/o/ index .htm#national, (*citing* CENTER FOR EDUCATION REFORM, THE NATIONAL CHARTER SCHOOL DIRECTORY 2003).

U.S. Charter Schools, *available at* http://www.uscharterschools.org/pub/uscs_docs/o/ index.htm# national.

U.S. Department of Justice, Office of Justice Programs, Bureau of Justice Statistics, *Prison and Jail Inmates at Midyear 2002, Table 13: Number of inmates in State or Federal prisons and local jails, by gender, race, Hispanic origin, and age, June 30, 2002*(Apr. 2003), *available at* http://www.ojp.usdoj.gov/bjs/pub/pdf/pjim02.pdf.

U.S. Dept. Of Educ. Institute of Educ. Services, Nat'l Ctr. for Educ. Statistics, *Status and Trends in Education of Blacks, available at* http://nces.edgov/pubs2003/ 2003034.pdf 38 (Sept. 2003).

Yale University *Ethnicity Report (Fall 2002) available at* http://www.yale.edu/oir/factsheet.html.

Young, Beth Aronstamm, *Public School Student, Staff, and Graduate Counts by State, School Year 2001-02, Table 5: Percentage of public school membership by race/ethnicity and state: school year 2001-02, available at* http://nces.ed.gov/pubs2003/2003358.pdf.

Index of Cases

Index of Names

General Index